CAIRO

PRINCETON STUDIES ON THE NEAR EAST

CAIRO

1001 YEARS OF *THE CITY VICTORIOUS*

JANET L. ABU-LUGHOD

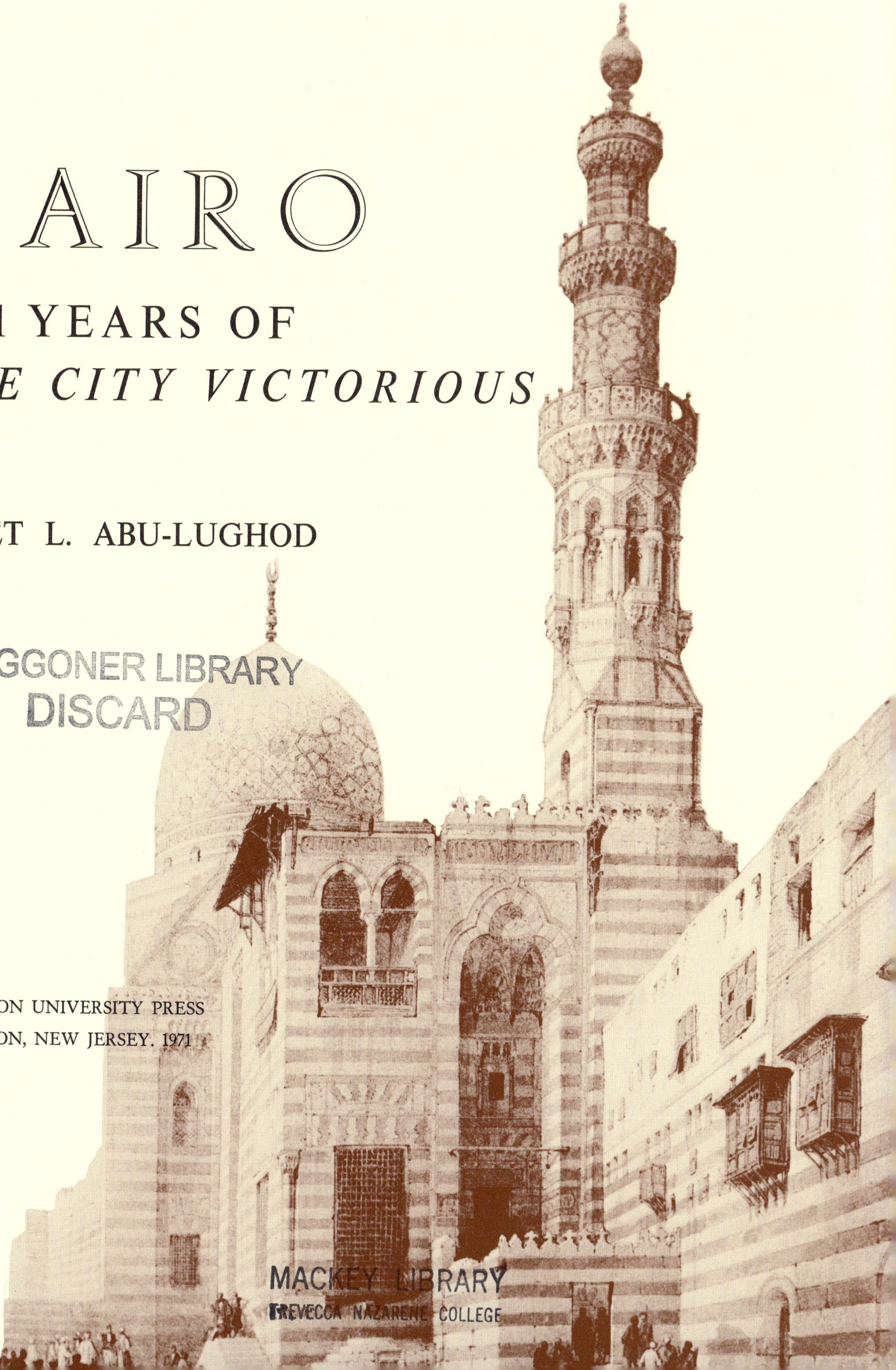

PRINCETON UNIVERSITY PRESS
PRINCETON, NEW JERSEY. 1971

L.C. Card: 73-112992

ISBN: 0-691-03085-5

A version of Chapter 7 appeared in slightly different form in *Comparative Studies in Society and History*, VII (July 1965), 429-457. It is used here with the permission of Cambridge University Press.

Parts of Chapter 12 have appeared in highly summarized form in J. Abu-Lughod, "Varieties of Urban Experience: Contrast, Coexistence and Coalescence in Cairo," in Ira Lapidus, ed., *Middle Eastern Cities* (University of California Press, Berkeley: 1969). Reprinted by permission of the Regents of the University of California.

Printed in the United States of America
by Princeton University Press, Princeton, New Jersey

Preface

Cities are, to paraphrase, all things to all men. Great symbolic cities such as Cairo, with their extended histories and current vitality, are even more likely than most to evoke diverse and conflicting responses from those who know them. To the contemporary inhabitant who lives out his daily routine along selected and repetitive pathways—to work, home, to visit friends and relations, to pray and to play—his "city" appears so mundane that he scarcely notes its all too familiar and thus invisible aspects. He envisages neither its extent and form nor its links with past and future. The tourist notes all with eager and undulled eyes, finding excitement but also bewilderment in the city's apparent formlessness and anachronistic contrasts. All modernity is dismissed by the antiquarian, who sees the modern metropolis merely as an inconvenient obstacle to a proper vantage point from which to explore this precious mosque or that priceless wall fragment. He moves selectively from one to the other, ignoring the contemporary form of the city in his effort to reconstruct an earlier life, still temptingly visible at times.

To the student of modern urbanism, however, Cairo presents primarily problems and an enormous challenge. Here admittedly is a city with pressing problems of land use chaos and inefficiencies, of human and vehicular congestion, of social disorder and poverty, striving vigorously to create a utopia. But here also is a complex city, a blend of old and new, of East and West, which must not be allowed to achieve its new order at the expense of its unique and poignant beauty nor its human warmth. The problem is one of balancing conservation and progress.

The challenge, on the other hand, is one of discovery. Can a pattern, a form, a rationale be extracted from what appears to the casual observer to be capricious disorder? For order there must be. Perhaps no creation of man is capable of retaining its underlying organization so obdurately in the face of dramatic shifts in culture and technology as the urban shell-home he has built over history. If order is to be found, however, more than the naked eye must be employed to uncover its hidden framework. Both the telescopic lens of history and the infrared lens of statistics are needed to separate the accidental from the essential and to trace the often devious chains that bind present with past and that link parts with the whole. If this book has an implicit goal, it is to uncover the orderly patterns and temporal sequences in Cairo's growth and development that have yielded the present form of the city and have given rise to its particular qualities.

There has been an ancillary objective as well. While every city constitutes a unique *Gestalt*, it also shares with others of its genre certain basic similarities. While explicit comparisons are eschewed in this book, it is nevertheless clear that Cairo was, to some extent, merely one example of genus "preindustrial city," species "Islamic." As such, an analysis of her experience can throw light on other communities whose growth and development have been conditioned by similar technological and cultural determinants. Furthermore, the modern bifurcation of Cairo into indigenous and "Westernized" quarters parallels the experience of many cities with a colonial heritage. The problems the city now faces in eliminating these divisions and building a unified physical form which reflects her recently regained cultural unity are problems being faced in other modernizing nations as well.

How shall a study of Cairo—a city of such venerable antiquity—cope with the question of historical data? How much should be included; what can be left out or glossed over; how shall the evidence be interpreted? There is no easy nor universally satisfactory solution. As a sociologist I make two assumptions: that historical writing, like every other kind, is always selective and, in ways, personal; second, that one's view of history is deeply affected by one's vantage point. The general historian, standing above the incredibly complex and sweeping movements encompassed within the more than one thousand years of Cairo's life, may be annoyed to find emphasis given to certain periods relatively insignificant on the larger canvas, or certain institutional arrangements and patterns treated to the exclusion of others of at least equal import to the larger society. My defense is to plead unabashed myopia. Viewing history not from the heights but from the narrow streets of Cairo yields a peculiarly distorted image. Throughout, my criterion has been to measure each period and development by its impact upon Cairo and its relevance in explaining the conditions and counterimpulses at work in the contemporary city (although some parts of the history are intrinsically so fascinating that I could not resist them). In this I have operated more in the manner of biographer than of historian, for the ultimate goal has been to understand the city, viewing the formative milieu selectively and in terms of its relation to the object of study.

This book, to which I owe so much of my education, has had a varied and overlong history. I began work on it in 1959 while associated with the Social Research Center of the American University at Cairo, and it is to the Director of the Center, Dr. Laila S. Hamamsy, that I must express my deepest appreciation, not only for her tangible contributions in making available financial support and assisting personnel but also for the faith she demonstrated by granting me a free hand to explore the subject and to shift the focus of the study. The project began originally as a statistical analysis of Cairo by census tracts. The results of that inquiry have already been published by the Social Research Center in 1963, under the title *Cairo Fact Book*. It became evident, however, that the ecology of the modern city laid bare by that analysis was static and still confused. Further statistical analysis was to clarify the picture, but the reasons for the ecological pattern could be grasped only within the longer perspective of the city's evolution. Thus, toward the end of my sojourn in Egypt I began the research and writing of this book, a project that in one form or another has taken a decade.

In this endeavor I have benefited from the generous support and encouragement of many. To the Radcliffe Institute for Independent Study I owe the time during which most of this manuscript was committed to paper. An appointment as Associate Scholar during 1963-1964 allowed me to devote more time to writing and gave me access to Harvard University's excellent library. The rather complex statistical operations required for the final portion of the book were made possible by a grant from the Milton Fund of Harvard and by the liberal amount of computer time granted jointly by Smith College and the University of Massachusetts. Additional machine time and skilled secretarial services were made available by the M.I.T.-Harvard Joint Center for Urban Studies. I owe Martin Meyerson, its first director, a special debt of gratitude, for he gave me my earliest training as an urbanist, was a stimulating guide and colleague for many years after that, and demonstrated his continued confidence by co - sponsoring this book with the Radcliffe Institute. Various other staff members of the Joint Center gave generously of their time and competence. Mrs. Johanne Khan, in particular, rendered significant and intelligent editorial services as she typed much of the manuscript.

Intellectual acknowledgments are sometimes more difficult to identify than practical ones, for they tend to become so deeply incorporated that we lose sight of their origins. This is not the case here. This book literally would never have been conceived, much less brought to fruition, without my husband, Ibrahim Abu-Lughod. Not only did he take me to Cairo, an irresistible stimulus to an urbanophile, but he generously gave of his vast scholarly store. He guided me to and through the original Arabic sources, translating, tracing usages and traditions, evaluating conflicting evidence. No less important were his contributions to my psychic stamina. A wise criticism or an optimistic encouragement at those recurrent moments of author's cramp are gifts for which no adequate recognition can ever be given.

I have not been the first to be charmed into bondage by the city of Cairo; she has captivated many before, and to these earlier writers each new student of the city must defer, recognizing that his endeavor has been built upon foundations laid by others. If and to the extent that my effort improves upon theirs, it is only because I have had the advantage of "standing on their shoulders," freed by their prior syntheses to pursue additional goals. While the number of books on Cairo is legion, two in particular have represented the culmination of their generation's knowledge of the city and have made these findings available to the western reader. The first was a small classic, *The Story of Cairo* (1902), written by Stanley Lane-Poole, nephew of childless Edward Lane and heir to his mantle as one of the first British scholars to study seriously the language, literature, and culture of Islamic Egypt. If my book does not duplicate his intriguing narrative, it is only because my ultimate orientation has been social and contemporary rather than historical and architectural. The revisions required by later knowledge have been amply supplied by the architectural histories of Sir K.A.C. Creswell, in whose debt we all remain. The second book, prepared one generation later and far broader in scope and temporal coverage, was the two-volume work by Marcel Clerget, *Le Caire; Étude de géographie urbaine et d'histoire économique*, published in Cairo in 1934 and now, unfortunately, out of print and difficult to find. Since its publication it has served as the standard Western-language source for information on Cairo and, in orientation and focus, approximates the present work more closely than does Lane-Poole's. If I appear in the course of this study to cavil with Clerget on points of fact or interpretation it is only because his comprehensive work has alerted me to many of the unresolved issues in Cairo's growth and development; I can only hope that my own synthesis will prove equally stimulating to the *next* reappraisal. Furthermore, Clerget's analysis terminated with the Egyptian Census of 1927, when Cairo had only little more than a million inhabitants and covered only a fraction of its present developed area. The city's population now exceeds 6 million, suggesting that a crucial phase still remained unexplored. From this newly gained hindsight I cannot help but reinterpret some of the past factors responsible for the contemporary city's organization. Not only has the city grown but our knowledge of societal organization during its earlier periods has similarly expanded. I have tried to incorporate these revised views of Islamic urban organization into the interpretation wherever they seem relevant, while recognizing that they still fall short of adequacy and may be significantly changed in the future.

Not only paper-and-ink friends but also more lively coworkers have aided me in fathoming Cairo. Numerous colleagues at the American University at Cairo contributed to initiating me into the intricacies of the city. The late Professor Alphonse Said, who generously shared his intimate knowledge of the city with me, and Ezz al-Din Attiya, who acted as my enthusiastic research assistant for almost two years, must be singled out especially, although there were many other Cairenes who assisted without knowing. From among the government officials shaping Cairo's future who were generous with their time and spirit, I must single out for special thanks Muḥammad Ḥāfiẓ 'Ali, Sa'īd al-Najjār, and Mahdi 'Arafah. The cooperation of the U.A.R. Ministry of Culture made it possible for 'Abd al-Fattāḥ 'Īd to contribute his exciting contemporary photographs as accompanying illustrations, and it was the generosity of Aḥmad Bahā' al-Dīn, chief editor of *Al-Muṣawwar*, that made inclusion of older photographs of Cairo, drawn from the archives of that magazine, possible.

Others have been equally generous in reading parts of the manuscript and, by their constructive comments, in protecting me from numerous but not all errors and inaccuracies. These include Sir K.A.C. Creswell, distinguished scholar and lifelong force behind the preservation of ancient Cairo, Roger Le Tourneau, Donald Little, Alan Horton, and Charles Issawi. Among the sociologists who have considered and commented on the manuscript itself or upon the statistical techniques utilized for the final section are Gideon Sjoberg, Hilda Golden, Thomas Wilkinson, and Peter Park. To all these I express my gratitude and appreciation.

This volume was no simple matter to produce. The accuracy of its expression and the beauty of its presentation owe a substantial debt to two members of the Princeton University Press. Manuscript editing was done meticulously, graciously, and with interest well beyond the call of duty by Eve Hanle, and the handsome design was created by Helen Van Zandt whose taste and judgment are revealed on every page. Their contributions should be a source of pride to them as they are pleasure to me. The assistance of the Program of African Studies of Northwestern University made possible the inclusion of maps and illustrations, and the erudition and judgment of Barbara Kalkas transformed the index into a true guide.

Perhaps my final acknowledgment must be to the city of Cairo itself. Had she not been so fascinating the impetus for this book could never have been sustained.

Janet L. Abu-Lughod

Wilmette, Illinois

Contents

List of Illustrations

Except where otherwise attributed, all photographs are from the author's personal files

List of Maps

List of Tables and Charts

CAIRO

If we would lay a new foundation for urban life, we must understand the historic nature of the city, and distinguish between its original functions, those that have emerged from it, and those which may still be called forth.

LEWIS MUMFORD

1 Introduction

IN THE YEAR A.D. 969 the lines of a small rectangular military capital were staked out by a Fāṭimid conquering army from North Africa. Set near an existing town founded more than three centuries earlier by another military conqueror imbued with similar religious fervor, the new bastide was named al-Manṣūrīyah, from the Arabic root signifying God-granted victory. Within a few years the name—but not its meaning—had been changed to al-Qāhirah (The Victorious), to celebrate the triumphal entry of the Fāṭimid Caliph into a city which was to serve as the seat of his Shi'ite dynasty for the ensuing 200 years and which was to persist to the present as one of the great cities of Islam.

The blend of religion and the military, characteristic of her origin, was to impart unique elements to the city's development; the meaning of her name was to augur accurately for the future. Despite wide oscillations in the fate and vigor of Cairo (the Western corruption of al-Qāhirah), she not only survived but developed into the present metropolis—home to more than 6 million Cairenes, symbol and center for more than one hundred million Arabs.

The colossus of Cairo today dominates the two continents Egypt bridges. Even as Africa and Asia Minor find their cultural and geographic nexus in the heartland of Egypt, so also do both continents turn inevitably toward its core, Cairo. One must go as far north as Berlin to find a competitor in size, as far east as Bombay and as far west as the Americas to find its equal, and one may travel to the southern Pole without ever meeting its peer. Within Egypt, the city's dominance is even more striking. One out of every seven Egyptians resides within her official boundaries; one in six lives in her metropolitan web. And, just as Egypt herself stands astride two continents, so Cairo stands astride Egypt, linking as well as dominating the two subregions—Upper Egypt to her south and Lower Egypt to her north. Her dominance is challenged only by the Nile, the river that bisects both Cairo and the nation but paradoxically unifies as it divides.

The geographic site of the city is strategic. Historically, the flow of things, peoples, and ideas in the Nile's narrow valley has always funneled eventually into the north-south, south-north axis. South to north is the natural flow of the country. Ancient and contemporary Egyptians alike describe south as "up" and north as "down," and by no capricious reasoning. South is the source of the river, the source of the very soil, and the power of the river's flow has dragged the country with it. It has even dragged Cairo herself downstream, as will be seen later.

1. Obelisk of ancient Heliopolis *ca.* 1860

Viewed from the south, Cairo is a prism through which the single stream of the Nile is refracted into the myriad channels which vein the Delta. Only ten miles north of Cairo is the barrage that regulates water flow into the two branches of the lower Nile, one leading to Damietta, the other to Rosetta (Rashīd). Thus, Cairo guards the gateway to the wide Delta and controls its destiny.

North, on the other hand, has been the soft underbelly which attackers, coming one after the other in dizzying succession, have invaded from three directions to reap the fruits of the black soil and the browned people. Here Egypt is virtually defenseless. Nowhere in the diffuse Delta can an enemy be repelled in force. But just as all streams lead out from Cairo, so all roads from the north converge inevitably upon her, and through her narrow bounds must pass any force intent on controlling the

2. Lane in walled Babylon today

headwaters and hence the country. So it is that invaders have traditionally moved on to establish military headquarters at strategic Cairo.

The first known settlement in the vicinity of modern Cairo was also one of the earliest urban settlements in the world, the ancient capital of Memphis. The ruins of that city lie a dozen miles south of contemporary Cairo on the opposite (i.e., western) bank of the river. Memphis flourished between perhaps 5000 and 2500 B.C., reaching its zenith during the thirtieth century before Christ when the Southern Kingdom extended its hegemony over the Delta and unified the two regions. This unity made centrally located Memphis a logical seat for a capital for the very same reason that Cairo now serves as one.[1] Pharaonic remains have also been found on the eastern bank of the river (the site of present Cairo), indicating similarly that this area contained early settlements of importance. Among these were the shrine city of Ôn, or Heliopolis, which now lies within the northeast extension of the contemporary city,[2] and the religious settlement at the river which guarded its approach, Khery-Aha, later called Babylon, which is now incorporated into the southern limits of the modern city.[3]

In later times, when Egypt had become merely a Mediterranean colony of the Greeks, the seaport of Alexandria usurped the title of primate city from Memphis and Thebes. Despite this loss in stature, the strategic

[1] James H. Breasted, *A History of Egypt* (Charles Scribner's Sons, New York: 2nd edn., 1956 imprint), pp. 5, 111. Marcel Clerget, in his *Le Caire; Étude de géographie urbaine et d'histoire économique* (Imprimerie E. & R. Schindler, Cairo: 1934), has also recognized the strategic importance of Cairo as a link between Upper and Lower Egypt from ancient times to the present. See, particularly, I, 14-15.

[2] An obelisk marking the site of this ancient shrine city, where once Plato had studied, can still be seen *in situ* in the village of Maṭarīyah which, since the 1920's, has been increasingly engulfed by the expansion of Cairo.

[3] While nothing remains of the earliest settlement of Babylon, remnants of the Roman fort there can still be seen in Miṣr al-Qadīmah (Old Cairo), although the lower ramparts are under water. Breasted mentions a shrine settlement during pharaonic times, calling it Babylon, but the origins of the community by that name are obscured forever. Conflicting accounts are found in the writings of Greek, Coptic, and Arab geographers and historians. One entire book, *Babylon of Egypt* (The Clarendon Press, Oxford: 1914), by Alfred J. Butler is devoted to untangling the various traditions and terms as they appear in Greek, Coptic, and Arabic manuscripts. Two major traditions prevail. The first places the founding of a fortified settlement on the eastern bank in about 1400 B.C. and suggests that it was founded by rebellious Babylonian captives. This account was found in earliest form in the work of Diodorus who wrote about 50 B.C. See Sidney Toy, "Babylon of Egypt," in *The Journal of the British Archaeological Association*, Third Series, I (January 1937), 53 especially. It was incorporated into the geography written by Strabo some twenty-five years later. See Horace L. Jones, trans., *The Geography of Strabo* (William Heinemann Ltd., London: 1932), VIII, 85-87. The second tradition dates the founding of the community from the sixth century B.C. and attributes it to Persian invaders under the leadership of Nebuchadnezzar. This was the account given by John of Nikiou, a seventh-century Coptic chronicler. See *Chronique de Jean, Évêque de Nikiou*, published in its Amharic version with a French translation by H. Zotenberg in 1883, p. 413 of the French translation. An English translation is also available, but some major discrepancies exist between the two versions. See R. H. Charles, *The Chronicle of John, Bishop of Nikiu* (Williams and Norgate, London: 1916), p. 55, for the founding of Babylon. While the fifteenth-century Arab topographer of Cairo, Taqi al-Dīn Aḥmad al-Maqrīzi, despaired of resolving the mystery of Babylon's origin, he favored the theory that it had been founded by the Persians under Nebuchadnezzar in the sixth century B.C. See Maqrīzi, *Al-Mawāʿiẓ wa al-Iʿtibār fi Dhikr al-Khiṭaṭ wa al-Āthār*, henceforth referred to simply as *Khiṭaṭ*, in two volumes (Būlāq Press Edition, Cairo: 1853), I, 296. Whatever the true origins of this first settlement, however, it is clear that by the time of the Romans little remained of either the original fortress or the community surrounding it.

position of Memphis assured continuity of settlement on the site. Thus, when the Greek geographer Strabo visited Egypt in 24 B.C., a few years after the Romans had conquered it, he found Memphis a thriving city, large and populous, ranking second only to Alexandria.[4] At Heliopolis he found only the ghost of a shrine city;[5] but, in the meantime, the settlement at Babylon had become more populous, since one of the three Roman legions guarding Egypt was encamped there on the defensible highlands overlooking the approaches to it and to Memphis across the river.[6] Had Strabo returned about a century later, he would also have observed the reopening of an ancient canal linking the Nile with the Red Sea and some new heavy fortifications on the site (later named by the Arabs and currently known as the Qaṣr al-Sham') contributed by Turbo[7] or even by Trajan himself.[8] A Greek contemporary of these developments was Ptolemy who, writing in the second century after the Roman conquest, described Babylon as a town surrounding the Roman fortress, through which passed the canal to the Red Sea. From his description, one gains the impression that there existed a fairly extensive settlement in Babylon at that time.[9]

3. Fortress of Trajan in Babylon

4. Fortress now far below ground level

Developments during the next few centuries are surprisingly shrouded from view. Following adoption of

[4] Jones, *Strabo*, VIII, 89.

[5] *Ibid.*, p. 79, where he relates that "the city is now entirely deserted." "In Heliopolis I also saw large houses in which the priests lived, for it is said that this place was in ancient times a settlement of priests who studied philosophy and astronomy, but both this organization and its pursuits have now disappeared," p. 83.

[6] The discrepancy between Strabo's account, which placed the fortress of the Persians on high land, and the known location of the later Roman fortress (still extant) at what was then the edge of the river, has led to an unresolved controversy concerning whether the latter could have been a reconstruction of the former or whether it was a new fortress on another site. Scholars writing early in the twentieth century were of the opinion that the Persian fortress had been located on al-Rashad hill, even though no remains of this building have ever been excavated there, and that Trajan's fortification was a new one relocated closer to the water. This is the interpretation of A. R. Guest and is accepted and amplified by Butler in his *Babylon of Egypt*, p. 87. This opinion is also accepted by a recent writer on the subject who, however, adds no new evidence to that of Butler. See Kenneth P. Kirkwood, *Preface to Cairo: A Survey of Pre-Cairo in History and Legend* (Mutual Press, Ltd., Ottawa: 1958), pp. 9-11, 28, 33-36. Butler claims that it was the new Roman fortress that was stormed by the Arabs during their conquest, the earlier Persian one having completely disappeared by that time. Edward Lane hypothesized that the Persian fortress, the "Ckusr Ba'beluyoo'n," as distinguished from the "Ckusr esh-Shem'ā," survived as the structure known in his time as the stable of "An'tar." See British Museum Manuscript No. 34,080, I, 196, which is Lane's handwritten manuscript, *Egypt*. This appears unlikely, however. On the other hand, Sidney Toy ("Babylon of Egypt," p. 54), citing only the Chronicle of John of Nikiu in his support, argues that Trajan's fortress was on the same site as the original Persian fortress observed by Strabo. Either explanation appears plausible, since a discrepancy between descriptions of the fort's position with respect to the water's edge could be explained easily by seasonal differences in flood stage. No true resolution of this controversy is likely unless earlier ruins are excavated.

[7] E. A. Wallis Budge, *Egypt* (Henry Holt & Company, New York: 1925), p. 242; and Clerget, *Le Caire*, I, 96.

[8] Alfred J. Butler, *The Arab Conquest of Egypt and the Last Thirty Years of the Roman Dominion* (The Clarendon Press, Oxford: 1902), p. 243. The evidence of John of Nikiu may be cited in this context. ". . . And Trajan came to Egypt and built a fortress with a strong impregnable tower . . . and he named it Babylon in Egypt. Nebuchadnezzar . . . was the first to build its foundations and to name it the fortress of Babylon. . . . And Trajan moreover added some buildings to the fortress and other parts in it." Quoted from the translated version of R. H. Charles, *The Chronicle of John*, p. 55.

[9] According to the *Master Plan of Cairo* (Government Printing Office, Cairo: 1956), p. 2, the testimony of Ptolemy can be used to substantiate the view that the Canal of Trajan *bisected* the city of Babylon, which would have made the latter an extremely large settlement indeed. However, a closer reading of the geographer's statement reveals that he merely noted that the canal flowed *through* the city; presumably it could have passed near its northernmost limit.

Christianity as the official religion of the Roman Empire came the mass conversion of Egypt's heterogeneous population. Babylon became the religious seat for a bishopric as well as an important defense fortification, but its economic base still remained—providing commercial and personal services to the Roman forces. Across the river on the western bank stood Memphis, much reduced in size and importance and, by then, subordinate to Jīzah,[10] which had the advantage of being in closer connection with the fortified island of Rawḍah and the armed camp at Babylon.

The opening decades of the seventh century saw Egypt an important battlefield. By 610, the forces of Emperor Heraclius held both ascendant Alexandria and declining Memphis, as well as Babylon—its protecting bulwark across the river. But fragmentation of the Empire had already occurred. Only a few years later, Egypt was wrested from Byzantium by the Persians who subdued Memphis in 617 and then consolidated their position by taking Alexandria. During the succeeding struggles, Heraclius recaptured Egypt in 629, only to lose it again, this time permanently, to the Arab invaders some eleven years later. These decades of strife, during which the environs of Babylon were a battlefield, undoubtedly drove much of the urban population out into the surrounding villages, leaving the city sadly deserted.

In 640 the Arab forces under 'Amr ibn al-'Āṣ reached the vicinity of contemporary Cairo. They encamped at the small settlement of Heliopolis, renaming it 'Ain Shams, an Arabic variation of the Greek term. To the southwest was a fortified port town called Tendunyas by the Romans (Umm Dunayn, but rechristened later by the Arabs as al-Maqs, meaning Customs House),[11] while still farther south lay the impregnable fortress of Babylon, or 'Alyūnah, according to the earliest Arab historians.[12] Gardens and monasteries were scattered on the plains between the fortress and the port on the north and between the fortress and the mountains to the east.[13] The

[10] Modern riverine Jīzah was founded in the fourth century, according to Clerget, *Le Caire*, I, 97. Pharaonic Jīzah (containing the pyramid of Cheops) was, of course, much farther west. It is presently four miles inland from today's narrower river channel.

[11] The Chronicle of John of Nikiou, as translated by Zotenberg, *Chronique de Jean*, p. 557, indicates that Tendunyas was a port, since 'Amr embarked from there, and that it also contained a contingent of Byzantine soldiers. Creswell states categorically that Tendunyas was Coptic for Umm Dunayn; see K.A.C. Creswell, *Early Muslim Architecture* (The Clarendon Press, Oxford: 1932), I, 27.

[12] The earliest Arab historians whose works have survived refer to the fortress of 'Alyūn (alternately 'Alyūnah), never to the fortress of Babylon. For example, see al-Ṭabari, *Ta'rīkh al-Rusul wa al-Mulūk* [Annals of the Apostles and Kings], in nine volumes (de Goeje edn., Leiden: 1877-1901); or al-Balādhuri, *Futūḥ al-Buldān* [The Conquest of Countries] (al-Mawsū'āt Press, Cairo: 1901), p. 220, where he says specifically that the area which later became known as Fusṭāṭ was then called 'Alyūnah. There is no doubt that Babylon and 'Alyūn were identical. The thirteenth-century Arab geographer, Yāqūt, in his geographical dictionary, *Mu'jam al-Buldān* (Beirut, 1957), used a cross reference to direct his reader from 'Alyūn to a later entry under Bāb 'alyūn; see I, 248, 311.

Alfred J. Butler, in his *The Treaty of Misr in Tabari* (The Clarendon Press, Oxford: 1913), says, "Bab al-Yun [sic] . . . is a mere blunder for Babylon," p. 21. If we recall Cortez's blunder in naming Yucatan, it is not difficult to hypothesize how the Babylon blunder may have arisen. Perhaps the Arabs approached the walled fortress, inquired after the name of the place, and were told that it was "Babylon." The Arabs assumed "The Gate of 'Alyūn" (since *bāb* is Arabic for a door or a gate in a wall), and hence assumed the name of the entire settlement to be 'Alyūn. There are certainly stranger occurrences in history.

[13] Maqrīzi, *Khiṭaṭ*, I, 286, describes the fortress of Babylon as surrounded by only gardens and monasteries at the time of the Arab conquest. As we have shown, Greek documents of an earlier period, of which he had no knowledge, demonstrate the existence of a town of Babylon in addition to the fortress. What had happened to that town during the interim? Either Maqrīzi's sources were incorrect or the settlement had declined by the time the Arabs arrived.

Another moot point in history is whether, at the time of the Arab conquest, there existed a town or city by the name of Miṣr in the immediate vicinity of Babylon on the eastern bank of the river. Among the historians who have subscribed to this view are: A. R. Guest, in an article, "The Foundation of Fustat and the Khittahs of that Town," *Journal of the Royal Asiatic Society* (January 1907), pp. 49-83, who Butler claims located this presumed city to the north of the Babylon fortress (although Guest does not actually state this view as his own); Butler, who argues, in his *The Arab Conquest* cited above, that this town must have been to the south and not to the north of the fortress; and Becker, in his article on "Cairo," in the *Encyclopedia of Islam*[1] (Luzac, London: 1913), I, 817, who accepts the existence of this community. The arguments use supporting evidence from a very small number of sources. Butler, for example, depends heavily on the Chronicle of John of Nikiu where, indeed, reference is made to the *city* of Miṣr. (See p. 180 of the English translation and p. 557 of the French.) However, it must be recalled that this often inaccurate and biased manuscript was originally written in a mixture of Coptic and Greek. It was then rendered in summary form into Arabic, after which the original copy was lost. Later, the Arabic paraphrasing was translated into Amharic and the Arabic version lost. The Ethiopian manuscript (two versions extant) was discovered in the seventeenth century. To depend exclusively upon a manuscript of such questionable accuracy seems foolhardy.

Butler also substantiates his position by evidence in the Treaty of Miṣr, reported by al-Ṭabari. In that document (a one-sided treaty since only the Arabs signed it), certain dispositions and terms were accorded the "people of Miṣr," but since Miṣr is also the name of the entire country of Egypt and the "people of Miṣr" are, in other contexts, merely the "Egyptians," this evidence alone is not conclusive proof that a city by that name existed then. In the Arabic versions of early historians (for example, al-Balādhuri, cited above), a distinction is made between Alexandria and Miṣr. In one translation of al-Balādhuri by Philip K. Hitti, *The Origins of the Islamic State* (Columbia University *Studies in History, Economics and Public Law*, Volume LXVIII, No. 163, New York: 1916), pp. 335-345, the term "Miṣr" is sometimes translated as "Egypt," and in other contexts

Byzantine stronghold of Babylon gave refuge to some of the frightened population which formerly lived outside the walls, while the rest presumably fled into the countryside. The defending army concentrated its forces within the Citadel of Babylon and in the complementary stronghold on the island of Rawḍah which was connected to the city during flood season by means of a floating bridge. Indeed, the chief of the defenders, al-Muqawqis (Patriarch of Alexandria), escaped from the landlocked fortress to the island as the invaders approached. The western bank of the Nile at that time was used primarily for agriculture, although an urban population lived in Jīzah and Memphis.

The seed from which the modern metropolis of Cairo sprang dates in reality from the time of the Arab conquest. The ancient historic significance of the site and the continuity of settlement from earliest times indicate that, whatever had been the course of history, some great city would have emerged in the general location. But modern Cairo is not merely "some" city; it is a unique city. The Arab conquest, while it did not interrupt the geographic continuity, created a marked break in the cultural continuity. Contemporary Cairo stands preeminently as a Muslim city, bearing neither the physical nor the cultural imprints of its pharaonic and Greco-Roman precursors.[14]

It was the conquering Arab general, 'Amr ibn al-'Āṣ, who also established the trend which for almost twelve centuries confined urban growth to the eastern bank of the Nile, a factor of lasting significance for contemporary Cairo. When he had subdued Egypt, 'Amr received instructions from the Caliph 'Umar to establish his headquarters in the country's interior and to protect his *land* lifeline to Arabia.[15] The strategic site of Cairo was his inevitable choice, both because of its central location and because of its position on the *eastern* bank of the Nile which assured access to Arabia by land and, later, by water as well, through the old Red Sea Canal which 'Amr reopened in 643. This preference for the eastern bank sealed forever the doom of Memphis and, until the present century, led to greater and greater concentration on that bank.

While successive and expanding settlements proliferated on the eastern side of the river, the area on the western bank stagnated, developing little beyond the few villages of Imbābah, Duqqi, and Jīzah which had existed before the time of 'Amr. It was not until numerous natural and man-made transformations had occurred—including the recession of the Nile into its present narrower channel, the increased control over the floods which annually covered much of the riverine plain, the construction of a ladder of connecting bridges linking the two shores, and, most recently, a pressing

is retained in its original form, which leads the reader to assume the separate existence of a city called Miṣr. It is difficult, however, to distinguish between the two (if there *are* two) uses of the term in the original manuscript, and there is nothing in the text to indicate the existence of a city of Miṣr comparable to the city of Alexandria. An alternative explanation, supported by the sources, would be that the people of Miṣr were all of the indigenous residents of the central portion of Egypt who were administered separately from the Greek and Roman populations which resided chiefly in Alexandria. Miṣr, then, might have referred at that time both to the ethnic classification of native Egyptians and to the region in which they resided, namely, from the Delta outside the walls of Alexandria southward beyond Memphis and Babylon. In fact, Butler himself, in *The Arab Conquest*, p. 221, undermines his own position by acknowledging that Memphis was sometimes called Miṣr and Stanley Lane-Poole, in *The Story of Cairo* (J. M. Dent & Sons, Ltd., London: 1902), p. 34, suggests that all the sprawling settlements from Memphis northwards and on both sides of the river were considered by the people as a unit.

The Latin documents on Roman administration in Egypt may hold the key to the usage of the term "Miṣr." Highly suggestive is the material presented in Prince Omar Toussoun, *La géographie de l'Égypte à l'époque Arabe*, which is Volume VIII of the *Mémoires de la Société Royale de Géographie d'Égypte* (Imprimerie de l'Institut Français d'Archéologie Orientale, Cairo: 1926). His description of Egypt prior to the Arab invasion has been taken from the account of Georges de Chypres, a Byzantine geographer who wrote a general description of the Roman Empire at the beginning of the seventh century. Fragments of this document have been preserved, and there is an edition by Heinrich Gelzer, *Georgii Cyprii, Descriptio Orbis Romani* (Bibliotheca Scriptorum Graecorum et Romanorum Teubneriana, Lipsiae: 1890), which is cited by Prince Toussoun. According to this, Lower Egypt under the Roman administration just prior to the Arab conquest was divided into two major parts, Éparchie Augustamnique and Éparchie d'Égypte (or Miṣr). While Toussoun hypothesizes that Éparchie d'Égypte was the western half of the Delta, I believe that it may have been the eastern half, which would have included Babylon. Further investigation is certainly warranted.

While a complete weighing of the evidence is beyond the scope or requirements of the present study, I would like to suggest that, at the time of the Arab conquest, there was no important settlement on the *eastern* bank of the river in the vicinity of the Babylon fortress which was known by the name Miṣr. The term "Babylon in Miṣr" (Egypt) was used merely to differentiate it from the original Babylon, *not* to locate it within a "city of Miṣr." This position agrees with that taken by A. J. Wensinck, in his article, "Miṣr," *Encyclopedia of Islam*[1], III, 520-521. The term "Miṣr," referring to a later settlement on the site, Fusṭāṭ, came into use several centuries *after* the Arab conquest, as is shown below.

[14] Le Tourneau notes a similar discontinuity between Islamic and pre-Islamic communities in North Africa as well, indicating that Cairo was hardly a unique case. See Roger Le Tourneau, *Les villes musulmanes de l'Afrique du Nord* (La Maison des Livres, Algiers: 1957), pp. 9-11.

[15] This injunction is reported by a ninth-century Arab geographer, Ya'qūbi. See his *Kitāb al-Buldān* (de Goeje edn., Leiden: 1892), I, 331, or the French translation by G. Wiet, *Livre de les pays* (Cairo, 1937), p. 185. The same account is repeated by Maqrīzi, *Khiṭāṭ*, I, 296. An English rendering of the story appears in Lane-Poole, *The Story of Cairo*, p. 40.

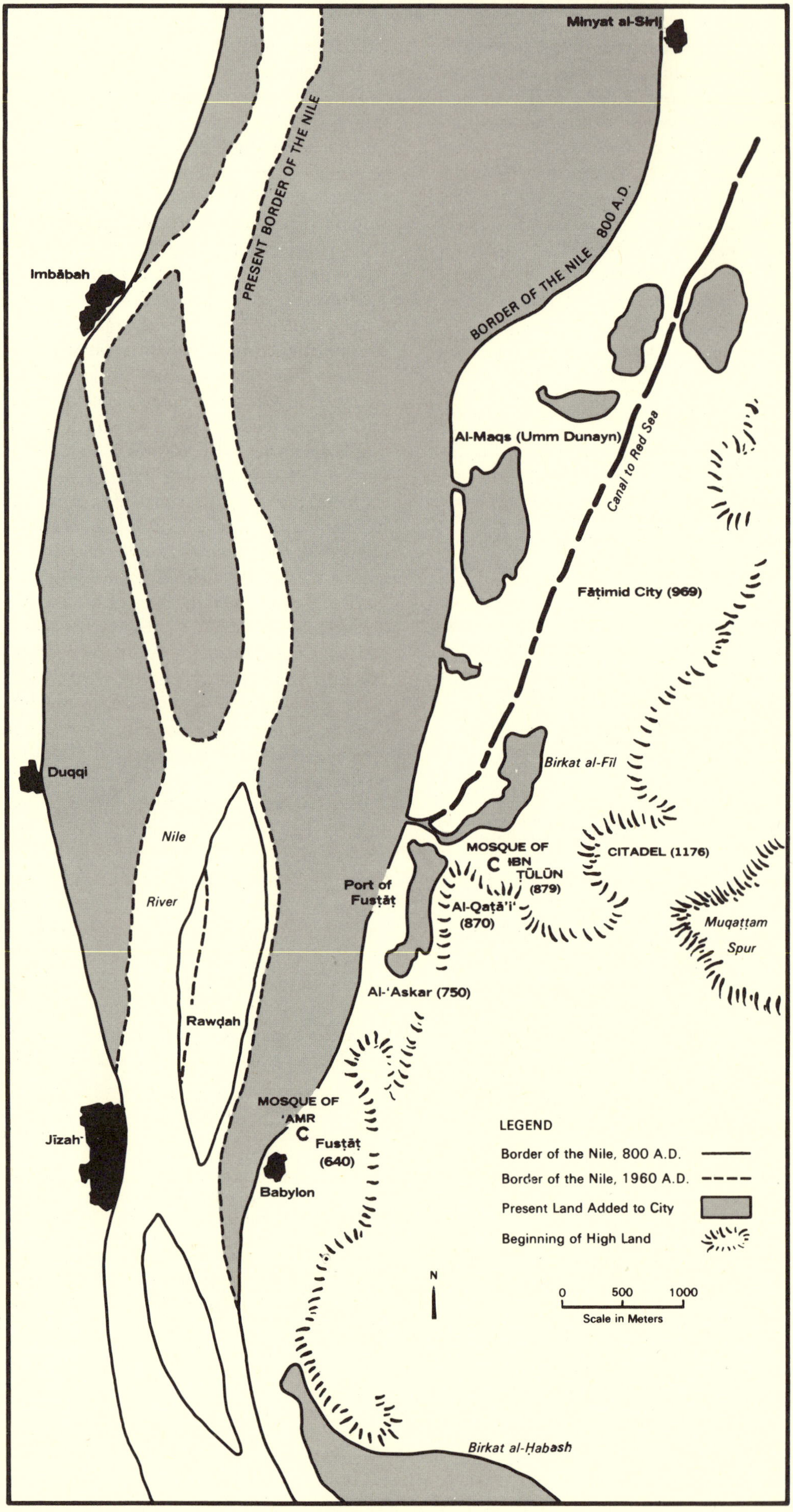

I. The Cairo area showing the location of major settlements and the land added through shifts in the channel of the Nile since A.D. 800

demand for new urban space—that a parallel growth on the western bank created what is now a true metropolitan region spanning the river. To understand how the Nile formerly constituted the insurmountable barrier which it no longer presents, a brief description of the regional terrain and of the changes in the course of that river is essential.

The Nile valley at Cairo is relatively narrow, but its usable width was once even narrower. Unchanged through the centuries are the two low mountain ridges whose sudden escarpments fix the boundary of the valley bed. The ridge which divides valley from desert on the western extremity follows a relatively smooth course, on a line even with the locations of the ancient pyramids of Jīzah and Saqqara. While a fairly wide alluvial plain presently stretches between these higher lands and the now-stable banks of the river several miles to the east, much of this plain had but a periodic existence in the past. In pharaonic times, the granite used for many of Memphis' monuments was floated down the Nile from the quarries of Aswān during the flood season, when the river's swelling brought water to the gates of the city. During the dry season, receding waters left a wide strip of rich river-bed land which was cultivated until the next flood.

On the eastern side of the river the width of this flood plain was not nearly so generous in earlier times, nor is the ridge dividing valley from desert so even and simply formed. Rather, the break between the two is achieved through a series of southeast to northwest projections. Instead of following a due north-south direction parallel to the present course of the river, the ridges take a southwest to northeast direction. What remains is a cone-shaped valley, narrowest at the southern extremity and becoming increasingly broader to the north, blending finally with the larger Delta. The apex of that inverted pyramid, where the low steps of the mountain projections approach the river, was the site of ancient Babylon, whose strategic position noted earlier now becomes clarified by topography. As was the case on the Memphis side of the river, during early times the river flowed up to the foothills during the flood season, inundating the valley land. But, unlike the fortunate state at Memphis, not all the present land was revealed when the water receded. Much of it lay permanently beneath the wider channel of the Nile. At the time of ʿAmr, only a relatively small alluvial plain existed on the eastern bank of the Nile.

Most of contemporary Cairo is built on land which lay either permanently or periodically submerged under the river in the seventh century. Map I, adapted from Haswell,[16] shows the land which has been added to Cairo since 800. As early as the tenth century, natural silting began to build up the land below water level. Later, diversion of flood waters, at first through a system of canals and ponds and later by complex dam storage upstream, finally permitted the emergence of much of the land on which modern Cairo stands. Map II, adapted from Haswell[17] and Clerget,[18] summarizes the topological and riverine features which underlie the natural history of Cairo.

The growth and expansion of the city of Cairo from the first small nucleus at Babylon to the sprawling giant of today can be understood only by tracing the interplay between socio-political and physical developments since the time of ʿAmr in the seventh century. Indeed, the ecological organization of the contemporary city appears confused and utterly capricious to an observer who fails to understand its previous natural and cultural history.

[16] C.J.R. Haswell, "Cairo, Origin and Development. Some Notes on the Influence of the River Nile and its Changes," *Bulletin de la Société Royale de Géographie d'Égypte*, Tome XI, Nos. 3 & 4 (December 1922), pp. 171-176; four plates, of which Plate II is particularly helpful. Mr. Haswell was for years the British Director-General of the *Tanẓīm* department.

[17] *Ibid.*, Plates II and IV.

[18] Clerget, *Le Caire*, I, 46.

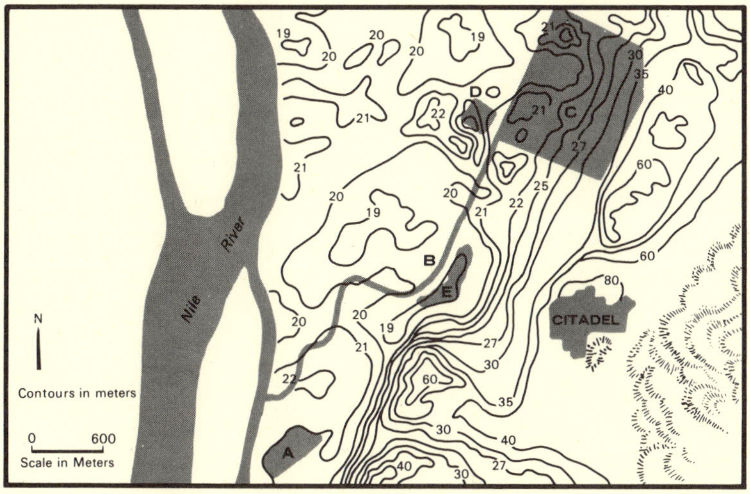

Landmarks:

A. Fusṭāṭ
B. Khalīj Miṣri
C. Fāṭimid al-Qāhirah
D. Birkat Azbakīyah
E. Birkat al-Fīl

II. Contour map of southern and central Cairo superimposed on historic landmarks

PART I · THE ISLAMIC CITY

5. Potters' quarter on buried ruins of Fusṭāṭ. Minaret is Mosque of 'Amr

6. Roofscape inside Babylon-Fusṭāṭ

2 The Legacy of the First Arab Settlements
640-1170

During the seven months that the Arab invaders under 'Amr besieged the Byzantine fortress at Babylon, they pitched their tents on the high dusty plain above riverine Babylon. Once capitulation was achieved, the troops were arranged somewhat more formally. Northeast of the fortress (renamed Qaṣr al-Sham' by the Arabs) at the firm bank of the Nile, 'Amr erected the first mosque in Africa. With the mosque at its core, flanked by the commercial markets which usually accompanied the central mosque in Islamic cities, a quasi-permanent army camp was established. It formed an elongated semicircle stretching as far north as the mouth of the Red Sea Canal and as far south as the inland lake, the Birkat al-Ḥabash.[1]

This was hardly a unique Arab settlement. Indeed, throughout the conquered territories, Arabs set up similar encampments, to which they gave the name *fusṭāṭ* (from the Latin *fossātum*, or the Byzantine Greek *φόσσατον*, meaning simply entrenchment).[2] Always located at the edge of the desert, each had a similar plan of widely scattered nuclei. The *raison d'être* of this physical design can only be understood in terms of the social characteristics of the founders. The Arab army consisted of diverse and often incompatible tribes and ethnic groups, was accompanied by a straggling retinue of women, children, and slaves, and was composed of men whose past nomadic life made close quarters repellent. Such an army was not likely to set up a permanent city of the Hellenic or Roman bastide type. The city of Fusṭāṭ, established by 'Amr around the Babylon fortress,[3] was originally, as Clerget has aptly described it, a "centre mi-sédentaire, mi-nomade, grand campement à proximité du désert. . . . Une sorte de ville en formation."[4]

At first, segregation was rigid, with each ethnic group or tribe assigned its own isolated quarter. However, during the sixty years following the conquest, as the temporary camp was transformed into a permanent commercial as well as military settlement, there was both a retrenchment toward the central nucleus at the Mosque of 'Amr and its radiating markets, and a filling in of the spaces purposely left open by the original plan. The ultimate result was a fairly compact town of a permanent nature, having little relation except in name to the army camp which had been its progenitor. An economic depression had also contributed to the physical retrenchment but, with the restoration of prosperity in the eighth century, Fusṭāṭ embarked on a new expansion in all directions: eastward to the higher land, westward to the new land left by an even-then receding Nile, southward to the banks of Birkat al-Ḥabash—deserted during the period of retrenchment but newly rebuilt—and, less markedly, northward to the vicinity of the more and more neglected canal. By mid-century, the time of its first major dynastic shift marked by the 'Abbāsid victory over the Umayyads, Fusṭāṭ was a somewhat provincial

[1] A. R. Guest has done a remarkable job of scholarship in reconstructing this early settlement. See his "The Foundation of Fustat and the Khittahs of that Town," *Journal of the Royal Asiatic Society* (January 1907), pp. 49-83. The article includes a valuable map, which has been reproduced in Carl Becker, "Cairo," *Encyclopedia of Islam*[1] (1913). Guest points to the basic similarities among Fusṭāṭ, Baṣrah, and Kūfah, each "a long straggling colony of mean houses and hovels . . . arranged irregularly in groups of loose order . . . ," p. 82. Each was also a *miṣr*.

[2] See K.A.C. Creswell, *Early Muslim Architecture* (The Clarendon Press, Oxford: 1932), I, 29, particularly note 7 on etymology. This derivation is also noted by Philip K. Hitti, *History of the Arabs* (The Macmillan Company, New York: 5th edn., 1951), p. 165, note 2; and by Xavier de Planhol, *The World of Islam* (Cornell University Press, Ithaca: 1959), p. 3. Historians of Cairo, such as Lane-Poole and Marcel Clerget, have translated Fusṭāṭ as "tents," without recognizing the military implications of the term. In this they have undoubtedly followed Maqrīzī's interpretation, as explained in *Khiṭaṭ* (Būlāq Press, Cairo: 1853), I, 285.

[3] As we have seen, Fusṭāṭ was a generic term referring to any army encampment. While eventually the name replaced Babylon or 'Alyūn, the distinction was retained in the papyri until the end of the seventh century. Becker suggests that the early distinction was probably more administrative than geographic. The name "Babylon" fell out of use among the Arabs soon afterward, but was retained throughout the Middle Ages by the Copts who sometimes used it with reference to all the settlements stretching between the fortress and Heliopolis. The term "Babylon" was also used in Latin manuscripts, in trade agreements with Europe, and in European literature by, among others, Mandeville and Boccaccio. See Becker, "Bābalyūn," in the new *Encyclopedia of Islam*[2] (Luzac, London: 1958), I, 844-845. European travel documents throughout the Middle Ages continue to refer to Babylon which, after the establishment of al-Qāhirah in the late tenth century, was used as the ordinary term for Miṣr al-Qadīmah, i.e., Old Fusṭāṭ. Some of these usages are supported by documents translated and incorporated into an article by P. Hermann Dopp, "Le Caire: Vu par les voyageurs occidentaux du Moyen Âge," *Bulletin de la Société Royale de Géographie d'Égypte*, XXIII (June 1950), 117-149, which deals with travelers to Cairo before the fifteenth century. In a fifteenth-century manuscript by a Venetian trader, a similar distinction is made between Babylon and Cairo. See P. Hermann Dopp, ed., *L'Égypte au commencement du quinzième siècle d'après le traité d'Emmanuel Piloti de Crète (Incipit 1420)* (Fuad 1st University, Cairo: 1950), pp. 11, 20, 26, 31, 38, for examples of this usage.

[4] Clerget, *Le Caire*, I, 106. See pp. 107-113 for the later evolution of this community.

but nevertheless important city serving both administrative and commercial functions. It continued in these functions until much later, even after the founding of new suburban communities by the succeeding 'Abbāsid, Ṭūlūnid, and Fāṭimid dynasties.

The new towns of Islam have been classified into two main types: army camps which eventually developed into permanent cities; and princely towns founded to "mark the birth of dynasties and to affirm their authority."[5] The city of Fusṭāṭ, which evolved from a coalescence of the army camp of 'Amr with the preexisting nucleus of Babylon, is an excellent example of the first type. Al-'Askar, founded by the triumphant 'Abbāsids in 750, al-Qaṭā'i', founded by the overambitious Aḥmad ibn Ṭūlūn in 870, and finally, al-Qāhirah (Cairo) herself, founded by the new Fāṭimid dynasty in 969, are all examples of the second type. While the former tend to be relatively unplanned, meager in public amenities and unembellished aesthetically, the latter, intended as symbols of status and display, are both well planned and handsomely constructed. By definition, however, a princely city remains somewhat outside the mainstream of economic vitality of a region, being a center of conspicuous consumption rather than one of trade and production. It was this very characteristic that permitted Fusṭāṭ to remain the commercial capital of Egypt, despite the series of princely cities developed on her northern border.

An internal struggle between the Umayyads and the 'Abbāsids for supremacy within the Islamic empire led to the first major discontinuity in the structure of Fusṭāṭ since 'Amr had given her life. The final scene of 'Abbāsid victory, in fact, was played out on the site of Fusṭāṭ, to which the Umayyad Caliph, Marwān II, had fled in hopes of eluding his pursuers. In the struggle, a large portion of Fusṭāṭ was burned, but this scorched-earth tactic did not prevent Marwān from being apprehended and beheaded. For the Islamic world outside of Spain this marked the end of Umayyad power and meant the removal of the seat of the Caliphate from Syria to Iraq where it later flowered in the new capital of Baghdad. For the smaller world of Egypt it meant the displacement of the governmental functions of the region to a newly built suburb just north of Fusṭāṭ, called al-'Askar (the Cantonment).[6]

A prototype of a princely town, al-'Askar was planned as a permanent settlement whose core was the official residence, the Dār al-Imārah, together with the central mosque around which the markets were concentrated. Surrounding this typical nucleus were the luxurious residences of members of the court and the various regiments whose double responsibility it was to defend the administrative suburb from popular uprisings and to repel any attack on Fusṭāṭ from the ridges above it. During the century or more which followed, the two communities fused so that the combined settlements of Fusṭāṭ and al-'Askar stretched in attenuated fashion along the axis of the Nile, occupying both the low riverine plain and the crest of foothills to its east and north.

The century which witnessed growing conurbation in the Fusṭāṭ region, however, also witnessed a growing decadence in the 'Abbāsid empire, a succession of governors of Egypt who remained for brief albeit profitable stays, and—the factor which led ultimately to the building of one of the grandest princely towns—a growing independence of parts of the far-flung and only loosely controlled empire. It was during this period of increased provincial autonomy and proliferation of feudalistic princedoms within the empire that Aḥmad ibn Ṭūlūn, of Turkish descent but raised in the Mesopotamian princely city of Sāmarra, came to al-'Askar as deputy for the governor of Egypt. Inspired perhaps by the luxurious court from which he had come, and aided immeasurably by the temporary autonomy bequeathed him by a fragmenting empire, he founded his own princely city in 870, two years after his arrival. Located on the higher land east and slightly north of al-'Askar, this community was called al-Qaṭā'i' (the Wards), reflecting its feudal base.

The pleasure city of al-Qaṭā'i' was, to that date, both the finest planned addition to Fusṭāṭ and yet the addition most isolated from the region's economic life which still centered in Fusṭāṭ. Set on the dry hills of Yashkur, overlooking not the Nile but the Birkat al-Fīl in the flood plain due north of the settlement, al-Qaṭā'i' represented a final thrust away from the promise and punishment of the river. In fact, so independent of that stream was it that fresh water was supplied from across the southern desert by an aqueduct which carried it from its intake tower at the Birkat al-Ḥabash all the way to the suburb,

[5] De Planhol, *The World of Islam*, p. 4.

[6] There is general unanimity concerning the violence of the struggle between the 'Abbāsids and the Umayyads and about the burning of a portion of Fusṭāṭ during the conflict. It is difficult to reconcile these facts with the version recounted by Clerget, *Le Caire*, who traces the foundation of al-'Askar to ". . . the accidental founding in 748 of a kind of small twin city by the 'Abbāsid generals, launched at the behest of the last Umayyad Caliph. The newcomers, rather than camp their army at Fusṭāṭ where the indigenous population had become predominant and where a fire, moreover, had destroyed a part of the buildings, preferred the neighborhood of Yashkur. . . ." (Translation from I, 113.) J. Jomier, in his article on "Fusṭāṭ," *Encyclopedia of Islam*², II, is more accurate in dating the flight of Marwān II and the fire in 750, and in dating the construction of al-'Askar after 751. Additional information on the town is found in Maqrīzi, *Khiṭaṭ*, I, 286; Becker, "Cairo," p. 817; Lane-Poole, *The Story of Cairo*, p. 65.

7. Aerial view of Mosque of Ibn Ṭūlūn, now surrounded by city

a considerable distance away.[7] While scholars have sought tortuous rationalizations for Aḥmad ibn Ṭūlūn's site selection, a glance at Map I reveals that, incommodious as its location may have been, it was a logical extension of the existing settlements, since many of the changes in the form of the land had not yet occurred. At the heart of this city were the palaces of the ruler and his deputies, central *maydān*s (open spaces) for sports and tournaments, and the awesome Mosque of Ibn Ṭūlūn, begun in 876 and finally completed in 878. Surrounding this area were the rectangular feudal fiefs granted to various groups of supporters. While al-Qaṭā'i' attracted to itself the markets for luxury consumer goods, the bulk of economic activity remained in Fusṭāṭ where a profusion of goods flowed in and out of the port, where production remained concentrated, and where the mercantile class ruled a commercial world quite removed from the aesthetic and sybaritic preoccupations of the princely city.

[7] Lane-Poole, *The Story of Cairo*, p. 72; Clerget, *Le Caire*, I, 115; Maqrīzi, *Khiṭaṭ*, I, 286. Ibn Ṭūlūn's intake tower has been located at Basātīn and its route to al-Qaṭā'i' traced by K.A.C. Creswell. See his *Early Muslim Architecture* (The Clarendon Press, Oxford: 1940), II, 331. These discoveries invalidate Lane-Poole's contention that the aqueduct delivered spring water.

8. Interior court and minaret of the Mosque of Ibn Ṭūlūn

The four successors of Ibn Ṭūlūn further embellished the family crown jewel of al-Qaṭā'i' but, during the brief reign of the last successor, Ibn Ṭūlūn's son Shaybān, the splinter state founded only a third of a century earlier reverted to 'Abbāsid control. To avenge the indignity which the Ṭūlūnid's abortive independence had inflicted, 'Abbāsid troops destroyed al-Qaṭā'i' in 905. Only that vast square courtyard surrounded by gracefully arched porticos—the Mosque of Ibn Ṭūlūn—still survives to mark the site of the dead city. Once again, the 'Abbāsids resumed their rule from the Dār al-Imārah in al-'Askar[8] which by this time had so merged with Fusṭāṭ that even the name had been dropped, the entire city again being identified simply as Fusṭāṭ.

At the same time the 'Abbāsids were reasserting their hold over Egypt and her principal city, Fusṭāṭ, the movement that was destined eventually to overthrow them in that region and to establish Cairo not merely as the largest city in Egypt but as one of the great cities of Islam had already begun. By 909-910 in Tunisia, Sa'īd ibn Ḥusayn ('Ubaydullah al-Mahdi) had established the Shi'ite Fāṭimid Caliphate that was to reach its fullest expression on Egyptian soil. Abortive attempts were made in 914 and again in 921 to press eastward to Egypt, but it was not until 969 that the movement gathered enough momentum to permit the conquest of Egypt. By then, the Ikhshīdis were in power at Fusṭāṭ which had become a bustling commercial metropolis.[9] At the head

[8] Maqrīzi, *Khiṭaṭ*, I, 286.

[9] It may have been at this time that the term "Miṣr" began to be applied to the settlement of Fusṭāṭ together with its offshore island of Rawḍah. Although Clerget suggests that this usage dates from the time of Ibn Ṭūlūn (*Le Caire*, I, 115), we have no evidence that the term "Miṣr" was used as a substitute for Fusṭāṭ before the end of the ninth century, and its usual application to Fusṭāṭ may date even later. My argument rests on the following evidence. In 889, Ya'qūbi wrote his *Book of the Countries*, a detailed geographic account of the regions of the Arab domain. He notes that "the districts of Egypt bear the name of their chief towns" and that one of the chief towns is Fostât sometimes called Babylon . . . [which is] also known by the name of Kasr." This translation is from Gaston Wiet, *Livre de les pays* (Cairo: 1937), pp. 184, 185. If Fusṭāṭ had also been called Miṣr at that time, presumably Ya'qūbi would have included this among the alternate names provided. However, in another work by the same author, his *Ta'rīkh*, the term "Miṣr" appears in infrequent contexts to mean the metropolitan area of Fusṭāṭ, rather than the country. See, for example, Ya'qūbi, *Historiae*, ed. T. Houtsma (Leiden, 1883), II, 402, 567, 600, 623. We have already seen that a contemporary of Ya'qūbi, al-Balādhuri, writing in the late ninth century, equated 'Alyūn with Fusṭāṭ but used the term "Miṣr" to refer to the larger region. See his *Futūḥ al-Buldān* (Cairo, 1902). This also tends to be the usage employed by a somewhat later writer, Mas'ūdi, who described the Egypt he knew during his visit in 941. In Mas'ūdi's epic work, *Les prairies d'or* (Arabic text edited and translated into French by C. Barbier de Meynard and Pavet de Courteille, published by the Société Asiatique, l'Imprimerie Nationale, Paris: 1861-1917), "Miṣr" is occasionally used as a possible substitute for the Fusṭāṭ region. In this work the confusion between Miṣr as the name of a country and Miṣr as the name of a district or city, which plagues even contemporary usage, remains compounded. In most contexts, when Mas'ūdi uses the term "Miṣr," he refers to the country of Egypt (see for example II, 360, 361, 366, 367, where Fusṭāṭ as a city is used in contradistinction to the country of Miṣr). However, there are at least three contexts in which the term "Miṣr" seems to refer to a city which included both Fusṭāṭ and the island of Rawḍah (Jazīrat al-Ṣinā'ah). For example, in II, 364-365, he describes the festivities on the night of the *ghatas*, using alternately the terms "Fusṭāṭ and Jazīrat al-Ṣinā'ah," and "Miṣr," and observing that none of the gates of the *durūb* are closed during that night. Gates were found only in cities. This, however, is far from conclusive proof that Miṣr was the common term for Fusṭāṭ. Another context appears in II, 406, when the name Miṣr is coupled with other towns, Ḥoms, Ma'rrah, and Antioch, as an equal. A third use of Miṣr as a city rather than a district or a country is found in V, 204-205, where he says "Marwān led his Zubayrite soldiers from Syria to Miṣr which he besieged and around which he dug trenches in the area adjacent to the cemetery; over them was Ibn Zubayr ibn Ḥajdam, and the leader and the master then of Fusṭāṭ was Abū-Rushd . . . al-Ṣabbāḥ." (Translated from the Arabic version.) Presumably only a city can be besieged. The conclusion from the above is that, as early as Ya'qūbi and certainly by the time of Mas'ūdi, the term "Miṣr" was in occasional use for the area of Fusṭāṭ; its application, however, was still fragmentary and without uniform meaning. Less than half a century after Mas'ūdi, the term "Miṣr" was a complete substitute for Fusṭāṭ, and is used by all later writers describing the community, as will be seen below. Between the time of Mas'ūdi (whose use of Miṣr is fragmentary) and 985, when al-Muqaddasi wrote his *Aḥsan al-Taqāsīm fi Ma'rifat al-Aqālīm*, which included a geographic description of Egypt and its cities, the term "Miṣr" had evolved into a popular substitute for the term "Fusṭāṭ," which evidently was falling out of use although still mentioned. It is in this work that a specific identity between the two terms appears. Note the following quotations translated from the Arabic text edited by de Goeje (E. J. Brill, Leiden: 2nd edn., 1906/1909). "The Miṣr region [i.e., Egypt] is divided into seven provinces, six of which are inhabited and have extensive developments [cities] and a beautiful countryside (p. 193). . . . [among the provinces he lists] Maqdūnya, whose central town [*qaṣabah*] is Fusṭāṭ which is al-Miṣr, and whose cities include al-'Azīzīyah [Memphis], al-Jīzah and 'Ain Shams [Heliopolis]" (p. 194). Elsewhere he says: "Al-Fusṭāṭ is Miṣr according to every authority because it includes the central ministries and the *Amīr al-Mu'minīn* [the Caliph]. . . . the region flourished and its name became famous and esteemed and therefore it had become Miṣr Miṣr, that which surpassed Baghdad, the pride of Islam, the market of mankind" (p. 197). It would not be unreasonable to connect this new usage with the founding in 969 of the new city of al-Qāhirah which had to be distinguished from the true metropolis, Fusṭāṭ—hence the term "Miṣr."

The position I have taken here is in contradiction to that subscribed to by, among others, A. J. Wensinck, in his article "Miṣr," *Encyclopedia of Islam*[1] (1913), III. Wensinck claims that "In the period between the Arab conquest and the foundation of Cairo the name Miṣr is *regularly* applied to the city just mentioned [southwest of later Cairo]. . . . After the conquest of Egypt by the Muslims there were two settlements only on the right bank of the Nile . . . *viz.* Babylon and Fusṭāṭ. The papyri

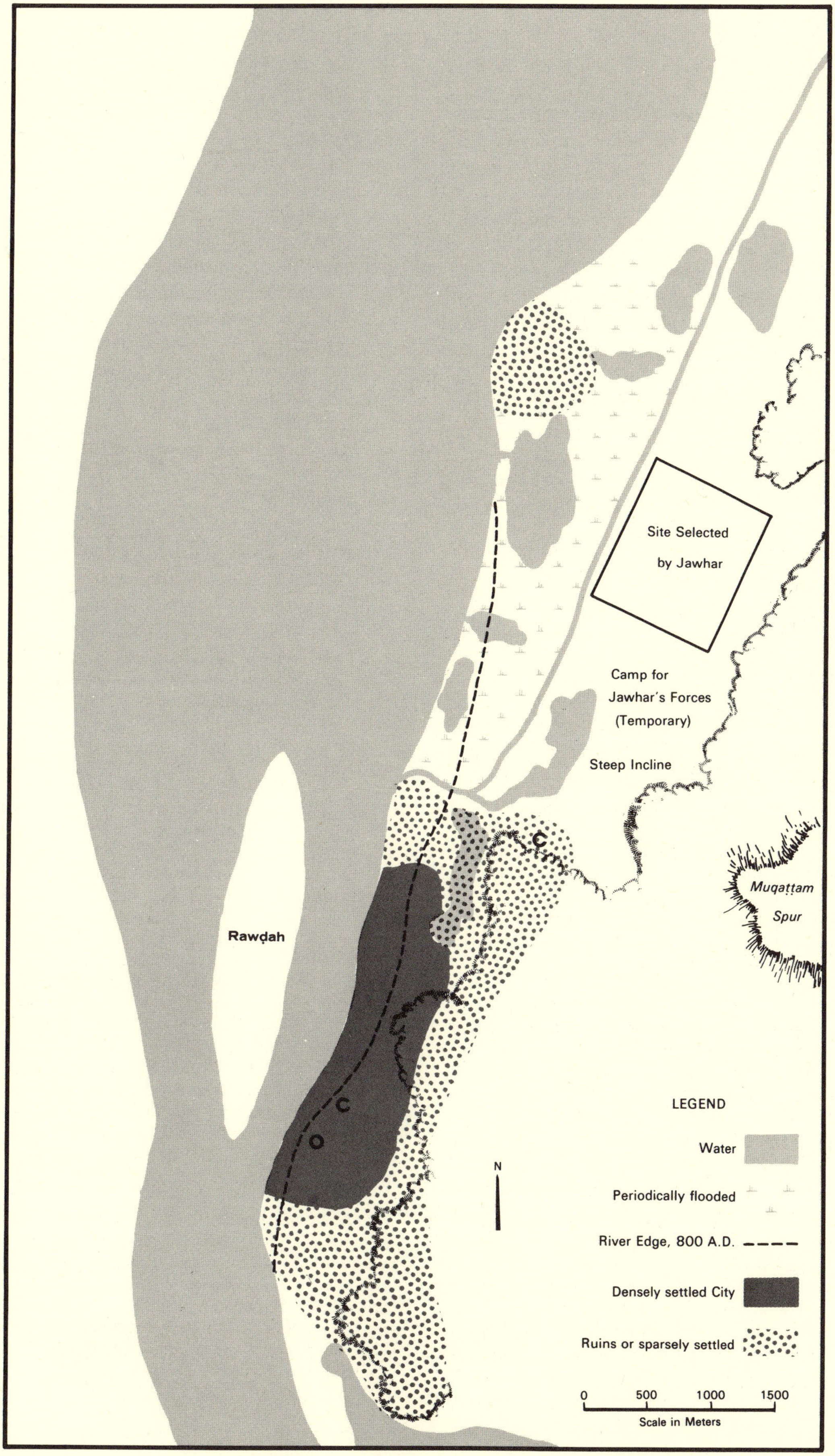

III. The site of Cairo and its development at the time of the Fāṭimid invasion and the founding of al-Qāhirah

of the Fāṭimid dynasty was its fourth Caliph, Mu'izz al-Dīn, who had selected to lead his forces for the Egyptian campaign a brilliant general and administrator, one Jawhar by name.[10]

The discontent of Fusṭāṭ's population with the arbitrary rule of the Ikhshīdis was so great that, once Jawhar had defeated the defending forces in a token battle at Jīzah in July of 969, the populace stood idly but curiously by as his troops crossed the river without difficulty and established their control over the capital. Leading his triumphant army through the city, Jawhar sought open land on which to quarter his troops. According to at least one account, he carried with him precise plans for the construction of a new princely city which Mu'izz envisaged as the seat of his Mediterranean empire and as a fitting rival to Baghdad.[11] Mu'izz entrusted to his general the selection of its site in the vicinity of Fusṭāṭ.

In order to visualize the paucity of alternatives open to Jawhar in executing this plan, one must reconstruct the geography of the Cairo area as it had evolved up to that time. Map III shows the riverine lands which had been ceded by the Nile between the beginning of the ninth century and the end of the tenth, the probable land uses of the occupied terrain, and the configuration of the vacant land near Fusṭāṭ.[12] If indeed Jawhar had to impose on the fragmented region his preexisting rigid plan with predetermined dimensions, he located his new city in the *only* space available to him.

Almost immediately after his arrival, Jawhar began to stake out the walls which were to enclose the new rectangular palace city, al-Manṣūrīyah. Four years later the city was renamed al-Qāhirah (The Victorious) al-Mu'izzīyah, to commemorate and celebrate the arrival of Mu'izz and, some say, to propitiate Mars, whose planet had been in the ascendant when the signal for groundbreaking was erroneously given.[13] Construction for troops was completed by 971, with blocks allocated to various categories of mercenaries, i.e., Greeks, Armenians, Berbers, Kurds, Turks, and Blacks, and the army was transferred from its temporary encampment near the Birkat al-Fīl to permanent quarters within the new city.[14] The

---

never mention Miṣr as the name of either of these settlements. Yet in the latter part of the seventh century A.D. the application of the name Miṣr to one or the other or to both must have begun, as is attested by John of Nikiu . . ." (pp. 520-521, italics added). As demonstrated above, the application of the term "Miṣr" to pre-Qāhirah settlements was not regular at all. Only the document of John of Nikiu, then, can be cited in evidence of this position, and I have already discussed the dubious reliability of this document (Chapter I, note 13).

[10] A brief account of the origins of this dynasty and its designs on Egypt may be found in Carl Brockelmann's *History of the Islamic Peoples* (Capricorn Books, New York: 1960), especially pp. 158-160. The origins and identity of Jawhar have been shrouded in mystery and subject to continuing controversy. Although it was formerly believed that he was a converted Christian slave from either Greece or Sicily (his name is Jawhar, the Sicilian), the most current opinion is that he was of Slavic origin, the freed son of a converted slave. This recent research has been incorporated in H. Monés, "Djawhar," *Encyclopedia of Islam*², II, pp. 494-495.

[11] Clerget, *Le Caire*, I, 123. It is Clerget's contention that Mu'izz himself had designed the proposed city. While it is impossible either to confirm or refute this hypothesis, the original plans as reconstructed by Ravaisse (reproduced as Figure 28 opposite p. 128 in Volume I of Clerget, and as Plate II in Haswell, "Cairo, Origin and Development") reveal a Hellenistic or Roman bastide symmetry of right angles and a central dominance *not* of the mosque, which would have been more typical of the Islamic genre, but of the palace. This deviation appears significant.

Although the authors of the *Cairo Master Plan* (Government Printing Office, Cairo: 1956) suggest that there was a striking resemblance between the city planned by Mu'izz and the Roman town of Timgad in North Africa, I have examined the latter, an aerial view of which is reproduced as Plate II in Arthur Korn's *History Builds the Town* (Lund Humphries, London: 1953), and find little similarity to the Fāṭimid plan. Professor Roger Le Tourneau has suggested to me that the prototype for al-Qāhirah might have been the Fāṭimid town of Mahdīyah. While the resemblance is greater in this instance, the fact that the latter city is located on a neck of land protected on three sides by water meant that the plan could not have been adapted easily to the landlocked site of al-Qāhirah, although the moats constructed outside the walls at Cairo may have represented an attempt to reproduce the defensive strength of Mahdīyah.

[12] This map compiles data formerly available in scattered sources. The base map follows Haswell, "Cairo, Origin and Development," Plate II. The river border in the Fāṭimid period was transcribed from Figure 27 opposite p. 119 in Clerget, *Le Caire*, I. Land use and the general extent of the city of Fusṭāṭ at that time have been estimated from the numerous verbal descriptions of site development that have served as general sources.

[13] The usual story associated with the change in Cairo's name is a mythical one, namely, that a crow accidentally tugged the string which the astrologers had devised to signal the most propitious moment for breaking ground. The change in nomenclature to al-Qāhirah was supposed to have been made immediately afterward for the reason given above. This myth has been accepted and repeated by practically all writers who have discussed the founding of al-Qāhirah, including Maqrīzi. However, K.A.C. Creswell, in his *The Muslim Architecture of Egypt: Ikhshīds and Fāṭimids, A.D. 939-1171* (The Clarendon Press, Oxford: 1952), has raised a legitimate objection to the authenticity of this account by pointing out that "an almost identical story is related by Mas'ūdi in his obviously legendary story of the building of Alexandria by Alexander the Great. Thus the story that is told by Maqrīzi seems to have been in circulation twenty-six years before the establishment of Cairo" (p. 23).

[14] Clerget (*Le Caire*, I, 124) and other scholars have raised the question of why Jawhar did not locate his city farther south near the Birkat al-Fīl, where it could have been in more proximate relationship to Fusṭāṭ. While this might have been a more logical choice, its possibility can be ruled out by a closer examination of his dilemma. The construction of the city required several years, during which the army had to be camped temporarily and near enough to Fusṭāṭ to retain control over her. To have camped

remainder of the royal city was not ready until October 974, when Mu'izz made his triumphal entry to be installed as Fāṭimid Caliph in his chosen imperial capital.

Despite the beauty, lavishness, and intellectual vitality of the Fāṭimid princely city, it remained simply a royal refuge within whose secure enclosure an alien Caliph and his entourage could pursue their lives.[15] Fusṭāṭ, already known by the alternative name of Miṣr, remained the dominant transport, productive, and commercial metropolis of Egypt, as was attested by several travelers who have given us eyewitness accounts of Egypt between the founding of al-Qāhirah and the middle of the eleventh century.

According to the description written by al-Muqaddasi sometime before 985, the city of Fusṭāṭ (Miṣr) was about two miles in length and built in tiers up the slope from the river. The buildings of the city impressed him by their height of five to seven stories, "like minarets," and the population was "thick as locusts." The most densely settled section of the city was in the neighborhood of the Mosque of 'Amr near the Dār al-Shāṭ and the warehouses. While he devotes much space to describing the city of Fusṭāṭ, calling it superior to Baghdad and larger than Naisapur, Baṣrah, and Damascus, he dismisses the new city of al-Qāhirah in a few sentences, noting merely that one cannot enter Fusṭāṭ from Damascus without passing through al-Qāhirah. He gives us one of the few available descriptions of developments around Fusṭāṭ, remarking that the city of Jīzah had a mosque and a larger population than the island of Rawḍah, that Heliopolis ('Ain Shams) was primarily an agricultural area, and that Memphis (then called 'Azīzīyah "which used to be al-Miṣr in olden times") had completely disintegrated by his time.[16]

During the next 65 years al-Qāhirah grew in importance and could no longer be dismissed so curtly in travel accounts. The Persian, Nāṣir-i Khusraw,[17] divided his attention more equally between the two competitors. Al-Qāhirah he described as an unfortified city (from which scholars have deduced that the original walls had deteriorated by the middle of the eleventh century) with buildings of five and six stories, each a veritable fortress. The city was divided into ten *ḥārāt* (wards or quarters), all on the eastern side of the Red Sea Canal (the Khalīj) which began at Miṣr. Less than a mile south of al-Qāhirah was the city of (Fusṭāṭ) Miṣr, built on a hill. The northern limit of Miṣr was the Mosque of Ibn Ṭūlūn. He describes seven- and even fourteen-story structures in Miṣr[18] and concurs with al-Muqaddasi in locating the center of the city at the Mosque of 'Amr which, by that time, was surrounded on all four sides by exceedingly prosperous markets.[19]

During the eleventh century, then, we reconstruct an image of two symbiotic cities: Miṣr-Fusṭāṭ, the larger of the two, occupied by the indigenous population and devoted to commercial and industrial activities; and al-Qāhirah, a well-designed community for the needs of a large and complex courtly society, divided into separate quarters according to ethnic lines and liberally endowed with gardens and palatial residences. The dual community was served by dual ports, the older one at Miṣr devoted to commercial ventures, and a newer one at al-Maqs (the revival of the pre-Islamic port of Tendunyas) where the military fleet of the Fāṭimids was anchored.

The glory depicted by the travelers was to vanish within little more than a century. While the first harbingers of disaster were "natural events"—the Great Plague of 1063, the seven-year famine beginning only a few years later, the earthquake in 1138—the final blow was administered in 1168 *deus ex machina* by larger scale religio-

his army north of the planned city would have meant a sacrifice of this proximity and a danger that the new city under construction might have been a barrier to troop maneuvering. Therefore, the army was placed on the southern portion of the plain, while the new city was located to its north.

[15] At this time the common people of Fusṭāṭ could enter the royal enclosure only by special permit. Note the parallel between this and the later case of the royal city of Fez Jadīd, which had a similar relationship in the fourteenth century to Old Fez, called al-Madīnah, as reported by Roger Le Tourneau, *Fez in the Age of the Marinides*, trans. by B. Clement (University of Oklahoma Press, Norman: 1961), pp. 12-18.

[16] Al-Muqaddasi, *Aḥsan al-Taqāsīm* (de Goeje 2nd edn.), pp. 193-200. In an English translation published by the Asiatic Society of Bengal, New Series, No. 899 (Baptist Mission Press, Calcutta: 1897), the relevant portions appear on pp. 316-329.

[17] Nāṣir-i Khusraw, *Safar Nameh*, written in Persian about 1048. I have used the Arabic translation (Cairo University: Cairo, 1945), of which pp. 48-61 describe Fusṭāṭ and al-Qāhirah. A French translation of this manuscript also exists. See *Sefer Nameh: Relation du voyage de Nassiri Khosrau en Syrie, en Palestine, en Égypte, en Arabie, et en Perse, 1035-42*, published, translated, and annotated by Charles Schefer (Publications d'École de Langues Orientales Vivantes, Series 2, Volume 1, Paris: 1881).

[18] While some have questioned the veracity of this report, it receives enhanced credence from the recent archeological excavations at the site of Fusṭāṭ. In his "Preliminary Report: Excavations at Fustat, 1964," George Scanlon suggests that the capacity and elaborate reticulation of the (probably) tenth-century sewerage system uncovered by the expedition would have been adequate to accommodate an extremely dense settlement of fairly high multi-story buildings. See the report reprinted from the *Journal of the American Research Center in Egypt*, IV (1965), 7-30 plus plates. See especially p. 17.

[19] *Safar Nameh* (Arabic translation), p. 59. There is another hint concerning the application of the term "Miṣr" which appears in this document. Nāṣir-i Khusraw uses Miṣr to refer to the central town of Fusṭāṭ plus the Jazīrah (the island of Rawḍah) and the development at Jīzah on the opposite side of the river (p. 61), and distinguishes this entire conurbation from al-Qāhirah, whose southernmost limit lay almost a mile north of the Mosque of Ibn Ṭūlūn.

political events, in which Fusṭāṭ was an innocent but perhaps inevitable victim.

It will be recalled that the area of al-Qaṭā'i' had never really recovered from its destruction in 905. The buildings still standing had been usurped by squatters who lived among the rubble. By the end of the tenth century it and also the sparsely settled borders of al-'Askar had become sites from which building materials were scavenged. The district had become so desolate that a wall was built during the eleventh century to hide these unsightly portions.[20] As the population of Fusṭāṭ was further decimated by the series of catastrophes which befell it at the end of the eleventh century, the abandoned areas grew larger. The reduced population huddled closer to the center near the Mosque of 'Amr or was drawn toward the port area which had been displaced westward by the receding river channel. Political power had long since shifted to the new city of al-Qāhirah, and gradually economic power began to move there as well, with the luxury markets transferred to the princely city and the Caliph controlling more and more of Fusṭāṭ's real estate.[21]

Thus, a decline in Fusṭāṭ's fortunes had already begun from within by the time the Franks launched their first crusade at the end of the eleventh century. Egypt's peripheral position, however, placed her outside the main path of European forays, and she remained relatively isolated from the upheavals occurring in the Fertile Crescent until she was disastrously drawn into them three-quarters of a century later. Between 1164 and 1169 she was at best a pawn in the complex and shifting alignments of the rival powers of the Seljuks in Syria (under Nūr al-Dīn) and the Christian forces of Amalric (Amaury) at Jerusalem, her young Fāṭimid Caliph a figurehead at the mercy of the changing *wazīrs* (viziers) who actually ruled the country.[22]

When the campaigns that had wracked the country for five bitter years ceased temporarily in 1169, the future of Cairo had been completely altered. Al-Qāhirah had been transformed from a princely city in symbiotic competition with commercial Fusṭāṭ-Miṣr to an overflowing metropolis inhabited by masters and masses alike. Although the city was nominally still ruled by the Fāṭimid Shi'ites, it was actually controlled by the new Sunni *wazīr*, Ṣalāḥ al-Dīn (Saladin), a participant in the campaign (led by his uncle Shīrkūh, whom he succeeded after the latter's death in 1169) which had rescued Egypt from the attempted conquest by the Crusaders. The next few years were to witness the final overthrow of the Fāṭimids in Cairo and the establishment of a new dynasty of Sunni Ayyūbids under the leadership of this same Ṣalāḥ al-Dīn.

How had this remarkable transformation in the nature of al-Qāhirah taken place? Quite simply through the virtual destruction of Fusṭāṭ, not the only but certainly one of the major casualties of the war. In 1168, Shawār, an opportunistic *wazīr* then siding with the Syrians against Amalric, feared that the crusader forces already occupying the Birkat al-Ḥabash would use indefensible Fusṭāṭ as a base from which to launch a fatal thrust to fortified Cairo,[23] and he therefore ordered the city burned to the ground. Burn it did—for 54 days and nights.[24] Borne by the prevailing winds, the smoke billowed southward, driving Amalric's forces into retrenchment while the people of Fusṭāṭ fled northward in great confusion to seek protection within al-Qāhirah. By the following year, when Amalric had been routed by the Syrian forces and Ṣalāḥ al-Dīn had assumed the office of *wazīr* in Cairo, much of Fusṭāṭ lay in ashes, her population crowded within the former princely city or living in temporary camps outside her walls.

While the disaster was not total it was irreversible. During the decade and a half following the holocaust, the riverine portions of Miṣr were rebuilt or restored, but the greatly reduced population no longer needed the higher land which was then abandoned. In an account of his pilgrimage to Mecca in 1183, Ibn Jubayr describes both al-Qāhirah and Miṣr, and from this we can derive an impression of the changes which had occurred. He notes, "we moved to Cairo, the Sultan's magnificent and extensive city [and] from there we passed to Miṣr . . . [where] we lodged at the inn . . . in the Lane of the Lamps beside the Mosque of 'Amr." His description of Miṣr is revealing. "In Miṣr too are the remains of the destruction caused by the fire. Most [*sic*] of the city has been restored, and buildings now adjoin each other without intermission. It is a large city but the ancient relics to be seen in

[20] Maqrīzi, *Khiṭaṭ*, I, 305.

[21] *Safar Nameh* (Arabic translation), p. 48, where it is reported that the Sultan owned 8,000 houses in al-Qāhirah and Miṣr (Fusṭāṭ).

[22] See Stanley Lane-Poole, *Saladin* (G. P. Putnam's Sons, New York and London: 1898), pp. 78-98, for a detailed if dizzying account of the rival factions, their shifting roles and the campaigns which inflicted such injury on the countryside which was, unwittingly, transformed into a battlefield. Much of his account is based on the original chronicle of Ibn al-Athīr, who lived between 1160 and 1234.

[23] Since the visit of Nāṣir-i Khusraw, the crumbled walls had been replaced and enlarged toward the end of the eleventh century by Badr al-Jamāli.

[24] The classic account of the destruction of Fusṭāṭ comes to us from the chronicle of a contemporary but scarcely an eyewitness, Ibn al-Athīr. In his *al-Kāmil fi al-Ta'rīkh*, he notes that 20,000 barrels of naphtha and 10,000 torches were used, and that the fire smouldered for 54 days. This same account is repeated by Shihāb al-Dīn Maqdisi al-Shāfi'ī (early thirteenth-century historian), in *al-Masālik wa al-Mamālik* (Cairo, 1879), pp. 170-171; by Maqrīzi, *Khiṭaṭ*, I, 286; by Lane-Poole, *Saladin*, p. 93, and *The Story of Cairo*, p. 169; and by Clerget, *Le Caire*, I, 138.

and about it attest the size of its former boundaries."[25]

The city of Miṣr, formerly almost contiguous with al-Qāhirah and of at least equal importance, had become a community separated from[26] and definitely subordinate to its magnificent neighbor. And so it remained. The area in the vicinity of the Mosque of 'Amr (restored under Ṣalāḥ al-Dīn) was the only surviving section of the great city which had once stretched from the Birkat al-Ḥabash to the Muqaṭṭam heights. The city of al-Qāhirah, on the other hand, profited from this change. Now the true center of the region, during the Middle Ages it expanded into a world capital, reaching its zenith under the Mamluks in the fourteenth century.

Before tracing these developments, however, it might be well to explore the ways in which the pre-Ayyūbid settlements not only helped shape the medieval capital that evolved from them but left permanent traces in the ecology of the modern city as well, for Fusṭāṭ, al-'Askar, al-Qaṭā'i', and Fāṭimid al-Qāhirah imprinted the city of the future both physically and socially. To identify these influences we must return to the present for a moment and preview some of the later conclusions of this study. Modern Cairo can be divided into three horizontal segments, the southern, the central, and the northern. Each of these segments has followed a separate pattern of growth during roughly different periods of time, each pattern being determined by a fairly distinct set of technological and social conditions. The earliest settlements founded during the opening centuries of Islam were confined to the southern third of the present city. The first nucleus in the central segment of the city was Fāṭimid al-Qāhirah, out of which the modern city developed in fairly consistent fashion until almost the end of the nineteenth century. The northern segment dates from the twentieth century, making a consideration of this latter zone premature here.

The influence of Fusṭāṭ, al-'Askar, and al-Qaṭā'i' on the ecology of the modern city of Cairo can be seen clearly on a land use map of the southern zone of the city (see Map IV). This influence has been essentially negative and yet, paradoxically, of utmost significance. The former settlements have rendered useless the land on which they stood and have effectively prevented an expansion of the city to the south. The barriers in the southern portion of the city are of two kinds: the *kharāb*, or mounds of debris which bury the former "live" cities; and the cemeteries or "Cities of the Dead," consisting of blocks and blocks of inhabited tomb-dwellings, which make up the modern district of al-Khalīfah.

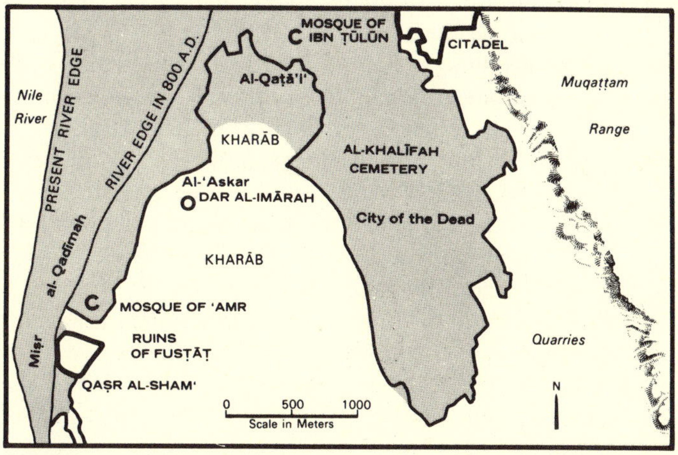

IV. The southern segment of contemporary Cairo showing early landmarks and present land uses

More than one-third of the southern segment of Cairo is given over to the mounds of ruins that began to form just south of the Mosque of Ibn Ṭūlūn as early as the opening of the tenth century as an aftermath of the 'Abbāsid destruction of al-Qaṭā'i'. By the next century, the outlying portions of al-'Askar had fallen into disuse as plagues, famines, and other disasters substantially reduced the population to be housed at Fusṭāṭ. The blight crept farther south during the twelfth century, finally absorbing those sections of Fusṭāṭ which had been destroyed when the city was set on fire in 1168.[27] As noted earlier, the only portions of Miṣr which were rebuilt after the fire were those located near the Mosque of 'Amr on the river-bottom lands. This new zone, developed chiefly on land which had been below water at the time Fusṭāṭ was founded, became known eventually as Miṣr al-Qadīmah (Old Miṣr), not because the buildings themselves necessarily predated al-Qāhirah, but because it became useful to distinguish between the old seat of central authority and the new capital (Miṣr), al-Qāhirah. Eventually, all the area east of the Qaṣr al-Sham' and the

[25] *The Travels of Ibn Jubayr*, trans. by R.J.C. Broadhurst (Jonathan Cape, London: 1952), quotations from pp. 36 and 46.

[26] From Ibn Jubayr it is clear that the distance between the two was considerable. The traveler states that Cairo consisted of two distinct cities, Miṣr and al-Qāhirah, with the Mosque of Ibn Ṭūlūn relatively deserted and midway between them. *Ibid.*, p. 44. Becker, in his article on Cairo, quotes the authority of Ibn Sa'īd who described the physical relationship between the two cities at the end of the Ayyūbid period, i.e., early thirteenth century. At his time, two miles of dusty road intervened between al-Qāhirah and Miṣr. Becker, "Cairo," *Encyclopedia of Islam*[1], p. 819.

[27] Clerget (*Le Caire*, I, 139) dates the formation of the *kharāb* from the time of Mustanṣir (late eleventh century) and remarks that little change in them could be noted until the time of Maqrīzi. Marius Schemeil, in *Le Caire: sa vie, son histoire, son peuple* (Dār al-Ma'ārif, Cairo: 1949), p. 91, follows Clerget in this, as he does throughout his book, scarcely altering the language of his unacknowledged source. Clerget's own evidence, however, indicates that the ruin-mounds began to form somewhat earlier, becoming progressively worse with time. Since much depends upon one's definition of "ruins," a controversy on this point would be sterile.

Mosque of 'Amr was swallowed up by the encroaching *kharāb*. To the present, with the exception of two post-1952 public housing projects on Tilāl Zaynhum and 'Ain al-Ṣīrah, these areas have remained absolutely closed to habitation, serving variously as a squatters' preserve, a municipal rubbish dump, and, most recently, as a site for archaeological excavations, although a major highway now traverses the zone.

Another third of Cairo's southern zone is made unfit for development by the extensive cemetery which occupies a wide swath of precious land. This cemetery is modern Cairo's other heritage from the pre-medieval period. Bounded by the *kharāb* on the west and the sharp incline of the Muqaṭṭam range on the east, the Khalīfah City of the Dead stretches in an elongated U from its gateway, the Bāb al-Qarāfah between the Mosque of Ibn Ṭūlūn and the Citadel, to its southernmost tip almost three-quarters of a mile away. This cemetery contains the tombs of religious and political dignitaries of the 'Abbāsid and later periods, including the sacred mausoleums of Imām Shāfi'i and Sayīdah Nafīsah which are, today as in the days of Ibn Jubayr, among the important meccas for pilgrims. The extension of this cemetery northward paralleled the extension of the city of Fusṭāṭ,[28] but it is significant that while the city of the living of Fusṭāṭ has long since disappeared, its city of the dead—much expanded—continues to house thousands of residents of the contemporary city.

The only land available for a southern extension of the city was the narrow strip abutting the Nile. This is the zone now called Miṣr al-Qadīmah, practically all of which was built on land that came into existence after the ninth century and was not fully ready for construction until the shifting of the shore had been completed in the fourteenth century. Abandonment of the land between central Fusṭāṭ and the new city of al-Qāhirah resulted in the gradual isolation of greatly deteriorated Fusṭāṭ which became merely an industrial port suburb of the new metropolis. By the time of the Napoleonic Expedition in 1798, al-Qāhirah had a population of more than a quarter of a million, while Miṣr al-Qadīmah had declined to an outlying town of no more than ten thousand inhabitants.

The present structure of Cairo, then, reveals a strangely stagnated development in the entire southern third of the city, indicating a complete breakdown of the usual processes whereby new land uses and developments supplant older ones to create an ever-renewing city. This breakdown, which has resulted in the disuse of large segments of southern Cairo, is one of the most striking elements in the pattern of the present city.

The Ayyūbid period ushered in a lengthy era during which much of the central segment of Cairo was de-

[28] See *The Travels of Ibn Jubayr* (Broadhurst translation), pp. 37-42, for an eyewitness account of the tomb city in 1183, and Clerget, *Le Caire*, I, 135, for a discussion of the early growth and divisions within this cemetery.

9. Urbanized section of the al-Khalīfah city of the dead, near the tomb mosque of Imām Shāfi'i

veloped. During the thirteenth, fourteenth, and fifteenth centuries, the city of al-Qāhirah expanded to almost five times the size of its original walled nucleus. And, perhaps of even greater significance, the area it encompassed by the end of the fifteenth century remained almost constant until the latter half of the nineteenth century. This much-expanded city, however, was shaped in part by the physical and social characteristics of its progenitor, the Fāṭimid princely city. Even today the physical pattern of that area shows elements that cannot be understood without an examination of their tenth- and eleventh-century roots. The city of the Fāṭimids had a social system and a physical shell—partly imposed but partly the inevitable counterpart of its system of social organization—that influenced the form the medieval city was to take.

One of the most striking elements of that social system was its internal organization according to occupation. During late Roman and Byzantine times, the various trades and crafts in urban centers throughout the empire had been organized into corporations or "guilds," in which membership was compulsory and through which commercial activities were closely regulated by the state. The Arab conquerors of Egypt left these inherited occupational corporations relatively intact, and they persisted through the end of the ninth century, chiefly as a means for maintaining public regulation over merchants, tradesmen, and artisans.[29] That this social organization was translated into a physical order was already evident in early Fusṭāṭ. Specialized markets were distributed within the city, each market being associated with its own quarter in which production and distribution were combined with residences for tradesmen and inns for transient merchants. Thus, even disorderly and crowded Fusṭāṭ represented an accretion of occupational cells, although some quarters, chiefly peripheral, appear to have been almost exclusively residential.

During the ensuing centuries this form of organization continued to play a role in structuring groups within the urban environment, thereby influencing the physical pattern of that environment. Unfortunately we still lack detailed knowledge of the institutional character of such occupational organizations and of the changes which these institutions appear to have undergone during their many centuries of evolution. Indeed, contemporary scholars specializing in the investigation of Islamic guilds (or occupational corporations) now vigorously deny that, prior to the Turkish period, anything analogous to the highly structured guilds that developed in medieval Europe ever existed in Middle Eastern cities.[30] However,

[29] On these earliest precursors, see A.E.R. Boak, "Guilds, Late Roman and Byzantine," *Encyclopedia of the Social Sciences*[1] (The Macmillan Company, New York: 1932), VII, 206-208. Given the common conditions, it is not surprising to find guild-like prototypes in even earlier societies, for they appear to have been known, in one form or another, in pharaonic, semitic, and other cultures of the area. It is irrelevant for our purposes whether the existence of precedents "accounts" for the emergence of occupational corporations in Islamic cities or even whether exact parallels are to be found or not. Obviously, we are dealing with a form of social organization congruent with the technical level of production, but one which was modified, shaped, and utilized in different fashion by different cultures and even by the same culture over time.

[30] In few other areas have the specialists in Islamic history been so involved in basic controversy as on the question of guilds. The present consensus is essentially negative, rejecting or at least calling into question previously accepted views. Earlier scholars, in refreshing if misleading contrast, offered rather firm positions. Foremost among the early scholars of the Islamic guilds was Louis Massignon, whose position can be found in his "Les corps de métiers et la cité Islamique," *Revue Internationale de Sociologie*, Volume 28 (1920), pp. 473-489 and in his summaries: "Ṣinf,"

āb al-Futūḥ at northern wall of Cairo, sketched in 1800

10b. Bāb al-Futūḥ today

even if occupational groupings were only loosely and informally constituted, there can be no denial that these affiliations were reinforced by functional affinities of interest and were consolidated—in the space-determined social world of the Middle Ages—by geographic proximities. Of significance to us in this study of Cairo's evolution is the fact that throughout her early history the organization of urban life was, at least in part, occupation-linked, and that this persistent linkage left definite traces in the physical form of the city.

Before demonstrating this linkage, however, we might pause for a moment to mention the *muḥtasib*, an agent who, through his supervision of the activities of the corporations and the morality of the market place, fulfilled certain functions generally assigned to administrators of the contemporary municipality. While the office of the *muḥtasib* evolved further in the ensuing centuries—and indeed continued into the nineteenth century until it was abolished by Muḥammad 'Ali and will therefore be treated in greater detail in a later chapter—it is important to stress at this point that it, too, was part of Cairo's pre-'Ayyūbid heritage. Here, again, the precedents went back to the pre-Islamic period, for the Roman and Byzantine inspector of the markets was a prototype for the *muḥtasib* whose role was formalized at the time of the 'Abbāsids. What Islam seems to have added was the religious sanction and sanctity, by classifying offenses against *ḥisbah* as morally reprehensible as well as legally inexpedient.[31]

Not only a social order but a physical pattern as well was central Cairo's heritage from the past. The original plan of the Fāṭimid suburb was regular and rectangular in the extreme. In addition to the extensive palaces, gardens, cemetery, mosque, and market squares, all of which were concentrated within the centermost core of the walled enclosure, there were ten to fifteen *ḥārāt* (pl.) or quarters in which members of the ethnically organized military units of Mu'izz were installed.[32] Physically, a *ḥārah* (sing.) is a subsection of a city. Having only limited access, usually through a street terminating in an open square, it is equipped with walls and gates which can be closed at night and, in addition, barricaded completely during times of crisis. Socially, the *ḥārah* is a group of persons usually unified by ethnic and/or occupational characteristics as well as by vicinal ties, and segregated physically and socially from other subgroups of the city. Politically, it is often a unit of administration and control. As the commercial life of al-Qāhirah diversified, and as occupational groupings came to dominate more and more of the essential loyalties and identification of the nonmilitary classes, the original *ḥārāt* and those established both north and south of the first walls were adapted to the requirements of craftsmanship and trade. Whereas the nomenclature of the earliest *ḥārāt* showed a preoccupation with ethnic and tribal affiliations, the names of later *ḥārāt* sometimes

---

Encyclopedia of Islam[1] (1913), IV, 436-437; and "Guilds, Islamic," *Encyclopedia of the Social Sciences*[1] (1932), VII, 214-216. It was Massignon who suggested that the Ismā'īli Fāṭimids introduced a new fervor of religious and even "secret society" internal cohesion into the professional, craft, and commercial corporations which had traditionally been utilized chiefly as agencies for state regulation, and drew a connection between the secret societies of the Qarmaṭians and the guilds of Fāṭimid Egypt. Detailed statements confirming this view of Fāṭimid corporate organization appeared in Bernard Lewis, "The Islamic Guilds," *The Economic History Review*, VIII (November 1937), 20-37, and in Clerget, *Le Caire*, II, 130-131. For many years this position was widely accepted by scholars, and is echoed in entries in the *Shorter Encyclopaedia of Islam* edited by H.A.R. Gibb and J. H. Kramers (Cornell University Press, Ithaca: 1965) under the "Ḳarmaṭians," pp. 218-223, and under "Ṭariḳa," pp. 573-578. The connection between the heretical Qarmaṭians and the Ismā'īli Fāṭimids is currently rejected, and even Bernard Lewis has recently disavowed his 1937 article, suggesting that it will require critical revisions.

[31] A brief reference to the role of the *muḥtasib* in Fāṭimid Cairo can be found in al-Qalqashandi, a contemporary of Maqrīzi, who described the administrative structure of the government under the Fāṭimids. The relevant section of his many-volume work has been edited and published by Marius Canard under the title *Al-Qalqachandi: Les institutions des Fâtimides en Égypte* (La Maison des Livres, Algiers: 1957). According to this description, in Fāṭimid times the *muḥtasib* was the third highest ranking official among the "men of the pen" (i.e., religious rather than military), inferior only to the chief *qāḍi* and the supervisor of religious knowledge (*Dār al-'Ilm*). So important was he that his appointment was announced from the pulpits of the Friday mosques in both al-Qāhirah and Miṣr (Fusṭāṭ), where he also sat in judgment on alternating days. His authority in moral matters was absolute (see Canard's edition, p. 16). A fuller treatment of the *muḥtasib*'s role, especially as it developed in Fusṭāṭ and Cairo, can be found in Émile Tyan, *Histoire de l'organisation judiciare en pays d'Islam* (E. J. Brill, Leiden: 2nd edn., 1960), pp. 616ff. Early prototypes are mentioned by Joseph Schacht, *An Introduction to Islamic Law* (The Clarendon Press, Oxford: 1964), and in the derivative work by Noel Coulson, *A History of Islamic Law* (University Press, Edinburgh: 1964). Ishaq Musa al-Husaini, "Ḥisba in Islam," *The Islamic Quarterly*, Vol. 10 (July and December 1966), pp. 69-82, argues for the critical distinction between the secular character of the Byzantine model and the sacred character of the Islamic.

[32] While I have not included a sketch map of the Fāṭimid city, a number of excellent reconstructions have been attempted. For example, K.A.C. Creswell, *The Muslim Architecture of Egypt: Ikhshīds and Fāṭimids*, includes a plan of Fāṭimid Cairo and a detailed description. See pp. 23-35. The reconstruction done by Ravaisse is reproduced on p. 129 of Clerget, *Le Caire*, I; and a third sketch is found in Haswell, "Cairo, Origin and Development," Plate III. The number of *ḥārāt* in the original city is not known with certitude. Clerget, following Maqrīzi, suggests fifteen; Ravaisse distinguishes seventeen within the first ring of walls; while Nāṣir-i Khusraw, writing in the mid-eleventh century, identified only ten, including the palace itself.

revealed the dominant occupational or commercial functions of the areas.

There evolved from the Fāṭimid beginnings a basic form of the city which reflected its social organization and which gave to medieval cities throughout the Islamic lands a similar physical pattern. This pattern has been described by a number of scholars, all of whom have stressed the intimate connection between the physical organization of the city and its social constitution.[33]

The heritage of medieval Cairo from its Fāṭimid antecedent was this essential social constitution which persisted, despite changes in the ruling dynasties and in the ethnic composition of the aristocracy, in shaping the old and new portions of the city according to a consistent principle. This principle of ethnic-occupational segregation was still operative in early nineteenth century Cairo.

Thus, from the earliest settlements Cairo inherited a pattern of land misuse in the southern section which has persisted into the present. From the Fāṭimid creation she inherited two equally important elements: the walled nucleus or core of a city which was soon to expand into a major preindustrial metropolis; and a form of social organization which was to make medieval Cairo an outstanding but hardly unique example of the Middle Eastern genre of city-building.

[33] Among the sources pointing out this basic uniformity of physical organization in such widely separated urban settlements as those of North Africa, Syria, Egypt, Ottoman Turkey, etc., are: Lewis, "The Islamic Guilds," *The Economic History Review*, pp. 20-37, where he says that the guilds were so important that the form which a city took was often determined by the needs of the guildsmen, p. 20; H.A.R. Gibb and Harold Bowen, *Islamic Society and the West*, Volume I, Part I (Oxford University Press, London: 1950), especially Chapter VI, "The City: Industry and Commerce," pp. 276-313; Massignon's article on the "Ṣinf," *Encyclopedia of Islam*[1], IV, where he says on p. 436 that "the study of the distribution of the different guilds in the Muslim cities, Fez or Baghdad, Damascus or Cairo, shows that as a general principle there was a fixed topographical distribution of the trade guilds in any particular Muslim city"; Xavier de Planhol, *The World of Islam*, who notes that: "The Moslem town obeys a number of well-defined general rules. These are a concentric arrangement and hierarchical division of the different quarters, topographic partitioning and corporative concentration in commercial districts, and ethnic as well as religious segregation in residential areas" (p. 9 but see also pp. 11-13); Gustave E. Von Grunebaum, "The Structure of the Muslim Town," in his *Islam: Essays in the Nature and Growth of a Cultural Tradition* (Memoir No. 81 of the American Anthropological Association, April 1955), pp. 141-158 but particularly pp. 145-146; Jean Sauvaget, *Alep* (Haut Commissariat de L'État Français en Syrie et au Liban, Service des Antiquités, Paris: 1941), where he describes the ecological structure of Aleppo, Syria; and his "Esquisse d'une histoire de la ville de Damas," *Revue des Études Islamiques* (Paris, 1934), pp. 421-480; Nicola Ziadeh, *Urban Life in Syria Under the Early Mamluks* (American Press, Beirut: 1953), see especially pp. 75-76 in which he describes the towns of Syria in the eleventh century; Georges Marçais, "L'urbanisme Musulmane," in the 5e *Congrès de la Féderation des Sociétés Savantes de l'Afrique du Nord* (Algiers, 1940) and his "La conception des villes dans l'Islam," *Revue d'Alger*, II (1945), 517-533; William Marçais, "L'Islamisme et la vie urbaine, *L'Académie des Inscriptions et Belles-Lettres, Comptes Rendus* (Paris, January-March 1928), pp. 86-97; and Roger Le Tourneau, *Les villes Musulmanes*, pp. 14-18, 20.

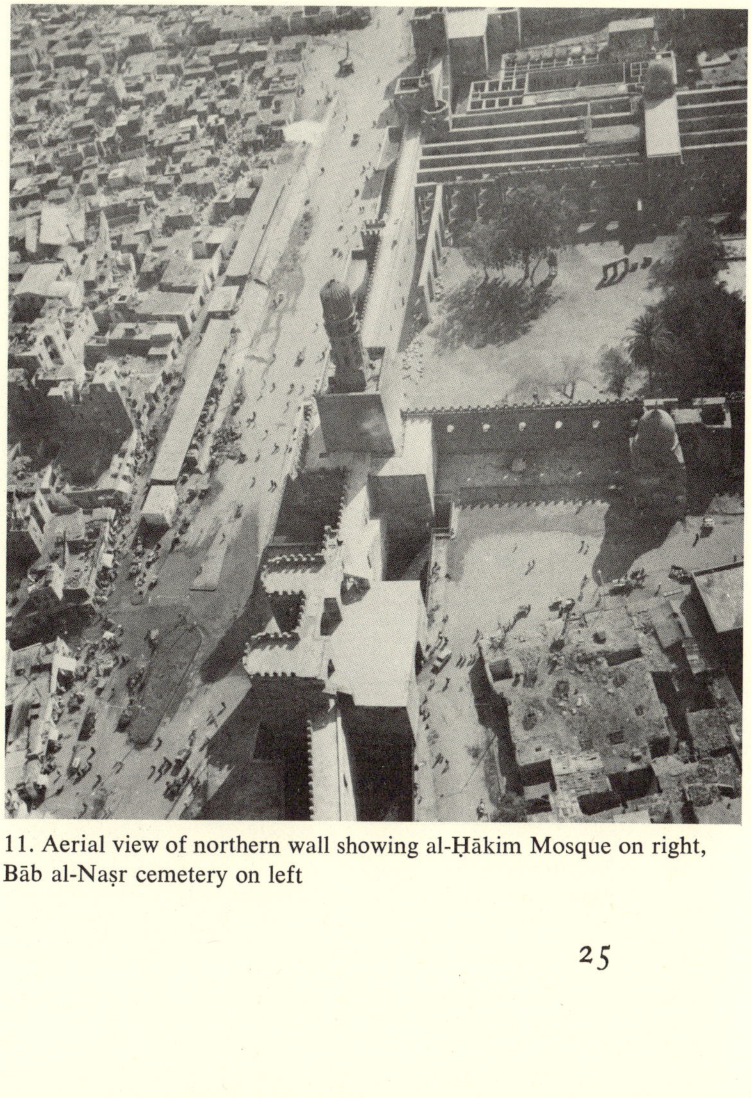

11. Aerial view of northern wall showing al-Ḥākim Mosque on right, Bāb al-Naṣr cemetery on left

12a. Bāb Zuwaylah in the southern wall *ca.* 1900

12b. Bāb Zuwaylah today: cars have replaced camels

13. The gate to the Citadel *ca.* 1857

3 Ascent to Medieval Capital

1170-1340

THE medieval cycle of Cairo's growth and decline begins essentially with the accession of Ṣalāḥ al-Dīn to the leadership of Sunni Islam. It rises sharply within the next century and three quarters, reaching an apogee during the reign of the Baḥri Mamluk Sultan al-Nāṣir ibn Qalāwūn before the middle of the fourteenth century. The city's fortunes closely reflect those of the empire, for as internal strife and external threats multiply, the expansion of the city comes to a halt. This decline, already perceptible in the early Circassian Mamluk period but masked by a temporary revival in the fifteenth century, is transformed into a precipitous descent during the centuries of Ottoman rule. The arrival in 1798 of the Napoleonic Expedition to Egypt brings the cycle to a close, the intrusion forming a bridge between a medieval Cairo much decayed and a modern Cairo yet to be.

The entire cycle was played out within the central section of contemporary Cairo (see Map V). Note that the boundaries of the city in 1800 are merely extensions of those perceptible at the time of Ṣalāḥ al-Dīn. Expansion occurred predominantly in two directions: southward, pulled by the concentration of political and military power in the Citadel, and westward, conditioned by a recession of the river. These centuries, during which political and economic changes of enormous magnitude took place, were those during which the course of the Nile underwent its most rapid and dramatic transposition. The marked shift of the river bed westward yielded contiguous land which doubled the width of the previous settlement, left the former port of al-Maqs (now occupied by the major railroad station of modern Cairo) completely landlocked, and exerted an irresistible westward pull on the city's center. Whereas at the time of Ṣalāḥ al-Dīn, the Khalīj Miṣri (abortive residuum of the former Red Sea Canal) constituted the occidental limit of the city, by the end of the Mamluk period its channel bisected the city, dividing the eastern from the western halves of settlement. Thus, political, economic, *and* physical developments combined to transform Cairo completely during the medieval epoch.

When Ṣalāḥ al-Dīn first came to power as governor of Egypt, however, there was nothing to indicate that he planned a total transformation of its capital. Little in fact was done immediately, except to refortify the city by a new set of walls to replace the former enclosures of Jawhar and Badr al-Jamāli.[1] Shunning the Fāṭimid palaces, which were turned over to lesser lords, Ṣalāḥ al-Dīn set up residence in the Dār al-Wazīr just north of the Great Eastern Palace.[2] It was not until after the death of Nūr al-Dīn in 1174 that Ṣalāḥ al-Dīn showed the independence of his hand and proceeded to conquer Syria. So successful were his rapid campaigns that only one year later he was invested with dominion over not only Egypt but the North African lands, Nubia, western Arabia, Palestine, and central Syria.

It was probably after his triumphant return from these campaigns that Ṣalāḥ al-Dīn first conceived the plan for his Citadel and for the gigantic walls designed to encircle the two cities of Miṣr and al-Qāhirah. The key-

[1] See Becker, "Cairo," *Encyclopedia of Islam*[1] (1913), I, 823, where he discusses the position taken by Casanova on this point.

[2] The site of the Dār al-Wazīr has been fixed exactly by K.A.C. Creswell, but was evidently unknown at the time of Clerget's writing, since the latter erroneously places it north of the city's walls. See Clerget, *Le Caire*, I, 144.

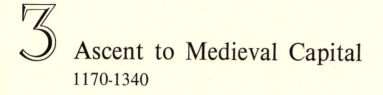

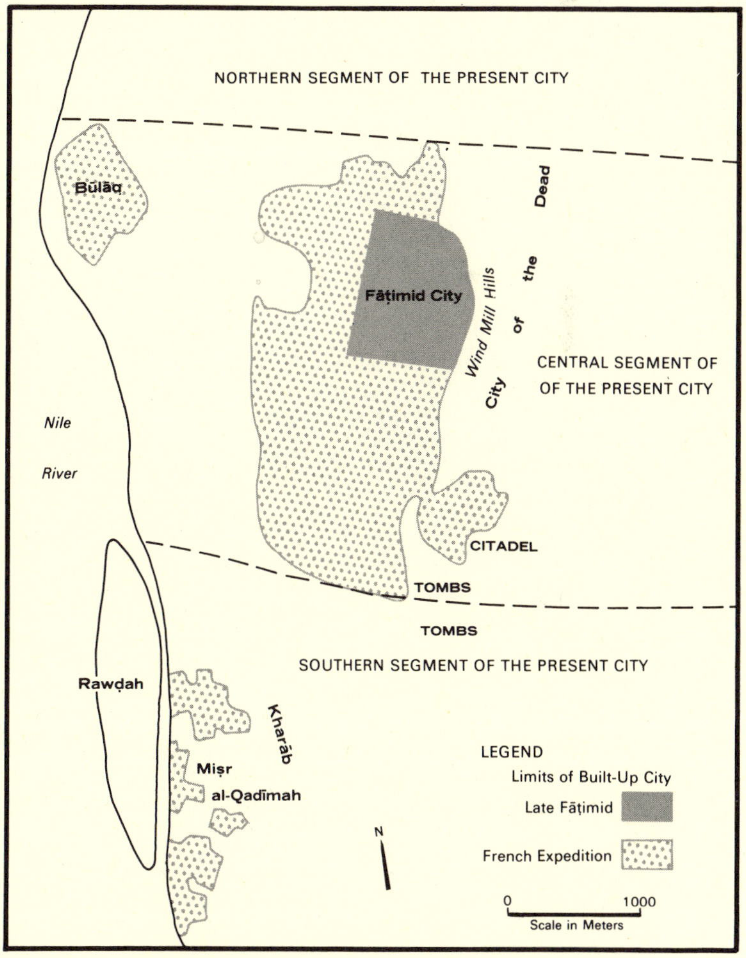

V. Expansion of al-Qāhirah during the medieval epoch

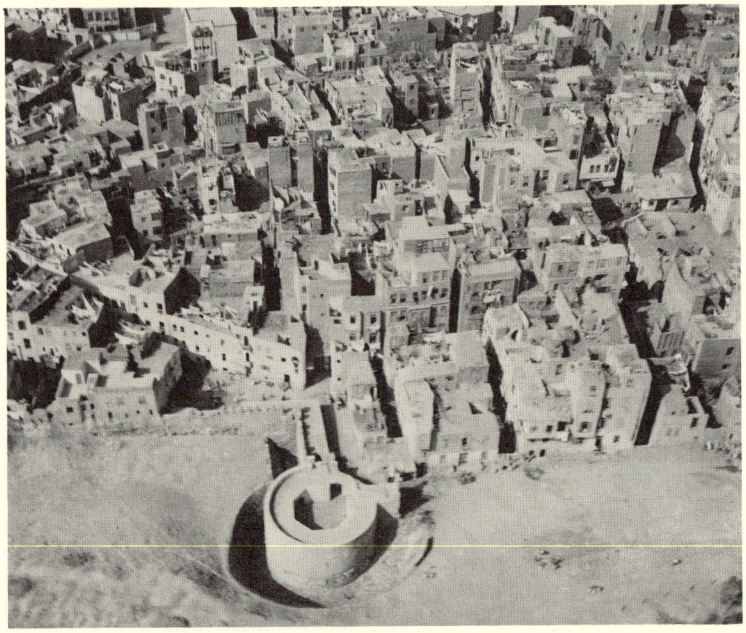

14. Citadel of Ṣalāḥ al-Dīn now crowned by Muḥammad ʿAli Mosque (early 19th century) 15. Burj al-Ẓafar in the eastern wall: desert to the east, al-Jamālīyah quarter to the west

stone of his defense system was to be the Citadel which he conceived originally not only as a fortress for his troops but as a residence for himself.[3] Begun sometime after 1175,[4] the Citadel was still under construction when Ibn Jubayr visited the capital in 1183 and reported that Crusader prisoners in "numbers beyond computation" were being used to construct an "impregnable fortress."[5] Ṣalāḥ al-Dīn was never to occupy his Citadel, however, for his numerous campaigns against Mesopotamia and then against the Crusaders kept him far from Egypt. Even before his death in 1193, construction ceased on the Citadel (by then substantially completed) and work on the ring of defensive walls was interrupted. Only portions of the walls[6] he envisaged were actually in place when he died. Attributed to Ṣalāḥ al-Dīn are: the wall which ran due west from Bāb al-Futūḥ across the Khalīj Miṣri to the tower on the Nile (Qalʿat al-Maqs) to enclose the port of al-Maqs; the eastern wall in two sections, the first of which stretched from the Bāb al-Wazīr to Darb al-Maḥrūq and the second extending it northward to Burj al-Ẓafar; a portion of the western wall parallel to the Khalīj Miṣri and only a narrow distance away from an earlier one, which gave rise to the name "Bayn al-Sūrayn" (between the two walls), still a street in today's Cairo. Planned but only partially built were the walls to connect the Citadel with the eastern borders of Fusṭāṭ and an extension of the western wall along the water's edge.[7]

Although the interior of the Citadel remained unfinished until Ṣalāḥ al-Dīn's successor oversaw its completion in 1207-1208 and work on the walls was still going on some 45 years after Ṣalāḥ al-Dīn's death,[8] other

[3] Becker, "Cairo," pp. 823-824; Yāqūt, *Muʿjam al-Buldān*, IV, 266.

[4] Yāqūt, *ibid.*, clearly dates its inception in the year 572 H. (1175-1176) when he states in his geographical dictionary that "In the year 572 [H] Ṣalāḥ al-Dīn came from Syria . . . and ordered the construction of a wall around Fusṭāṭ and al-Qāhirah and the citadel which is on the top of the Muqaṭṭam," IV, 266. This is the same year given by Maqrīzi, *Khiṭaṭ*, II, 203. However, Lane-Poole dates it from 1176-1177, see *The Story of Cairo*, p. 176; D. Margoliouth, in *Cairo, Jerusalem and Damascus* (Dodd, Mead & Co., New York: 1907), p. 51, places its commencement some time after 1175; Hitti, *History of the Arabs*, p. 652, gives the year 1183, undoubtedly too late.

[5] *The Travels of Ibn Jubayr*, p. 43.

[6] Yāqūt, *Muʿjam al-Buldān*, IV, 266, gives the extent of the walls completed by the time of Ṣalāḥ al-Dīn's death as 2.5 *farsakhs*. On flat terrain, a *farsakh* is roughly equivalent to three miles, but since the measure is based on the distance an ass can traverse within a given time period, a *farsakh* on hilly terrain would be considerably less than three miles.

[7] For a detailed architectural description of both the walls and the Citadel of Ṣalāḥ al-Dīn, see K.A.C. Creswell, *The Muslim Architecture of Egypt; Ayyūbids and Early Bahrite Mamlūks, A.D. 1171-1326* (The Clarendon Press, Oxford: 1959), pp. 6-59. For the walls, see pp. 41-59. At an earlier time it was believed that the southern wall designed to connect the Citadel and Fusṭāṭ was never built. See Lane-Poole, *The Story of Cairo*, p. 175, for this view. However, Yāqūt, writing in the early thirteenth century, noted that Fusṭāṭ and al-Qāhirah were "both surrounded by a wall" (*Muʿjam al-Buldān*, IV, 301). Maqrīzi also described a wall near the southern cemetery which appears to be the abortive beginning of the wall planned to surround Miṣr. Excavations in the twentieth century have uncovered parts of this wall, conclusive proof that at least a part of the Fusṭāṭ wall was constructed, even though perhaps not during Ṣalāḥ al-Dīn's lifetime. The final wall along the Nile bank was probably never begun.

[8] Lane-Poole, *The Story of Cairo*, p. 179, suggests that the Citadel was completed in 1208 by al-ʿAdil, although Creswell, *The Muslim Architecture of Egypt* (1959), p. 9, states categorically that the supposed "completion" was merely the addition of defense towers astride the original wall. On the subsequent construction of the walls, see *ibid.*, p. 59.

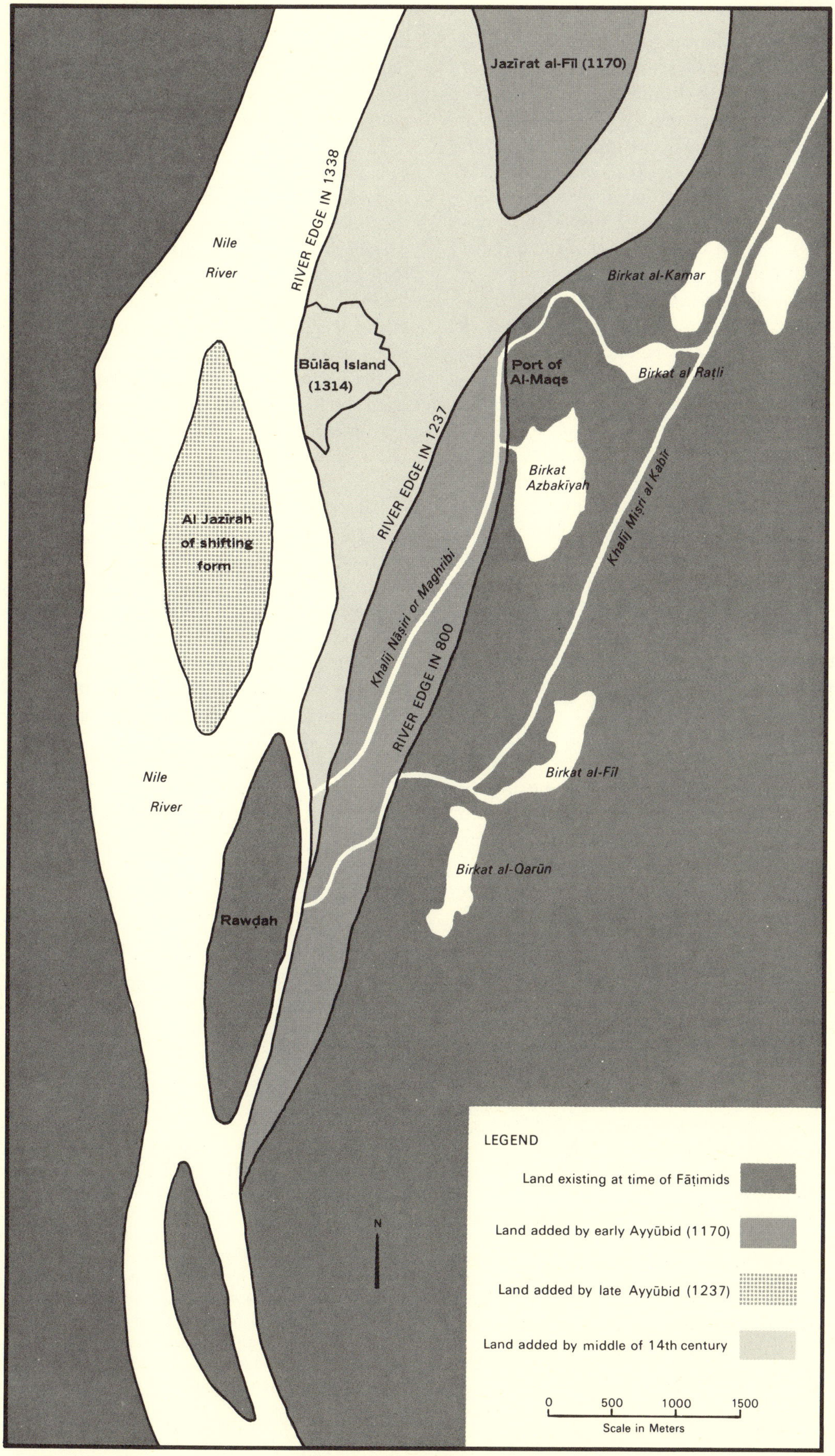

VI. Changes in the river's course during the twelfth, thirteenth, and early fourteenth centuries

changes of note were made in Cairo during his lifetime. It will be recalled that the burning of Miṣr had crowded the Fāṭimid city with excess residents, only some of whom moved back to Miṣr during its reconstruction. Having little interest in preserving al-Qāhirah as a sacrosanct refuge for the court and contemplating his own private domain in the Citadel, Ṣalāḥ al-Dīn opened the city to the masses who, in their need for space, constructed everywhere within the larger streets and *maydāns*, gradually effacing the basic outlines of the original symmetrical plan. The major palaces were torn down and replaced by schools and mosques, and former Fāṭimid villas were converted into commercial structures as the economic life of the area revived after its transplantation from Miṣr to al-Qāhirah.

The extension of the northern wall from the Khalīj Miṣri to the Nile at al-Maqs had important repercussions for the city's expansion to the west. Now relatively secure from invasion, the port area on the opposite side of the canal offered an attractive building site for a fast-growing and overcrowded city. Nor was the area adjacent to Miṣr neglected during the early Ayyūbid period. Prior to the completion of the Citadel, the largest contingent of the army was quartered on the island of Rawḍah where Ṣalāḥ al-Dīn had constructed a fortress. Even after the Citadel had become the true seat of government during the reign of his successors, troops continued to be concentrated on the island.[9] This tended to pull the city toward the southwest, but the lack of flood-free land in the intervening space meant that only gardens and winter residences could be laid out in that section. Only later, after a change had taken place in the Nile's course, were more permanent forms of land use possible there.

But, by far, the greatest transformations took place in the area south of the Fāṭimid city. Beyond the southern wall, outside the Bāb Zuwaylah, had been the quarter of the Sudanese militia of the Fāṭimids. To subdue an insurrection, Ṣalāḥ al-Dīn burned their barracks bordering the Shāri' al-A'ẓam, the Bāb Zuwaylah, and the Sitt Nafīsah tomb and redeveloped the area with parks and gardens.[10] This laid the base for future developments and, during the reigns of his successors, this section grew to be one of the most populated districts of the city. As more activities concentrated in the Citadel south of it, the impetus for growth increased.

Thus, during the reign of Ṣalāḥ al-Dīn, most of the forces which were to shape the pattern of future growth had been set in motion. It was during his time also that the Nile began to give up her gifts, at first only periodically during the dry seasons between floods, and then permanently as more and more high land was left behind following each inundation. By then the Elephant Island (Jazīrat al-Fīl in present-day Shubra) had already made its appearance, but its location considerably to the north of the existing settlement and its isolation from the firm bank of the Nile prevented its exploitation until much later. In the four decades following Ṣalāḥ al-Dīn's meteoric rise, perhaps twice as much land was ceded along the borders of the Nile as had materialized in the preceding four centuries. Map VI shows the changes in the land which took place during the Ayyūbid and later periods. Note the rather minor changes in the coastline that occurred between 800 and 1170 in contrast to the radical changes which had become evident by the end of the Ayyūbid epoch. Here apparently was one of those fortunate coincidences of history. At the very time an expansion of the empire and a growth in commercial activity made the enlargement of the city mandatory, the stock of Cairo's habitable land was expanding commensurately. While neither the politico-economic nor the physical development was to follow a steady pattern of advance, the net result was a tremendous gain in both.

The reunification of Egypt with the larger Sunni community, the continued vitality of the East-West spice trade now channeled more securely through a subdued Yemen and a thriving Fusṭāṭ, and the existence of a comparatively well-administered state all contributed to Cairo's prosperity and expansion during the later years of Ṣalāḥ al-Dīn's rule and the reigns of the first few dynastic successors following his death in 1193. However, by the fourth decade of the next century, the family solidarity that had held the various provinces of the Ayyūbid empire together began to dissolve into a host of petty rivalries, and the governorships devolved more and more upon military subordinates of the Sultan

[9] Clerget, *Le Caire*, I, 142, 144; Maqrīzi, *Khiṭaṭ*, I, 286; Becker, "Cairo," p. 823, notes that from 1208 on, all the rulers of Egypt resided in the Citadel, with the sole exception of Ṣāliḥ (the last Ayyūbid Sultan before the transition to Mamluk rule, 1240-1249), who built a fortress and a royal residence on Rawḍah. Margoliouth dates the quartering of Mamluk troops on Rawḍah from the reign of Kāmil (1218-1238), see *Cairo, Jerusalem and Damascus*, p. 60. The location of Mamluk troops on the island of Rawḍah was significant, because it was from their location that the first Mamluk dynasty derived its name, the *Baḥri*, or water (Nilotic) Mamluks. This was in contradistinction to the later Circassian Mamluks whose power was concentrated in the Citadel, from which they also derived their name, *Burji*, or Mamluks of the Fort. It was at the time of Qalāwūn that the first barracks for slave troops were constructed within the Citadel.

[10] Maqrīzi, *Khiṭaṭ*, II, 110. See also Clerget, *Le Caire*, I, 146-147; Schemeil, *Le Caire*, p. 144. The destruction of the Sudanese militia had more than mere topographic implications. Ṣalāḥ al-Dīn abolished the Fāṭimid army of black slaves and substituted a special force of Kurds and Turks, thus laying the ground for the Mamluk dynasty which followed the Ayyūbid period. See the discussion in Reuben Levy, *The Social Structure of Islam* (Cambridge University Press, Cambridge: 1957), p. 447.

in Cairo, al-Malik al-Kāmil. When he died in 1238, disintegration began in earnest with a battle for succession among his descendants and those of his brother. One of the latter, al-Ṣāliḥ, was eventually invested as Sultan in 1240, but the days of the Ayyūbids were already numbered, for it was he who shifted military dependence from Kurdish mercenaries to the Mamluks who were to assume lordship over Egypt for the ensuing several centuries. When al-Ṣāliḥ died in 1249, his widow, Shajart al-Durr, in an unprecedented move, mounted the throne for eighty days, finding a temporary ally in her chief Mamluk minister, Aybak, whom she married and with whom she briefly shared her shaky sovereignty. Displacing her, Aybak and his praetorian guards assumed command and continued to rule, despite the temporarily reinstated puppet Ayyūbid heirs. The years between 1250 and 1260, when the Mamluk general Baybars finally consolidated the new dynasty, were ones of recurring chaos and violence, perhaps symptomatic of the fluid social state of the country.[11]

The shift to Mamluk rule was much more than a simple change in dynasty; it represented, rather, a social revolution of deep significance which, while facilitating a flowering of medieval Cairo, contained within it the seeds of its own (and Cairo's) eventual decline. Although from one point of view Egypt had rarely been ruled by indigenous elements, earlier conquerors had eventually been absorbed into or at least coalesced with the population they ruled; the Mamluks, on the other hand, remained a military caste, each generation recruited anew from abroad. Although intermarriage and offspring created some roots through kinship, and conversion to and education in Islam helped strengthen the bonds to the native population through a religious community, the peculiar institutions of the Mamluks (in particular, the special variation of feudalism they evolved) tended to insulate rulers from the ruled to an unprecedented degree. Not since the first days of the Arab conquest, when Muslims governed a predominantly Christian populace, had so great a cleavage existed. But whereas the former cleavage had eventually been bridged by the gradual conversion of most Egyptians to the religion of their conquerors, such assimilation was impossible during the later era when the ranks of the Mamluks were, by definition, closed to local recruits.

Even feudalism, which in the absence of ethnic assimilation might have acted as a bridge by involving the Mamluk princes with a clientele of dependent villagers, also operated in this instance against an identification of interests. At the time of the Arab conquest, all lands taken by force belonged, in theory at least, to the Caliph who distributed some among his military chiefs and the descendants of the Prophet and permitted the remainder, as residual crown lands, to be farmed by their former proprietors in return for the head tax upon non-Muslims. After the ninth century, political and fiscal administration became more and more coordinated, as conversions made deep inroads on the formerly lucrative head tax. Some fiefdoms became hereditary, and landlords began to assume political powers and administrative responsibilities in addition to their financial role. During Fāṭimid rule, fiscal responsibilities rendered as tithes sufficed, but more and more the Ayyūbids used the *iqṭāʿ* (fief) system to administer the state while making the enjoyment of feudal rights more dependent upon centralized dispensation. By the late Ayyūbid period the seeds of the feudalism hybrid that was to prevail under the Mamluks had already been planted, for fiefs were already being assigned as sources of revenue rather than units of administration. Under the Mamluks this was carried to its ultimate form, with the rights to the produce of given areas being assigned to the manumitted slaves who constituted the aristocracy of the system (the amirs, of whom more will be said later), in return for their obligation to maintain a military force commensurate with their status. Agricultural areas and even commercial enterprises yielding profits were assigned and often quickly reassigned, dependent upon the whims of lotteries or the expediencies of political infighting. This insured the consolidation of a military caste system without deep or lasting roots in the countryside,[12] a situation which prevailed until and even beyond the Ottoman conquest of 1517.

Just as succession in feudal proprietorship was divorced from heredity, so also succession to the Sultanate conformed less and less to this principle. While the Baḥri Mamluks did not abandon it completely—fictive kinship in many cases being substituted for biological—the Circassian Mamluks who assumed power by the late fourteenth century owed the recurrent internecine convulsions which beset them to their almost total renunciation of hereditary succession, in practice if not in theory.

[11] See Lane-Poole, *Story of Cairo*, pp. 198-202; Hitti, *History of the Arabs*, pp. 671-672; Sir William Muir, *The Mameluke or Slave Dynasty of Egypt, 1260-1517 A.D.* (Smith, Elder & Company, London: 1896), pp. 8-11.

[12] I have simplified here a complex set of institutions and their changes. More detailed treatment can be found in Paul Wittek, "La féodalité musulmane," *Revue de l'Institut de Sociologie* (January-March 1936), pp. 97-101; the first third of A. N. Poliak, *Feudalism in Egypt, Syria, Palestine and the Lebanon, 1250-1900* (Royal Asiatic Society, London: 1939); Claude Cahen, "L'evolution de l'iḳṭāʿ de IXe au XIIIe siècle," *Annales: Économies, Sociétés, Civilisations*, VIII (January-March 1953), 25-52. On the Mamluk system itself, see particularly the work of David Ayalon, especially his articles on "The System of Payment in Mamluk Military Society," *Journal of the Economic and Social*

There was yet another consequence of this system, perhaps of even greater relevance. The Mamluks' lack of involvement with the land, except as a form of wealth to be exploited, tended further to concentrate all power in Cairo, where the important Mamluk amirs lived during intervals of peace. The wealth, then, of the entire countryside tended to converge upon the capital city which also monopolized the buying power of an empire. Enjoying such a position of central dominance, the city of Cairo was able to grow and to flourish, even after economic decline had already begun to wither the agricultural hinterland upon which she ultimately depended.

It was during the period that roughly corresponds to the rule of the Baḥri Mamluks, or the Turkish Slaves of the Nile (1260-1382), that Cairo experienced her greatest growth and development during the medieval era. This growth was stimulated in part by the growing trade between East and West in which Egypt—and indeed the entire Middle East—was both a critical link in the geographic route and, thanks to the vigorous activities of her merchants (the so-called Kārimis), the reaper of economic profits from each commercial transaction.[13] Despite occasional threats from the last Crusaders still entrenched on the coast of the Fertile Crescent and more serious incursions by invigorated Mongol tribes from the Eastern steppes, and despite the periodic plagues and other natural disasters which from time to time took unbelievable tolls in the urban population, the city of Cairo not only survived but reached the pinnacle of her development.

It was General Baybars' victory over the Mongols, who had succeeded in destroying the seat of the Caliphate at Baghdad and had even reached Syria before they were repelled, that led eventually to his assumption of the throne in 1260 as the first real Mamluk Sultan.[14] To bolster his legitimacy he had the 'Abbāsid Caliphate transferred to Cairo in 1261, where it remained up to the Ottoman period, an empty figurehead chiefly of ceremonial significance. While Baybars' contributions to the architecture of Cairo were mostly military (he restored the barracks on Rawḍah and added to the Citadel),[15] the enlargement of the empire and the greater

History of the Orient, Volume 1, Part 1 (August 1957), 37-65, and Volume 1, Part 3 (October 1958), 257-296.

[13] The spice trade was always an important aspect of Cairo's economy, and even during the era of the Fāṭimids important trade routes linked Egypt with the Far East. Under the Ayyūbids this commerce flowered, particularly through the Red Sea ports of the Ḥijāz and Qulzum (Suez). Under the Mamluks, despite the loss of control over the Arabian shore of the Red Sea, commerce was vigorous, with the trade route diverted to Aden and then to the west shore at Quṣayr, where goods were transferred by caravan to the up-Nile port of Qūṣ, from whence they were transported by boat to the port at Miṣr (Fusṭāṭ). Critical in the transactions were the spice merchants who linked Yemen-Aden with Cairo; their great wealth not only permitted them to maintain luxurious *funduqs* in Miṣr and to endow many religious facilities but made them a mainstay of government finance, helping to sustain the regimes of Ṣalāḥ al-Dīn and his later successors as well as the Mamluks who followed. Information on the characteristics and activities of these spice merchants can be found in S. D. Goitein, "New Light on the Beginnings of the Kārim Merchants," *Journal of the Economic and Social History of the Orient*, Volume 1, Part 2 (April 1958), pp. 175-184, which treats their appearance and role during Fāṭimid times as revealed through the Geniza documents. See also Gaston Wiet, "Les marchands d'épices sous les sultans Mamlouks," *Cahiers d'Histoire Égyptienne*, Series VII, Fasc. 2 (May 1955), pp. 81-147, and Walter Fischel, "The Spice Trade in Mamluk Egypt; A Contribution to the Economic History of Medieval Islam," *Journal of the Economic and Social History of the Orient*, Volume 1, Part 2 (April 1958), pp. 157-174, both of which deal with developments during Mamluk times.

[14] See S. Fatima Sadeque, *Baybars I of Egypt* (Oxford University Press, Dacca, Pakistan: 1956), which includes a short biography as well as an English translation of *Sīrat al-Malik al-Ẓāhir*, a contemporary account of his exploits. See also Muir, *The Mameluke or Slave Dynasty of Egypt*, for a chronology of Mamluk successions; and, for an overview of the relationships between Mongol incursions and repercussions in the Mamluk empire, see F.R.C. Bagley, trans., *The Muslim World* by Bertold Spüler, Part II, *The Mongol Period* (E. J. Brill, Leiden: 1960).

[15] Margoliouth, *Cairo, Jerusalem and Damascus*, p. 71; Becker, "Cairo," p. 824.

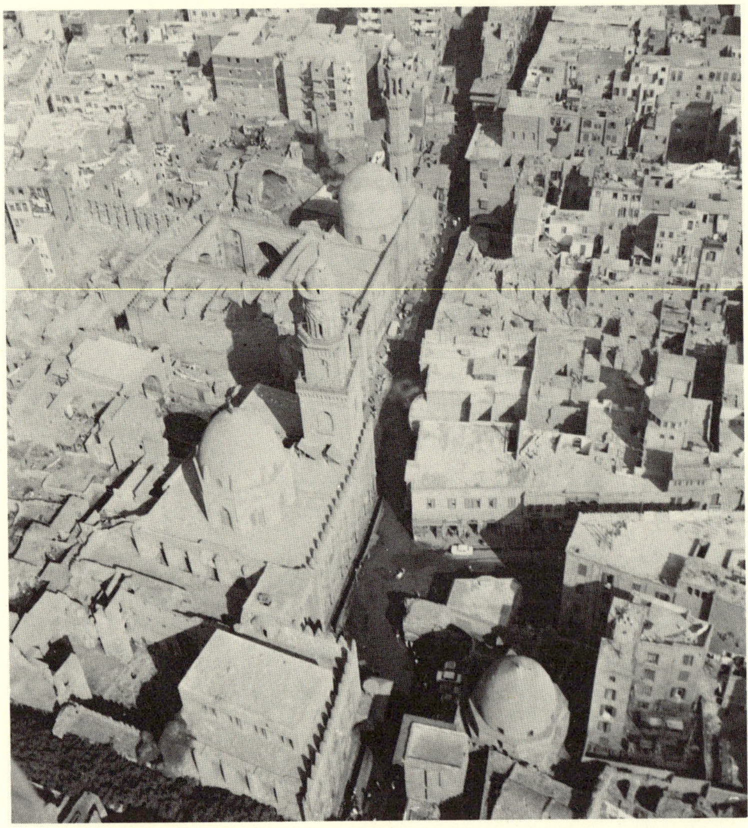

16. Aerial view of the *qaṣabah* showing hospital and mausoleum of Qalāwūn and college mosque of Ibn Qalāwūn

internal stability and external security he achieved encouraged the growth of the city. Development in the area north of Ṣalāḥ al-Dīn's walls (Ḥārat al-Ḥusaynīyah) was aided by his construction of a mosque (al-Ẓāhir) and a palace there. Land formerly in agricultural use began to be converted to urban purposes, particularly in the al-Lūq section west of the Khalīj Miṣri and in the Sayīdah Zaynab area southwest of the walled city.[16] It was in this latter district that Baybars constructed his famous Lion's Bridge over the Khalīj.

The forays against Crusaders and Mongols, which had preoccupied the Mamluks during the reign of Baybars, continued through the Sultanate of his second successor, Qalāwūn. But, as in the case of Baybars, the campaigns still left time for the development of Cairo, including the famous hospital which Qalāwūn had erected in the heart of the walled city.[17]

It was, however, during the reign of Qalāwūn's son and second successor, al-Nāṣir, that relative tranquillity and peace permitted a true flowering of Mamluk culture and a major expansion of the Mamluk capital, Cairo. Enjoying the longest reign of any Mamluk ruler, al-Nāṣir first became Sultan in 1293 as a boy of about nine under the control of powerful amirs. Twice replaced, each time he returned to power stronger than before, and during his third reign (between 1310 and his death in 1341), Cairo knew its period of greatest security and calm. Peace had finally been concluded with the troublesome Mongols from whose threats the Mamluk state was freed until the rise of Tamerlane two generations later.

These were critical years, not only for Cairo's development but for the entire Islamic empire. This was the age of the tireless traveler, Ibn Baṭṭūṭah, the birth era of Ibn Khaldūn, of the life described in the *Arabian Nights*. Cities throughout the empire, secure at last from invasion, began to expand beyond their fortifications. In Syria, towns such as Aleppo and Damascus grew rapidly outside their walls.[18] What was happening in the provincial cities, however, was but a dim reflection of the glory of the capital. Some of Cairo's most beautiful architectural constructions date from that era,[19] and much of the settled land outside the walled city received its first impetus to growth in the first four decades of the fourteenth century.

Cairo's phenomenal expansion during the early decades of the century has been well-chronicled by her topographer, Taqi al-Dīn Aḥmad al-Maqrīzi,[20] and it is to his monumental, detail-choked history and description of the city that all writers must turn for information on this and later periods.

From his study one can reconstruct the extent of greater Cairo and the new areas opened to settlement during the reign of al-Nāṣir. Madīnat al-Qāhirah, the city contained within the stone walls, was by this time clearly distinguished both from Miṣr, the independent industrial port-suburb to its south, and from what was known as Ẓāhir al-Qāhirah—literally, the unfortified portions of Cairo, the sections outside the walls.[21] Al-Qāhirah proper contained most of the population and, concentrated near and along its north-south thoroughfare between Bāb al-Futūḥ and Bāb Zuwaylah, most of the major markets (sing. *sūq*; pl. *aswāq*) of local, regional, and international trade. Maqrīzi tells us that during the height of good times (al-Nāṣir's rule), this commercial zone, the *Qaṣabah*, bustled with 12,000 shops in addition to numberless itinerant vendors who blocked the public way and shop entrances with their wares.[22] Only a handful of the 35 major *aswāq* enumerated by Maqrīzi dated from the Fāṭimid period. Some were added during the era of Ṣalāḥ al-Dīn, only one during the time of Qalāwūn. Many, however, had been established during the reign of al-Nāṣir, including Sūq al-Jammālīn al-Kabīr, Sūq al-Kharrāṭīn, and Sūq al-Kutubiyīn.[23] In addition, all of the markets *outside* the walled city were developed after 1300, i.e., during the period of al-Nāṣir.

It was in these areas outside the walls that the greatest changes were taking place. Before the time of al-Nāṣir there had been some development north of the city, somewhat less construction south of the city walls, hardly any growth to the west, and no development east of the walled city. By the end of al-Nāṣir's reign, the northern and southern districts were heavily populated, the western region had been transformed entirely, and a new City of the Dead had begun to form in the eastern section. Maqrīzi proves an invaluable guide in tracing these changes.

When Jawhar first built his city, all the land between

[16] Margoliouth, *Cairo, Jerusalem and Damascus*, pp. 71-72. A group of Tatar colonists settled in this district.

[17] Maqrīzi, *Khiṭaṭ*, II, 406-408; Margoliouth, *Cairo, Jerusalem and Damascus*, pp. 75-77; Lane-Poole, *The Story of Cairo*, p. 212.

[18] Nicola Ziadeh, *Urban Life in Syria Under the Early Mamluks*, pp. 81-82.

[19] Lane-Poole, *The Story of Cairo*, enumerates them on pp. 220-224; see also Margoliouth, *Cairo, Jerusalem and Damascus*, pp. 89-92.

[20] Maqrīzi was born in Cairo in 1364 during the last period of al-Nāṣir's Baḥri successors. His life span witnessed the rise of Tamerlane, the shift in Cairo from the Turkish to the Circassian Mamluk State, the pain and chaos of Mongol victory in the empire, and civil strife, plagues, and famine in his beloved Cairo. He died in 1442, having written, in addition to an historical work of great magnitude, his famous *Khiṭaṭ*, which was both a history and topography of Cairo.

[21] Maqrīzi, *Khiṭaṭ*, I, 360.

[22] *Ibid.*, II, 95.

[23] See *ibid.*, pp. 95-106, where he enumerates and describes the major markets of the city.

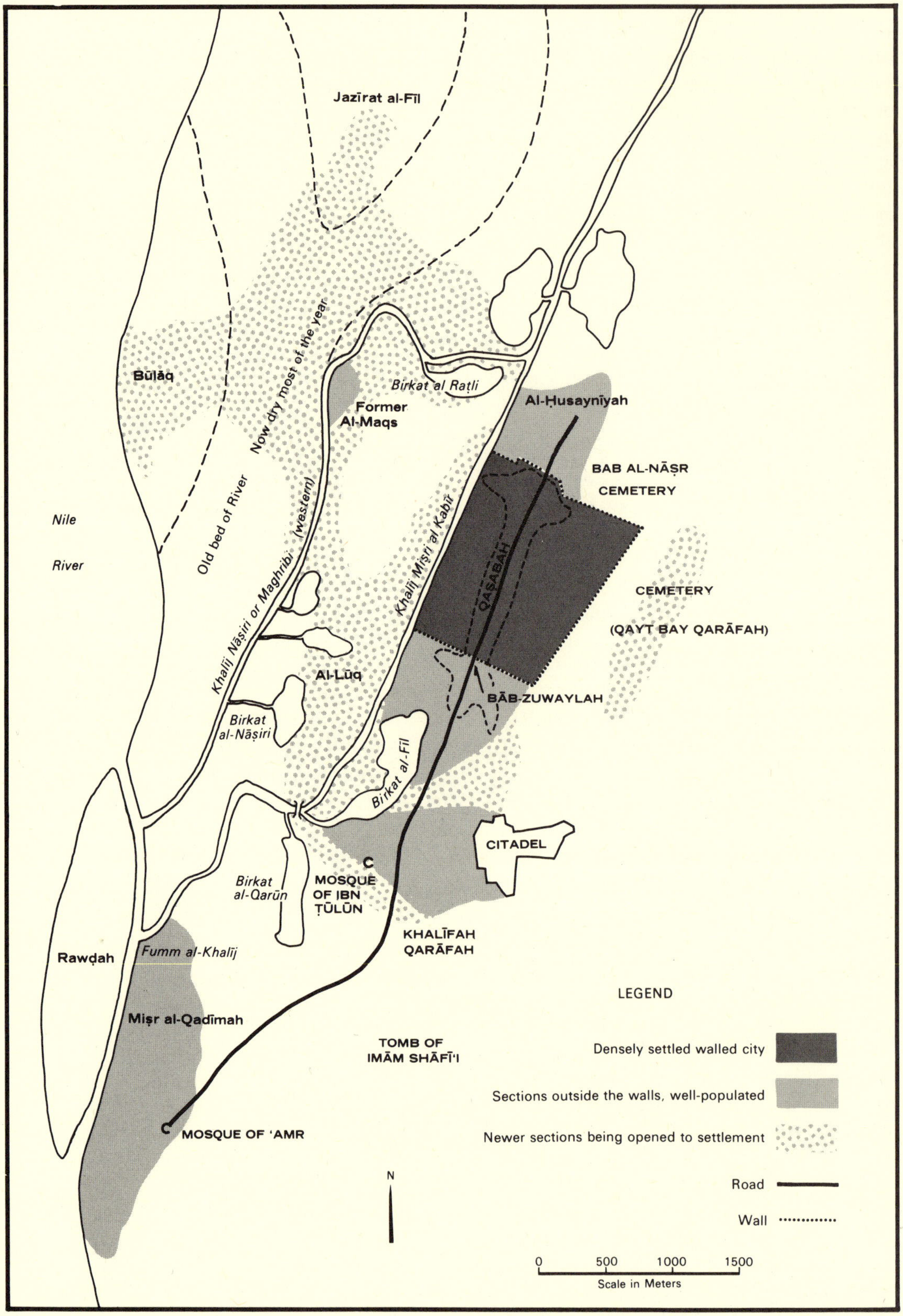

VII. Cairo's development at the time of Sultan al-Nāṣir ibn Qalāwūn

17. Tomb city (probably Bāb al-Naṣr cemetery) *ca.* 1800

18. Bāb al-Naṣr cemetery today

the northern wall and the agricultural suburb of Maṭarīyah (near Heliopolis) was empty desert.[24] During the Fāṭimid era some soldiers were quartered in the western half of this area while the eastern section served as a stopping place for caravans. It was not until the middle of the eleventh century, at the death of Badr al-Jamālī, that part of the eastern section was converted into a cemetery (the Bāb al-Naṣr cemetery containing the tomb of Badr al-Jamālī, which can still be seen from the north wall). The area, however, received its strongest impetus to growth during the period of Baybars, when it became "one of the greatest sections of Miṣr and al-Qāhirah." By al-Nāṣir's time, the entire area between Bāb al-Naṣr and the troop assembly grounds at al-Raydānīyah was completely covered by buildings, interspersed with tombs.

Developments in the north, however, were quite overshadowed by those occurring outside the southern wall of the city.[25] This had become, by the end of al-Nāṣir's reign, the most populous district of Ẓāhir al-Qāhirah. It will be recalled that this area had once housed the Sudanese soldier-slaves of the Fāṭimids, whose *ḥārah* was destroyed by Ṣalāḥ al-Dīn. In the late Ayyūbid period, the amirs constructed palaces and luxurious villas along the shores of Birkat al-Fīl (midway between the southern wall and the Citadel), but it was not until the third reign of al-Nāṣir that systematic and vigorous construction in this district began. The result was an intensive development stretching from Bāb Zuwaylah to the Citadel-Mosque of Ibn Ṭūlūn-Sitt Nafīsah tomb limits on the south, and from the Muqaṭṭam mountains to the shore of the Nile on the west. Even the Great Qarāfah (the Khalīfah City of the Dead parallel to Fusṭāṭ) became a popular residential zone all the way from the Bāb al-Qarāfah southward to the Tomb of the Imām Shāfi'i.

Maqrīzi tells us that before the third reign of Sultan al-Nāṣir there were no buildings at all in the hilly area east of the city which today contains the Mamluk City of the Dead (including the masterpiece mausoleums of Barqūq, Ināl, Qayt Bay, and other Circassian Mamluk rulers).[26] It was not until 1320, when al-Nāṣir abandoned the use of a *maydān* which formerly stretched between the Bāb al-Naṣr cemetery and the mountain, that buildings began to be constructed in this area. However, developments during his reign were minimal in comparison to the growth that was to take place during the following centuries.

Whereas the growth in the northern and southern suburbs was but a more vigorous continuation of previous developments, the western section truly owed its transformation to the public works of al-Nāṣir. Most of the buildings in that section were constructed after 1312; before that time the area had been occupied by seasonal gardens or submerged under water. Beginning at the time of Ṣalāḥ al-Dīn, the Nile's recession exposed the Jazīrat al-Fīl and later stranded the port of al-Maqs. In this process, many islands and sand bars were formed, more in each successive year, until some of the higher points in the drying riverbed were flooded only a few days each year. The Mamluks used the newly vegetating lands for hunting, archery practice, and other sports. In 1313, al-Nāṣir proclaimed the area open for settlement, and all the high lands along the new river edge at Būlāq and the Jazīrat al-Fīl, from al-Lūq to the village of Minyat al-Sīrij, began to be filled with orchards, farms, and palatial residences.[27]

The chief factor that encouraged the growth of the western suburb was the canal which al-Nāṣir ordered to be dug there. Sultan al-Nāṣir was justly famous for his public works,[28] but none had as much impact on the

[24] Maqrīzi's account of developments in the northern suburb is found chiefly in *ibid.*, I, 360; II, 22, 110-111.

[25] Scattered references to the southern zone in *ibid.*, I, 360; II, 110, 161, 444.

[26] For the eastern cemetery zone, see *ibid.*, I, 360; II, 463.

[27] *Ibid.*, I, 361; II, 131. To illustrate the extent of these developments, Maqrīzi cites the case of the Jazīrat al-Fīl (present-day Shubra); on that tremendous island in 1311 there were only 20 *basātīn* (orchards or gardens) whereas in Maqrīzi's day about a century later, the area contained more than 150.

[28] See Muir, *The Mameluke or Slave Dynasty of Egypt*, pp. 79-81, for a partial enumeration.

growth of the city as this canal which, from its mouth at the Nile, followed a course parallel to and due west of the older Khalīj Miṣri, which it later joined north of the walled city. Al-Nāṣir had built a palace at Siryākis for which he wanted access from the Nile. The engineers selected the lowest land (the center of the old bed of the Nile) and, with the forced labor of innumerable peasants, the digging of a new canal was completed within two months of its commencement in 1325. Its course was specially designed to pass just north of the Birkat al-Raṭli in order to supply this pond with water. Originally the new canal was known as the Khalīj Nāṣiri, although later it came to be referred to more simply as the Western Canal (Khalīj Maghribi). Once the canal was completed, al-Nāṣir issued proclamations inviting the people to construct in the vicinity and, within a short time, the competition for space resulted in a profusion of building on both sides of the canal "so that all the land between al-Maqs and the shore of the Nile in Būlāq was built upon." Orchards, elaborate villas, mosques, dwellings for ordinary persons, markets, and other urban features filled the area from the high dike at Birkat al-Raṭli in the north to the al-Lūq zone in the south.[29]

South of al-Lūq, urban development was also encouraged by another of al-Nāṣir's public works. The area in the vicinity of Birkat Qārūn had been relatively deserted since the time of al-'Askar's destruction, but, reactivated by the excavation of Birkat al-Nāṣiri in the vicinity and the establishment of a checkpost on the main road between Cairo and Miṣr, it began to show the first stirrings of urban growth. At Maqrīzi's time, all the buildings in that section dated from the period of al-Nāṣir.[30]

Map VII summarizes the major developments which resulted, by the end of Sultan al-Nāṣir ibn Qalāwūn's lengthy reign, in a Cairo which had attained almost the same dimensions she had by the time of the French Expedition at the turn of the nineteenth century. A community of vast extent and enormous population, sustained by international commerce, nurtured by a rich agricultural hinterland, and protected by an era of peace, she had become the foremost capital of the East. This was the city which the Baedecker of the time, Ibn Baṭṭūṭah, called "Mother of cities . . . mistress of broad provinces and fruitful lands, boundless in multitudes of buildings, peerless in beauty and splendour . . . she surges as the sea with her throngs of folk and can scarcely contain them for all the capacity of her situation and sustaining power."[31] This glowing description of Cairo, written at the pinnacle of her development, may perhaps serve also as her epitaph, for only a short time later she was to begin her long descent.

[29] Maqrīzi's account of the canal and its impact upon urban expansion in the western zone is found in *Khiṭaṭ*, II, 131, 145 (most detailed), and 162. Quotation taken from p. 145.

[30] *Ibid.*, II, 161.

[31] Taken from Ibn Baṭṭūṭah's description of his first voyage to Egypt during the time of Sultan al-Nāṣir. See *The Travels of Ibn Batuta*, H.A.R. Gibb, trans. (Issued by the Hakluyt Society and published by Cambridge University Press, Cambridge: 1958), I, 41.

4 Decline and Fall

Alas, it is all gone, except for very little . . .
deteriorated . . . ruined . . . deserted. . . .
What remains of it pains me to see.

These are the lamentations which appear as dismal choruses throughout the voluminous *Khiṭaṭ* of Maqrīzi who described the city he knew in the second and third decades of the fifteenth century.[1] Less than a century had passed since the panegyric of Ibn Baṭṭūṭah.

The decline of Cairo had, in fact, taken much less than a century. Only sixty years of political dissension at home, of plague and famine throughout the empire, and of renewed Mongol invasions had been sufficient to undo much of the progress that had been achieved by 1340. Just as the zenith had been reached during the era of Sultan al-Nāṣir ibn Qalāwūn, so the penultimate nadir at the turn of the fifteenth century coincided with the reign of Sultan al-Nāṣir Faraj ibn Barqūq. The intervening events read as an unrelieved chronicle of doom.

Political instability was certainly a chief factor in the decline. After al-Nāṣir's death in 1341, one after another of his very young sons was elevated to the Sultanate, each a pawn of powerful but disunited amirs, each speedily and bloodily deposed as the factions gained and lost.[2] So disorganized a state was in no position to resist when natural disaster struck. Disaster, world-wide in extent, came stealthily, clothed as the Black Death. While the history of Egypt is rife with plagues and epidemics, this was a plague "the likes of which had never been known before in Islam." Arriving in autumn of 1348 from China by way of Asia Minor, Syria, and the Mediterranean region, the bubonic plague spread from the coast through the Delta until it reached Cairo. While by the first month of the Arab year it had contaminated all of Egypt, it did not reach its peak in the city until between the sixth and ninth months. By spring, Cairo's "streets and market places were piled high with unburied corpses." A few weeks later, "Cairo had become so desolate . . . [that] a person might walk all the way from the Bāb Zuwaylah to Bāb al-Naṣr [i.e., the busiest street of the city] without even being jostled." Whole streets and quarters were deserted and all the cemeteries were filled to overflowing, burial trenches and communal graves an unavoidable expedient.[3] That the bubonic plague, which returned twice more within the decade, took an incredible toll in lives is unquestionable. While Maqrīzi's estimates are ludicrous exaggerations,[4] the mortality in Cairo alone must have reached 200,000, a not insubstantial figure for a city which at its height had a population of perhaps half a million.[5] When to this is added the flight of many residents into the countryside and the deaths from the famine that followed, one can well believe that Cairo, at least temporarily, was reduced to a ghost city.

The crisis brought about by the plague seems to have done little to assuage the political difficulties. Four more ineffective successors of the house of Ibn Qalāwūn followed one another, compounding pestilence and famine with rebellion and misrule. And then, as if these burdens were still too light, in 1380 the Mongols under Tamerlane again commenced their small forays, presaging a future threat to the empire. It was at this point that the amirs turned in desperation to the talented general, Barqūq, who became in 1382 the first Circassian Sultan and the founder of the Burji (Citadel) Mamluk dynasty that was to rule Egypt until the Ottoman conquest in 1517.[6]

[1] Maqrīzi began writing his *Khiṭaṭ* during the reign of Mu'ayyad (1412-1421) and completed the manuscript in the fourth year of the reign of Barsbay, i.e., in 1424. In the 1853 Būlāq edition of the manuscript (reputed to be the most accurate), the editors have identified portions concerning later epochs as presumed forgeries. The quotations have been taken from II, 95 *re* the *qaṣabah*; pp. 94, 104; p. 97 *re* Sūq Bayn al-Qaṣrayn.

[2] See Muir, *The Mameluke or Slave Dynasty of Egypt*, pp. 86-94, for a quick review of the succession during the first seven years after al-Nāṣir's death.

[3] Maqrīzi gives a graphic account of this plague in his *Kitāb al-Sulūk li Ma'rifat Duwal al-Mulūk*, ed. M. Ziadeh (Cairo, 1958), Volume II, Part III, pp. 770-791. The quotations and details cited appear on pp. 772-773, 781-783.

[4] According to his account, 10,000 to 20,000 persons died daily in al-Qāhirah and Miṣr (*ibid.*, p. 772), and within the two most disastrous months, 900,000 funerals were held in the two cities, not including the suburbs (*ibid.*, p. 782).

[5] These are my very rough estimates. The population of Cairo at the time of the French Expedition was between 250,000 and 260,000. During the reign of al-Nāṣir ibn Qalāwūn, it undoubtedly exceeded this number, but not by more than double. Statistics on deaths were not kept during this plague in Cairo. However, statistics which are reported for the city of London when it experienced the last of its bubonic plagues in 1665 indicate that, for a city of that size taking minimum health precautions, mortality ranged from several thousand to 6,000 dead each week during the height of the plague. Even doubling these figures yields a total which does not exceed 200,000. See the semi-fictional account of Daniel Defoe, *A Journal of the Plague Year* (A Signet Classic, The New American Library of World Literature, New York: 1960), which also conveys an emotional understanding of a plague's impact.

[6] Muir, *The Mameluke or Slave Dynasty of Egypt*, pp. 100-101, 105-116. An indispensable source on the Circassian Mamluk period is the Annals of Abū al-Maḥāsin ibn Taghri Birdi, which have been translated by William Popper under the title *History of*

Irrepressible Cairo, despite her continuing problems, had already begun a remarkable recovery from the plagues[7] and, during the reign of Barqūq (1382 to 1399, with only one brief interruption), reconstruction went on at an even faster rate. Most of the rebuilding, however, was concentrated in the central portion of the walled city, with the areas outside the walls still abandoned or severely depopulated. In 1384 work began on the Barqūq college mosque in Bayn al-Qaṣrayn.[8] Several of the *aswāq* of central Cairo were rebuilt by Barqūq, and a new commercial area, known to all tourists of modern Cairo as the Khān al-Khalīli, was developed at this time.[9] The condition of both al-Qāhirah and Miṣr-Fusṭāṭ at the time of recovery under Barqūq has been described in detail by Ibn Duqmaq, the teacher of Maqrīzi, who wrote his series on the cities of Islam some thirty years before his pupil.[10]

Egypt, 1382-1469 A.D. Part I covers the years 1382-1399 and is Volume 13 of the University of California Publications in Semitic Philology (University of California Press, Berkeley: 1954); Part II chronicles 1399-1411 and is Volume 14 of the same series (1954); Part III covers the period 1412-1422 and is Volume 17 of the same series (1957). Subsequent parts are noted below.

7 Just as two centuries earlier Ibn Jubayr described a prosperous Miṣr only fifteen years after the "Great Fire," so in 1383 Ibn Khaldūn came to post-plague Cairo to extol this "metropolis of the universe, garden of the world, swarming core of the human species . . . ; a city embellished with castles and palaces, bedecked with convents and colleges, illuminated by the moons and stars of knowledge." My translation from the French quotation appearing in Clerget, *Le Caire*, I, 152. Nor can Ibn Khaldūn's account be dismissed as mere poetic excess. Three accounts written by Italian travelers at almost the same time (1384) are equally glowing. Frescobaldi, for instance, notes that "the imperial city of Cairo is rich and abounds with all sorts of sugars, spices, and food from all places. . . . This city of Cairo has a population greater than all of Tuscany, and there is one street more populated than all of Florence. . . ." Translated from the French rendering by Dopp, "Le Caire: Vu par les voyageurs occidentaux du Moyen Âge," p. 135. His companion, Simone Sigoli, showed even more enthusiasm, although less intelligence, when he noted that "the city of Cairo is more than twelve miles long and its circumference is thirty miles around. . . . In the city there is a great abundance of merchandise of all kinds, above all spices of all varieties which come from the Indies by the Ocean Sea, entering into the Red Sea and being discharged at the Port of Saint Catherine. . . ." Again translated from Dopp, p. 141. The original Italian accounts can be found in Carlo Gargiolli, *Viaggi in Terra Santa di Leonardo Frescobaldi e d'altri del Secolo XIV* (G. Barbera, Florence: 1862). It is difficult to make a transition from Maqrīzi's description of plague-desolated Cairo to the city described above.

8 William Popper, *History of Egypt*, Part I (1954), p. 12.

9 See Maqrīzi, *Khiṭaṭ*, II, 95-106, for the reconstructions of Barqūq. Maqrīzi tells us that the Khān al-Khalīli was established under the reign of Barqūq by the Amir Jakārkus al-Khalīli, who removed the bones from the old Fāṭimid cemetery to gain the site for Cairo's still thriving bazaar area (*ibid.*, II, 94).

10 Ibn Duqmaq (d. 1406) wrote an encyclopedic work on ten cities of Islam, the *Kitāb al-Intiṣār li Wāsiṭāt 'Iqd al-Amṣār*, de-

19. Mausoleum mosque of Barqūq in the eastern cemetery *ca.* 1840

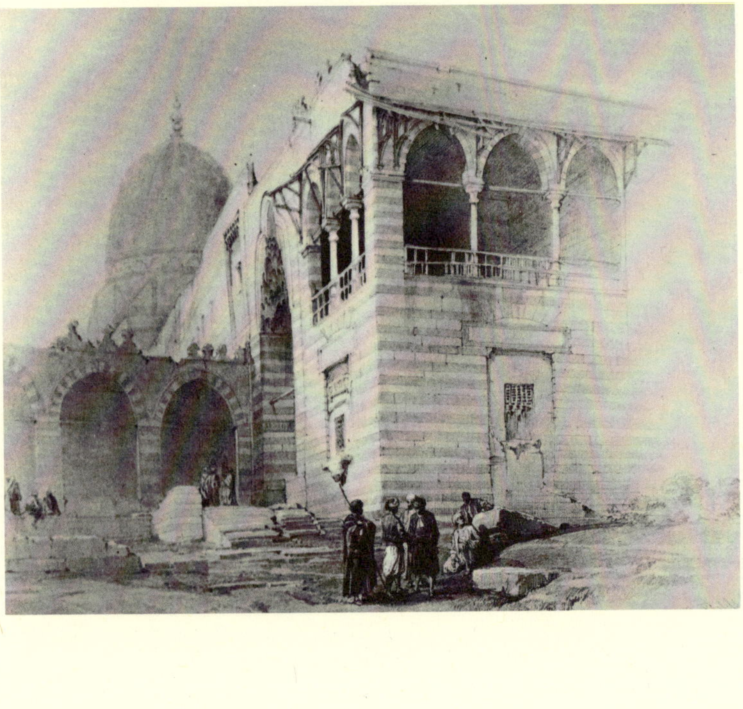

20. Bazaar of the Coppersmiths in early 19th century

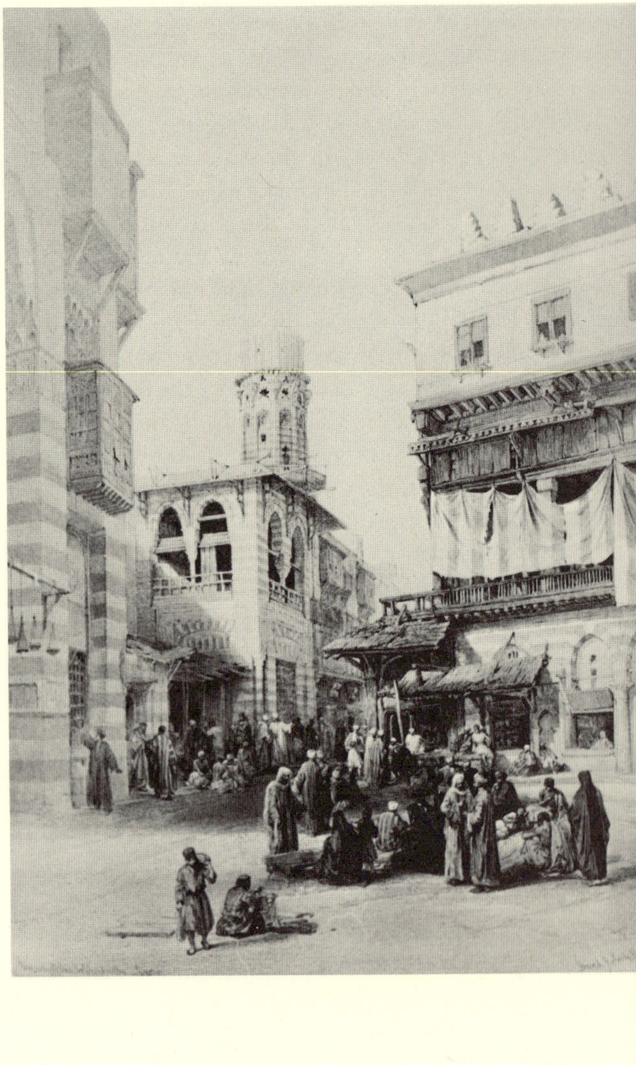

21. The Khān al-Khalīli (14th century) still frequented by tourists

The revival under Barqūq, however, proved to be but a respite rather than a reversal of Cairo's fortunes. The plague returned in 1388-1389,[11] and an insurrection in the latter year, in which Barqūq was temporarily overthrown, turned the city again into a battlefield.[12] Barqūq was restored to power in 1390, but dissension and economic difficulties continued to harass him, as they did his successors for years to come. Furthermore, the Mongols were approaching. By 1393 they held Baghdad, poised for their invasion of Syria in 1400. Thus, an empire on the verge of disaster was the bequest which Barqūq left to his thirteen-year-old son, al-Nāṣir Faraj, when he died in 1399.[13]

Maqrīzi's verdict on al-Nāṣir Faraj is harsh indeed, and from what we have seen above, somewhat unjust. In his words:

> An-Nasir was the most ill-omened of all the rulers of Islam, for by his mismanagement he brought ruin upon all the land of Egypt and all of Syria from the source of the Nile to the outlet of the Euphrates. And the tyrant Tamerlane invaded Syria in 803 (1400) and reduced to ruins Aleppo. . . . Famine struck Egypt from 806 (1403) on. . . . More than half of Cairo, its estates and environs, were ruined; two-thirds of the population of Misr died of famine and plague; and innumerable others in Cairo were killed in insurrections during his reign.[14]

While these occurrences can hardly be blamed on the agency of one man (particularly a young boy), there is little doubt that Cairo did reach a low ebb at this period of history. What the plague had begun was completed by the Mamluk defeat at the hands of Tamerlane, by the economic depression that followed, and by the civil strife which endangered life and property within Cairo as fighting took place around the periodically besieged Citadel.

The northern suburb of al-Ḥusaynīyah, which had become relatively deserted after the Black Death, was utterly desolate by 1403. The western suburbs, sorely decimated during the preceding fifty years, were reduced to scattered dwellings and a few orchards. Birkat al-Raṭli, the former resort area to the northwest, was deserted, and even the once-populous industrial district of al-Maqs was in ruins, with only a few markets and mosques still functioning.[15] Ruins bordered the Citadel,[16] and al-Qāhirah and Fusṭāṭ were once again separated by dusty plains and rubble. In the brief thirty years between the works of Ibn Duqmaq and Maqrīzi, Fusṭāṭ had undergone a rapid decline, with a devastation of the famous Sūq al-Qanādīl (the covered bazaar so dark and dense it was lit by candles) and the Khiṭ al-Muṣāṣah, and with many buildings destroyed by scavengers.[17] Only the cemetery cities south and east continued to grow,[18] ironically confirming the macabre state of the city.

Furthermore, the blight which had hitherto been confined to the suburban ring now spread into the very heart of the central city. Once-bustling markets were abandoned as poverty and depression inhibited commerce. The caravan market had still not recovered from the sequestrations of al-Nāṣir Faraj, and the luxury mar-

---

voting one volume to each city. While much of his work was lost, the volumes describing Cairo (including Miṣr) and Alexandria are preserved. The Cairo manuscript has been edited by Karl Vollers and published under the title, *Description de l'Égypte* (Imprimerie Nationale, Cairo: 1893).

[11] Popper, *History of Egypt*, Part I (1954), pp. 19, 33.

[12] *Ibid.*, pp. 32-38, 60-104.

[13] Faraj's reign is covered in Part II of Popper, *History of Egypt* (1954).

[14] As quoted by Ibn Taghri Birdi, *ibid.*, pp. 197-198. Ibn Taghri Birdi is far more measured than Maqrīzi in his view, all the more remarkably since it was at the hands of al-Nāṣir Faraj that his family was victimized. He calls attention to the poor flood in 1403, the famine, and then the plague, which introduced "a series of events and trials in which most of Egypt and its provinces were ruined, not only because of the failure of the inundation but also because of the lack of harmony in the government. . . ." *Ibid.*, p. 80.

[15] Maqrīzi, *Khiṭaṭ*, II, 23, 111, 162, 124.

[16] Popper, *History of Egypt*, Part II (1954), p. 179.

[17] See A. R. Guest and E. T. Richmond, "Misr in the Fifteenth Century," *Journal of the Royal Asiatic Society* (London, 1903), pp. 791-816, which compares the descriptions of both topographers. See especially p. 809.

[18] On the growth of the eastern cemetery (the so-called Tombs of the Caliphs), see Popper, *History of Egypt*, Part II (1954), p. 166. It was in this zone that al-Nāṣir Faraj built the exquisite mausoleum for his father which still dominates the district. On developments in the southern or Great Qarāfah, see Guest and Richmond, "Misr in the Fifteenth Century," p. 810.

22. Mu'ayyad Mosque and the twin minarets above Bāb Zuwaylah *ca.* 1840

kets—fur, candles, gold and silver armor and ornamented bridles for horses—closed for lack of customers; even the prostitutes felt the impact of the depression. Residential quarters suffered a similar fate. The *ḥārāt* within the eastern and northern sections of the walled city (for example, Ḥārat al-'Uṭūfīyah, Ḥārat al-Barqīyah, see Map IX) were deserted at their fringe and decayed into slums near the city's center.[19]

It is perhaps significant that almost all the *ḥārāt* of the city and its environs listed by Maqrīzi were located within the longitudinal belt stretching between al-Ḥusaynīyah north of the walled city and the Citadel due south of the walled enclave. It is perhaps also significant that only 31 of the 37 *ḥārāt* identified by Maqrīzi were noted as still in existence. (See Map IX and its accompanying key for the names and locations of the *ḥārāt* enumerated by Maqrīzi.) Thus, by the opening decades of the fifteenth century, if we are to be guided by the famous topographer, Cairo had diminished in extent and population, had retrenched toward the portions settled before the expansive era of al-Nāṣir ibn Qalāwūn, and had suffered a severe setback in prosperity and commercial activity.

The fifteenth century did witness a temporary economic revival which again filled the markets with goods, the streets with tradesmen, and the coffers of the government with customs fees. Toward the end of his lifetime, Maqrīzi himself saw and acknowledged the beginning of this revival and noted the reconstruction of certain areas which had formerly been desolate.

This revival was sluggish and faltering during the harassed reigns of Barqūq's two young heirs and their successor, al-Mu'ayyad, a leading amir and manumitted Mamluk of Barqūq's household. His accession marks the demise of the hereditary principle of succession to the Sultanate of Egypt, for thereafter, although lip service continued to be paid to natural (and often infant) heirs, who were occasionally elevated to the throne, real power lay in the hands of those princes fortunate enough to consolidate their strength—by murder or imprisonment of weaker rivals or by uneasy alliance with those whom they could not eliminate—in a precarious bid for legitimacy. One of the most successful of these new rulers was Barsbay, another manumitted slave from the house of Barqūq. By 1421 he was the regent for an infant heir soon to be displaced when he had himself proclaimed Sultan in 1422.[20]

While Barsbay was powerless to undo the disastrous effects of the bankrupting campaigns and natural catastrophes that were irreparably undermining Egypt's economy,[21] he was successful in gaining time before the eventual collapse through his exploitation of the renewed trading opportunities facilitated, ironically, by Tamerlane's victories. Since it was Egypt's monopoly of the East-West spice trade that helped maintain fifteenth-century Cairo's prosperity and that led to a final change in the ecology of the city, we must digress here to trace the relevant shifts in the trade route.[22]

[19] The foregoing has been reconstructed from the account of Maqrīzi contained in *Khiṭaṭ*, II, 95-106, 2-23.

[20] See Popper, *History of Egypt*, Part III (1957), *passim* for the sordid history of succession through Barsbay. An excellent study of developments under Barsbay is to be found in Aḥmad Darrag (Darrāj), *L'Égypte sous le règne de Barsbay: 825-841/-1422-1438* (Institut Français de Damas, Damascus: 1961), upon which the following section depends.

[21] See Chapter III of Darrag, *L'Égypte sous le règne de Barsbay*, pp. 57-107. Government funds were squandered in financing al-Mu'ayyad's foreign campaigns in 1413, 1415, 1416, and 1418. Distributions to the Mamluks were again required for Ṭaṭar's campaign of 1421. Plagues, famines, and fiscal shortages recurred in 1403-1407, 1415-1416, 1419, 1427, 1429, 1430, 1437-1438, 1445, and again in 1449. They were to become an endemic condition of Egypt throughout the successive centuries of depopulation.

[22] I draw heavily upon Darrag's account, *L'Égypte sous le*

Tamerlane's advances had disrupted the arteries over which most of the trade between China and the Crimea had flowed, causing it to be deflected once again to its older route through Aden (Yemen) and the Red Sea. Unsuccessful attempts were made to reopen the central land route, but by the second decade of the fifteenth century virtually the only access from China to the West was through the Red Sea. This was, however, still an insecure passage not yet firmly under Egyptian control. The ruler of Aden had imposed "a virtual reign of terror," causing the Kārimi merchants to flee northward to Jiddah. The Chinese emperor lodged vigorous protests against his interference with trade. Thus commerce was already being channeled through the Ḥijāz ports when Barsbay strengthened his hold over them. With Yemen no longer an important rival in the spice trade, traffic flowed into the restored and improved ports of Jiddah, Ṭor, and Qulzum (Suez), where it came under the government monopoly established by Barsbay. The Kārimi merchants, formerly an independent economic force, were reduced to middlemen who transacted business for the Sultan;[23] the southern trade route (from Aden to Quṣayr to Qūṣ and from thence, by boat, to the old port of Miṣr) was abandoned in favor of a more northerly course from Qulzum across the eastern desert to Cairo, a shift that was to have radical implications for the city's port facilities.[24] These changes bolstered the economy of Egypt, despite the growing decadence of its underlying agricultural base, and created a superficial glow of health upon her visage to the world, the capital city of Cairo.

Nor had that city ever been in as dire a state as Maqrīzi claimed. It was perhaps only to one who glanced backward and compared her present with her former glory that she appeared so decadent. Certainly the rest of the world viewed fifteenth-century Cairo in a more favorable light, recognizing her still as one of the most important cities of the world. To European travelers who began to visit Cairo in small but increasing numbers she represented a wondrous achievement exceeding anything which Europe had yet produced.

This was literally true. Despite the decline in population from its fourteenth-century peak, Cairo was still greater in extent and population than *any* city of Europe. It must be remembered that not until the following century did Europe begin to experience a spurt in urbanization. For example, it was not until the end of the sixteenth century that London's population grew to a quarter of a million or that the population of Paris approached 200,000.[25] The enthusiastic comments of European visitors must be viewed in the context of this real contrast. Thus, when Pero Tafur marvels at the markets of "Babylonia"[26] or when Meshullam Menahem writes in 1481 that "if it were possible to place all the cities of Rome, Milan, Padua and Florence together with four other cities, they would not . . . contain the wealth and population of the half of Misr [al-Qāhirah],"[27] these are not rhetorical exaggerations. These and other visitors[28] during the fifteenth century confirm the power and renewed vigor of the Mamluk capital, particularly when viewed within the perspective of the medieval world.

During the revival of the mid-fifteenth century much of the area which had been abandoned at the turn of the century began to be redeveloped. This was particularly true of the western section, i.e., the territory between the Khalīj Miṣri and the Western or Maghribi Khalīj which had been dug by al-Nāṣir ibn Qalāwūn. Once again this area was covered with palaces, dwellings, and gardens, and long-dormant markets and mosques were reactivated. The city also continued to grow on the eastern extreme, with the tombs of the Caliphs and Sultans interlaced

règne de Barsbay, pp. 195ff., for this discussion, although the evaluation of its implications for Cairo remains my responsibility.

[23] See Fischel, "The Spice Trade in Mamluk Egypt," p. 172. He notes that "in 1428 . . . [Barsbay] prohibited the Karimi merchants to sell spices to the Italian merchants in Alexandria, and forced them to buy the spices from the government directly at a much higher price. . . . Thus the Karimi were eliminated as the chief merchants and became agents and employees of the government." Barsbay collected one-tenth of the value of all merchandise passing through the port of Jiddah, a practice continued by his successors who further regularized Mamluk administration of port revenues. See Popper, *History of Egypt*, Part v, Volume 19 of the University of California Publications in Semitic Philology (University of California Press, Berkeley and Los Angeles: 1960), pp. 79-80, 99.

[24] See below on the development of the port at Būlāq.

[25] See Lewis Mumford, *The Culture of Cities* (Secker and Warburg, London: 1944), pp. 80-81. Mumford gives the following comparative figures: London, 250,000; Naples, ca. 240,000; Milan, ca. 200,000; Palermo, Rome, Lisbon, Seville, Antwerp, Amsterdam, each ca. 100,000. At the turn of the sixteenth century, Paris had only 180,000 inhabitants.

[26] *Pero Tafur, Travels and Adventures, 1435-1439*, trans. and ed. by Malcolm Letts (George Routledge and Sons, Ltd., London: 1926), see pp. 72-100. Chapters 8 and 11 contain material on Cairo. Note the use of the term "Babylonia" to refer to the entire area including Fusṭāṭ-Miṣr and Miṣr al-Qāhirah.

[27] See the account of Meshullam Ben R. Menahem in Elkan N. Adler, ed., *Jewish Travellers* (George Routledge and Sons, Ltd., London: 1930). Quotation appears on p. 166, and description of Miṣr continues through p. 171. It is from his description that we learn the significant fact that "old Misr . . . is all in ruins and few people live there . . . (p. 167) . . . [while in New Misr] there is not even a single house in it in ruins" (p. 168).

[28] Among these are Piloti, *L'Égypte au commencement du quinzième siècle*, ed. Dopp; Obadiah Jare da Bertinoro, whose letters are preserved in Adler, *Jewish Travellers*, pp. 223-230; and Friar Felix Fabri, whose impressions of Cairo have been reconstructed in Hilda Prescott, *Once to Sinai; The Further Pilgrimage of Friar Felix Fabri* (Eyre & Spottiswoode, London: 1957), see particularly Chapters 9, 10, and 11.

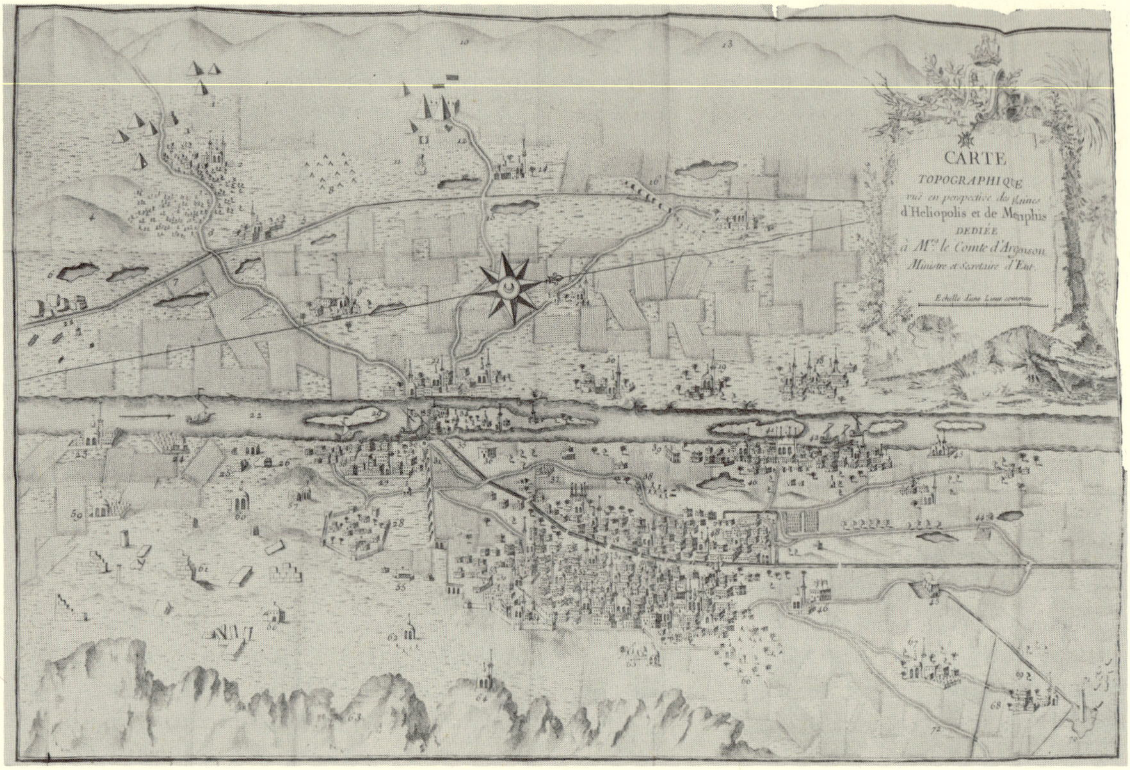

VIII. Plan view of Cairo and environs in the middle of the eighteenth century

Key to the *Ḥārāt* Enumerated by Maqrizi and Located on Map IX*

Location Shown	*Key No.*	*Name and Description*
Yes	1.	*Ḥārat Bahā' al-Dīn.* Formerly Ḥārāt al-Rīḥānīyah and al-Wazīrīyah during the Fāṭimid period.
Yes	2.	*Ḥārat Burjuwān.* Named after former Fāṭimid palace servant.
Yes (?)	3.	*Ḥārat Zuwaylah.* An ethnic group following Jawhar. Location not definite. Presumably the Jewish quarter.
Yes	4.	*Ḥārat al-Maḥmūdīyah.* Fāṭimid soldiers.
Yes	5.	*Ḥārat al-Jūdarīyah.* Soldiers of the Fāṭimid ruler, Ḥākim.
Yes (?)	6.	*Ḥārat al-Wazīrīyah.* Formerly known as Ḥārat Bustān al-Maṣmūdi and Ḥārat al-Akrād.
No	7.	*Ḥārat al-Bāṭilīyah.* The quarter of those who were treated unjustly by Mu'izz. Was in ruins at the time of Maqrīzi and considered part of Ḥārat Kutāmah (No. 11).
Yes	8.	*Ḥārat al-Rūm.* Known as the "lower" Greek quarter. Formerly outside the original southern wall of al-Qāhirah but, after the new walls were built, within the city.
Yes	9.	*Ḥārat al-Daylam.* Turkish.
Yes	10.	*Ḥārat al-Atrāk.* The quarter of the Turks near al-Azhar Mosque; known in Maqrīzi's time as Darb al-A and sometimes combined wi Ḥārat al-Daylam (No. 9).
Yes	11.	*Ḥārat Kutāmah.* This was formerly adjacent Ḥārat al-Bāṭilīyah but, by Maqrīzi's time, the two we combined.
No	12.	*Ḥārat al-Ṣaliḥīyah.* No descriptive or locational information.
Yes	13.	*Ḥārat al-Barqīyah.* Fāṭimid soldiers.
Yes	14.	*Ḥārat al-'Uṭūfīyah.* Formerly one of the best qua of al-Qāhirah but by Maq time all the better houses deteriorated and the distric housed the poorest people o the city.

* Source: *Khitat*, II, 2-23.

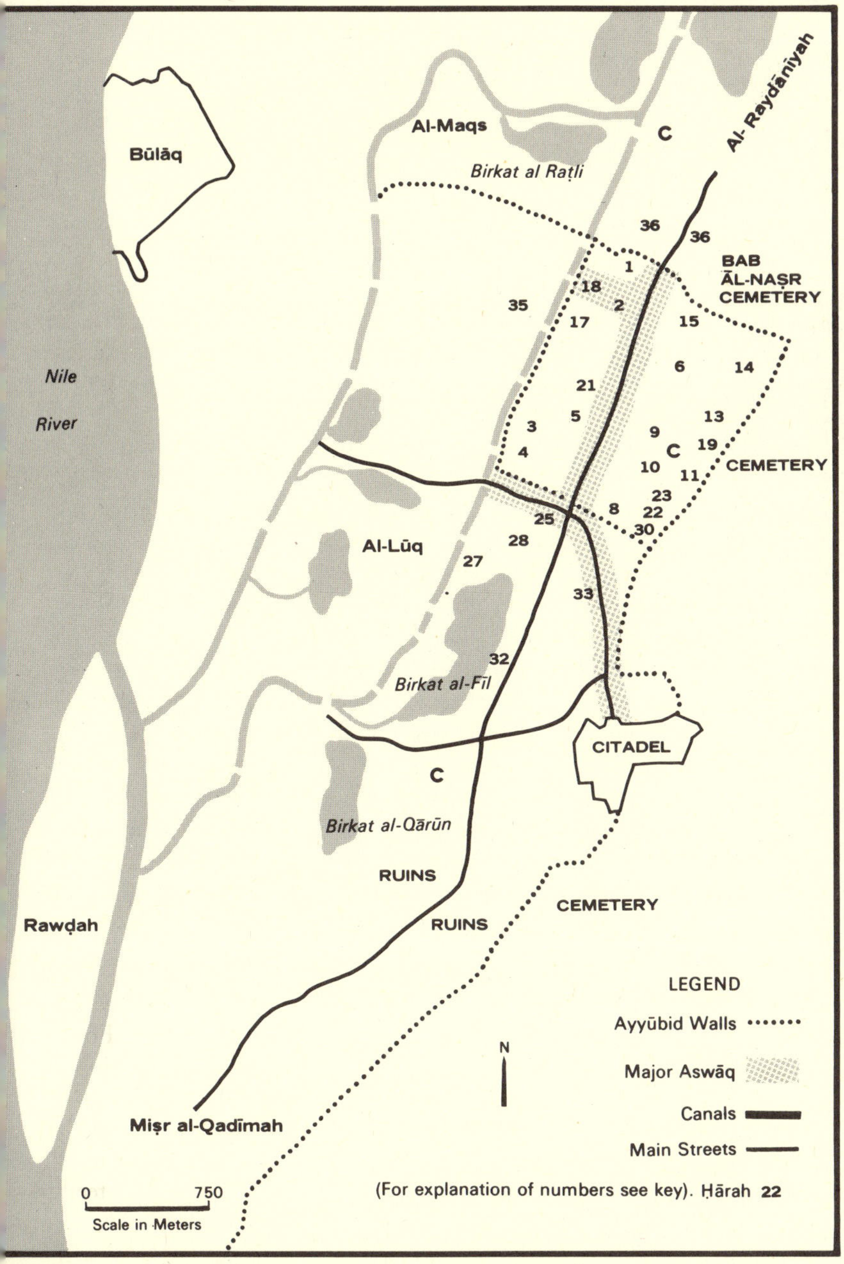

. The *ḥārāt* of al-Qāhirah *ca.* 1420 (based upon Maqrīzi)

ɔca- ion own	*Key No.*	*Name and Description*
s (?)	15.	*Ḥārat al-Juwwānīyah.* The second Greek quarter, formerly known by its full name, Ḥārat al-Rūm al-Juwwānīyah. Located near the palace.
•	16.	*Ḥārat al-Bustān.* Now merged with Ḥārat al-Wazīrīyah and Ḥārat al-Akrād. Maqrīzi gives no additional location.
s	17.	*Ḥārat al-Murtāḥīyah.* Named after a group of soldiers; formerly included the Bāb al-Qanṭarah.

Location Shown	*Key No.*	*Name and Description*
Yes	18.	*Ḥārat al-Farḥīyah.* Adjacent to No. 17.
Yes	19.	*Ḥārat al-Faraj.* Part of the section known as Qaṣr al-Shawk.
No	20.	*Ḥārat Qā'id al-Quwwād.* Formerly where Jawhar lived; in the time of Maqrīzi known as Darb Mulūkhīyah. Exact location is not given.
Yes	21.	*Ḥārat al-'Umarā'.* The quarter of the Nobles, also known as Darb Shams al-Dawlah.
Yes	22.	*Ḥārat al-Tawāriq.* On the way from Bāb Zuwaylah to Ḥārat al-Bāṭilīyah.
Yes	23.	*Ḥārat al-Sharābīyah.* Between Ḥārat al-Tawāriq and Ḥārat al-Bāṭilīyah.
No	24.	*Ḥārat al-Dimīri* and *Ḥārat al-Shāmīyyīn.* By the time of Maqrīzi, both were part of No. 14.
Yes	25.	*Ḥārat al-Muhājirīn.* The Quarter of the Immigrants, a part of the market of hides near the Bāb Zuwaylah.
No	26.	*Ḥārat al-'Adawīyah.* No location or description given.
Yes	27.	*Ḥārat al-'Īdānīyah.* Outside the walls; some of its buildings overlook the Bustān al-Ḥabbānīyah; others overlook the Birkat al-Fīl.
Yes	28.	*Ḥārat al-Ḥamziyīn.* Outside the Bāb Zuwaylah; formerly known as the Bustān al-Ḥabbānīyah until an ethnic group, the Ḥamzi, settled there.
No	29.	*Ḥārat Bani Sūs.* No information or location given.
Yes	30.	*Ḥārat al-Yānisīyah.* Named after a group of soldiers.
No	31.	*Ḥārat al-Muntajibīyah.* No location given.
Yes	32.	*Ḥārat al-Manṣūrīyah.* This was the Sudanese militia quarter destroyed by Ṣalāḥ al-Dīn in 1168.
Yes (?)	33.	*Ḥārat al-Maṣāmidah.* To the left of the Bāb al-Jadīd and the right of those leaving the Birkat al-Fīl.
No	34.	*Ḥārat al-Hilālīyah.* This quarter was apparently no longer in existence by the time of Maqrīzi who speculated that it might be the same as Ḥārat al-Maṣāmidah.
Yes (?)	35.	*Ḥārat al-Bayāzirah.* Outside the Bāb al-Qanṭarah on the eastern (sic?) bank of the Khalīj; near Ḥārat Bahā' al-Dīn.
Yes	36.	*Ḥārat al-Ḥusaynīyah* (in two sections, including the cemetery of Bāb al-Naṣr).
No	37.	*Ḥārat Ḥalab.* Maqrīzi quotes Yāqūt in locating it outside Bāb Zuwaylah on the way to Fusṭāṭ; unlikely that it still existed by Maqrīzi's time.

23. "Port" of Būlāq at time of French Expedition. Sixteenth-century Turkish mosque of Sīnān Pasha at center

with those of more modest status and with monasteries, markets, and schools as well.

Only the northern suburb, al-Ḥusaynīyah, never recovered fully from its earlier desolation. Its exposed position, directly in the indefensible path of any invader from the north, must have been the underlying cause of its stagnation. Nor was Cairo ever again contiguous with Miṣr to her south as she had been during the early fourteenth century. In fact, although the city of Miṣr (now known as "the Old Miṣr," Miṣr al-Qadīmah) had been deteriorating steadily over the centuries, it was during the latter half of the fifteenth century that she was finally divested of the last remnants of her economic base. While as late as 1435 visitors to Cairo still disembarked at the port of Miṣr (al-Qadīmah), after the middle of the fifteenth century, goods and passengers were served by a new port at Būlāq.[29]

Map X shows one reconstruction of the physical extent of Cairo at the middle of the fifteenth century. It is taken from the work of William Popper, editor and translator of the chronicles of Ibn Taghri Birdi, to whom we have had occasion to refer earlier.[30] As can be seen from this reconstruction, by mid-century practically all of the southwest quadrant of the city had been redeveloped. The lengthy belt between al-Ḥusaynīyah and the Citadel was intensively settled and, in fact, beginning to deteriorate with age. The least developed quadrant of the rectangular city was the northwest section, but this was soon to be built up.

It was during the latter half of this final century of independent Mamluk rule that two developments of lasting significance transformed Cairo. These were the port development at Būlāq, already noted above, and the settling of the district called Azbakīyah, in the northwestern section of the city. It is also of utmost significance that these were the very last additions to the medieval city. The preindustrial city which evolved into its final form after these developments remained virtually constant in extent and size for the ensuing 300 years. For all purposes, the city found by the French Expedition in 1798 and mapped by them with such detailed precision was almost identical in shape to the medieval city of the late fifteenth century. A comparison of Map X, which reconstructs the city *circa* 1460, with Map XI, prepared by the French Expedition at the turn of the nineteenth century, gives dramatic proof of this remarkable fact.

Būlāq (see Map V for location) first emerged as an island in the Nile during the opening decades of the fourteenth century. Under the encouragement of al-Nāṣir ibn Qalāwūn's development policies it became an upper-class suburban area where princes and wealthy government officials built winter palaces amid the orchards of their agricultural estates. Gradually, these expansive uses gave way to more intensive developments, including year-round residences and auxiliary commercial services. But Būlāq was not yet a port, even after the eastern arm of the Nile had dried completely, although sailing vessels often anchored along it. At the time of Maqrīzī's *Khiṭaṭ* the semi-detached mainland of Būlāq was well populated, primarily by the well-to-do, but the topographer assigns neither industrial nor transport functions to it.

We first learn of its port functions in conjunction with the launching of a newly built navy dispatched by Bars-

[29] One can trace this transition clearly, although the historians and chroniclers are unaccountably vague on the details of the port development at Būlāq. During the time of Piloti, i.e., ca. 1400-1420, the main port was still at Miṣr (or Babilogne, as he calls it). Goods coming by caravan across the desert from Mecca came first to Cairo and then passed on to Miṣr for the levying of customs and for trans-shipping. See *L'Égypte au commencement du quinzième siècle*, pp. 46-47. When Pero Tafur came to Egypt in 1435-1439, he disembarked at Miṣr, spent the night in that city, and then proceeded by donkey to present his credentials at the Citadel. See *Pero Tafur, Travels and Adventures*, pp. 72-73. It is significant that none of the later European visitors to Cairo mentions a port at "Old Miṣr" or Babylon. By the second half of the fifteenth century, overland caravans crossed directly to Būlāq from north of the city, and all goods and passengers from or to Europe passed through the port at Būlāq. Those travelers who specifically mention disembarking at Būlāq are: Friar Felix Fabri (1483), see H. Prescott, *Once to Sinai*, p. 175; Bertinoro (1487-1490), see Adler, *Jewish Travellers*, p. 223; and Domenico Trevisan (1512), see Jean Thenaud, *Le voyage d'outremer*, published and annotated by Charles Schefer (Leroux, Paris: 2nd edn., 1884), pp. 35 and 179; and all later visitors to Cairo.

[30] See W. Popper, *Egypt and Syria under the Circassian Sultans, 1382-1468 A.D.; Systematic Notes to Ibn Taghri Birdi's Chronicles of Egypt*, Volume 15 of the University of California Publications in Semitic Philology (University of California Press, Berkeley and Los Angeles: 1955), assembled from Maps 8, 9, 10, and 11.

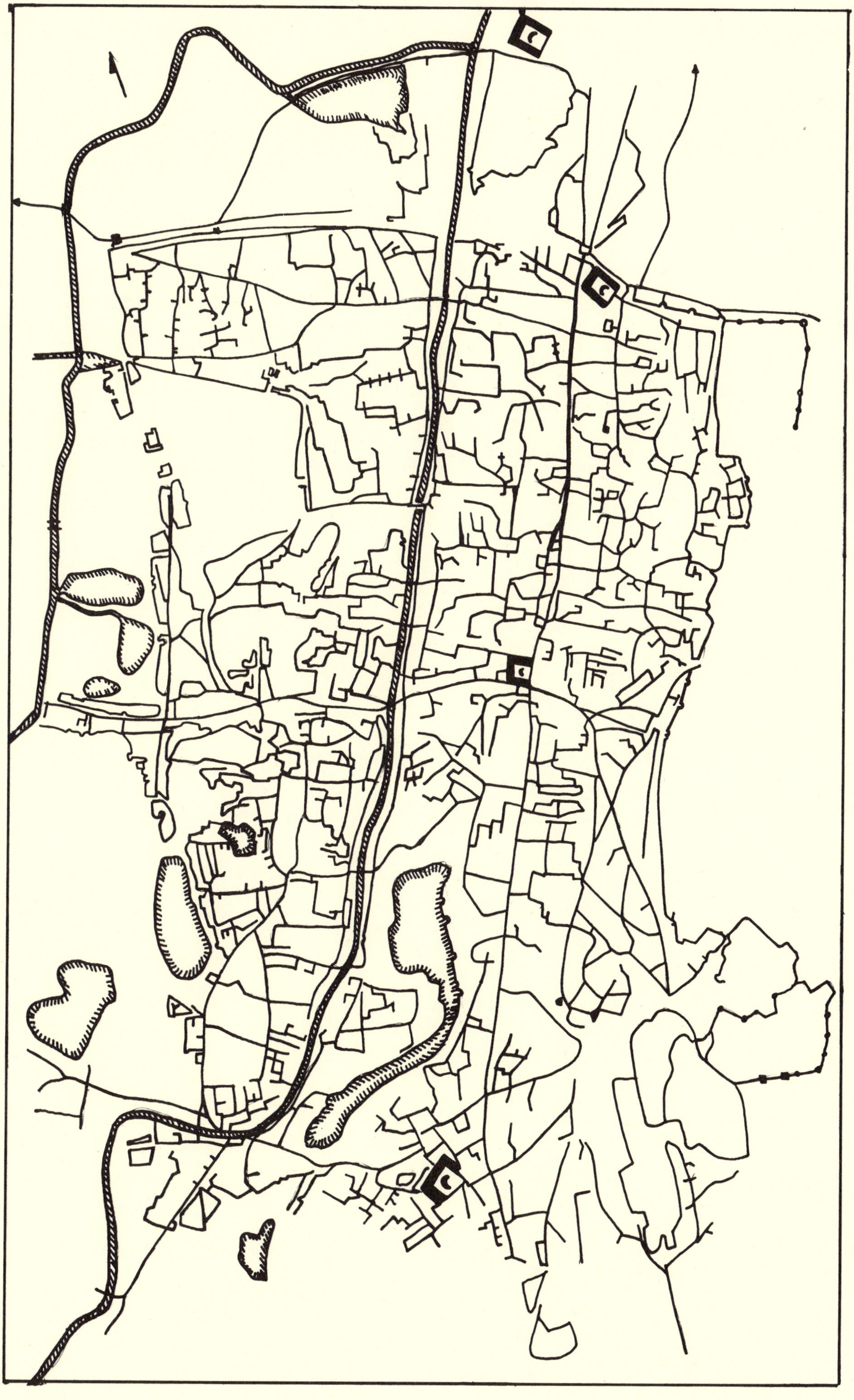

X. The built-up area of Cairo *ca.* 1460 (based upon Popper)

XI. The built-up area of Cairo *ca.* 1800

Qarameydân
I
II
III
Place birket el Fyl
Gamiʿ Touloun
Kymân Toulaun
Birket Sitty Nasrah
es el Saqqâyn
Etang de l'Institut
Birket Abou l Châmât

bay in 1425 to conquer Cyprus; after 1438, when control over the trade at Jiddah became absolute, it is increasingly mentioned as a port and as a dispatching point for the navy. By the middle of the fifteenth century, the former island, by then joined to the mainland even in flood season by two raised causeways, had become the major port serving the city of Cairo and had begun to develop the wholesale and industrial character which the area retains to this day. This transition continued despite, or perhaps even facilitated by, a fire in 1458 which virtually destroyed the town, permitting it to be rebuilt in a form more suited to its changing function.[31]

It would not be unreasonable to link the expansion of this port to the alteration in the main route of the spice trade, for with the decline in the previous Nile route downstream from Qūṣ, the port at Miṣr was no longer conveniently located; a more northerly location was called for, accessible to the eastern desert caravan route that terminated north of Cairo at the Pilgrims' Lake (Birkat al-Ḥujjāj). When this change first occurred at the time of Barsbay, Miṣr al-Qadīmah still remained the commercial port of the city, but by the end of the century all boats carrying wares between Cairo and Alexandria (and beyond, to Europe) docked at the new port facilities at Būlāq, a mile-long donkey ride through farmland to the built-up part of al-Qāhirah. In Būlāq also were constructed the warehouses, inns, and other facilities for the great caravans that carried goods overland between Cairo and the Red Sea ports. Thus Būlāq became the key link and break-in-bulk point for the East-West spice trade which in large measure underlay the comparative prosperity of the fifteenth century. Despite a decline in trade during the centuries that followed, Būlāq continued to serve this function. When the French arrived at the end of the eighteenth century, they found this port town still intact and still separated from the city of Cairo by agricultural lands.

The settling of Azbakīyah, now part of the central business district of the "Westernized" city and the geographic heart of the metropolis, also occurred toward the end of this last century of growth. Its site, midway between the abandoned industrial port of al-Maqs on the north and the rich agricultural lands of al-Lūq to the south, had been a wasteland before its development into an upper-class suburb during the later decades of the fifteenth century. In early times the land just south of al-Maqs, between the Nile's former shore and the Khalīj Miṣri, had been occupied by a large plantation called the Bustān al-Maqsi. In 1019 the trees of this orchard were cleared to make room for a large pond (*birkah*) which was excavated there. However, during the difficult times of Mustanṣir toward the end of that century, the deserted banks of the pond became a thieves' quarter and the area was otherwise abandoned. Over the centuries, yearly silt deposits gradually filled in more and more of the pond until, by the time of Maqrīzi, the zone (Kaum al-Jāki) had become almost entirely sand dunes. Only a tiny remnant of the pond still survived.[32] A few decades later, when Ibn Taghri Birdi was writing, evidently even that last remnant of the pond had disappeared.[33]

So the area remained until 1470 when Azbak, an amir of the Sultan Qayt Bay, built a stable and then a residence in the zone which today still bears his name. He had the sand heaps removed and the land excavated anew for the Birkat Azbakīyah which was flooded by waters from al-Nāṣir's Western Canal. Along the banks of this beautiful pond many of Cairo's merchants and princes built luxurious dwellings, and the area—whose growth must have been stimulated by its proximity to the new port activities in Būlāq—eventually rivaled the Birkat al-Fīl in prestige. By the end of the fifteenth century, Azbakīyah had become one of the most fashionable districts of suburban Cairo, a veritable "city in itself," serving all the daily needs of its wealthy residents.[34]

These developments were, perhaps, the last burst of energy before final stagnation. Certainly the two factors that were to bring the medieval cycle to a close were already at work. One was the shift in world trade routes which undermined irreversibly the last economic base of the community; the other was the rise of the Ottoman Turks whose conquest of Egypt deprived Cairo of her political hegemony. The sixteenth, seventeenth, and eighteenth centuries were to reduce Cairo to a provincial capital of declining importance, and not until the nineteenth century would Cairo be revitalized.

We have seen that the element which had sustained

[31] The above has been reconstructed from the chronicles of Ibn Taghri Birdi. See Popper, *History of Egypt*, Part IV, Volume 18 of the University of California Publications in Semitic Philology (1958), pp. 32-34, for the Cyprus expedition departure from Būlāq; see Part V (1960) for Sultan Jaqmaq's Rhodes campaign; and Part VI, Volume 22 of the University of California Publications in Semitic Philology (1960), pp. 76-79, on the conflagration in Būlāq. It must be acknowledged that since no other maps of early Cairo are extant prior to the French Expedition survey, Popper has depended heavily on the latter in his reconstruction of the street system of Ibn Taghri Birdi's Cairo. However, the very fact that the French map could be used retrospectively to locate with accuracy the areas, monuments, and land uses identified verbally by the chronicler is in itself an indication of how little the city had changed during the interim.

[32] Maqrīzi, *Khiṭaṭ*, II, 163.

[33] See Popper, *Egypt and Syria under the Circassian Sultans* (1955), Map 10, where the entire area is identified as Kaum al-Jāki. This area was, of course, far more extensive than the current designation of Azbakīyah would indicate. The Baṭn al-Baqarah included this as well as the eastern portion of what is now known as 'Abdīn.

[34] Margoliouth, *Cairo, Jerusalem and Damascus*, pp. 128-129.

Cairo even up through the fifteenth century—despite political disorders, declining agricultural production, currency debasement, and recurrent plagues—was the Oriental spice trade with Europe, still virtually monopolized by Venetian traders who routed their commercial exchanges through Egypt. This concentration of the East-West trade through the heart of the Mamluk empire not only brought income directly to the Mamluks, who charged high customs fees at each of the several ports through which goods passed, but exerted a multiplier effect on the economy by stimulating the demand for ancillary goods and services. However, the profits gathered so greedily into the purses of the Mamluk lords weighed heavily upon the foreign merchants who found the route growing costlier and more perilous each year. Complaints about the high duties charged in Egyptian ports and of the dangers of transporting goods through poorly policed territories became more and more frequent.[35]

The prosperity of Cairo hung on a narrow thread, a monopoly that was soon to be broken by that rival to the Italian city-states, Portugal. Vasco da Gama's successful circumnavigation of Africa and his triumphant arrival in India in 1498, more than any other discovery of the closing years of the fifteenth century, snipped this thread, stranding Cairo in a backwater of the rapidly changing world. The effects of this discovery were immediate and irremediable. Within only a decade the Portuguese had taken much of the East-West trade out of the hands of the Venetians. By 1503 commerce through Egypt had decreased perceptibly; in the following year practically the only goods entering the Mamluk empire were those intended for local consumption. The discriminatory policies imposed by the Portuguese in India established a virtual monopoly for their traders. The latter also gained control of the access to the Persian Gulf and the Red Sea, and when one of the last Mamluk Sultans, al-

[35] I avoid here any detailed coverage of routes and their shiftings back and forth, for this would involve us in the complex history of an area far wider than Cairo. Among the sources which can be consulted are Archibald Lewis, *Naval Power and Trade in the Mediterranean, A.D. 500-1100* (Princeton University Press, Princeton: 1951) and George Hourani, *Arab Seafaring in the Indian Ocean* (Princeton University Press, Princeton: 1951) for the earliest period; Albert H. Lybyer, "The Ottoman Turks and the Routes of Oriental Trade," *English Historical Review*, Volume 30 (October 1915), pp. 577-588 (who dates the shift to the southern route through Egypt earlier than Darrag); and George W. Stripling, *The Ottoman Turks and the Arabs, 1511-1574* (The University of Illinois Press, Urbana: 1942), who gives excellent evidence in support of the contention that customs fees were excessive, see especially pp. 27-28. Piloti, in *L'Égypte au commencement du quinzième siècle*, p. 52, complains bitterly about the exorbitant tariffs imposed by Barsbay and about the piracy of the undisciplined beduins who ruled the routes between cities, two problems which became even greater in the years that followed.

24. Birkat al-Azbakīyah still flooded *ca.* 1800

25. Azbakīyah environs *ca.* 1857

26. Thoroughfare now bisects Azbakīyah Gardens

Ghūri, launched a newly built Egyptian fleet to break this hold, it was destroyed by the Portuguese in 1509.[36]

Thus, the shifting of the trade route removed the foundation stone of Mamluk prosperity, left Cairo with a depleted economic base, and, in so doing, reduced Mamluk power to its lowest ebb. This decline was well under way by the early sixteenth century, so it is not surprising that the new Venetian ambassador to Cairo wrote in 1512 that the city was much "inferior to her reputation," albeit still very wealthy and "with money in abundance."[37] Nor is it any wonder that, with their coffers so depleted, the Mamluks were unable to raise a sufficient force when the Ottoman Turks turned their attention from Europe and Persia to the lands of the Mamluks.[38]

Some eleven years after the death of Maqrīzi and forty-five years before Vasco da Gama's historic voyage, the rising Ottoman Turks took Constantinople, signaling a new balance of power in the eastern Mediterranean. The Mamluks of Cairo rejoiced, little realizing that the event augured ill for their future. The impact of this victory was not soon felt in Egypt, however, since for more than half a century the Ottomans directed their efforts toward Europe and then toward their eastern rivals, the Persians. Only in the sixteenth century did they concentrate their attention on Egypt. In 1516 Sultan al-Ghūri led his Mamluk forces to Syria for a disastrous encounter with the Ottomans near Aleppo, in which al-Ghūri was slain and his forces routed. They returned in disorder to make a final defense of Cairo. Tumanbay, the newly appointed (and last) Mamluk Sultan, refused to capitulate, and within five months the Turks had pursued the Mamluks to their capital. An extremely high Nile that year had driven many of the inhabitants of the lower lands of western Cairo into the city proper and, when it was reported that the Turkish troops of Salīm were approaching, panic drove the remainder of the suburban residents into the confines of the walled city.[39] The Turks arrived and speedily vanquished the Mamluks in a decisive battle, thus gaining possession of the city and, with it, the land of Egypt. Perhaps the mundane eyewitness account of Ibn Iyas conveys better than any rhetoric the full impact of that defeat.

> *On Wednesday* . . . news arrived that Ibn 'Othman's advanced guard was at Birkah al-Haj, which put the military in Cairo into an advanced state of great consternation. They closed the Bab al-Futuh and Bab al-Nasr and the Bab al-Sha'riyyeh, also the Bab al-Bahr and the Bab al-Kantarah, and the other gates of the town. The markets in Cairo were closed, the mills were stopped, and bread and flour became scarce. . . .
> *On Thursday* . . . a tremendous engagement took place. . . . In the short space of about sixty minutes the Egyptian army was defeated and in full retreat. . . .
> *On Sunday* . . . it was reported that the Sultan Selim Shah had moved his camp from Raidaniyyeh [the scene of the major battle, north of the walled Cairo] to Bulak, where it occupied the ground from the embankment to the end of the central island, and that *the keys of the citadel were brought there. . . .*[40]

In such a manner did Cairo—which had ruled for almost 550 years over the prosperous and extensive Fāṭimid, Ayyūbid, and Mamluk empires, which had been an unrivaled center of world commerce, which had been the undisputed model of culture for the Islamic world, and which was still the largest city of the Middle East and Europe—pass into the hands of the Turks, to become a mere provincial capital subordinate to Constantinople. With the passing of the keys to the Citadel went the symbol of the city's independence and supremacy.

For the next few centuries without interruption, Egypt remained nominally under Turkish rule, although after only two generations of vigorous Ottoman leadership, the old Mamluks regained much of their former power. By the seventeenth century the country was little changed administratively from what it had been under independent rule (with the exception of the annual tribute), and by mid-eighteenth century the Mamluk *Shaykh al-Balad* held almost as much power internally as the Sultan had formerly. What had changed, however, was that Cairo was no longer at the head of an empire. The court of Constantinople attracted to itself the intellectual and artistic talents of the empire, talents which had formerly

[36] Information on this later period is to be found in Stripling, *The Ottoman Turks and the Arabs*, and in R. B. Serjeant, *The Portuguese off the South Arabian Coast* (The Clarendon Press, Oxford: 1963).

[37] In Jean Thenaud, *Le voyage d'outremer* (1884), p. 207. In all fairness, however, it should be pointed out that his account suggests that trade had not entirely dried up by 1512 since, according to him, "the city is very commercial; all the spices and all the merchandise from India, Mecca and Persia are transported there by caravans." See p. 208.

[38] Ibn Iyas graphically describes the fiscal difficulties of financing the war against the Turks and chronicles the periodic revolts of the unpaid soldiers. See Lt. Col. W. H. Salmon, trans., *An Account of the Ottoman Conquest of Egypt in the Year A.H. 922 (A.D. 1516), Translated from the Third Volume of the Arabic Chronicle of Muhammed ibn Ahmed Ibn Iyas, an Eyewitness of the Scenes He Describes* (Royal Asiatic Society, London: 1921). David Ayalon, in his *Gunpowder and Firearms in the Mamluk Kingdom, A Challenge to Mediæval Society* (Vallentine, Mitchell, London: 1956) argues, however, that the reluctance of the Mamluks to adopt firearms must share with insolvency the responsibility for their eventual defeat.

[39] Ibn Iyas, *An Account of the Ottoman Conquest*, pp. 28, 106.

[40] *Ibid.*, excerpted from pp. 110-112. Italics added.

concentrated in and glorified Cairo. Furthermore, as Turkish supplanted Arabic as the language of intellectual endeavors, the Arabic-speaking provinces were excluded more and more from the stimulation of the capital.

There is no doubt that Cairo deteriorated gradually but greatly during the period between the Turkish conquest and the Napoleonic Expedition. Enduring a steady decline in population and economic viability, she grew older and shoddier. While the built-up surface of the city neither expanded nor appreciably contracted (see Maps X and XI), over the years more and more individual houses and shops became deserted. Crumbling buildings, instead of being repaired or replaced, were left to the ravages of the elements. Top stories of dwellings tumbled one by one, leaving the lower floors still inhabited but exposing the walls of abandoned upper sections. A kind of creeping blight set in (quite different from that known in Western cities of the industrial era) which, over the years, reflected the diminution of Cairo's population.

While we lack accurate population statistics for the country as a whole, estimates based on the head tax suggest that Egypt had a population of perhaps 4 million when the Arab conquerors first arrived in the seventh century. During times of greater prosperity, when irrigation canals were well maintained and being extended, presumably the population of the country approached 8 million or even more. Such a populous country might well have supported a capital city of half a million persons, particularly when that city served not only local central-place functions but empire-administrative- and international-trade functions as well. During the era of Turkish domination, however, there was a dramatic drop in the carrying capacity of the country. As public works and maintenance were neglected, marginal lands went out of cultivation. This inhibited population growth which in turn led to an even greater reduction in cultivated areas. Thus, by 1800 the total population of Egypt, including the beduins, was estimated at no more than 3 million persons, i.e., considerably less than the present population of the city of Cairo alone!

Whether the deterioration so noticeable in the city of Cairo can be blamed entirely on the "evil" administration of the Turks, as has sometimes been claimed, is open to very serious question. First, as we have seen, the reorganization of world trade was beginning to exclude Cairo as an important commercial center even before the Turkish conquest. And second, although the Turks and their fairly autonomous Mamluk deputies can be held responsible for the neglect of public works and therefore indirectly for the population decline, they were themselves victims of a decline in vigor and prosperity which set in soon after the conquest and was certainly well established by the end of the sixteenth century.[41] Not only Cairo, not only Egypt, but indeed the entire Turkish empire was left behind as the world moved forward. Both absolutely and in relation to the tremendous strides taken by an awakening Europe during the sixteenth, seventeenth, and eighteenth centuries, the Mediterranean world was dying. The decline in Cairo was but a reflection of this more general and all-pervasive decay.

While the boundaries of the city did not change significantly during the several centuries of Turkish rule, there was a shift in the internal organization of the urban community over the years as the center of the city continued to move westward toward the new sections.[42] The *qaṣabah*, formerly the unrivaled *sūq* of the entire city, became somewhat less important as specialized markets on the western side of the Khalīj Miṣri began to compete for business. And as an area of elite residence, the zone of Azbakīyah gradually usurped prime position in the ecological hierarchy from its nearest competitor, the quarter around the Birkat al-Fīl. In the opening years of the sixteenth century, the preferred residential area of the Mamluk aristocracy was in the vicinity of the Citadel, that is, the southeastern quadrant of the city beyond the walls of the al-Qāhirah nucleus; only a minor fraction of the aristocracy had built homes in the Azbakīyah area which was then chiefly a zone of merchant and bourgeois elements. Gradually, however, the recurrent insecurity of the Citadel region led many of the aristocracy to remove themselves from the "line of fire," most of them preferring the greater tranquillity (and beauty) of the Birkat al-Fīl which, by the late seventeenth century, contained almost half of the identifiable homes of important Mamluk Bays.[43] Deserted by its aristocratic clientele, the

[41] W.E.D. Allen, *Problems of Turkish Power in the Sixteenth Century* (Central Asian Research Centre, London: 1963).

[42] The following account is based largely upon the remarkable reconstructions of André Raymond, "Essai de géographie des quartiers de résidence aristocratique au Caire au XVIIIème siècle," *Journal of the Economic and Social History of the Orient*, Volume VI, Part I (May 1963), pp. 58-103. On the early period, see particularly Table I, p. 59, and pp. 61 and 73. The decline of the *qaṣabah* area is illustrated by the fact that many of the bourgeois families occupying the Azbakīyah region had moved there from the old city's center.

[43] Raymond, *ibid.*, p. 69, has carefully chronicled some of the disturbances that encouraged the flight of former residents from the area around the Citadel: for example, those in 1698, 1709, 1711, 1715, 1719, 1726, 1736, and 1747. Only a courageous or very foolish resident would remain on a battlefield to court accidental or intended disaster. The late seventeenth- and early eighteenth-century shift to Birkat al-Fīl quarter is well documented in *ibid.*, Table II, p. 67. If the impetus to leave the Citadel was fear, the attraction to the Birkat al-Fīl was undoubtedly beauty, as attested by this description by a contemporary observer writing in about 1700. Fulgence, in his *Description de la situation de l'Égypte* (MS. No. 524 in the Bibliothèque de Lille, pp. 206-207), noted that "The most beautiful houses

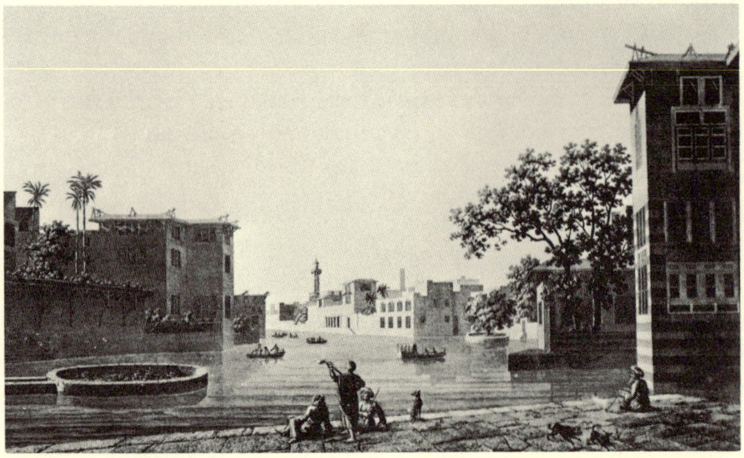

27. Birkat al-Fīl in 1800

southeastern extremity deteriorated, and by the end of the Turkish period it was inhabited mainly by the city's destitute, who had no other choice.

The significance of Azbakīyah and its gradual attraction over the Birkat al-Fīl region did not begin much before the eighteenth century, but, once launched as an aristocratic zone, it soon surpassed all rivals. By mid-eighteenth century, the area was shared by the original bourgeois residents, by lower-ranking officers, and by the newest comers, the aristocracy. This gradual transformation was sharply accelerated by a fire in 1776 which destroyed numerous merchants' residences. In the rapid rebuilding that followed the fire, many Mamluks at all levels of status took their cue from the leading Bays who hastened to reclaim the land and construct elegant palaces. By the time the French arrived in 1798, the district was the undisputed elite area of the city,[44] into which they moved without hesitation, Napoleon himself occupying the most beautiful home of them all, the one Muḥammad Bay al-Alfi had constructed only a year before on a site overlooking the lake.

Just as growth was most vigorous on the western edge of the city, so, conversely, decay was most pronounced at the extreme eastern edge. While the area just inside the eastern wall had been decaying since before the time of Maqrīzi, this trend became even more evident during the Turkish epoch. The very poorest quarters of the city were located in the tumbling-down eastern fringe of the city, to which unskilled village migrants gravitated. By the Turkish era also, the northern suburb of al-Ḥusaynīyah, containing the Mosque of Baybars—which soon after its construction had stood midst a prosperous and populous suburb—was left stranded, encircled by plowed fields. The older aristocratic zone within the walled city, just south and west of the Mosque of al-Azhar, was also much deteriorated, although numerous old mansions there attested to its past elegance.

Much of the decline in Cairo can be traced in the increasingly unenthusiastic accounts of travelers who came to the city during the Turkish regime. Domenico Trevisan and his companion, Jean Thenaud, were the last European visitors to describe Cairo before the Turkish conquest. From their joint account one reconstructs a city that was about three times the extent of Paris and that contained about five times as many inhabitants. Trevisan recounted that, although some believed the population of Cairo to be about 1.5 million, he did not believe it exceeded 750,000.[45] Neither of the travelers mentioned any ruins to be observed in or about new Cairo, although most of Old Cairo was acknowledged to be deserted. A few decades later another visitor, Greffin Affagart, concurred in estimating Cairo's size as three times as great as Paris, but qualified this by including Old Cairo and other suburban developments within the circumference.[46]

---

of Cairo surround this birkat [al-Fīl] . . . [which] is inundated during eight months of the year; and it is a perpetual garden during the other four; during the flood one sees a large number of gilded vessels on which important personages and their wives promenade in the evening. . . ." As cited by Raymond, "Essai de géographie," pp. 72-73; my translation from the French.

[44] *Ibid.*, pp. 74 *et seq.*, especially Table III, p. 79, and Table IV, p. 83. The fire in Azbakīyah, documented by Djabarti, has been recognized by Raymond, "Essai de géographie," p. 87, and by Clerget, *Le Caire*, I, 182, as a critical turning point in the history of Azbakīyah's development. However, while it appears to have facilitated a more rapid population succession in the area, it can scarcely be credited with either having initiated the trend, which began before the fire, or having "caused" it. Raymond includes a map (p. 94) of the Great Homes in 1798 which depicts the situation clearly. By that year, almost all the important Bays were living in homes within the *western* half of the city, i.e., along or west of the Khalīj Miṣri.

[45] Thenaud, *Le voyage d'outremer*, pp. 46, 207-208. I do not believe it could have been even as high as Trevisan's conservative figure. Delimiting the area of the city at that time and calculating the population within it in 1947, one gets a total of 640,000 persons living at the extremely high average densities made possible by modern building techniques. It is doubtful that this area contained more persons in 1512 than it did in 1947, especially since land coverage is greater today than it was then, due to the disappearance of the ponds. Hence my estimate is at the maximum 500,000, but probably lower.

[46] See Greffin Affagart, *Relation de Terre Sainte, 1533-1534*, ed. and annot. by J. Chavanon (Librairie Victor Lecoffre, Paris: 1902), p. 170. However, the report of this traveler should perhaps be discounted, since he is otherwise so inaccurate. Other sixteenth-century travelers included several Englishmen whose descriptions are disappointingly brief and irrelevant. For example, see "The Second Voyage of M. Laurence Aldersey to the Cities of Alexandria and Cayro, in Aegypt, 1586," in R. Hakluyt, *The Principal Navigations Voyages Traffiques and Discoveries of the English Nation*, VI (Glasgow Extra Series, Glasgow: 1904), 39-46; and "The Voyage of M. John Evesham by Sea into Aegypt," also written in 1586 and found in *ibid.*, pp. 35-38. Another disappointing account is found in "A Report of the Voyage of Master

While in retrospect we can reconstruct that Cairo declined precipitously after these reports were written, we have no one to chronicle the descent. Our only knowledge is that by the seventeenth century Cairo was no longer the object of admiration which she had formerly been to all visitors. Several European accounts, written in 1630, 1636, and 1652, give us graphic albeit *ex post facto* evidence of this decline, as well as a fairly clear picture of what Cairo was like in the seventeenth century.

The earliest report was the joint work of several Frenchmen, notably Fermanel, Fauvel, and others. They note that although the city of Cairo was as famous among Europeans as she was among Easterners, she "had not been able to prevent the changes and deterioration wrought by time." By that era, Cairo was well developed into her three major sections, central Cairo, suburban Būlāq connected by a bridge with the mainland, and Old Cairo, by then more or less in ruins. Noteworthy were the many short and narrow streets within the city, estimated at over 20,000. One of the most valuable descriptions contained in this account gives us our first clear image of the developments which had taken place since Azbakīyah was founded 160 years earlier: "There are large open spaces within the city which resemble ponds when the Nile is high: when the water recedes they use these spaces to grow herbs and vegetables. The most important and largest of these places is called Ezbekiah, which is surrounded by the most beautiful houses of the city." The area just west of the canal was already beginning to house the minute but growing foreign community in the city—merchants engaged in trading cotton, leather, wax, rice, and medications and their protective consuls, including French, English, Venetian, and Dutch representatives.[47]

Sir Henry Blount, an English magistrate who journeyed to the Levant in 1634-1636, gave as one of his chief justifications for traveling his intent to "view Grand Cairo . . . it being clearly the greatest concourse of mankind in these times, and perhaps that ever was," indicating that Cairo's reputation had withstood the ravages of time more hardily than had her physique. Once there, however, Blount used more subdued language to describe the city's actual state. "This city [*Elkhayre,* i.e., al-Qāhirah] is built after the *Egyptian* manner, high and of large rough stone, part of brick, the streets narrow. It hath not been yet above an hundred years in the *Turks* possession, wherefore the old buildings remain; but as they decay, the new begin to be after the *Turkish* manner, poor, low, much of mud and timber. . . ." He too remarked on the "many spacious places in the city, which in the rivers overflow, are dainty pools called birkhaes, and of great refreshment, as also the calhis [khalīj], which is a channel cut through part of the city, from the Nile into a plain on the north. . . . In these birkhaes and calhis, towards evening, are many hundreds washing themselves; in the mean while divers pass up and down with pipes and roguy fiddles in boats full of fruits, sherbets, and good banqueting stuff to sell. After the rivers fall, those places are green for a while, then burnt to sand."[48]

An even more thorough account of the city is given by Monsieur de Thevenot, who left France in 1652 for a trip to the Orient. It was clear that by this time Europe's cities had so expanded and Cairo had so declined that, like Blount and Fermanel, Thevenot was not very impressed with Cairo. Whereas fifteenth- and even sixteenth-century European visitors were still overwhelmed by the metropolis, Fermanel had found it a most unpleasant place, while Thevenot said, with undisguised condescension that "they are in the wrong, who persuade themselves that Caire is bigger than Paris. . . . Those who would have Caire to be bigger than Paris, when they speak of Caire, comprehend therein Old Caire and Boulac . . . but that cannot rationally be done . . . for Old Caire is separated from the New by Fields; and Boulac is another Town, divided from Caire by several ploughed Grounds."

Perhaps a few more quotations from Thevenot's description can give depth to our impressions of Cairo in the seventeenth century. He tells us that the high walls surrounding the city "are at present all covered with Ruines, which are so high, that I have passed over some places where they wholly hide the Walls. . . . And though it would be very easie to clear the Rubbish, and by repairing what is wanting, make the Walls appear beauti-

Henrie Timberley from Cairo in Egypt to Jerusalem in Fiftie Dayes" (1601), in S. Purchas, *Purchas His Pilgrimes,* IX (Glasgow Extra Series, Glasgow: 1905), 487-492.

[47] *Voyage d'Italie et du Levant, de Messieurs Fermanel, . . . , Fauvel . . . , Baudouin de Lavney, et de Stochove* (Chez Jean Viret, Rouen: 1670). My description summarizes items appearing on pp. 412, 420, 426, and 417, from which the quotation on Azbakīyah has been taken. Information on the foreign quarter is given on p. 435. The existence of this nucleus of a "Frankish" quarter along the Khalīj is acknowledged by an even earlier French traveler, Henri de Beauveau, who in September of 1605 arrived from Rosetta by boat, entering the city by way of the Fam al-Khalīj and continuing northward on the Khalīj Miṣri "between gardens planted with tamarisks" and under seven bridges, until he reached the Frank quarter which abutted the west bank of the canal. See his *Relation journalière du voyage du Levant* (Nancy, 1615), p. 158, as translated and cited by Robin Fedden, "Notes on the Journey from Rosetta to Cairo in the Seventeenth and Eighteenth Centuries," in *Bulletin de la Société Royale de Géographie d'Égypte,* Volume 21 (1943-46), pp. 99-107. Citation on p. 107.

[48] Quotations have been taken from *A Voyage into the Levant: A Brief Relation of a Journey Lately Performed by Master Henry Blount, Gentleman* (Printed by R. C. for Andrew Crooke, London: 1650), pp. 513, 525-526.

ful and high, yet the Turks make no Reparations, but suffer all to run to decay. . . ." Concerning the street plan of the city, Thevenot notes that "all the streets of Caire are very short and narrow, except the street of the Bazar and the Khalis, which is dry but three months of the year . . .; there is not a fair street in all Caire, but a great many little ones that go turning and winding."[49]

Again, it is from the account of Thevenot that we derive a picture of the changing role of Europeans in the city of Cairo. Before the days of the Turks, few foreigners lived in the city except for the Venetian merchants active in the spice transactions of the India trade. Those few foreigners who passed through the community came under the exploitive supervision of specially appointed dragomen during their brief sojourn in the city.[50] By the time of Thevenot, however, the number and variety of European residents had increased to the point where a special quarter of the city was devoted to their residence, from which even the chief official of the city was enjoined from entering without permission.[51]

The disappointment which European travelers universally experienced upon seeing eighteenth-century Cairo was due to something more than the relative improvements on the continent of Europe. While this was a century of city expansion and improvement in the latter,[52] it was also a period of accelerated decline in the Ottoman empire. The combination of the two had a double impact. While the basic problems of Cairo changed little in essence between the seventeenth and eighteenth centuries, they undoubtedly increased in severity. Particularly during the latter half of the eighteenth century, the physical condition of Cairo deteriorated rapidly, reflecting a general trend in the country.

The rule of the Porte, never strong, had by then become an open mockery. The Mamluks who had recovered power not long after the Ottoman conquest were now sufficiently in control to accept or reject Turkish figurehead governors at will. As early as 1734 an English observer noted that "the Government of *Egypt* . . . is in the Hands of a Bashaw [Pasha] . . . sent to *Cairo* from *Constantinople*, who having in reality but very little Power, his Business seems chiefly to consist in communicating the Orders of the *Grand Signior* to his Divan of Beys," and whose continuance in office was contingent upon their "interests."[53] By 1762 the Dane, Niebuhr, reported that the Turkish Pasha was completely dependent upon the Mamluk Bays for his power, a fact described less politely but with infinitely greater élan by the excitable Eliza Fay in a letter from Egypt dated 1779. This situation was similarly remarked on by both Savary and Volney, who complained that the Pasha was a virtual prisoner of the Bays.[54]

[49] His book describing the trip was translated almost immediately into English, indicating a widening interest in the Orient within England. See *The Travels of Monsieur de Thevenot into the Levant,* as translated by A. Lovell (Printed by H. Clark for H. Faithorne, J. Adamson, C. Skegnes and T. Newborough, London: 1686-1687), particularly Part I, Book II, Chapters IVff. The quotations reproduced here have been taken from pp. 128-129.

[50] Some rather unpleasant aspects of this institution are recounted in Hilda Prescott, *Once to Sinai.*

[51] *The Travels of Monsieur de Thevenot* (English trans.), Part I, Book II, p. 254.

[52] It is important, in order to regain perspective, to realize that medieval cities throughout the world were characterized by those very qualities which European travelers, from the vantage point of their Renaissance- and Baroque-transformed communities, found so distressing in Cairo. The following description of German cities during the Middle Ages may remind us that Cairo was still superior to the conditions from which most European cities were gradually emerging. "The visitor from the suburbs or the outer districts near the fortifications was struck, in approaching the center of town, by the narrow and tortuous streets and lanes that were laid out without any apparent system. Regulations regarding width existed only for the principal streets. . . . Most streets remained unpaved . . . in general, the streets were extremely dirty. Nobody went out without wooden-soled overshoes; even the saints depicted in paintings by the earlier German masters were apt to wear some sort of protection over their shoes. . . . The gutters were mostly in the middle of the roads, thus making them still less passable. Watering places for animals were dispersed all over the town, and draw wells spilled their water unchecked into the streets. Sweepings, remains of food, even dead animals were thrown out of the houses; this habit assumed such proportions that some cities resorted to the institution of communal dumping places. In addition to all these unpleasant features, there were numerous vacant lots and dilapidated houses that also served as dumping grounds for all sorts of rubbish. . . ." The illustrative quotation has been taken from E. A. Gutkind's *International History of City Development,* Volume I, *Urban Development in Central Europe* (The Free Press of Glencoe, New York: 1964), 172.

[53] See *The Travels of the Late Charles Thompson, Esq.,* which contains a lengthy account of Egypt which he visited in 1734 (J. Newbery and C. Mickelwright, London [?]: 1744), III, 253-404. The quotation is found on p. 387. A contemporary of his was the Danish Navy Captain, Frederick Ludvig Norden, who wrote and illustrated *Travels in Egypt and Nubia,* based upon his trip of 1738, in two volumes, trans. by Dr. Peter Templeman (Lockyer Davis and C. Reymers, London: 1757).

[54] See Carsten Niebuhr, *Voyage en Arabie et en d'autre pays circonvoisins* (Amsterdam, 1776-1780), Tome I, 74, for his remarks. Eliza Fay puts it more vividly: "In order to be a check upon these gentlemen [i.e., the contending Mamluk Bays], the Grand Signor sends a Bashaw, to reside among them, whom they receive with great respect and compliment with presents of value, pretending the utmost deference for his authority, but at the same time a strict eye is kept over him, and on the least opposition to their will, he is sent in disgrace away—happy if he escapes with his life, after refunding all his presents and paying enormous sums besides. By the above statement you perceive that, the Beys are in reality independent, and likewise discern the hinge on which their politics turn, for as long as under colours of submission, they consent to receive a Bashaw, it is in their power

The years of the last quarter of the eighteenth century were thus difficult ones. The once bounteous countryside was in ruins; brigands ruled the roads between towns with complete audacity, exacting tribute or heads with equal freedom from Mamluk intervention. Taxation, which had never been light, became more and more oppressive as the economic base of trade and cultivable land contracted. To escape their tax arrears, farmers deserted their villages. A famine left the public granaries of Būlāq empty, and, if this were still not sufficient, a plague imported from Constantinople in 1783 and an inadequate flood in the same year further decimated the population. The abortive attempt of the Mamluk Bays to overthrow the Porte also drew further pain, since it was put down rather oppressively by a Turkish reoccupation of Egypt in 1786 and 1787, when the innocent were almost as likely to be punished as the guilty.[55]

With so chaotic a state of local affairs, it was perhaps inevitable that the capital should decline in amenities. The unattractiveness of the city which Thevenot noted was even more advanced when Monsieur Volney, a French traveler, described Cairo as he saw it in 1783. He noted that "Its environs are full of heaps of dirt, formed by the rubbish. . . . Within the walls, the streets are winding and narrow . . . unpaved."

By this time the French had definitely come to dominate the foreign community, competing successfully with the earlier arrivals, the Venetians and English, in furnishing European goods.[56] However, the insecurities of the foreign traders were also increasing. Whereas in 1630 Fermanel reported that European merchants enjoyed great liberty, later restrictive policies of the Ottomans and hostility on the part of the inhabitants were driving the Europeans out of the country. Thus, Sonnini, sent by Louis XVI to "investigate" Egypt in 1780, reported that after a brief sojourn in the capital he was made to feel so uncomfortable and confined that he escaped to Rosetta where, along with Alexandria, the former foreign community of Cairo had repaired.[57] Volney reported that by 1785 there were only three French mercantile houses left in the city of Cairo, whereas there had been at least nine only a decade and a half earlier.

Indeed, it was this harassment of foreign, i.e., French, merchants that Napoleon used at home to rationalize his need to invade Egypt in 1798, although his real aim was to strike against the British. While the results of the French Expedition were disastrous for Napoleon,[58] any student of Cairo's development must be eternally grateful for his military blunder, for a permanent by-product of the three-year French occupation was *Description de l'Égypte*,[59] a work of enviable scholarship and precision. The text and plates from the particular series devoted to *État moderne* constitute an indispensable bench-mark study of Cairo just as it was poised to emerge from the medieval into the modern world.

constantly to throw the odium of every disagreeable occurrence on his shoulders, under pretense of Orders from the Porte." See her *Original Letters from India (1779-1815)*, ed. E. M. Forster (Harcourt, Brace and Company, New York: 1925), p. 95. See also Claude Savary, *Lettres sur l'Égypte*, in three volumes (Onfroi, Paris: 1785-1786), I, 102; and M. Volney (pseud. for Constantin-François Chassebeuf), *Travels through Syria and Egypt in the Years 1783, 1784, and 1785 . . .*, in two volumes, the first of which refers to Egypt (trans. from the French, G. G. and J. Robinson, London: 1787).

[55] For the general condition, see H.A.R. Gibb and Harold Bowen, *Islamic Society and the West*, Volume I, *Islamic Society in the Eighteenth Century*, Part I (Oxford University Press, London: 1950) and Part II (Oxford University Press, London: 1957). For its specific effects on Cairo, see Marcel Colombe, *La via au Caire au XVIIIe siècle* (Conférence de l'Institut Français d'Archéologie Orientale, Cairo: 1951).

[56] Volney, *Travels through Syria and Egypt*, I, p. 234 for quotation, p. 226 on foreigners.

[57] C. S. Sonnini, *Travels in Upper and Lower Egypt: Undertaken by Order of the Old Government of France*, trans. Henry Hunter (John Stockdale, London: 1799), I, 214-215. He notes that "while at Cairo, the European, confined to his own home or, at least, to a narrow quarter of the town, trembling every moment for his life, durst not shew his face amidst a confusion, an uproar, of which it is impossible to form an idea, without having lived in this capital of Egypt."

[58] Not only did Napoleon waste his troops by bringing them to a land which, while promising milk and honey, delivered only dysentery and deprivation, but he also courted disaster by attracting the British fleet which, under Lord Nelson, destroyed French sea power at Abukir Bay and cut off his retreat. While much has been written on these events, I have found Percival Elgood's book, *Bonaparte's Adventure in Egypt* (Oxford University Press, London: 1931) and J. Christopher Herold, *Bonaparte in Egypt* (Harper and Row, New York: 1962) among the more interesting accounts. Also helpful in seeing the human dimension of the expedition is the three-volume collection of letters sent by members of the French Expedition, *Copies of Original Letters from the Army of General Bonaparte in Egypt, Intercepted by the Fleet Under the Command of Admiral Lord Nelson*, with an English Translation (3 vols., London: 11th edn., 1798).

[59] See *Description de l'Égypte: ou Recueil des observations et des recherches qui ont été faites en Égypte pendant l'expédition de l'armée Française* (L'Imprimerie Royale, Paris: 24 volumes published between 1818 and 1828). Information on the various French scholars involved—their recruitment, activities, and achievements—is available in Jean de Metz and Georges Legrain, *Aux pays de Napoléon. l'Égypte* (Jules Rey, Grenoble: 1913), pp. 73 *et seq.*, and in J. Christopher Herold, *Bonaparte in Egypt*, Chapter 6 especially.

5 The Heritage from the Medieval City

In contrast with the meager and essentially negative elements modern Cairo received from her pre-Islamic and early Arab past, her inheritance from the medieval period has proven both rich and vital. The earliest developments, which were concentrated in the southern third of the modern metropolitan region, left their mark chiefly in the form of ruins and "dead" land uses which have prevented expansion without shaping or contributing to the functional order of the contemporary city. On the contrary, with certain modifications, medieval Cairo has been incorporated into the modern metropolis as a living and still vigorous entity.

At present several square miles of the east-central section of Cairo constitute a relatively self-contained community of essentially medieval character, standing in bewildering contrast to the newer city against which it is juxtaposed. Strange anachronisms there are: cheap manufactured goods heaped high on the backs of donkeys or the heads of men; patent leather pumps flashing beneath the long black gowns of veiled women; staccato sounds of typewriters issuing from ancient *mashrabīyah* windows. But without the extensive and all-pervading reminders of the medieval past, these would scarcely attract attention.

The reminders are all about one. Remnants of Ṣalāḥ al-Dīn's walls still stand sentinel at Bāb al-Futūḥ, Bāb al-Naṣr, and Bāb Zuwaylah. His Citadel, much embellished, still dominates the city skyline from above. Street names, such as Bāb al-Baḥr, al-Mu'izz li-Dīn Allāh, the Bazaars of the Coppersmiths, of the Grilled Foods, and of the Armor Makers, Between the Two Castles (Bayn al-Qaṣrayn), Between the Two Walls (Bayn al-Sūrayn), all have their origin in the history recounted here. Sections are still known by their early landmarks: Birkat al-Fīl and Birkat al-Raṭli (both dry and densely developed now), Bāb al-Wazīr, Bāb al-Ḥadīd (Cairo's present rail terminal), al-Ḥusaynīyah, al-Ḥabbanīyah, al-Darb al-Aḥmar, Khān al-Khalīli, al-Jamālīyah. Studding the area are mosques built by Barqūq, Qalāwūn, Mu'ayyad, al-Ghūri, al-Nāṣir, and other sultans whose turbulent careers were enmeshed in the city's development.

But the heritage from medieval Cairo is much more than the monuments which lure tourists. They are the superficial elements, mere symptoms and signs that attract the eye. Underlying them is a pattern of social and physical organization which persists from the medieval period and, even today, exerts a powerful if declining influence on the city. And underlying not only the older sections but the entire city of Cairo are principles of organization derived from the medieval progenitor.

Born in the nineteenth century, adolescent in the twentieth, modern Cairo had as its birthright four distinct elements: (1) the basic framework of its regional pattern—three centers which were to coalesce but never quite blend; (2) the basic framework of its social and ecological organization—diverse ethnic, religious, and class divisions which were to subdivide the modern city in much the same way they had fragmented the medieval one; (3) the basic determinants of its physical structure—streets ill-adapted to modern transport requirements and chaotic mixtures in land use which were to plague the planners of its modern destiny; and (4) a form of municipal administration which, perhaps more than any other heritage, obstructed the way to reform.

Each of these has given way gradually to change. The regional pattern, encouraged by the creation of new nuclei of attraction, has now spread far beyond the original triad. The social system based on regional, national, and religious differences is slowly giving way before the nonethnic cash nexus. Radical surgery has opened up the narrow streets of medieval Cairo, and modern principles of land use segregation now govern the location of new industries. Municipal reform, the achievement of home rule, and the beginnings of city planning have made Cairo somewhat more the master of its own house. However, most of these changes are fairly recent. They began to occur only *after* the medieval heritage had left its deep imprint on the face of the metropolis.

When the scholars attached to the Napoleonic Expedition began their monumental study of Cairo at the turn of the nineteenth century (and incidentally prepared the first accurately scaled map of the city), the metropolitan area of Cairo consisted of three separate but functionally related communities: al-Qāhirah, plus her two port suburbs of Būlāq and Miṣr al-Qadīmah. (See Map XII, based on the French Expedition Regional Map.)

The largest and dominant member of the triumvirate was the city of al-Qāhirah itself, whose name had been distorted in Italian to Kayro and in French to Le Caire. On the north, the urbanized portion of the city terminated abruptly at the wall of Ṣalāḥ al-Dīn which extended from the edge of the eastern desert to the Bāb al-Ḥadīd at the former port of al-Maqs. One thick arm of urban development stretched northward beyond the Bāb al-Futūḥ to form the district of al-Ḥusaynīyah, remnant of the earliest suburban quarter of post-Fāṭimid Cairo. The eastern border of the city was not as well defined since, while desert and blight had encroached within the walls, beyond these ruins lay the Mamluk funereal city with its small resident population. On the south, the city was limited by yet another cemetery beneath the Citadel and by the rim of ruins which had formed south of the Mosque of Ibn Ṭūlūn. On the west, urban forms decreased gradually as the seasonally unstable flood plain was approached.

This main complex comprised a little less than five square miles of land in the form of an irregular rectangle, roughly three miles long and a mile and a half wide.[1] Within this area, which had once contained perhaps half a million persons, the French academicians estimated a population of only 250,000 to 260,000.[2] Thus, even then Cairo had an average density of over 50,000 persons per square mile, moderately high for a preindustrial city where most houses were only two or three stories high[3] and where the general outline contained very large pockets of uninhabited land. It will be recalled that included in the area were several substantial lakes (notably Azbakīyah and Birkat al-Fīl) and numerous smaller ponds, all of which were inundated during the late summer and fall and planted to legumes and grains when the water receded. In addition, the city also contained scattered small cemeteries and many semi-deserted and ruined districts. Surrounding the major rectangle, as a decayed epidermis, was a ring of high rubble mounds—compost heaps of crumbled mudbrick buildings and rubbish which had formed primarily but not exclusively during the Turkish era. This ring was broken only on the western and northwestern extremities where the rich alluvial soil supported agricultural estates and a peasant population to tend them.

Beyond the rubble and the rural lay the two major suburbs of the city: Būlāq, due west of al-Maqs at the new shore of the Nile; and Miṣr al-Qadīmah, southwest of the city near the Mosque of 'Amr, once the thriving core of

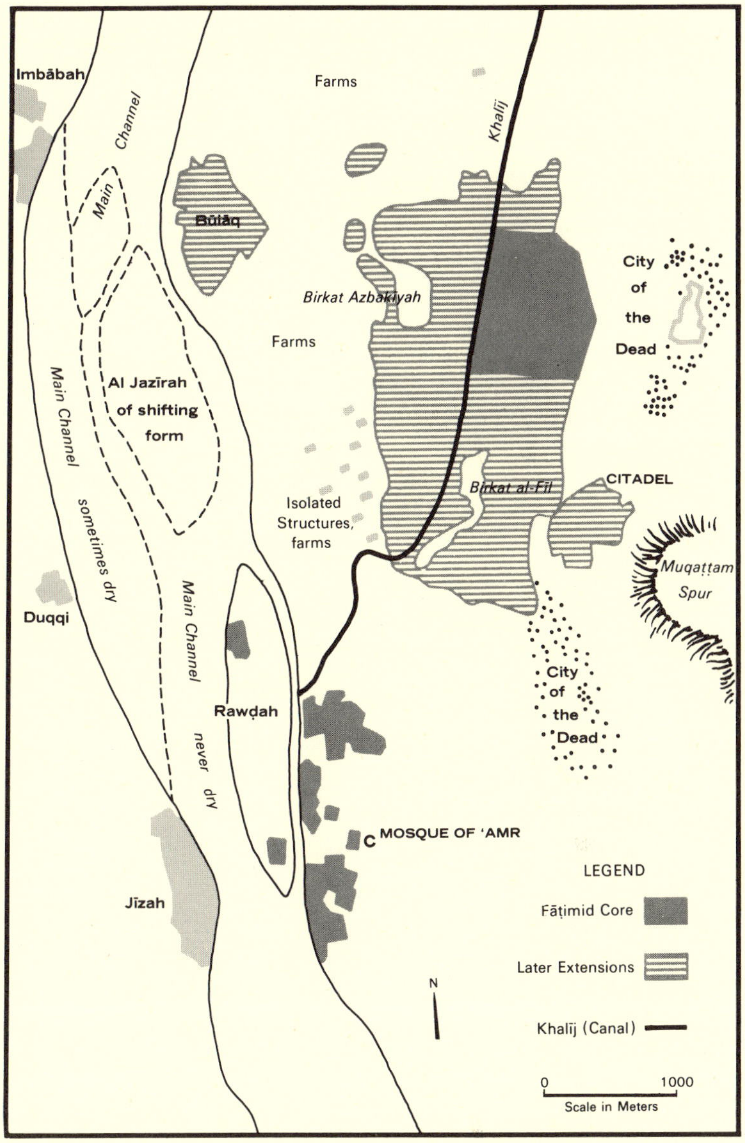

XII. Regional map of Cairo and its environs (based upon *Description de l'Égypte*)

[1] *Master Plan of Cairo* (Government Printing Office, Cairo: 1956), p. 22. Detailed measurements also appear in E. Jomard, "Description abregée de la ville et de la citadelle du Kaire," in *Description de l'Égypte: État moderne* (L'Imprimerie Royale, Paris: 1822), Tome II, Part II, pp. 579-783. Jomard gives the area of al-Qāhirah as 793 hectares and her circumference as 24,000 meters, the latter extremely large because of the irregularity of the borders. See p. 580.

[2] Two methods of estimating Cairo's population were used by the French. First, for purposes of taxation the French made a house count of the city. Then, multiplying the number of houses by estimated average size of household (26,000 dwellings by 10 persons per dwelling), they arrived at an estimated population total of 260,000. The second method was somewhat more sophisticated. The French introduced a system of recording births and deaths to the city which formerly had kept no vital statistics. The total number of deaths during 1798 was recorded. Later, when a firmer population base was established, the death rate of later years was applied to 1798 to estimate the population base during the earlier year. This retrospective method yielded an estimated population of 263,700 in 1798. See Jomard, "Description abregée . . . du Kaire," pp. 585-586. Somewhat different figures, however, appear in the same volume. V. de Chabrol, in his "Essai sur les moeurs des habitants modernes de l'Égypte," in *Description de l'Égypte: État moderne,* Tome II, Part II, says that "in 1798 Cairo had 250,000 to 260,000 persons, including the Mamluks and foreign traders. According to another computation made prior to the expedition, there were 300,000 persons . . ." (my translation), p. 364. One must marvel at the perspicacity (or sheer luck) which led W. G. Browne in the last decade of the eighteenth century to estimate Cairo's population at over 300,000 and the country's at 2.5 million. See his *Travels in Africa, Egypt and Syria from the Year 1792 to 1798* (Printed for T. Cadwell and W. Davies by T. N. Longman and O. Rees, London: 1799), p. 71.

[3] Jomard, "Description abregée . . . du Kaire," p. 585.

28. Cairo stops abruptly at the walls in the 1800's

29. Northern gate to Miṣr al-Qadīmah *ca.* 1800. Island of Rawḍah to right

Fusṭāṭ. Of the two, Būlāq was larger and more important, reflecting the long centuries during which trade with Europe had taken precedence over commerce with the African inland. Būlāq's population totaled 24,000 in 1818,[4] which may have represented a reduction from her population a score of years earlier, since the French had burned parts of the town during an 1800 campaign to recapture the rebellious city. Between Būlāq and Cairo intervened a wide plain,[5] on which corn and beans were grown between floods. Two roads connected the suburb with Cairo. One was the northern diagonal used by the caravans; the other, leading into the Azbakīyah quarter, was elevated and stabilized by the French to give them an all-weather connection between the quasi-island port and their headquarters. Būlāq's functions were, even then, chiefly transport and wholesale.

Somewhat farther removed from the core city was Miṣr al-Qadīmah, reduced to a ghost town of only 10,000 or 11,000 souls.[6] Once the most important city of the Muslim world, by 1800 this town had practically reverted to its pre-Islamic composition and function. A large number of its inhabitants were Copts, a Christian sect dating back to the era of Diocletian, while another large minority were Jews. One subgroup of the population was concentrated near the shrines of the Qaṣr al-Sham', the rest farther north in the port area. This port, through which the trade of a vast empire formerly passed, had been reduced to a mere landing for sailboats arriving from and departing to Upper Egypt. History had dealt most cruelly with this city which, some eight centuries earlier, had been described in such glowing terms by Nāṣir-i Khusraw and al-Muqaddasi. The populated city, like the Delta, had edged inexorably downstream.

During the ensuing century of growth, these three communities—al-Qāhirah, Būlāq, and Miṣr al-Qadīmah—served as the triangulation points of the regional pattern. Throughout the nineteenth century, expansion was almost entirely confined to filling in the connective tissue between the three nuclei. By the end of that century the city still retained her rectangular shape, but by then the rectangle stretched westward from the northern tip of al-Ḥusaynīyah to the Nile shore at Būlāq, southward along the river from Būlāq to Miṣr al-Qadīmah, northeastward to the Citadel, and then due north again to complete the form. It took only one century to transform these three functionally interdependent but physically separated communities into a contiguous whole.

Perhaps one of the most significant differences between cities of the industrial era and those of the feudal or preindustrial order[7] is the critical role which subgroup identification plays in sorting and segregating the inhabitants of the latter type. In the preindustrial city, not income but "ethnic" division according to the dual criteria of religion and place of origin is the basis for social class, occupation, and place of residence within the community. The ecological organization of pre-modern Cairo conformed well to this hypothesis. The distribution of population within the city was governed by the principle of social rather than economic segregation, although economic distribution was often a function of this social identity.

What were the major groups in the city and how were they distributed? From the researches conducted by the French scholars there emerges a fairly clear picture of the social composition of Cairo as the city neared the end of its preindustrial phase of development.[8] Of

[4] *Ibid.*, p. 748.

[5] Jomard, *ibid.*, estimated its width at 1200 meters.

[6] V. de Chabrol, "Essai sur les moeurs," p. 366; Jomard, "Description abregée . . . du Kaire," p. 744.

[7] My use of this term follows the typology developed by Gideon Sjoberg in "The Preindustrial City," *American Journal of Sociology*, Volume 60 (March 1955), pp. 438-445, and his later elaboration in book form, *The Preindustrial City: Past and Present* (The Free Press, Glencoe: 1960).

[8] The following figures have been derived from the tables appearing in Jomard, "Description abregée . . . du Kaire," p. 694.

her total population, some 90 per cent were Muslims, the remaining 10 percent being divided among Jews and Christians of various persuasions and sects. Among the latter were about 10,000 Christian Jacobites (Copts), 5,000 Greek and Maronite Catholics, 5,000 other Greek splinter sects, 3,000 Jews, 2,000 Armenian Christians and 400 Roman Catholic and Protestant Europeans.

While, with the exception of the Copts, all religious minorities were also national minorities, no such easy congruence characterized the Muslim majority which included several national and regional minorities. Egyptian-Arab Muslims made up less than four-fifths of the total population. Included in the remainder were not only Christians and Jews (essentially extraneous to the class hierarchy) but also Muslim foreigners of both highest and lowest status who accounted for some 13 percent of the total population. At the top of the pyramid was the ethnically divergent elite, consisting of 10,400 Mamluks and 10,000 Turks. At the base were 12,000 Blacks, Nubians and Ethiopians, many of whom had originally been brought to the city as menial rather than military slaves.

Careful scrutiny reveals certain discrepancies between the figures appearing in his two separate tables of nationality and religion. However, despite these, the tables are in general agreement and must serve as our guide, since they are the only ones available.

30. Street in the Coptic quarter in the 19th century

Occupationally, the city was similarly divided. A computation made prior to the French Expedition, when the city had an estimated 300,000 persons, gave some labor force figures. Of the 99,000 adult males (no definition of adult given), some 12,000 were Mamluks, the ethnically distinct ruling class. Of the remainder, perhaps 11 percent could be classified as middle class, being either proprietors, landlords, or international traders. Another 35 percent might be called upper-lower class, being small merchants or artisans. Well over half (54 percent) were lower-lower class, engaged in agriculture, unskilled labor, domestic service, etc.[9]

There was close congruence between occupation and ethnic identity, with Turks and Circassians constituting the military and governing elite, with foreigners and members of religious minorities overrepresented in the trading professions, and with African and rural Egyptian "imports" concentrated in the lower levels of domestic service and unskilled labor. Because of this close congruence, we shall use ethnic identity as the chief criterion of ecological distribution. (It is not possible to investigate "place of origin" and its influence upon social subdivisions within the Muslim-Egyptian majority because these data have been lost. However, since this is *still* important in contemporary Cairo, we must assume that it was even more significant and operative at an earlier stage of the city's existence.)

Each ethnic-religious group occupied its own quarter in the city. Just north of Azbakīyah, on the site of the former port town of al-Maqs, was the main Coptic quarter. Most of the city's Copts lived either in this area or within the Qaṣr al-Sham' portion of Miṣr al-Qadīmah. It is interesting to speculate on the causes of this coincidence. The answer probably lies in the close connection between ethnic identity and occupational function. Among the traditional Coptic occupations were those of scribe, account-keeper, and customs official (except for those periods when the position of customs official was entrusted to Jews). One can readily see how involvement in these occupations might lead, in a city in which place of work and place of residence were intimately connected, to a concentration of Copts in port and former port areas.

Adjacent to the northern Coptic quarter were the smaller sections occupied by Christian Syrian and Ar-

[9] The results of this earlier study were reported by V. de Chabrol, "Essai sur les moeurs," p. 364. The total population consisted of 99,000 adult males, 126,000 females, and 75,000 children. No definition of children is given, but these may have been only males. Otherwise the city would have been quite heavily female, an unlikely statistical occurrence, especially since one would expect greater underreporting of females than males.

menian merchants whose wealth, great as it may have been, was still insufficient to allow them to escape the limits imposed by a deviant religion. They formed a transitional group, as well as occupied the transitional zone, between the native Copts and the primarily mercantile Europeans who inhabited the Mūski (Frankish) quarter between the Birkat Azbakīyah and the Khalīj Miṣri.[10] Thus, in 1800, the northwest corner of Cairo housed most of the "minorities" of the city, who were excluded by and in turn excluded the majority, and who were held in loose alliance by similar if rival religions.

Two of the oldest ethnic minorities, however, remained within the walled city in approximately the same locations which they had been assigned in the early plans of the city. These were the Greeks and the Jews. Ḥārat Zuwaylah (later renamed, more descriptively, Ḥārat al-Yahūd) remained the chief Jewish quarter up to 1956.[11] Its location, near the Fāṭimid Great Western Palace on land formerly occupied by the Gardens of Kāfūr, was not an unusual one in Islamic cities. Since the Jewish community tended to grow up in the service and under the protection of the ruler, the Jewish quarter was often located within the walled city not far from the palace. Not only in Cairo, but in the Islamic cities of North Africa, such as Fez, Rabat, and Casablanca, as well as those in the Fertile Crescent, such as Damascus and Aleppo, this coincidence of location prevailed. Traditionally, also, the markets for money changing and goldsmithing were located within the Jewish quarter. The only unusual feature in the case of Cairo was the persistence of the original location, even after the religious-secular authority had removed itself from the walled Fāṭimid city to the Citadel. Instead of being relocated with it, the Jewish community remained where it had been.

The two Greek settlements had an even longer and certainly more complex history in the city. Maqrīzi's description (see Map IX above, *ḥārāt* Nos. 15 and 8) leaves little doubt concerning either their locations or early origins. Dating from earliest settlement was the Ḥārat al-Rūm, located just northeast of the Fāṭimid Eastern Palace. Some time before the eleventh century, a second Greek quarter began to develop south of Jawhar's Bāb Zuwaylah along the southern wall of the city, and thus it became necessary to distinguish between the two Greek quarters. The former became known as the "Inner Greek Quarter" (Ḥārat al-Rūm al-Juwwānīyah) while the latter was referred to as the "Outer Greek Quarter" (Ḥārat al-Rūm al-Barrānīyah), a distinction that soon lost its relevance when Badr al-Jamāli enlarged the walls to include the latter within the city's circumference. By the time of Maqrīzi, Ḥārat al-Rūm al-Barrānīyah had become the chief quarter of Greek residence, a supremacy it still retained at the coming of the French almost four centuries later. However, by this time another colony of Greeks had begun to form nearer to the foreign and native Christian communities in the northwestern quadrant.

The remainder of the city was occupied by the Muslim community which dominated it both numerically and socially. The Mamluks were concentrated, as before, within the southern portion of the city which contained not only the Citadel but also the assembly grounds and the markets catering to the military needs of the group. The great mansions of the elite were located around the Birkat al-Fīl or on the borders of the Birkat Azbakīyah which, together, constituted the most desirable residential zones of the city.[12] During the time of Maqrīzi, the main Turkish quarters of the city had been in the vicinity of al-Azhar Mosque, primarily to the south and west of that religious center. However, with the increase in the Turkish population after Salīm's conquest, the Turkish community spread out to encompass areas previously the exclusive domain of the Mamluk elite. Many of the Turks, however, were itinerant merchants who came and went without establishing permanent headquarters in Cairo.

Within the heart of the Fāṭimid city, throughout the *qaṣabah* and its surrounding fringes, were the Egyptian merchants, master craftsmen, journeymen, and artisans who made up the bulk of what might be termed the upper-lower class, for middle class there was little. These were the groups upon whose life the industry of the city depended, and these were the groups most involved in the vicinal, occupational, and religious fraternities of the city. The northern and eastern fringes of the Fāṭimid city had been declining in importance and prestige since before the fourteenth century, and to these sections were relegated the Muslim masses—the new migrants, the destitute, the unskilled laborers. These classes also occupied the semi-rural peripheral areas, such as al-Ḥusaynīyah north of the wall and a squatters' preserve on the east. Farther south, at the foot of the Citadel, was another

[10] Jomard, "Description abregée . . . du Kaire," p. 586.

[11] Ḥārat Zuwaylah is easily located through Maqrīzi. In his time, five of the six synagogues of al-Qāhirah were to be found in that quarter. See Maqrīzi, *Khiṭaṭ* (Būlāq Press: 1853), II, 471-472. The nomenclature is somewhat confusing because the Ḥārat Zuwaylah was *not* in the vicinity of the Bāb Zuwaylah. A Jewish settlement also persisted in Miṣr al-Qadīmah, descendant from the prosperous Jewish community of Fusṭāṭ. It was there that the famous Geniza documents were found.

[12] Clerget, among others, has pointed out that a principle which still governs the ecological structure of contemporary Cairo was operative throughout her early history, i.e., the tendency of the best residential areas to be located near water. See *Le Caire*, I, 265. His description of the various quarters of Cairo at this period is found on pp. 264-265.

31. Along the *qaṣabah* in the early 19th century

32. Along the *qaṣabah* today: the Spice Market

33. Along the *qaṣabah* today: clothing

"popular" quarter of similar composition. The southwestern quadrant contained a population drawn from both extremes of the class distribution. "Landed" gentry of Circassian and Turkish origin were settled amid a native Egyptian peasant population in this area of semi-agrarian character. In this peripheral section also lived the volatile gangs of the demimonde who preyed upon the city dwellers, and the poorer workmen who, while occupied in the city each day, were attracted by the lower rents at the fringe.

This was the ecological organization of Cairo at the turn of the nineteenth century. In a fashion almost uncanny to observe, the ordering of these subcommunities in the preindustrial city has determined the distribution of religious and ethnic groups in contemporary Cairo, despite the fact that the city's area has increased more than tenfold in the past 150 years. Although the details of this distribution are reserved for the final section of this book, it should be pointed out here that the functions of many older areas have changed little in the interim, while the newer areas owe much of their current character to the particular old quarter from which they radiated. Thus Shubra, a relatively new area just north of the old Coptic quarter, became the chief area of Egyptian Christian resi-

34. Bazaar of the Silk Merchants *ca.* 1840. Note roof

35. Textile *sūq* in al-Jamālīyah today

dence. Ismā'īlīyah and Garden City, newer areas of European-type residence, trace their roots to the Mūski-Azbakīyah quarter out of which they expanded. Ẓāhir and 'Abbāsīyah represent extensions of the populous al-Ḥusaynīyah quarter, while the popular zone at the foot of the Citadel has spread westward to Sayīdah Zaynab. Indeed, it is difficult if not impossible to understand the intricacies of modern Cairo's ecological pattern without a knowledge of the city's organization in medieval times.

If residential segregation on religio-ethnic lines is one crucial trait of the preindustrial city, another equally important element is the relative *lack* of such segregation with respect to land uses. Mixed land use seems to be a universal characteristic of cities in the medieval, feudal, or preindustrial period.[13] The modern industrial city, with its highly differentiated pattern of land uses and its planners' preoccupation with separating mutually offensive activities, bears little relation to cities of an earlier era. Types of land uses usually distinguished in a modern city are: (1) residential zones of various quality; (2) retail commercial and personal service uses; (3) wholesale commerce and storage; (4) light industrial uses, including assembling, small-scale fabrication, and minor repairs; (5) heavy industrial production and noxious processing industries, such as tanning, pottery kilns, abattoirs; (6) transport terminals and affiliated storage and trans-shipment installations; (7) religious edifices, often associated with (8) educational, health, and other public services; (9) governmental and administrative

[13] I use these terms somewhat interchangeably, following the definitions of Sjoberg, *The Preindustrial City*, pp. 9-11.

uses; (10) recreational facilities, both open peripheral land and more centralized commercial recreation; and (11) cemeteries.

When one states that preindustrial Cairo had little or no segregation of these uses, the standard of comparison is the modern industrial city. Segregation, though minimal, was not entirely lacking. On the contrary, certain uses were even more rigidly segregated in eighteenth-century Cairo than would be deemed necessary or desirable in a modern city. Uses were hardly distributed at random, nor do I want to imply that there was no area specialization. Indeed, nothing could be farther from the truth. The medieval city of Cairo demonstrated concentrations and specializations which continue to influence land use patterns down to the present. By exploring some of these in greater detail here it is possible to show in which ways use-segregation was present and in which ways absent in preindustrial Cairo.

Among the uses as rigidly segregated in medieval Cairo as in a modern city were the open recreational uses, the governmental administrative uses, and the cemeteries. The recreational areas, primarily those used by the Mamluks, were located outside the city in the semi-marshlands west and north of the city. Governmental offices were concentrated in the Citadel, with the notable exception of those dealing with the regulation of commerce which were located on site. (For example, the official weights and measures administration was, and still is, located within the *qaṣabah.*) Segregation of cemeteries was even more marked than in a modern Western city. While there were a few small cemeteries scattered within the city, the major installations were, and still are, located east and south of the urban complex. It is difficult to give a reader who has not seen them some idea of their extent. In 1800, for example, these two major funereal quarters occupied land equivalent to one-fourth of the area of Cairo.[14]

One should not imagine, however, that these cemeteries were (or are) used exclusively as burial sites. Although physically segregated, they were never functionally segregated. From early times, among the shrines were found monasteries and schools for various religious and mystic orders. Some of these served as free hostels for itinerant scholars or travelers. In addition, guarding each family tomb was a resident retainer and his dependents. To this population must be added a few temporary and permanent squatters who found the rent-free stone and wooden structures of the "tomb city" more spacious and substantial than the mudbrick huts available to them within the city proper. With such a resident population, it was perhaps inevitable that some artisans and shopkeepers should gravitate to the area to fulfill the demand for daily goods

[14] Jomard, "Description abregée . . . du Kaire," p. 582.

36. Unchanged landmark: al-Ghūri aqueduct near Fam al-Khalīj *ca.* 1840

37. The aqueduct today, surrounded and functionless

and services. Nor were these the only functions of this unique land use. Just as the marshlands provided open recreational space for the militaristic sports pursued by the Mamluks, the Cities of the Dead provided recreational facilities for the bulk of the population who repaired there weekly and, in even greater numbers, on the major festival occasions.[15] While this custom originated as a means of paying respect to the tombs of saints and relatives, it attained a momentum of its own, with festivities rather than solemnity usually accompanying the exodus.

Similarly, noxious industrial uses, transportation terminals, and wholesale uses were assigned to specialized sections of the urban complex. For example, the pottery kilns, the slaughterhouses, and the tanneries were segregated near Miṣr al-Qadīmah where, indeed, they still remain. Transport terminals had specialized locations, although the technology of the times required extensive

[15] For a description of this behavior as it persisted into the nineteenth century, see Edward Lane, *The Manners and Customs of the Modern Egyptians* (3rd edn. of 1908 as reprinted by J. M. Dent Ltd., London: 1954), p. 485.

installations only for maritime transport. Traffic to and from the city went overland on animate carriers or went by water in wind-driven craft. Terminal facilities for caravans were located north of the city at Birkat al-Ḥujjāj and also in Būlāq where connections could be made with the water-borne network. Storehouses, wholesale firms, and inns for itinerant traders were also to be found near the port. Within the city itself, no specialized facilities were required, since legs and donkeys were the major means of internal circulation, but combined storehouses and inns dotted the *qaṣabah*.

Commercial functions also were scarcely distributed at random in the city. The pulsing heart, or rather artery, of medieval Cairo was the market zone, the linear strip of *qaṣabah* which extended from the Bāb al-Futūḥ to beyond Bāb Zuwaylah, supplemented by horizontal out-pockets both east and west of the thoroughfare. Within this central business district, specialization was even more extreme than in the business zone of an industrial city. Each trade, each product, had its own area within the market complex.[16] The ordering of the various trades followed functional necessity, with items related by raw material or associated use grouped in close proximity. Books, religious artifacts, and candles were associated with the most important mosque, al-Azhar. Yard goods, sewing findings, and tailoring establishments formed another subsystem. Armor, metal items, accoutrements for war horses, and special apparel for the Mamluk masters were clustered together in the southern segment near the areas of Mamluk concentration. Precious metals and costly silks occupied the most central location in the *qaṣabah*, anticipating the land economists' theory of highest use. Fruits, vegetables, and poultry had their own market areas near the northern gates of the city by which peasants entered to deliver their produce. Grouped functionally near the point of departure of caravans (in Jamālīyah) were the markets for beasts of burden, saddles, and other travel accessories. European imported goods were sold in the Mūski.[17]

Thus, when scholars note that the preindustrial city had "no real specialization of land use," they must refer to quite a different matter. The modern city which segregates place of residence from place of work and production from point of sale (and then squanders time and money relinking the fragments) is the antithesis of the preindustrial city. The latter, dependent upon animate energy sources and on the walking radius, combined these functions the modern city seems intent on pushing farther and farther apart. It is in this sense only that preindustrial Cairo had little land use specialization. To a degree inconceivable to the resident of a modern industrial city, homes, workshops, and retail outlets were combined in medieval Cairo, if not within the same structure then within the same small *ḥārah* (quarter) or *darb* (alley).[18]

It was this intermixture which made rigid segregation by income impossible in the city. At the time of the French Expedition, the city of Cairo was divided into 53 *ḥārāt*,[19] each of which in turn consisted of several *durūb* (sing., *darb*), i.e., perhaps 30 dwellings grouped around common access alleys which were barricaded nightly. In the more commercialized sections of the city, each *darb* or group of *durūb* was devoted to a particular craft or product. Not only were goods produced and sold there, but, in addition, residing there were some of the individuals involved in production and distribution. Hence, the same unit might contain the luxurious home of a prosperous merchant, the humbler but still substantial dwelling of the master craftsman, and poorer quarters for apprentices, porters, unskilled laborers, and menials. Within the same unit were shops and dwellings for small tradesmen catering to daily needs of residents, at least one coffee shop for recreation, and in the larger units a public bath,[20] a small mosque with an associated *kuttāb* (Koran school), possibly a meeting hall, and warehouses and inns for the convenience of visiting merchants. Even outside the commercial hub of the city similar admixtures of workshops, stores, and residences were to be found.

Thus, the very principle which militated against segre-

[16] The following is based chiefly upon Maqrīzi's topography of the *aswāq* of Cairo, as given in the *Khiṭaṭ*, II, 96-106. While his description deals exclusively with Cairo, it could easily be used to describe most Islamic cities and a good number of medieval European and Far Eastern towns as well. The works of G. Von Grunebaum, on the "Structure of the Muslim Town," of Georges Marçais, and of Roger Le Tourneau, all cited earlier, permit a comparison with other Islamic cities; the writings of Sjoberg, especially "The Preindustrial City," p. 439 and his *The Preindustrial City*, Chapter IV, pp. 80-107, suggest a parallel with preindustrial cities elsewhere in the world.

[17] The latter point supplied by Jomard, "Description abregée . . . du Kaire," p. 582.

[18] Apparently the Islamic preindustrial city had a somewhat greater separation between domicile and place of work than did the European medieval city, a fact not unrelated to the eastern pattern of female seclusion. Only unmarried workers were free to live in the workshops; men with families often commuted (but not far) to homes in more exclusively residential zones. This was particularly true of the proprietors who could afford the added expense of the protected *harīm*. Germain Martin, in his *Les bazars du Caire et les petits métiers arabes* (Université Égyptienne, Cairo: 1910), p. 74, calls our attention to Nāṣir-i Khusraw's description in the eleventh century of the daily entry and exodus of the merchants into and out of the *qaṣabah*, suggesting that "this custom of living outside the centers of industry and commerce is very ancient."

[19] Jomard, "Description abregée . . . du Kaire," pp. 580 *et seq.*, enumerated the major *ḥārāt* of the city.

[20] V. de Chabrol, "Essai sur les moeurs," noted the existence of some 1200 cafés (p. 437) and nearly 100 public baths (p. 435) in Cairo alone at the time of the French Expedition.

'offee shop in the early 19th century

gation of land uses, i.e., area specialization by product, also prevented the pure operation of the principle of segregation by economic level or income. When the residential population of a subarea of the city was partially determined by its involvement in a particular industry or trade, it was impossible for individuals also to be sorted neatly according to their relative prosperity. (While this was true for those involved in artisan, craft, and commercial activities, it was less applicable to the large "army" of the unskilled and irregularly employed, often only temporarily resident in the city, who tended to be segregated by income in the most deteriorated peripheral quarters east and south of the city's core.)

It was perhaps inevitable also that such an arrangement should be reflected in a unique street system. Concerning this street system, Jomard noted that "the interior arrangement of the city has hardly any resemblance to European cities; not only are its streets and public squares extremely irregular, but the city is almost entirely composed, with the exception of a few very long avenues, of extremely short, broken, zig-zag streets with innumerable dead ends. Each of these off-shoots is closed by a door that the inhabitants open when they wish; the result is that the interior of Cairo is very difficult to know as a whole. . . ."[21]

Only eight avenues of any length could be found in the city. Three ran north-south, while three of the five transversals connected the all-important Citadel with points along the Nile shore. With these notable exceptions, few streets followed a simple course for more than a quarter of a mile, and most ended abruptly before they had passed by more than four or five buildings. It is to these short streets that the term *darb* is applied, although the concept refers more to the unit of structures than to the actual street itself. Map XI, reproduced from the plan prepared by the French Expedition, shows the course of the major thoroughfares, but also demonstrates the remarkable complexity of the smaller components of the circulation system.

How had this pattern developed? And to what type of technology was it adapted? Certainly, the original princely city of al-Qāhirah was not planned in such a fashion. The relatively simple, rectangular design of the Fāṭimid capital contained, in addition to the main longitudinal procession-way between the two palaces, at least two other straight north-south parallels and five or possibly six east-west streets of similar directness. How had this pattern degenerated into the rabbit-warren convolutions of a later era?

First, it must be recognized that this street system was not unique to Cairo. Just as a practiced observer can examine a map of modern Cairo and distinguish the medieval from the modern portion *solely* on the basis of street pattern, so the same observer can make a similar judgment for every compound North African and Middle Eastern city. The contrast is everywhere the same. Nor is this phenomenon confined to Islamic cities, although some scholars of the Islamic city form seem to stress this as a unique quality. Actually, many plans of medieval European towns show a similar configuration and, if we accept the evidence of Sjoberg, Islamic and medieval European towns were but subspecies of the genus preindustrial city, with its common manifestations in such diverse locations as China, India, and South America as well.[22]

Most phenomena have both particular and universal elements in their constitutions, and the street system of preindustrial Cairo exemplifies this dualism. The universal, that which it shares with other cities at a similar stage of development, can best be understood in terms of technology, which determines the functions a circulation system is called upon to fulfill.

Transportation on foot (the masses), on donkeys and camels (middle-class riders and bulk goods), or on horses (reserved for Mamluks), requires neither broad avenues

[21] Jomard, "Description abregée . . . du Kaire," pp. 580, 581 (my translation). He might well have added that such an arrangement also made the interior of Cairo very difficult to control militarily, a consideration which led the French to dismantle forcibly the gates to the individual *durūb*.

[22] Illustrations of medieval towns may be found in Mumford, *The Culture of Cities*; in Arthur Korn, *History Builds the Town*; in Arthur B. Gallion, *The Urban Pattern* (D. Van Nostrand, New York: 1950), pp. 33-39; and in F. Hiorns, *Town Building in History* (G. G. Harrap, London: 1956), to mention but a few sources. Actually, the plans of medieval European towns exhibit a somewhat less intricate maze of streets than preindustrial Cairo, although they lack the symmetry of either their Roman forebears or their later Renaissance reconstructions. For non-European examples, see also Sjoberg, *The Preindustrial City*, pp. 91-93.

39. A typical street in the medieval core *ca.* 1840

nor elaborate traffic separations. Travel at such low speeds requires neither crow-flight directness nor a hard, smooth pavement. Given this technological level, the circulation requirements of the community follow. Proximity for convenience takes precedence over land use segregation, with which it is in conflict. The principle of least effort, operating within the primitive transport technology of the preindustrial city, leads to roughly circular time-cost belts of access. The city attempts to minimize the need for mobility of all kinds. As against these, there are only two opposing forces to encourage the long, wide avenue: (1) the need to connect one urban community with another; and (2) the internal need to provide an impressive procession-way for an occasional display of political power and the periodic need to marshal and dispatch the army. But these limited and only occasional demands can be met quite satisfactorily by a handful of such avenues. The remainder of the streets are called upon to serve merely as limited accessways rather than thoroughfares. No more than a pathway between buildings is essential for residents to reach their doors and, in medieval Cairo, no more than this minimum was usually retained.

Thus, the multiple functions of the modern street are reduced, under the technological conditions of the feudal city, to the bare minimum of access, and access on foot or animal at most. These were elements which medieval Cairo had in common with other communities of similar technical advancement. However, the three particular elements which helped shape her street pattern are in many ways more interesting, and in the final analysis, crucial. In order of increasing specificity, they are climate, social structure, and political organization.

The direct overhead sun of Cairo, the lengthy eight-month summer, the lack of clouds or rugged terrain to cast natural shadows, all lead to a similar imperative: create artificial shade. In Islamic cities, this goal was achieved by narrow streets covered by either rush mats or wooden roofs, or protected by overhanging balconies. Placing buildings close together insulated against unwanted sunlight for all but a short period each day. The same effect was achieved by building the second stories wider than the first. This was one of the most striking architectural forms employed in preindustrial Cairo, often so extreme as to make opposing balconies almost touch. While this form also appeared in the populous districts of Tudor London and other cities of northern latitude, the impulse to open the streets, felt by most of the latter, was absent in cities of the Middle East to whose climate they were emi-

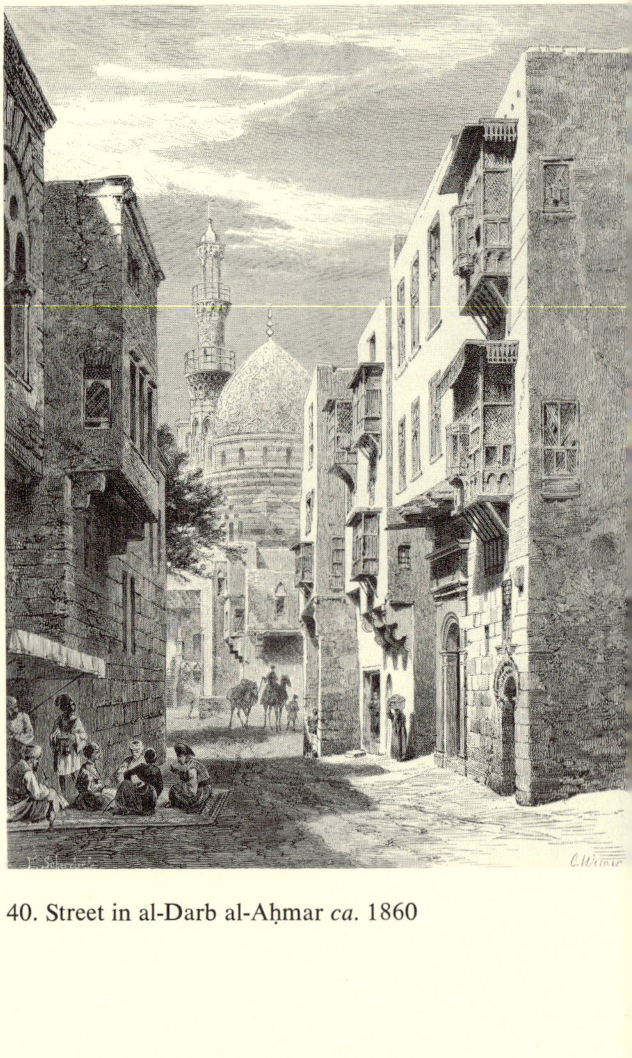

40. Street in al-Darb al-Aḥmar *ca.* 1860

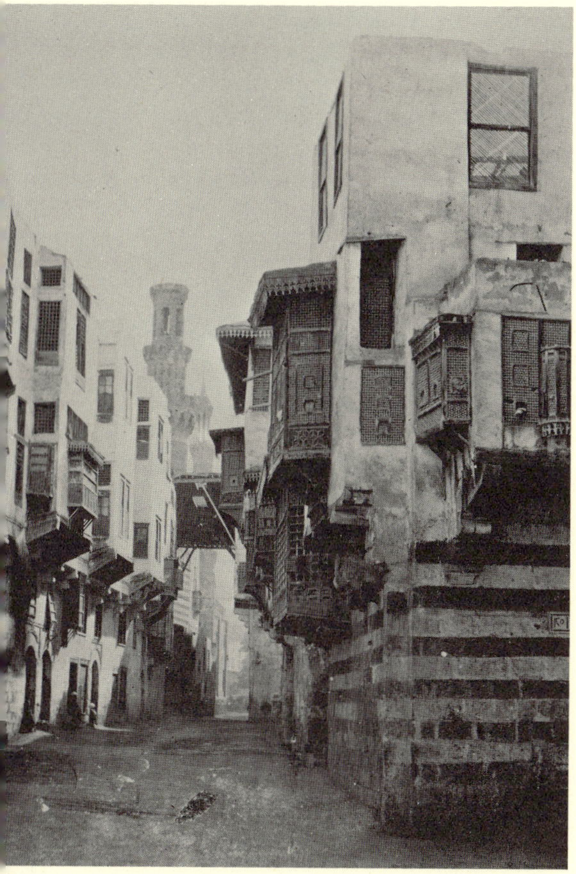

41. Street scene in medieval quarter *ca.* 1857

42. Covered *sūq* in al-Darb al-Aḥmar, 1960

nently suited. (In fact, during periods of intense heat, the architecturally protected *aswāq* of the older city are far more comfortable than the air-conditioned shops of the modern quarter.) Where narrow streets and building overhangs were insufficient to create the needed coolness, mat coverings and later wooden roofs were erected, particularly in the market districts. Thus the narrow street was not only a natural concomitant of the limited functions it was called upon to serve but was also a highly functional adaptation to climatic requirements.

The street system reflected not only geographic climate but the social climate as well, and in this respect was equally functional. The division of the city into *durūb* was not dictated solely by technology or temperature. The *darb* was a social unit as much as it was a physical and industrial unit. True, economic function unified the inhabitants but, given the relationship between trade and ethnic identity, it was also inevitable that religious and regional ties should strengthen the cohesiveness of the area. Nor was it accidental that the essence of the *darb* was its capacity for defense. The barricades between *durūb* reflected not only the lack of a reliable municipal police force but an entire society in which diverse groups existed perpetually in uneasy symbiosis and uncertain security. There was constant danger of explosion, particularly during the later periods of Mamluk and Ottoman rule when contending factions of soldiers rampaged through the city and when undisciplined gangs from among the populace fought each other over "turf."[23] Limited access, a solid wall of peripheral buildings, and a narrow defensible point of penetration were the strategies of protection.

All these considerations, however, still do not answer the question originally posed, namely: by what process was the finely planned, right-angled palace city of Fāṭimid al-Qāhirah transformed into the maze-like combina-

[23] A discussion of these gangs, the so-called *zu'ar*, during Mamluk times can be found in the study by Ira Lapidus, *Muslim Cities in the Later Middle Ages* (Harvard University Press, Cambridge: 1967), particularly Chapter v. Parallel institutions in more eastern-situated parts of the Arab empire are discussed by Claude Cahen in his *Mouvements populaires et autonomisme urbain dans l'Asie Musulmane du Moyen Âge* (reprinted from his articles in *Arabica* by E. J. Brill, Leiden: 1959). Whether these were exactly comparable is not clear. What is clear, however, is that the commercial classes in Cairo, especially during times of civic disorder, found it necessary to solicit or to succumb to the "protection" of these local "toughs," regardless of their exact origin and organization.

tion of small cells which characterized it by the late medieval period? Technology, climate and even social tension may explain the teleological aspect, the "why," but they do not illuminate the process, the "how." For this one must turn to the Islamic concept of property and the legal system which presumably was called upon to enforce it.[24]

It is perhaps ironic that Roman (and from thence, Western) law, which emphasized private property rights, should have been so much more successful in preserving the sanctity of the public ways than Islamic law which emphasized the public and communal rights over land, i.e., favored state domains and trusteeship over freehold tenure. While Islamic law acknowledged in principle the inviolable sanctity of, if not all streets, at least public thoroughfares, in actual practice several factors intervened to make preservation difficult and to soften the penalties for encroachment. First, within an alley, *cul de sac*, or other limited accessway, the abutters alone were responsible for maintenance and for keeping the passageway clear of obstructions; unless a neighbor complained, there was nothing to be adjudicated. Second, even on the thoroughfares or public ways, the air rights over the street and a basic easement around the building plot itself, including the street side, "belonged" to the owners of abutting property. Owners, then, retained preferential rights to the street which they were free to exercise, so long as they did not "unreasonably" block traffic (and this was a matter for *ex post facto* legal opinion, not of prior legal specification) and so long as their exercise did not infringe on the equally valid rights of other owners along the street. In short, whereas Western law sought to prohibit all encroachments upon the public way except where specifically exempted, the law in Islamic cities tended to permit encroachments, except when these were judged to interfere with the rights of others. Therefore, while a watchful neighborhood and a zealous government might guard the public way by requiring the demolition of obstructing constructions, neither could prevent their existence a priori. And third, once an obstruction had been in existence for a lengthy period of time and been uncontested, the right to its continuance was assured. Thus, the results of a period of public neglect could not later be remedied; constant vigilance was required.

With these as the governing legal principles, it is not difficult to reconstruct the process whereby Cairo was allowed to develop her complex pattern. Whenever the city experienced a rapid rise in population, probably beginning from the time of the massive influx that followed the burning of Fusṭāṭ, unpreempted open spaces—whether *maydāns*, interior courts, or wide public roads—were gradually encroached upon. Shops added temporary extensions onto the street which were transformed, step by step, into more permanent structures. In front of these, benches may have been placed for temporary use. Again, these were later transformed into the *masāṭib* (stone benches) which permanently obstructed passage until Muḥammad 'Ali, in the best tradition of former rulers, summarily ordered their removal.[25] A man might set up a vending stand in the middle of a street, later building on a sleeping room for his family, then adding a wing or second floor, until the building choked the thoroughfare entirely. Single actions, multiplied by the hundreds, gradually sealed off one after another straight path, causing traffic to be deflected around the new building or creating yet another of the numerous dead-end alleys which abound in the "old" city.

That inadvertently the city transformed itself is not noteworthy. What does appear remarkable to the modern reader is that there does not seem to have been much concerted or sustained effort on the part of the political authorities to prevent or punish these actions. Rather, when deemed necessary, ameliorative steps were taken in somewhat arbitrary fashion. The Sultan, who found that the chandelier for his new mosque was too wide to be delivered there by any existing route and who therefore ordered the demolition of intervening obstructions, was operating in the best tradition of local municipal administration. The power of the burghers, which in Europe gave rise to a municipal government preoccupied with protecting property rights, seems to have been an irrelevant force in the military feudalism of Egypt, where even the wealthiest merchant adopted poor dress to escape the confiscation which might well follow, should his prosperity attract the attention of the Mamluks.

The failure to preserve an orderly street system was not necessarily, then, the result of incapacity or inefficiency. It was due rather to a failure to value such orderliness, reinforced by the complacency that, should access ever be needed, it could be achieved immediately, merely by using randomly conscripted labor. History, however, has proven this complacency unfounded. On the contrary, with the passing of despotic regimes it has become more and more difficult to alter the street pattern which is modern Cairo's most crippling heritage from the medieval epoch. As any city planner is aware, a basic reorgani-

[24] In the following discussion I depend heavily upon the article by Robert Brunschvig, "Urbanisme médiéval et droit Musulman," in *Revue des Études Islamiques*, Volume 15 (1947), pp. 127-155, which unfortunately draws largely upon North African rather than specifically Egyptian examples. However, I have attempted to allow for this by stressing the broad lines of agreement among the schools of jurisprudence rather than their points of controversy.

[25] Lane, *The Manners and Customs of the Modern Egyptians* (3rd edn.), p. 322.

zation of a circulation system is the most difficult problem faced in replanning, since, of all the elements which make up a city, the streets are least amenable to change.[26] Proof of this is easy to find. In the past 150 years, only three major thoroughfares have ever been cut through the maze of medieval Cairo, and each was achieved by fiat and at tremendous cost—both financial and in terms of the priceless monuments which were razed to make room for the mechanical transport that came with modernism.

To recapitulate, three basic ecological characteristics of preindustrial Cairo have been found, each of which has had a lasting effect on the city. First, the distribution of population within the city was determined by the principle of ethnic and religious segregation. This in turn prevented pure segregation according to income or economic class and, in addition, encouraged the development of a second basic characteristic of the preindustrial city, i.e., land use mixture. This intermixing of residential, industrial, and commercial uses in each cellular unit of the city was not only a concomitant of congruity between ethnic and occupational status but also a natural consequence of the technology which dictated small-scale enterprises and minimal transport distances. The primitive level of technology tended to reduce the function of most streets to mere access, a tendency encouraged both by the climatic functionalism of the narrow street and by the utter lack of interest in preserving the public right of way. Out of these factors grew the third ecological characteristic of preindustrial Cairo, its tortuous and intricate street pattern. Nor was this final characteristic independent of the first. The sharp cleavage between subgroups organized by locality, which led each to barricade itself against potential threats by limiting and controlling entrance to the *darb*, reinforced the existing impulse to fragment and individualize the circulation pattern. The net result was a city form probably quite well adapted to life in the Middle Ages but eminently unsuited to the industrial era.

These three physical characteristics were not only linked one to the other but were, in turn, products of the socio-political order which modern Cairo inherited along with the more tangible aspects of city form. While this political order has been hinted at throughout, a somewhat fuller explanation now seems necessary.

It is in political form that the medieval Islamic city diverged most radically from the European model, thus necessitating a somewhat more detailed discussion than would otherwise be required. Rather than attempt the ambitious project of summarizing municipal administration[27] as it evolved through centuries of changing leadership and alterations in the precarious power balance between sacred and secular hierarchies, this discussion will be confined merely to certain salient elements which have had permanent effects on the growth and development of Cairo.

One of the most significant elements of the political system was the existence of the Mamluk elite. The vast and originally unbridgeable ethnic, economic, and social cleavage between this alien ruling class on the one hand and the masses and bourgeoisie on the other hand negated the possibility of a municipal "corporation" which placed the well-being of the community above the vested interests of an unrelated ruling class.[28] Since the middle of the thirteenth century, Cairo had been ruled by a praetorian guard which had assumed independent power. This group, largely proscribed from maintaining itself through reproduction, had to be continually replenished by foreign youths, converted to Islam and raised in the traditions and loyalties of military feudalism. Even before the Ottoman conquest their dominant language was Turkish, and many spoke or read Arabic with great difficulty if at all. It was hardly to be expected that such a group would develop deep loyalties to its adopted home or feel compassion for its "lowly" inhabitants.

Furthermore, the mediating force of religious congruence seems to have been less effective in the Mamluk state than elsewhere in the Islamic domains. In early Islam the sacred and secular hierarchies had been subsumed together under the Caliphate. While this unity had already begun to fragment before the Mamluks came to power, under them the religious hierarchy became more and more subservient to the Sultan, with the Caliph being retained merely as an ineffectual figurehead. The Mamluk Bays and their dependents, then, occupied the elite position relatively unfettered by the religious hierarchy. They were separated by a wide gulf from the Arabs and Egyptians whom they at best governed but more often merely exploited. During the medieval period and even before, Cairenes had become accustomed to a wealthy, capricious, unsympathetic governing elite whose relationship to the indigenous popu-

[26] Even in cities virtually destroyed by bombs, fires, earthquakes or floods, it has proven almost impossible to change the basic street system when rebuilding. Property lines, underground utility installations, and sheer inertia operate to frustrate such attempts.

[27] I apologize without guilt to the Orientalist scholars who will find their special areas of concern ignored or grossly oversimplified in this account. Out of a highly complex field in which the specialists themselves are in doubt and disagreement, a very few items have been selected for treatment here, from the single-minded criterion of their relevance to Cairo's present difficulties.

[28] Von Grunebaum, "The Structure of the Muslim Town," in *Islam: Essays in the Nature and Growth of a Cultural Tradition* (1955), p. 142, has pointed out that the Muslim town never was a *polis*, even under non-Mamluk rule.

lation was minimal—and, insofar as they were concerned, the more minimal, the better.[29]

During the Ottoman period the great distance between rulers and ruled narrowed somewhat, due to the enhanced status accorded sons of Mamluk-Egyptian marriages, who had formerly been excluded from any rights of succession. Before, these so-called *awlād al-nās* (children of good descent) could at best hope to join the ranks of the inferior foot soldiers; under the Ottomans, however, they were accepted more fully into the chain of descent, were no longer given discriminatory names (formerly, Mamluks had Turkish names, their children Arabic names; later all were to share in Arabic names), were eligible to join the privileged Janissary corps and even to inherit their fathers' positions in Mamluk society.[30] The strengthened kinship link, by sustaining ties throughout several generations and involving Mamluks in a more widely ramified set of blood connections with the indigenous population, must have helped to bridge the wide and formerly absolute break between the alien elite and the remainder of society, although it could not eliminate it.

In Europe, however, it was the development of an urban bourgeoisie that played so important a role in the growth of municipal government. Such a bourgeoisie did indeed make its appearance in Cairo during the early centuries of Islam, but its ascendancy (which coincided interestingly enough with the advent of the Mamluks) never led it to become an independent class or to obtain political power.[31] It is difficult to explain why this should have been the case, but I might suggest the following partial explanation. While in Europe cities were founded and grew chiefly as escape havens from the rural-situated feudal aristocracy, in Egypt the Mamluks concentrated in preexisting Cairo, rarely leaving the city except for campaigns. Although the agricultural estates of Egypt were nominally in their ownership, in practice they were farmed out to administrators, while their products were exploited commercially by the urban amirs. Thus, rather than serving as a refuge from the feudal lords, the city was their chief province or domain; rather than a rival to feudal power, the city was the kingpin in the system.[32]

Two elements may be distilled from these brief remarks. First, the indigenous population of Cairo never had the opportunity to develop municipal self-consciousness or a system of self-government because a foreign elite ruled without distinction both the city and the country. Home rule and self-government, considered to be two essential elements in modern municipal administration, were both aborted before they began. The shift during the nineteenth and early twentieth centuries to a different type of elite, composed chiefly of Europeans, tended to perpetuate rather than remedy these lacks. Second, the bourgeoisie and masses, proscribed from assuming either loyalty to or responsibility for the city as a whole, remained withdrawn in their own more primary units of identification—the religious community (subdivided in the case of Muslims into brotherhoods that at their height evidently embraced almost all urban males), the extended family, the town-of-origin group, the ethnic class, the occupational group, the neighborhood unit. There they remained, and in large measure *still* remain, cooperating with one another on the achievement of some small measure of security in a basically unpredictable and hostile system, and reacting to the "public good" with suspicion and subterfuge, since it so often implied a confiscation of their money (in taxation, tribute, and special levies), their time and labor (in the corvée), or their prerogatives (dress, customs, religious observances, and the like).

These were hardly ideal conditions under which the "delicate blossom" of good city government could even sprout, much less flower. The wonder is not that a municipal administration dedicated to the protection of

[29] While in most preindustrial cities there was a similar wide gap between the elite and the masses, the situation in Mamluk Cairo differed in two important respects from the more typical case. First, the elite was not merely different in degree but in kind: ethnically, linguistically, racially, and culturally. Furthermore, for hundreds of years it remained a caste rather than a class, because entry was closed to indigenous peoples. Second, whereas in most preindustrial cities the religious and secular hierarchies were intimately combined, this was only superficially true in the Mamluk state where religious offices were either subordinated to the military or exploited as "patronage" and a means of secular control.

[30] See the excellent analysis by David Ayalon, "Studies in al-Jabarti I: Notes on the Transformation of Mamluk Society in Egypt under the Ottomans," *Journal of the Economic and Social History of the Orient*, III (August 1960), 148-174, and continued in III (October 1960), 275-325.

[31] S. D. Goitein, "The Rise of the Near Eastern Bourgeoisie in Early Islamic Times," *Cahiers d'Histoire Mondiale*, III (1957), 583-603.

[32] Two factors intensified this situation. First, important fiefs often consisted of several widely separated rural territories, which obviated the possibility of a Mamluk amir playing "seignior" to a community of peasants, even if he did manage to retain the same fief over a lengthy period of time, which was uncommon also. See the discussion on fiefs by William Popper, *Egypt and Syria under the Circassian Sultans*, Volume 16 of the University of California Publications in Semitic Philology (University of California Press, Berkeley: 1957), pp. 109ff. And secondly, fiefs yielded not currency but produce, which the amirs marketed chiefly in Cairo, maintaining large granaries and frequently manipulating prices. This involved them in mercantile operations of an urban type which in Europe were seldom considered appropriate functions for a feudal lord. The medieval Arabic chronicles have been carefully combed by Ira Lapidus, who has presented convincing descriptions of Mamluk involvement in urban trade in *Muslim Cities in the Later Middle Ages*, Chapter II.

public rather than private interests failed to materialize, but that so fragmented a set of private ones ever managed the minimal coordination necessary for the bare survival of the city. Part of the answer lies in the fact that very few of what we would now consider "public facilities," except for the great mosques and associated schools, were actually provided on a city-wide basis in the medieval Islamic city.[33] Instead, each quarter of the city tended to provide for and look after its own. Another part of the answer lies in the peculiar system upon which the Turkish administration depended more and more in its later years, i.e., the system of "farming." Tax farming in rural areas had been practiced for many centuries as a means whereby feudal "owners" could administer their holdings *in absentia.* During Mamluk rule and even more during the Ottoman era, in Cairo this system was extended to more and more municipal services. Thus, the "farming" of the customs offices in Cairo and Būlāq offered a lucrative opportunity to the highest bidder. What might elsewhere have been considered "public services" or governmental functions were, in this late period of Cairo's development, treated as "private enterprise"; the "entrepreneur" paid a fixed sum to the imperial treasury for his right to perform the service and received in return all the net profit the traffic would bear.[34] Still another part of the answer lay in the paradoxical fact that coordination was possible only because of the "lack of a complex, all-embracing political organization."[35] Little coordination was required because the elite lived in an entirely different world from the bourgeoisie and the masses, each group being independently organized for continuity and having fairly superficial and formal relations with the other. This minimal contact was channeled through a few significant institutions which had been evolved to link the central elite with the masses, not as individuals but as members of apolitically organized groups.

Just as the physical city was an accretion of cells only loosely linked by walls and a common dependence upon a minimum number of central facilities, so the political community of the Islamic city was an accretion of groups —organized on religious, occupational, and proximity lines—through whose representatives the directives of the state were channeled downward and the responses channeled upward. The two major "building blocks" of this system were the *ḥārah*, which grouped persons on the basis of place of residence, and the *ṣinf* (trade), which grouped persons on the basis of occupation.[36] Although the reader is, by now, familiar with both these institutions, it must still be demonstrated how these groupings were utilized in municipal administration.

By the time the French arrived, Cairo was divided for administrative purposes into 53 *ḥārāt.* Each of these was represented by a *shaykh al-ḥārah,* who was primarily responsible for the police functions in his district and who acted as an intermediary between the quarter's residents and the chief of police.[37] During Mamluk times, the chief of police was actually the military governor of the city, responsible directly to the Sultan for the maintenance of order. Under the Turks, the chief of police was a subordinate responsible to the governor or *wāli.* The latter, in turn, was theoretically superior but in actual fact accountable not only to the 24 Bays who

[33] Le Tourneau has noted the conspicuous absence of public municipal buildings (such as forums, agoras, etc.) in the medieval Islamic cities of North Africa, explaining their absence by the cellular nature of those cities in which public facilities were provided separately within each quarter. See his *Les villes musulmanes de l'Afrique du Nord* (La Maison des Livres, Algiers: 1957), pp. 20-21. Sauvaget reached the same conclusion about Damascus, noting that each cellular quarter had its own peculiar life, each *ḥārah* being almost a miniature town with its own religious and civic facilities.

[34] See Stanford Shaw, *The Financial and Administrative Organization and Development of Ottoman Egypt, 1517-1798* (Princeton University Press, Princeton: 1962), pp. 155ff.

[35] This is the argument advanced by Gibb and Bowen, *Islamic Society and the West,* Volume I, Part I (Oxford University Press, London: 1950), p. 209. Toynbee has accepted and incorporated this view into his own theory, noting that in Egypt the Ottoman conquest simply added a new alien ruling class but did not essentially alter society, since "underneath this exotic military crust, the indigenous Arabic Society . . . still continued to lead its separate and self-sufficient life, in which the peasantry and the 'ulamā' and the urban guilds of merchants and artisans each played their interdependent parts. . . ." See *A Study of History* (Oxford University Press, London: 1956), IV, 113.

[36] Actually, the underlying and prime "building block" was the religious community, governed by its own canonical law and granted far greater internal autonomy than a modern state could tolerate. Even within the three major religious communities, however, smaller units of organization were the effective means of cohesion and control. Among Muslims, the religious brotherhoods seem to have served the function of social cohesiveness, but since there is no evidence that these were exploited by the governing class in the way that professional corporations were, I shall omit them from the discussion.

[37] The functions ascribed to this official and the means by which he was selected seem to have varied over the centuries, reflecting his shifting identification with the central power and with his "constituents." At the end of the Turkish era, he not only played a political role but a crucial economic one as well, that of real estate agent in his district, a role he exercised by virtue of his intimate knowledge of his quarter. Later, in the nineteenth century when the registration of births and deaths became mandatory, the *shaykh al-ḥārah* was made responsible for the collection of vital statistics in his quarter. This office continued to exist beyond the medieval period, although police subchiefs gradually assumed more and more of the duties formerly exercised by the *shaykh al-ḥārah,* until the role was reduced to that of a clerk without honor. In recognition of the low state to which the office had fallen and in protest against quite unsavory practices in extorting bribes in return for local exemptions or privileges to which the incumbents had turned for financial support, the Nasser regime finally did away with the office in 1962.

actually governed the province of Egypt (in return for a substantial tribute to Constantinople), but also to their "leader among equals," the *shaykh al-balad*, who was the prime power in both the nation and its capital city.[38] From this involved structure we learn the futility of trying to separate municipal from national administration for purposes of analysis. The two were, in fact, inseparable.

The occupational organizations constituted the second administrative system within the city. While it would be beyond the scope of this study—and indeed beyond the state of our present knowledge—to detail this critical institution in all its changing complexity, some salient features that survived through the Ottoman period might be noted. First, Islamic trade organizations, unlike the guilds that developed in medieval Europe, were apparently not confined to the artisan class but embraced virtually the entire working population of the cities, whether engaged in commerce, crafts, or services—legitimate or even illegitimate. Only members of the ruling elite and the *'ulamā'* (intelligentsia) appear to have remained outside the syndical structure. Second, at least during certain phases of its existence, the institution was endowed with religious significance and had ties with the various mystical-religious brotherhoods, although a simple correspondence between the two types of "cells" seems to have been the exception rather than the rule in Egypt. Because of this, sacred rituals perhaps played a more significant role in creating and reinforcing the natural occupational and consanguineous social cohesion of Islamic occupational organizations than was typical in their European counterparts. And finally, the fact that the occupational corporations were made responsible to external authorities for fiscal and regulatory functions helped to sustain the forms and activities of the corporations, perhaps even after internally generated cohesion and conviction had waned.

Despite the fact that the institutional forms of corporations had altered markedly over the centuries, there were still close to 300 professional organizations in the city of Cairo and its two port suburbs when the Turkish traveler, Evliya Çelebi, enumerated them in the 1670's. This was not much more than the total listed by the French savants almost a century and a half later, indicating a persistence of the form if not the content of the institution. At the time of the French occupation, the corporations were still active enough to occupy 12 great bazaars or *khāns* and about 80 markets or *aswāq*, and to control from 1200 to 1300 individual premises within the city.[39]

[38] The governor of the city had different titles in different places and at different times, but one recognizes a certain congruence of roles. In North African cities he was called the *qā'id* or *'āmil*, and, in Fez at least, he was merely the executive of the Sultan. See Le Tourneau, *Les villes musulmanes*, p. 34. The term used during Mamluk times to designate this officer was usually *qā'id*, but by the Turkish era *wāli* was the term most frequently used. By that time, the *wāli* was assisted by the *kikhyet al-moyoualli* (as he is called by V. de Chabrol, "Essai sur les moeurs," p. 515), or, more commonly, the *khikhya* (the term still used at the time of Edward Lane), who was, in fact, the chief of police.

A most valuable source is W. G. Browne, *Travels in Africa, Egypt*; see especially p. 52, where he attempts to describe the governmental structure of Egypt. While his details may be somewhat confused, they do capture the conditions during the final years of Mamluk control, just prior to the reorganization that followed French occupation.

Again, Mrs. Eliza Fay's description, uninhibited by scholarly pretensions, adds color and insight. She notes: "Egypt, then, is governed by twenty-four Beys, of whom one presides over the rest, but this superiority is very precarious; for he holds it no longer than 'till some other of the number thinks himself strong enough to contend with him; and as they have here but two maxims in War, the one to fly, the other to pursue, those contests last not long: the vanquished, should he escape assassination retires up the country, 'till Fortune changes her aspect; while the victor takes his place. Thus do their lives pass in perpetual vicissitudes. Today a Prince, to-morrow a Fugitive, and next day a Prince again. *These things are so common, that nobody notices them; since they never disturb the inhabitants or compel them to take part in their disputes.*" Italics added. Quoted from Mrs. Eliza Fay, *Original Letters from India*, ed. E. M. Forster (Harcourt, Brace and Co., New York: 1925), pp. 94-95.

[39] Concerning the abysmal lack of knowledge on the early corporations, Gabriel Baer has complained that "long periods of their history are still completely obscure, and only a few detailed studies have been published on guilds in single countries—mainly about the later periods of their development." See Gabriel Baer, *Egyptian Guilds in Modern Times* (The Israel Oriental Society, Jerusalem: 1964), my quotation from the opening page. Ignorance is compounded by controversy. Although Baer claims that the *futuwwah* (chivalrous brotherhoods) and the professional organizations (*aṣnāf*) were somewhat separate institutions, the most authoritative annotated bibliography on Islamic materials, updated to 1965, still gives only a few references to outdated studies on the guilds and combines these with several more current ones on the *futuwwah*. This same bibliography despairs, noting that "economic and social history is a particularly neglected branch of Islamic studies." See Jean Sauvaget's *Introduction to the History of the Muslim East; A Bibliographical Guide*, based on the second edition as recast by Claude Cahen (University of California Press, Berkeley and Los Angeles: 1965). Furthermore, although there is clear evidence that some form of guilds existed in Egypt during the Ottoman period and even beyond, Ira Lapidus (*Muslim Cities in the Later Middle Ages*) has questioned the existence of guilds in Mamluk times, although he has based his position primarily on negative evidence, i.e., that references to the guilds have not been found. Given the confused state of our knowledge, then, these remarks must remain tentative. Later research may require a basic revision of this section.

Certainly, Baer has few sources upon which to base any discussion of pre-nineteenth-century guilds in Cairo. The two upon which he depends almost exclusively are a manuscript (Gotha) dating from the late sixteenth or early seventeenth century, exhorting the guilds to *return to* their former traditions and high moral solidarity, and the tenth volume of Evliya Çelebi's travel account dealing with Egypt. While the quality of this

Each profession or trade in the city had its own corporation—or several, if physically separated—at the head of which was a *shaykh*, generally assisted by a *naqīb* or ceremonial organizer. As the corporations came increasingly under external regulations, the roles of the *shaykh* and his deputy seem also to have undergone redefinition. Originally the *shaykh* was selected from among the elder members. He was a respected leader who, by virtue of the veneration accorded him, was able to wield considerable power in supervising the ethical dealings of the profession, in adjudicating between members in cases of internecine disputes, and in gaining cooperation for mutual welfare needs. In addition, as titular head, he presided over periodic meetings, initiations, and other ceremonies, represented the trade in city-wide processions and, most important, acted as its intermediary in dealing with the central administration. Gradually, however, as the ruling elite succeeded in exploiting the structure for its own purposes—chiefly to collect the professional capitation tax, to sequester labor for "public" ventures, and to disseminate rulings and regulations—the role of the *shaykh* changed to a more ambiguous one, not dissimilar to that of the foreman in a factory who must please two masters. The tensions inherent in his position as both representative and defender of the profession vis-à-vis the central administration and, on the other hand, as an enforcement agent of the government, must have done much to undermine his effectiveness and eventually his prestige. In certain occupations, it must be pointed out, the *shaykh* had always been an agent of government regulation, namely in the quasi-legitimate occupations supervised by the police. This seems to have extended to more and more occupations, until by the nineteenth century only exceptional occupations retained the older form of solidarity.[40]

When the system operated in an ideal manner, the *shaykhs* of the individual professions were connected to the central administration through a government-appointed religious officer, the *muḥtasib*, an official whose role can be traced back in Fusṭāṭ to as early as 'Abbāsid times and who had his secular counterpart even earlier in the cities of Greece, Rome, and Byzantium. Originally, the task of the *muḥtasib*, as deputy of the chief *qāḍi* (religious judge), had been nothing less than to oversee the moral life of the community in *all* its aspects. One can see clearly how this made his position one of highest religious esteem and one which required recruitment from among the most religious and learned elders of the Islamic community. We have already noted the high rank accorded to the *muḥtasib* in Fāṭimid Cairo. Apparently this revered status was retained during the Ayyūbid epoch and, even under the Mamluks, the office of the *ḥisbah* still occupied the fifth highest rank of religious functions and was, at least initially, staffed by persons with impeccable credentials. By this time the national office was subdivided regionally, with the *muḥtasib* of Miṣr responsible not only for that city but in charge of appointing and supervising subordinates in the towns and provinces of Upper Egypt. The *muḥtasib* of al-Qāhirah was similarly responsible for the administration

evidence leaves much to be desired, it does not permit one to question whether or not corporate occupational organizations existed. They existed; the only quarrel is their exact nature and function and a terminological one, i.e., whether or not one chooses to use the word "guild" to describe them or whether one prefers to use another term with fewer connotations derivative from the European form of the institution.

By the turn of the nineteenth century—the point in time we are primarily concerned with—the sources become fuller. The articles by Girard and de Chabrol in *Description de l'Égypte* are the starting point for all inquiry. The French Expedition material is organized by André Raymond, "Une liste des corporations de métiers au Caire en 1801," *Arabica*, Volume IV, Fasc. 2. That some trades still had formal initiation ceremonies for apprentices as late as the nineteenth century is attested by Lane's description in *The Manners and Customs of the Modern Egyptians* (3rd edn.), pp. 515-516. According to one observer writing on the subject in 1910, the professional corporations persisted in Egypt—perhaps hollowed out in function but still visible in form—until about 1880. See Germain Martin, *Les bazars du Caire*, p. 27.

Despite the improved sources, however, conclusions remain far from self-evident and controversy persists in interpretation. Three basic works are in general disagreement: Moustafa Fahmy, *La révolution de l'industrie en Égypte et ses conséquences sociales au 19e siècle (1800-1850)* (E. J. Brill, Leiden: 1954); Nada Tomiche, "La situation des artisans et petits commerçants en Égypte de la fin du XVIIIe siècle jusqu'au milieu du XIXe siècle," *Studia Islamica*, XII (1960), 79-98; and G. Baer, *Egyptian Guilds*, cited above. My summary draws primarily on Baer, for his arguments appear the most convincing. The sample French Occupation figures given in the text appear in Massignon, "Guilds, Islamic," *Encyclopedia of the Social Sciences* (1932), VII, 215.

[40] For comparative material, see Le Tourneau, *Les villes musulmanes*, pp. 47-53, for a description of how this system was applied in North African cities. Cairo under the Mamluks, however, paralleled Damascus more than the cities of North Africa. A description of the latter can be found in Ziadeh, *Urban Life in Syria*, pp. 124ff. By Ottoman times the office of *shaykh* of the trade had undergone a demeaning of status, for he was often used merely to collect the tax assessed against the profession as a whole. With the era of the house of Muḥammad 'Ali, corporate organization itself began to disappear rapidly, and by the end of the nineteenth century only a few professions (notably the barbers, a quasi-medical occupation) retained vestiges of their former organization. See G. Baer, *Egyptian Guilds, passim.* To a large extent one sees a parallel between the decline of the *shaykh* of the guilds and the *shaykh al-hārah.* Each played an essential role in the cellular social system we have been describing. But, as this fragmented cellular organization of the premodern period gradually gave way to a widening network of direct municipal administration, their functional value declined. They had formerly been indispensable middlemen; their role became less and less crucial as the city changed from an organization of communal cells to an organization of individual citizens.

of *hisbah* in the towns and provinces of the Delta, while a third *muhtasib* was responsible for the autonomous municipality of Alexandria.[41]

Quite early, however, the enormous scope of the *muhtasib*'s potential functions came to be somewhat more narrowly defined. Rather than total morality, his chief concern became that morality which was exercised in the economic sphere of life, i.e., the market place. (That this was not strictly correct is seen by the fact that the *muhtasib* in Cairo was the overseer of the public baths, of the prostitutes and the entertainers, as well as of the more "normal" trades and industries.) It was he who set the "just price," enforced accurate weights and measures, checked the scales of the "house of money," punished the adulteration of products and otherwise controlled their quality, adjudicated in economic disputes between one trade and another, oversaw the cleanliness of the market places and even, at one time, the upkeep of the mosques, the walls, the water system, and other public facilities. In Cairo he apparently also supervised roads and construction and could even order the demolition of dangerous structures. Furthermore, he was sometimes charged with collecting the professional taxes and with encouraging the attendance at the Friday prayers of workers in the *aswāq*.[42]

In fulfilling these responsibilities he was assisted by various subordinates and, in addition, by individuals selected from each of the corporations themselves whose task it was to report to the *muhtasib* on the state of affairs in the profession and on any problems being encountered. Enforcement of the *muhtasib*'s judgments was sometimes obtained through his own quasi-police agents but also, especially in later Mamluk times, through the *shurtah* (municipal police) under the authority of the Governor of Cairo. During the Mamluk era, there was a marked tendency for the offices of the *muhtasib* and the military governor of the city to be tightly linked—if not in the hands of the same person then at least administratively. But by this time the office had become quite venal and was often a "tax farm" of or a forced assignment to a person lacking the prerequisite religious qualities.[43]

In Cairo this gradual subordination of the *muhtasib*—originally a revered "man of the pen"—to the Mamluk "men of the sword" resulted in a steady decline in the *muhtasib*'s authority and the scope of his powers, in addition to a reduction in his prestige and importance. The growing size of the city, the increasing complexity of its economic operations, and the perhaps inevitable "specialization" which resulted from that growth in scale and complexity, all operated to undermine the general jurisdiction of the *muhtasib* and to force him to share his prerogatives with other "economic administrators." Additional inspection officers were added one by one, quite without logic or plan.

This process seems to have been speeded up under Ottoman rule, as the offices of the *muhtasib* as well as the other inspectors were "farmed out" to Janissaries who, in return for a fixed fee to the treasury, collected what revenues they could through licensing, fines, and bribes. By the eighteenth century the *muhtasib* of Cairo, although still conspicuous by his dress and entourage and still a major ceremonial participant, had been divested of most of his powers and jurisdiction. He was responsible only for supervising the merchants of edible goods. Other officials, such as the *shaykh* of the baths (who supervised 24 trades, including the tentmakers and the street minstrels), the *shaykh* of public spectacles (who supervised a variety of corporations, including those of the tin and ironmongers, the makers of sugar and sweets, tobacconists, camel sellers and saddlers, etc.) had equal if not superior status to the *muhtasib*.[44]

[41] J. Schacht, *An Introduction to Islamic Law*, pp. 25, 52; Tyan, *Histoire de l'organisation judiciare en pays d'Islam*, pp. 622-630, especially.

[42] Much has been written on the *muhtasib*, but often a specific role found at one period of history or in one particular place has been taken as typical, which has greatly compounded the confusion which surrounds this topic. Note the variety of roles that have been ascribed to him. In the thirteenth and fourteenth centuries in Syria, for example, the *muhtasib*, in addition to his other duties, even inspected lonely lanes for secret lovers, controlled boats and harbors, and supervised the schools—tasks which he does not seem to have been assigned in Cairo. See Ziadeh, *Urban Life in Syria*, p. 122. Von Grunebaum includes, among the functions of the *muhtasib*, the cleaning of streets, the protection of the public way against building encroachments, overseeing the water supply, maintaining the condition of the walls and even, on occasion, regulating the mutual responsibilities of tenants and landlords—many of which were responsibilities of the *qāḍi* himself in Cairo. See his *Islam: Essays in the Growth of the Cultural Tradition*. While these functions may have been performed by the *muhtasib* in early Islamic times and in the very small towns and cities, there is no evidence that the *muhtasib* of Mamluk Cairo had an office so broadly defined.

[43] See Tyan, *Histoire de l'organisation . . . en pays d'Islam*, pp. 635-645; Lapidus, *Muslim Cities in the Later Middle Ages*, *passim*; and especially the multitude of separate references to the *muhtasib*, the conditions of his appointment and the deteriorating quality of the incumbents, found in the chronicles of Abū al-Maḥāsin ibn Taghri Birdi, as translated by Popper, *History of Egypt, 1382-1469 A.D., passim.*

[44] Certainly, by late Turkish times Cairo's *muhtasib* was responsible only for the comestibles market, and his was one of the least powerful and lucrative of the urban offices. In Browne's description of the late eighteenth-century municipal administration of Cairo (*Travels in Africa, Egypt*) the *muhtasib* is totally ignored. Stanford Shaw, *The Financial and Administrative Organization and Development of Ottoman Egypt*, pp. 182-183, concludes on the basis of Turkish archival material that the *muhtasib* in eighteenth-century Cairo was relatively insignificant in power and prestige. V. de Chabrol, "Essai sur les moeurs," p. 515, stresses that by the time of the French Expedition his role was confined

This fragmentation of the *muḥtasib*'s coordinative role and the gradual divestment of his authority over municipal facilities seem to have left a serious vacuum in the system which was never completely filled, if the widespread deterioration of these facilities can be taken as an indirect proof of ineffectiveness. Any "farming out" of municipal and government services leads to a deterioration of facilities, due to the tendency of "farmers" to avoid reinvestment of capital in plant and maintenance, unless specifically required by law. This impetus to deterioration operated unchecked under Ottoman administration. Nevertheless, the system remained nominally in existence up to the middle of the nineteenth century. It was not until after the reign of Muḥammad 'Ali that the position of *muḥtasib* in Cairo was abolished and his responsibilities assigned directly to the municipal police.

Two other city-wide offices might have filled the vacuum created by the *muḥtasib*'s failure, one in the "secular" hierarchy, the other in the religious, but, as we shall see, these were also victims of the general disregard of overall welfare goals. The governor of the city of Cairo was the first, the chief *qāḍi* the second. To the Western scholar bound by his ethnocentric tendency to "read into" the past and into another culture the assumptions of his own world view, the official obviously in the best position to guard the interests of the city as a whole was the Governor of Cairo. The temptation is to project upon this officer the role and functions of a municipal mayor—but no inference could be farther from reality. Despite his elegant title and his apparent city-wide responsibilities, in practice this official was a military figure whose chief responsibility was that of military governors everywhere, namely to ensure discipline over the populace. He represented the coercive power of the rulers vis-à-vis the residents, rather than the executive arm of an organized community.

There was, then, only one city-wide office which continued to exercise significant power over municipal affairs throughout Cairo's history, and this was the office of the chief *qāḍi*, later called the *mulla* in Ottoman-administered Cairo. The judicial system supervised by the chief *qāḍi* (and since the time of al-Nāṣir ibn Qalāwūn shared jointly but not equally by the heads of the four schools of Islamic jurisprudence) and administered by his district subordinates[45] tended to overlap the realms of both the police power (exercised under the military governor) and the *ḥisbah* (exercised by the *muḥtasib*s and their surrogates), since it was the mediator and interpreter of law, both Koranic and *qānūn* (canon). During the height of Mamluk power when the office of the governor of the city was more and more subordinated to the palace and when the role of the *muḥtasib* was losing its authority through fragmentation and venality, the *qāḍi* seems to have become by default the *only* official still charged with guarding the general public welfare. His role was enhanced by the fact that he was an important figure in the administration of *waqf* (pl. *awqāf*, mortmain) properties, i.e., literally all the public facilities of the city and much of its real estate.

Ideally, then, the *qāḍi* should have been a key figure in municipal administration.[46] Had the judiciary system been above corruption, which it notoriously was not, this municipal institution might have been able to guard the community in a way that the more specialized agencies could not. In Cairo, at least, this proved not to be the case. In actual fact, the very power vested in the judiciary made it a highly attractive office to those with financial ambitions. Since the income of the *qāḍi* amounted to one-tenth of the value adjudicated, supplemented of course by any sums proffered to tip the scales of justice, many individuals were willing to offer heavy bribes to gain an appointment. When the religious

solely to supervising prices, weights, and measures in the food markets of Cairo. For a somewhat different evaluation of the *muḥtasib* of Cairo, see Clerget, *Le Caire*, II, 131-138.

[45] The place of the *qāḍi* in the administration of Islamic law has been dealt with extensively in the literature. The basic sources are the works of Tyan, *Histoire de l'organisation . . . en pays d'Islam*, throughout, and Schacht, *An Introduction to Islamic Law*. See also the remarks of Claude Cahen in his *Mouvements populaires*, especially pp. 7-9. Concerning the specific administrative hierarchy by the end of the Turkish era, which is our chief concern in this chapter on the "heritage," Browne, *Travels in Africa, Egypt*, p. 53, tells us that in 1792 each of the more than 200 subdistricts of Cairo had its own *qāḍi*. This system seems to have been simplified by the French soon afterwards, since de Chabrol, "Essai sur les moeurs," p. 473, noted that the chief *qāḍi* had under his jurisdiction not only Cairo but the twin suburbs of Būlāq and Miṣr al-Qadīmah. The two latter communities each had their own special judges, as did the major subdistricts of Cairo, all in turn responsible to the chief *qāḍi*.

[46] Since this section was originally written, Roger Le Tourneau published a book on Fez lucidly describing the municipal administration of that North African city during the fourteenth to sixteenth centuries. In his analysis he makes a number of points which parallel arguments developed here, particularly connecting the institution of the *awqāf* with municipal services and budgeting. According to his account, in fourteenth-century Fez the chief *qāḍi* of that city had so much centralized authority over the *awqāf* that he could serve as a kind of bureau of the budget for the city. See his *Fez in the Age of the Marinides*, trans. Bessie A. Clement (University of Oklahoma Press, Norman: 1961), particularly Chapter II, pp. 35-36. This does not seem to have been equally true in medieval Cairo. For one thing, Cairo had greater conflict between the military caste and the *'ulamā'*, which prevented the jurisdiction of the latter from interfering with the wishes of the former. Second, the control of *awqāf* properties in Cairo was much more diffuse and decentralized, which would have prevented the *qāḍi*, even with more power than he in fact possessed, from planning or budgeting municipal services.

hierarchy was strong, this potential threat could be repulsed, but sooner or later the institution succumbed to baser influences. The eventual sale of the position to the highest bidder could not escape notice, and thus the prestige of this religious office, which touched the life of the people perhaps more intimately than any other, was greatly reduced in their eyes by its crass exploitation.

Matters seem to have deteriorated during the centuries of Ottoman supremacy. By the end of the sixteenth century the chief *qāḍi* of Cairo had been stripped of his last residual power over the *awqāf*, this lucrative administration being assigned to the Chief Eunuch of the Porte. Wherever parts of this control were wrested back they went to the powerful Mamluks rather than reverting to the *qāḍi*. As the Mamluks regained their former privileges, the *qāḍi* became more and more of a figurehead, a powerless representative of the Porte. Toward the end of the premodern epoch the Turks sent out a new one from Constantinople each year; his sole aim became the rapid accumulation of wealth, while the courts were administered by local civil servants.[47]

Thus we have the second political heritage from the medieval Ottoman city—if not municipal anarchy at least a low level of corporate coordination. There was no single administrative structure which combined police power, market supervision, and the judiciary into a municipal government, and thus these three elements tended to remain fragmented and uncoordinated in Cairo. Even if there had existed a concept of the public good and a unified set of municipal goals, these could hardly have been executed through the diffuse system of municipal administration which sufficed only for the "do-nothing" approach of the medieval city. To build an administrative structure capable of assuming welfare and planning responsibilities remained a task for the distant future.

The Islamic city, however, was not entirely devoid of public facilities. True, Cairo had no public water system—water being provided by numerous vendors who carried Nile water in goat skins throughout the quarters. True, Ottoman Cairo had no municipal street cleaning and waste disposal system. Private enterprise again partially met this need by carting off, for a price, the refuse which was then dumped at the edge of the city, forming the high mounds on which every visitor of the Turkish period remarked. However, mosques and related schools, baths, public drinking fountains, roads, bridges, hospitals, orphanages, almshouses, and many other amenities did exist in the city. While a few of these had been built by the *ḥārāt* and the trades, the majority had been constructed and maintained through the institution of the *awqāf*, i.e., properties of sultans, princes, and other wealthy individuals deeded to and administered by religious foundations, the profits of which were devoted to providing many of the facilities which in a contemporary city are considered to be within the public domain. Whether municipal government failed to grow because its functions were being performed by the *waqf* institution, or whether the *waqf* was stimulated to expand because of the vacuum left by the absence of municipal government will forever remain unknown. But it must be noted that the two were, in a way, mutually exclusive substitutes.

Even before Islam, land in Greek and Byzantine cities was often bequeathed to religious organizations supervised by the church hierarchy, the proceeds of which were marked for charitable purposes. While this procedure does not seem to have been a part of original Islam, it was quickly incorporated into the religion within a century of the Prophet's death as a means of fulfilling one of the basic pillars of Islam, the giving of alms.[48] As originally conceived, *waqf* was the land and buildings owned by mosques and other religious foundations, usually granted by the sovereign. In much the way that European monasteries supported their activities by their land holdings, the mosques and schools were expected to maintain themselves and offer charity from the proceeds of their possessions. In time, these original holdings were augmented by the bequests of private individuals who willed their property to religious organizations with the understanding that any profits over and above those needed to maintain the fruitfulness of the lands and/or buildings would be devoted to specific charitable purposes, generally spelled out in great detail in the *waqf* document.

Quite early in Egypt the supervision of all properties so bequeathed was vested in the chief *qāḍi* who, in turn, appointed administrators (called *mutawalli* and *nāẓir*) who received a small stipend for their services. It was natural, however, that, given the reciprocal relationship between sacred and secular power that seemed to characterize the division of labor in Mamluk Egypt, with the decline in the *qāḍi*'s importance came his divestment of real control over *waqf* administration and the assign-

[47] See S. Shaw, *The Financial and Administrative Organization and Development of Ottoman Egypt,* pp. 63-69. See also Chapter VI below.

[48] On the early history of the institution, see Heffening's article on "Waḳf," in *Encyclopedia of Islam*¹, IV (E. J. Brill, Leiden: 1934), 1096-1103, especially 1098. Claude Cahen has argued convincingly, in his "Réflexions sur le waqf ancien," *Studia Islamica*, XIV (1961), 37-56, that although religious donations were an early part of Islam and although mortmain property deeded for the support of religious edifices preexisted Islam in those parts of the Byzantine empire conquered by the Arabs, the peculiar development of *waqf* in Islam can only be understood with reference to its specific functions of "protecting ownership" and granting flexibility to bequests, which grew out of the Islamic social order.

ment of this authority to agents of the political state, the *siyāsah*.[49] Furthermore, although originally *waqf* was chiefly urban property, after a while agricultural land and even buildings and movable wealth (with the sole exception of money which had no legal usufruct) were added to the institution.

Long before the founding of al-Qāhirah, at the height of Fusṭāṭ's development, a new aspect of *waqf* was added, i.e., family or private *waqf* (*waqf ahli*), which differed in kind rather than degree from the early "public" character of original *waqf*.[50] In a family endowment, the owner of a property could relinquish his title (*raqabah*) to a religious foundation but continue to receive its profits personally during his lifetime. When he died he could bequeath the profits from the property to his descendants, merely making an arrangement for their eventual disbursement to a charitable purpose if and when his line of descent died out. Often the "owner" himself was appointed to administer his property, although after several generations this administration generally passed into the hands of the more professional *mutawalli*.

The family *waqf* scheme was particularly appealing to Muslims for a variety of reasons. First, *waqf* property was held in perpetuity by the religious foundation and theoretically could under no circumstances be confiscated by the temporal powers. (In actual fact, however, there were many periods of Mamluk and Turkish rule during which this principle was violated.) Particularly during periods of insecurity, there was a great incentive to create family endowments which could protect ownership and future rights while in no way interfering with present enjoyment. Second, the rather inflexible laws of Muslim inheritance (whereby each descendant received a fixed proportion of the estate depending solely on his or her status as wife, daughter, son, uncle, etc.) could be avoided if the property in question were made into *waqf*. Therefore, anyone wishing to deviate from the traditional pattern of inheritance could, by signing over his ownership to a religious foundation, apportion the usufructs of that property in any way he wished. Finally, it was an excellent device for preventing the fragmentation of holdings which eventually occurs when property must be divided and subdivided among increasing numbers of descendants.

Family endowments, despite their great usefulness to the individuals concerned, had a negative effect on the city which should not be underestimated. Whereas true *waqf* had a compensating value in that, theoretically, its proceeds had to be used to provide and maintain needed public services, there was no such compensating value for the alienation of ownership from use which occurred in the case of family endowments. Furthermore, outside of confiscation or complete depletion of the worth of the property, there was no provision for returning *waqf* property to free circulation. This tended to insulate the use and development of *waqf* land and buildings from the normal processes of economic incentive which elsewhere have proven essential to encourage reinvestment and renewal of urban property. This alienation, then, was responsible for the well-known and universally observed phenomenon in Islamic cities: that *waqf* property tended to deteriorate faster than non-*waqf* property.

The explanation for this is not difficult to find. Let us consider the most typical kind of *waqf* property, urban commercial establishments.[51] Ownership of land

[49] According to al-Kindi, *waqf* agreements were originally between the beneficiary institutions and the guardians, without interference from outside. Tawbah ibn Nimr, the *qāḍi* of Fusṭāṭ in 736, was the first magistrate in Egypt to place the *awqāf* under "public justice." Tyan, *Histoire de l'organisation . . . en pays d'Islam*, p. 380. During Fāṭimid and Ayyūbid times the administration of *waqf* properties was independent but still under the rubric of "qāḍial" powers. By the Mamluk epoch in Cairo one finds three types of *waqf* administrations: (1) those bequests placed under the supervision of a high functionary of the palace, the *dawādār al-Sultān*; (2) the so-called *ḥukrīyah waqf* properties whose revenues were earmarked for Mecca and Madīnah as well as other charitable purposes, still placed under the authority of the chief Shāfi'i *qāḍi*; and (3) the family or *ahli waqf* bequests which, though administered privately, came under the ultimate control of the judge. *Ibid.*, pp. 383-384, 451. By later Mamluk times the *waqf* institution had been corroded by the general venality of the society, for Abū al-Maḥāsin ibn Taghri Birdi complains bitterly about the abuses of the terms of *waqf* bequests, abuses he attributes as much to the active collusion of the *nāẓirs* whose official task it was to supervise and prevent them as to the unscrupulous character of the administrators. While neglect of the terms of endowment deeds was evident as early as the beginning of the fourteenth century, this merely signaled the beginning of problems which were to become increasingly common in the centuries to follow. See W. Popper's *Egypt and Syria under the Circassian Sultans* (1957), p. 122.

[50] The oldest *waqf* document concerning a family endowment was that in which the Imām Shāfi'i made his house in Fusṭāṭ and its belongings into a *waqf* for his descendants (Heffening, "Waḳf," p. 1100). It would be difficult to find a more convincing precedent for its legitimation in Egypt.

[51] Heffening notes that business properties were most frequently made into *waqf*, followed by tenements and industrial uses. See *ibid.*, p. 1099, for a list of varieties. Gibb and Bowen, *Islamic Society and the West*, Volume I, Part II, p. 174, present figures on the *waqf* created in the province of Aleppo in the eighteenth century, noting that their distribution was typical. Of the 485 new *waqf* properties registered between 1718 and 1800, over 400 were urban buildings and more than half were family endowments. Lapidus, *Muslim Cities in the Later Middle Ages*, pp. 195-198, includes an appendix in which he enumerates some 81 charitable *awqāf* created in Aleppo and Damascus between 676 and 921 H. (Mamluk times), an examination of which reveals that the deeded properties are chiefly urban commercial. Unfortunately, we do not have a comparable listing for Cairo,

and buildings was in the hands of a religious foundation. Management services were performed by an administrator who, if he were one of the beneficiaries of the property, tended to withdraw maximum profits, or, if simply a civil servant (who had probably paid for the right to administer the property), tended to withdraw maximum returns from the property without transmitting all the profits to the beneficiaries. In either case, the administrator was tempted to mulct the property. The original requirement, that maintenance and reinvestment take priority over the distribution of profits, was virtually impossible to enforce. Therefore, "dead hand" ownership could not be depended upon to supply the reinvestment necessary for property upkeep or improvement.

Nor could the tenant be expected to provide what the owner did not. Originally *waqf* property could be rented only for one to three years at a time. Any improvements the tenant added to his leased premises became part of the original *waqf*. Here certainly was no incentive for investment! It was not until the sixteenth century that, in an effort to arouse the interest of tenants in the maintenance and improvement of *waqf* property, it became possible to obtain a lease in perpetuity.[52] Since these leases could be bought and sold, this reform tended in practice to return dead land to the market place where it was once again sensitive to economic incentives for development and change.

We have noted above some of the factors that encouraged the creation of *waqf* and some of the unanticipated failures of this system, but we can have no idea of how pervasive this institution was without recourse to some actual statistics on land and property ownership in Egypt. Maqrīzi tells us that in 1339 some 130,000 feddans (a feddan is approximately an acre) of land were held in public *awqāf*, the proceeds of which were to be used for the upkeep of mosques and other religious institutions. These were directly supervised by the Sultan's personal secretary (the *dawādār al-Sultān*). In addition, there were the town lands in Miṣr and al-Qāhirah, the proceeds from which were devoted to the upkeep of Mecca and Madīnah as well as for charitable purposes within the city itself. These were controlled by the *qāḍi* and supervised by special *dīwān* in each section of the city. Finally, there were the innumerable family endowments. Combined, they accounted for the overwhelming majority of the real estate of Miṣr and al-Qāhirah. Maqrīzi, even then, noted with alarm the corruption and mismanagement which led to a deterioration in all forms of *waqf* property. Even as late as the early twentieth century in Egypt, despite confiscations of unclearly titled agricultural lands by Muḥammad 'Ali, about one-eighth of the cultivable land of Egypt was held as *waqf*, and much of the property in the older portion of Cairo (untouched by Muḥammad 'Ali's reforms) came under the administration of the Ministry of *Waqf*.

What were the implications of this inheritance from the medieval period, whereby a large proportion of all real property in Cairo was either government-owned or held by religious foundations of various kinds? The major unanticipated consequence has already been indicated: the accelerated rate of property depreciation which, despite reforms, persisted in causing blight in the city. Every visitor to Cairo during the late medieval period commented on the large sections of that community which showed signs of former dense occupancy but which were by then relatively deserted, the tumbled-down structures being occupied by occasional squatters. It will be recalled that this was particularly true in the northeastern section just within the walls, although the phenomenon was by no means confined to that section. We are now in a better position to understand this condition and must ascribe a major responsibility for it to the institution of *awqāf*.

Let us take an hypothetical example to trace the operation of the process. A tenement dwelling was made into *waqf*, either public or family. A tenant or group of tenants leased and occupied the building, but neither "owner," administrator, nor tenant felt responsible for the condition of the structure. Finally, the building, typically constructed of unstabilized mudbrick (the universal Egyptian building material), was unable to withstand further abuse and toppled. The tenant was free to move elsewhere. The administrator of the property had of course failed to set aside a sum for depreciation and could not be expected to supply out of his own pocket the money necessary to recreate the value of the property. It was simpler for him to seek a new sinecure. In times of prosperity, when demand for city land was high and the population expanding, this land might revert to private ownership (since its value had dissipated) and be redeveloped. However, in times of depression or a static or declining population base, the property might simply remain deserted until a squatter established his rights by moving into the debris.

Thus a system which could, with later reforms, cope with the problem of urban renewal during prosperous days, was totally incapable of sustaining property conditions during eras of contraction, i.e., during the Turkish era. The institution of *awqāf*, which had begun so auspiciously and which promised so reliable a means for

---

but there seems to be no reason to assume that it departed radically from the experience of other Islamic cities of the times.

[52] See Heffening, "Waḳf," pp. 1097, 1099. See also Chapter x below for a much more detailed discussion of the long-term lease on mortmain property as this developed in more recent centuries.

supporting municipal facilities and services, had deteriorated by the late medieval and Turkish periods into a self-defeating agency which merely accelerated the deterioration of the city.

These, then, were the three chief handicaps of the political order which Cairo, about to enter the modern era, inherited together with her physical ecology and social organization. The discrete and alien elite was to remain with her far into the modern era. While the composition of the elite changed periodically, it remained through the twentieth century a pressing problem which prevented the emergence of a broad-based and responsible form of municipal government. It served to fragment the city and the society and to act as a focus of hostility for growing nationalist sentiments.

Anarchy in municipal administration, another heritage, was attacked earliest and most successfully. And yet, even in this area, despite an increasing indigenization of the process of administration, home rule proved virtually unobtainable. It was not until 1949 that the government of Cairo was truly separated from national administration, and even today, it lacks many of the attributes and powers normally considered part of "home rule."

The diffuse control of lands officially part of the *awqāf* of Cairo, the widespread corruption and inadequate regulation of the activities of *waqf* administrators, and the disastrous effects such a system had on the maintenance of urban property were early recognized as evils needing correction. Reforms, however, came late and gradually. Attempts were made to deal, piecemeal, with specific abuses and inefficiencies, but it was not until the middle of the nineteenth century that a more concerted approach was attempted. And not until the complete abolition of the *waqf ahli* and the concentration of all *waqf k͟hayri* under a central ministry by the revolutionary reforms of 1952 was a true solution found to the problem that had plagued Cairo's development throughout the medieval period.

Each of these developments will be considered in greater detail in the discussion of modern Cairo, a city that came into being after 1798.

PART II · THE MODERN ERA: A TALE OF TWO CITIES

6 Cleansing the Augean Stables

1800-1848

While it is conventional for historians to date Egypt's entry into the modern era from the French Expedition or a few years later at the accession of Muḥammad 'Ali, neither is strictly correct. In reality, the discontinuity between a medieval past and a modern future had already begun before the appearance of French soldiers,[1] and the movement toward "modernization" or "Westernization" was not truly under way until the reigns of Muḥammad 'Ali's successors during the second half of the century.[2]

This was particularly true in the case of Cairo which changed little in tangible attributes during the first half of the nineteenth century. Modern Cairo is only one hundred years old and came into being after the death of Muḥammad 'Ali. The outlines of Cairo and her two port suburbs were roughly the same in 1848 as they had been in 1798.[3] Nor had the population experienced an appreciable net change during those fifty years.[4] But despite this superficial stability, a revolution had already begun, without which later developments in Cairo could not have occurred. Thus, no chronicler of Cairo's history can ignore the germinal effects of both the brief French occupation of the city and the more extended rule of the Albanian soldier of fortune who was elevated in 1805 to the Pashalik of Egypt.

In trying to understand the nature of contemporary Cairo one is faced with an inscrutable paradox. One knows that French troops were present on Egyptian

[1] Gibb and Bowen have astutely recognized that "many of the tendencies and factors . . . in Meḥmed 'Alî's administration of Egypt—the economic exploitation, the military reorganization, the introduction of European technical experts, the attempt to shake off Ottoman suzerainty and to extend Egyptian control over the neighbouring provinces—are already visible in Egypt and Syria during the last decades of the eighteenth century." See *Islamic Society and the West*, Volume 1, Part 1 (Oxford University Press, London: 1950), p. 231.

[2] With respect to Cairo, Muḥammad 'Ali's grandson, the Khedive Ismā'īl (1863-1879), must be credited with transforming the city.

[3] Compare Map XI showing Cairo in 1798 with Map XIII of the city in 1868, below.

[4] This cannot be ascertained exactly because few demographic records were kept during this period. However, if one accepts the French estimate of between 250,000 and 263,000 persons for Cairo alone in 1798, and if one accepts the figures variously presented from Muḥammad 'Ali's census of 1846 of between 253,000 and 257,000 for the city, one must conclude that, whatever the fluctuations in the interim, the net change was minimal. The figure of 253,000 is given by Edward Lane in Appendix F of the third edition of his *Manners and Customs* (J. M. Dent and Co., London: 1908), p. 584, and is identified as having been taken from the census of 1847-1848. Lane believed the figure to be an underestimate. The official report of the Muḥammad 'Ali census, as of December 16, 1846, has been reproduced in the Egyptian Ministry of the Interior, Bureau of Statistics, *Éssai de statistique générale de l'Égypte, années 1873, 1784* (sic), *1875, 1876, 1877* (Imprimerie de l'État-Major Général Égyptien, Cairo: 1879), p. 7, where the population of Cairo is given as 256,679, and that of the entire country as 4,463,244.

Fluctuations in the intervening years appear to have been rather extreme. During the earliest period of Muḥammad 'Ali's reign, the general insecurity undoubtedly depressed the urban population of the country. Félix Mengin, in his *Histoire de l'Égypte sous le gouvernement de Mohammed-Aly* (A. Bertrand, Paris: 1823), estimated the population of Cairo alone (excluding Miṣr al-Qadīmah and Būlāq) in 1823 at about 200,000. It probably remained fairly constant until about 1830, when increased stability and a flight from the farms pushed the population up. In the first edition of Edward Lane, *An Account of the Manners and Customs of the Modern Egyptians, Written in Egypt During the Years 1833, -34, and -35, partly from notes made . . . in the years 1825, -26, -27, and -28* (Charles Knight and Co., London: 1836), 1, 26, the author states that by about 1834 the population had risen to 240,000 for Cairo alone, but that this increase had taken place within only the preceding few years. In 1835, however, Cairo suffered from a severe plague (the last *catastrophic* one) which, according to official estimates, reduced her population by at least a third. This is noted by Lane in a footnote to his manuscript added to p. 26 between 1835 when the manuscript was completed and 1836 when it went to press. Again, massive migration from the rural areas seems to have repaired this loss shortly, although it is unlikely that the population ever reached the optimistic figure suggested by Clot-Bey in 1840. See Clot-Bey, *Aperçu général sur l'Égypte* (Fortin, Massin et Cie., Paris: 1840), 1, 204, where he estimates the number of houses in Cairo at 30,000 and then, using the assumption of an average occupancy of 10 persons per dwelling, reaches a total population for Cairo of 300,000. It is generally acknowledged that Clot-Bey's work heavily gilds the lily, being more a panegyric to his patron, Muḥammad 'Ali, than an objective or cautious evaluation. Given a government preoccupied with inflating the population, it is logical to see this optimism incorporated into Clot-Bey's estimate.

How are we to weigh these various attempts to establish Cairo's population? Logic points to the approximate figures of about 250,000 as an upper limit and 200,000 as a minimum during periods of population decrease. A substantial growth of Cairo's population would have been unlikely during the reign of Muḥammad 'Ali, since, at least during the first half of his rule, the total population of the country did decline, a fact that has not been debated as much as Cairo's population figure. Some population estimates are given in A. E. Crouchley, "A Century of Economic Development, 1837-1937," in *L'Égypte Contemporaine* (February-March 1939), pp. 133-155.

soil for only three brief years, while the British occupied and administered the country for forty. Yet twentieth-century Cairo, where it deviates from the Oriental genre, is stamped in the French rather than the British mold. What impresses the visitor to modern sections of the city is its resemblance—albeit imperfect and perhaps shabby—to Paris. As recently as a dozen years ago the French language was prominent on newsstands, in advertisements on billboards, and even in conversation, although this has since declined rapidly. Commercial enterprises are set up and run on the French pattern. However, one can scarcely attribute these pervasive signs of French influence to the earliest period of contact. These indirect indications of France must be distinguished clearly from the more limited direct effects of the Napoleonic occupation which were, in the long run, minimal.

The French occupation, which destroyed or severely damaged large sections of Cairo,[5] also imposed a number of "improvements" on the city. Scholars of Cairo's history have made much of these positive efforts, but what has been overlooked, unfortunately, is their very short-lived existence. Of all the reforms instituted by the French, only two were to persist beyond the actual physical presence of their troops. One was the reorganization of Cairo's administrative districts. The French, by judiciously combining the 53 existing *ḥārāt* of Cairo, created 8 large *arrondissements*, each known as a *thumn* (Arabic for one-eighth). These basic divisions established by the French more than a century and a half ago have been retained, with certain boundary modifications, in the present administrative organization of the city,[6] although obviously they have been supplemented by the *aqsām* (districts) of the newer quarters of Cairo.

The second impact of the French occupation was on the street pattern of the city. For purely military reasons the French began to regularize a number of important communicating streets in the city, since European armies could not cope with the confusions and potential ambushes of Cairo's maze-like system. In this process, al-Fajjālah Street was cleared of obstructions, to allow the French readier access to the strategically important gates along the northern wall of Cairo (Bāb al-Naṣr and Bāb al-Futūḥ).[7] The ancient pathway which connected Azbakīyah to the medieval city at the Mūski Bridge over the Khalīj (mentioned by Maqrīzi) was similarly widened and straightened to permit the maneuvering of troops.[8] The old road between Azbakīyah and Būlāq was elevated and stabilized, again for purely tactical purposes.[9] These streets have since become major thoroughfares of the city, indispensable to the present circulation system of contemporary Cairo.

The remainder of the French reforms were obliterated directly after their departure. However, they evidently left germinating seeds, since one reform after the other was reinstituted in the decades that followed. So it was with the French attempts to clean Cairo's streets, to introduce minimal sanitation measures, and to require the registration of births and deaths. Street cleaning was not undertaken again until three decades later; refuse removal was reintroduced at that same time, and the keeping of accurate vital statistics had to wait even longer for reactivation. French regulations which had required householders to keep lanterns burning throughout the night to illuminate the treacherous streets of Cairo did not outlast their presence. As soon as the French withdrew, the streets were again plunged into darkness. Within a decade or two, however, they had been relit to some extent, since Muḥammad 'Ali required pedestrians to carry their own lanterns when venturing abroad at night. Municipal gaslighting of public thoroughfares was not undertaken until the closing decades of the century.

For ease of control the French commandant had also ordered the removal of all internal fortifications and gates in the numerous *durūb* and *ḥārāt* of the city. And yet, even during the occupation, many of these gates had evidently been overlooked or rebuilt, since they were used

[5] Among these were the *Ḥusaynīyah* suburb, the central or *qaṣabah* area near the al-Azhar mosque, Būlāq which was burned, and the Azbakīyah and Birkat al-Raṭli sections.

[6] The eight divisions introduced by the French were: al-Azbakīyah, Bāb al-Sha'rīyah, al-Jamālīyah, al-Darb al-Aḥmar, al-Khalīfah, al-Mūski, 'Abdīn, and al-Sayīdah Zaynab. These eight major districts still appear as *aqsām* in the census of Cairo. By 1947, in addition to the eight original districts, Miṣr al-Qadīmah and Būlāq had been added, as well as four zones settled during the late nineteenth and early twentieth centuries.

[7] This street runs parallel to the older Bāb al-Baḥr Road over which traffic to the port of al-Maqs had traveled during Fāṭimid times. Bāb al-Bāḥr Street, just inside Ṣalāḥ al-Dīn's extension of the northern wall, had become completely congested. (It is now absolutely impassable for vehicles.) Shāri' al-Fajjālah (now called Shāri' Kamal Sidqy Pasha on modern maps) was a newer thoroughfare just outside the wall. It is now the *only* street capable of carrying heavy traffic between the northern portion of the medieval city and the major rail and bus terminal at Bāb al-Ḥadīd, and is thus an indispensable element in the street network of today's city.

[8] This was the beginning of the famous Mūski Street, destined to become the first Westernized commercial zone of Cairo in the latter half of the nineteenth century when French, Greek, and other European merchants established non-Oriental shops in Cairo. It has since lost its upper-class status. Mūski Street now caters to the native demand for domestic manufactured goods of low and moderate quality.

[9] French innovations have been enumerated by Jomard in "Description abregée de la ville et de la citadelle du Kaire," *Description de l'Égypte: État moderne* (L'Imprimerie Royale, Paris: 1822), on p. 585; by 'Ali Mubārak in *Al-Khiṭaṭ al-Tawfīqīyah al-Jadīdah* (Būlāq Press, Cairo: 1888), I, 61; and by Clerget, *Le Caire*, I, 190.

by the rebellious townsfolk in the 1800 uprising. After the French withdrew, occupants of the various *durūb*, *ḥārāt*, and even *aṭfāt* (narrowest alleys) lost no time in reconstructing their gates. European visitors in the early nineteenth century remarked on their ubiquity and, as late as the 1870's, they were still occasioning comment.[10]

Again, during a minor plague which made its unwelcome appearance during the French occupation, burials within the built-up section of Cairo were prohibited. From this many have assumed that intramural interments never again took place in Cairo. And yet we later learn that the interior cemeteries at Azbakīyah and Munāṣirah were still being used for burials as late as 1845. It was only when Muḥammad 'Ali acquired this land in preparation for his planned boulevard connecting Azbakīyah with the Citadel that these cemeteries were closed, the area razed, and the bones removed to exterior cemeteries.[11]

Thus, of the direct reforms introduced to Cairo by the French, few had any permanent effect, apart from suggesting procedures which were later followed. The most important effect—albeit unintended—of the French campaign was that it brought to Egypt's soil the founder of the hereditary line which was to govern Egypt during a critical phase of her modernization, from 1805 until the Revolution of 1952. Cairo's development during the nineteenth century is inseparable from that dynasty and, in particular, from its two major figures: Muḥammad 'Ali (1805-1848), the founder; and Ismā'īl (1863-1879), the builder or the profligate, depending upon one's prejudices.

Just as Ṣalāḥ al-Dīn had been brought to Egypt, almost by chance, by the Syrian force which expelled the crusaders, so Muḥammad 'Ali had come, equally capriciously, as lieutenant commander of a small corps of Albanians in the Turkish army which helped repel the French.[12] In both instances, Cairo's development was shaped, so to speak, by military chance. Of the two leaders, however, Ṣalāḥ al-Dīn arrived at the more propitious moment. Whereas he inherited a city on the verge of becoming a world metropolis, Muḥammad 'Ali inherited an unattractive and senile provincial capital.

The interregnum years following Ottoman reoccupation of Egypt were dark ones. Townsfolk, who had been pillaged by the French soldiers, were victimized doubly when at the mercy of the undisciplined and rivalrous factions of the Turkish army. Anarchy was even greater outside the cities, with villages despoiled by beduins and Mamluks alike. This anarchy seems to have extended to the very gates of Cairo, since at one point beduins even controlled the mile-long road between Būlāq and the city. Several years of struggle over booty and power in Cairo had made the Albanians a leading faction. By then, Muḥammad 'Ali's astuteness (and the death of his competitor) had catapulted him to the head of this unruly but powerful group. Finally, the Porte, to restore order and placate the Cairenes, recognized the *de facto* control of the Albanians by appointing Muḥammad 'Ali as Pasha.

But it was a piteous prize. Muḥammad 'Ali had been elevated to the Pashalik of a country but had become thereby the reluctant heir to its host of woes. The problems were both political and physical. The country itself was divided, with the Mamluks in control of Upper Egypt and another Turkish faction holding Alexandria. Even within Cairo there was a precarious balance and the threat of renewed Mamluk strength. Law and order, never secure, had become virtually nonexistent during the decades of shifting elite power. Within the countryside this breakdown was evident in the frequent raids on settled communities and the total disruption of lines of communication between cities. Within Cairo to venture out at night was to court certain plunder or worse. It had become accepted custom for Janissaries and Mamluks, then French, and finally the Albanian successors, to help themselves openly from the shops of Cairo, sometimes even repaying an accommodating merchant with a gratuitous beheading. Given this situation, it was hardly surprising that Muḥammad 'Ali's first efforts should have been directed toward the consolidation of his position in Cairo and the unification of the remainder of the country under his rule. The first decade or more of his reign was devoted almost exclusively to this difficult but essential task.

The physical and economic problems of the country and Cairo were no less pressing, but they could be approached only after political stability had been achieved. Three centuries of neglect had led to the gradual silting

[10] As early as 1814 their large number is noted. See Henry Light, *Travels in Egypt, Nubia, Holy Land, Mount Libanan, and Cyprus in the Year 1814* (Rodwell and Martin, London: 1818). They are also described by a visitor a few years later. See Edward de Montulé, *Travels in Egypt During 1818 and 1819* (Volume 5 of the *New Voyages and Travels* series) (Phillips and Co., London: 1821), p. 9. As late as 1867, John Wilkinson, in his *A Handbook for Travellers in Egypt* (Murrays, London: Revised edn. of 1867), mentions these gates in every part of the city *except* the new.

[11] For the French order prohibiting intramural interment, see Mubārak, *Al-Khiṭaṭ*, I, 61, and Clerget, *Le Caire*, I, 190. However, in his discussion of the history of the Muḥammad 'Ali Boulevard (now Shāri' al-Qal'ah), Mubārak noted that the Azbakīyah and Munāṣirah cemeteries were still used for burials until the terminal years of Muḥammad 'Ali's reign. See *op.cit.*, III, 65.

[12] For an account of Muḥammad 'Ali's life and activities, based on archival research, see Henry Dodwell, *The Founder of Modern Egypt: A Study of Muhammad 'Ali* (Cambridge University Press, Cambridge: 1931. For a brief account of his rise to power, see pp. 9-21.

up of the canal system, so essential for irrigating agricultural lands. In the process, at least one-third of the land had gone out of cultivation. To restore the productivity of the land, it was first necessary to clean, excavate, and extend the irrigation canals.

The physical neglect of the countryside was more than matched by the physical deterioration of the capital city. For three centuries she had been falling imperceptibly into ruin. House after house in the older quarters had crumbled and been neither cleared nor rebuilt. For centuries rubbish had been disposed of in the most primitive manner: it had been dumped into the Khalīj (long since dry for all but a few months during high flood) or thrown over the city walls. This process had turned the once-charming canal into a fetid stream or, during the dry season, into an offal-laden offense to eye and nose. This process had also resulted in the accretion of an almost continuous band of high mounds which virtually surrounded the city on all sides, breeding flies, rats, and disease. Interspersed among these unnatural hills, particularly on the western extremity, were lowlands, swamps, and periodic ponds which harbored the mosquitoes and other insects whose contribution to Cairo's recurring epidemics still went unrecognized. Until these areas could be cleared and leveled, there was no real hope of tackling the serious health problems of the city or of making room for future expansion.

43. A *masṭabah* of the early 19th century

The situation on the periphery, however, was no worse than that in the city's center. Within the city, street confusion had degenerated into chaos. Not only were the streets unpaved, unswept, and unwatered (even during Maqrīzi's time water had been sprinkled on the streets to keep down the dust), but they were also becoming increasingly impassable. Many structures had ground-level appendages which jutted out into the narrow lanes. In addition, each tiny cubicle of a shop had its own massive stone bench (*masṭabah*) extending out into the roadway in front, on which customers and tradesmen sat to talk and smoke, and where the proprietor performed his ritual prayers. So congested were the streets and alleys that often only one donkey could proceed down them at a time, and a loaded camel had to choose its route with care. The houses were as unkempt as the public ways, and the mosques and other public facilities—the *sabīls* (drinking fountains), baths, and schools—had inevitably deteriorated. *Waqf* revenues had for too long been diverted into the pockets of their administrators. Industry and trade, the economic bases of the city for more than six centuries, had stagnated and declined; they were ill-adapted, in addition, to the needs of a modern age. Trade with Europe was minimal and a knowledge of Western technological advances utterly lacking.

This was hardly an enviable inheritance for the ambitious founder of a modern state. The stable was filthy; no new growth could take place until the Herculean task of cleansing had been carried out. It was to Muḥammad 'Ali that this task fell.

There is no need to describe here the vast program of reforms—some wise, some foolish, most uncoordinated—instituted by the Albanian ruler, but a few might be mentioned because, for several decades, they took priority over improvements in Cairo. First came the consolidation of power, culminating in the destruction of the Mamluks who, after six centuries, were finally divested of their power.[13] Then came a confiscation of illegally constituted agricultural *waqf* lands and eventually a monopolization of all cultivable land.[14] To bring this land back into

[13] In 1811, six hundred chief Mamluks were invited to participate in the procession organized to celebrate the appointment of Muḥammad 'Ali's young son, Ṭūsūn, as head of the army being sent against the Wahhābīs in Arabia. As the procession filed solemnly out of the Citadel, the Mamluk princes were trapped between the upper and lower gates of the narrow passageway and, by prearranged plan, slaughtered by Muḥammad 'Ali's soldiers. Those still remaining in Upper Egypt were relentlessly pursued until the surviving remnant took refuge in Ethiopia.

[14] Much of the rural land of Egypt had been granted not as freehold property but as military fiefs. Gradually, however, these had been converted (with the authorities looking the other way) to private property and later further secured as family endowments. In 1808 Muḥammad 'Ali ordered a checking of titles and added to the crown lands all properties of dubious title. By 1814

productivity—and later to devote some of it to the new crop, long staple cotton, that was to play so vital a role in the economic future of Egypt—virtually the entire irrigation system of the Egyptian Delta had to be rebuilt. Thousands of villagers were conscripted to perform this back-breaking work, and between 1814 and 1820 hundreds of canals were made functional. Not the least important of the canals constructed was the Maḥmūdīyah navigation canal[15] which permitted water-borne traffic to ply between Alexandria and Būlāq with only one break-in-bulk stop beyond Rosetta.

And finally, in a parallel program to foster industrial and military development, Muḥammad ʿAli introduced European-modeled schools and factories, importing foreign teachers and advisers for the former and foreign machines and technicians for the latter. A number of these schools and factories were located in or near Cairo and inadvertently exerted an "ecological pull" which encouraged city expansion in their vicinity. Furthermore, the use of French experts and the sending of educational missions to France by the Pasha tended to establish Paris as the first model of "Western" ways. When, almost two decades after Muḥammad ʿAli's death, his grandson Ismāʿīl sent for one of the chief landscape architects of Paris to help redesign the city of Cairo, à la Haussmann, he was not so much innovating as he was carrying to its logical conclusion a pattern that had been established during the early decades of the nineteenth century.[16]

It is therefore perhaps ironic that Muḥammad ʿAli, famed for his imaginative and dynamic reforms, noted for his ambitious and visionary innovations, should go down in the history of Cairo in the rather prosaic role of housekeeper. Cairo and its problems never seemed to have captured his imagination. During the first two decades of his rule changes in the city were minimal and were more the by-product of other activities than ends in themselves. The chief changes which occurred during this period were a reorganization of governmental administration, in which Cairo profited but no more than any other part of the country; a restoration of peace and order following the reorganization of police and military forces, in which Cairo profited primarily because such forces happened to be concentrated in the capital; a spotty development of certain outlying suburbs of Cairo, as a by-product of Muḥammud ʿAli's predilection for bucolic atmosphere; and a rather intensive development of Būlāq, chiefly again as a by-product of his industrial and educational ambitions.

It was only during the last two decades of his rule that Cairo began to receive direct attention and that the amelioration of her difficulties became an end in itself. In these later reforms the hand of Muḥammad ʿAli's adopted son and brief successor, Ibrāhīm Pasha, is seen with increasing frequency. Although history is mute on this point, credit for the conception of many of these projects, as well as their execution, perhaps should go to Ibrāhīm rather than his father.

During these later decades, changes in the city were directed toward cleaning up the abuses which had rendered the older city less and less habitable. Among the changes introduced in this era were the leveling of the rubbish mounds on the western edge of the city; the filling in of the ponds, depressions, and swamps, and, in general, the preparation of land for the future expansion of the city; sweeping, dusting, painting, and otherwise "window-dressing" the older city; and, at the very end, the first tentative start in opening up the circulation system of the city in preparation for a revolution in transport.

During the first few decades of Muḥammad ʿAli's rule, the most pressing urban as well as national problem was the need to restore order and security. Consequently, one of the first reforms affecting the city was the suppression of its disorderly troops and the constitution of a strong, well-disciplined, quasi-military police force.[17] All the older gates to the various streets and quarters had been replaced and private watchmen once again stood guard over their entrances; this had been the security

this pretense was dropped and all agricultural land was made a government monopoly. The urban *awqāf*, however, was left untouched by Muḥammad ʿAli's confiscations, thus perpetuating the problems of urban renewal caused by this institution. Recent studies dealing with agricultural reforms include Helen Rivlin, *The Agricultural Policy of Muhammad ʿAli in Egypt* (Harvard University Press, Cambridge: 1961) and Gabriel Baer, *A History of Land-ownership in Modern Egypt, 1800-1950* (Oxford University Press, London: 1962), the latter touching only lightly on this early phase. See Clot-Bey, *Aperçu général sur l'Égypte*, II, 195-196, on the status of urban property.

[15] This canal seems to have been built and rebuilt a number of times but never functioned in the manner planned. Mubārak, *Al-Khitat*, I, 72, tells us that it was first built in 1814 under the supervision of French engineers. Yet we read elsewhere of the ceremonial opening of this canal in 1818, and still later it appears that for much of the year it was impassable and a break-in-bulk stop was necessary not too far beyond Alexandria.

[16] I am ignoring in this discussion all reference to Muḥammad ʿAli's various military campaigns and his partially successful efforts to free himself from the Porte at Constantinople. While these are undoubtedly extremely significant and would have been ranked of utmost importance by Muḥammad ʿAli himself, they had little significance for the city except for the fact that they often kept Ibrāhīm Pasha out of Cairo.

[17] This reform was effective quite early in transforming Cairo into a safer and more secure environment. Legh, as early as 1812, was impressed with the vigor of Muḥammad ʿAli's police force and with the effectiveness of the lantern regulation. See Thomas Legh, *Narrative of a Journey in Egypt and the Country Beyond the Cataracts* (M. Thomas, Philadelphia: 1817), pp. 43-44.

system from time immemorial. Muḥammad 'Ali supplemented this system by assigning his Albanians, and later joint military and civilian patrols, to make nightly rounds throughout the city to protect the populace. In addition, all pedestrians were required by law to carry their own lanterns after dark to light the streets and facilitate the work of the patrols. Police posts were established in all quarters of the city. The uniformed police were assisted by a roving contingent of plain-clothes police (perhaps identified by a small badge, although reports vary) who were posted during the daytime throughout the markets, coffee houses, and other public places to help keep the peace.[18]

Until about 1830 the office of chief of police was held by the governor (*wāli*) and the *ẓābit* jointly, but shortly thereafter authority was concentrated in the *ẓābit* alone who, from his central office in the Frankish quarter, dispensed summary justice wherever possible, referring only the more difficult and serious cases to the Pasha's court at the Citadel, where they were usually handled by Muḥammad 'Ali's deputy. After this, the office of *wāli* became less and less important and was eventually reduced to a merely honorific position. The role of the *qāḍi*, once a principal municipal officer in the Middle Ages, had also been reduced by this time to an absolute minimum. He was appointed for a year's term from Constantinople and, since the price of his office was high, had to recoup his investment in haste. Having neither continuity in office nor sufficient familiarity with the language, laws, or customs of the people, he could scarcely perform his essential role of adjudicating lawsuits, settling inheritances and other family disputes. In effect, the office was administered by his local and permanent assistant.[19]

In addition to these changes in affairs of justice, a number of other administrative reforms were made early in Muḥammad 'Ali's rule to facilitate more efficient management of the city and country.[20] But, as in the past, the administration of Cairo was not really separate from the administration of Egypt. Both came directly under the authority of the Pasha, now assisted by the various councils and ministries he established and by numerous staff officers to whom he delegated limited authority. Although Cairo was given, together with Rosetta and Damietta, the special status of *muḥāfaẓah* (governorate) and was therefore administratively independent of the provincial chiefs, she was still a long way from home rule. She has enjoyed this status of governorate ever since, although only recently has it meant any degree of autonomy.

As noted earlier, the few physical changes in Cairo which were made during this early period were each more by-products of other ends than outgrowths of direct concern with the city. Like Ṣalāḥ al-Dīn before him,

[18] As noted earlier, the lighting regulation was already in force in 1812 and continued without change throughout the reign of Muḥammad 'Ali. For the period before 1836, see Lane, *Manners and Customs* (3rd edn.), pp. 122-123; for its continuation until 1840, see Clot-Bey, *Aperçu général sur l'Égypte*, II, 188; and until 1847, John Wilkinson, *A Handbook for Travellers in Egypt (Being a New Edition, Corrected and Condensed, of "Modern Egypt and Thebes,")* (John Murray, London: 1847), p. 145.

It is impossible to determine exactly when the police reform was instituted. Lane, writing in 1835 but basing his material on a former trip in the 1820's, noted the existence of this new police force. See *Manners and Customs* (3rd edn.), pp. 114, 122-123. Later confirmation is found in Clot-Bey, *op.cit.*, II, 188.

[19] See the treatment of these matters in the cited works of Lane, Clot-Bey, and Wilkinson (1847 edn.).

[20] These are discussed by Dodwell, *The Founder of Modern Egypt*, pp. 192-241; Lane, *Manners and Customs* (3rd edn.), pp. 113-135; and Clot-Bey, *Aperçu général sur l'Égypte*, II, 171-196.

44. Muḥammad 'Ali's palace in Shubra

45. The fashionable carriage-way of Shāri‘ Shubra *ca.* 1860

ree-lined Shubra Street at the turn of the century

47. Shāri‘ Shubra just after installation of tramway tracks in 1903

48. The indispensable traffic artery of Shāri‘ Shubra today

49. Būlāq *ca.* 1857

Muḥammad 'Ali tended to ignore the existing metropolis and establish himself beyond its confines. One of his very first construction projects was a palace for himself in the retreat of Shubra, several miles north of the city near the banks of the Nile. Begun in 1808, this European-designed palace and its extensive formal gardens were completed a year after. Later, a wide avenue flanked by fast-growing sycamore and flowering trees was laid out to connect the palace with the northern tip of Azbakīyah.[21] Although a half century later this road was destined to serve as an upper-class carriage promenade, at the time it was constructed its *only* function was access to the palace—this at a time when the older city was choking for lack of major thoroughfares! Present-day Cairenes, however, must acknowledge with gratitude the somewhat accidental "planning" of Muḥammad 'Ali, since Shāri' Shubra, as this road is still called, remains the major access route to the heavily populated districts of Shubra and Rawḍ al-Faraj, twentieth-century additions to the metropolis.

As Ṣalāḥ al-Dīn had done, Muḥammad 'Ali turned his attention to the Citadel, which again became the site of intensive construction. Large sections were ruthlessly cleared of older monuments to make room first for Muḥammad 'Ali's new palace and later for his mosque, whose dome and twin minarets still dominate the skyline of Cairo. Walls and fortifications were reconstructed in the European manner and, when an explosion of a powder magazine destroyed a large segment of the old walls in 1824, they were promptly replaced by ones of Western design.

Other royal palaces were scattered throughout the environs of the city. The western edge of Azbakīyah and to a lesser extent the open area to its south, Būlāq, and the land intervening between the port and Shubra were preferred sites. Although none of these palaces seems to have been located with any idea of determining or influencing future urban development, each later constituted a nucleus for a future residential zone of Cairo.

Only in the development of Būlāq does there seem to have been any conscious plan. Every previous ruler of Cairo had his own favorite section which therefore tended to absorb a disproportionate share of urban growth. Ṣalāḥ al-Dīn had the Citadel which pulled the city southward; Baybars had preferred the Ḥusaynīyah section which stretched the city northward; al-Nāṣir ibn Qalāwūn had favored the western bank of the Khalīj which led to that area's growth. Muḥammad 'Ali's clear preference was for the extreme northwest corner of the city, demonstrated by his palace at Shubra and even more by his policies in Būlāq, which was transformed during his era.

In 1812 Būlāq still bore the marks of French destruction; two years later recovery was underway, aided by the presence of the Pasha's naval arsenal and docks, renewed trade, and a small construction boom.[22] Within the en-

[21] Mubārak, *Al-Khiṭaṭ*, I, 68, gives information on the palace. St. John, who traversed Shubra Road on his way to Cairo in 1832, estimated its width at 90 to 100 feet. See James Augustus St. John, *Egypt and Mohammed Ali: or Travels in the Valley of the Nile* (Longman, Rees, London: 1834), I, 102.

[22] Legh, *Narrative of a Journey in Egypt*, p. 34, described the destruction in Būlāq still evident in 1812, but note the contrast between Būlāq and Cairo in the comments of Henry Light just two years later. "Each year takes away from its [Cairo's] population and adds to its ruins; nothing is repaired that grows old; but . . . Whilst Cairo appears neglected, Boolac, its port, increases. New houses are built by merchants, . . . some of them . . . large . . . ; it contains the naval arsenal and dockyards of the Pasha. . . ." Henry Light, *Travels in Egypt*, pp. 21-22. The continued decay in al-Qāhirah is described by Count de Forbin, who visited Egypt in 1817-1818. See his *Travels in Egypt, Being a Continuation of the Travels in the Holy Land, in 1817-18* (Volume 2 of the *New Voyages and Travels* series) (Sir Richard Phillips and Co., London: 1820).

suing decade Būlāq became the site for many of the new industrial establishments set up by Muḥammad 'Ali as part of his plan to modernize the economy. In 1818 a wool factory was established in Būlāq, and other textile factories for cotton, linen, and lighter weight wools followed. By 1820 Būlāq proudly contained the first iron foundry of Egypt. That year also marked the laying of the foundation stone for the National Press, in operation by 1822. To this nucleus were added improved naval installations and enlarged facilities for riverboat construction. Spinning mills went up in Sabtīyah on the northern fringe of Būlāq, and still farther north, between Būlāq and Shubra, an enormous bleaching plant was built to service the various textile factories.[23] Būlāq was, in addition, a favored location for Muḥammad 'Ali's new schools. As early as 1821 a civil engineering school specializing in roads and bridges was opened in Būlāq. By 1823 this school had been transferred to the palace of Ismā'īl (a deceased son of Muḥammad 'Ali) in that quarter and, in 1834, finally expanded into a full-fledged Polytechnic Institute. Other schools were opened in Shubra for agriculture and veterinary medicine.[24]

On the intervening land between Būlāq and Shubra, Muḥammad 'Ali encouraged the elite to build palaces and summer residences in addition to their homes in the city. This had already begun to occur by about 1830, since St. John passed a number of new dwellings on his way into the city in 1832, and the trend was well advanced by the early 1840's as attested by others.[25]

From its inception, Būlāq had labored under a conflict between two incompatible land uses. One impulse had been to exploit the port functions fully by making the area a center of commerce, manufacture, and transport. The other had been to take advantage of its riverine location and the fresh northerly breezes and keep Būlāq a pleasant, bucolic suburb. This conflict was resolved essentially during the Muḥammad 'Ali period. One glance at current Būlāq suffices to indicate the outcome of this competition. Today Būlāq is a densely settled indigenous quarter filled with moderate-scale workshops and warehouses and populated by a heterogeneous working class drawn from all parts of Egypt. To the north of this district now stretches a fan-shaped sector of the city in which is concentrated the bulk of the city's newer industrial plants. Muḥammad 'Ali's premature attempts to industrialize Egypt may have ended in abortion but they established Būlāq unequivocally as a future industrial zone of Cairo.

50. Small-scale industrial workshops in Būlāq today

The capital itself, which had been sorely neglected during the first part of Muḥammad 'Ali's rule, became the scene of intensive efforts during the terminal half. Beginning in earnest in the 1830's, one after another of the city's sanitary and aesthetic affronts was attacked with vigor. One of the very first reforms instituted aimed directly at cleaning the streets of the city which for generations had been known as the "dirtiest in the world," a sad distinction. A contemporary observer wrote in amazement:

> I have not been many days in Cairo, and yet I discover that many changes have taken place in its appearance ever since the descriptions of the very latest travellers were written. The streets, formerly disgustingly filthy, *are now remarkable for their cleanliness*, being all swept three times a day.[26]

[23] Enumerations of Muḥammad 'Ali's industrial establishments can be found in Clot-Bey, *Aperçu général sur l'Égypte*, I, 212 and II, 289-295; in Clerget, *Le Caire*, I, 190-191; and in the *Master Plan of Cairo* (Government Printing Office, Cairo: 1956), pp. 88-89.

[24] On the Polytechnic Institute, see J. Heyworth-Dunne, *An Introduction to the History of Education in Modern Egypt* (Luzac, London: 1939), pp. 108, 142-144; and also Clot-Bey, *Aperçu général sur l'Égypte*, I, 212. For a firsthand account of it and particularly its "strange" library, see M. Sherer, *Scenes and Impressions in Egypt and in Italy* (Longman, Hurst et al., London: 1825), pp. 189-190. On the other schools, see Heyworth-Dunne, *op.cit.*, p. 134.

[25] Wilkinson, *A Handbook for Travellers in Egypt* (1847 edn.), p. 114; St. John, *Egypt and Mohammed Ali*, I, 104; D. Millard, *Journal of Travels in Egypt, Arabia, Petrae, and the Holy Land, During 1841-42* (Printed by E. Shepard, New York [Rochester]: 1843), p. 70. Edward Lane and his sister, Sophia Poole, occupied one such house in 1842, until the "Effrit" forced their removal. See Sophia Poole, *The Englishwoman in Egypt; Letters from Cairo* (Zieber, Philadelphia: 1845).

[26] Written in 1832 by St. John, *Egypt and Mohammed Ali*, I, 140. Italics added.

Ibrāhīm Pasha had ordered each householder to sweep the area in front of his building, and hundreds of bullock-driven carts were employed to collect the refuse and remove it beyond the city. Furthermore, it was no longer simply dumped in piles to rot. At the outskirts it was sifted, combustibles salvaged for fuel, and the remainder used to fill in existing depressions and swamps.[27]

Another element in this program to clean the city and its environs involved the rubbish mounds which had grown to impressive heights on the northern and western perimeters of the city.[28] These were to be leveled and the materials taken from them used to help fill the swamps and several marshy ponds in their vicinity. This work seems to have been well under way by the early 1830's, particularly in the southwestern section between the city and the Nile. Again, this was primarily the work of Muḥammad 'Ali's adopted son, Ibrāhīm. In the area now known as al-Insha and Dawāwīn, Ibrāhīm planned a plantation and, on the site of present Garden City, a palace. To prepare these areas, the mounds had first to be leveled, trees planted, and roads constructed. These improvements had already been made by the time Ibrāhīm constructed his new palace compound (with white exteriors and, a marvelous innovation, glass windows) north of the preexisting Qaṣr al-'Ayni in 1835.[29] The transfer of Muḥammad 'Ali's medical school to the latter in 1836-1837 and the opening of an 800-bed military hospital there contributed further to the growth of the area. It may have been at this time also that the Birkat Qāsim-Bay in the southern section was filled. The mounds on the northern and northwestern edges of the city were removed a few years later as part of the same program. Much of the material from these mounds was used to improve the major thoroughfare connecting Būlāq with Azbakīyah and to fill in the low lands which had formerly flanked the causeway.[30]

To this period of municipal improvement belongs one of the most dramatic changes effectuated—the filling in of the Birkat Azbakīyah. For centuries this vast pond had been inundated during flood season by water from the Maghribi Canal. When the water receded the area was planted to crops. Today, only a portion of the area of this former *birkah* has been retained as the formal garden of Azbakīyah, which comes as a welcome green oasis in the solidly built-up downtown business district of the modern city. The first step in this transformation was taken by Muḥammad 'Ali during the 1830's, although the area did not begin to assume its present appearance until the reign of Ismā'īl several decades later.

The draining of Azbakīyah, rather than an isolated project, was a subsidiary part of a wider plan to reorganize the canal system of the city. The Maghribi Canal, first constructed by Sultan al-Nāṣir ibn Qalāwūn in the fourteenth century, had completely silted up at its intake point on the Nile. Even before the French Expedition, it had been reduced to a mere branch of the Khalīj Miṣri, its reversed flow drawing water southward. Thus, the diminished flow of the Khalīj was required to keep the Maghribi Canal filled, to provide sufficient water for the flooding of Birkat Azbakīyah and, in addition, to deliver water north of the city that was required for the irrigation of agricultural lands near Heliopolis and the Birkat al-Ḥujjāj. It served none of its functions well and the agricultural lands were experiencing critical shortages. To increase the amount of water supplied to these outlying areas, a new and more direct canal beginning at the Nile just south of Būlāq and merging with the northern arm of the Maghribi Canal was constructed in 1832-1833.[31]

[27] Lest one conclude from this that Cairo had "solved" her sanitation problem, a quotation presumably written about 1847 must be included: "All the animals that die in Cairo are cast upon the mounds of rubbish, where they are quickly devoured by vultures, kites and dogs." This is taken from p. 128 of Edward Lane, *Cairo Fifty Years Ago*, edited from notes of the author by his nephew, Stanley Lane-Poole (John Murray, London: 1896). From the context it is clear that this observation postdated the construction of Ibrāhīm's palace in 1835.

[28] The mounds on the southern and northeastern fringes of the city were possibly even higher, and their presence is noted by Lane in *Cairo Fifty Years Ago*, p. 37, after the leveling of the western mounds. Evidently, no attempt was ever made to clear them, since the area was unattractive to urban settlement, being desert land with no access to water. Some of these may still be seen in present-day Cairo, although a post-Revolution project undertaken in 1960 has already redeveloped parts of the eastern chain of eminences.

[29] In 1832, St. John observed Ibrāhīm's workmen engaged in clearing the high mounds in the southwestern section. See his *Egypt and Mohammed Ali*, I, 141-142, for a description of this operation. Another firsthand account, written perhaps in 1842, described the area as follows: "You pass by the Kasr el Ainee, one of the colleges or schools established by Mohammed Ali, and the Kasr or palace of Ibrahim Pasha; the neighborhood of which has been greatly improved within the last ten years, by the planting of trees, the removal of mounds of rubbish, and the formation of roads by which it is approached." See Sir John Wilkinson, *Modern Egypt and Thebes* (John Murray, London: 1843), the original source for the later Murray Handbooks (guides) referred to throughout this chapter. Quotation has been taken from Volume I, p. 285. This refers to the completion of a task that St. John had observed in its initial stage. Ibrāhīm's palace remained in that location until 1906, when a private firm bought the land, tore down the palace, and sold subdivided lots for the modern development of Garden City. See *Master Plan of Cairo*, p. 31.

[30] These had also been observed *in situ* by St. John in 1832, *Egypt and Mohammed Ali*, I, 103. Work on their clearance evidently did not begin until several years later. For a description of changes in this area, see Wilkinson, *Modern Egypt and Thebes* (1843), I, 199.

[31] For information on this new canal, see Wilkinson, *A Handbook for Travellers in Egypt* (1847 edn.), p. 146. The Khalīj Miṣri was then used *only* to supply water to the city itself. At one

Functionally this replaced the old Western Canal, the southern portion of which was allowed to dry, and also relieved the Khalīj Miṣri of its extraneous irrigation duties.

These projects all increased the feasibility of draining Birkat Azbakīyah. This was easily achieved by digging a small diversionary canal around the Azbakīyah, sufficient to absorb the decreased quantity of flood water still percolating through to the depression. Although one source suggests that this was accomplished as early as 1827 or 1828, this is extremely unlikely. Perhaps some small beginning in the project was attempted that early, but it is clear from contemporary descriptions that Azbakīyah was still a flooded pond as late as 1835 or possibly even 1838.[32] Wilkinson, writing in the early 1840's, stated that "*within the last few years* a canal has been cut around it [Azbakīyah], in order to keep the water from the centre, though from the lowness of its level much still oozes through and partially covers it, during the high Nile; and it has been laid out partly as a garden, and partly as fields, with trees planted on the banks of the canal that surrounds it."[33]

Azbakīyah was not the only pond to be filled during this period. Similarly, Birkat al-Raṭli (now Shiyākhat Ẓāhir just north of Shāri' al-Fajjālah) and the southern-situated Birkat Qāsim-Bay were both filled from nearby rubbish mounds. The Birkat al-Fīl—certainly the oldest and most famous of the interior ponds—was also partially filled, its tributary canal permanently sealed and its new regularized shoreline planted in gardens and orchards which surrounded the palace of Maḥmūd, Kikhya Bay under Muḥammad 'Ali.[34] In brief, land throughout the city but particularly on the western fringe was being prepared for future urban expansion.

It was also in the 1830's that a number of superficial changes were introduced which, nevertheless, began to alter dramatically the appearance of Cairo. The domestic architecture of that city, which had evolved little during the later centuries of Turkish rule, slowly yielded to Western influence. The first signs of dissatisfaction with Cairo's appearance are hinted at in the 1830's. When Ibrāhīm returned victorious from his Syrian campaign, many of the houses in the city were whitewashed and decorated in his honor. Evidently this so pleased him that a few years later an order was issued making it mandatory for every householder to whitewash the exterior of his building. This practice persisted—despite the horrified gasps of Westerners—until well past mid-century, although the buildings of older Cairo have long since reverted to their original dun and mud hues.[35]

time Muḥammad 'Ali had evidently considered keeping the canal filled permanently, to facilitate the distribution of water. (While in flood, the Khalīj provided the water source for the ubiquitous water carriers who, during the dry seasons, still had to haul their wares from the river bank.) Unfortunately, this project was never executed. See Mubārak, *Al-Khiṭaṭ*, I, 82. The alternative to permanent flooding would have been to dry the canal entirely. This does not seem to have been considered by Muḥammad 'Ali, perhaps because the ancient ritual of the yearly dam-cutting by the temporal ruler of the country had too great symbolic significance. Wilkinson suggested draining the canal as the most logical solution, and it is interesting to note that it was the British who did finally follow this course—but not until 1898, by which time the city was partially served by a municipal water system.

[32] Clerget, *Le Caire*, I, 191, gives the earlier date but his chronology in this section seems generally untrustworthy, and he gives no sources for this allegation. Lane, writing the first version of his *Manners and Customs of the Modern Egyptians*, in 1835, refers to the pond of Azbakīyah and mentions nothing of a program to drain it. Had it been drained in 1827, certainly he would have noted this spectacular change between his first and second visits. Nor does the circular canal appear on the map he prepared for his sister's (Sophia Poole) book. In 1838-1839, Azbakīyah is still described as wet by one source. See *Egypt: Familiar Description of the Land, People and Produce*, no author given (William Smith, London: 1839), p. 43. It is questionable whether this secondary source should be given credence, however. Observations varied during different seasons of the year. St. John, arriving toward the end of the flood season, reported partial flooding in Azbakīyah, with other sections given to corn crops. See *Egypt and Mohammed Ali*, I, 104.

[33] Quoted from Wilkinson, *Modern Egypt and Thebes* (1843), I, 199, italics added. Partial flooding is still reported by Mrs. Poole in a letter dated 1842. See her *The Englishwoman in Egypt*, pp. 87-88.

[34] Clerget, *Le Caire*, I, 191, is the source for this information on the filling in of the Raṭli and Qāsim-Bay ponds. Evidence indicates that the Birkat al-Raṭli was seasonally flooded through the 1840's. Mrs. Pool described the beauty of its flood-time appearance, as did Edward Lane. The latter notes that in the Birkat al-Raṭli, "many lotus plants are seen in blossom in the month of September. The Lake at that season is quite full; soon after it dries up, and the ground is sown with corn. The water flows into the bed of this lake from the western canal, during the season of inundation." See p. 119 of Edward Lane, *Cairo Fifty Years Ago*, as edited by Stanley Lane-Poole. On the Birkat al-Fīl, see *ibid.*, pp. 72-73.

[35] This custom was of early origin and is still practiced in the villages and small towns of Egypt, where a return from the Pilgrimage is frequently celebrated by whitewashing and even painting colorful murals on the exterior walls of the pilgrim's house. In the first writing of Lane's *Manners and Customs* in the 1820's, no mention at all is made of whitewashing. In a note added just prior to the publication of the first edition in 1836, the whitewashing of houses in honor of Ibrāhīm's return is acknowledged. See note † in Volume I, p. 6, of the 1836 edition. By the third edition of his book, prepared in the 1840's (and reprinted in the 1908 edition cited earlier), an additional note had been appended to the effect that the Pasha had since made whitewashing mandatory. See note 2, p. 6, and note 2, p. 564, of the 1908 edition. Sophia Poole, *The Englishwoman in Egypt*, in her letter July 1843, states that ". . . at last a proclamation has been issued by the Pasha for extensive alterations and repairs throughout the city. The houses are to be whitewashed within and without; those who inhabit ruined houses are to repair or sell them; and uninhabited dwellings are to be pulled down for

51. *Mashrabīyah* work on old house near al-Azhar Mosque

52. Windows and balconies of a house in Būlāq

Other changes in architectural values were also becoming evident. It was within the next decade that the order was issued making it illegal to enhance new buildings with *mashrabīyah*, those delicately turned wooden lattice windows which for centuries had graced even the dullest and least attractive buildings.[36] While the rationale for the ruling was that they constituted a potential fire hazard, one must look deeper to recognize this also perhaps as a rejection of traditional values. In place of the Arabian and Mamluk styles, a mixed southern European and Turkish style, often not in the best of taste, was gaining ascendance. One of the first examples of this "new" style was the palace of Ismā'īl in Būlāq (which later housed the Polytechnic Institute), built in a "strange mixture of Italian, Greek and Arabian styles."[37] In this and other houses for nobles which were contructed in the early 1830's, the arched apertures of the Oriental genre had been replaced by stark rectangular windows copied from Europe. Always covered by iron grillwork, they were sometimes also equipped with glass panes—a style that became increasingly common as the decade advanced. By 1840 the trend that was to fill many of the "early modern" sections of Cairo with architectural monstrosities and melanges seems to have been well established—and irreversible.

It is perhaps strange that only at the very end of

the purpose of forming squares and gardens; meshrebeeyahs are forbidden and mastabahs are to be removed." Quoted from page 154. That such an order was enforced is attested by Wilkinson's 1847 edition of his *A Handbook for Travellers in Egypt*, where, on page 115, he states that "all . . . houses of Cairo have been lately whitewashed by order of the Pasha."

[36] *Ibid.*; and the letter of 1843 from Mrs. Poole, an extract of which appears in note 35, above.

[37] *Egypt: Familiar Description*, p. 43. See also description in M. Sherer, *Scenes and Impressions*, p. 154. There is no doubt that this set the "tone" for later additions. Mubārak, *Al-Khiṭat*, I, 83, acknowledges that Muḥammad 'Ali was the first to introduce "Western" structures to the city. It will be recalled that St. John observed several of these new buildings just north of Azbakīyah as early as 1832. However, they seem not to have become very common until the very last years of the decade. Thus, Lane in the first edition of *Manners and Customs* (1836) does not consider them significant enough to mention. By 1843, however, they had evidently grown in importance, and in his third edition Lane has added a note to the effect that "windows with European sashes of glass, each with a sash of close trellis-work outside the lower half, have lately become common in new houses, in many parts of Cairo. They are mostly houses built in the Turkish style, more or less approaching to European fashions; not well adapted to a hot climate. . . ." See Lane, *Manners and Customs* (3rd edn.), p. 8. Clot-Bey, writing in 1839, is harsh indeed in his evaluation of the "new" architecture. He states: "In the last few years, the style of construction [Arab] has been considerably modified. The Constantinoplean style, a bastard genre, mixing in the very worst taste a degenerate Greek style with the Arab, has been adopted. Many wooden buildings have been constructed according to this system, in which the arched windows have been replaced by rectangular ones and in which arabesque reliefs have been sacrificed to more uniform surfaces" (my translation). See *Aperçu général sur l'Égypte*, I, 179.

Muḥammad 'Ali's reign did he finally address himself to the problem which modern observers, from their advantage of hindsight, would have given highest priority, namely the need to improve the antiquated and impossible street system. Apart from regulations related to street cleaning and face lifting, undertaken as part of the other schemes described above, no direct attack on the convoluted circulation pattern of the city was attempted until 1845. One ought not be too harsh in judgment, however. Despite the tremendous technological progress achieved during this era, no change in the technology of transportation had yet occurred. Massive introduction of wheeled vehicles had not yet compounded the difficulties of the past. True, Muḥammad 'Ali himself possessed a carriage, "a cardinal's at second hand, similar to our Lord Mayor's waggon," an English visitor was to note as early as 1823. But, considering the state of the roads, he added: "How fortunate it is that there are not two carriages in Egypt."[38] Nevertheless, by 1840 the Pasha had imported a number of these outmoded vehicles from Europe, although they still numbered perhaps a little over thirty in all of Cairo and her environs. It was illegal, in fact, for anyone outside the royal family to purchase a carriage, and the Pasha had bestowed only a few as rewards to his most trusted ministers.[39] The "wheels" of the future, however, were not to be halted and even by the end of Muḥammad 'Ali's reign, although the basic rule remained in force, the number of carriages continued to increase.[40] Even so, no overwhelming traffic congestion resulted from the fact that the city contained hardly any streets broad enough to accommodate one, much less two passing carriages. But even the royal coach could not proceed down the few thoroughfares of the city without colliding with flimsy appendages or being halted altogether by a more recalcitrant projection into the street. It was on these streets—and these streets only—that Muḥammad 'Ali reclaimed the public way from the private usurpations made during centuries of *laissez faire*.

In the opening years of the fourth decade, *masāṭib* and other projections still impeded traffic with impunity. Streets were becoming cleaner but were still dusty, unwatered and, of course, unpaved. Above the bazaars, tattered awnings still gave way occasionally, depositing accumulated dirt on the heads of unsuspecting passers-by. Shops were unpainted, cluttered, and unrepaired. Most of these abuses had received some attention but results were spotty and impermanent. A new concerted effort was made in the opening years of the 1840's to end them once and for all. *Maṣṭabāt* on the major streets were summarily ordered removed, and only later were a few in the wider portions of the thoroughfares allowed to be rebuilt. An order was similarly issued to require replacement of the flimsy *sūq* coverings with more substantial wooden planks, although this order seems, in the main, to have been ignored. Also resumed was the earlier practice of sprinkling the unpaved streets to help settle the dust.[41]

Commendable as they were, these piecemeal efforts failed to provide a basic solution to the growing problem

[38] Quoted from page 58 of Sir Frederick Henniker, *Notes, During a Visit to Egypt, Nubia, The Oasis, Mount Sinai and Jerusalem* (John Murray, London: 1823).

[39] This remarkable fact is so significant that I quote at length from Clot-Bey. "Before Mohammed Ali, this means of transportation [*voitures*] was virtually unknown. One might cite how remarkable an object was the carriage which Ibrahim Bey received from France; and during the French Expedition, the carriage of Napoleon, drawn by six horses and racing down the straighter streets of Cairo and Boulaq, was one of the wonders of the country." *Aperçu général sur l'Égypte*, II, 456. "Since that time, the vice-roy has begun at first to use this equipment for his own service and that of his Hareem. After him, Ibrahim Pasha, Abbas Pasha and all the rest of his family have adopted this convenient means. It cannot become popular, nevertheless; because, reserved for the royal family, no one can use one except many of his ministers to whom he has given them. . . . (T)oday, *one counts in the Cairo environment only thirty people who have carriages*." *Ibid.*, p. 457. Translation and italics mine.

[40] Harriet Martineau, who visited Egypt at the end of 1846, commented upon the recent increase in carriages in that city. "Carriages are quite alarming in Cairo, which was not built for the passage of anything so large. They are very peremptory, having no idea of stopping for anybody. . . . The keeping of carriages was much on the increase. . . . A friend of mine found one on his street when he went to live there, four and a half years before my visit; and now there are twenty-four or twenty-five, making the passage of the street very hazardous." See her *Eastern Life* (Roberts Brothers, Boston: new edn., 1876), p. 224. The modern reader can but wish that Miss Martineau could see the present traffic congestion of Cairo.

[41] Lane, in the text of his first edition (1836) of *Manners and Customs*, takes cognizance of the ubiquitous *masāṭib* and the tattered condition of the street awnings. In portions of his book prepared during the 1820's these problems are described. See the 1836 edition, Volume II, p. 10. In a note added between the first writing and the book's publication, Lane informs us that Muḥammad 'Ali "has lately caused the *mus'tub'ahs* in most thoroughfare streets to be pulled down, and only allowed them to be rebuilt in the wider parts, generally to the width of about two spans. At the same time, he has obliged the tradesmen to paint their shops, and to remove the unsightly *sackee'fehs* (or coverings) of matting which shaded many of the *soo'cks*; prohibiting the replacing of them unless by coverings of wood. Cairo has, in consequence, lost much of its Arabian aspect." *Ibid.*, p. 351. That the removal of the *maṣṭabāt* was not totally successful is attested by Clot-Bey, see *Aperçu général sur l'Égypte*, I, 179, and by Mrs. Poole's mention of another order to that effect in 1843. Additional removal of street obstructions in the 1840's is noted by Wilkinson, *A Handbook for Travellers in Egypt* (1847 edn.), p. 139. Wilkinson also noted the persistence of the tattered *sūq* coverings, although by 1846 some wooden roofs were also in evidence. Both materials are still in use in the narrower alleys of Cairo's older market areas. Hourly sprinkling of the streets is first noted in *Egypt: Familiar Description*, p. 41.

53. Shāri' al-Mūski (the "New Street") *ca.* 1935

54. Shāri' al-Mūski today, relatively unchanged

of circulation and, by 1845, Muḥammad 'Ali was ready with a more direct approach. A *tanẓīm* (plan) for the city was drawn up, providing for a number of new or enlarged streets.[42] Among these was a design to widen and extend the latitudinal thoroughfare through the Frankish quarter (Shāri' al-Mūski and its eastern extension, originally named al-Sikkah al-Jadīdah or Rue Neuve, now called Shāri' Jawhar al-Qā'id). Also proposed was a much more ambitious new diagonal to be cut like a surgical incision through the densely packed residential quarters between Azbakīyah and the Citadel (Boulevard Muḥammad 'Ali, now more descriptively named Shāri' al-Qal'ah, or the Street of the Citadel). Neither of these ambitiously conceived arteries was destined for completion during his lifetime.

The need for Shāri' al-Mūski was related to recent changes in the status of foreigners. From its tiny original nucleus, the Frankish quarter expanded during the reign of Muḥammad 'Ali to encompass the alleys and byways on both sides of the Mūski. European merchants, encouraged by the Pasha's protection and a burgeoning taste among the elite for goods of Western manufacture, migrated to the capital to open shops along the Mūski.[43] Although this street had been regularized by Napoleon, it was still too narrow to accommodate the cart traffic generated by a thriving trade. To answer the vociferous complaints of the foreign merchants, Muḥammad 'Ali condemned and then purchased all land and buildings in the path of a broad (all of eight meters!) thoroughfare. Demolition began in 1845 when the partial plots abutting the street were resold to private investors. Progress was evidently slow—to which Muḥammad 'Ali's declining health may have contributed—for at the accession of 'Abbās in 1849 only a small portion of the street had been completed. The Mūski itself was widened, but the extension of the path into the Jewish quarter east of the Khalīj had barely begun. By 1848 the road had inched its way to the Maydān Qanṭarat al-Mūski where it ended in a confusing maze. It remained for Muḥammad 'Ali's successors to complete its route to the edge of the eastern desert.

The second road presented even greater obstacles, involving as it did a longer distance and a more congested path and having perhaps a somewhat less compelling rationale. It was desired chiefly to facilitate the ruler's access between his palaces at Azbakīyah and the Citadel. Nevertheless, 1845 marked the beginning of land acquisition for the Boulevard Muḥammad 'Ali. The two cemeteries blocking the westernmost segment of the road were razed, houses were purchased, and some demolition

[42] Amīn Sāmi, in *Taqwīm al-Nīl* [Almanac of the Nile] (Cairo: 1936), II, 547-552, notes that by 1847 there existed a *majlis tanẓīm al-maḥrūsah* (council of *tanẓīm*) of Cairo which recommended that many of the streets be given names, that houses be numbered, and that street signs be installed. These suggestions do not seem to have been followed very enthusiastically, if at all.

[43] Lane, in *Cairo Fifty Years Ago*, p. 70, described the new Mūski: "In this, as well as in some of the neighboring streets, most of the shops are constructed and fitted up as in Europe, with glass fronts, and stocked with almost all the luxuries of western countries; these are occupied by Franks and Greeks."

begun. But no construction was ever undertaken and the project remained abandoned until Ismāʿīl tackled it anew and carried it to completion a generation later.[44]

Despite these few attempts to open the circulation system within the city and to extend its lines of communication outward, at midcentury Cairo still remained an insulated and inward-looking community. Throughout the suburban hinterland were villages and small towns that were destined to become an integral part of the city during the next century but, as yet, these remained unconnected with the capital and led independent existences. One might mark their presence, however, since they will figure in our later discussions of Cairo in the modern era.

Making a full circuit of the city, one notes to the east the high mounds (the so-called windmill hills) which still separated the medieval walled core from the Mamluk tomb city in the desert beyond. Few persons then lived in the cemetery area, except in the vicinity of the mausoleum of Qayt Bay.[45] Northeast of the city were a few scattered villages, Maṭarīyah, Heliopolis, and Dimardāsh, whose inhabitants were engaged in agrarian pursuits. Agriculture also predominated due north of the city walls, with the inlying villages of Maḥmāshah and Jazīrat al-Badrān and the more peripheral ones of Shubra and Minyat al-Sīrij surrounded by fields. In the northwest corner was the expanding but still ecologically discrete town of Būlāq, already taking on an industrial character.

Southward, along the eastern shore of the Nile, all mounds had been cleared; in their place stood scattered palaces amid rich plantations but, as yet, no urban forms. Already existing were: the Qaṣr al-Dūbbārah, a palace built originally by Muḥammad ʿAli's son-in-law and later occupied by the Pasha's *Ḥarīm*, which gives its name to the *maydān* near which the American Embassy now stands; the Qaṣr al-ʿAyni, an early palace around which the present medical complex of public hospital and medical school grew and evolved; another palace, al-Qaṣr al-ʿĀlī, built by Ibrāhīm Pasha in the zone known today as Garden City, near his extensive plantations on the linear strip destined to become the government ministry zone of a later era. This entire eastern area was already served by a tentative system of roadways, although not yet hard-surfaced.

Several miles to the south and still separated from the main complex by rubble and swamp land was the small independent suburb of Miṣr al-Qadīmah. While she had lost much population, even since the time of the French,[46] she had established her future character as host to the less attractive industries of the city and to a reviving Christian community. East of the town were the *kharāb* covering the still unexcavated remains of Fusṭāṭ, and beyond them, the Khalīfah cemeteries.

Out into the Nile and across the river on the western bank were other small settlements—each more forlorn than the last. Half of the once-populated island of Rawḍah was occupied by a botanical forest laid out in the 1830's for Ibrāhīm Pasha by a Scotch horticulturist, while the remainder was but sparsely and spottily occupied. The three islands strung out in a row opposite Būlāq (which had been mapped by the French and were referred to collectively as Jazīrat al-Būlāq) had finally coalesced into a single larger one. While this island was destined to become one of the prime residential quarters of twentieth-century Cairo, Zamālik, it was then still subject to periodic flooding and inaccessible except by boat. It remained deserted except for the seldom-frequented retreat which Muḥammad ʿAli had constructed there in 1830. On the western bank of the Nile, stretching from north to south, were the small villages of Imbābah (where Napoleon had won his decisive victory over the Mamluks), Būlāq al-Dakrūr, Duqqi and, farthest south, the ancient town of Jīzah, which had declined from the luxurious summer resort favored by the Mamluk lords to a handful of houses, a mosque, and a pottery works.

Throughout the environs, then, there was room for potential growth. The city, however, had not yet even expanded to encompass the preexisting settlements. The era of building had to await a population explosion and a technological revolution—both of which began during the second half of the nineteenth century but were not fully underway until the twentieth. The work of Muḥammad ʿAli had been to clear the preindustrial city of her encrustations; the modern city came into being in the age that followed, but it would not have taken the form it did without the preparatory efforts of Egypt's first "modern" ruler.

[44] For information on the former road, see Mubārak, *Al-Khiṭaṭ*, III, 82-83. Details on the latter diagonal to the Citadel are given in the same volume, pp. 63-68.

[45] Lane, *Cairo Fifty Years Ago*, pp. 122-123, describes the eastern cemetery.

[46] According to Lane (*ibid.*, p. 139), its population in 1847 was no more than 4,000.

7 The Origins of Modern Cairo

A PERCEPTIVE visitor to Cairo just after the turn of the twentieth century noted that "European Cairo . . . is divided from Egyptian Cairo by the long street that goes from the railway station past the big hotels to Abdin [palace]. . . . And it is full of big shops and great houses and fine carriages and well-dressed people, as might be a western city. . . . The real Cairo is to the east of this . . . and . . . is practically what it always was."[1] The insulation between the two Cairos was so absolute that an English visitor in 1889 could remark with matchless condescension that ". . . with the polo, the balls, the races, and the riding, Cairo begins to impress itself upon you as an English town in which any quantity of novel oriental sights are kept for the aesthetic satisfaction of the inhabitants, much as the proprietor of a country place keeps a game preserve or deer park for his own amusement."[2]

Thus, by the end of the nineteenth century Cairo consisted of two distinct physical communities, divided one from the other by barriers much broader than the single street that marked their borders. The discontinuity between Egypt's past and future, which appeared as a small crack in the early nineteenth century, had widened into a gaping fissure by the end of that century. The city's physical duality was but a manifestation of the cultural cleavage.

To the east lay the native city, still essentially pre-industrial in technology, social structure, and way of life; to the west lay the "colonial" city with its steam-powered techniques, its faster pace and wheeled traffic, and its European identification. To the east lay the labyrinth street pattern of yet unpaved *ḥārāt* and *durūb*, although by then the gates had been dismantled and two new thoroughfares pierced the shade; to the west were broad straight streets of macadam flanked by wide walks and setbacks, militantly crossing one another at rigid right angles or converging here and there in a *rondpoint* or *maydān*. The quarters of the eastern city were still dependent upon itinerant water peddlers, although residents in the western city had their water delivered through a convenient network of conduits connected with the steam pumping station near the river. Eastern quarters were plunged into darkness at nightfall, while gaslights illuminated the thoroughfares to the west. Neither parks nor street trees relieved the sand and mud tones of the medieval city; yet the city to the west was elaborately adorned with French formal gardens, strips of decorative flower beds, or artificially shaped trees. One entered the old city by caravan and traversed it on foot or animal-back; one entered the new by railroad and proceeded via horse-drawn victoria. In short, on all critical points the two cities, despite their physical contiguity, were miles apart socially and centuries apart technologically.

The history of the second half of the nineteenth century is essentially the history of the new western city. At the end of Muḥammad 'Ali's rule in 1847, Cairo was still a single city with somewhat fewer than 300,000 inhabitants, including her port suburbs of Būlāq and Miṣr al-Qadīmah. By 1897, Cairo was composed of two symbiotic communities whose combined population approached 590,000. In 1847 the number of European foreigners in Cairo was still insignificant, comprising chiefly the old but expanding Greek community to which had been added a small number of Italian and French "adventurers." By 1897, Cairo's European population exceeded 30,000. Numbers, however, tell but part of the story. In 1847 Egypt was still a semi-autonomous member of the Ottoman empire, ruled in Eastern fashion by an Easterner. Westerners were still barely suffered, despite the handful of trusted advisers retained by the Pasha. By 1897, although still nominally within the Ottoman fold, Egypt had been governed by a representative of the British government for some fifteen years. European nationals monopolized the important government posts and enjoyed privileges, exemptions, and a style of life that made them the envy not only of Egyptians but of their countrymen at home as well. In 1847 Europe and Egypt were first becoming acquainted,[3]

[1] Augustus Lamplough and R. Francis, *Cairo and its Environs* (Sir Joseph Causton & Sons, London: 1909). Quoted from p. xv of the Introduction.

[2] William Morton Fullerton, *In Cairo* (Macmillan and Company, London: 1891), pp. 6-7. An earlier observer to whom the coexistence of two distinct cities appeared equally obvious was Gabriel Charmes. See his *Five Months at Cairo and in Lower Egypt*, an authorized translation by William Conn (R. Bentley and Son, London: 1883), especially pp. 52 *et seq.*

[3] The 1830's saw the publication of two remarkably parallel books. The English introduction to Egypt, Edward Lane's magnificent *The Manners and Customs of the Modern Egyptians* was first published in 1836 and proved so popular that it was reprinted several times. At that very time, educated Egyptians were avidly reading the first account of the manners and customs of the modern French, *Takhlīṣ al-Ibrīz ila Talkhīṣ Barīz*, by Rifā'ah R. Ṭahṭāwi, first published by the Būlāq Press in 1834 and reprinted in numerous editions.

the first transportation links were being forged,[4] and trade had barely begun. By 1897 the destinies of Egypt and Europe had become inextricably intertwined.

The fifty years had been critical ones. They witnessed not only an agricultural and demographic revolution within the country but also the transformation of Egypt's status vis-à-vis the world. They also witnessed an expansion of the city of Cairo, a phenomenon that had not occurred since the fourteenth-century reign of Sultan al-Nāṣir ibn Qalāwūn. During that earlier period Cairo had, in a brief span, doubled in width, incorporating the parallel strip just west of the Khalīj Miṣri which had hitherto marked its western boundary. During the latter half of the nineteenth century Cairo again widened to encompass a third band beyond the western limit of the city, edging toward but not quite reaching the river's bank. This new strip included portions that had been developed in the fourteenth century but which had long since been abandoned.

The reigns of Muḥammad 'Ali's first three successors contributed little to city development, although they were marked by events that exerted important if indirect influences on the city's future. By 1847 Muḥammad 'Ali's advanced age and declining mental powers left the administration of the country in the hands of Ibrāhīm, a *de facto* situation finally recognized late in 1848 when the latter confirmed himself officially as Pasha. But by the end of that year Ibrāhīm had predeceased his father and the succession fell to Muḥammad 'Ali's nephew, 'Abbās I, Pasha until his death in 1854.[5] It is difficult to believe that any ruler could have been as completely unattractive as 'Abbās Pasha is pictured, for one searches in vain in Western literature for a sympathetic word or a redeeming virtue. While it is true that many of 'Abbās' contributions were, from a European point of view, negative, two of his policies did leave permanent marks on the city. The first was the construction of a railroad between Alexandria and Cairo; the second was his founding of a small military city in the desert outpost of 'Abbāsīyah, now a well-populated quarter in northeast Cairo that bears the name of its founder.

Even before his accession, 'Abbās had been approached by the British who solicited his support for their scheme to connect Alexandria and Suez by rail. The suggestion was hardly novel. Indeed, for as long as the French had pressed for a seaway canal through the Isthmus of Suez, the British had been advocating the rail alternative to carry mail and passengers between Europe and India without jeopardizing Britain's sea-freight monopoly around the Cape of Good Hope. At one time the British had come close to success, when Muḥammad 'Ali agreed in 1834 to the plans of an English engineer to build what would have been one of the first railroads in the world, had the scheme been carried out. But bungling on the British side, coupled with the inopportune death of the engineer, Galloway, aborted the plan, and when Muḥammad 'Ali was approached again in 1847 he was no longer amenable.[6]

'Abbās was scarcely more enthusiastic but, for reasons of his own,[7] finally succumbed to the pressure and signed the railway agreement in the summer of 1851. In the hope of minimizing foreign control he specified that only Egyptian capital and labor were to be used; and to help placate the irate French he stipulated that the line should not be a direct connection between Alexandria and Suez but rather should be built in two segments, the first from Alexandria to Cairo, the second between Cairo and Suez. Construction of the Alexandria to Cairo leg was completed in 1854 just prior to 'Abbās' death, and the railroad was officially opened to through traffic at the end of the following year. The second part, between Cairo and Suez, was opened in 1858 but proved so poorly designed that it was abandoned ten years later.

Although Britain thus failed to achieve her objective, Cairo was left the unintended beneficiary. The trip between Alexandria and Cairo, which had formerly taken four days, was reduced to a matter of hours. The access of Cairo to the world and of the world to Cairo was thus drastically altered. During the age of Muḥammad 'Ali, Cairo had been relatively isolated and inward-look-

[4] In the early 1830's not a single steamship plied regularly between Alexandria and European ports. By the end of that decade there were "eighteen regular opportunities to and fro every month from Alexandria." See *Egypt: Familiar Description of the Land, People and Produce* (William Smith, London: 1839), p. 294.

[5] A partisan biography of Muḥammad 'Ali's adopted son, Ibrāhīm, is Gabriel Enkiri, *Ibrahim Pacha, 1789-1848* (Imprimerie Française, Cairo: 1948). For the succession of Ibrāhīm, see Henry Dodwell, *The Founder of Modern Egypt: A Study of Muhammad 'Ali* (Cambridge University Press, Cambridge: 1931), p. 261. There is a difference of opinion concerning the death of 'Abbās. While the official medical report gave natural causes, the generally accepted opinion at the time was that he had been murdered by his guards. Various contemporary versions are recounted in *Conversations and Journals in Egypt and Malta by the Late Nassau William Senior*, based on his trip of 1855, edited by M. Simpson (Sampson Low, *et al.*, London: 1882).

[6] A rather complete analysis of the British rail *vs.* French canal rivalry is contained in Charles Hallberg, *The Suez Canal: Its History and Diplomatic Importance* (Columbia University Press, New York: 1931). For information on the early railway, see especially pp. 101-113.

[7] Mougel-Bey claimed that the concession to the British was granted in return for a "bribe" which was none less than influential British support of Egyptian autonomy vis-à-vis the Porte, a not unlikely explanation. See *Conversations and Journals . . . by Nassau William Senior*, p. 28.

ing; with the advent of the railroad she began to look—and then to stretch—outward.

The terminus of the new railway was constructed on the site of the former Fāṭimid port of al-Maqs, more recently marked by the westernmost bastion of Ṣalāḥ al-Dīn's wall, the Bāb al-Ḥadīd. Although this historic gateway had been demolished by Muḥammad 'Ali only a few years earlier in 1847,[8] the station took its name from the former landmark. The location of the terminal at Bāb al-Ḥadīd, then the outer limit of the city, determined the ecological future of the surrounding land. Not only did its presence stimulate development, but around this "port of entry" assembled many of the later immigrants (both European and native) to the city. In the old Coptic quarter between it and the Azbakīyah grew up a zone of marginal uses, including rooming houses, coffee shops, and later, the prostitution district of the city.

In the northeast quadrant of the contemporary city, surrounded by middle-class zones, is a small slum pocket known today as 'Abbāsīyah Baḥrīyah. Its isolated position cannot be understood unless one knows that its development began in 1849, whereas the surrounding sections remained unsettled until the twentieth century. This was the area contributed by 'Abbās. Muḥammad 'Ali had rid himself early of the troublesome Albanian mercenaries, by means of whom he had gained power, and had substituted a conscript army of Egyptian *fallāḥīn.* 'Abbās reverted to imported troops but, perhaps remembering their undisciplined nature, decided to station them outside the city. In 1849 he had built for them a series of barracks on the desert edge along the route to the outlying villages of Maṭarīyah and Heliopolis. Soon a complement of businesses and dwellings began to grow up around this core. To encourage their development, 'Abbās gave free land to those wishing to build, and houses for tradesmen and officers went up rapidly. A hospital, a school, and a palace for the Pasha added further vigor to the section whose population was swelled by that of the neighboring village of al-Wāyli, settled by a beduin tribe (the Bani-Wā'il). In short, a sort of royal suburb—that recurring phenomenon of Cairo's history—began to take shape.[9]

It is difficult to predict what might have been the pattern of Cairo had 'Abbās lived long enough to put his "town" on a firmer footing. But his unexpected death only five years later condemned the settlement to stagnation. His successor sent the mercenaries packing, stationed his new troops in barracks on the shore of the Nile, and 'Abbāsīyah was abandoned as abruptly as it had been founded. Only fifteen years later the area was described as a "miserable memorial . . . of its founder . . . [which] in a few years . . . will be an unsightly mass of ruins."[10] This prediction proved overly pessimistic, for 'Abbāsīyah remained a somewhat forlorn outpost until infused by British troops after 1882. It was finally incorporated into the city during the first decade of the twentieth century when a great speculative boom swept urban forms about it like a flood.[11]

The creation of one of Cairo's most famous landmarks, Shepheard's Hotel, also dates from the era of 'Abbās, and therefore cannot be left out of any discussion of contemporary developments. Samuel Shepheard, who had gone to sea to escape the drudgery of apprenticeship to a pastry cook, landed somewhat fortuitously in Egypt in 1842, having been put ashore there in consequence of a minor mutiny. After some years as assistant and then manager in several small British hotels in the Frankish quarter, his opportunity came through a meeting with 'Abbās over their shared interest in hunting. This initial contact was exploited until, as Samuel Shepheard wrote to his brother in November 1849, the Pasha "has given me a grant of a large college to build an Hotel on the site. I am now busy making a plan." The site granted to the hotel-keeper was none other than the Palace of Alfi Bay, overlooking the Azbakīyah, which had been requisitioned by Napoleon during the French occupation and later, during the educational exuberance of Muḥammad 'Ali, had housed his famous School of Languages. 'Abbās, having little use for such fripperies, had closed the school, thus making it available for the hotel that was to attain such real and symbolic fame.[12]

These seem to have been the sum total of 'Abbās's contributions to the city. True he had considered water

[8] Edward Lane, *Cairo Fifty Years Ago* (John Murray, London: 1896), p. 43.

[9] Fragmentary accounts of this settlement appear in Louis Bréhier, *L'Égypte de 1798 à 1900* (Combet et Cie., Paris: 1901), p. 150; Clerget, *Le Caire*, I, 197; Fu'ād Faraj, *Al-Qāhirah* (Ma'ārif Press, Cairo: 1946), III, 527; Amīn Sāmi, *Taqwīm al-Nīl* [Almanac of the Nile], Volume III, Part I (Cairo, 1936), pp. 21-22; and *Master Plan of Cairo* (Government Printing Office, Cairo: 1956), p. 31.

[10] Wilkinson, *A Handbook for Travellers in Egypt* (John Murray, London: Revised edn., 1867), p. 151.

[11] Lamplough and Francis, *Cairo and its Environs*, pp. 28-34, describe graphically the jerry-building of that period.

[12] A full and fascinating account of the hotel and its founder can be found in Michael Bird, *Samuel Shepheard of Cairo* (Michael Joseph Press, London: 1957). Quotation has been taken from a letter dated November 1849, appearing on p. 46. The Shepheard's Hotel known to twentieth-century visitors would not have been recognized by Samuel, since he sold his interest in 1860 and retired to England to live out his few remaining years in country-squire style. Another enlarged Shepheard's Hotel was built on the same site soon afterward, where it remained until burned in the Cairo riots of 1952. A final successor now exists in Cairo, but it is a modern building on the shore of the Nile and bears no resemblance to the earlier models.

55. Palace of Muḥammad Bay al-Alfi: first Shepheard's Hotel

56. Second Shepheard's Hotel on same site, late 19th century

57. Shepheard's Hotel, early 20th century

58. Third Shepheard's Hotel on same site, mid-20th century

59. Shepheard's Hotel: burned in the 1952 riot that ignited the Revolution

60. Fourth Shepheard's Hotel at the Nile shore near the Qaṣr al-Nīl Bridge

distribution (mostly for his arid 'Abbāsīyah) but, in fairly typical fashion, abandoned the plan upon seeing the first cost estimates.[13] Nor did he neglect entirely the project begun under Muḥammad 'Ali to extend Shāri' Mūski into the heart of the old city, but progress was so desultory that, by 1854, the Rue Neuve extended only up to the Bazaar of the Brassworkers, Sūq al-Naḥḥāsīn.[14]

There were many who rejoiced at the death of 'Abbās and the appointment of Muḥammad 'Ali's youngest son, Muḥammad Sa'īd, as his successor, but perhaps none was as jubilant as Ferdinand de Lesseps, the "father" of the Suez Canal. Sa'īd's education had been entrusted to French savants and among his instructors had been the son of the French Consul in Cairo, young de Lesseps. Upon Sa'īd's accession, de Lesseps wrote his congratulations and in turn received an invitation to visit Egypt, a bid he accepted with alacrity and *not* with empty hands. With him he brought fairly detailed plans for the projected canal, elaborations of those first proposed in 1834 and refined further by the Société d'Étude du Canal de Suez, organized by Enfantin in 1846.[15]

De Lesseps reached Alexandria on the seventh of November and by the last day of that month had Sa'īd's signature on the canal concession.[16] All that remained was to obtain the Sultan's ratification of the agreement—a simple matter which, in fact, required almost a dozen years to negotiate. British opposition, through the unusual influence which Lord Canning exercised in the Constantinople court, placed obstacle after obstacle. In desperation, de Lesseps raised his capital and began construction by 1859, all without Porte sanction.

Ratification by the Porte and completion of the canal did not occur until years after Sa'īd's death, and yet to him must be assigned responsibility for this single most important event of nineteenth-century Egypt—an event which altered the entire future of the country and, with it, that of the capital city of Cairo. The canal thrust Egypt onto the center of the world's strategic stage, a position she had not occupied since the fifteenth century. But it also enmeshed her in the rivalries and machinations of the empire builders and led eventually to British occupation and the growth of "colonial" Cairo.

While these were to be the long-term effects of the decision, the short-term impact was relatively negligible. The years between 1854 and Sa'īd's demise in January 1863 witnessed few alterations in the structure of Cairo. 'Abbāsīyah was neglected when troops were rehoused in newly constructed barracks at Qaṣr al-Nīl (the site of the present Hilton Hotel) just south of Būlāq.[17] The gradual development northward along the finger of Shubra Road continued in undramatic fashion, aided somewhat by the construction of Sa'īd's Nuzhah Palace there in 1858.[18] The second leg of the railroad, between Cairo and Suez, was completed in that same year, which tended to encourage scattered growth along its route, notably at Maḥmāshah.[19] But in general, the city, like the country, seemed to be marking time, thanks in part to the ruler's paradoxical tendency first to monopolize all govern-

[13] 'Ali Mubārak, *Al-Khiṭaṭ al-Tawfiqīyah al-Jadīdah* (Būlāq Press, Cairo: 1888), I, 82; Amīn Sāmi, *Taqwīm al-Nīl*, Volume III, Part I, p. 26.

[14] Mubārak, *Al-Khiṭaṭ*, III, 83. This was still less than half the distance to the eastern desert.

[15] Bréhier, *L'Égypte de 1798 à 1900*, p. 158, gives the early history.

[16] Hallberg, *The Suez Canal*, pp. 117-118.

[17] Mubārak, *Al-Khiṭaṭ*, I, 83.

[18] This palace is now occupied by the Tawfīqīyah Secondary School. See Faraj, *Al-Qāhirah*, III, 529.

[19] Mubārak, *Al-Khiṭaṭ*, I, 84. One should not overemphasize the "pulling power" of the railroad, however, since this area still remains one of the least developed sections of Cairo.

61. Qaṣr al-Nīl barracks in the 1940's

62. The same view showing the new Hilton Hotel along the post-1952 Corniche Drive

mental responsibility and then to devote minimal time and effort to the business of governing. The staticism of these mid-years of the century is made even more conspicuous by contrast with the sudden explosion of activity that followed. It was possibly the proverbial calm before the storm.

Ismā'īl, son of Ibrāhīm, inherited his father's drive and love of urban embellishments. He also inherited Egypt at a moment when many events, some planned, others coincidental, converged to stimulate the most dynamic era of city building that Cairo had experienced in hundreds of years. He came in on the crest of a cotton boom caused by the withdrawal of American supplies during the Civil War.[20] He came in just as Egypt's population was experiencing its first upsurge of the modern era after centuries of decline.[21] The pace of growth was quickening but, in forcing that pace, he helped to precipitate foreign intervention.[22]

In the past, canal building and land stabilization of the flood plain had always preceded urban development. This period was to be no exception. Just as Sultan al-Nāṣir ibn Qalāwūn first constructed the Maghribi Canal to allow the city to expand onto land between it and the Khalīj Miṣri, so Ismā'īl's construction of the Ismā'īlīyah Canal helped prepare for the settlement of the new quarters of Ismā'īlīyah and Fajjālah (the latter named for *fijl*, the radish which had until then been cultivated there). The Ismā'īlīyah Canal was but a part of a broader program of public works which was energetically launched. One of the very first acts of the new Pasha had been to abrogate several clauses of the concession granted to the Suez Canal Company, the most important of which was the agreement governing a fresh water connection between Cairo and the Isthmus at Lake Timṣāḥ.[23] Ismā'īl reclaimed the right to construct the fresh water canal which had formerly been granted to the company. Construction of the Ismā'īlīyah Canal began shortly thereafter, together with related embankment reinforcements at Cairo. In charge of these projects was the French engineer, Brocard. By 1866 not only had the major canal been completed and opened to traffic but the shoreline north of Būlāq (Rawḍ al-Faraj and Sāḥil) had been stabilized[24] and, in addition, the island opposite Būlāq (originally Jazīrat al-Būlāq, then al-Jazīrah, and, finally, Zamālik, its present designation) was made almost entirely flood free.[25]

With these engineering feats accomplished, the adjacent areas underwent significant changes. The Maghribi Canal, long an unimportant backwater channel for the Khalīj, was finally filled in completely and, with the loss of its source, the smaller canal that Muḥammad 'Ali had used to divert the flood around the Azbakīyah also dried. Birkat Azbakīyah was no more, and roads replaced the path of the Qanṭarat al-Dikkah Canal and the circular one around the former marsh. The adjacent lands of al-Fajjālah, Ismā'īlīyah, and the two triangular tracts remaining from Birkat Azbakīyah once the smaller rectangular park was delimited, were all ripe for the development which was soon to take place.

Hand in hand with these public works went an attempt to provide Cairo with water and gas—municipal utilities which were becoming the *sine qua non* of the modern European city. (Drainage was also contemplated, but its price was so prohibitive that it was not introduced until some fifty years later.) The year 1865

[20] The Civil War which cut off supplies of American cotton created a heavy demand for the Egyptian substitute whose price tripled and then quadrupled on the international market. In 1861 Egypt exported less than 600,000 *ḳantars* of cotton, selling at an average of 14 *tallaris* per *ḳantar*. By 1863 the quantity exported had more than doubled, and the average price had tripled. By 1865 Egypt exported in excess of two and a half million *ḳantars* at a similarly high price. But, with the end of the war and the rapid recovery of the lost markets, demand for Egyptian cotton fell off. By 1867 the price of Egyptian cotton tumbled to only half of what it had been the preceding year. See Georges Douin, *Histoire du règne du Khédive Ismail, les premières années du règne, 1863-1867*, Tome I (Istituto poligrafico dello stato per la reale società di geografía d'Egitto, Rome: 1933), 257-259.

[21] At the end of Ismā'īl's reign the population of Egypt was probably in excess of 7 million. Two generations earlier at the time of the Napoleonic Expedition, the population had been estimated (variously) at between 2 and 3 million, a figure which did not begin to mount until about 1840.

[22] The claim that Ismā'īl's irresponsible borrowing and excessive spending were the major reasons for Western intervention in the affairs of Egypt is one-sided if not naïve. Perhaps the fairest appraisal of Ismā'īl is given by George Young, in *Egypt* (Charles Scribner's Sons, New York: 1927), who points out that the mulcting of Egypt to pay for the Suez Canal, from which she could not profit, and the unscrupulousness of both foreign contractors and financiers must share this responsibility.

[23] For other concessions revoked and compensations agreed upon, see Hallberg, *The Suez Canal*, especially pp. 197, 207, 212-214; Douin, *Histoire du . . . Khédive Ismail*, Tome I, 19-52, 188-201.

[24] All the land west of Shāri' Abū al-Faraj had hitherto been subject to periodic flooding and could be used only for agriculture. Between 1863 and 1865 the embankments were improved and, with the Ismā'īlīyah Canal siphoning off Nile water south of Būlāq, this land was permanently added to the city. See Faraj, *Al-Qāhirah*, III, 529. After that, the area served as a northern extension of the river port of Būlāq. Today, long after the closing of the main installations at Būlāq, sailboats still deposit their wares and service the *shūnah* and warehouses that stretch along the shore at Sāḥil.

[25] Eventually a permanent separation between al-Jazīrah and the west bank was accomplished by the channeling of the "Blind" Nile. Even before this, however, the island was raised and protected from flood. See, for example, the account in Baedecker's *Guide to Egypt* (Karl Baedecker, Leipzig: 2nd edn., 1885).

marks the establishment of both the Cairo Water Company and the Cairo Gas Company. In February the company of M. Charles Lebon, already engaged in supplying the city of Alexandria, was granted the concession to provide gas to Cairo and the suburbs of Būlāq and Miṣr al-Qadīmah.[26] The following year government land in Būlāq was donated to the company for its plant and, in April of 1867, the train station at Bāb al-Ḥadīd was symbolically lit to celebrate the inauguration of this service. Gradually, Azbakīyah and its vicinity, the new quarter of Ismāʿīlīyah, the major thoroughfares, and the Khedive's palaces were brought into the network which eventually extended into parts of the older city as well.

The work of the water company proceeded less efficiently. In May of 1865 the concession to provide Cairo and her suburbs with municipal water was granted to M. Cordier, who had successfully provided water to forty French towns and was engaged in a similar operation for Alexandria. Late in the year a joint stock company was formed to raise capital for the venture. The city donated land near the Qaṣr al-ʿAyni at the mouth of the Khalīj for the major pumping station and, by the summer of 1867, the first conduit (to the Citadel and thence to ʿAbbāsīyah) was laid. But financial and/or engineering inefficiencies aroused the ire of both shareholders and Ismāʿīl Pasha, and Cordier was finally discharged. The company was then reorganized and its deadline extended until 1874.[27] The pumping station was relocated to a site near the Ismāʿīlīyah Canal and conduits were laid to serve Azbakīyah and Ismāʿīlīyah. Only gradually and incompletely were these extended to other parts of the city.

Thus by 1867 Cairo was physically prepared to enter a new era of city building. An event of that year provided a model for the new city and stimulated the motivation for it: the Exposition Universelle held in Paris in the spring of 1867. The exposition was Baron Haussmann's[28] *pièce de résistance*, the climax of his career which was fated to end in calumny and rejection only two years later. By then, Haussmann had been Préfet de la Seine for more than a decade and a half, during which he had transformed the Ile de la Cité, planned the peripheral zones, and ruthlessly imposed formal parks and broad boulevards on the antiquated street plan in a manner so associated with his name that even today this method of planning is referred to as "haussmannizing." Municipal utilities had been installed on a grand scale, including the famous sewers of Paris through which visitors to the Exposition were conducted with pride.

63. Ismāʿīl Pasha

The Universal Exposition was designed to display Paris' accomplishments to the world. Even the site of the exhibit, the Champ de Mars, was redesigned for the event in the same grand style. The impact of the Paris Exposition Universelle on European city planning of the nineteenth century was as significant as it was unquestioned. It set the style and served as the model for numerous countries for decades to come, just as the Chicago World's Fair of 1893, with its return to the classic mode, set the style for the "city beautiful" movement which dominated American city planning for decades. It is perhaps testimony to the new relationship of Egypt to Europe that she, too, was so deeply affected by the ideal incorporated in the Exposition Universelle.

To establish Egypt among the concert of "important" nations and to establish himself, perhaps, as a peer of European royalty, Ismāʿīl accepted the invitation of Napoleon III to participate in the Exposition. Indeed, the Egyptian display was one of the most elaborate, includ-

[26] See Douin, *Histoire du . . . Khédive Ismail*, Tome 1, 265. It is difficult to understand where M. Clerget obtained his information that the Cairo Gas Company was not founded until 1873. See his peculiar statement in *Le Caire*, 1, 194. This later date is an anachronism since we have ample evidence to indicate that the entire vicinity of Azbakīyah, the train station, as well as the palaces and hotels to which guests were assigned, were already illuminated by gas when the Suez Canal opening was celebrated in 1869.

[27] See Douin, *Histoire du . . . Khédive Ismail*, Tome 1, 266; Bréhier, *L'Égypte de 1798 à 1900*, p. 177.

[28] See the fascinating narrative of *The Life and Times of Baron Haussmann*, by J. M. and Brian Chapman (Weidenfeld and Nicolson, London: 1957), in its entirety.

ing a full-scale model of the Temple of Philae, a populated bazaar and *funduq* of Arab style, a beduin encampment, and other reconstructions of Egyptian life and culture.[29] The effort was not unrewarded. The Egyptian exhibit attracted tremendous interest and received numerous medals and citations. It was, perhaps, even worth the loan which Ismā'īl contracted to help defray its expense.

In June 1867, accompanied by a massive entourage, Ismā'īl reached Paris, where he was received personally by Haussmann. The day after his arrival he opened the Egyptian exhibit at the Champ de Mars and, in the afternoon, visited the Bois de Boulogne.[30] While the question must remain forever unanswered, could it have been on this day that Ismā'īl met the landscape gardener, Barillet-Deschamps, who had executed the plans for both the Bois de Boulogne and the Champ de Mars? And could it have been then that he first resolved to create in the Birkat Azbakīyah a formal garden modeled on them? One may merely note the circumstantial evidence that two years later he engaged the services of this same Barillet-Deschamps to help him in his schemes to beautify Cairo.[31]

During the remainder of his sojourn in Paris, Ismā'īl was entertained repeatedly by Haussmann and, like the other royal visitors, given extensive guided tours through the "new" Paris. This was, of course, not his first visit to the French capital. As a young man he had attended the military academy of Saint Cyr and in 1854 had returned to that city on a mission for Sa'īd Pasha. These trips, however, predated the revolutionary changes introduced by Haussmann. That Ismā'īl was deeply impressed by the city's reconstruction is attested by reports in contemporary French journals. Thus, while his trip of 1867 cannot be credited with being Ismā'īl's first introduction to a European capital nor even with creating his interest in city development—which predated his trip—the visit did give Ismā'īl renewed inspiration and motivation, a fact that can be surmised from the events which directly followed it.

[29] See Charles Edmond (pseud. for Karol Edmond Chojecki), *L'Égypte à l'exposition universelle de 1867* (Dentu, Paris: 1867), for a full description.

[30] Douin, *Histoire du règne du Khédive Ismail, l'apogée, 1867-1873,* Tome II (Istituto poligrafico dello stato per la reale società di geografía d'Egitto, Rome: 1934), 5-8.

[31] There is no documentary evidence of such a meeting. However, that Barillet-Deschamps was the landscape gardener for the Bois de Boulogne and assistant to Alphand in preparing the Champ de Mars for the Exposition is incontestable. See, for example, Chapman, *The Life and Times of Baron Haussmann*, p. 201. Both the 1885 edition of Baedecker and 'Ali Mubārak in his *Al-Khiṭaṭ* confirm Barillet-Deschamps' later role in designing extensive parks and gardens in Cairo between 1869 and his death in 1874.

After stopping at Constantinople to obtain a long-desired *firman* from the Porte that elevated his title from Pasha to Khedive, Ismā'īl returned to Cairo and surveyed its depressing dinginess. Where, in his crumbling capital, was there anything to rival what he had seen in Paris, or even in London which he had visited afterward? And how could he invite the crowned heads of Europe to a city which reflected so poorly on its ruler? For he had already conceived his plan to mark the opening of the Suez Canal with a gigantic celebration that was to be his own, personal, Exposition. Even Azbakīyah, then the finest section of the city, dimmed in beauty when compared with Europe.

The solution to this problem was obvious. Cairo must be cleaned, polished, and given at least a façade of respectability. There was no time to dig deep into the eastern city. He was realistic enough to know that even with maximum effort this was too ambitious a project. The façade of a new Cairo on the western edge of the city would have to suffice. Visitors could be kept to planned itineraries that would show them only the new vigorous Cairo, comparable to their own capitals. The utmost haste was required, however, if this enormous task was to be completed before the planned opening of the Suez Canal. Progress on the latter was rapid after the Porte finally ratified the agreement in 1866, and de Lesseps anticipated the completion of construction by the end of 1868. As it was, however, delays granted Ismā'īl a slight reprieve, and the opening date was postponed to November 1869.

The two intervening years were marked by an almost frantic pace of municipal improvement.[32] Two months after Ismā'īl's return from abroad he shuffled his ministries and appointed 'Ali Pasha Mubārak as Minister of Public Works. He commissioned him with the gargantuan responsibility of (1) supervising the execution of plans for the quarter of Ismā'īlīyah; (2) redeveloping the older and vacant lands peripheral to Azbakīyah; and (3) drawing up a master plan for the entire city in accordance with the style of Paris.

He had chosen a remarkable man for the job. Born of humble origins in a Delta village, 'Ali Mubārak had been one of the very few native Egyptians included in Muḥammad 'Ali's educational missions to Europe. Between 1844 and 1849 he had studied military and civil

[32] The modern reader, familiar with fiscal controls, vested property interests, and legislative bottlenecks which impede urban improvements, may find it difficult to accept the fact that the whim of any ruler could play so crucial a role in altering a city. Yet this was the last era of royal prerogatives, when the will of the sovereign was supreme. His personal purse was the entire wealth of the country, and his powers included the right to mortgage the future tax revenues of the state even for personally incurred debts.

engineering in France but had been recalled when 'Abbās suspended these activities. Under Ismā'īl he had served first as a member of the Privy Council engaged in Cairo development and later as director of the Qanāṭir Barrage and chief of the engineering subsection of the newly constituted Ministry of Public Works. In 1867 he was sent to Paris on a brief mission to study (with enviable virtuosity!) both the educational and sewerage systems of that city. His appointment as Minister of Public Works, and concurrently as Minister of the *Awqāf* as well, therefore, was hardly illogical. He continued to occupy the former position with only brief interruptions during most of his later career. Periodically he served also as Minister of Education and, in addition, found time to write books on military engineering, educational theory, and the work for which he is deservedly most famous, his twenty-volume *Al-Khiṭaṭ al-Tawfīqīyah al-Jadīdah*, sections of which are devoted to an historical and topographic description of Cairo.[33]

'Ali Mubārak tells us that the planning of Ismā'īlīyah took place at the same time plans were made to subdivide the two triangular plots remaining once the smaller rectangle of Azbakīyah Gardens was demarcated and fenced. After these plans had been drawn up, Ismā'īl issued a further order to replan the remainder of the city according to the same principles.[34] Both of these events appear to have occurred in 1867 but, because the first set of improvements involved new or raw land whereas the latter required land acquisition and demolition of existing structures before plans could be executed, it was natural that progress should have been faster on the former. By the grand opening of the Suez Canal, considerable headway had been made in developing the new sections; the plans to redevelop the older city were never fully executed, and it was many years before even those few parts of the plan that were executed showed any results.

Even before Ismā'īl's trip to Paris he had evidently conceived the idea of a new city addition to be built in the area bounded on the north by the road to Būlāq, on the west by the main road to Miṣr al-Qadīmah (today Shāri' al-Qaṣr al-'Ayni), on the south by the lands of al-Lūq, and on the east by the built-up edge of Cairo. While an attempt *may* have been made to encourage settlement in the area known as Ismā'īlīyah as early as 1865, the area remained unimproved by streets and unserved by utilities until its intensive planning and development after 1867. Before 1869, wide streets flanked by sidewalks had been laid out according to plan, and the district, about one square mile in area, was subdivided. The Khedive offered the royal lands without charge to those princes and wealthy merchants agreeing to build substantial villas surrounded by gardens.[35] Although public improvements were in place by the opening of the Canal, the actual settling of the section proceeded much more gradually, and for many years it retained the appearance of a premature subdivision rather than a substantial community. An observer in the winter of 1870-1871 described its still unfinished state, noting that ". . . the Viceroy has here, for the space of about a square mile, laid out broad macadamized streets with broad trottoirs on each side, *as if he were contemplating an European city*, [but] . . . not much, however, with the exception of these roadways, has yet been done towards carrying out his grand designs, except around the Ezbekiah."[36]

[33] We are fortunate to be able to rely heavily on this firsthand source of data on developments in Cairo under Ismā'īl. Much of the preceding information about 'Ali Mubārak has been taken from his autobiography, included in *Al-Khiṭaṭ*, IX, 52-53. Details of his career were also traced in scattered references contained in the archival documents reproduced in Amīn Sāmi, *Taqwīm al-Nīl*, Volume III, Part II.

[34] For the orders relevant to the former, see Mubārak, *Al-Khiṭaṭ*, III, 67, 119. Concerning the replanning of the old city, see his I, 83, and IX, 53.

[35] Many versions of the founding of Ismā'īlīyah are extant in the literature. According to the 1885 edition of Baedecker, "the new town of Ismailia was begun about the year 1865, when the Khedive presented sites there gratuitously to anyone who would undertake to erect on each a house worth at least 30,000 francs within eighteen months." See *Guide to Egypt*, p. 259. Clerget, who unfortunately fails to cite his sources here, seems to accept this version, noting merely that the land was unoccupied until 1865, after which "Ismail Pasha gave gratuitously land to anyone willing to construct there a dwelling worth at least 2,000 Egyptian Pounds." See *Le Caire*, I, 198 (my translation). The version of 'Ali Mubārak (which I accept as authentic) is at variance with both these secondary sources. 'Ali Mubārak states categorically that the offer of free land was made *after* the area had been improved. See *Al-Khiṭaṭ*, IX, 53. We know that streets had not yet been laid out in the Ismā'īlīyah quarter by 1867, both from the testimony of 'Ali Mubārak and from the graphic evidence of a map of Cairo prepared by the Ministry of Public Works to facilitate its planning. This map, which is evidently the one reproduced in Clerget and dated 1868 (see *Le Caire*, I, insert before p. 193), shows no streets for the Ismā'īlīyah quarter and no subdivision of the vacant triangles adjacent to the Azbakīyah. It was obviously made at the end of 1867 or the beginning of 1868, since it shows the Ismā'īlīyah Canal (opened in 1866) and the rectangular enclosure of Azbakīyah Gardens (made in 1867). Therefore, to date the founding of Ismā'īlīyah as early as 1865 is to anticipate it prematurely.

[36] See F. Barham Zincke, Vicar of Wherstead, *Egypt of the Pharaohs and of the Khedive* (Smith, Elder and Company, London: 1871), p. 405. Italics added. This book covers the author's trip to Egypt made in the winter of 1870-1871 and makes it possible to establish the exact date of his observations. A map dated 1872 (but undoubtedly later, because it shows Boulevard Muḥammad 'Ali, not constructed until 1873-1875) and serving as an annex to a *Guide annuaire d'Égypte* by François-Levernay, which I had occasion to examine and transcribe in Cairo, shows graphically the limited extent of the buildings in

Streets and utilities could be and were created by royal edict, but private demand could not be manufactured by decree. By the end of the Ismā'īl period there were only some 200 houses and palaces in the entire "western" zone from Shubra down through Ismā'īlīyah.[37] The street plans for the new areas, however, provided a framework which remained relatively unchanged throughout the later period of intensive settlement. The British built their colonial city within the lines of the French-styled town begun by Ismā'īl, lines which are still easily detected on a map of the contemporary city.

It was in the vicinity of Azbakīyah, however, that the most obvious changes were made during the busy period between 1867 and 1869. Within the small triangular patch north of the gardens new hard-surfaced streets were laid out and the remaining land subdivided for apartment houses. Roads supplanted the Qanṭarat al-Dikkah (between Bāb al-Ḥadīd and the Azbakīyah) and the old bed of the circular canal which passed north and east of the new gardens. A bold new thoroughfare (Shāri' 'Abdul-Azīz, after the Ottoman Sultan) set out from al-'Atabah al-Khaḍrā' at the southeast corner of Azbakīyah and followed a diagonal course to the square and palace of 'Abdīn to its southwest. The entire triangle cut off by this diagonal was replanned. To the north of it had been vacant land once submerged as part of the *birkah*. Along the irregular border of the former pond had been a number of large but shabby palaces in varying stages of deterioration. These palaces and adjacent structures were demolished to make way for the thoroughfares[38] and for the many public buildings planned for the triangle. In this section were placed the National Théâtre de Comédie inaugurated in January 1868; the elaborate rococco opera house, erected within the short span of five months and completed barely in time for the première performance during the November canal celebrations;[39] and other public edifices built in the European style. The remaining structures in the vicinity of the Azbakīyah were whitewashed and renovated; gaslights were installed along all adjacent streets; Shāri' Mūski was "upgraded" and Europeanized on the extremity closest to the Azbakīyah; and even the minarets of the nearby mosques were given gaily painted red and white stripes for the occasion.

64. The Cairo Opera House *ca.* 1946

The central park of Azbakīyah, however, still remained in only partially finished form. Its preliminary design of a large circle at the core and straight radiating spokes was, to say the least, somewhat unimaginative. In a bold move, Ismā'īl imported the French landscape architect whose work he had admired in the Bois de Boulogne and Champ de Mars and commissioned him to redesign Azbakīyah as a Parc Monceau, complete with the free-form pool, grotto, bridges, and belvederes which constituted the inevitable clichés of a nineteenth-century French garden. Thanks to the fast growing season of Egypt, shrubs and flowers were already blooming when the guests arrived in November.[40]

The need to prepare the city for the coming celebra-

the new quarter. Numerous structures, including the "New Hotel," occupy the eastern border of the Azbakīyah as well as the small triangular patches north of the central *maydān* (Falaki) of Bāb al-Lūq and both north and south of the Azbakīyah. In contrast, except for a few preexisting palaces, the entire new quarter to the south is absolutely vacant. A slightly later description of the "modern bricklayer's paradise," Ismā'īl's city, is found in Colonel Wilson, *Picturesque Palestine, Sinai and Egypt* (D. Appleton Company, New York: 1883), Division 4 dealing with Cairo. See especially p. 374.

[37] Mubārak, *Al-Khiṭaṭ*, I, 85. The estimate includes the section of al-Fajjālah.

[38] The Khedivial order to acquire this land was issued just before Ismā'īl's second trip to Paris in 1869, which he made for the purpose of extending personal invitations to the opening of the Suez Canal. See Amīn Sāmi, *Taqwīm al-Nīl*, Volume III, Part II, p. 87.

[39] The opening performance, *Rigoletto*, was given for the Empress Eugenie and others on November 1, 1869. Ismā'īl commissioned Verdi to write an opera on an Egyptian theme, and two years later *Aida* was performed at the Cairo Opera House. The Opera House still stands, anachronistically, in its currently not too fashionable district, but there have been rumors of its planned demolition.

[40] For a description of the completed Azbakīyah, see on the complimentary side, H. de Vaujany, *Description de l'Egypte: Le Caire et ses environs* (E. Plon et Cie., Paris: 1883), pp. 129-130. Less enthusiasm was shown in the acid comments of Rhoné presented later in this chapter.

65. Ismā'īl's palace on al-Jazīrah, converted into a hotel after his bankruptcy. Now the 'Umar Khayyām Hotel

66. Tourists lounge in the 'Umar Khayyām Hotel today

tions also provided the impetus for changes on the Jazīrah and on the western bank of the Nile. As early as 1863 Ismā'īl had engaged the services of a German architect to design his palace on the Jazīrah, but construction had been halfhearted and intermittent. Now the palace was required as a temporary residence for Ismā'īl's most distinguished visitor, the Empress Eugenie herself, and it was completed with dispatch by 1868. Within, the palace was fitted with all the latest luxuries Paris could provide; without, Barillet-Deschamps began his ambitious scheme to cover almost the entire island with a formal park, incorporating the existing palace and kiosk of Muḥammad 'Ali into the new gardens of Ismā'īl's palace.

Across the river from Cairo another problem pressed for expeditious solution. Access from Jīzah to the pyramids was still negotiated during the "wet" season over a circuitous series of dikes via uncomfortable donkeys. Certainly the royal guests could not be expected to bear such indignity, even for a view of one of the world's wonders. Within a matter of months a wide and elevated causeway suitable for carriages was constructed which led directly to the base of the largest pyramid. Barillet-Deschamps was assigned the task of transplanting shade trees to line it and, when the visitors arrived, they were escorted out in style, as if there had never been any other way to reach the pyramids.[41]

These developments on the Jazīrah and the western bank, plus the construction of another Khedivial palace at Jīzah and the location there of the terminus of the new rail line serving Upper Egypt, all contributed to a growing need for a bridge to connect the two banks of the Nile. Ferries and small wind-propelled craft were the only means for crossing from one side to the other, a fact which intensified the contrast between the rural western shore and the urban eastern bank. It was perhaps natural that the idea of a bridge should suggest itself at this time.

In the spring of 1869, just before setting out again for Europe, Ismā'īl contracted the French firm of Fives-Lille to construct a massive iron swing-bridge between the eastern shore at Qaṣr al-Nīl and the southern tip of the Jazīrah, a span of over 400 meters. A smaller span across the Blind Nile (the Kubri al-Jalā') was also planned at this time to complete the connection with the western shore. Neither of these bridges, however, could be completed in time for the opening of the Canal and the temporary expediency of a floating boat-bridge was resorted to in order to give the Empress Eugenie access to her apartments on the Jazīrah. By 1871, the smaller bridge over the Blind Nile was completed and, in the following year, the finished swing-bridge was demonstrated before an incredulous audience.[42] The knitting

[41] One visitor who recorded her experiences was the Honorable Mrs. William Grey, in her *Journal of a Visit to Egypt, Constantinople, the Crimea, Greece, etc. in the Suite of the Prince and Princess of Wales* (Harper and Bros., New York: 1870). Included in her account of the trip made by the Prince and Princess was the following concerning their visit to the pyramids on March 15, 1869. "Off we drove over a rather rough road, which has only lately been made to the Pyramids. . . . Our road led through a most beautiful acacia avenue almost all the way. . . ." Quoted from p. 518.

[42] For information on the palace at Jīzah and the extensive gardens designed by Barillet-Deschamps, see Mubārak, *Al-Khiṭaṭ*, I, 84. The railway between Jīzah and Imbābah and the Upper Egyptian terminus at al-Minyah was begun in 1865 but was not

together of the two sides of the river was thus begun. For many decades these bridges constituted the sole link between east and west. Not until the twentieth century were they supplemented by a series of additional connections which finally and forever joined both shores, permitting the development of a single metropolis spanning the river.

It was not only the new areas that received attention in these busy years, however. In accordance with Ismā'īl's request, a master plan for the entire existing city was drawn up with incredible speed by 'Ali Mubārak's subordinate in the Ministry of Public Works, Maḥmūd Falaki. It was a plan that would have elicited Haussmann's most enthusiastic support, although it evoked a reverse response from the contemporary French architect, Rhoné, who romanticized medieval Cairo and deplored its mechanical modernization.[43]

67. First Qaṣr al-Nīl Bridge to al-Jazīrah

68. Second Qaṣr al-Nīl Bridge

69. Cloverleaf with underpass: present approach to the Qaṣr al-Nīl Bridge

completed until several years later. See Amīn Sāmi, *Taqwīm al-Nīl*, Volume III, Part II, p. 632, and Wilkinson, *A Handbook for Travellers in Egypt* (1867 edn. with addendum to 1869), pp. 2, 7. A rail bridge to connect the Delta Line terminating at Bāb al-Ḥadīd with the Upper Egyptian line terminating on the west bank was not constructed until the twentieth century. For information on the first Qaṣr al-Nīl Bridge, see Amīn Sāmi, *op.cit.*, Volume III, Part II, p. 815 for contract and p. 919 for demonstration of opening.

[43] One of the most acid critiques ever leveled against any master plan was that of Arthur Rhoné concerning Cairo's. He recalled the early days of Ismā'īl when "the Viceroy and his ministers spoke then with glowing enthusiasm of the rebirth of

The plan advocated a direct attack upon what was becoming Cairo's most pressing problem—traffic. Carriages were multiplying at an "alarming" rate, while there remained only a few streets wide enough to admit one, much less two vehicles abreast. It will be recalled that in 1823 Cairo had but one carriage, the Pasha's. By 1840, while ownership remained a royal prerogative, there were some thirty to forty carriages at large in the city. By the time of Ismā'īl, however, the monopoly had been broken, with carriages available for hire and private ownership extending to the merchant as well as to the lower echelons of the ruling class. Mubārak's census of vehicles about 1875 enumerated almost 900 passenger carriages and twice that number of transport carts.[44]

Clearly there was a need to "break into" the medieval city. Muḥammad 'Ali had already begun this process by opening the first section of the Rue Neuve (al-Sikkah al-Jadīdah). Ismā'īl continued the efforts of his predecessors and finally extended that road all the way to the edge of the eastern desert. Now the master plan contemplated a network of supplementary latitudinal and longitudinal thoroughfares as well as numerous connecting diagonals.

Map XIII that follows shows my reconstruction of the *maydāns* (open spaces) and the thoroughfares projected in the master plan for the old city.[45] These were to be superimposed on the maze-like pattern of the preindustrial city. The motif was everywhere the same. At the core of the system were the open spaces out of which were to radiate wide straight streets cutting through the old *ḥārāt* like the boulevards of Haussmann's Paris. Among the *maydāns* anticipated by the plan were those of (1) al-'Atabah al-Khaḍrā', (2) 'Abdīn, (3) Khāzindār, (4) Bāb al-Ḥadīd, (5) Sayīdah Zaynab, (6) Bāb al-Lūq, (7) Bāb al-Futūḥ, (8) Muḥammad 'Ali, (9) Sultan Ḥasan, (10) Qaṣr al-Nīl, (11) Theatro or Opera, (12) Birkat al-Fīl, (13) al-Azhar (not near the mosque of that name but in Bāb al-Lūq). Each of these was in turn to be connected with others, a plan which, had it been carried out, would have given to Cairo the pattern shown in broken lines on the map.

But this was not meant to be. It was quite possible to impose this system on the *tabula rasa* of the new quarters. Thus, most of the streets and squares projected for the western section of the city were built according to plan, including the *maydāns* of Kūbri Qaṣr al-Nīl, Bāb al-Lūq, al-Azhar (now Falaki Square), 'Abdīn (fortuitously open, thanks to a preexisting *birkah*) and their connecting streets. The three *maydāns* bordering the Azbakīyah Gardens—Khāzindār, Opera, and al-'Atabah al-Khaḍrā' —were also completed with little difficulty, since they were located on essentially vacant land. But in the older areas the need to survey properties, to settle on compensation, to acquire the plots and demolish the existing structures made the process lengthy, expensive, and uncertain. While a small beginning was made in the early 1870's to actualize the plan for the existing quarters, the difficulties proved overwhelming and, of the ambitious program, only two *maydāns* and two thoroughfares saw fruition. The *maydāns* were those of Bāb al-Ḥadīd (which required no clearance) and Muḥammad 'Ali (which required only peripheral land acquisition since it was located on the site of the old Qaramaydān). The two thoroughfares, Shāri' Clot-Bey connecting Bāb al-Ḥadīd with Maydān Khāzindār, and its continuation, the Boulevard Muḥammad 'Ali, between Maydān al-'Atabah al-Khaḍrā' and the yet-unfinished *maydān* beyond the Mosque of Sultan Ḥasan at the foot of the Citadel, were not undertaken seriously until 1873 and were not completed until two years later. Despite this overall failure of Ismā'īl's master plan, the scheme continued to exert a lasting influence on later attempts to open up the old city, and a number of projected streets and *maydāns* were eventually constructed almost as Falaki had designed them.

This tremendous flurry of municipal planning and

Cairo according to the expeditious methods of Paris. They displayed with pride their plans for new quarters laid out in checkerboards, and for bold new thoroughfares that could evoke in one only a shudder. In all directions, the ancient city of the caliphs and sultans was criss-crossed by straight and endless incisions which formed patterns like those emblazoned on coats of arms . . . [as if they were planning] the eruption of an American city in the heart of a virgin forest." See Arthur Rhoné, *Coup d'oeil sur l'état du Caire, ancien et moderne*, extracted and reprinted from the November 1881, and February 1882, issues of *La Gazette des Beaux Arts* (A. Quantin, Paris: 1882). The quotation is my translation of an excerpt from p. 1.

[44] In his edition of 1867, Wilkinson remarks sarcastically on the outmoded style of many of these vehicles. "Many of the private carriages are curiosities. They might be supposed to have come from some European museum, which had preserved them unchanged for a century or two, and had taken advantage of the new want in Cairo, and of the inexperience of the purchasers, to sell off all of the duplicates that could be spared." *A Handbook for Travellers in Egypt*, p. 113. Mubārak, *Al-Khiṭaṭ*, I, 103, lists 174 carts for water; 1,675 carts for goods, 400 privately owned passenger carriages and 486 passenger carriages for hire.

[45] This map of Cairo at the end of Ismā'īl's reign shows the new quarters of Ismā'īlīyah (west and south of the Gardens of Azbakīyah) and al-Fajjālah (north of al-Maqs, east of the train station and south of the Ismā'īlīyah Canal), the replanned triangles north and south of Azbakīyah, as well as the area covered by the medieval city of Cairo. My reconstruction of the partially executed master plan is shown in broken lines and the *maydāns* listed above have been located by their corresponding numbers. Actually no map of the master plan has survived. This tentative reconstruction is based on the verbal descriptions given by Mubārak. See his *Al-Khiṭaṭ*, I, 83; III, 63, 67-68, 82-83, 118-120ff.; IX, 53.

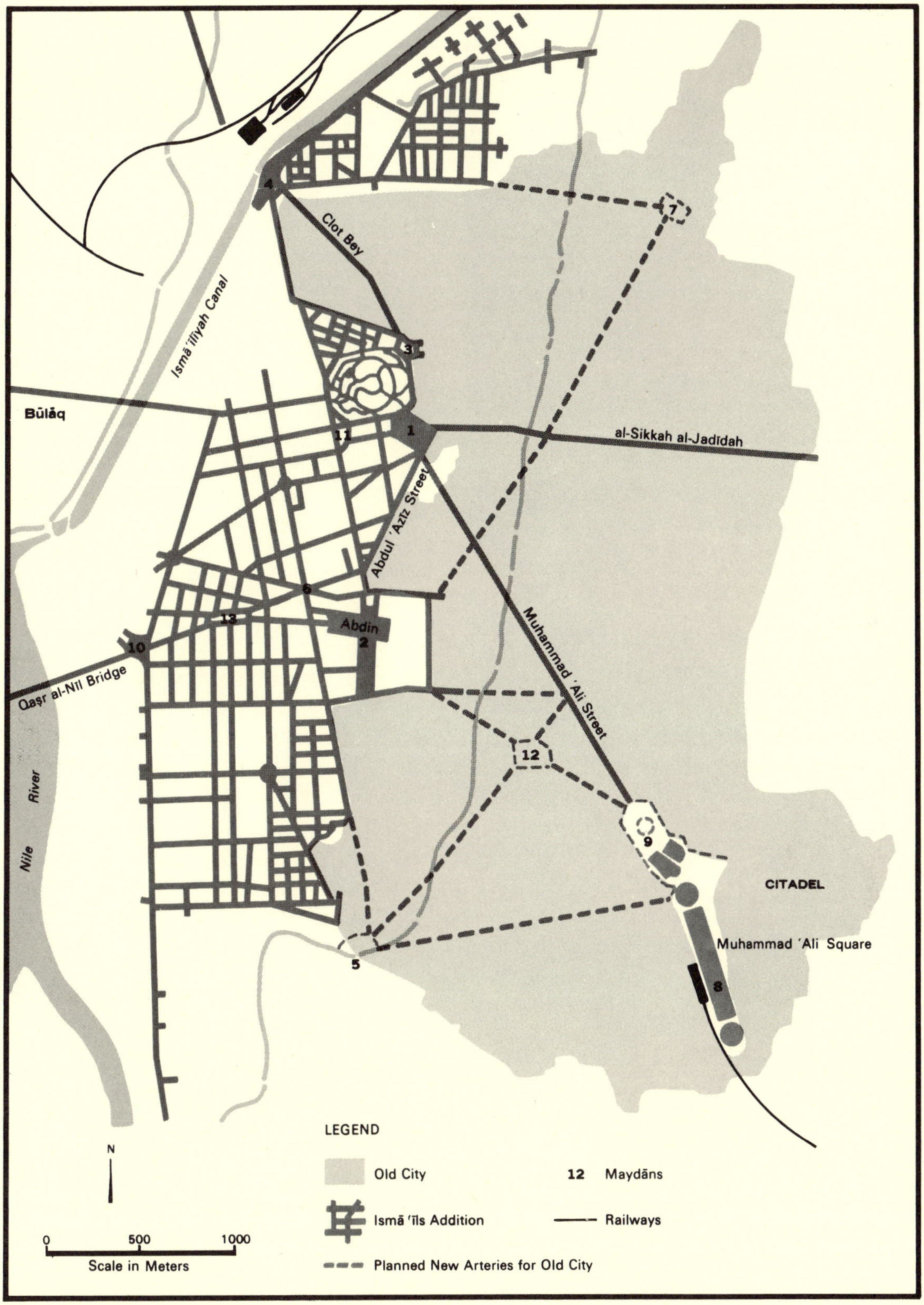

XIII. The city developments added by Ismā'īl, 1869-1870

70. The Orman Gardens of Barillet-Deschamps

71. The Jīzah campus of Cairo University

city building culminated in the fall of 1869 with the festivities which attended the dramatic opening of the Suez Canal on the 17th of November. From October through December, Cairo, Alexandria, Upper Egypt, and the new Canal town of Ismā'īlīyah were thronged with European visitors. Not only royalty but journalists (including Théophile Gautier), physicians, savants and archaeologists, government officials, and military officers filled the streets, consumed the banquets, clambered up the pyramids, and in general enjoyed the planned and unplanned spectacles before them. In reading Western accounts of the fêtes, one senses that guests and host operated somewhat at cross purposes. Ismā'īl did his best to create a European image of himself and his country; the Europeans wanted only the exotic. Gautier glanced distractedly past the Parc Monceau bordering his veranda at Shepheard's Hotel, seeking the world of the *Arabian Nights*. The guests at Ismā'īl's grand reception at the Qaṣr al-Nīl Palace were treated to a chamber concert and a performance of the Comédie Française; they had looked forward to an evening with Scheherazade. Despite this minor communication failure, the celebration went off successfully. There is no doubt that these months marked the apogée of Ismā'īl's career.

The climax came, then went. It was perhaps natural that it was followed by a relaxation of the tension that had driven Cairo's improvement at such a frantic pace. 'Ali Mubārak, who complained that for two years he had not enjoyed a full night's sleep, was eased out of office (although he was reappointed again in 1872). The master plan was filed away. The works already undertaken were to be completed but at a more leisurely pace. Barillet-Deschamps alone seems to have continued as before, embellishing his gardens, methodically planting street trees, and designing his *magnum opus*, a park five and a half miles long and three miles wide covering the entire western bank of the Nile from Imbābah to Jīzah, a work which was destined to remain incomplete when he died in 1874.[46]

There were still other reasons for a retrenchment in the program of public improvements. Difficulties with the Porte and a new program of judicial reform were absorbing more and more of Egypt's attention. Financial insolvency was increasing. Time had begun to run out for Ismā'īl.

One final effort seems to have been made in Cairo between 1873 and 1875 to return to the enthusiastic plans of former years. The subdividing of the Fajjālah section probably was begun then, stimulated perhaps by the construction of Shāri' Clot-Bey which gave the quarter bordering the Ismā'īlīyah Canal direct access to the business district of al-Mūski. By then, 'Ali Mubārak was again Minister of Public Works or, what was functionally the same, advisor to Prince Ḥalīm who was its honorary chief. Under him, plans were again advanced to construct the Boulevard Muḥammad 'Ali, by far the most ambitious of the replanning projects. 'Ali Mubārak tells us that to make room for the 2-kilometer-long street almost 400 large houses, over 300 smaller dwellings, plus mills, bakeries, baths, and not a few mosques had to be demolished.[47] While the street's course may not have been as capricious as Rhoné's sarcastic description,[48] its toll in

[46] See Baedecker's 1885 edition of the *Guide to Egypt*, pp. 76, 329. This park formed the nucleus for the present Zoological Gardens and the Jīzah campus of Cairo University.

[47] Mubārak, *Al-Khiṭaṭ*, III, 69.

[48] Rhoné caustically described it as follows: "Like a shot, one fine day it [the Boulevard] took off from the garden of Ezbekiah,

priceless mosques and monuments was so high that many wish its arrow-straight path had been deflected here and there to spare some of the most precious. Nevertheless, once the final plans were drawn in 1873, the remaining plots of land were speedily acquired and construction began. The street was considerably wider than al-Sikkah al-Jadīdah and, unlike that prototype, was provided with wide sidewalks, shaded in part by trees and in other sections by the arcades of buildings that were swiftly built to line it. Gaslights were installed along the entire length of the road which, being the pride and joy of the monarch, was compulsively swept thrice daily to keep it immaculate. The dream of Muḥammad 'Ali was thus finally realized.

One last project was also completed about this time. Ismā'īl replaced the old palace at 'Abdīn with an enormous horseshoe shaped structure which he considered to be in the "best" European style, a project finished in 1874. It is perhaps ironic that events which helped to precipitate the downfall of independent Khedivial power were soon to take place outside this structure which represented one of Ismā'īl's last contributions to the city. The two were not unrelated.

The building of the canals, railroads, telegraphs, etc., the creation of a Western-type city with all the "symbols" of culture, the lavish entertainments and luxurious palaces, plus the heavy tributes exacted by Constantinople in return for each new concession of autonomy[49] had all raised the expenditures of the Egyptian government to unprecedented high levels. At this very time, reforms such as the return of much royal land to private ownership, the failure of the state monopolies, and the cracking down on the illicit slave traffic were all serving to decrease, relatively, the resources of the state. The expanding gap between revenues and expenditures was being methodically filled by loans from the financial houses of Europe, a process that led to mortgaging not only future revenues but even Egypt's share in the profits of the Canal, the initial cause of much of her borrowing. The first loan had been negotiated one year before Ismā'īl took office. In 1862 Sa'īd had borrowed over 3 million pounds, primarily to help finance the Canal. Ismā'īl simply continued this precedent, contracting substantial debts in 1864, 1865, 1867, 1868, and in following years with disquieting regularity.

Financial difficulties approached a crisis in 1875 as creditors became more insistent. Having little else left to pawn, Ismā'īl considered borrowing on Egypt's shares in the Canal itself. Knowledge of his negotiations with a French firm came to the attention of Disraeli, then Prime Minister of Victoria's England, who pulled off what must be considered one of the most fantastic financial *coups* of history. Prior to Cabinet approval, he purchased *all* of Egypt's shares in the Suez Canal with only 4 million pounds of Rothschild's money. The results of this bargain were to be even more far-reaching than Disraeli could have predicted, for they led to England's immediate involvement in the financial management of Egypt and, some seven years later, to her actual military occupation and governing of the country.

The camel's nose was already within the tent in 1876 when Mr. Stephen Cave, selected by the British government as "financial adviser" to the Khedive, recommended the consolidation of all Egypt's debts—which by then amounted to some 91 million pounds—and the appointment of a commission of financial control. This commission was soon replaced by the Dual Control, with a British official supervising revenues and a French representative auditing expenditures. In 1878 this system was relinquished in favor of a basic reorganization of the Egyptian government. Ismā'īl was demoted to constitutional monarch and real power was given to the cabinet which included an English Minister of Finance and a French Minister of Public Works. This Alice-in-Wonderland situation proved too much for the Khedive who made a last feeble effort to evict the camel, but it was already too late. He dismissed his ministers in April of 1879 and in June he was in turn deposed by the Sultan in response to English and French pressure. The tent belonged to the camel.

Thus ended rather ignobly the Age of Ismā'īl. In twelve years he had altered the face of Cairo; within sixteen he had lost his country. His son, Tawfīq, inherited his hollow throne, his public debt amounting by then to almost 100 million pounds, and inherited the virtual management of Egypt by a revived Dual Control, the English member of which was Evelyn Baring (later elevated to the title Lord Cromer) who in a few years became the British agent and Consul General, and virtual ruler during the occupation. He also inherited a country on the verge of revolution. A revolt in the army, led by ex-peasant Colonel 'Urābi, began in 1879 with riots around the 'Abdīn Palace and culminated on September 13, 1882, with 'Urābi's defeat at Tal al-Kabīr by English forces under General Wolseley. A few days later British troops entered Cairo.[50]

without knowing where it was going, and landed some two kilometers away, at a formidable angle from the Sultan Hassan Mosque, which it could not avoid encountering." My translation from A. Rhoné, *Coup d'oeil*, p. 23.

[49] The last of these concessions, purchased at a high price, was the *Firman* of 1873 which made the hereditary line of succession pass from the Khedive to his oldest son and so on. Before this, succession had been to the oldest male of the Muḥammad 'Ali line.

[50] The complex and still-beclouded events transpiring between 1879 and 1882 cannot be treated here. This brief summary of

Thus began a new phase of Cairo's history, a phase marked by the final evolution of a self-contained colonial city on the west, by a total revolution in the technology of transportation, and by the development of an Egyptian middle-class city on the north. During the next decades, barrages, canals, and the dam at Aswān (first completed in 1902) helped to reorganize Egyptian agriculture, creating an agricultural surplus which permitted Cairo's population to grow faster than the country as a whole. During the ensuing decades mass transit and then the automobile made their appearances, permitting the physical expansion of the city along the newly created axes of transportation. The next decades also saw an intensification of nationalist sentiment and ideology which led eventually to Egypt's independence.

These momentous events were sluggish in starting, however, and few of their results became apparent until the terminal years of the nineteenth century. The first decade of British occupation witnessed no drastic alterations in the development of the metropolis but merely a continuation of the trends that had already been set in motion during the later years of Ismā'īl's reign. Whether stagnation was due to the fact that power was concentrated in the hands of a foreign group that viewed its responsibilities as "temporary" and "custodial" rather than developmental, or whether it was an inevitable retrenchment after insolvency (the years between 1883 and 1888 were characterized accurately as a "race against bankruptcy") is, for our purposes, irrelevant.

When Britain stumbled into the affairs of Egypt in 1882 her initial reaction was to feel martyr to French interests and to hope for a speedy withdrawal. Throughout the first decade her official documents always refer to the temporary nature of the occupation and reiterate her intent to evacuate as soon as order and self-rule were restored. Beneath these protestations—which seemed to have grown more vociferous as Britain became more firmly entrenched—there was an increasing reconciliation to her role, aided not a little by her realization that Egypt offered richer booty than insolvency had hinted and by her increasing dependence upon the Suez Canal for her Indian traffic. These "forced" her to tighten her hold over Egypt even as she paid elaborate lip service to evacuation.[51]

The situation was anomalous. Officially, Egypt remained a member of the Ottoman empire subject to the ultimate authority of the Porte; at her helm she had Khedive Tawfīq (1879-1892), son and successor to the exiled Ismā'īl. In reality, however, decisions were made by the British Consul General (Lord Cromer between 1883 and 1907), often subject to the approval of as many as fifteen other European powers. Theoretically, a parliamentary government with ministries staffed by Egyptians administered the country, but Cromer's slogan of "English brains and Egyptian hands" was perhaps a truer reflection of reality. Neither the attempts to set up local government (embodied in the Organic Law of 1883) nor the efforts to deal one by one with the specific abuses of the Capitulations[52] seem to have altered the basic untenability of the arrangement.

British efforts during the first tentative years of occupation were directed toward agricultural reorganization, chiefly of cotton cultivation. One of the first public schemes undertaken was the reactivation of the barrage at Qanāṭir which, since its inception under Muḥammad 'Ali in the 1830's, had proved a disappointing failure.[53] Twice commenced under that ruler, it remained incomplete until Ismā'īl oversaw its final stages. But poor design and materials resulted in the appearance of serious breaches in the foundation when a full load was placed against the structure in 1863 and again in 1867. Since that time it had stood sentinel over the forking of the

very controversial material, gleaned primarily from the account in Hallberg, *The Suez Canal*, pp. 230-265, has been presented merely to indicate why few changes occurred in Cairo after 1875 and to prepare the reader for the new era which British occupation introduced in the development of Cairo. Controversies still rage as to the causes and significance of the 'Urābi rebellion. For our purposes, its significance was that it provided a convenient rationalization for British intervention.

[51] These conflicts in the British position are painfully obvious in the writings of the time. Among the sources are: The Earl of Cromer, *Modern Egypt*, in two volumes (The Macmillan Company, London: 1908); Sir Alfred Milner, *England in Egypt* (Edward Arnold, London: 7th edn., revised, 1899); Francis Adams, *The New Egypt* (T. Fisher Unwin, London: 1893); Lord Lloyd, *Egypt Since Cromer*, in two volumes (The Macmillan Company, London: 1933 and 1934); and, of course, the innumerable Government Blue Books on the Egyptian question (98 of which appeared in the first 3-year period following Tal al-Kabīr alone!). French-English conflicts of interest are treated in L. J. Ragatz, *The Question of Egypt in Anglo-French Relations, 1875-1904* (Pembroke, Edinburgh: 1922). Complete documentation now exists to support my contention that between 1888 and 1890 evacuation "hopes" were abandoned by even the most reluctant British occupiers. See the book by Robert Tignor, *Modernization and British Colonial Rule in Egypt, 1882-1914* (Princeton University Press, Princeton: 1966), especially pp. 88-93, 391-392.

[52] These were concessions granted by the Ottoman Porte to Europeans, including exemptions from various local laws and financial responsibilities. More will be said of them later.

[53] The purpose of a barrage, unlike a dam, is to maintain a relatively constant height for water downstream to permit year-round irrigation. For an early firsthand account of the barrage, see *Conversations and Journals . . . by Nassau William Senior*, various scattered notes. For later developments and an evaluation of this scheme, see Milner, *England in Egypt*, pp. 232-245; William Lawrence Balls, *Egypt of the Egyptians* (Charles Scribner's Sons, New York: 1916), pp. 150-151; and Tignor, *Modernization and British Colonial Rule in Egypt*, pp. 116-120.

river, mocking its builders' hopes to revise the system of Delta irrigation. Declared valueless in 1883, the barrage lay idle until a few years later when the newly appointed British Minister of Public Works, Sir Scott-Moncrieff, began the task of reconstruction. By 1891 the barrage was operating in the fashion first envisaged sixty years earlier, bringing perennial irrigation (and its by-products of soil depletion and *bilharzia*) to the Delta.

This and other irrigation projects helped to increase Egypt's agricultural productivity and expand the area under cultivation. Coupled with the establishment of elementary health and sanitation measures, this seems to have been responsible for the substantial population increase which Egypt experienced between 1882 and 1897. During that decade and a half, the number of inhabitants increased from about 6.8 million to over 9.7 million.[54]

Cairo shared in this population increase, growing from over 400,000 (my revised estimate) in 1882 to almost 600,000 by the end of the century. As before, her growth came not from natural increase but from migration, since deaths still outnumbered births in the capital, making it impossible for the city to maintain even a constant population without continuous replenishment from the countryside.[55] The demographic revolution that was to drive down urban death rates faster than rural ones had not yet occurred. Some of Cairo's increase resulted from foreign immigration, as Greeks came in search of commercial opportunities and Italians to man the machine shops and minor industries being established. French, Swiss, Swedish, Belgian, and English entrepreneurs and just plain adventurers were attracted by expanding opportunities which, thanks to the immunities granted them under the Capitulations, they were privileged to exploit. To these must be added British military and civilian personnel assigned to protect the country and help administer its government. Other minority groups, such as Armenians, Jews, and Syrian Christians, also grew in number as their power increased. But the bulk of the city's new population came, as before, from the rural hinterlands of Egypt.

Given the pressure of this substantial population increase, it was natural that Cairo expanded physically during this epoch. However, all expansions took place in those areas immediately adjacent to the built-up city, areas that had been blocked out for development under Ismā'īl but had failed to fill up for lack of population. The region just west of Azbakīyah Gardens experienced the most intensive development, with taller and more tightly spaced commercial, financial, and consular buildings supplementing the villas, small apartment houses, and gardens of the previous decades' growth. The major commercial zone had leaped from the Mūski just east of the Gardens to the vicinity of Maydān Opera on the western border; the older center of European commerce in the Mūski was given over more and more to Greek, Armenian, and Jewish merchants who provided cheap Western goods to the indigenous population.

To the south, the area of Ismā'īlīyah, which had been open subdivision land as late as 1870, was now converted to urban uses. Villas mushroomed in the southern half while higher density developments proliferated to the north, particularly in the neighborhood of the new commercial cores at Maydān Opera and along Shāri' Būlāq. Despite these changes, however, the area retained much of its suburban aspect, with buildings still interspersed by the gardens and agricultural plots which diminished in extent year by year.[56] It was at this time also that government buildings and ministry offices began to gravitate toward the linear strip east of and parallel to the Shāri' al-Qaṣr al-'Ayni south of Bāb al-Lūq. This land, originally the site of Ibrāhīm Pasha's plantations during the first half of the century, had been retained in royal ownership. As early as the time of Ismā'īl it contained the Ministry of Public Works; during the later period many additional ministries were grouped around it. These later nineteenth-century constructions formed the nucleus of the present governmental zone, known as al-Insha and Dawāwīn (pl. of *dīwān*). The concen-

[54] It is unlikely that the population growth was as great as these figures indicate. The 1882 Census is generally admitted to be inaccurate and an underestimate of true population. It is my considered judgment that the population was already in excess of 7 million at the early date. Even so, the increase is sizeable and neither the influx of foreigners (small, absolutely, although large relative to the past) nor the settling of the beduins can account for more than a fraction of the increment. Although reliable death rate statistics are unavailable for the period, it is an inescapable indirect conclusion that *some* net decrease in mortality must have occurred during these years, although such a decrease is certainly not apparent in the Cairo data. My best judgment on this is that the period was marked by a decline in the average mortality rate, achieved primarily through control over the "catastrophic" death rate, i.e., that sudden inflating of the "normal" rate due to periodic disasters such as floods, famines, and epidemics. These matters are dealt with in much greater detail in the chapter that follows.

[55] In the 1897 Census the population of Cairo is given as 570,000. The 1947 Census reestimates this at 589,000. A higher death rate in urban than in rural areas seems to be universally characteristic of the preindustrial and early industrial eras. In Cairo between 1882 and 1897 the average estimated CDR was about 46.6/1000/year, as contrasted with an average CBR of 45/1000/year. See Clerget, *Le Caire*, II, 24, and Chapter VIII, below.

[56] A discussion of these developments, including changes in land values in the newly developing sections of western Cairo at that time, may be found in Yacoub Artin Pasha, *Essai sur les causes du renchérissement de la vie matérielle au Caire dans le courant du XIXe siècle (1800 à 1907)*. See Tome V, Fasc. II, *Mémoires présentés à l'Institut Égyptien* (Imprimerie de l'Institut Français d'Archéologie Orientale, Cairo: 1907), pp. 111ff.

72. 'Abdīn Palace

tration of civil servants to staff these ministries led naturally to an increased demand for housing in the vicinity. Large white Victorian mansions, designed chiefly for the foreign "advisers," began to be constructed along the western edge of the governmental zone while, due east of the strip, new apartment houses were built for higher-ranking Egyptian officials. Darb al-Jamāmīz in the Sayīdah Zaynab section owed its upgrading to this new demand, and the Ḥilmīyah quarter (on the site of the former Birkat al-Fīl) was later developed in response to these same pressures.

Only along the shore of the Nile did former patterns of land use persist. These riverine lands were still not completely free of flood danger. In addition, the Khedivial family still held title to the palaces and royal gardens that stretched all the way from the Qaṣr al-Nīl barracks southward to the Qaṣr al-'Ayni Hospital. Farther south near the Fam al-Khalīj, the land formerly ceded to the Water Company and then abandoned was in disputed ownership, which precluded the possibility of its subdivision and sale. The expansion of the city into the riverfront strip, which is now the luxurious façade of the contemporary city, had to await the great speculative boom of the next century.

To the north of the existing city, parallel developments were taking place, particularly in the Fajjālah district, that triangular plot wedged in between the old Coptic quarter, just north of the Azbakīyah Gardens, and the diagonal course of the Ismā'īlīyah Canal. By 1880 this area had already been tentatively subdivided and, in the decade that followed, row apartment houses architecturally reminiscent of the Passy Quarter of Paris began to be constructed. This area provided a safety valve for the heavily overcrowded and obsolescent Coptic quarter. Wealthier Christian merchants joined the recently arrived European migrants there to create a new middle-class zone which, via the roads built by Ismā'īl (Shāri' Clot-Bey and Shāri' Nubar Pasha, formerly the Qanṭarat al-Dikkah), was directly connected to the newly evolved business district near Azbakīyah.

Only one large pocket of potential settlement within the circuit of the existing city remained completely unexploited until the 1880's. This was the broad triangular plot bounded on the south by Shāri' Būlāq, on the east by Shāri' Nubar Pasha (now Shāri' 26 Yūlyū and Shāri' Jumhūrīyah, respectively) and on the northwest by the Ismā'īlīyah Canal. This area had once been submerged beneath the main channel of the Nile before the river shifted its course. It still remained a deep depression in the terrain where swamps combined with the concentration of canals in the vicinity to make it an ideal breeding ground for mosquitoes. The neglected wasteland became more and more conspicuous as the city gradually encompassed it. The draining and leveling of this site and the filling in of the superfluous canals was undertaken by Khedive Tawfīq in the mid 1880's, thus creating the quarter known today as al-Tawfīqīyah, an integral part of the present central business district. When the land was finally subdivided and sold in 1889-1890, it found an eager market due to its proximity to the very heart of the new "western" city. Plots in the district brought prices well above those in the more peripheral zone of

Ismā'īlīyah, and it was not long before large blocks of apartment houses sprang up on land formerly vacant or occupied by destitute squatters.[57] Only a few isolated tracts of hovel-covered *waqf* land detracted from its opulent appearance.

Thus, up to 1896, the developments which took place in Cairo were entirely predictable within the framework of growth that had been established by Ismā'īl's planners. The promise and potential inherent in the city of Ismā'īl were being methodically fulfilled during the decade and a half that followed his exile, due to the pressures exerted by a steadily increasing population and to the changing demands of a still small but infinitely powerful foreign community. By the end of the nineteenth century Cairo's population was approaching 600,000, and the city had completed its physical and ecological mitosis into two distinct communities. The old native city had been left relatively intact from the premodern age, its abandoned areas reconstructed on the medieval pattern to house the thousands of rural migrants who had been drawn to the capital. A new European-style city had developed parallel to it on the west and had begun to encircle it on the north, but this community remained socially and physically distinct. Each city had a predictable continuity of its own.

This continuity was abruptly shattered just as the nineteenth century drew to a close. The cause was a total revolution in both the demand and supply elements of urban growth. The demographic revolution in the country finally reached Cairo, and, combined with an unprecedented trend toward urbanization, served to swell the demand for capital city residence. At the very same time, a revolution in the transport technology of the city (tramways) opened vast peripheral areas to urban settlement, creating, as it were, a new supply of land to meet the demand pressures of population. The combined impact of these changes stampeded into existence within the span of a single lifetime the vast attenuated metropolis known to us today.

[57] Clerget, *Le Caire*, I, 202.

8 The Exploding Demand for Capital City Residence

By 1957 Cairo contained within her boundaries at least as many persons as had inhabited *all of Egypt* when the French Expedition made its population estimate little more than a century and a half earlier. Within that relatively brief span of history, the Egyptian population had increased eightfold—from 3 to 24 million—while Cairo's population had become fully twelve times greater than it had been in 1800.

It is impossible to comprehend the explosion that occurred within the city of Cairo without recognizing that Egypt's demographic structure and her entire pattern of urbanization had been totally transformed within that critical century and a half. From an underpopulated country whose major barrier to economic development appeared to have been a shortage of labor,[1] Egypt became one of the world's most frequently cited examples of an overpopulated nation whose rapid rate of natural increase is considered by many as a serious obstacle to her industrialization and a rising standard of living. During the same span of time, Egypt was gradually transformed from an almost entirely agrarian country to one in which more than a third of the population lived in urban areas. Given the importance of Cairo in the national economy, it was not unnatural that she absorbed a substantial portion of this newly urbanizing population. She exploded from a compact rectangle, only 5 square miles in extent, housing a "mere" quarter of a million inhabitants to an immense metropolitan conurbation whose millions of inhabitants and over 75 square miles of area still do not totally comprehend the urbanized region of which she is the center.

This expansion was the result of a demographic revolution that began in the nineteenth century (and still has not fully run its course), compounded by a trend of urbanization that began early in the twentieth century. Before tracing Cairo's growth decade by decade in the present century, therefore, it is necessary to paint with rough brush strokes the broader background of national growth against which the Cairo foreground may be placed.

Although Egypt had experienced recurrent cycles of demographic growth and decline during her earlier history, it was not until the nineteenth century that her population began its first upswing in the contemporary cycle. The "revolution" that occurred in that century was essentially agricultural, rather than urban or industrial, and represented the regaining of a former position rather than a catapulting into a new or "modern" one. During the first half of the century the reactivation of the country's system of irrigation brought back into cultivation lands that had gradually been abandoned to desert encroachments during the preceding centuries of economic decadence. This expanding resource base, coupled with the restoration of law and order under the firm if somewhat oppressive hand of Muḥammad 'Ali, led to a larger carrying capacity of the country and to moderate population increase. Between 1798 and 1848 this amounted to perhaps 35 percent, bringing Egypt's population to over 4 million by midcentury.[2]

Cairo did not share proportionately in this population increase. Within the city itself, more residents died each year than were born to replace them, a situation common in preindustrial cities where, due to the absence of sanitation, recurring epidemics always took a higher toll among the vulnerable, densely packed urbanites than among the "healthier" farmers. On the other hand, the expanding opportunities on the land discouraged rural persons from seeking their fortunes in the city. Migration to the capital was barely sufficient to compensate for the annual deficit created by the excessive death rate and to add perhaps 20 percent to the city's population in the fifty-year period.

The agricultural revolution begun in the opening half of the century gained momentum during the terminal half and, with it, the pace of population growth quickened. Changes and expansions in the irrigation system, improved methods of cultivation and, not least, the introduction and extension of long staple cotton as a major crop, all contributed to the expanding economy. This agricultural revolution must be credited with permitting much of the population increase that occurred during this period, although by the final decade of the century a supplementary element had been added in the form of epidemic control. Between 1848 and 1897 the population of Egypt more than doubled, exceeding 9 million just before the turn of the century. It is significant to note

[1] At the time of Muḥammad 'Ali it was even suggested—although one cannot know with what degree of seriousness—that Chinese laborers be imported to help meet Egypt's military, agricultural, and industrial needs.

[2] At the end of 1846 Muḥammad 'Ali took the first census in the country. Very little is known about it, except that its dubious results were revised upward several times to placate the ruler who felt his prestige enhanced by a larger number of subjects. The final revision suggested a total population of almost 4.5 million, but this exceeds all other estimates made at the time. See p. 83 above. Chart 1 suggests that Muḥammad 'Ali's census erred in overestimating the population in that year.

that this population was roughly equivalent to the level that some scholars have estimated as a maximum during pharaonic and, later, medieval times. It appears to have been the saturation level of the country when the economy was based upon agriculture and when the exploitation of the natural irrigation powers of the Nile was at an efficient level. Only in the twentieth century, when the technological revolution of dams and barrages permitted the wide-scale conversion from basin to perennial irrigation, was this asymptotic ceiling exceeded.

This increase within fifty years is impressive and can be accounted for only partially by the settling of the beduins, which took place at this time, and by the immigration to Egypt from other parts of the Ottoman empire and from Europe. While the latter was substantial in comparison to the past, it was numerically insignificant in terms of total growth. Even in the absence of reliable vital statistics for the era, the conclusion is inescapable that the *increase was primarily the result of a rather marked decline in mortality rates* and, consequently, of a sharp increase in the rate of natural increase, since there was apparently no change in fertility.[3]

The declining death rate was experienced first in the rural sections of the country where dependence upon subsistence farming made numbers immediately responsive to the increasing food supply. In Cairo, where famine was a less effective killer than environmental and contagious diseases, the high death rate persisted. Throughout most of the nineteenth century, deaths continued to exceed births in the capital, since epidemic fatalities periodically and methodically wiped out any population gains achieved through the operation of uncontrolled fertility. During the five-year period between 1872 and 1877, for example, deaths in Cairo exceeded births by 3,301, although in the rural provinces of the country, the balance for the period was consistently in favor of an excess of births.[4] This deficit was still apparent even after an improvement in reporting. Thus, in a sample five-year interval between 1882 and 1887, the average CBR for Cairo was computed to be 44.8, while the average CDR during the same interval was 45.3.[5] Whatever growth the capital experienced was dependent *entirely* upon her capacity to attract a continuous stream of migrants from the rural areas, and even this attraction was insufficient to keep pace with the overall rate of population increase. Thus, while the country as a whole was swollen by an increment of 130 percent between 1847 and 1897, Cairo's population grew by only 90 percent. Although this was, in comparison to the country, a relatively "small" increase, in actuality it represented a rather sizeable addition to the city that more than justified the physical expansion of Cairo planned by Ismā'īl.

The twentieth century witnessed a total reversal of the demographic balance between city and countryside that had prevailed during the preceding century of growth. By the turn of the century, Cairo's growth rate had begun to catch up with the country as a whole. It soon pulled ahead, each year increasing its lead. For at least the last fifty years, Cairo has been growing faster than Egypt and has been absorbing a larger and larger proportion of the country's rapidly multiplying inhabitants. Between 1897 and 1947, when Egypt's total population doubled, the number of persons living in Cairo tripled to reach 2 million. That this trend has shown no signs of weaken-

[3] The only source this author has located which attempts to reconstruct the growth variables during the pre-British era of the nineteenth century is a publication of the Egyptian Ministry of the Interior, Bureau of Statistics, in 1879, entitled *Essai de statistique générale de l'Égypte, années 1873 . . . 1877* (Imprimerie de l'État-Major Général Égyptien, Cairo: 1879). Vital statistics used to derive the population estimates in this publication were provided by l'Intendence Générale Sanitaire. According to Table I on p. 6 of this report, between 1846 and 1877 deaths exceeded births in the country *only* during the years 1847, 1848, 1849, 1850, 1853, and 1854, i.e., in the very opening years of that era of growth. From 1855 onward, there was no year in which the total number of recorded deaths exceeded the total number of recorded births, although in 1865, due to a particularly virulent cholera outbreak, the excess was minimal. Not too much credence can be given to these figures in themselves, since many of the observed changes may be attributable to changes in the degree to which births and deaths were reported. Death reporting (except in the very youngest age groups) was probably fuller than birth reporting at the beginning of the period studied, since burial permits were required. *Op.cit.*, p. 7. Over the years, the reporting of births, although still far from complete, undoubtedly improved, as can be seen from the "order of magnitude" of the reported numbers: about 42,000 births per year ca. 1846-1847, 80,000 by 1850, and about 100,000 by 1851-1854. It jumps to 140,000 by 1855, to 160,000 ca. 1857-1858, and then steadies at 170,000-190,000 per year for the remainder of the period. According to the authors of this report, between 1846 and 1861 Egypt experienced an annual net increase of population of 0.44 percent per year (compounded), while, during the next period of 1861-1876, her annual growth rate was 0.92 percent per year. See explication on p. 18. Growth rates after 1876 were even higher.

[4] See Table II of *Essai de statistique générale*, pp. 8-9, which presents the results of the informal census of 1877 and birth and death records for the period of 1872-1877, for the country as a whole, the governorates (including Cairo) enumerated separately, and the individual provinces of Upper and Lower Egypt. It is possible to compute the annual crude death rate for Cairo in 1877 on the basis of information presented in this table, supplemented by detailed death figures for the city as presented in Table XI, p. 21. On the basis of this information, one estimates Cairo's CDR in that year at over 50/1000. As would be expected, deaths were particularly heavy in the youngest age groups. Of the 18,879 deaths reported in Cairo during the year 1877, 7,432 were children under one year of age, and almost half of all deaths occurred within the age group under three years.

[5] See Clerget, *Le Caire*, II, 24, which includes a table comparing vital statistics rates for Cairo and Egypt, from which my figures have been computed.

ing is evident from the most recent intercensal periods when Cairo grew almost twice as fast as the country (see Chart 1).

Table 1, which summarizes comparative growth rates for Egypt and Cairo since 1897, demonstrates this proposition beyond any question.

The spectacular growth of Cairo in the twentieth century—growth that has taken place within the lifetime of her oldest inhabitants—resulted not only from the general demographic "revolution" in the country but from what might be termed an "urbanization revolution." Cairo along with other urban centers throughout the country experienced the impact of a massive movement of population off the land and into the cities.[6] In 1897, less than 15 percent of the Egyptian population resided

[6] For reasons that will be presented in greater detail below, it would be false to assume that all, or even most, of this urbanization involved the physical displacement of persons, although actual migration did play an extremely important role, particularly in the growth of the very largest cities, such as Cairo, Alexandria, and the new towns that developed along the Suez Canal. First, the high rate of natural increase in the country and the pattern of dense settlement on limited land have tended to raise a number of former villages to the urban size class without a relocation of population or, indeed, an acculturation to "urban" ways or an urban economic base. Second, growth in even the largest cities is now coming increasingly from natural increase, as will be shown.

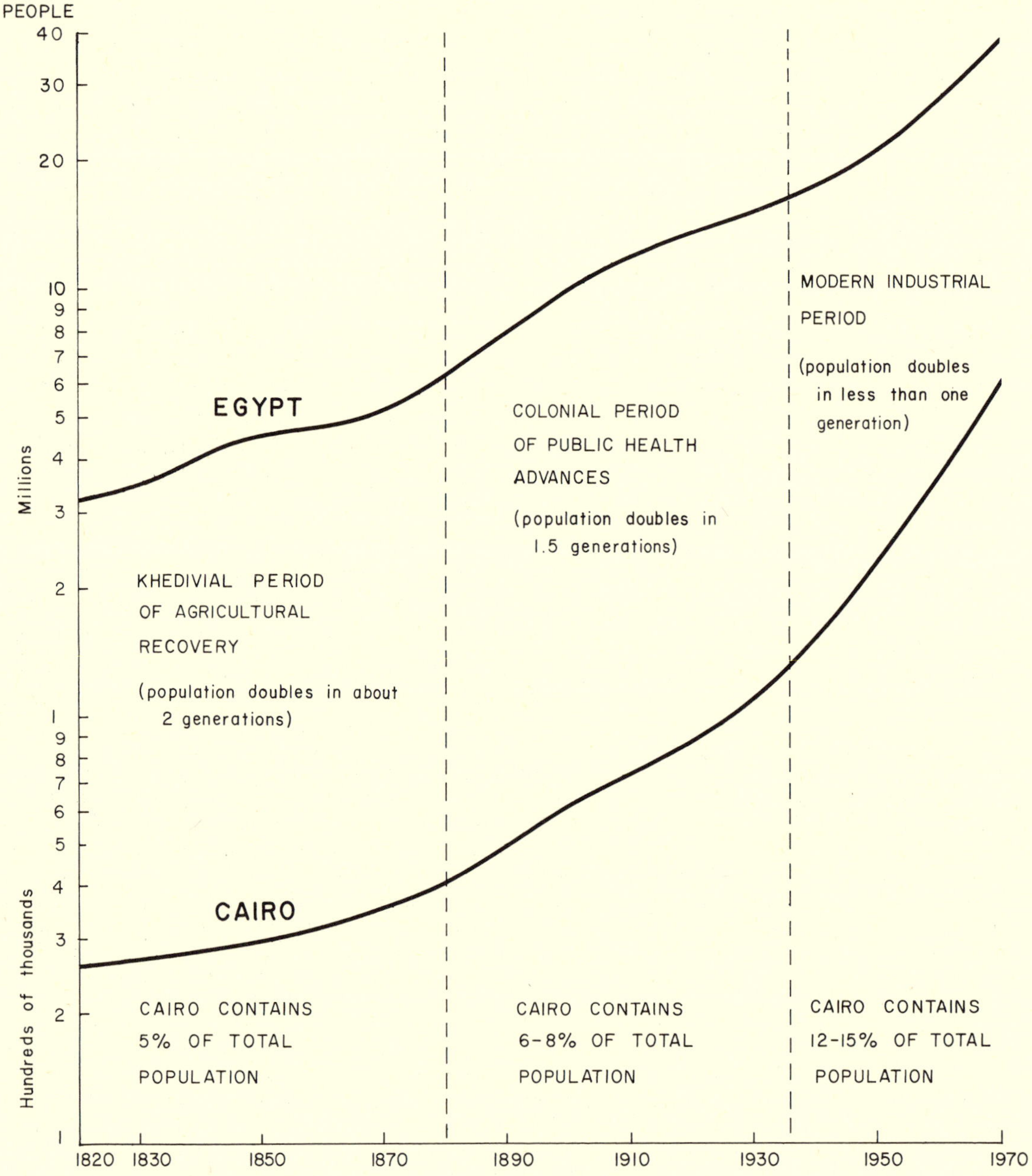

CHART I. Population Growth of Egypt and Cairo, 1820-1970

TABLE 1. ANNUAL RATES OF POPULATION INCREASE FOR EGYPT AND CAIRO, BY INTERCENSAL PERIODS, 1897-1960

Intercensal Period	*Computed Annual Rates of Increase* *Egypt (%/yr)*	*Cairo (%/yr)*	*Cairo Excess*
1897-1907[a]	1.5	1.4	−0.1
1907-1917	1.3	1.6[c]	0.3
1917-1927	1.1	3.0[d]	1.9
1927-1937	1.2	2.1	0.9
1937-1947	1.8	4.8[d]	3.0
1947-1960[b]	2.5	4.0	1.5

[a] Intercensal growth rates for the ten-year periods between 1897 and 1947 have been taken from Table 3 in the Appendix of Alphonse M. Said, "The Growth and Development of Urbanization in Egypt" (multigraph report published by the Social Research Center, The American University at Cairo, in 1960). The discrepancy between these computed rates and those presented by I. A. Farid in his monograph, *Population of Egypt* (Cairo, 1948) and reproduced in Gamal Hamdan, *Studies in Egyptian Urbanism* (The Renaissance Bookstore, Cairo: 1959), p. 12, cannot be explained, since Farid and Hamdan do not give the basis for their computations.

[b] The estimated intercensal growth rate for the period between 1947 and 1960 has been computed by the author. Cairo boundaries have been corrected to make them roughly comparable to those of earlier periods.

[c] This rate is inflated somewhat by a redefinition of Cairo's boundaries which occurred between the censuses of 1907 and 1917. In the 1907 Census, Cairo was confined to the eastern bank of the river. In the 1917 Census, a portion of territory on the western bank was added to the corporate limits, where it remained until Cairo was again deprived of this zone between the censuses of 1947 and 1960.

[d] The extremely high rates of increase during both these periods must be attributed to wartime migrations. These patterns will be explained in fuller detail below.

in the 17 cities and towns with at least 20,000 inhabitants in that year. Fifty years later almost 30 percent of the population was living in the 57 communities of urban size.[7] A quickening of this long-term trend had resulted by 1960 in a situation in which more than 36 percent of the population was to be found in the 86 urban-sized communities of Egypt.[8] It is even greater by now.

Throughout this long period of increasing urbanization, Cairo attracted a disproportionate share of the newly urbanizing population. The city of 1897 contained somewhat less than 8 percent of the country's population; by 1947, about 11 percent of the nation's population was residing in the capital city, a proportion that had increased to over 13 percent by 1960. Present trends suggest that by 1970 Cairo should have contained 17 percent of the Egyptian population. Cairo is still growing at about twice the national rate and faster than all urban areas combined.[9]

During the twentieth century, Cairo's growth can be traced to three relatively independent sources whose separate contributions must be distinguished. In the analysis that follows, intercensal population increments are broken down into three components: (1) natural increase, the excess of births over deaths occurring within the city limits; (2) migration, the net change in population due to the excess of persons moving into Cairo from other areas over the number of Cairenes emigrating from the city; and (3) annexation, the incorporation of nonmobile persons into the city due to an expansion of city limits. Whereas the first two sources represent a true increase in the *demand* for urban expansion, the third is a by-product of that expansion. Statistically speaking, the former have been responsible for the major share of population increase, while the contribution of the third has been relatively insignificant.

During the decade between 1897 and 1907, insofar as the situation can be reconstructed from admittedly inadequate data, Cairo's population grew from 589,572 to

[7] See Alphonse Said, "The Growth and Development of Urbanization in Egypt," Tables 4 and 9, Appendix, for a convenient summary of the raw data which these figures have been derived.

[8] My computations from the Census of 1960. Much more detailed information on the towns and cities of Egypt and their growth during the twentieth century appears in J. Abu-Lughod, "Urbanization in Egypt: Present State and Future Prospects," in *Economic Development and Cultural Change*, XIII (April 1965), 313-343.

[9] All of the preceding computations have been made from figures appearing in the published official census reports. Several words of caution concerning these figures must be introduced at this point. There are a number of discrepancies in the reporting of total and Cairo populations in various census editions. For example, the total population of Egypt, as reported in the original *Census of Egypt, 1897*, has been revised in later editions. In the *Census of Egypt, 1907* (National Printing Department, Cairo: 1909), the 1897 figure was adjusted downward to eliminate the area that had been ceded to the Sudan during the intervening decade. The *Census of Egypt, 1937* (Government Press, Cairo: 1942) reports a further downward revision of the population total in 1897. Similarly, the 1897 figure for Cairo is given at about 570,000 in an earlier edition but 589,000 in a later revision. In these cases, I have used the most current revision of the figure in question. Therefore, individuals wishing to recompute or check the statistics presented in this chapter are urged to examine all relevant sources. The *Preliminary Returns* of the Census of 1960 have been used to compute the figure of 13 percent. A small degree of variation may be introduced if computations are made from final returns. However, on the basis of these tentative figures, it appears that the total population of Egypt increased by about 38 percent over the thirteen years since 1947. During this same interval, the total *urban* population (i.e., population in communities containing 20,000 or more inhabitants) increased from 5,474,000 in 1947, to about 9,300,000 in 1960 (computations mine). This represents an increment of 69 percent over the earlier figure. Cairo's increase—from 2 million in 1947 to almost 3.5 million in 1960 (my boundary correction)—was, in contrast, on the order of 75 percent. The projections for 1970 can be derived from Chart I. Since this section was written, Cairo's population has been dramatically inflated by at least half a million refugee-migrants from the Canal Zone cities, as a result of the 1967 war.

678,423.[10] Since, to the best of our knowledge, the boundaries of the city did not alter during that interval, this would indicate that the entire increase of close to 90,000 was attributable to the combined effects of natural increase and in-migration. This was a unique period of Egyptian history when she was attracting a surprisingly large number of foreign immigrants, not only Ottoman subjects from other parts of the empire but also many southern Europeans and a lesser number from northern Europe who were drawn to her by the promise of commercial gain. These foreign immigrants concentrated, not illogically, in the major cities, and while Cairo never contained as dominant a foreign minority as Alexandria, her share of the new population was impressive. In 1897, some 35,000 of Cairo's population had been born outside of Egypt, a number that only ten years later had increased to over 75,000. All of this increment must be treated as "migration," since the births and deaths of foreign nationals in the city were not recorded. (Because of this fact, it is necessary to treat births as part of "immigration" and to include deaths within the foreign community as equivalent to "emigration.") Thus, out of the total intercensal increase, slightly under one-half must be attributed to an influx of foreigners. Never again was foreign immigration to play so important a role in the city's expansion.

The remainder of the increase was due to an excess of births over deaths among the indigenous inhabitants and to a less marked movement of Egyptians from rural regions within the country to the capital city. While it is impossible to gauge the precise proportion due to each, one can reach a tentative estimate based on internal logic. An examination of the vital statistics for Cairo during the period leads us to conclude that the net rate of natural increase could have been no higher than 5/1000/year, the result of a new and still barely perceptible decrease in the urban death rate that made its appearance during that decade. Applying this rate of natural increase to the indigenous population, one estimates that perhaps 28,000 of the addition to Cairo's population might have come from natural increase. Estimating internal migration indirectly as simply the residual between total growth minus foreign migration and indigenous natural increase, one arrives at an estimate of some 22,000 native Egyptians who moved to Cairo from other parts of the country during the decade between 1897 and 1907. In summary, then, during the opening decade of the twentieth century approximately 30 percent of Cairo's growth could be attributed to natural increase while, of the remaining 70 percent due to in-migration, almost two-thirds was due to an influx of foreigners.[11]

The decade between 1907 and 1917 was, by contrast, a period of much slower population growth which coincided with a financial retrenchment (precipitated by the "crash" of 1907) and a dramatic cessation of many of the employment opportunities that the preceding boom had nurtured. Economic recovery did not begin until the World War I years, and this recovery, in Egypt at least, was really not experienced until about 1917 when Britain concentrated many of her installations and personnel in the Cairo region. This slowing down of urban growth is masked, statistically, by a boundary expansion of the city which must be isolated before internal developments can be evaluated.

Between 1907 and 1917, the boundary of Cairo, which had formerly included only that portion of the urban region on the east bank of the Nile, was expanded to include the settled portion on the west bank as well, which increased the area of the city from 108 to 161.7 square kilometers. By 1917, therefore, the city included 34,620 persons living in the primarily agricultural communities and estates that dotted the western shore. When one eliminates this "fictitious" growth from the intercensal increment, one discovers that the population on the eastern shore had increased by only about 78,000; that is, the absolute increase was even less than the preceding decade of expansion and the relative growth rate was substantially lower.[12]

The major reason for this decrease in the rate of growth appears to have been a virtual cessation of foreign immigration to Egypt. The Bourse crash in 1907 (which previewed similar bank failures in Europe and America several months later and was not unrelated to them causally), with its attendant foreclosures, mortgage defaults, and contraction of credit, served notice that Egypt was not to be another "America." Fortunes were not to be made on a speculative shoestring, the myth that had attracted so many of the foreign immigrants during the

[10] These figures have been taken from the Summary Table I, p. 2, contained in the *Census of 1947, Governorate of Cairo* (Government Press, Cairo: 1954). Evidently, Egyptian demographers have corrected material which appeared in earlier documents. Both population figures are higher than those recorded in the *Census of Egypt, 1907*, Table v, p. 30.

[11] My analysis of the proportion of Cairo's growth attributable to natural increase and immigration is in complete disagreement with the estimates suggested by the demographers compiling the *Census of Egypt, 1907*. Their estimates appear on pp. 26-27 of that document.

[12] This point, so obvious from a critical examination of the statistical sources, seems to have been totally overlooked by other students of Cairo's growth. It will be particularly important to bear this in mind when the actual pattern of the city's physical expansion is discussed in the next chapter. The great period of speculative building and of opening up new areas to urban settlement occurred between 1897 and 1907, *not* in the depressed decade that ensued.

previous decade.[13] While the Census of 1917 does not contain data comparable to that of 1907, which makes impossible a direct comparison between the number of foreigners resident in both years, one can, through indirect manipulation, estimate the number of foreign-born persons residing on the eastern bank of the city in 1917 at about 76,660.[14] This represents an increase over 1907 of only about 1,650 persons and leaves more than 76,000 of the intercensal increment still unaccounted for. This latter increase was due solely to natural increase and internal (native) migration.

But how much of this increase was due to each? Here again the statistics leave much to be desired and the situation must be reconstructed indirectly. The rate of natural increase was slightly higher during this decade than it had been in the preceding one, but I would estimate that it was no greater than 7/1000/year on the average.[15] (The

[13] Among the sources that treat the causes and events leading to the crash are: Edwin Lévy, "Les événements de 1907 et la situation actuelle de l'Égypte," in *L'Égypte Contemporaine*, Volume III (November 1912), pp. 503-530; and F. Legrand, *Les fluctuations de prix et les crises de 1907 et 1908 en Égypte* (J. Coubé, Nancy: 1909), particularly the introduction and Chapter I, pp. 1-25. See Chapter 9, below, for additional details.

[14] Table VII of *Census of Egypt, 1907*, pp. 36-38, presents data on "place of birth" for all residents in Cairo in that year. The figure of foreign born may be obtained by summing all residents born in a country other than Egypt. No comparable table appears in the *Census of Egypt, 1917*. Our estimate of the foreign-born population resident on the east bank portion of Cairo in that year was derived in the following manner. First, the population on the west bank of the Nile was subtracted from the total. Second, the not unreasonable assumption was made that the number of foreign-born persons residing in the predominantly agricultural western district was so minimal that, for practical purposes, this group could be ignored. Third, Table XVII, Volume II, *Census of Egypt, 1917*, was consulted. (See pp. 574-575.) This table shows "Local-Born Population Classified by Birthplaces," and includes an entry for Cairo. According to this table, 714,281 of Cairo's residents had been born in Egypt and, of these, 38,805 had been born in the Province of Jīzah (of which the west bank had been a subregion prior to the redistricting of Cairo). Present residents on the west bank were therefore subtracted from this subtotal, yielding an estimated Egyptian-born population on the east bank of 679,661. Subtracting this figure from the total population on the east bank in 1917, one estimates that there were approximately 76,661 foreign-born residents in the city in that year. The reader is cautioned here concerning the distinction between "foreign-born" and "foreign national." The *Census of Egypt, 1917* does present information on the nationality of Cairo residents in that year, but this is *quite* different from "foreign-born." It should be noted that the foreign communities in Egypt tended to retain their inherited nationalities (the principle of blood rather than soil having been the determinant of citizenship) even after generations of residence in that country and, in addition, due to the special privileges accorded foreign nationals under the Capitulations, natives often sought the "protection" of a foreign consular authority. Because of these factors, I have been forced into the rather circuitous methodology explained above.

[15] The basis for this assumption is, in part, intuitive, in the sense that it is the assumption which best reconciles existing vital statistics data available for the period with known intercensal growth rates. While no absolute proof can be offered, the following is presented in support of the assumption. In 1908 the Ministry of Interior, Department of Public Health, issued a set of vital statistics on *Births and Deaths in the Principal Towns of Egypt During the First and Second Quarters of 1907-1908* (National Printing Office, Cairo: 1908). Cairo data are presented separately. In January-March of 1907, the CBR for Cairo was computed as 44.7 and, since that season is the most healthful during the year, the CDR was 28.6. During April-June, the computed CBR was 40.2 while the CDR was 50.7. For the comparable quarters of 1908, the rates were respectively: CBR 49.9 for the first quarter and 44.4 for the second quarter; CDR 26.6 for the first quarter and 43.6 for the second quarter. Averaging the natural increase rates for each quarter in each year, one arrives at about 7/1000, a figure quite consistent with evidence from other sources.

While I shall attempt to avoid too technical a discussion of Egyptian statistics, some explanation of why I have interpreted existing data rather "freely" must be given to the specialist. Vital statistics, that is, annual births and deaths from which mortality and fertility rates can be computed, have been collected in Egypt since the period of Ismāʿīl. The quality of this reporting, particularly in rural areas and until very recently even in urban ones, has left much to be desired. Underreporting has been the rule rather than the exception. While this is no longer of statistical significance today in major cities such as Cairo, underreporting may still be as high as one-third outside of the major towns. Series of crude birth and death rates for Egypt and for Cairo may be found in a variety of sources. The Department of Statistics publishes summary volumes of vital statistics as well as a *Quarterly Return of Births, Deaths, Infectious Diseases, Marriage and Divorce*, covering the major cities and all other areas served by health bureaus. Clerget, *Le Caire*, II, 24, has conveniently compiled the series of crude birth and death rates for Cairo between 1875 and 1930, which is easily brought up to date by the government publications noted above.

I have not included these figures in this volume because they would require substantial revision. The major conclusion that can be reached by a demographer when confronted with these figures of "misplaced concreteness" is that they are patently incorrect, and that the constants that would be required to correct them cannot be reconstructed from the past. For example, if we accept the figures at face value, it would appear that Cairo's crude birth rate has increased over the past century from 40-45/1000 to 50-55/1000. Without examining data on completed fertility and comparing these over time, one cannot conclude that such an increase in fertility has occurred. To investigate even this simple problem involves research of impressive magnitude. Only small beginnings, however, have been made in answering this question. To take an even more obvious example, one can compare fertility rates in rural areas with those in urban areas and conclude, on the basis of published statistics, that the urban birth rate is almost twice as great as the rural rate. This, from the few careful demographic analyses that have thus far been made, is certainly untrue. Among the studies that may be consulted for "true" rates are Hanna Rizk, "Fertility Patterns in Selected Areas in Egypt" (unpublished Ph.D. Dissertation, Princeton University: 1959); Mohammed El-Badry, "Some Demographic Measurements for Egypt Based on the Stability of Census Age Distributions," *Milbank Memorial Fund Quarterly*, XXXIII (July 1955), 268-305; S. H. Abdel-Aty, "Life Table Functions for Egypt Based

average recorded CDR during the decade was about 35/1000 while the average recorded CBR remained fairly constant at about 42/1000; both figures for Cairo are underestimates of the true situation, due to the still widespread degree of underregistration of both births and deaths.) Applying this estimated rate of natural increase to the base of Egyptian-born residents on the east bank, one can estimate that approximately 43,000-44,000 of the intercensal increment could be attributed to an excess of births over deaths in the capital while the remaining 32,000-33,000 resulted from the migration of rural Egyptians into the city.

Thus, the growth during the second decade of the twentieth century was the result both of an improved health situation in the city which permitted Cairo's population to expand through natural increase—a trend that was to become even more marked in the years that followed—and of an increased rate of migration to the capital city from within Egypt. Excluding the population increase between 1907 and 1917 that was due solely to the boundary revision, one arrives at the estimate that some 55-60 percent of the true growth was probably due to natural increase while the remaining 40-45 percent was attributable to internal migration. Each of these points requires further explanation.

It will be recalled that during the nineteenth century Cairo's death rate had been so high that none of her growth could be attributed to natural increase. And yet, by the turn of the century it was clear that the urban death rate had begun a slow decline, making it possible for the first time for the city to increase through natural growth. This reversal of an age-old pattern can be traced to the greater control over epidemic disasters that had been achieved by the final years of the century. The British occupying troops were made painfully aware of the health hazards in the country to which they had fallen heir by the outbreak in 1883 of a particularly virulent cholera epidemic, similar to ones that had ravaged the country in 1856, 1855, 1848, 1831, and on back into dim history. It was natural that epidemic control should have received top priority in British policy, since cholera was no respecter of the uniform, and, with most of the foreign population concentrated in Cairo and Alexandria, that these two cities should have received the most attention.[16]

Beginning at the end of the nineteenth century, numerous reforms were instituted to prevent or control the spread of contagious diseases. By 1885 the Sanitary Service of Egypt had been reorganized under the Englishman, Greene Pasha, and Europeans manned most of the posts of responsibility. A decree of December 17, 1890, made vaccination against smallpox mandatory for Egyptians and Europeans (although ironically, due to the "rights" accorded under the Capitulations, this could not be enforced against the latter), and clinics were set up to administer the vaccine without charge. Another edict on June 13, 1891, made it obligatory for physicians to report immediately any cases of infectious disease to the Sanitary Department, which also undertook to disinfect houses and effects without fee. By 1895 the quarantine station (governing pilgrims returning from Mecca, who had often been carriers of infection in the past) was reorganized and traveling hospitals for infectious diseases had been set up. By the time cholera recurred in 1896 and again in 1902, its toll had been cut at least in half.[17] The effects of these and other measures can be seen in the decreased fluctuations of yearly death rates. The annual death rate of Cairo, which from year to year had varied as widely as 20 to 25 per thousand due to periodic epidemics, began to swing with less amplitude as one after another of the unpredictable killers came increasingly under control. While the "steady killers," such as infant digestive disorders and diarrhea, tuberculosis, pneumonia, dysentery, typhoid, measles, etc. still showed no signs of yielding, their relatively regular toll was no longer periodically inflated by plagues.

Less progress, however, was evident in the realm of environmental sanitation. A slow beginning was made

on Model Life-Tables and Quasi-Stable Population Theory," *Milbank Memorial Fund Quarterly*, XXXIX (April 1961), 350-377; J. Abu-Lughod, "Urban-Rural Differences as a Function of the Demographic Transition: Egyptian Data and an Analytical Model," *American Journal of Sociology*, LXIX (March 1964), 476-490; J. Abu-Lughod, "The Emergence of Differential Fertility in Urban Egypt," *Milbank Memorial Fund Quarterly*, XLIII (April 1965), 235-253.

While the above examples might be multiplied many times to indicate the impossibility of using uncorrected rates, the conclusion remains the same. Informed "guestimates" by persons who have worked intimately with Egyptian data are probably more reliable than published figures. Furthermore, census counts are more reliable than vital statistics rates. This does not mean, however, that every rate is as unreliable as every other one. The rate of natural increase, for example, appears to be more reliable than either the birth or the death rates from which it is computed. In addition, the rate of natural increase, in a country such as Egypt where external migration is minimal, may be checked against rates of intercensal increase to test consistency. For all these reasons I have felt it necessary to take certain "liberties" in analyzing the dynamics of Egyptian and Cairo growth rates, although no liberties in overlooking potential sources of statistical data have been taken.

[16] For a fuller account of British policies with respect to epidemics, see Robert Tignor, "Public Health Administration in Egypt Under British Rule, 1882-1914" (unpublished Ph.D. Dissertation, Yale University: 1960).

[17] This chronicle of health regulations has been compiled from information appearing in *ibid.* and *An Almanac for the Year 1902* (National Printing Department, Cairo: 1902), p. 39, but is available in numerous other sources.

at the turn of the century to establish standards for food preparation and service and to enforce these through market inspection. But contravention of requirements had always been simple in Egypt, especially since Muḥammad 'Ali curtailed the often inhumane punishments which the *muḥtasib* had formerly used to gain compliance through fear. The expansion of the system of purified water had gradually decreased dependence upon the brackish and often polluted shallow wells within the city, and in 1903 the intake source for the city was switched from the Nile to deep wells in the Rawḍ al-Faraj section (although protests concerning its mineral taste finally led in 1912 to a reversion to the Nile source with improved filtration). Regular trash collection was attempted from 1895 onward, but the system was primarily confined to the newer sections of the city. In addition, the filling in of some of the more offensive canals, culminating in 1898 with the disappearance of the famous Khalīj, helped to remove some of the more blatant sources of contamination and mosquito breeding.[18] It was to the above advances that the moderate decline in Cairo's average death rate must be ascribed. A major decline was to occur during the next decade as a result of the completion in 1915 of a sewerage system for the city, but this will be treated below since its impact was felt chiefly after the war.

The remainder of the 1907-1917 increase resulted from rural-to-urban migration, a process that began slowly but more than compensated for its sluggish start during the war and postwar periods. With the outbreak of World War I, the anomalous position of Egypt as an Ottoman domain under British rule was "regularized" by the unilateral English declaration that Egypt was to be, henceforth, a British Protectorate. The uncooperative Khedive, 'Abbās Ḥilmi II, was unceremoniously removed from office, his place taken by the short-lived Ḥusayn Kāmil (d. 1917). Particularly after 1915, Egypt became an important base for Britain's Middle East operations, with a sizeable armed force quartered there and with much of her agricultural and infant industrial productivity geared to supplying British requirements.[19] It was inevitable that some portion of the rural population should be attracted to Cairo, Alexandria, and the Canal cities by the expanding demand for service and other workers, and the response was not long in coming. The cityward migration which began during this period intensified and, during the next decade of growth, increased still further.

During the decade between 1917 and 1927, Cairo grew faster than ever before. Within barely ten years the *increment* to her population *exceeded the total population of the city in 1800*. Some 273,600 residents were added, bringing Cairo's population to over one million by 1927. Furthermore, this growth was due neither to statistical fiction nor to foreign sources. The boundaries of the city remained constant (161.7 square kilometers in area) while the number of foreign residents was approximately the same as it had been in 1917. Two indigenous forces had become totally responsible for her growth: a rapidly rising rate of natural increase within Cairo; and a heightened migration out of rural areas into the cities, of which Cairo proved by far the most attractive.

The stream of migrants that had begun to head for Cairo during the early war years increased to flood proportions during the last years of the war and the several years of economic prosperity that ensued. Employment opportunities were excellent, not only attached to the British forces but also in the industries that had been established to meet shortages created by the interruption of world trade. Opportunities remained even after the withdrawal of troops, since construction, which had been halted during the war due to material shortages, provided a healthy outlet for economic activities. (A backlog, coupled with the burgeoning demand, had led to a serious housing shortage in Cairo and to such rent increases that rent control had to be imposed on residential structures in 1920 and further extended in 1921.) General prosperity, and its step-sister, inflation, which placed an unanticipated burden on the poorer newcomers to urban life,[20] remained high throughout most of the 1920's, thanks to a sustained demand for high-priced

[18] The foregoing information has been compiled from a variety of sources, including the annual issues of the *Almanac*, cited above; *Egypt No. 1 (1909): Reports by His Majesty's Agent and Consul-General on the Finances, Administration, and Condition of Egypt and the Soudan in 1908* (His Majesty's Stationery Office, London: 1909); supplemented by accounts of travelers. Among the latter sources, the book by Alfred Cunningham, *To-Day in Egypt: Its Administration, People and Politics* (Hurst and Blackett, Ltd., London: 1912), is particularly valuable, since it contains chapters on "Public Health and Sanitation," pp. 92-122, and "Public Services," pp. 123-155, which are as critical as they are informative.

[19] For an account of the economic effects of World War I on Egypt, see A. E. Crouchley, *The Economic Development of Modern Egypt* (Longmans, Green and Co., London: 1938), pp. 182-209; and Charles Issawi, *Egypt at Mid-Century: An Economic Survey* (Oxford University Press, London: 1954), chiefly, p. 40 *et seq.*

[20] The index numbers (1913-1914 wholesale prices = 100) of certain staple commodities in Cairo in 1919 afford some measure of the increased cost of living which affected primarily the poorer classes of the city. The index of the price of wheat was 234; lentils, 207; sugar, 294; and soap, 373. See *Egypt No. 1 (1920): Reports by His Majesty's High Commissioner on the Finances, Administration, and Condition of Egypt and the Soudan for the Period 1914-1919* (His Majesty's Stationery Office, London: 1920), p. 3.

cotton[21] and to the favorable balance of payments that was Egypt's legacy from wartime. Only during the upheaval of the General Strike in 1919, protesting Britain's failure to include an Egyptian settlement on the agenda of peace treaty negotiations, and during the catastrophic recession in world cotton prices during 1921 was there any general setback to the Egyptian economy.

On the other hand, the balance between people and resources within the rural sections of the country was being altered, due to the rapid rate at which population had been increasing. The labor shortage that had characterized nineteenth-century Egypt was rapidly being transformed into a labor surplus. Although Issawi dates this transition from the turn of the century,[22] it is likely that "population pressure" did not begin to be felt in the rural areas until several decades later. In any case, the migration that took place during the war and particularly the postwar periods was not due only to the attractions of the capital but also to an expulsion from oversaturated rural areas. This marks the beginning of a problem that has grown more and more severe as the century advanced.[23]

At the very time migration had increased, health conditions in the capital were improving so rapidly that each year witnessed a further decline in the city's crude death rate. Since no real change in the birth rate was observable (except a slight increase that might be attributed to improved reporting), this meant a significant rise in the rate of natural increase. It is my conservative estimate that the rate of natural increase altered from about 7/1000/year at the beginning of the intercensal period to at least 12/1000/year by the end. The decline in death rates was interrupted only briefly, though catastrophically, by the influenza epidemic that hit the city at the end of 1917 and the beginning of 1918. One may legitimately question why the death rate in Cairo dropped so dramatically during this decade. Was it a mere statistical illusion or had health conditions in the city really improved markedly? The latter explanation appears the more probable, especially when one examines the specific change—the introduction of a drainage-sewerage system for the city—that occurred in the urban environment just prior to the observed drop in death rates.

A safe and sanitary means for disposing of human and animal wastes, as well as a system for draining water (particularly in those areas served by the water system) became more and more necessary as the size and density of the city increased. From time to time during the nineteenth century proposals to drain the city had been advanced, but each time cost factors intervened. Some sewers of obscure origin had evidently already been installed, since on occasion they were unearthed when foundations were dug, but, outside of an uncoordinated network along the Khalīj, no city system existed.

It was toward the very end of Ismā'īl's reign, under the influence of the French representative of the Dual Control, that the Ministry of Public Works undertook the construction of a system of storm drains to remove surface water from the major streets of the new quarters on the west. From what can be reconstructed today, it appears that these drains were never intended for sewage.[24] Nevertheless, they were in fact used for this purpose by residents in the abutting houses who made illegal connections to drain their cesspits into the sewer system that debouched in the Nile.[25] This created a health hazard of such magnitude that, during the later British administration, many had to be destroyed to eliminate the foul sources of infection.[26] As one contemporary observer noted: "Whether these egregious sanitary failures were responsible for the aristocratic epidemic of typhoid fever or not, it is certain that the disease ceased to commit ravages in the European community as soon as the French drains were abolished. . . ."[27]

[21] A table illustrating the close connection between the Egyptian economy and the world agricultural market is found in Issawi, *Egypt at Mid-Century*, p. 79.

[22] *Ibid.*, p. 35.

[23] One of the most sensitive indirect measures of the rate of rural to urban migration in Egypt is the sex ratio (the number of males per 100 females within a given population) of the urban population, since migrants tend to be drawn from among the younger adult males of any community. It is therefore perhaps significant that Cairo experienced a rather sharp increase in its sex ratio in the decade between 1917 and 1927. In 1897, 1907 and 1917, this sex ratio remained constant at 113 males per 100 females, indicating a steady but gradual migration to the city. By the 1927 Census, this sex ratio had increased to 144, the highest it ever reached either before or afterward.

[24] While the scheme was conceived under Ismā'īl, its execution, according to 'Ali Mubārak, was not undertaken until 1880. The French representative in the Ministry of Public Works at that time was de Blignières. See Mubārak, *Al-Khiṭaṭ al-Tawfīqīyah al-Jadīdah* (Būlāq Press, Cairo: 1888), IX, 55-56. The term used by Mubārak implies rain water drainage, not removal of sewage wastes.

[25] A description of the "five separate and distinct sewers of modern construction" that existed in Cairo when Dr. Greene Pasha became Director of the Sanitary Service is included in his article, "The Sanitation of Cairo," in *The Provincial Medical Journal*, Volume VII, No. 73, January 2, 1888, pp. 9-10. He recommended that the sewers be condemned, noting that "owing to faulty construction, absence of means for flushing, fissures in the masonry, and unauthorized communication of house drains, these so-called sewers and the soil surrounding them have attained such a degree of foulness as to render them veritable 'foyers d'infection' . . ." (p. 9).

[26] That these drains were opened and destroyed only ten years after their installation, due to their hazardous nature, is attested by the anonymous author, Pyramid (pseud.), "The Drainage of Cairo," in *The Provincial Medical Journal*, Volume XIV, No. 162, June 1, 1895, pp. 298-301.

[27] *Ibid.*, p. 299.

Most of the city, however, did not benefit even from inadequate drains. Outside the "modern" or western district, cesspits for the reception of nightsoil were common, "the greater number [of these being] . . . simply holes dug in the ground, occasionally lined with porous masonry, but never floored, and for the most part placed either entirely or in part within the buildings."[28] The nightsoil and other wastes that accumulated in this fashion (and, admittedly, in even less savory ways) were periodically removed by independent contractors, either to be discarded beyond the city limits or, more profitably, sold to the public baths, bakeries, and other fuel-using industries within the city where they were stored on the premises, dried, and then burned in the ovens.[29]

There was never any real controversy about whether Cairo *needed* a better system; that was a given. But the question of finance was another matter altogether. Had Ismā'īl installed a system before his bankruptcy, the medical history of Cairo might have been totally different, but once the country had reached the economic plight of the 1880's, this opportunity could not be recaptured. While the major obstacles to sanitation were undoubtedly financial, they were further complicated by the Capitulations, which placed tedious hurdles in the pathway of municipal reforms of all kinds. Here, then, a slight digression is required to explain why Cairo was forced to wait until 1915 for a modern drainage system.

In a series of agreements with various European powers, the Sultan in Constantinople had granted to foreigners in the Ottoman domains virtual exemption from the laws of the empire, a fact that in large measure was responsible for the "success" with which foreign nationals engaged in commercial ventures closed to natives. These Capitulations—which remained in force in Egypt until the 1937 Convention of Montreux—provided that foreigners could be tried only in their own consular courts or later, and only in certain cases, in the Mixed Tribunals that had been established in Egypt toward the end of Ismā'īl's reign. Furthermore, no laws, even those passed in the interests of the foreign communities themselves, had any binding power unless and until the foreign governments concerned gave their express consent. And, what was perhaps of greatest importance in terms of municipal development, *real estate taxes, special assessments, and any other techniques for raising funds for needed facilities could not be imposed on foreigners*, despite the fact that the demand for amenities and modernization in Cairo came chiefly from these quarters.

[28] Dr. Greene Pasha, "The Sanitation of Cairo," p. 9.

[29] For some of the less attractive details of this system, see Cunningham, *To-Day in Egypt*, pp. 101-104, where he quotes at length from the report of a special sanitary commissioner who was dispatched to Cairo in 1909 by the British Medical Association's official journal, the *Lancet*, to study conditions.

This had not posed any particular problem during the era of Muḥammad 'Ali, since foreigners were relatively few and were, furthermore, proscribed from owning real property in Cairo. However, with the liberalization of land policy under Sa'īd and Ismā'īl, and with the increasingly important role played by foreign capital in the country's development as the century drew to a close, more and more urban property was controlled by individuals and corporations that remained beyond the reaches of government regulation and were exempted from the financial responsibilities which otherwise accompany ownership. The situation was so unworkable that in 1885 England obtained the signatures of involved European governments on an agreement authorizing the extension of the 8.5 percent house tax formerly levied only against Egyptian property owners in Cairo to foreign landlords as well. The justification for this was to provide sufficient revenues to finance needed municipal improvements. The significance of this innovation can be appreciated from the fact that, when foreigners first paid this tax in 1887, receipts were double what they had been before the agreement.[30] Unfortunately, even this increased revenue proved insufficient to finance all the desired capital improvements and the prospects for a drainage system remained dim.

Drainage schemes had been proposed in 1885, 1889, and with ever-hopeful regularity in the years that followed, but no plan was ever capable of mustering the necessary foreign support or of solving the budgetary problems. Finally, with the signing of the Anglo-French Entente in 1904, the rivalries that had formerly obstructed agreements in even simple matters were partially resolved, and soon afterward, in 1906, the British sanitary engineer, Carkeet Jones, was retained to design the system. At the same time, negotiations were begun to gain the needed approval of the Capitulatory Powers to an increase in the house tax of Cairo to 10 percent, the additional funds to be specially earmarked for the drainage of the city.

[30] For information on these tax receipts, see Sir Alfred Milner, *England in Egypt* (Edward Arnold, London: 7th edn., revised, 1899), p. 50. Cairo was never fortunate enough to obtain the degree of self-government accorded to Alexandria. At the initiation of European traders resident in the latter community, Alexandria received in 1890 from the Capitulatory Powers the right to establish a municipal corporation with authority to impose and collect special assessments in addition to the house tax. The Municipality of Alexandria was governed by a mixed European and Egyptian council. Following this precedent, other Egyptian towns set up similar systems of modified "home rule," although none enjoyed the autonomy granted to Alexandria. Of all the major cities, only Cairo never succeeded in establishing its corporate identity, until 1949 when a change in the laws accorded her some degree of self-government. See Chapter 10, below, for a more complete discussion of the evolution of municipal government.

By early 1909 all signatures had been secured, and by June of the same year the Governorate of Cairo formally adopted the plans drawn up by Mr. Jones and recommended by both the ministries of Public Works and Health. Among the expenditures authorized in 1909 was the preliminary sum of *LE* 70,000 from the Reserve Fund for the Cairo Drainage Scheme. Two contracts were awarded: one to an English firm for the surface water drainage of Cairo, the sewerage of Zaytūn and other suburbs, the construction of the main collector, and the building of purification works at Khānkah fifteen miles north of the city; the other to a French firm for the construction of the rising main from the central pumping station to the purification works.[31]

With financial support assured, execution of the drainage system was begun, although progress was slow and intermittent. By 1914, however, most of the system had been completed, including the main collector, the purification works, the sewage farm at Khānkah, the main pumping station, the compressed air station and 63 ejectors. The system was officially inaugurated by the Minister of Public Works in March of 1915.[32] Although the system was designed to cover all the newer quarters of the western and northeastern sections of the city as well as substantial portions of the medieval town (excluding the funereal quarters of the east and south, the island of Rawḍah, the western bank, and the northern zone beyond the more inlying portions of Shubra), sewer reticulation and house connections lagged behind, due to the interruption of the war. It was only after the war that intensive work was resumed, with an additional 22 kilometers of sewers laid in 1919 and some 27 more, primarily in the older quarters, installed in 1920. And while in the newer quarters many owners availed themselves of the option to connect with the system, participation in the older quarters was extremely spotty.[33]

The effects of even this incomplete sewerage system in depressing mortality rates within Cairo were not long in appearing. I believe that it was not accidental that the 1920's witnessed such a rapid decline in the death rates prevailing in Cairo and that, after the initial and rather sharp descent, the change in rate leveled off somewhat. The inauguration of the drainage system, supplemented by later extensions and by the establishment of a parallel system at Jīzah on the western bank, contributed to the creation of a healthier urban environment and thus to the increased chances of survival of the urban population.

While it is impossible again to separate precisely the portion of Cairo's growth attributable to increased rural-to-urban migration from the portion due to her improved potential for natural increase, some rough estimates may be offered here. In 1917, there had been some 230,791 Cairo residents born in other parts of Egypt and an additional 76,660 born outside the country. By 1927, these figures had increased to 368,691 and 81,825 respectively. Weighing these increments against a total population gain during the decade of 273,628, and cross-checking this against the estimated rate of natural increase, I conclude that, during this period of extremely rapid urban expansion, a little under half of the increase was due to an excess of births over deaths while the remainder was the result of net immigration to the city. The fact that most of the migrants arrived early in the intercensal period helped to swell the increment due to natural increase.[34]

The prosperous 1920's were succeeded by the depressed 1930's, in Egypt no less than in the rest of the world. Egypt experienced a severe recession in 1926, due to a temporary drop in cotton prices, from which she had not fully recovered when the 1929 New York crash reverberated on the Egyptian stock exchange. In Egypt, as elsewhere, this economic state was rather directly reflected in both a slower rate of population growth and a depressed rate of urbanization. In fact, it appeared to contemporary observers[35] that Egypt's rate of population growth might actually be stabilizing at a maximum of 1.2 percent/year, since the death rate showed no signs of further decline. During the 1927-1937 decade, population increase was moderate, the total rising from 14,217,864 at the beginning of the period to only 15,962,694 at the end. A somewhat similar situation prevailed within the

[31] Among the more useful sources of information on the development of the Cairo drainage system are: Clerget, *Le Caire*, II, 8-10 plus the map opposite p. 16; various annual editions of the *Almanac*, cited above; Cunningham, *To-Day in Egypt*, pp. 97-101; *Egypt No. 1 (1909): Reports by His Majesty's Agent . . . in 1908*, pp. 15, 25, 35.

[32] *Egypt No. 1 (1920): Reports by His Majesty's High Commissioner . . . for the Period 1914-1919*, p. 44.

[33] *Ibid.*; and also *Egypt No. 1 (1921): Reports by His Majesty's High Commissioner on the Finances, Administration, and Condition of Egypt and the Soudan for the Year 1920* (His Majesty's Stationery Office, London: 1921), p. 66.

[34] The figures on both internal and international migration used in this computation have been taken from the following official sources: unnumbered table on pp. 44-45, *Census of Egypt, 1927*, Volume I, presenting information on native-born residents by place of birth and place of residence for both 1917 and 1927; and the tables appearing in *Census of Egypt, 1927*, Volume I, 40-41, and in the *Census of Egypt, 1917*, Volume II, 574-575, presenting data on current residence of all foreign-born persons.

[35] The conditions of this time undoubtedly account for the complacent attitude toward Egypt's "population problem" taken by W. Wendell Cleland in the mid-1930's. See primarily the final chapter of his *The Population Problem in Egypt; A Study of Population Trends and Conditions in Modern Egypt* (Ph.D. Dissertation, Columbia University, 1936, privately printed by the Science Press, Lancaster, Pennsylvania: 1936).

city of Cairo. The momentum of the previous drop in the urban death rate appeared to have played itself out, and the rate of natural increase by the end of the decade was only slightly higher than it had been ten years earlier. Furthermore, migration from the rural areas to the cities was temporarily suspended. Poor as conditions may have been in the villages, many persons preferred the marginal subsistence of farm areas to precarious employment in urban centers. A very similar phenomenon was noted during the depression era in other parts of the world, including such highly industrialized countries as the United States where urban growth rates received a temporary setback. Thus it was that the population of Cairo grew from 1,064,567 in 1927 to only 1,312,096 by 1937. Of this relatively small increment, approximately two-thirds can be attributed to the effects of natural increase, which by then was slightly higher in the city than in the remainder of the country, while the remainder was due to an inevitable migration trickle.

Despite the comparatively slow rate of population increase during this decade, there was little doubt that pressure was building to explosive levels in the rural areas. The standard of living, which during the nineteenth century had shown a fairly constant rise, dropped faster and faster as population outdistanced resources. While some land was added to cultivation with the successive heightenings of the Aswān Dam, this did not keep pace with population increase, and each year the existing land was subdivided into smaller plots to accommodate the inhabitants of the swollen villages. Cairo, with its lack of demand, could no longer serve as a safety valve although migrants still straggled into the city as a last resort, crowding into the older districts of the city or seeking squatter's rights on still-vacant *waqf* land or in makeshift tomb dwellings in the funereal cities on the eastern and southern fringes of the city.

Such was the situation of country and city when World War II began. Rural pressures on the land found a welcomed outlet in the major cities where industrial and military demand had been generated by the war. An exodus from village to city began in the early 1940's and continued in unprecedented fashion. The internal migration that had occurred toward the end of World War I and its aftermath, substantial as it had been, was in retrospect a minor current when contrasted with the flood of migrants who invaded Cairo and other major Egyptian cities in the early 1940's. Between 1937 and 1947, with only a minor boundary adjustment that increased her area from 164 to 178 square kilometers (and that of land still predominantly in agricultural use), Cairo was called upon to absorb more than three-quarters of a million additional inhabitants. By 1947, her population exceeded 2 million and had been growing at a rate close to 5 percent per year. It was inevitable that this enormous population growth not only led to astronomical densities within the older quarters but set in motion new urban expansions which totally transformed the outlying sections.

It would be incorrect, however, to assume that migration accounted for all of this urban increase. As before, a substantial portion of the growth came from natural increase, the dynamics of which were changing radically. The stability of the death rate throughout the 1930's proved illusory, for with the return of prosperity came another decline in mortality rates that forced population up at the rate of about 1.8 percent per year. Cairo, due to her superior standard of living and health care and to the fact that the migrant population swelled the ranks of the fecund 15 to 49 age groups, experienced an even higher rate of natural increase than did the remainder of the country. It is possible to estimate that, even in the total absence of in-migration, Cairo was capable of growing at the rate of at least 2 percent per year, *solely* from an excess of births over deaths. When one adds to this the immigration of several hundred thousand villagers, one begins to appreciate why Cairo's population grew so rapidly during the war and postwar years. Between 1937 and 1947, of 778,558 new Cairenes, some 45 percent had been added through natural increase while the remaining 55 percent had entered the city through migration.

As had been true during World War I, residential construction virtually ceased at the very time when the city was attracting so many new residents. Thus, by 1947, the city's facilities were badly strained. Older quarters that had been fully built up and overcrowded even during the preceding decades became even more densely packed, with inhabitants piling up at the rate of 300,000 per square mile and higher in certain of the inlying subareas. Close to 50,000 persons were living in the cemetery zones alone. Peripheral areas which at the beginning of the war had been vacant or in agricultural use were converted to urban uses, and other built-up fringe sections doubled and trebled their populations. The prosperity brought about by the war was sustained into the postwar decade which saw construction undertaken on an unprecedented scale.

Even before Cairo could begin to assimilate the increased population that had been her legacy from the war, she and Egypt were faced with a new demographic crisis, the continued effects of which dominate the present era. The national death rate, which had shown only a small net decline during the preceding few decades, suddenly began a steep descent. Beginning with 1946-1947, health conditions in Egypt experienced a notable improvement, the result not only of extended and better medical facilities but of the wider availability of new wonder drugs and insecticides.[36] While infant mortality rates enjoyed the maximum impact, all age groups benefited from the decline. Cairo shared in this improvement if, indeed, it did not lead the way, experiencing a rapid decrease in her death rate from about 30/1000 in the mid-1940's to about half that rate by the mid-1950's. Since the crude birth rate remained impervious to change,[37] this resulted in an even more rapid rate of natural increase than had obtained during wartime. While migration from the rural areas declined somewhat (proportionately, although *not* absolutely) after the war, this was more than offset by the new demographic imbalance between births and deaths.

Since 1947 Egypt's population has been growing by more than 2.5 percent per year, as compared to the world growth rate of about 2 percent per year. This resulted in a total population of over 26 million by the date of the Census of 1960 and about 33 to 35 million by 1970. Cairo's population has been expanding even faster. Since 1947 the number of city residents has increased by about 4 percent per year, yielding a 1960 total of close to 3½ million.[38] Cairo's population, as projected to 1970, reached 6 million, exclusive of the rapidly developing industrial suburbs of Jīzah to the west, Ḥalwān to the south, and Ḍawāḥi Miṣr to the north.[39]

Of perhaps even greater significance is the fact that, unlike earlier decades, much of this growth has been unavoidable, since it came more from internal demographic potential than from migration. Of Cairo's growth between 1947 and 1960, at least three-fifths was due to an excess of births over deaths in the city itself, a phenomenon which shows no signs of diminishing. Even if the attempts of Egypt's planners to deflect migration streams from Cairo and channel them to other industrial centers are totally successful,[40] this will curb only a small fraction of the city's anticipated increase. The excess of births over deaths within Cairo will be sufficient to sus-

[36] The effects of DDT, penicillin, and other antibiotics on the crude death rates in underdeveloped countries throughout the world since 1946 have been noted by numerous demographers. Thus, this phenomenon was not unique to Egypt but was worldwide in its impact. In general, a differential decline in death rates has been noted within these countries, favoring the population in the younger age groups over those in the older ages and favoring the urbanized population over that in rural areas.

[37] Recorded crude birth rates for Cairo have actually been rising over the years; during the most recent period they have ranged between 50 and 55. Older deficiencies in reporting have been almost totally rectified, which accounts in part for the ostensible increase. It now appears unlikely that the crude birth rate was ever much less than 48, despite recorded rates in the low 40's. Part of the recent observed increase is real, however, even though it does not necessarily indicate greater fecundity. The crude birth rate should be used with caution since it is affected by the age and sex distribution of the population. For example, some increase in the crude birth rate—independent of a fertility change—will appear when the sex ratio of the population changes from a heavy excess of males to a more balanced relationship between males and females, a change that has recently occurred in Cairo. At the beginning of the twentieth century, the city was weighted toward males. Since about 1927, the ratio has been equalizing, having been approximately 103 in 1947 and only 101 in 1960. In addition, one can expect a higher crude birth rate, *ceteris paribus*, when a large percentage of the total population is in the childbearing years of life than when the population contains greater proportions of very young and/or very old persons. Thus, when the age distribution of the population changes, this can affect the crude birth rate without indicating a fertility increase. This change has also occurred in Cairo. The percentage of young adults to the total in Cairo has been increasing, just as the proportion has been diminishing in the rural parts of the country, due to the selective character of the rural-to-urban migration. Thus the observed increase in Cairo's recorded birth rate appears to be due to (1) improved and fuller reporting; (2) a shift to a more balanced ratio between the sexes, i.e., an increase in females; and (3) an increase in the percentage of the population in the childbearing years of life. It may be that very recently these factors have been supplemented by a drop in the age at marriage and an increased survival of embryos to full term, leading to a real increase in fertility and fecundity linked to economic advance.

[38] A boundary change between 1947 and 1960 has affected the totals and must be taken into account when computing the growth rate of the city during the intercensal period. In brief, the official boundary of the city in 1960 differs from that in 1947 as follows:

1. The western bank settlements have been eliminated from the city limits.
2. The eastern bank settlements down to and including the suburb of Ḥalwān on the south have been included with the city in 1960, although Ḥalwān was a separate census entry in 1947.
3. The city limits have been extended on the northeast to include areas beyond Heliopolis.

According to the official returns of the 1960 Census, Cairo contained 3,348,779 inhabitants. However, if one adjusts the boundaries to conform roughly with those of 1947, one estimates the total at closer to 3,500,000.

[39] Bandar Jīzah's population in 1960 was about 145,000 in addition to the 105,000 inhabitants residing in areas formerly within the city limits of Cairo. Ḥalwān in 1960, when her total was recorded as part of Cairo, had some 94,000 inhabitants, as compared to only 24,000 in 1947. Ḍawāḥi Miṣr, no longer a distinct census-enumeration district, contained the city of Shubra al-Khaymah with over 100,000 inhabitants in 1960.

[40] One notes the pathetic irony of the *Master Plan of Cairo* (Government Printing Office, Cairo: 1956), which advocated that a ceiling of 3.5 million be placed on the city's population. This number has already been surpassed. Nor do the five- and ten-year development plans drawn up by Egypt's national planners seem likely to achieve decreased migration to Cairo. The further concentration of industrial establishments planned in and around the major city of the country will undoubtedly encourage additional underemployed farmers to "try their luck" in the capital.

tain a growth rate of at least 3 percent per year, an increase impervious to migration controls and other devices of growth limitation. It is therefore safe to predict the continued growth of Cairo in the decades to come, a growth which, since it cannot be prevented, must at least be planned for.

The demographic and urban revolutions that began in Egypt during the nineteenth century but reached full strength only in the twentieth operated to concentrate within the capital city a population of several million persons, many of whom were actually newcomers to an urban way of life. However, over this period, Cairo's growth pattern was transformed from one in which the dominant—and indeed only—source was migration to one in which the major source of population increment has become natural increase.

Until the closing years of the last century, the increasing demands upon city resources imposed by the rapidly growing population could be met in a manner not dissimilar from that employed during earlier periods of expansion. Medieval Cairo, at the peak of her prosperity and grandeur, had contained almost as many residents as the 590,000 persons who lived in the city of 1897. And medieval Cairo, during the fourteenth century, had covered almost as extensive an area as that staked out for urban development by the end of the nineteenth century. Thus, while the character of parts of the city had changed markedly in the interim, the basic factors of supply and demand had not. Only with the fantastic expansion of demand in the twentieth century came problems that could not be solved within the framework of the older technological order. The revolutionary demands generated in the present century required a commensurate revolution in supply. Urban space—both horizontal and vertical—was required to accommodate millions of new urbanites, and modern facilities were required to permit the larger and infinitely more complex metropolis to function and survive.

9 The Increased Supply of Urban Land

JUST as the expansion of Cairo during the Middle Ages was preceded by the recession of the Nile which made available new contiguous land suitable for development, so the twentieth-century expansion was also facilitated by the addition of land. But whereas nature had been the active agent in the former case, during the present century it was man, armed with a newly gained power over nature, who "created" the lands by making them accessible to the city and by draining or irrigating them—thus converting them into that precious commodity, urban land. This transformation was accomplished within a relatively brief moment in Cairo's long history, between about 1897 and 1917.

Peripheral land to the north and northeast of the city had always been in existence but, as long as transportation was by human or animal means, such land lay beyond the limits of reasonable accessibility. Separated from the heart of the city by several hours of tedious travel, the land was suitable only for truck gardening and other nonurban uses. Once transportation links were forged that brought them within an hour or less of travel time from the city's core, these lands became sites of potential urban expansion.[1]

Similarly, there was land to the east of the city, but its elevation on the plateau and foothills of the Muqaṭṭam range placed it above the valley floor and rendered it a useless desert. Urban expansion into this area—or indeed any settled habitation—was precluded by the character rather than the location of the land. Only artificial irrrigation could convert this land into a site for potential city growth.

If too little water prevented expansion to the east, its opposite hindered the settling of land to the west along the borders of the Nile. Up to the twentieth century, this land was still threatened by periodic flooding, causing structures to be confined to isolated high points in the terrain and consigning the bottom lands to winter cultivation. Until the fluctuations in the level of the Nile could be controlled with greater skill, this land also remained unavailable for urban growth.

Farther west, on the two islands formed in the center of the Nile (Rawḍah and al-Jazīrah) and on the fertile broad valley of the western bank, were additional lands not yet functionally related to the city. It was not distance per se that prevented the city's expansion into these areas but the barrier of water. So long as access to the western bank could be gained only by wind- or muscle-driven ferries or over the single thin strand of bridgework built by Ismāʿīl, these lands could not be developed as an integral part of Cairo.

Distance, drought, flood, and the river, then, were the four forces which prevented Cairo's physical spread, which hemmed the city in at all compass points and confined urban development to the region already settled by the end of the nineteenth century. During the opening two decades of the twentieth century each of these barricades was stormed, leaving the surrounding terrain almost defenseless against the tide of urban expansion demanded by Cairo's population explosion. In the history of these campaigns is found the key to the modern ecological structure of metropolitan Cairo.

The only meaningful measure of distance in a city is the amount of time, effort, and expense required to travel from one point to another; anything that reduces these "costs" shrinks distance. In this sense, nineteenth-century Cairo shriveled to less than a third of its original size (or, looked at from the opposite point of view, tripled her area without increasing her size) within the two decades between 1896 and 1916. For in those twenty years a system of mass transit was installed which connected even the most distant points of the expanding city with the central core in a complex network upon which the present city is still heavily dependent.[2]

Cairo inaugurated her first electric tramline several years before New York City was to take advantage of this means of transportation. The initiative and the capital came from Europe, a phenomenon we shall note over and over again as we examine the technological changes that took place in Cairo in the early decades of the twentieth century. In December of 1894, the Baron

[1] A case study of the effects of the transportation system on the conversion of nonurban to urban land has been done for the city of Boston, which offers an interesting parallel to the situation in Cairo. See Sam Warner, Jr., *Streetcar Suburbs* (Harvard University Press, Cambridge: 1962).

[2] Modern Cairo, more than an American city of comparable size, is essentially a mass transit city. The private automobile (which made its Cairo debut in 1903) has never played the crucial role in Cairo that it has, to the despair of planners, in Western cities. The high cost of cars and gasoline coupled with the low level of income protected Cairo until fairly recently from a surfeit of automobiles but made her dependent upon a now obsolete and overburdened mass transit system. The backbone of that system is the electric tramcar that clangs its preordained course down the center of most wide thoroughfares. Beginning in the 1930's, this was supplemented by buses. Gradually, trolley tracks have been removed from many routes as the trams have been converted to overhead wires.

Empain (better known in his capacity as the founder of the modern suburb of Heliopolis) was granted a concession to establish a tramway system for the city of Cairo. The following year he assigned this concession to a joint stock company which had been organized for that purpose by his fellow countrymen in Brussels. Funds were readily raised as European speculative capital was attracted to Egypt in anticipation of a boom. The original agreement had specified eight lines or routes, of which six were to radiate from the central terminal of Maydān al-'Atabah al-Khaḍrā' at the southeast corner of the Azbakīyah Gardens. Between 1896 and the opening month of 1898 all eight lines, having a total track length of 22 kilometers, were inaugurated. The aim of this initial system was to create an internal network linking important points within the built-up portion of the city, not to extend the boundaries of that area. This fact is seen clearly in a catalogue of the routes themselves.

The First Eight Tramlines in Cairo[3]

Description of Route	*Date of Inauguration*
1. Line from al-'Atabah al-Khaḍrā' via the Boulevard Muḥammad 'Ali to the Maydān Muḥammad 'Ali (the old Qaramaydān below the Citadel).	August 1896
2. Line from al-'Atabah al-Khaḍrā' via Shāri' Būlāq to the original Abū al-'Alā' Bridge over the Ismā'īlīyah Canal near the shore of the Nile at Būlāq.	August 1896
3. Line from al-'Atabah al-Khaḍrā' via Shāri' 'Abdul 'Azīz to Bāb al-Lūq and from there south to the Nāṣrīyah (pond) section.	September 1896
4. Line from al-'Atabah al-Khaḍrā' via Shāri' Clot-Bey north to al-Fajjālah and then eastward to 'Abbāsīyah.	September 1896
5. Line from al-'Atabah al-Khaḍrā' southwest to Bāb al-Lūq and from there to the Qaṣr al-'Ayni complex.	December 1896
6. Line from al-'Atabah al-Khaḍrā' via Shāri' Clot-Bey to the railway station at Bāb al Ḥadīd.	December 1896
7. An extension of Line 5 (above) from the Qaṣr al-'Ayni southward to Miṣr al-Qadīmah.	December 1896
8. An extension of Line 4 (above) from 'Abbāsīyah westward to the railway.	January 1898

Another fact is equally obvious from the catalogue. It would not be an exaggeration to claim that Cairo's mass transit system, at least in this initial stage, *could not* have been installed without the prior replanning of the city executed under Ismā'īl and his chief engineer, 'Ali Mubārak. Note how each of the *maydāns* and new streets created in the 1860's and 1870's was pressed into service as an essential link in the evolving transit system. There is no doubt that without the farsighted efforts of that earlier period such rapid installation of a transit system would have been impossible. Certainly, areas that lacked straight thoroughfares of modern dimensions were simply and totally ignored. Thus, the entire medieval core city was left out of the network, to this day a defect only partially remedied.

Initial progress was rewarded and, in 1897 and again in 1902, the concession of the company was extended to additional lines that were more ambitiously conceived than the first eight. The transit system was to be extended to areas beyond the built-up borders of the city and, within the city, was to be channeled along newly created routes. In this process Cairo's oldest landmark, the Khalīj, disappeared, leaving a less picturesque but infinitely more functional thoroughfare and tramline as its substitute.

[3] A number of sources have been consulted to build up a comprehensive description of Cairo's evolving transport system as presented in this chapter. Among the more valuable are: Clerget, *Le Caire*, II, particularly the table compiled from the transit records that appears on pp. 107-108, and which has been adapted for use here; Fu'ād Faraj, *Al-Qāhirah* (Ma'ārif Press, Cairo: 1946), III, 561-563; Émile Boulad, *Les tramways du Caire en 1919* (Imprimerie Barbey, Cairo: 1919); and several chapters in Muṣṭafa Niyāzi, *Al-Qāhirah: Dirāsāt Takhṭīṭīyah fī al-Murūr wa al-Naql wa al-Muwāṣalāt* [Cairo: Planning Studies in Traffic, Transport and Communications] (Anglo-Egyptian Library, Cairo: 1958-1959).

73. Ceremonial cutting of the dike to the Khalīj *ca.* 1800

74. The Khalīj during flood season *ca.* 1800

75. Khalīj Street *ca.* 1930, long after its filling

76. Port Sa'īd Street, today's widened thoroughfare, follows the pathway of the Khalīj canal and street

The reader will recall the long history of the Khalīj. The canal connecting the Nile with the Red Sea had first been dug in the days of the pharaohs; it had been reopened by Trajan during Roman times and had been reactivated by 'Amr after the Arab conquest. But gradually it ceased to be a link with the Red Sea and was reduced in function to irrigating the northern outskirts of Cairo and providing water to the city. Its ceremonial importance, however, exceeded its functional significance. For untold centuries (certainly predating the Arabs), religious ceremonies and great festivity had attended the annual cutting of the dike of the Khalīj at Cairo. (At first, when the water level was higher, the canal was navigable all year and the flood stage was marked by construction of a dike. Later, as the land dried, this procedure was reversed, with the dike opened at flood time.) By this ceremony the head of the Egyptian state signaled to the entire Delta the moment after which the Nile's replenishing flow could be released over the parched earth. But, little by little, the Khalīj was divested of its functions and, with the introduction of perennial irrigation, even its ceremonial importance was undermined. On the other hand, increased dessication had changed the canal into an unattractive and dangerous source of infection. The time was ripe for it to be filled.

In 1897 the Tramway Company agreed to compensate the city for converting the ancient canal bed into a level and wide thoroughfare and to construct a tramline along its entire length from Ẓāhir (Mosque of Baybars I, north of al-Ḥusaynīyah) to its bend at Sayīdah Zaynab (near the site of the seven water wheels of early history). Filling began the following year. By the summer of 1900 the course which had once carried white-sailed boats was being noisily traversed by rattling trolleys, horse-drawn victorias, donkey-drawn carts and carriages, camels, and even water buffaloes being driven to the abattoirs south of Sayīdah Zaynab. At last Cairo had a centrally located north-south thoroughfare extending almost the entire length of the city.

Many of the other tramlines opened during the first decade of the twentieth century stretched out beyond the city proper, for the first time making peripheral sections accessible to the city's center. The first of these was the line constructed between the Qaṣr al-Nīl Bridge and the pyramids along the route laid out by Ismā'īl just prior to the opening of the Suez Canal. Next came a tentacle of the system extending north of the city into Shubra along the route established by Muḥammad 'Ali, the Shāri' Shubra. One branch of this was later extended westward into the Rawḍ al-Faraj section at the Nile north of Būlāq, while another extension carried the line all the way to the village of Shubra farther north. By 1907 many of the peripheral areas north and northeast of the city destined to become populous quarters had been brought within reach of urban expansion by the new tramlines.

Tramlines Added Between 1899 and 1907

Description of Route	*Date of Inauguration*
9. From the Qaṣr al-Nīl Bridge (west bank) to the pyramids and the new Mena House Hotel.	Portion opened in September 1899; remainder in August 1900
10. Line extending from Maydān Ẓāhir due south along the old bed of the Khalīj Miṣri (now filled) to Sayīdah Zaynab.	June 1900
11. From the Pont Limoun near the Bāb al-Ḥadīd railroad station westward along the Ismā'īlīyah Canal and then south to Maydān Ismā'īlīyah at the Qaṣr al-Nīl barracks at the Nile.	May 1902
12. From the Bāb al-Ḥadīd railroad station due northward along Shāri' Shubra and thence to Sāḥil Rawḍ al-Faraj.	May 1903
13. A small connecting loop between al-'Atabah al-Khaḍrā' and the eastern side of the Azbakīyah Gardens via the Mixed Courts Building.	October 1903
14. From Ghamrah to Ẓāhir and then, continuing northeast through 'Abbāsīyah via Boulevard 'Abbās (later known as Shāri' Ghamrah; currently as Shāri' Ramses).	June 1906
15. From the Trade School in northern Būlāq due north along Shāri' Abū al-Faraj to Rawḍ al-Faraj.	February 1907
16. From the Bāb al-Ḥadīd railroad station to the industrial quarter of Sabtīyah in northern Būlāq.	March 1907
17. Extension of Line No. 12, northward along Shāri' Shubra to the outlying village of Shubra al-Khaymah.	May 1907

As can be seen from the table and from Map XIV opposite, while a few of these newly inaugurated lines were directed toward the elaboration of the interior circulation system, five of them (Nos. 9, 12, 14, 15, and 17) pierced deep into the surrounding countryside. And wherever the tramlines blazed a trail the land speculators followed with predatory greed. Astute financiers, many of them foreign, recognized that the city's form was about to be revolutionized by the new transportation system that was evolving. Farm land and squatters' preserves abutting the new tramlines were quickly bought up, often to be resold at a profit immediately afterward. Marginal investors lacking sufficient funds to cover even the negligible purchase prices took options in the hope of a quick killing. Few of the participants in the boom were disappointed. Within the first several years the value of lands adjacent to the new tramlines had doubled, trebled, and even quadrupled.

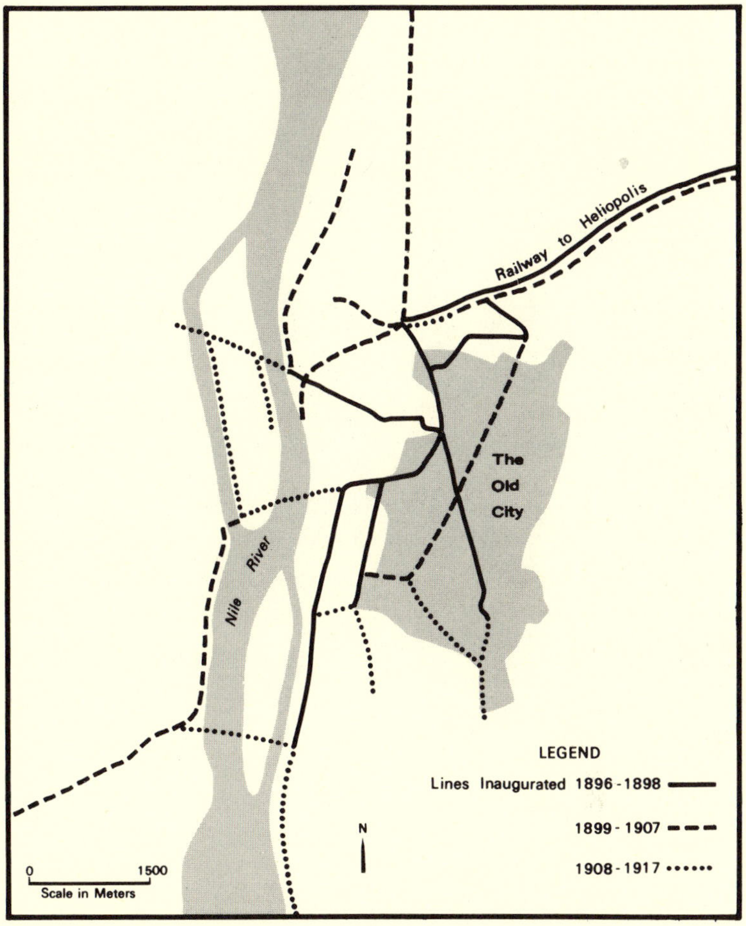

XIV. Extension of the electric tramway lines of Cairo, 1896-1917

77. Al-'Atabah al-Khaḍrā', hub of the modern transit system, in the 1930's

78. The older "mass transit system" *ca.* 1900

79. Al-'Atabah al-Khaḍrā' *ca.* 1960

80. Al-'Atabah al-Khaḍrā' in the 1940's

The process was one very familiar to students of urban land economics, one which has been replicated in every Western city under similar circumstances, and one which still continues, although superhighways have now superseded streetcar lines as the stimulus. It is significant to note that speculation began well in advance of a population growth that would have permitted urban development of all lands taken out of agriculture. Land was simply held vacant, even including plots in the central portion of the city, in anticipation of future gains. In the decade that followed, the character of land use began to change; wholesale and storage warehouses gravitated northward from Būlāq into the Sāḥil Rawḍ al-Faraj (as the former port at Būlāq was relocated farther north), casinos and resorts were established at the ends of lines, and "speculator" houses were jerry-built along the northeast axis toward and beyond 'Abbāsīyah.

Other lines were soon added, either to fill in the interior network or to reach across the river over the series of new bridges that had been constructed. By 1911, 58 kilometers of tramlines were in use, over which rolled some 483 trolleys serving about 55,700,000 passenger-fares yearly.[4] Thus, in the brief span of only fifteen years, Cairo had become a mass transit city. The Baedecker edition of that period assured its readers of Cairo's ubiquitous and convenient system of transportation. By that time, one could travel between al-'Atabah and Miṣr al-Qadīmah in less than forty minutes on tramcars that passed every six or seven minutes. This was the trip that had taken several hours over a dusty donkey path less than fifty years earlier! At twelve-minute intervals a tram ran between the Sporting Club on the Jazīrah, the Azbakīyah Gardens in the heart of "downtown," and the Citadel—a journey which, again, had required several hours and several modes of transportation in earlier days. Every three minutes a tram was dispatched from al-'Atabah al-Khaḍrā' to the railway station and, from there, to 'Abbāsīyah, once the desert outpost near which

[4] Figures on rolling stock and passenger-fares used throughout have been assembled from various issues of *Annuaire Statistique*, issued biennially until 1960-1961 by the Government of Egypt, Department of Statistics and Census. See issue of 1914 as well as later editions.

beduins encamped. Within five minutes one could catch the tram that left from the Mosque of Baybars (at the time of Napoleon isolated amidst cornfields, now the heart of the well-populated district of Ẓāhir) for Sayīdah Zaynab and the slaughterhouses beyond, traveling along the course of the old Khalīj Miṣri. Every six minutes trams served the growing suburbs of Shubra and Rawḍ al-Faraj on the north. Only the west bank of the river remained relatively inaccessible; the single line between the Qaṣr al-Nīl Bridge and the pyramids carried only one car every twenty to thirty minutes.[5]

Final Additions to the Tram System, 1908-1917

Description of Route	*Date of Inauguration*
18. Line connecting Jīzah on the western shore with Miṣr al-Qadīmah via the new bridges (see below).	March 1908
19. Connection between Sayīdah Zaynab and al-Khalīfah cemetery.	May 1908
20. Between the Qaṣr al-Nīl Bridge (east bank) and Maydān 'Abdīn and Maydān 'Abdul 'Azīz.	March 1910
21. Along Shāri' al-Fajjālah to the *maydān* (Karacol) near Bāb al-Ḥadīd and then northeast to Sakākīni.	Between August 1910 and January 1911
22. Connection between Sayīdah Zaynab and Nāṣrīyah.	June 1911
23. Sayīdah Zaynab southward to the abattoirs.	September 1911
24. From Būlāq over the new bridge to the Jazīrah.	July 1912
25. Between the two western bridges on the Jazīrah.	October 1912
26. A short feeder-line connecting the Sporting Club with Line No. 24 on the Jazīrah.	February 1913
27. Connection between the Jazīrah and the village of Imbābah on the western bank via the Zamālik Bridge.	March 1913
28. Extension of the northern lines to Rawḍ al-Faraj and Sāḥil Rawḍ al-Faraj.	November 1913
29. Line from the Citadel southward into al-Khalīfah cemetery as far as the Tomb of Imām Shāfi'i.	December 1916
30. Southern extension from Miṣr al-Qadīmah to outlying Athar al-Nabi.	September 1917

81. Streetcar line to the pyramids

Between 1908 and 1917 thirteen new lines or extensions to existing routes were added to the system, many of them to incorporate the islands and the western bank into the network which already served most of the city and its protrusions to the north, northeast, and south.

The mass transit system as it had evolved by 1917 established the framework within which the twentieth century city grew. Only two additional lines were added to the tram network after that date, both in 1931, on thoroughfares especially created to permit easier access through the older parts of the city, namely, Shāri' al-Azhar and Shāri' al-Jaysh. (The Bus Company, organized in 1930, supplemented the carrying capacity of the system but did not change its essential pattern.) By 1917,

[5] Baedecker's *Guide to Egypt* (Charles Scribner's Sons, New York: 7th edn., 1914), p. 38.

82. The Shāri' al-Azhar shortly after it was opened

83. Aerial view of Heliopolis today

there were 65 kilometers of electric tram tracks criss-crossing the city, over which rolled some 500 tramcars carrying more than 75 million riders annually.[6]

Within twenty years the physiognomy of Cairo had been revolutionized. Measured by travel time, the city had been compressed so that even its most outlying settlements could be reached from the center within less than an hour, and most points in the built-up zone were within a fifteen- to twenty-minute radius of the hub at al-'Atabah al-Khaḍrā'. By measure of distance, therefore, the city was ready for expansion. Areas which, under older means of transportation, could be used only for truck gardening were ready to be converted into valuable urban sites. Later improvements in the transport system simply confirmed without basically altering this fact.

To the east of the city, outlining the fanning Delta, were desiccated plateau lands which prevented the city's expansion in that direction. Up to 1952, only one attempt had been made to crash through the desert barrier[7] and that attempt, a prototype for all to come later, resulted in the creation *in vacuo* of Cairo's most impressive suburb, Heliopolis. Its development was intimately tied to the expansion of the mass transit system in Cairo.

In 1906, the Tramway Company bartered its concession for an extension of the 'Abbāsīyah line to the suburban villages of 'Ain Shams and Maṭarīyah in return for 5,000 shares in the newly organized Miṣr and 'Ain Shams Oasis Electric Railroad Company. It was an exchange it never needed to regret. The latter company contemplated a scheme so unique at the time that, had it ended in disaster, it could easily have been dismissed as "Baron Empain's Folly." The plan was to construct a *new* Cairo (Miṣr al-Jadīdah) on the desert plateau northeast of and quite beyond 'Abbāsīyah.

Heliopolis was to be a garden satellite town designed in the latest manner of British town planning, but it would have been impossible to find a site less garden-like in its original state![8] In May of 1905 the Oasis Company obtained a license from the Egyptian government to build its city and received permission to purchase the valueless desert land at the nominal price of one Egyptian pound per acre. Within the first few years of its existence, the company exercised its option on almost 6,000 acres. But without capital investment on an impressive scale this land was not even worth its bargain price. Not only did the new area require extensive irrigation, but a full complement of municipal services—roads, water lines, sewers, electricity, and other site improvements—was needed to convert the raw land to urban use. As in the case of the transportation system, the capital came from European sources. By 1906 the capitalized value of the company was on the order of 15 million francs. Five years later, when the operation

[6] See *Annuaire Statistique*. In 1915, prior to the completion of the last few lines, the length of tram tracks was 63 kilometers, a figure increased to 65 by 1917. After that date, the figure remains constant until the addition of the lines on Shāri' al-Azhar and Shāri' al-Jaysh, in 1931. By then the trackage had increased to 71 kilometers; the present length is 70 kilometers. In various issues of *Annuaire Statistique*, figures are also given concerning rolling stock and passenger-fares. From these we learn that by 1915 the number of tramcars had reached 498, a stock which was preserved unchanged until the 1920's. We also see the impact that Cairo's rising population had on the use of this stock. In 1915, 50,489,000 passenger rides were recorded. This was increased to 82,733,000 passengers by 1920 and, with only a small increment to rolling stock, to 93,265,000 five years later.

[7] Since the Revolution of 1952, several more attempts have been made to utilize the dead land east of the city for urban purposes. The most impressive of these has been the creation of Naṣr City, on the desert land between 'Abbāsīyah and Heliopolis. In addition, in 1960 the government began the clearing and leveling of the so-called windmill hills just east of the city, the squatters' preserve which had grown up on the artificial mounds intervening between the medieval city and the Mamluk City of the Dead, i.e., the Qayt Bay cemetery, and this zone is now being redeveloped. Perhaps the most ambitious of the recent projects has been the construction of a residential suburb on the heights of the Muqaṭṭam range, since the technical problems of laying utilities and constructing houses on the rocky promontory there presented an unusual challenge to ingenuity and finance. See Chapter 13, below, for details on some of these projects.

[8] Among the sources which can be consulted for information on the founding of Heliopolis are: Clerget, *Le Caire*, I, 205-206; the *Cairo Master Plan*, pp. 31-32.

was beginning to show tangible results, some 50 million francs had been invested.

Even a well-designed and improved city could not exist, however, without a lifeline to the economic heart, Cairo. Rapid transit connections between the dormitory suburb and the city were essential. The tramline along the northeast axis had already been extended as far as ʻAbbāsīyah, but there was as yet no means for continuing the journey beyond to the outlying site of Heliopolis. As part of the initial concession, the Oasis Company had agreed to construct and equip an electric street railroad (Metro) which would serve its new community. By 1908 the outermost portion of this line was already in operation, connecting the new city with the terminus of the tram tracks at ʻAbbāsīyah. In the following year another line was inaugurated to link Miṣr al-Jadīdah with the other outlying suburban community of al-Qubbah, where the residential palace of the Khedive was located. In 1910, the system was completed by an extension which continued the Miṣr al-Jadīdah-ʻAbbāsīyah line all the way to the terminus at Pont Limoun station, just across the Ismāʻīlīyah Canal from the rail terminal of Bāb al-Ḥadīd. Other feeders carried traffic into the very heart of the city, although these have since been removed.[9] It was this transportation link which permitted the growth of Heliopolis and which resulted, much later, in a continuous band of urban settlement stretching all the way from ʻAbbāsīyah to Heliopolis and beyond. The gigantic gamble undertaken in the opening decade of the twentieth century by a Belgian "robber" Baron recompensed its foreign investors beyond their wildest hopes.

Some indication of the venture's success is that by 1947 the suburb in the desert contained a resident population of almost 50,000 persons and now houses more than twice that number. Nor is it any longer a mere dormitory suburb. Close by are three airports, extensive military installations, and numerous factories offering local employment. In addition, an important secondary government center is located within the town itself as well as a fairly self-sufficient central business district. While large numbers of its residents still commute the half-hour to Cairo, the community has gradually taken on many qualities of the satellite town initially envisaged by its founders.

Thus, within the opening two decades of the twentieth century the desert barrier had been pierced, although admittedly the single breach at Heliopolis was far from

[9] By 1911, 24 kilometers of Metro lines were in operation. After that date, only 3 kilometers of feeder lines were added, the maximum being reached about 1930. After that, the extent of trackage was reduced to 22 kilometers, its present length. See *Annuaire Statistique*, various issue from 1914 *et seq.*

84. Bāb al-Ḥadīd railway station about 1920. Note Jisr Shubra to left of station

85. Widened Shāriʻ Ramses in front of Bāb al-Ḥadīd station in the early 1960's

86. Aerial view of the train station, the metro terminus, and Shāriʻ Ramses

a decisive victory. It proved, however, that expansion into the desert was feasible and economic; further conquests required merely the stimulation of demand.

These were also the decades during which Cairo conquered the barrier which the Nile had always presented. Although the opening skirmish had taken place in the nineteenth century when Ismāʿīl installed the first iron bridge of Qaṣr al-Nīl, it was not until the first years of the twentieth century that the city was able to break through the riverine barrier sufficiently to permit urban development of river-margin land, of the islands in the middle of the river, and of the agricultural land on the western bank.

The decisive "battle of the Nile" was not fought at Cairo but more than 500 miles upstream at the cataract above the small provincial town of Aswān, not far from the Sudanese border. In February of 1898 a group of British financiers combined to underwrite the costs of constructing a dam and reservoir at that site, engaging the firm of Sir John Aird and Company to execute the massive engineering project. By December of 1902 a dam, a mile and a quarter in length and capable of maintaining a 65-foot head of impounded water, was dedicated and placed in operation.[10] This low Aswān Dam with its associated reservoir gave Egypt some measure of control over the river at whose mercy she had existed since earliest recorded history. During the late summer flood and the winter months, the reservoir stored the excess water which formerly had roared and eddied downstream, overflowing the banks before being lost finally into the Mediterranean. These impounded waters could now be released gradually during the drought months of late spring and early summer to maintain a water supply for year-round cultivation in the Delta. While this was the major purpose of the dam, one side effect at Cairo was the reduction in flood damage on both margins of the river. Once the banks of the river had been stabilized it became possible to develop them more intensively and also to throw bridges across from one firm shore to the other.

It is therefore not accidental that the year 1902, which marks the inauguration of the first dam at Aswān, also marks the initiation of plans for several bridges spanning the tamed waterway. Three bridges begun in that year were completed and opened for traffic in 1907. These were the ʿAbbās Bridge, 535 meters long and stretching between the western edge of the island of Rawḍah and the west bank of the Nile at Jīzah; the Malik al-Ṣāliḥ Bridge, spanning the short distance between the eastern edge of Rawḍah and Miṣr al-Qadīmah; and the Muḥammad ʿAli Bridge, connecting the Qaṣr al-ʿAyni with the northern tip of Rawḍah. These three bridges created a southern route to supplement the central connection originally achieved in 1872 by the Qaṣr al-Nīl Bridge and its extension across the Jazīrah.

The dam at Aswān, hailed at the turn of the century as the "final" solution, soon proved inadequate for the task assigned to it and, in 1909, over the protests of concerned archaeologists, plans were made to heighten the crest to increase its storage capacity, a scheme finally completed by 1912. Following this new heightening a third bridge connection between the eastern and western banks at Cairo was added, this time to the north of the existing bridge at Qaṣr al-Nīl. In 1908 work was begun on the Abū al-ʿAlā' Bridge connecting Būlāq with the northern half of the Jazīrah, a span some 274 meters in length. By 1912, this bridge (now known as the 26th of July Bridge) and its western extension to Imbābah (called the Zamālik Bridge) were both completed and opened to wheeled and tramway traffic. Two years later, the older Jalā' Bridge (western extension of the Qaṣr al-Nīl Bridge originally constructed in 1872) was replaced by a wider and sounder structure. With these final additions, the bridge building phase came to a halt temporarily.[11]

Thus, by 1914, there were three alternative routes connecting the banks of the river, two using the Jazīrah as a stepping stone to link east and west at the northern and central sections of the city, the third employing the island of Rawḍah in similar fashion to effect a connection between the southern sections. No basic additions to the system were made after that date, although the bridges were rebuilt or improved from time to time. It was not until after the Revolution of 1952 that a fourth route was created by the construction of the Jāmiʿah Bridge between northern Rawḍah and Cairo University on the western bank.

In much the same manner in which the tram system, completed substantially by 1917, opened up the northern and northeastern suburban regions to urban development, so the completion of the system of bridges by

[10] The number of sources concerning the Aswān Dam is legion. However, some idea of the response of contemporaries to the bold project can be gained from F. C. Penfield, *Present-Day Egypt* (The Century Company, New York: Revised and enlarged edn., 1903), pp. 145-165.

[11] Omitted from this discussion is the long and varied history of the railway bridge of Imbābah, designed to carry rail traffic between the Delta line terminus at Bāb al-Ḥadīd on the eastern bank and the Upper Egyptian line terminus at Imbābah on the western bank. This bridge had first been undertaken in 1889 and completed in 1892. It was demolished in 1898 and then replaced by a more modern structure. Also, in 1933, the Qaṣr al-Nīl Bridge replacement was installed and opened for traffic while Ismāʿīl's structure was simultaneously demolished. Neither of these affected the basic transportation connections in the city.

1914 made possible the expansion of the city onto the two islands in the midst of the Nile and, beyond, onto the western shore. Note that here again the "creation" of additional land preceded the phenomenal upsurge in demand of the 1920's.

The disappearance during this period of one further landmark of the city must also be noted. With the filling in of the Khalīj Miṣri, Cairo was left with only one major canal to remind her of the medieval period when her canal system had been likened to Venice. This was the broad Khalīj Ismā'īlīyah, built less than fifty years earlier as a replacement for the Maghribi Canal and as a fresh water link with the Suez Canal. With only a handful of bridges crossing it (notably the Qanṭarat Būlāq near the shore of the Nile; the Pont Limoun at the railroad station of Bāb al-Ḥadīd; and a final one over its juncture with the Khalīj Miṣri), the canal presented a serious barrier to the integration of nineteenth-century Cairo with the still-independent community of Būlāq and with the northern suburbs that were developing in Shubra and Rawḍ al-Faraj. On the other hand, the functions which the canal had originally been designed to serve had become irrelevant. Shipping technology had so altered that the canal was useless as an interior waterway. Furthermore, the port of Būlāq had gravitated northward to Sāḥil Rawḍ al-Faraj and was no longer vitally connected with Mediterranean traffic, again due to the disappearance of smaller vessels from world commerce. A water system supplanted its irrigation functions, while the filling of the Khalīj Miṣri before the turn of the century eliminated even its limited role in the water-borne internal transportation system of the city itself. The filling in of the Ismā'īlīyah Canal in 1912 was, then, a logical and final step in the centuries-old process of converting Cairo from a city at the mercy of her river to a city functionally independent of the river.

Within the broad strip of land bequeathed by the filled canal a major transportation axis was created, upon which the present circulation pattern of the city depends. Thus, the canal which had formerly served to divide the city became, after 1912, a critical link in her unification, giving simplified access to the settlements proliferating between the railroad station and Heliopolis.

The construction of a dam at Aswān was not only associated with the development of bridges in the Cairo area but also with the development of the narrow strips of land bordering the hitherto unstable edges of the river, strips which have since become the most exclusive residential quarters of the contemporary city. Their development also dates from the opening decade of the twentieth century.

In the nineteenth century as well as earlier, the predominant land use found along both shores and on the islands within the Nile was royal. Here were scattered the numerous palaces of a large ruling family, interspersed by gardens, plantations, and orchards. Particularly at the time of Ismā'īl these areas had received preferential development. By 1897 the following were located on the east shore southward from Būlāq: (1) the barracks of Qaṣr al-Nīl, originally constructed by Sa'īd; (2) the palaces of Ismā'īlīyah and Dūbbārah, surrounded by their gardens, in the general area known as Qaṣr al-Dūbbārah extending between the street leading to the Qaṣr al-Nīl Bridge on the north and the Shāri' Dākhilīyah on the south; (3) the plantations north of and associated with the two palaces of the Queen Mother and the older palace built by Muḥammad 'Ali's son, Ibrāhīm, al-Qaṣr al-'Ālī; (4) vacant land which had been ceded to the Water Company for its pumping station but abandoned after the pumping station was relocated near Būlāq; and finally (5) the Qaṣr al-'Ayni of Muḥammad 'Ali, which had been serving as a military and public hospital for many decades.

On the Jazīrah opposite Būlāq there was the palace which Ismā'īl had built just prior to the opening of the Suez Canal and, north of it, the gardens designed and executed by Barillet-Deschamps. In 1880, when Ismā'īl's creditors claimed many of his possessions, the palace itself had been sold to a hotel chain and after 1893 transformed into the luxurious Jazīrah Palace Hotel, rival to the famous Shepheard's and under the same management. (After a generation as a private residence, it has recently been converted back to a hotel, the 'Umar Khayyām.) Around the palace lay the race course, polo fields, and gardens which became the elite Khedivial Sporting Club (now known as the Jazīrah Club), while to the west of the palace was Ismā'īl's fish grotto, later opened to the public as an aquarium and park in 1902. Circling the island was a shaded carriageway which had displaced Shāri' Shubra as the favored promenade of the fashionable.

On the island of Rawḍah to its south the uses remained a strange combination of rural and regal. At the southern end was a park belonging to the heirs of Ḥasan Pasha and the ancient Nilometer; in the northern and eastern parts of the island were several royal family palaces and the remnants of Ibrāhīm's famous botanical forest. Intervening were small rural settlements (including the village of Manyal) in which lived a peasant class which cultivated the island.

On the western bank of the Nile was a similar compounding of uses. The villages of Imbābah, Mīt Kardak, Mīt 'Uqbah and their surrounding fields and *'izab* (feudal settlements) preempted the northern portion.

87. Aerial view of the Garden City Gold Coast

South of them came the still periodically flooded, undeveloped *waqf* land of al-Ḥūtīyah containing fishermen's shacks. Between this and the old town of Jīzah opposite the Nilometer were the grounds of the Orman Gardens which had been incompletely executed by Barillet-Deschamps and, to their south, the Jīzah Palace built by Ismā'īl. Since 1889 the Egyptian Museum of Antiquities had been housed in this structure (having been moved there from the original museum site in Būlāq) where it remained until the completion in 1902 of the new (and present) Museum of Antiquities near the Qaṣr al-Nīl barracks. In 1891 a section of the Orman Gardens was converted to a public zoological garden and today the zoo, slightly enlarged, still occupies the same spot.

Practically all these areas were opened to urban development during the boom years of the 1900's, thanks in part to the demand exerted by an influx of foreigners and in part to their final freedom from flood. On the east bank of the Nile the area of Qaṣr al-Dūbbārah was the first section to be transformed. Following the location there of the British Consulate General, the area became particularly attractive to high-ranking foreigners who, beginning at the turn of the century, constructed elaborate villas in the vicinity. After 1906, when a syndicate purchased Ibrāhīm's palace and planned its demolition, the section newly named Garden City came into being. The complex, winding circulation system of the new quarter was distinctly British in conception, reflecting the then popular clichés of Ebenezer Howard in the same way that Ismā'īl's contributions had reflected the Haussmann approach to city design. Development of Garden City, however, took place only gradually, since the economic crisis of 1907 and the deflation of speculative demand which followed inhibited the construction of many of the homes planned for the area. By the World War I period, although streets had been laid out all the way from Qaṣr al-Dūbbārah south to the Qaṣr al-'Ayni Hospital and although several intervening palaces had been demolished, there were only a handful of elaborate villas sprinkled over the extensive quarter. Not until the more prosperous 1920's did the area begin to fill in, and not until the even more active 1940's and 1950's were these villas replaced by the tall apartment houses which now predominate in the quarter.

Developments on the Jazīrah date from the same era of speculative expansion. Between 1905 and 1907 the Baehler Society purchased and subdivided the portion of the island north of the Jazīrah Palace Hotel. Houses were constructed on the lots closest to the center of the island, while more peripherally located sites were held vacant or still farmed in anticipation of future demand. What was true of the Jazīrah was even more typical of the western bank of the Nile. There, speculators had purchased all lands not usurped by the royal domains or tied up in *waqf* but, except for the very narrow strip between the river and the major tramline which contained a string of elegant homes, only spotty building gave evidence of fulfilled promise.

Thus, by the end of the second decade, all the barriers which had prevented the city's expansion before the twentieth century (except the still-extant *kharāb* south of the major nucleus) had been methodically demolished. Distance had been compressed by mass transit; the desert had, in places at least, been irrigated and developed; bridges spanned the river at three important points, bringing the islands and the west bank into the potential circumference of the city; and drainage and flood control had made possible the subdivision and sale of lands bordering the no-longer capricious river.

These lands had been added to the city's supply during an era of unprecedented foreign investment, real estate speculation, and unguarded optimism concerning Egypt's economic future and her secure position as a British colony, in fact if not in name. The tremendous population boom experienced in the 1920's had not yet occurred. Nor was it then predictable that by 1922 Egypt would gain some greater measure of autonomy under a constitutional monarchy. Nor could the world-wide depression which inhibited urban growth during the decade of the '30's have been predicted during the revolutionary opening decades of the twentieth century.

All these events were yet to come. The evolution of every quarter of the city was to be affected differentially by them, but it is important to note that without the new urban framework established between 1897 and 1917 none of these developments would have taken the form they did. Later we shall trace the evolution of each of the quarters to show how both supply and demand interacted to yield the particular ecological pattern of contemporary Cairo. However, before proceeding to this final section, we might summarize some of the problems of urban growth and control as they evolved during the modern era, indicating which of the problems inherited from the past had been solved during the nineteenth and early twentieth centuries, which residual difficulties persisted into the modern era, and what new kinds of problems were created by the process of modernization.

10 Urban Problems: Old, Persistent, and New

By 1917 Cairo was prepared to embark upon a new phase of development destined to transform her perhaps into a more prosaic but certainly more familiar model of a modern metropolis. The groundwork for this transformation had been laid during the nineteenth century and the opening decades of the twentieth. Within that span of time many of the older problems that had been her legacy from medieval and Turkish times had, in large measure, been solved. A significant few, only slightly modified or ameliorated, persisted to hinder her metamorphosis. Finally, and perhaps of greatest importance, it was at this time that new and unprecedented problems came to be recognized, ones which were not unique to Cairo as a Middle Eastern city, nor an Islamic one, nor even as a prototype of a preindustrial city but familiar problems faced by any major city in the twentieth-century Western world. The emergence of these problems indicates that Cairo was, indeed, evolving into an industrial metropolis. While the unique history of the city's development shaped the particular form the problems were to take, the problems themselves signaled the passing of uniqueness.

Most of the problems resolved by the early twentieth century may be classified as physical and technological, rather than social or institutional. The preceding chapters have explored in some detail the physical advances made in the critical century between the later decades of Muḥammad 'Ali's reign and the opening years of World War I. Thus, only a very brief recapitulation is necessary here.

Among the earliest improvements were the removal of most of the rubbish mounds that had surrounded the city (all but those in the vicinity of Old Cairo and on the eastern border of the walled city) and the successive filling of the numerous *birak* and marshlands that had constituted major barriers to the expansion of the city. This was followed by a stabilization of the banks of the Nile at Cairo, a process which although it began in the 1860's was not completed until the inauguration of the first low dam at Aswān in 1902, and not fully perfected until the subsequent heightening of that dam in 1909-1912 and, again, in the early 1930's.

A road system in many new sections of the city had been substantially achieved by the early twentieth century. The planning of the Ismā'īlīyah quarter, the Fajjālah section and the area of Tawfīqīyah, followed by similar innovations on the Jazīrah, along the banks of the Nile in Qaṣr al-Dūbbārah and Garden City, as well as on the Jīzah side, and culminating in the subdivision of the northern quarters, such as Shubra, Ẓāhir, Sakākīni, and extending to 'Abbāsīyah, Qubbah, Maṭarīyah, Zaytūn, and Miṣr al-Jadīdah on the northeast—all these represented a "final" solution to the old problem of space. The solution was facilitated by major technological innovations in the form of bridges and, most important, a network of electric tramlines that threaded the newer districts and joined each to the city's center.

Not only had the city successfully coped with the problems of space and accessibility, but by 1917 a safe and relatively sanitary urban environment—notoriously absent as late as the nineteenth century—had been achieved, even though much room for improvement remained. While the political stability attained during the Muḥammad 'Ali era must be credited with having initiated this process, the safer environment could not have been created without the institutional innovations of hospitals and clinics, the regulatory innovations in the field of public health, and, finally, the physical addition of the drainage-sewerage system for the city. Although there were areas in which inadequate efforts had been made and although only a relatively tiny proportion of the national budget was still allocated to these ends, the fact remains that, even with the minimal and inexpensive means employed, Cairo by 1917 had become an infinitely safer place in which to be born and live than she had been a scant fifty years earlier.

While most of the solved problems may be classified as "physical," most of the yet unresolved ones were to be found in the social, economic, and institutional aspects of urbanization. Although some small beginnings had been made in ameliorating these remaining impediments to modern development, their ultimate solutions lay in the future. Perhaps the most basic unsolved problem was the most ancient. Egypt, on the eve of World War I, still lacked political autonomy and was still governed essentially by an alien elite, even though its nature had altered significantly since the days of the Mamluks. As we have seen, this situation was scarcely initiated by the British occupation of 1882 which, rather, must be viewed merely as a culminary continuation—albeit different in kind as well as degree—of the pattern which for centuries had separated governmental and social decision-making from the indigenous population.

The problem of political autonomy had once come close to solution. The military exploits of Muḥammad

'Ali and Ibrāhīm Pasha had been attempts to establish Egypt's independent status vis-à-vis the Ottoman Sultanate, a goal foiled largely by European intervention in 1840-1841. Thereafter, fiscal rather than forceful means were employed to the same end, particularly by Ismā'īl, in an effort to extract in piecemeal concessions what had been denied in principle and *in toto*. The autonomy so dearly "purchased" from the Porte, however, was ceded to the British Consul General after 1882, so that little net gain could be recorded. Ironically, Egypt's declaration of independence from Constantinople came in 1914 with the unilateral British creation of a protectorate status for Egypt—a step which was an inevitable consequence of the state of war existing between the two "partners" in Egypt's rule. Thus, while autonomy was theoretically achieved, self-government by native Egyptians remained if anything an even more remote possibility.

Self-government and the elimination of alien elements from the control of national affairs, however, were becoming the goals of an increasingly articulate Egyptian nationalist movement. It is certainly beyond the scope and requirements of the present study to trace the development of this movement from its modern beginnings during the second half of the nineteenth century.[1] We need note merely that many decades of preparation and built-up pressures lay behind the "crisis point" that was reached at the end of World War I, when Egyptian nationalist leaders claimed the concessions they believed Britain had promised to grant once hostilities ended. The formation of the Wafd by Sa'd Zaghlūl, the frustrations that exploded into the national strike of 1919, the "investigating committee" appointed by Great Britain, the initiation, breaking-off, and resuscitation of negotiations—these are merely some of the landmarks in the crisis that led, early in 1922, to the British declaration officially terminating the protectorate and recognizing the status of Egypt as an independent sovereign State.[2]

Not that the establishment of an independent political entity indicated fulfillment of nationalist demands or aspirations. While the agreement of 1922 opened the way for a constitution (1923) and a good measure of *de jure* independence, the continued presence on Egyptian soil of a substantial British military force (one of the rights reserved in the agreement) tended to detract from the *de facto* exercise of self-determination. It was not until the Anglo-Egyptian Treaty of 1936 that physical and numerical limits were imposed upon the British military forces, even though the exigencies of World War II soon invalidated the terms of these restrictions. The final evacuation of all British troops from Egyptian soil did not take place until 1956, when Egypt became sovereign in the fullest sense of that term. Nevertheless, the 1922 agreement did contribute substantially to the "nativization" of the governmental if not the social elite, by eliminating foreign nationals from many top positions in the bureaucracy and by turning over the administration of the country to its inhabitants. This was as true with respect to the administration of Cairo as it was with respect to the country.

The alien elite, however, had never rested its powers on governmental participation alone. Indeed, the ethnic groups in the strongest financial position (Belgians, French, and Swiss) and those with the greatest numerical strength (Greeks, Italians, and the oddly designated "Levantines") had scarcely been involved in the British-directed administration of the country and were thus untouched by the concessions granted to the nationalists in 1922. The Capitulations, which had given to these groups their favored and protected status and had aided them in their accumulation of economic and social power, remained unaffected by the agreement of 1922. For example, the Mixed Courts, which had been established in 1875 for the ostensible purpose of regularizing within a unified legal system the multiplicity of jurisdictions permitted under the Capitulations, remained in force. These continued to place native Egyptians at a practical if not legally sanctioned disadvantage in litigations with foreign nationals. While British policy occasionally chafed under the diffusive powers of the Capitulations, and while certain modifications and concessions were sought and even obtained—notably the power to impose "voluntary taxes," by consent, within specified municipalities—Britain neither desired nor sought a basic modification of the Mixed Courts system. It was not until the Convention of Montreux in 1937, whose success the British had "guaranteed" in the treaty of the preceding year, that the concessions under the Capitulations were finally abrogated and foreigners lost some of their long-sanctioned privileges within Egypt. However, even this did not lead to an immediate disbanding of the Mixed Courts, since a transitional period of twelve years was allowed which delayed the establishment of a single-standard unified judicial system in Egypt until 1949.

Not unrelated to the problems outlined above were two additional institutional difficulties that still beset Cairo in 1917 and were not to be solved so easily. One was the lack of home rule (that is, municipal status with its attendant power to finance locally determined improve-

[1] For this development, see Jamal Ahmed, *The Intellectual Origins of Egyptian Nationalism* (Oxford University Press, London: 1960); and Nadav Safran, *Egypt in Search of Political Community* (Harvard University Press, Cambridge: 1961). A contemporary account of some aspects can be found in Wilfred Blunt, *Secret History of the English Occupation of Egypt* (Alfred Knopf, New York: 1922).

[2] A succinct account of the actual events, then and later, together with reproductions of the relevant documents, can be found in John Marlowe, *A History of Modern Egypt and Anglo-Egyptian Relations, 1800-1953* (Praeger, New York: 1954).

ments from an independent budget) and local representative government through which local aspirations could be translated into community goals. The other was the lack of local institutions for financing private urban developments on a modern scale. Each of these requires more detailed analysis.

It must be admitted at the outset that the issue of local government has not the emotional commitment in many parts of the Orient that it has in the West. While in Europe local administrations often preceded—and jealously guarded their rights against—the establishment of a central or national government, the process was generally the reverse elsewhere. Certainly, in Egypt the central administration always took precedence and local subdivisions were often created primarily for the purpose of ensuring the execution of policies that had already been determined.

Cairo, as the capital city, was in an even more anomalous situation than most other local communities. Although since Mamluk times at least she had always been administered by special city officials—a quasi-military governor subordinate to the ruling House, a chief security officer, and at least two chief *qāḍis* (one for al-Qāhirah, the other for Fusṭāṭ)—in practice a separation between local and national politics was hardly feasible. To control the capital was, in fact, to control the country. And the converse was so compelling that the security of the capital always became the critical issue during the power struggles that recurred regularly throughout the centuries. It was perhaps due to this fact that, even after other local communities in Egypt began to enjoy a greater degree of autonomy and home rule, Cairo was consciously excluded from their ranks.

It is conventional to attribute the inauguration of a modified system of decentralized government in Egypt to the passage of the 1883 First Organic Law. In actuality, however, the administrative subdivisions utilized in this system had been delimited in 1820 by Muḥammad ʿAli in accordance with a reorganization that was taking place throughout the Ottoman empire. Furthermore, the British administration continued to use their newly established provincial councils *not* to initiate policies (which had been their ostensible purpose in the law) but, rather, in the same manner in which their predecessor-institutions had been used, i.e., chiefly as agents of execution.

Even before passage of the Organic Law, however, the foreign communities in several Egyptian cities had seeded the ground for local government. As in the medieval cities of Europe, the pressures toward self-government were "burgher" in their origins and "commercial" in their motivations. Thus, in 1869, the cotton export merchants of Alexandria agreed to contribute taxes or, more accurately, to pay assessments to improve the road between Mīnat al-Baṣal and the port, a venture the government helped to support by an annual subvention. This nucleus of organization grew into a town council by 1885 and was finally succeeded in 1890 by a municipality (*baladīyah*), the first to be established in Egypt.[3] While merchants in other communities also appear to have made some efforts in a similar direction, the practical difficulties involved in setting up a municipal structure, which in the case of Alexandria had required the signature of all Capitulatory Powers, were sufficient to guarantee Alexandria's uniqueness until 1893.

In that year, the Minister of Interior authorized nine cities to form local commissions for the purpose of planning municipal improvements that were to be financed by subventions from the national government.[4] These "local governments" were to confine their attentions, however, to apolitical housekeeping functions, such as arranging for the installation of water and electrical systems, overseeing the maintenance and cleaning of streets and public gardens, regulating public facilities, and the like. Eleven more communities were added to their ranks in the next three years. However, the uncertainties of planning for even these minimal services without some guaranteed form of locally raised revenues, coupled with the legal impossibility of collecting taxes from foreigners, were problems unsolved in the local commission. The Local Mixed Commission, in which foreigners were given equal representation in return for their voluntary com-

[3] A comprehensive account of the evolution of municipal government in Egypt between those early years and 1922 appears in M. M. Delcroix, then Director of the Municipalities' Service of the Egyptian government, "L'Institution municipale en Égypte," *L'Égypte Contemporaine*, No. 65 (April 1922), pp. 278-323. The following section depends heavily on this source. The question might be raised concerning connections between early municipal development in Egypt and similar developments in Turkey, for presumably Egypt, as a province of the Ottoman empire, should have been affected by events in the capital. This appears not to have been the case. As early as 1858, a model district (the Sixth District, covering the European quarters) was established in Istanbul as an experimental municipality, but its inspiration and execution were apparently by and for foreigners. In this it parallels the case of Alexandria rather than Cairo. Again, in 1868 a municipal code of regulations in Istanbul was promulgated, extending the application of the model district system to the remainder of the city, but, as R. L. Hill has pointed out, "the Ottoman municipal legislation of 1864-1877 was applied throughout the Arabic-speaking provinces of the Empire *except . . . in Egypt* where municipal development was following a different course." See R. L. Hill, "Baladiyya: Arab East," *Encyclopedia of Islam*², I, 975-976, from which the quotation, with italics added, has been taken, and Bernard Lewis, "Baladiyya: Turkey," *ibid.*, pp. 972-975.

[4] In November 1893, local commissions were authorized for Maḥallah al-Kubra, Asyūṭ, Damanhūr, Ḍimyāṭ, Manṣūrah, Fayūm, Suez, Ṭanṭa, and Zaqāzīq, which were to consist of four elected representatives plus, ex officio, the local *mudīr*, the inspector of sanitation, and the building inspector.

pliance with local taxation, was initially set up in 1896 in Manṣūrah as a way out of this dilemma, and other communities with powerful foreign minorities were quick to convert to this new form.

By 1908, three dozen Egyptian cities had local or mixed commissions—but Cairo was still conspicuously absent from their number. Despite the reforms of 1909[5] and the gradual increase in the number of communities coming under this system to 43 by 1912, 62 by 1921, and even more in the years that followed, Cairo's name does not appear on the list. Even the Constitution of 1923, which established the provinces, cities, and villages of Egypt as juristic personalities and enabled the enactment of several basic local government laws,[6] did not lead to the establishment of a separate municipal charter for Cairo.

In fact, it was not until 1949 (Law 145) that the Municipality of Cairo was created, as distinct from the provincial government. Since then there has been a total reorganization of the system of local government in the United Arab Republic, as promulgated in Law 124 of 1960 and amended by Law 151 of 1961, and many of the provisions of the 1949 law have been superseded. The details concerning the present administration are reserved for a later chapter, but it is legitimate here to examine the intriguing question of how, in the absence of an autonomous municipal structure until 1949, Cairo managed to govern, administer, and coordinate a metropolitan conurbation that was expanding so greatly and modernizing at so rapid a pace during the preceding century. The system that evolved to meet these exigencies had its own particular problems, of which two were perhaps of greatest significance: one was its circumscribed scope; the other the diffuseness of responsibility within it.

With education primarily the responsibility of the religious hierarchy or, later, a national ministry, with defense and security too crucial to be left to a local unit, with charitable institutions, hospitals, and other "public services" supported and administered under the *awqāf* or, later, the direct aegis of the ruler or the national government, there were only a few nonsensitive managerial functions which remained purely local in character and could be entrusted to local administrators. These were functions which in the past had often fallen within the jurisdiction of the *muḥtasib* and which, in the modern era, came under the rubric of the Cairo City Service. This apolitical unit of urban management substituted, in many ways, for the missing municipal government.

While the origins of this unit are somewhat obscure, there is no doubt that it represented an expansion of a basic local responsibility that had been recognized throughout Cairo's history, namely, the protection of the "public way" and of private property lines. While this responsibility may on occasion have been more honored in the breach than in the performance, it was never questioned in theory.[7] Its modern roots may be traced more specifically, however, to the *Tanẓīm* created under Muḥammad 'Ali during the last years of his rule, primarily for the purpose of executing the Rue Neuve (al-Sikkah al-Jadīdah) and other street projects. The function took on new significance at the time of Ismā'īl, due to the stepped-up pace of municipal improvements, at which time the responsibility for designing and constructing public roads and new subdivisions was assigned to a special subsection of the Ministry of Public Works. When that ministry was reorganized in 1879-1880,[8] this *Tanẓīm* section was revitalized and a special subunit of it was given its own staff and a separate budget in order to coordinate road planning for both Cairo and outlying Ḥalwān. It was from this subunit of this subsection in the ministry that the Cairo City Service evolved.

With British occupation, however, there was a temporary loss of its relatively independent status. The *Tanẓīm* section of the ministry became merely a staff aid to the minister, as decision-making powers were concentrated more and more in the hands of Sir Scott-Moncrieff, the Undersecretary of State responsible for all national public works.[9] When the Cairo *Tanẓīm* was reorganized again in the late 1880's, it emerged as an easily recognized

[5] By 1908 the European Bureau of the Ministry of the Interior was in reality supervising the work of the local and mixed commissions with respect to water, lighting, and alignment (*tanẓīm*) regulations, even though the 1893 legislation had set up a "Commission Supérieure" specifically for that purpose. In an attempt to coordinate the activities of the various ministries of the central government with reference to local improvements, the reforms of 1909 established in the Commission's place a "Consultative Committee of Municipalities," charged with overseeing the activities of the local governments, made up of representatives from the ministries of the Interior, Finance, and Public Health, as well as the Director of the Section of Municipalities and Local Commissions of the Ministry of Interior.

[6] For more detailed information on these early developments in local administration, see Institute of Public Administration, U.A.R., *Development of Local Government in the United Arab Republic* (Cairo, October 1959), pp. 1-4; and its revised version by Harold Alderfer, M. F. el Khatib and M. A. Fahmy, *Local Government in the United Arab Republic* (Institute of Public Administration, U.A.R., and the United Nations, Cairo: 1963), pp. 3-4.

[7] The powers invested in the City Service were those which, legally and in practice, had always resided in the government. For earlier precedents during Mamluk times, see Ira M. Lapidus, *Muslim Cities in the Later Middle Ages* (Harvard University Press, Cambridge: 1967), *passim.*

[8] 'Ali Mubārak, *Al-Khiṭaṭ al-Tawfīqīyah al-Jadīdah* (Būlāq Press, Cairo: 1888), IX, 55. He notes that, in the reorganization of the ministry in that year, three major subsections were established: (1) Administration and budgets; (2) Maintenance and planning of projects; and (3) *Tanẓīm* for Cairo and other cities.

[9] Clerget, *Le Caire*, I, 257.

"British" institution, whose functions were threefold. First, it was a regulatory agency, promulgating and enforcing minimum standards of location, safety, and construction of buildings; second, it was a "planning agency," concerned primarily with the preparation and enforcement of the Official Map (although it was not so designated in the laws); and third, it was an action agency, involved chiefly with the construction and improvement of public streets and roadways. However, since the *Tanẓīm* department had no capital improvements budget of its own, it could only recommend to the Minister of Public Works that money be allocated for these purposes. This lack of fiscal capacity was a rock upon which many a development scheme in Cairo foundered. In addition, several functions that had formerly been performed by the *Tanẓīm* Service were disengaged and assigned to other agencies, which resulted in increased problems of coordination. The Governor of Cairo assumed responsibility for supervising public lighting, the Department of Sanitation was charged with street cleaning and watering, and a private firm was engaged to repair and maintain the existing public ways. The coordination of all these activities in Cairo was presumably to be maintained through the Council of *Tanẓīm*.[10]

A sorely inadequate budget, however, was the chief obstacle to the proper functioning of the Cairo *Tanẓīm* even in the single major function left to it by the reforms of 1889. And this inadequate budget was partially the result of Cairo's lack of municipal independence. Clerget has pointed out, with considerable justification, that lesser communities such as Ḍimyāṭ, Manṣūrah, and Alexandria, *because* they enjoyed municipal status, were all freer to allocate proportionately greater funds for street improvements than Cairo, which lacked fiscal independence. For example, in 1902 when Alexandria budgeted some *LE* 40,000 for streets, Cairo, with her much larger area and population, had to manage on a budget of only *LE* 15,000 for that purpose.[11]

These inadequacies became increasingly obvious during the expansive era between 1895 and 1907. Due to public pressure, the proportion of the *Tanẓīm* budget allocated to Cairo[12] was increased substantially and, in 1905, some of the fragmented services were recombined. However, the basic dilemma still remained: on the one hand, the *Tanẓīm* department was concerned not with Cairo alone but with the remainder of the country as well; and, on the other hand, it did not control all the public services and utilities in the city but was substantially limited to buildings and the public ways. Furthermore, not only was a unified government that could have coordinated the various projects undertaken by the separate ministries totally lacking, but also there was no citizen representation in the governing of the city. These deficiencies are summarized in the report of the Consul General to the British Parliament in 1908:

The municipal services in Cairo are at present carried

[10] A full reproduction of the texts of the decrees promulgated in 1889 relating to the *Tanẓīm* can be found in Ministry of Finances of the Egyptian Government, *La législation en matière immobilière en Égypte* (The National Press, Cairo: 1901), pp. 81 *et seq.* Some extracts from these documents may serve to illustrate the scope of the *tanẓīm* and to bring out parallels to Western institutional forms. Thus, Article 1 of the Decree of August 26, 1889, notes, in language very familiar to the contemporary reader: "In the cities and towns where the Tanzim Service exists or will be created by ministerial order, nothing may be constructed, enlarged, elevated, reconditioned, repaired or demolished in the way of . . . houses, buildings, enclosing walls, balconies, steps, sidewalks or other works bordering the public way without having received from the Tanzim Service an authorization and an alignment . . ." (my translation from p. 81). Further, Article 10 provided that "Any construction that the Tanzim Service designates as requiring repairs from the point of view of public safety or because it threatens collapse, must be repaired or demolished in the manner determined by the service" (my translation from p. 83).

In the Ministry of Public Works' decree of September 8, 1889, Councils of *Tanẓīm* were instituted in many local communities, the Cairo council to be composed as follows: *President,* a functionary of the Ministry of Public Works designated by the minister; *Vice President,* the Director of Services (Head of the City Service) for the city of Cairo; *Members,* one delegate each from the Cairo Governorate, from the Sanitary Service, and one engineer from the *Tanẓīm* subsection (*ibid.,* pp. 85-86). The functions of the Council were specified as follows (p. 87):

1. To establish the outline of alignments on their plans or on general maps.
2. To classify the streets and give them official names.
3. To fix the width of streets.
4. To remove unnecessary streets from official designation.
5. To propose to the minister the purchase of lands required for the construction or widening of streets, and to sell roadways no longer officially designated.
6. To establish the width of plantings adjacent to the public ways.
7. To notify the minister of expenses required by urban streets.
8. To present plans concerning the establishment of public ways.
9. To issue orders concerning structures in need of repair whenever they endanger the public safety or threaten collapse.

The Official Map submitted by the Council of *Tanẓīm* had to be approved by the Minister of Public Works; once approved, all construction on lands slated for expropriation was forbidden. Control was obtained through a system of licensing (*rukhṣah*) (p. 89).

[11] Clerget, *Le Caire,* I, 258.

[12] It must be remembered here that the *Tanẓīm* department of the Ministry of Public Works was responsible not only for services in Cairo and other communities lacking municipal status but also for planning and executing public buildings and roads throughout Egypt, as well as supervising plans submitted by local and mixed commissions, wherever these existed.

> out by three different Departments, *viz.*: (1) The Public Works Department which is in charge of the construction and maintenance of roads, building regulations, and the lighting of the town; (2) the Public Health Department which controls the watering and scavenging of the streets; and (3) the Gouvernorate which issues licenses for temporary occupation of the public ways. It is clear that this triple control of the affairs of a large city is conducive neither to economy nor efficiency, and that the *municipal work of Cairo would be carried out in a much more satisfactory manner if it were managed by one central body on which the different departments interested, and also the inhabitants, were represented.*[13]

The report might also have added that, as before, policing and security in the city, as well as the Governorate office itself, came under the jurisdiction of the Ministry of Interior. A committee was appointed in 1907 to study the question of reorganizing Cairo's management and, in 1911, "the creation of a municipality for Cairo" was again under discussion.[14] However, such a reorganization never did take place and, in lieu of a basic restructuring of Cairo's administration, reforms and expansions of responsibility and budget took place within the same fragmented framework.

Despite the inherent unworkability of the system, much progress was made in providing paved roads and other services to the expanding metropolis during the decades that followed, thanks to the more generous budgets allocated to the *Tanẓīm*. Table 2, which assembles budget figures for selected years, illustrates both the gradual increase in resources as well as the periodic setbacks experienced during wartime and depression.[15]

While to some extent the larger budgets paralleled population increases, they primarily reflected the addition of new services to the expanding scope of the unit. For example, in 1924, the Cairo Cleansing Service, charged with scavenging and watering public streets and squares, was reunited with the *Tanẓīm*. By 1927, the *Tanẓīm* of Cairo had been made responsible for the outlying towns of Heliopolis and Ḥalwān and for the provision of water and electricity to Jīzah and the Jazīrah. By 1936 the Cairo *Tanẓīm* had expanded so much in scope that one could identify it quite legitimately as the agency that "to a great extent *exercises the municipal control of Cairo* and outskirts including the town of Helwan." In addition to its original functions (street alignment regulations, building permits, enforcement of standards of safe construction and adequate maintenance of buildings, and the construction and maintenance of public roads), it was also responsible for street trees, the planting and maintenance of public gardens, and the watering and cleaning of streets and open spaces. From the standpoint of Cairo's physical development, perhaps the most critical function was entrusted to a subunit entitled the Town Planning Service. This division was charged with applying the "principles of town and country planning and of the garden city movement to the future development of Cairo," as well as with studying the traffic conditions in the city and recommending needed streets, bridges, and other public works. In addition, the unit supervised the activities of the public utility companies (i.e., the tramway, Metro, water, gas, and electricity companies) operating in the city.[16]

Thus, in effect, many of the functions which would have been performed by a municipal government, had one existed, were actually concentrated in a bureaucratic agency that was, in turn, part of a ministry of the national government. This agency was neither politically responsive (nor responsible) to the citizens of the community it "served" nor fiscally independent of the national budget and the share allocated to public works in general. The Cairo City Service was, at best, an ingenious solution to the problem which the lack of a municipal body had created and perpetuated. It was not a total substitute, however, even in the circumscribed area of apolitical management. Other functions which a municipal government might have coordinated and controlled remained dispersed.

TABLE 2. BUDGET ALLOCATIONS TO THE CAIRO CITY SERVICE IN SELECTED YEARS

Year	*Appropriation (LE rounded to nearest 10,000)*	*Year*	*Appropriation (LE rounded to nearest 10,000)*
Prewar		Postwar	
1912	300,000	1919	310,000
1913	350,000	1920	580,000
		Then, gradually increasing to peak in	
War (curtailed)			
1915	180,000	1927	1,000,000
1916	140,000		
1917	180,000	Depression	
1918	200,000	1931	700,000

[13] See *Egypt No. 1 (1909): Reports by His Majesty's Agent . . . in 1908* (His Majesty's Stationery Office, London: 1909), p. 24. Italics added.

[14] See Émile Boulad, "La voirie et l'esthétique de la ville du Caire," *L'Égypte Contemporaine*, No. 5 (January 1911), p. 34.

[15] The figures in Table 2 have been assembled from various sources. See *Egypt No. 1 (1920): Reports by His Majesty's High Commissioner . . . for the Period 1914-1919* (His Majesty's Stationery Office, London: 1920), pp. 44-45; Clerget, *Le Caire*, I, 259; Egyptian Ministry of Finance, *Budget of the Egyptian Government, 1922-23*, especially under the heading of Ministry of Public Works; Egyptian Ministry of Finance, *Budget of the Egyptian Government, 1932-33*, which gives the appropriations between 1927 and 1932.

[16] Government of Egypt, *Almanac of 1937* (Government Printing Office, Cairo: 1936), pp. 354-355. Italics added.

Just as the Ministry of Public Works became, by design or default, responsible for Cairo's public works, so also the other expanding ministries of the national government each took on responsibility for planning, executing, and administering Cairo's various public facilities. Hospitals, clinics, and other medical units were provided under the auspices of the Ministry of Health. Primary and secondary schools, as well as colleges and universities, were constructed according to priorities established by the Ministry of Education. Public security and the Cairo police came under the jurisdiction of the Ministry of the Interior, etc.

This structural fragmentation based on "function" rather than "locality" had important implications for the type of local planning that could be done. When the locality is the basic unit of planning, a given budget must be allocated among competing community goals. Decisions cluster around such questions as: how much for education balanced against how much for health balanced against how much for highways or recreation, etc. On the other hand, where function (on the national level) is the basic unit of planning, the allocation decisions revolve to a large extent around competing localities. How much of the given public works budget can be allocated to Cairo and how much to other localities? What proportion of the public health budget should be spent on Cairenes? In this case, each community attempts to maximize its share in each separate budget, without necessarily considering the effect of each upon "balanced" community development. Furthermore, the diffusion of responsibility among separate ministries intensifies the problem of coordination within localities. Efficient management requires that separate programs be "timed" in their execution and that goals, if not coordinated, at least ought not to conflict. In Egypt, the institution of the provincial and local councils, on which sat representatives of the concerned ministries, was designed to achieve this coordination, but practice often fell short of theory.

In Cairo, public facilities that were not provided by the City Service or by the other national ministries were left to private concessionaires, a procedure which further compounded the fragmentation and intensified the need for coordination. The status of the "concession" in nineteenth-century Egyptian law, and some of the consequences for public welfare of so heavy a dependence upon this method of providing municipal services, therefore, cannot be ignored in any study of Cairo's development. However, since the general topic has been thoroughly explored elsewhere,[17] only a brief résumé is required for our purposes.

[17] By far the most detailed and scholarly study is Tawfiq Chehata, "La concession du service public: Étude comparée de droit administratif Français et Égyptien," entire issue of *L'Égypte Contemporaine*, Nos. 197-198 (March-April 1941), pp. 205-496.

During the second half of the nineteenth century when municipal service concessions of a modern type were first being granted in Egypt, this method was being used throughout France and other Western nations to achieve similar municipal goals. That is, there was nothing particularly unique about the institution, nor were the concessions granted in Egypt basically different in form from those concluded on the European continent. In fact, many of the French and Belgian firms engaged to provide Egyptian cities with water and gas systems, with public transit, etc., were well established at home and had had extensive experience with local communities in their own countries. (The firm of Lebon, given the concession for the gasworks, was as famous in France as the company of Bell, granted the Egyptian telephone concession, was in the United States.) It is true that by the end of the nineteenth century some of the abuses of the concession system were coming to be recognized in Europe and governments were attempting to impose more stringent regulations on standards and rates, but if the abuses were more rampant in Egypt than elsewhere, no more than a time-lag was involved.

A second point to be remembered is that the concession per se did not represent a significant departure from earlier Egyptian precedents for handling what modern public administrators might term "governmental functions." Throughout the Ottoman lands, the institution of "tax farming" offered the prototype of and precedent for the modern public utility concession. Reduced to its simplest terms, under this system the tax farmer (concessionaire) received from the governor the right to conduct a "government" function, whether to collect taxes in a given area, to administer the customs house and collect duties, to run a postal service, etc. In return for his fixed payment to the government, he was granted wide latitude in recovering his "investment" from users, his profit being the difference between his receipts and his initial investment. Thus, in an essential sense, the modern public utility concession was merely an extension of a preexisting and accepted pattern.

Nevertheless, dependence upon this method for the modern development of Cairo had certain serious consequences which were not completely ameliorated until drastic nationalization policies were instituted by the post-1952 revolutionary regime. One of the most serious problems was that virtually all the concessions were granted to foreign nationals. The terms of the agreements included clauses granting very lengthy duration but remarkably few specifications or performance guarantees. For example, the original water concession in Cairo (in actuality soon abrogated) was to have remained in force for 99 years, and other concessions were granted for periods of 50, 75, and 80 years. One searches almost in vain for evidence that concessions were ever granted to native Egyptians. A rare exception was the formation in 1897 of an Egyptian syndicate to construct a railroad in the Fayūm but, significantly, "the results were not brilliant and the concession had to be transferred to an Anglo-Belgian firm."[18] Thus it was that decisions made in the nineteenth and very early twentieth centuries were to bind Egypt to foreign control over her public utilities, long after political independence had been achieved and after a competent cadre of indigenous financiers and administrators had evolved.

In addition, the fact that the original agreements had failed to reserve to the government the right to establish standards, to control performance, and, in some instances, to set rates—powers which a modern government expects to exercise over public utilities and services—led to continual friction. Periodic renegotiations of the concessions were attempted throughout the years between 1920 and 1950. While the original arrangements had not necessarily appeared disadvantageous at the time they were concluded, the evolution of a modern political philosophy which viewed government as the protector of the public welfare made the concession approach increasingly anomalous.

On the public level, therefore, Cairo's basic problem was one of coordination. Activities relating to urban development were divided, with responsibility for certain aspects concentrated in the separately administered *Tanẓīm* department, but with responsibility for other basic services scattered among ministries of the central government. On top of this, still other urban services were being provided by private firms financed with foreign capital and administered by persons whose connection with the indigenous community was so tenuous that, in the absence of legal control, not even social pressures could be brought to bear upon them to temper the profit motive with a spirit of public service.[19]

Not only were functions thus fragmented in Cairo but conspicuously absent was an independent municipal entity that could have been expected to take an overall view of the city, that could have helped to establish a set of compatible community goals, and that could have served as coordinator, urging or requiring the separate agencies and private companies to modify their own plans in accordance with this set of unified community goals. It is highly significant that when the Cairo *Baladīyah* was established in accordance with the Municipality Law of 1949, one of its first acts was to commission a group of engineers, architects, and other experts to formulate a master plan for the city—the first since the abortive attempt of Maḥmūd Falaki and 'Ali Mubārak almost a hundred years earlier. The preliminary surveys—covering residential distribution, industrial location, labor conditions, transport and communication, streets and highways, trade, commerce, recreation and education—were begun in 1953 and recommendations were issued in a published version of the *Master Plan of Cairo* in 1956. Although it would be too extreme to claim that the lack of an adequate governmental structure prevented the solution of many of Cairo's problems, there can be no doubt that it constituted an unnecessary hindrance.

If the lack of a coordinated municipal organization in Cairo presented a major deterrent to urban development on the public level, the lack of financial institutions to permit large-scale development presented a parallel impediment on the private level. Modern city building depends in large measure upon the institution of credit, more specifically, upon mortgage financing. Not only does this system permit rapid expansion of the housing stock in response to demand, but it also facilitates large-scale subdividing according to relatively coordinated plans. Both of these became increasingly necessary in Cairo during the period of urban expansion ushered in at the turn of the twentieth century.

Up to the middle of the nineteenth century, modern banking and mortgage financing, in the Western sense, were virtually unknown and apparently unmissed in Egypt.[20] While the reasons for this are complex, two underlying factors often suggested are: (1) that the basic premise of banking offended the Islamic injunction against usury; and (2) that a long history of property insecurity (and, indeed, the weakness of the institution of private property itself) led to investment in real property (land) whenever possible or to gold-hoarding rather than savings. Institutions for credit extension, for deposit savings, and for organized (corporate) investment were slow in gaining acceptance in Egypt and, when first established, were used almost exclusively by members of the foreign communities.

The rulers, it is true, recognized the virtues of credit and, indeed, became heavily dependent upon it. Muḥammad 'Ali, for example, had from time to time been forced to issue treasury bonds to cover salary payments. In fact,

[18] *Ibid.*, see pp. 226-231 for data on a number of these concessions. The quotation is my translation from p. 230.

[19] This was, perhaps, the most basic difference between the older (Mamluk) and newer alien elites. In the final analysis, the Mamluks did consider themselves a part of the Islamic community, within which some social control existed, whereas the new European elite shared no moral bond with the indigenous population that might have transcended their alien identity and limited the full exercise of their power.

[20] A history of the development of modern banking in Egypt can be found in 'Ali al-Giritli, "Taṭawwur al-niẓām al-maṣrafi fi Miṣr," in *Buḥūth al-'Īd al-Khamsīni* (Cairo, 1960), pp. 197-302; and in Charles Issawi, *Egypt in Revolution: An Economic Analysis* (Oxford University Press, New York: 1963).

the failure of Egypt's first bank, which had been founded in 1837, has been blamed on the fact that it became so involved in discounting these bonds that it had no funds left for banking operations![21] Another bank, founded in the 1850's by a group of European financiers, also foundered on a similar reef at the time of Sa'īd. During the reign of Ismā'īl, deficit financing became an entrenched and indispensable part of state policy, and several European firms and branches were in operation in Egypt—not as public institutions but, more properly speaking, as "financial houses" specializing in interest-bearing loans to the government.[22] At the opposite extreme, each year thousands of petty loans were negotiated individually on agricultural lands in order to meet ill-timed tax levies, but such disorganized and small-scale operations could scarcely qualify as mortgages; in fact, they were highly irregular procedures since, until the reform in land laws in 1858, very little of the land in Egypt was in freehold tenure, so that it could not even be pledged legally against a loan.

Apparently, there were two prerequisites to the emergence of modern mortgage institutions in Egypt, both of which had been attained by 1880. The first was unequivocal and regularized laws governing the private ownership of real property; the second was European motivation for mortgage institutions, understandably absent until European nationals were permitted to own real estate. Both were initiated in 1858. The Sa'īdīyah Code of that year recognized hereditary rights to agricultural land formerly considered part of the state domains, thus facilitating the extension of private freehold ownership over much of the country. In addition, under the Code, foreign nationals were given the right to purchase land that had been abandoned by its cultivator or forfeited for tax arrears.[23] Subsequent reforms and a major simplification in land tenure categories that had been progressively complicated by accretions of Islamic and Ottoman precedents, as well as the institutionalization of a system of recording land titles in various courts, resulted by 1880 in a totally revised system of land ownership, in which the unchallenged dominance of private property provided a marked contrast to the state monopoly system that had prevailed under Muḥammad 'Ali. By then, only land within the much-circumscribed public domain and land held in *waqf* remained ineligible for mortgage borrowing.

It is therefore hardly accidental that the year 1880 witnessed the inauguration of the first mortgage bank in Egypt, the Crédit Foncier Égyptien, supported by French capital.[24] Its success encouraged the founding, soon afterward, of the English-financed Land and Mortgage Bank, also specializing in loans against land security. Thus, prototype institutions already existed when the completion of the Delta barrage in 1891 touched off an influx of foreign speculative capital directed chiefly toward land. During this period of expansion were founded the National Bank in 1898 (and its land subsidiary, the Agricultural Bank, in 1902), the Caisse Hypothécaire d'Égypte in 1903, the Land Bank of Egypt in 1905, and the Mortgage Company of Egypt in 1908.

The existence of institutions, however, is no guarantee of effective functioning and, during the first few decades of mortgage financing in Egypt, the system was characterized more by its abuses than by its constructive contributions to the economy. The chief abuse seems to have arisen from the unrealistic dreams of spectacular returns that lay behind the massive movement of foreign capital into Egypt. As one contemporary economist analyzed it, "The memory of the mushrooming cities and prodigious fortunes of America was in everyone's mind. . . . Each was convinced that the valley of the Nile would march in the footsteps of the United States . . . [but] the illusion . . . had little justification."[25] Another economist, writing just after the crash of 1907, also attributed the causes of the boom to psychological rather than real factors, noting that it was part of the same impulse that had led to the founding of great fortunes, based upon real estate speculation, in other "new" countries during the late nineteenth century.[26]

No matter how ill-founded these hopes, the massive influx of foreign capital into Egypt inflated all values in the short run, thus yielding very real returns to the

[21] A. E. Crouchley, *The Economic Development of Modern Egypt* (Longmans, Green and Company, London: 1938), p. 105.

[22] For some insight into their operations, see the fascinating correspondence between one of Ismā'īl's "bankers" and his Paris banking connection, as reported in David S. Landes, "Bankers and Pashas: International Finance in Egypt in the 1860's," in *Men in Business*, ed. W. Miller (Harvard University Press, Cambridge: 1952), pp. 23-70. A fuller account appears in D. Landes, *Bankers and Pashas* (Harvard University Press, Cambridge: 1958).

[23] See Crouchley, *The Economic Development of Modern Egypt*, p. 130. He notes that although Muḥammad 'Ali had permitted foreigners to hold *Ab'ādīyah* land since 1829, thus confirming their right to ownership, it was not until 1858 that their right to *purchase* land was granted. The parallels to more general Ottoman reforms are obvious here. See Roderic Davison, *Reform in the Ottoman Empire, 1856-1876* (Princeton University Press, Princeton: 1963), especially pp. 99-100.

[24] The importance of this institution cannot be overestimated. As late as 1920 it still held half of the mortgage indebtedness of the entire country. See Issawi, *Egypt at Mid-Century: An Economic Survey* (Oxford University Press, London: 1954), p. 223.

[25] Edwin Lévy, "Les événements de 1907 et la situation actuelle de l'Égypte," in *L'Égypte Contemporaine*, Volume 3 (November 1912), pp. 503-530. Quotation is my translation from p. 507.

[26] F. Legrand, *Les fluctuations de prix et les crises de 1907 et 1908 en Égypte* (J. Coubé, Nancy: 1909), pp. 1-7.

speculator which, in turn, served to attract even more risk capital. One finds in the process an almost classic case of unregulated boom and bust. Thus, the paid-up capital of companies operating in Egypt increased from some 7 million Egyptian pounds in 1892 to over 26 million in 1902 and to 87 million by 1907, excluding the Suez Canal and the branches of European banks and companies. Almost all of this increase came from foreign sources.[27]

Since much of this new capital was in the form of loans on land rather than investment in productive facilities, it was natural that land values should have "benefited" most dramatically from the heightened competition. While agricultural lands, particularly those enhanced by the new irrigation system created by the Aswān Dam after 1902, experienced some of the sharpest upturns,[28] all forms of speculation in land and buildings —especially on the outskirts of Cairo and Alexandria— yielded substantial profits. Land and building societies were founded in increasing numbers between 1901 and 1907, each following approximately the same procedure: "to buy, wait for an increase in values, and then sell." As Legrand put it:

> The new societies, buying without regard to price in order to employ their capital, contributed to the sentiment that the prices of land and buildings had no limit. . . . Sales were so extensive that there was almost no one in the European colonies of Cairo and Alexandria who did not own some land. . . . Those who could not purchase an entire lot bought a part-interest.[29]

Those purchasing in newly subdivided urban quarters had the greatest chance for a financial coup. For example, in a new subdivision in outlying Zaytūn along the road toward Heliopolis, land values increased from 2-15 *milliemes* per square meter before the 1890's to over 2,000 *milliemes* per square meter by about 1910.[30]

A boom of this variety, built on the capricious sands of "psychological" confidence, is particularly vulnerable to the second thoughts of investors and to any contractions in credit. Both seem to have occurred in the European markets during the opening months of 1907. Recognition that credit had been overextended, coupled with the general tightening of money that was later to result in worldwide panic selling and bank runs, led to the abrupt suspension of Egyptian credit in both Paris and London. The effects of this sudden prick upon the speculative bubble were as immediate as they were catastrophic. The April panic was precipitated by the closing of a bank in Cairo. Therewith, the Egyptian Bourse, an amateur operation that had never been able to control the wild speculations that ruled it, crashed, with shares depreciating by December of 1907 over 250 percent from what they had been a scant year before.[31]

Urban development in Cairo, which had been closely tied to the general boom, experienced a deep setback from which it was not to recover until after World War I. Land companies entered into bankruptcy, titles were forfeited, and a virtual moratorium on construction ensued. One reads in the descriptive accounts of contemporaries the sorry tragedy of abortive ventures. An observer of 1912 notes that "During the boom a few years ago a building frenzy seized the country, and buildings were run up everywhere. *There is a wilderness of half-finished buildings in Cairo* rivalling that of the archeological remains of Upper Egypt. . . ."[32] Another calls attention to the "hideous spectacle of grubbed-up trees and foundations" along the once-famous Shubra Road, and to the island of Rawḍah where the pashas had "allowed the Levantine speculator to tear most of their beautiful villas and gardens to pieces before he paid them the purchase price; and as the slump came before he had time to clear out of his gambles, they never did get the money, and *no one ever did build a mushroom suburb*."[33]

[27] The following quotation from Issawi, *Egypt at Mid-Century*, p. 39, presents a concise summary of the role played by foreign capital during this era. "The first twenty years of the occupation saw little foreign investment. After 1900, however, following the reconquest of the Sudan, the completion of the Aswan Dam, and the signature of the Anglo-French agreement, there was a spectacular investment boom. Between 1900-7, 160 companies with a capital of *LE* 43 million were formed . . . the nominal value of securities quoted in Cairo rose from *LE* 10,700,000 in 1903 to over *LE* 51 million in 1907. . . . In that year a world slump began and . . . . The rest of the pre-war years were spent in liquidating the 1907 boom. Nevertheless in 1914 the total value of the capital of joint-stock companies operating in Egypt was *LE* 100 million, of which *LE* 92 million was foreign owned. . . . The distribution of foreign capital in 1914 was . . . French, *LE* 46,267,000; British, *LE* 30,250,000; Belgian, *LE* 14,294,000. . . ."

[28] Legrand, *Les fluctuations de prix . . . en Égypte*, p. 17, notes that the prices of land located along the Ismā'īlīyah Canal increased 100 percent in value between 1901 and 1905, and that the average sale price per feddan (about one acre) of the State Domains land doubled between 1900 and 1906.

[29] *Ibid.*, pp. 18-19 (my translation). Almost 300 companies of this type were founded during the boom decade alone. Some insight into the rather wild speculative games afoot in Egypt—often promoted by Levantine or European adventurers with little financial and even less moral capital—is found in the marvelous (if tragic) satires written by Lord Cecil who, in his capacity in the Ministry of Finance, often had to pass on matters relating to them. See Lord Edward Cecil, *The Leisure of an Egyptian Official* (Hodder and Stoughton, London: 2nd edn., published posthumously *circa* 1921), especially Chapters III and IV, pp. 30-78.

[30] Cited by Boulad, "La voirie et l'esthétique de la ville du Caire," p. 35. There are 1000 *milliemes* to an Egyptian Pound.

[31] See Legrand, *Les fluctuations de prix . . . en Égypte*, p. 21; and Lévy, "Les événements de 1907," p. 511, for fuller details.

[32] Alfred Cunningham, *To-Day in Egypt* (Hurst and Blackett, Ltd., London: 1912), p. 138 (italics mine).

[33] Quoted from Douglas Sladen, *Oriental Cairo: The City of*

Thus, the first fruits of the mortgage institution in Cairo were speculation and premature subdivisions. Obviously, sound urban development required more than the institution itself. It required *indigenous* economic strength, based upon real rather than spurious improvements in productivity and demand, and it required a rational and creative rather than a wildly speculative use of the new tool. Evidence of the emergence of sound mortgage practices and of vigorous local investment does not appear in Egypt until after World War I. At that time Cairo entered another period of boom in land values and experienced a new spurt in building activity somewhat reminiscent of the earlier inflation. However, in very basic terms, this new expansion differed radically from the one that had ended so disastrously only a dozen years earlier. First, it was based upon demand whereas the earlier one had been based upon anticipation. By then, Cairo was suffering from a severe housing shortage since wartime migration had swelled the population just at the time construction was halted because of competing war requirements. Furthermore, prosperity had nurtured a rise in standards and expectations in housing which stimulated additional demand. Not only was the demand real, but the supply of capital this time was abundant, indigenous, and attracted to investment in land and buildings. Much of it had been accumulated locally through wartime profit taking. While some of this new capital was used to "buy back" Egypt's debts from abroad and some flowed into the industries sponsored by the newly organized Bank Miṣr, a substantial portion helped to sustain the high level of construction in Cairo. During the 1920's, areas that had been subdivided fifteen to twenty years earlier were finally developed with apartment houses and office buildings, many containing shops or even small industrial workshops on the ground level.

In this development, mortgage financing played a constructive if limited role. While Egyptians continued to prefer outright ownership of a single building to encumbered title to several, which meant that mortgage financing never became as important in Cairo as it did in Western cities, nevertheless, the Cairo real estate market was freed from its earlier subjection to fluctuations on the bourses of Europe and thus gained a greater flexibility than it had had earlier. It would be a gross oversimplification, however, to conclude that the basic problem had been solved. It must be borne in mind that mortgage and land companies in Egypt were primarily interested in rural agricultural holdings, *not* in urban development, which is one reason why so little has ever been written on their activities in urban areas.[34] The major credit institutions had only minor interests in urban construction, and it was only during a few brief years of the 1930 depression, and again in the late 1940's, that urban properties constituted a sizeable proportion of the outstanding mortgage debt. For the most part, real estate in Cairo constituted a form of savings for the upper classes, a pattern that has persisted even beyond the Revolution, when Saudi Arabian and Kuwaiti capital became a substitute source. This meant primarily small-scale development—a single structure at a time, very often containing an apartment for the owner or his relatives. And, as in many other cities, it meant a preoccupation with construction of luxury housing and a neglect of middle-income and "popular" housing.

The private mortgage institution never did contribute to construction of the latter type. It was the Ministry of *Waqf*, later joined by other governmental agencies, that has been responsible for whatever large-scale moderate-priced developments have taken place in modern Cairo. Whether this positive effect of *waqf* outweighed its negative influence, however, is debatable. Certainly the existence of *waqf* property severely limited the extent to which the institution of mortgages could be used to develop and modernize Cairo during the nineteenth and twentieth centuries. It will be recalled that over the centuries rather extensive portions of the city had been placed in mortmain—either in the form of charitable (*khayri*) or private family (*ahli*) endowments. By legal definition, property in *waqf* cannot be mortgaged, since its unalienable title cannot be pledged against a loan.[35] Only the usufruct "belongs" to the beneficiary(ies) and can be negotiated, pledged, rented, or otherwise transferred. In short, an unknown but probably substantial proportion of the urban real estate in Cairo was ineligible for mortgage financing. (The reader should bear in mind here that, under Islamic property law and convention,

the "Arabian Nights" (Hurst and Blackett, Ltd., London: 1911), pp. 37 and 280-281 (italics mine).

[34] For example, Gabriel Baer, *A History of Landownership in Modern Egypt, 1800-1950* (Oxford University Press, London: 1962), deals almost exclusively with rural Egypt, and only passing mention is made of the role mortgage financing played in the ownership and development of urban real property. See p. 100 for an isolated reference.

[35] The difference between freehold (*mulk*) property and mortmain (*waqf*) property has been summarized in modern legal terms as follows: "Lands held in waqf constituted a separate form of land tenure, distinct from private property. On a basic theoretical level, the *raqabah*, or title, was immobilized in perpetuity; as a result, the only property interests existing in waqf land were limited to, and based on, the usufruct." See Richard Debs, "The Law of Property in Egypt: Islamic Law and Civil Code" (unpublished Ph.D. Dissertation, Princeton University: 1963), p. 31. For comments on the connection between mortgageability and *waqf* status, see Issawi, *Egypt at Mid-Century*, p. 132. See also Gabriel Baer, "Waqf Reform in Egypt," *St. Anthony's Papers*, No. 4 (Chatto and Windus, London: 1958), pp. 61-76, particularly p. 64.

ownership titles to land and buildings do not necessarily go together. Separate forms of tenure, and indeed separate parties with property rights, were common on the same parcel. The land itself might be owned by or in *waqf* to one party while the building and even separate floors of the structure might be held by others.)

Ineligibility for mortgage finance was, of course, no problem with respect to lands and buildings in the quasi-public domain of religious *awqāf*. Some of it had been deeded in very large parcels, and additional land assembly was facilitated, once the separate holdings of individual beneficiary institutions were combined within a centralized administration or Ministry of *Waqf*. Furthermore, the operating budget of this central body was quite liberal. The chronic capital shortage which characteristically interfered with the maintenance and redevelopment of private *waqf* properties was not felt within the *waqf khayri*. The religious authorities had the power to enforce reinvestment in a depreciating property and could, if they chose, decide upon new construction or major rehabilitation. It was not accidental that one of the only attempts in nineteenth-century Cairo to reclaim a blighted area and to reconstruct a residential quarter according to a unified plan was the project 'Ali Mubārak had executed on *waqf khayri* land south of Sayīdah Zaynab. Indeed, as a contributor to sound urban development, the institution of the public *awqāf* was in a potentially enviable position.

Real estate that had been constituted into family trusts presented entirely different and much more complicated problems. Inherent in the system of the family or private *waqf* was the basic point that development, improvement and/or redevelopment could rarely be financed by internal means, and that the property itself could not be used to obtain development capital. The bequest specified that the "profits" from the property, after maintenance and administrative expenses had been deducted, were to be distributed among the beneficiaries, *not* reinvested in the property. Although beneficiaries could voluntarily choose to reinvest, no sanctions were available to encourage compliance. And, since the property itself could neither be pledged against a loan nor parts of it sold for the purpose of accumulating the capital required to develop the remaining portions, the system was by definition at best a static one in which adequate maintenance was all that could be hoped for. Even this minimal goal, however, became increasingly difficult to attain with each passing year after the demise of the original creator of the *waqf*. As beneficiaries multiplied and interests became more fragmented, responsibility for administering the property fell inevitably to salaried functionaries (the *nāẓir*, for example) whose short-term goals dominated development decisions. The sole criterion of successful administration was a regular payment to the beneficiaries, rather than the long-term preservation of the property value.

Three ways out of this impasse were possible. Either (1) the beneficiaries died, at which point the property was absorbed into the *waqf khayri*; (2) the property deteriorated to the point where the original value was totally dissipated, at which time it was returned to the open market as freehold; or (3) long-term leases on the property could be granted to investors with capital. Ever since the seventeenth century, leasing had become more and more prevalent in Egypt and, by the nineteenth century, three basic lease forms—the *ḥikr*, the *khūlū*, and the *ijaratayn*—were in use.[36] Each was an ingenious device designed to circumvent the restrictive terms of the *waqf* by attracting outside growth capital. Not only private *waqf* could be rented on these terms but even parts of the *waqf khayri* as well.[37] Naturally, these devices were most effective during periods of economic expansion and healthy demand; in ways, dependence upon them created a much more volatile real estate market than would have resulted from simple private ownership.

Early in the nineteenth century, attempts were made to reform some of the abuses deriving from the *waqf* form of tenure, to convert some *waqf* lands to other forms of ownership, and to adapt the system to modern requirements. Thus, when Muḥammad 'Ali commenced his land reforms after 1812, many parcels of land that had previously been constituted into *waqf* but which had never been held as freehold (*mulk*) by the original bequestors

[36] Debs, "The Law of Property in Egypt," p. 35. He defines each as follows. *Ḥikr*: "In return for the possession of waqf property, the recipient of a right to ḥikr undertook to make improvements on that property and to pay an annual rent that varied in accordance with current property values. Once he had made such improvements, his rights in the land continued as long as he paid the rent. All improvements made on the property, including, for example, buildings or plantations, became the property of the lessee." Quoted from p. 106. *Khūlū*: Under this arrangement, the lessee "undertaking the rehabilitation of a parcel of waqf land, took the property for an indefinite period of time in return for the payment of annual rent," p. 107. *Ijaratayn*: This was another arrangement also employed to rehabilitate buildings on waqf land, in which the lessee paid "a lump-sum . . . based on the value of the buildings and then . . . an annual fixed rent based on the value of the land," p. 107.

[37] An illustration of how the *ḥikr* was used for the development of *waqf khayri* land in the Ma'arūf quarter of Cairo, and how it permitted partial simulation of the market place, is found in Yacoub Artin, *Essai sur les causes du renchérrisement de la vie matérielle au Caire* (L'Institut Français d'Archéologie Orientale, Cairo: 1907), p. 114. There we learn that "the hikr itself which, since the beginning of the nineteenth century, had not changed in price, was revised by the Waqf Administration, and altered, in about a score of years, to 200 and 500 times its original price, according to the situation in which each piece of land bound by hikr found itself." My translation.

were confiscated or, with only minimal compensation, were absorbed into the crown lands. This action was justified on the grounds that only *mulk* property can be converted into a legally valid *waqf*. From this confiscation some have drawn the erroneous conclusion that Muḥammad ʿAli attempted to abolish the *waqf* system itself. Actually, only private *awqāf* of dubious authenticity were involved in this early reform. A more basic change was introduced in 1835, when a State Administration was set up to oversee many *waqf khayri* properties. It was this organization that constituted the nucleus—or rather the prototype, since it lasted only a few years[38]—of what was later to develop into the Ministry of *Waqf*. A direct attack on the *waqf* institution itself, and a remarkably restrained one at that, was not ventured by Muḥammad ʿAli until the end of his reign when, in the Land Law of 1846, he forbade the future creation of *awqāf*. But an institution so deeply ingrained and so legitimized by religion as the *waqf* was not to be abolished that easily. "In the case of waqfs of buildings and of urban land, it appears never to have been executed; in the case of agricultural lands, it was effective for a short time only."[39]

Waqf developments during the second half of the nineteenth century were characterized by two somewhat antithetical trends. On the one hand, there was an increase in the amount of *waqf* property. Paradoxically, the conversion of much of the country's land to freehold tenure that had been facilitated by the Saʿīdīyah Code of 1858 made possible the creation of legitimate *waqf* on many lands and buildings which were ineligible under their previous forms of tenure. This led inevitably to a steady increase in *waqf* holdings which, by 1900, involved over 300,000 feddans or acres. On the other hand, the government attempted to extend its control over *waqf* holdings and to channel their charitable intentions into governmentally approved ventures. Realizing perhaps that the *waqf* was potentially a "government within a government," it sought to coordinate its resources with the goals of the state. Thus, the State Administration that had been founded by Muḥammad ʿAli was reestablished by ʿAbbās I in 1851. In 1864 Ismāʿīl decreed that this administration should succeed every *nāẓir* of a charitable *waqf* upon his death or removal from office, which resulted in further centralization. Soon afterward, the administration was elevated to an official ministry of the government. It appeared that, within the *waqf khayri* at least, progress was being made in incorporating an anomalous institution within the framework of modern government.

This trend was reversed, however, when Britain entered the affairs of Egypt after 1882. The advantages of subsuming the *waqf* under the general rubric of government were less attractive, once the secular government came under the effective control of the colonial power. Rather, a *waqf* administration with an independent budget could constitute an immune subgovernment, through which, ideally, policies and programs could be pursued independent of foreign control. Thus, control over the *waqf* came to be viewed by the Egyptian Khedive as the last incontestable refuge of his autonomy and royal prerogative. In January of 1884, Tawfīq revoked its ministerial status and again made it an independent administration to be headed by a Director-General responsible only to himself.[40] In the decades that followed, conflicts between the Khedive and the British administrators often focused upon the *waqf*. Each feared and impugned the motives of the other. The delicacy of the conflict, verging as it did on the sensitive issue of religion, led to a virtual stalemate and a stagnation of reform. Cromer noted at the time that:

> Of late years the abuses [in the administration of the *awqāf*] have been singularly flagrant, the Khedive having practically taken the Administration into his own hands. I was well aware of these abuses but I postponed taking any drastic steps to reform them. My reasons were two-fold. . . . [First, the] institution . . . is invested with a semi-religious character. . . . [and second,] in view of the growing demand for Egyptian autonomy, I thought it desirable that a very long and patient trial should be given in order to see how far the Egyptians themselves . . . could reform.[41]

Gradually, however, British pressures succeeded in bringing this autonomous unit more and more within the jurisdiction of the regular government apparatus. Official regulations governing the *waqf* administration were promulgated in a decree of July 13, 1895, and finally, by 1913, under heavy pressure from Lord Kitchener, the Khedive reluctantly consented to a basic change. The *waqf* administration was once again designated as a ministry, although it still retained its separate budget and was still headed by a minister appointed directly by the Khedive.

None of these changes, however, had touched upon the institution of *waqf ahli* or had brought about a decrease in the quantity of urban property immobilized in mort-

[38] *Almanac of 1937*, p. 115.

[39] Debs, "The Law of Property in Egypt," p. 70.

[40] *Almanac of 1937*, pp. 115-116 gives a summary account of this and later administrative restructuring.

[41] Quoted from the Earl Cromer, in his *Abbas II* (Macmillan and Company, Ltd., London: 1915), p. 70. From the context it is obvious that he is discussing the situation as it existed before the turn of the century. It should be noted here that ʿAbbās II came under attack not only from Cromer but from the Muslim reformers as well, who resented his personal appropriation of *waqf* revenues. Muḥammad ʿAbduh, in fact, clashed with ʿAbbās over this very issue.

main. Nevertheless, there was some tendency for the Ministry of *Waqf* to have its jurisdiction extended to private trusts. Whenever legal complications arose, as, for example, when no heirs to a family *waqf* could be found or where malpractice was proven, the courts could turn over the administration of a *waqf ahli* to the government. In addition, it was permissible for bequestors or benefactors of a private *waqf* to assign the administration of the property to the central ministry, in return for payment of a set fee. Through these processes, the ministry accumulated quasi-control over a sizeable proportion of the private *awqāf*. By 1917 the ministry was administering over 70,000 feddans of land in *waqf ahli*, and in 1933 some 1,193 separate family bequests came under the jurisdiction of the ministry.[42] This was the outcome, however, not of reform but of simple convenience.

The unnatural hiatus in *waqf* reform, which one must attribute in part to the cross-pressures of the colonial situation, persisted until independence was attained. Then, the impulses to internal reform which Cromer had awaited burst forth. It was during the decade of the 1920's—a period of heightened *waqf* creation—that proposals of all sorts were advanced to deal with the institution, including the bold suggestion that the *waqf ahli* be abolished entirely! These efforts were continued in the 1930's and 1940's, as sporadic recommendations were set forth to control the ill effects of or to reduce the institutional incentives to create *waqf*. Finally, they culminated in 1946 in the passage of a law restricting the terms of bequests made under private *waqf* in the same way that ordinary forms of inheritance were restricted, "thus limiting, to a large extent, the motive for turning property into waqf."[43]

None of these various reform measures, however, was drastic enough to eliminate the impediments to modern development that the institution of the *waqf* had created. This remained a basic unsolved problem until 1952 when the revolutionary regime promulgated its radical and long-overdue land reform law. A few days later, it abolished the *waqf ahli* in unequivocal terms, forbidding the creation of new *awqāf* and providing for the conversion of all existing *waqf ahli* to freehold status by a system which recompensed beneficiaries in accordance with their proportionate share in the income.[44] The tremendous fluidity of urban change and redevelopment which has taken place in Cairo since the early 1950's must, in part, be attributed to the return of many properties from the dead hand of the family *waqf* to the mainstream of the urban real estate market. A detailed study of this phenomenon has not yet been made, but it is safe to venture that the rate of change in Cairo would have been considerably less impressive had the *waqf ahli* remained in force.

While the Revolutionary government proceeded far more cautiously in dealing with the *waqf khayri*, even this yielded to increased supervision and control by the central government. Distribution of agricultural lands in *waqf khayri* under land reform laws has already taken place. And while the Ministry of *Waqf* was permitted temporarily to retain some of its urban properties, this retention was made conditional upon upgrading and redeveloping them. Commercial properties situated in prime downtown locations, which had remained relatively undeveloped because their owners or renters paid below market *waqf* rental fees, are undergoing reconstruction by the ministry or are being charged such high rentals that their proprietors must either upgrade or get out. In addition, neglected residential areas in *waqf*, such as those in the Ma'arūf quarter adjacent to the central business district, and sites along the riverfront in 'Ajūzah, which had been preempted by squatters, are now being redeveloped. Since the reforms, the Ministry of *Waqf* has already constructed several thousand dwelling units for low-income families in Cairo, and additional projects are on the drawing boards.[45] But its days appear numbered and the ministry, as will be shown later, has

[42] Figures as cited in Debs, "The Law of Property in Egypt," p. 109 and in *Almanac of 1937*, p. 116.

[43] See Debs, "The Law of Property in Egypt," pp. 140-141 for details of the attempts at legislative reform. After numerous debates, a committee was appointed in 1936 to study the legal system and make recommendations in many areas, including the law of *waqf*. Progress was slow, evidently, since this committee did not submit its final draft until 1942, and the recommendations were not acted upon by the legislature until 1946. Among the changes introduced was the stipulation that family *waqf* could no longer be created in perpetuity; it could run only for sixty years or two generations of beneficiaries. See also G. Baer, "Waqf Reform in Egypt," p. 71, from which the quotation has been taken.

[44] See Articles 1 and 2 of Law 180, 1952. See also R. Debs, "The Law of Property in Egypt," pp. 179 *et seq.*; and G. Baer, "Waqf Reform in Egypt," pp. 71 *et seq.*

[45] The change with respect to urban properties has been less one of power than of purpose. The Ministry of *Waqf* was always free, within limits, to allocate its profits in the pursuit of developmental goals. But what was formerly permissible has now become mandatory. Gradually, the revenues of the ministry derived from urban properties are being deflected from precise and petty allocations into charitable ventures on a larger scale, for example, the city for vagrants at al-Marj. As the Ministry of *Waqf* has begun to sponsor social services and low-cost housing, its plans have inevitably been more and more coordinated with those of other ministries and with the goals of national economic plans. Some information on current Cairo projects appears in "Moslems Give up Holdings in Egypt," *New York Times*, April 1, 1962, p. 27; in *United Arab Republic: Achievements and Future Development Plans* (Cairo, 1960), pp. 108-109, containing a report by the Ministry of *Waqf*; as well as in isolated references in the various issues of the United Arab Republic, *Annual Year Book* [*Al-Kitāb al-Sanawi*].

gradually been shorn of more and more of its resources and independence.

The final persisting problem which Cairo inherited from the nineteenth century was, of course, the social and functional bifurcation of the city into its two basic components—the old city and the new. Instead of being resolved in the first part of the twentieth century this problem became, in fact, more severe. It also differed in very essential fashion from the types of problems that have been discussed above, for this bifurcation was no mere "abuse" which hindered development. It was no superficial "problem" that could be solved directly through institutional or governmental reforms or edicts. This condition was nothing less than the physical reflection of *the problem that afflicted Egyptian society itself*. It was tangible and graphic evidence of that rent in the social fabric which new societies, emerging from a colonial past, must everywhere seek to mend, eliminating the threads which cannot be incorporated into the new warp and woof, and strengthening those which, from disuse, have broken or frayed. A union between the two cities of Cairo was not likely to occur unless and until the deep cleavages within Egypt's entire social structure—those which separated class from mass, alien or alienated elite from indigenous proletariat—were somehow mended or bridged.

The eighteenth-century city had been all of one piece. While certain subareas of the city ranked above others socially, and whereas the segregation of subgroups persisted along lines established during the Middle Ages, these represented gradations in a single dimension of social space. Even the new city added by Ismā'īl in the 1860's might have been absorbed into this common framework had it remained merely "Western-influenced," rather than been transformed, during the colonial decades, into "Western-dominated." The Western forms of city structure, had they been inhabited by Egyptians, might have gradually been assimilated to Eastern needs, and the cleavage between the two cities might never have become so extreme. However, with colonial rule and the influx of large numbers of Europeans, this new portion of the city was increasingly marked off as a "foreign" preserve. Azbakīyah, the center of the new city, contained over 56,000 inhabitants in 1917, of whom only under 14,000 were Egyptian Muslims![46] The discontinuity between the two cities had ceased to be one of degree and had become one of kind.

While the underlying causes of Cairo's dual structure, then, must be traced ultimately to the very organization of Egyptian society, the duality itself was encouraged and intensified by the processes of modernization and technological change that, at an ever-increasing pace, proliferated during the twentieth century. These processes in themselves "created" new problems for the city, or led to the recognition of new areas of difficulty. Wherever their impact was felt—and this was chiefly in the newer quarters of the city, because only there were the new technologies demanded and only there could they be accommodated and absorbed—one physical part of the city and one social portion of the community raced ahead, leaving greater and greater distance between itself and the remainder. In the short run, technological developments created new problems for the city, but problems that were felt selectively and primarily within the new city that grew up to the west and north of the original nucleus. In the long run, they created the major problem which Cairo now faces, namely, how to reunite the fragmented community and upgrade that portion of the city hitherto ignored in the process of modernization.

If one were to single out the two most important aspects of modernization that have affected Cairo's twentieth-century metamorphosis and have offered some of her most pressing challenges, one might easily select the car and the factory. Obviously, these are the very same elements that one might also select in discussing the evolution of any other modern city. But whereas the stimuli are perhaps the same, the problems generated and the solutions attempted must be viewed in the context of Cairo's specific character.

In 1903, when the first automobiles were introduced to the streets of Cairo, few could have foreseen the consequences of this innovation. The immediate impact, it must be admitted, was minimal. Cars neither displaced the usual wheeled vehicles nor inhibited their increase, as can be seen from Table 3.[47] This was just as well, since Cairo's streets were in no way prepared. They were primarily unpaved and often deeply rutted, making them uncomfortable for animal-drawn vehicles and virtually impassable for vehicles of greater speed. In 1900, just prior to the "auto age," of the 2.78 million square meters of Cairo's area devoted to public roads, more than half were merely unimproved, mud-surfaced pathways! Even of the "improved" roadways, most were minimally improved by a macadam base covered with gravel. Macadam roads covered by basalt and fully modernized roads paved with asphalt constituted only 9 percent of the total area in streets. Thus what few cars were introduced were confined to a tightly circumscribed circuit. In addition, most streets in the city, even if they had been paved, were much too narrow to admit a fair-sized vehicle. At the turn of the twentieth century, 58 percent of the entire length of

[46] *The Census of Egypt Taken in 1917* (Government Press, Cairo: 1921), Volume II, Table VII, p. 482.

[47] Boulad, "La voirie et l'esthétique de la ville du Caire," p. 36.

the circulation system consisted of streets so narrow that the passage of automobiles and trucks was absolutely impossible; about one-third could admit one-way traffic at best; and only 8 percent were wide enough to accommodate two-way traffic.[48] That few Cairo streets had separate sidewalks for pedestrians, that tram tracks often preempted most of the roadway of the wider streets, and that the dominant means of transportation in the city was still by foot or donkey, merely intensified the inadequacy of the circulation system for modern means of transportation. The situation had all the ingredients of an impending catastrophe. If the 1880's were the years of the "race against bankruptcy," the twentieth century was to be the era of the race between cars and roads.

TABLE 3. INCREASE IN VEHICLES IN CAIRO, 1900-1910

Type of Vehicle	*Number of Vehicles in Cairo* 1900	1910
Passenger carriages	1,600	2,000
(Coachmen)	(2,000)	(4,940)
Carts, wagons, and tipcarts	10,000	16,000
(Drivers of carts)	(10,200)	(16,000)
(Wheelbarrow operators)	(2,500)	(2,000)
Taxi autos	none	80
Private automobiles	none	619
Motorcycles	none	182

At first it appeared that the street builders might emerge victorious. A Herculean effort was made during the first two decades of the twentieth century to outstrip vehicular growth and to convert the roads at least in the western and northern portions of the developing city to modern requirements. Particularly in the flush years between 1900 and 1906 much progress was recorded. By the latter year, despite an overall expansion of the circulation system, unimproved roads had been reduced to 43 percent (from 54 percent in 1900), while those paved with basalt or asphalt increased from 9 percent to 31 percent only six years later. Gravel, which was of course totally inappropriate for automobile traffic, was abandoned. The proportion of the system with gravel surfacing was reduced to 25.5 percent, as many of the roads were converted to harder surfacing. This remarkable rate of progress continued into the next decade and, by 1919, the Cairo street area that had been provided with modern paving amounted to 2.5 million square meters.[49] Unimproved roadways persisted chiefly on the outskirts or in the heart of the medieval core.

This expansion kept pace with the rapid increase in automobiles and trucks and, except in the oldest quarters of the city, the city streets proved adequate to accommodate their needs. However, in the 1920's there appeared signs of a slackening pace of street improvements just at the moment when the demands generated by the mass-produced automobile became more insistent. By the 1930's, matters had begun to get "out of hand," with motor vehicles increasing far more rapidly than streets could be widened and redesigned to accommodate them. The late 1940's witnessed a wheeled "population explosion" in which vehicles doubled in number while street conditions remained constant. By the time wide-scale reconstruction and ambitious highway projects were undertaken in the 1950's, Cairo had become so congested that she required the kind of drastic surgery familiar to metropolitan dwellers all over the world.

A few illustrative figures may help to paint this picture more vividly. In 1930 there were perhaps 7,000 or 8,000 private cars in Cairo plus a small number of taxis, trucks, and buses. Five years later the number of private cars exceeded 10,000, supplemented by some 2,000 taxis, trucks, and buses. By 1940, there were over 14,000 cars registered in the city, and, although their number had declined somewhat by 1945, due to the unavailability of new cars during the war years, this decrease was more than compensated for by the increased number of taxis (1,400), trucks (2,200), and buses (720) on the roads. Motorcycles as well had begun to join the crowded traffic stream and by 1945 there were over 1,000 of these in Cairo. The temporary setback of the war years was soon overcome and, in the single decade between 1945 and 1955, the number of private automobiles in Cairo almost trebled. By the latter year, there were over 34,000 private cars in addition to more than 5,000 taxis, over 7,000 trucks and lorries, well in excess of 3,000 buses, and close to 8,000 motorcycles—all competing with pedestrians and animals for space on the streets of Cairo![50]

[48] Muṣṭafa Niyāzi, *Al-Qāhirah: Dirāsāt Takhṭīṭiyah fi al-Murūr wa al-Naql wa al-Muwāṣalāt* [Cairo: Planning Studies in Traffic, Transport and Communications] (Anglo-Egyptian Library, Cairo: 1958-1959), pp. 31-32.

[49] *Ibid.*, p. 34.

[50] Figures are adapted from those appearing in Niyāzi, *Al-Qāhirah*, Table 8, p. 55, and Table 18, p. 118. Either there has been an interruption in the rate of increase, possibly due to restrictions imposed after the Suez War of 1956 or Niyāzi's figures include more than Cairo registrations of vehicles. The last issue of *Annuaire Statistique, 1960/1961* (Government Printing Office, Cairo: 1963), p. 302, gave the following figures for licensed vehicles in Cairo in 1959 and 1960:

	1959	*1960*
Private cars	31,333	32,891
Taxis	4,034	4,235
Buses, Total	1,718	1,698
Public	(938)	(848)
Private	(281)	(292)
School	(391)	(405)
Tourist	(108)	(153)
Trucks	5,805	5,729
Motorcycles	13,914	14,108

While this vehicular density may not appear particularly impressive to readers familiar with comparable figures for New York City, it takes on greater significance when one remembers that traffic in Cairo had to be concentrated within only a fraction of the city's total extent. First, the entire old city—with the exception of those few streets which had been violently imposed—was closed to motor traffic. In addition, extremes of income distribution and a concentration of the wealthier classes in just a few of the newer areas led to extremely heavy concentrations of private cars in selected sections of the city. What was true with respect to residential areas was even truer of the commercial zones. Although trucks serviced the newer "western" business district, they remained an irrelevant mode of transportation for the older commercial areas. Therefore, the vehicles reported above were all concentrated within a relatively small portion of the city, increasing the actual if not the statistical density of traffic to congestion heights. Furthermore, most of these vehicles were likely to be out on the streets at the same time, since virtually no provisions had been made for off-street parking in the commercial zones and, until quite recently, almost no apartment buildings were constructed with subsurface garages.

In addition, just at the time when traffic was becoming more dense, the feasibility of widening existing ways or of cutting new arteries was diminishing. Methods of house construction had changed. Whereas low-value, replaceable mudbrick structures might have been built a century earlier, the new construction favored stone and reinforced poured concrete. These new buildings lined the roads, presenting a solid phalanx against the encroachments of potential thoroughfares. They sprang up along each new street, rigidifying the pattern before second thoughts could be entertained. It is perhaps a commentary on the situation that, between 1897 and 1947, when the problem of circulation took on the character of a disaster, only four major roadways were added to the circulation system within the built-up portion of the city. Of these, two were dependent for their rights of way upon filled-in canal beds (the Shāriʿ al-Khalīj, added before the turn of the century, and the [now] Shāriʿ Ramses, constructed during the second decade of the century along the course of the Ismāʿīlīyah Canal), while the other two (Shāriʿ al-Jaysh and Shāriʿ al-Azhar) were both constructed in the late 1920's at the expense of and for the use of the Tramway Company.

In brief, an enormous backlog had accumulated by the 1950's and strangulation appeared imminent. When the revolutionary regime took over in 1952, it was faced not only with the problem of planning for future urban expansion but with making up a deficit that had been allowed to accumulate over the preceding decades during which motor vehicles had finally come to dominate. While a later section will describe the major street projects executed within the past decade in Cairo, it is significant to note that they far exceeded the accomplishments of the full half-century before. Between 1952 and 1958, some 5.5 million square meters of Cairo's street system were paved, and among the more important thoroughfares added or enlarged were the Corniche, the Khalīj, Turʿah Ghamrah (Shāriʿ Ramses), Shāriʿ Shubra, al-Turʿat al-Būlāqīyah, the road to the pyramids, etc.[51] It is virtually impossible to consider traffic movement within Cairo without reference to these essential thoroughfares. Much still remains to be done in untangling Cairo's perpetual traffic snarl, but there at least appears hope that the problem will receive the attention it deserves.

If automobiles introduced one new major problem, industrialization introduced the other. Although the modern, large-scale, assembly-line factory has just recently emerged as an eye-catching embellishment on the Egyptian landscape and small firms (employing under ten persons) still dominate the Cairo industrial picture, the gradual transition from tiny workshop to factory dictated rather dramatic alterations in the land use pattern of the city. Indeed, this trend is creating problems which are likely to be felt with increasing intensity as it gains momentum in the coming few decades.

The trend in itself is a composite of several types of changes. First, within the metropolitan area of Cairo, there has been a noticeable shift from agriculture—as *the* source of livelihood for most of the population—to commerce and industry. It is important to recall that as late as 1877, when Ismāʿīl collected some "labor force" data in his Muqābalah survey, some 56.6 percent of the city's active labor force was still engaged in farming.[52] Most of the land within the official city boundaries was used not for urban purposes but for agriculture. By 1907, primary production had been reduced to a minor element in the economic base of the community, both proportionately and numerically. According to the census of that year, only 16,144 persons (about 7 percent of the active labor force) were engaged in agriculture. By 1917, the percentage had dropped to six while the number of farmers remained constant.[53] Since that time, there has been a

[51] United Arab Republic, Ministry of Information, *Al-Kitāb al-Sanawi 1959* (Cairo, 1959), pp. 614-615. See also Ministry of Information, *Al-Kitāb al-Sanawi 1962* (Cairo, 1962), p. 292, which reports that since 1952 some *LE* 5,800,000 have been expended on street paving and sidewalks in Cairo.

[52] The source for this figure, which must be used with caution since adequate operational definitions are not given, is *Essai de statistique générale de l'Égypte, années 1873 . . . 1877* (Imprimerie de l'État-Major Général Egyptien, Cairo: 1879), Tables LIV and LV, pp. 115-121.

[53] Computed from *The Census of Egypt Taken in 1917*, Volume II, Table III, pp. 380-405. Since in this table the total labor

steady decrease until, at present, under 3 percent of the Cairo labor force earns its living from full-time farming.

Second, there has been a gradual increase in the average size of commercial and industrial firms employing the nonfarming portion of the labor force. The typical firm, in nineteenth-century Cairo as well as in the preceding centuries, was a family-size enterprise; furthermore, many persons worked either without fixed premises ("entrepreneurs" offering itinerant services or engaged in small-scale distribution) or on premises which required less space than the average dwelling. With the exception of the slaughterhouses, the pottery kilns, the quarries, and a few of the specialized industries that had been commenced under Muḥammad 'Ali, which required larger plots, there was no industry—even metal-working and fabricating—that could not easily be fitted into small undifferentiated spaces as they became vacant. Except in the case of bakeries and baths, which required large fixed ovens, industry and commerce were highly mobile. Tools were portable and inventories virtually nonexistent. If firms tended to remain immobile, which they did, this was due to social rather than technological factors.

It was these characteristics that made possible the intimate intermixing of land uses that prevailed in Cairo from its earliest history up to the present century. As changes occurred, greater differentiation and specialization of land uses resulted, due both to the larger scale of enterprise and more elaborate capitalization. These increases in scale coincided with the expansion of the city from the original medieval nucleus to the regions both north and west of it. Since by this time the older commercial and industrial districts were fairly well saturated, and since, in any case, the newer forms could not be crowded into the tiny premises available there, it was inevitable that the commercial and industrial establishments being added to the city's economic base gravitated to the open land of the developing quarters. Initially, they were located within the central portions of the new city with almost as much residential intermixture as prevailed in the medieval core. Commercial premises were slightly more commodious, to accommodate the larger inventories demanded by a "Westernized" clientele, and the modest production and repair centers that began to dot the newer quarters had to be somewhat larger to make room for "new-fangled" motor driven machines; but, still, the scale remained small.

Little if any attempt was made to segregate these uses.

88. Family-size industrial workshop in Būlāq, 1969

89. New iron and steel mill in Ḥalwān

To a population which took mixed land use for granted as an essential characteristic of urban life and which was well accustomed to a fairly high level of background noise, the existence of small repair and machine shops, of stores and service establishments studded throughout even chiefly residential areas was no cause for concern. Their distribution was dictated more by ecological convenience than regulation. Thus, concentrations of particular industries arose in districts occupied by ethnic groups engaged in special trades, i.e., machine shops in the Italian

---

force includes housewives, people in institutions, school children, and the like, I have excluded them to obtain an "active labor force" base comparable to that evidently used in the Muqābalah survey. The number of persons in agricultural employment was computed against this reduced base to derive the percentage in agriculture.

90. Family-size commercial premise in al-Mūski, photographed in the 1930's but unchanged today

91. One of Cairo's earliest "new style" department stores: Sednoui's

quarter, groceries and coffee shops in the Greek zone, ribbons and sewing findings in the Mūski. Those few developing industries that required larger sites and heavier installations, or whose raw materials and products were bulkier, tended to segregate themselves in the northern portion of Būlāq, not because they were relegated to this region by design or because they wished to isolate themselves, but simply because access to port facilities and later to the major rail sidings there (in Sabtīyah) gave this location its competitive advantage.

It was not until the 1920's, and even more in the decades that followed, that larger-scale commercial establishments began to be segregated in the central business district of Azbakīyah (including the first "department stores"), and that certain new "factories," employing more than the traditional minimal labor force, began to seek peripheral locations where land costs were lower and where production lines could be spread out according to crude assembly-line principles. Even then, however, the general scale of both commercial and industrial plants remained small, not only in comparison with industrialized nations but even in comparison with rival Alexandria.

This situation, to a large extent, persists to the present. The overwhelming majority of Cairo's industrial and commercial firms are still extremely modest operations, which permits them a diffuseness of location unanticipated in a modern city. According to a survey of 1957, 55 percent of the industrial labor force of Cairo was employed by the 87.5 percent of all firms consisting of four or less persons! One- and two-person businesses accounted for two-thirds of all industrial firms and employed almost one-third of the industrial labor force of the city. The average size of a firm was only 3.6 workers. The average size of commercial establishments was even smaller and, in addition, over one-third of these latter firms were engaged in "personal service" (many requiring no fixed premise) while more than half were retail stores,[54] the majority of which occupied no more space than a one-car garage. Thus, even in the present era, the small size and lack of specialized requirements of nonresidential premises permit a headier intermixture of land uses than could be tolerated in a Western city of comparable complexity.

Nevertheless, the very fact that there are now even a small number of industrial plants that employ over 500 workers indicates a new set of problems that are likely to grow more severe as these plants become not the exception but the rule under current programs of industrialization. During World War II and again after 1952, a substantial number of large factories were constructed on the periphery, chiefly in new industrial estates, first

[54] My computations are based on data presented in *Annuaire Statistique, 1960/1961*, pp. 266 and 400.

north (Shubra al-Khaymah) and then south (Ḥalwān) of the built-up city. While these modern establishments resemble those constructed elsewhere, they generate problems which are significantly different. The laborers they employ must either be housed adjacent to the plant, often on land better suited to agriculture or industry than to residence, or they must be transported by bus from distant points, often along routes which cannot sustain sufficient demand to warrant public service. The proliferation of the private automobile, which went hand in hand with industrial decentralization in the United States and upon which the labor forces of American factories often depend for their journey to work, is and for some time will remain unknown in Egypt. In some instances, firms must actually construct housing estates for their workers, estates which share the drawbacks of all company towns. This task has now fallen to the government since the factories, even those constructed originally by private enterprise, are administered under the nationalization program. In other instances, where the public transportation system has not yet been extended, special company buses must be used to transport workers.

In essence, the modern, large-scale, decentralized factory, introduced at this stage of Cairo's development, has imposed certain requirements which the society has not yet been able to meet. While from one standpoint this may be viewed simply as a problem, from another it offers creative possibilities. One of the best proposals that has been very seriously entertained—and which figures prominently in the 1956 Master Plan—is that a series of satellite towns be constructed around these new industrial complexes. This solution would both relieve the factories of their present responsibility for providing housing or transport and, in addition, help relieve the center city of some of the population increments that otherwise threaten to strain its already overcrowded residential and transportation facilities.

Not only industry but another of Cairo's major economic bases, government, has experienced a dramatic shift in the scale of its operations in recent years. This expansion in the public sector has required a greater degree of land use specialization than was previously necessary. Again, the solution has been in the direction of the satellite town (this time adjacent, however, to built-up Cairo), within which the major government offices are to be concentrated, supplemented by residential and commercial quarters.

A number of problems have been raised in this section, for which no simple solutions exist. What is required is a balance between competing pressures. On the one hand, especially in the older quarters but also in the central portions of the newer quarters as well, the persistence of many small-scale enterprises has resulted in too much and too capricious an intermixing of land uses. On the other hand, too much rather than too little land use segregation is the critical problem on the periphery of the city, where a dramatic leap to very large-scale enterprises has created a reverse difficulty. If new and old quarters are to be fused into a unified urban community, policies to redevelop the older zones by sorting out land uses and assembling larger sites must go hand in hand with policies designed to provide the new peripheral zones with a fuller and more balanced complement of land uses. And these policies must, in turn, be related to plans for improvement in the circulation system itself. Opening access to the old city is just as essential as linking the new peripheral zones to the city core, if efficient land use patterns are to be encouraged.

One might with ease devote this entire volume to a study of contemporary Cairo's "social" problems, for they both allow and deserve such treatment. However, upon reflection it is apparent that they have always been present, in one form or another, throughout the city's history. Numerically they may loom larger by virtue of the heightened scale of urban concentration at Cairo, but the major difference is to be found not in scale but in the evolution of a philosophy of social welfare in which they have become identified as "problems" requiring solutions. This recognition of the "problems" is, in itself, testimony to the modernization of the city.

The case of housing can be singled out as an illustration of the magnitude and complexity of some of these new problems. Isolation of this problem is virtually impossible, since rapid urban growth, inadequate employment opportunities, low incomes, and the lack of adequate housing are all linked together in a depressing but indivisible chain of causation. To really understand and evaluate Cairo's housing problem and its possible solution requires no less than an understanding of Egypt's economic dilemma, which is again beyond the scope of our inquiry. Nevertheless, even a superficial discussion will alert the reader to the nature of the problem.

Throughout history Cairo has suffered from an inadequate supply of housing even by the most minimal standards. Some of the very earliest travel accounts remarked on the large numbers of city "residents" whose only bed was a doorway or street. Others noted the incredible densities at which Cairenes were housed, 200 or more persons crowded into the cubicles of a single "apartment" hive. While these conditions are now exceptions, standards of adequacy have gone up faster than actual improvements could be made. And, in addition, the enormous number of urban newcomers that Cairo has been called upon to absorb during the present century would have presented a formidable challenge even if standards and expectations had not risen in the mean-

92. Crowds in al-Ḥusayn Square near al-Azhar after the noon prayer on Friday

time. Two separate elements must be distinguished in analyzing the "housing problem" of Cairo—each in the context of rising standards. The first is housing volume, i.e., the rate at which additions are made to the housing stock in relation to population growth; the second is housing demand, i.e., the financial capacity of Cairo families to demand and pay for adequate housing. Neither of these elements offers much encouragement to those seeking simple solutions.

The volume of housing construction in the present century has never been able to keep up with population increases in Cairo and, in recent years, there has been a monotonous gap annually between additions to population and additions to the housing stock. While we lack the data to trace this phenomenon back into the early years of the century, figures from recent years are unequivocal in supporting this depressing statement. In 1947, the 2,090,064 residents of Cairo were housed at an average of 4.6 persons per family within 448,333 dwelling units

93. People dot Maydān al-Taḥrīr on a hot summer afternoon

which, in total, contained 1,039,742 rooms.[55] The average number of persons per room in Cairo was, therefore, two. Construction had been halted during the war—the years of the greatest migration to Cairo—and all observers at the time were aware that, whatever its statistical magnitude, there could be no denial of the very real housing shortage that afflicted the city. Since 1947, the population of Cairo has been climbing at the rate of about 4 percent per year, until, by 1960, the population of the newly delimited metropolitan district was 3,348,779. This population, divided into family groups which by then averaged 4.8 persons (in part due to lowered infant mortality rates), was housed in 687,858 dwelling units comprising a total of 1,439,158 rooms. Whereas in 1947, the average dwelling unit contained 2.3 rooms and was expected to accommodate a family of 4.6 members on the average, by 1960 the average size of dwelling unit was only 2.0 rooms despite an increase in average family size. Density had mounted to 2.3 persons per room. Furthermore, because of extreme inequities in the distribution of housing space in Cairo, the detailed picture was even less attractive than the overview. Almost half of the occupied dwelling units in Cairo in 1960 consisted of only *one* room, and these were not necessarily or even overwhelmingly occupied by small families. The median size of households occupying one-room units was in excess of four, and families consisting of as many as ten or more persons were to be found in units of this size.[56]

[55] A difference between the Egyptian procedure for counting rooms and that followed by Western countries in their housing censuses must be pointed out here. The kitchen in Egypt is extremely small even in the most luxurious Cairo dwellings and is limited in function solely to the preparation of food. It is *not* included in a room-count in the Egyptian census, although it is almost always counted as a room in a Western census. Therefore, strictly speaking, density comparisons are not legitimate.

[56] Persons-per-room ratio in 1947 was computed from Kingdom

As modern standards of density have come to be accepted by Egypt's planners, the definition of the problem has been formulated in terms of a reduction in density. International comparisons may help to place this problem in context. In the United States in 1950, less than 2 percent of the dwelling units, urban and rural, were occupied at densities exceeding two persons per room, and even in urban Czechoslovakia, despite the enormous housing stock loss sustained in the war, only 28.6 percent of the dwelling units in that year were occupied so intensively.[57] Thus, what is now the exception in Western industrialized countries is still the rule in Cairo. Nevertheless, it would be both unrealistic and economically self-defeating to attempt any substantial reduction in Cairo densities. This must be accepted as a problem whose solution must be put off until some of the underlying causes of it have been approached.

In the meantime, however, it would be desirable to prevent a further deterioration in standards, and it is legitimate to ask whether additions to the Cairo housing stock are now being made at rates sufficient to replace units lost through demolition as well as to absorb, at standards not inferior to those already existing, the new population increments that inevitably flow into the city. Evidence indicates that this has not been taking place and that, in fact, the trend of deteriorating density conditions has persisted into the 1960's. This can be simply stated. In 1960, slightly under 3,000 building permits were issued in the Governorate of Cairo for the construction of an additional 48,550 rooms. In 1961, the comparable figures were 3,235 building permits for the construction of 50,910 rooms.[58] It is impossible to determine from these figures what proportion of the authorized rooms were designed for residential use and what proportion for industrial or commercial purposes, but even if we assume that all of them were actually built and all of them were for residential use (and neither is a valid assumption), their contribution to the housing stock would have been insufficient to absorb the new population added to the city in those two years, much less compensate for an unknown number of demolitions. Assuming a conservative population growth rate for Cairo of 4 percent per annum, some 136,000 additional residents in 1960 and another 140,000 residents in 1961 had to be absorbed. This was equivalent, at an average family size of 4.8, to adding 28,000 and 29,000 families respectively in the two years. If we can, for the sake of argument only, conceive of these newcomers being housed in these new rooms, the density of occupancy would have been 2.7 persons per room, i.e., considerably higher than the already-existing densities of the city. The evidence thus leads to the conclusion that the housing shortage in Cairo has not only

94a, b. Modern housing built by time-honored construction methods

of Egypt, Ministry of Finance and Economy, *Census of Egypt, 1947*, Volume 15, *Governorate of Cairo* (Government Printing Office, Cairo: 1952), Table III, summarized on p. 11. The comparable figure for 1960 was computed from the United Arab Republic, Department of Census and Statistics, *The Population Census of 1960*, unnumbered Arabic volume, *Governorate of Cairo* (Government Printing Office, Cairo: 1962), Table 29, summary on p. 256. The median size of households occupying one-room dwellings was computed from *ibid.*, Table 57, p. 472.

[57] Comparative figures have been taken from Louis Winnick, *American Housing and Its Use* (John Wiley & Sons, Inc., New York: 1957), Table 1, p. 2.

[58] A complete table of building construction licenses issued from 1955 through 1961 within Egypt as a whole and within selected urban centers appears in Federation of Industries in the United Arab Republic, *Yearbook July 1960* (Société Orientale de Publicité, Cairo: 1962), pp. 65-66. Whether the number of construction licenses is an accurate reflection of construction depends upon whether (1) all licenses are used, and (2) all construction is confined to licensed operations. Since these two specifications are never totally fulfilled, construction licenses may be taken as only a rough index to actual construction.

95. Workers' City in Imbābah: Cairo's first public housing

persisted since World War II but has actually become worse.

To some significant extent, inadequate housing in Cairo must be traced to inadequate demand. Needs there may be, but economic demand there is not. Again, by way of illustration, sample family budgets may give the reader some sense of the magnitude of the problem. In 1958/59 the Egyptian government conducted a sample survey gathering detailed family budgets from 3,284 families.[59] The results revealed that, for most urban families, food alone required so large a share of the family's income that, once that need had been met, very little indeed was left to cover all other necessities of life, including housing. Within the entire urban sample, almost 56 percent of all expenditures was for food. And, as is true everywhere, the lower the income, the higher the proportion absorbed by this basic item (see Table 4). Given these patterns of expenditure, it would be unreasonable to apply the "Western" standard of expecting that a fifth to a fourth of family income will be allocated to rent. In Egypt, expenditures in the neighborhood of 5 to 10 percent are closer to reality. And this, in combination with the low incomes of most urbanites, means that,

TABLE 4. THE SHARE OF FAMILY BUDGET ALLOCATED TO FOOD WITHIN SELECTED INCOME GROUPS. URBAN EGYPT, 1957/1958

Income Class (selected)	*Percent Spent on Food*
Under *LE* 25/annum	74.10 (primarily cereals)
LE 100-150/annum	69.67
LE 200-250/annum	62.51
LE 400-600/annum	51.41
LE 1,000 or more/annum	36.65

if adequate housing is to be provided for Cairo's population, it cannot be left to the economic market place. Direct government subsidy is inevitable.

Recognition of the government's responsibility in this area has appeared only very recently in Egypt's long history. Prior to the Revolution of 1952, only one publicly subsidized low-rent housing project was constructed in Cairo, namely the "Workers' City" in Imbābah, consisting of some 1,100 dwelling units. Since the Revolution, construction of "popular" housing has become an essential element of government policy, in which the Ministry of Housing and the Ministry of *Waqf* have been vitally involved. Housing units for the middle classes are also needed, and several projects have already been executed to provide reasonable housing for the "salaried middle class," many of whom are government employees in Cairo. Whether these ventures will be sufficient to compensate for a reduction in housing offered through the private sector cannot be judged at this early date. Raising the housing standards of a minority of Cairo's low-income families without substantially adding to the entire housing stock may benefit a small portion of the population without contributing to a rise in general standards.

The foregoing remarks are not to be taken as a definitive statement of *the* housing problem, but merely as an indication of the nature of the new social problems coming to the fore as Cairo enters its second millennium. Even as older problems have been "solved," new ones have come to take their place which are, if anything, even more challenging than the ones which have preceded them. But the reader will note that the new problem areas somehow appear more familiar to him, that they strike a responsive chord absent in, for example, a discussion of the role of the *muḥtasib* or the *awqāf*. Cairo, as a contemporary city and the capital of an industrializing nation, now shares with other major cities throughout the world the pains and perplexities of the modern metropolis.

[59] Some of the results of this study, including the figures from which Table 4 has been constructed, appear in *Annuaire Statistique, 1960/1961*, p. 104. I have merely combined the percentages to obtain the food total. Unfortunately, the table does not show the distribution of the sample by income class nor does it show a specific breakdown for housing expenditures as distinct from other nonfood consumption items. Both of these would be needed to estimate housing demand for Cairo.

PART III · THE CONTEMPORARY METROPOLIS

An Epilogue and an Introduction

All the problems discussed in the preceding chapter had more than tangential significance in shaping the form Cairo was to take in the twentieth century. Each, either directly or, more commonly, by default, affected the differential rates of growth in various quarters of the city and, by influencing the types of residential facilities available or newly provided, helped to bring about concentrations of persons with varying social characteristics in one district or another. While natural topographic and man-made technological factors circumscribed and channeled the explosive growth of the twentieth century into specific reservoirs, the social history of the community and the existing types of institutional forms acted more directly to distribute population within the metropolis and to give to each quarter its own unique functions and its own characteristic inhabitants.

Thus, decisions made by the autonomous concessionaires who built the tramlines served to encourage urban development in certain directions while consigning land off the major routes to continued agricultural exploitation. In a similar manner, decisions made by other foreign companies concerning the extension of service utilities into certain quarters enhanced the attractiveness of these zones—but only for a special clientele. The uneasy developments in mortgage financing coupled with the specific values of the investors, in similar fashion, shaped the kinds of subdivisions that flourished in the newly opened zones, serving, with the sole exception of Heliopolis, to fragment the newer additions to the city into tiny and uncoordinated patchworks of intensive construction. The small scale of private developments precluded coordination, a tendency that was compounded by the lack within the municipal superstructure of home rule and the attendant powers over land use necessary to guide development within an orderly pattern.

Lack of conscious control over development, however, did not mean capricious intermixing. In ways, the absence of planning allowed the subconsensual forces full play, and from their operation evolved a pattern within the newer parts of the city which was nonetheless marked for having been unplanned and which was clearly related to the divisions and specializations within the urban structure that were already apparent at the turn of the century.

In the older portions of the city, as well, the factors we have called "problems" in the above discussion served as "forces" which molded these historic quarters, condemning some to stagnation and further decline, encouraging the metamorphosis of others into shoddy Western imitations. Even the housing problem, that is, the lack of residential facilities for many of the new migrants to the city, returned its own ingenious solution, namely the conversion of the cemetery zones into residential quarters, thus expanding the population of the living city into areas which no plan could have foreseen.

Most of these changes had an air of caprice about them. Here, a decision of the Tramway Company led to an upgrading of some small linear strip within the old city; there, the accidental distribution of *waqf*-encumbered property led to a further deterioration of another section; here a shift in the methods of production in a certain industry led to its relocation, while the persistence of traditional techniques in others left a residual concentration in an older quarter; sometimes a politically motivated expulsion or restriction of some ethnic group resulted in residential succession in one subarea but not in adjacent ones. These are only a few of the many types of random influences that played upon the structure of the old city during the fluid years of the twentieth century. But again, despite the unplanned nature of the changes and the often accidental impulses that activated them, the most impressive fact to be observed is that continuity far outweighed drastic shifts, and that a knowledge of an area's earlier history enables one to predict quite accurately the general direction of change. Only occasionally has that direction been altered by a more recent opposing force.

The essential purpose of this book thus far has been to provide the reader with sufficient background to understand the city of Cairo as it is today, to see each part of the city as a subarea sharing much in common with the rest of the city but also retaining with remarkable persistence its own distinguishing characteristics—characteristics that mark it off as a relatively independent "natural" area. The present structure of the city is so tied to its past historical development that, for any given subsection of the city, to know the period in which it was first settled and to know the social and ethnic characteristics of its earlier residents (or, in the case of the most recently settled zones, the social and ethnic characteristics of the older part of the city out of which it radiated) is to know a good deal about its present inhabitants, and to be able to predict quite accurately many elements of its physical appearance. In order to complete the prediction, however, one needs also to know the relationship of each subarea to the transportation network of the city and, further, to know any special modifying or extenuating influences, particularly of an institutional nature, that made the area more or less responsive to the crosscurrents of stability and change that operated within it.

While this has been, perhaps, a relatively long introduction to the central purpose of this volume, we are finally ready to proceed to an analysis of contemporary Cairo. In this analysis we shall be able to employ not the fragmented verbal accounts of history—which often leave unanswered many of the most crucial questions—but the fuller, though still incomplete, records of the decennial censuses of Cairo. These records allow us to trace quite precisely the vicissitudes of the various quarters of the city and to measure growth and transformation in those peripheral areas of more recent settlement. Population figures, combined with an "imaginative reading" of specially computed indices of socio-economic status, of family life, of social organization or disorganization, and other indicators of differences in the way life is lived within the city's various quarters, can give us a new way of examining the complex structure of the modern city of Cairo and of abstracting from that complexity the underlying simplicities and patterns.

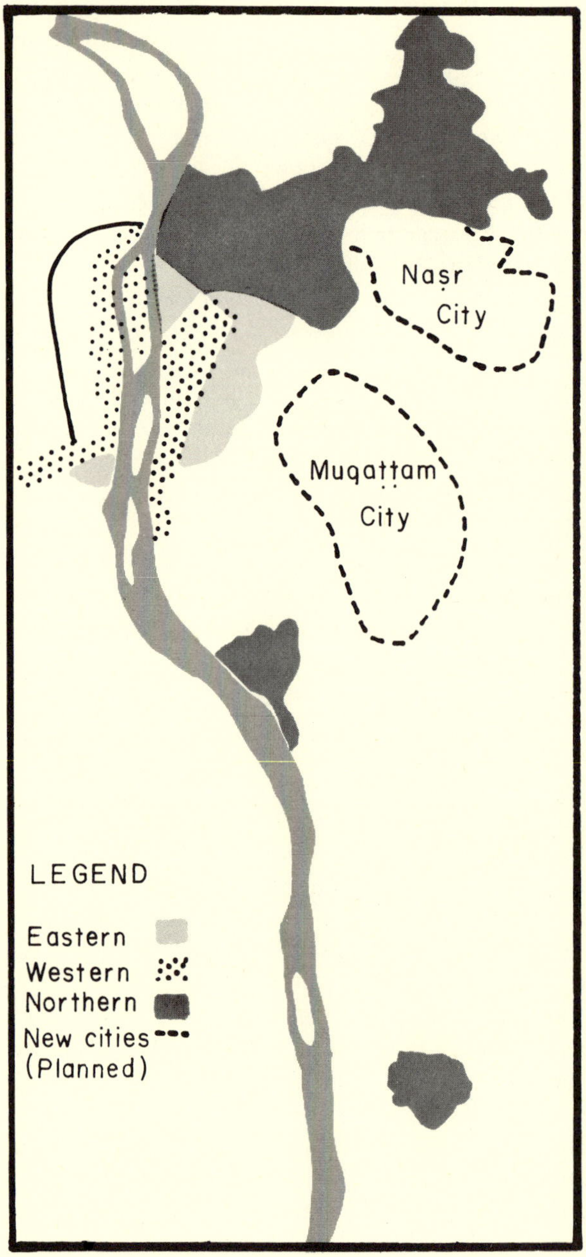

XV. The three major geographic divisions of Cairo

11 The Emergence of the Northern City: Comparative Growth Rates

Archaeologists have long used the strata of human and natural deposits to "peel the onion" of history and to assign contemporaneity to items within the same stratum. I propose to use this same approach but to reverse the procedure by using known historic developments to separate the series of urban accretions that, in the aggregate, constitute the present city of Cairo. For, just as the dimension of depth lays bare to the archaeologist distinctive, successive strata of time, so the horizontal dimension of surface space reveals to the urban ecologist the successive models of urbanism, each conditioned by roughly similar factors, that have followed one another in Cairo's progression from desert encampment to modern metropolis and which, to a limited extent, still stand side by side in the city of today.

We have already noted that, by the end of the nineteenth century, Cairo consisted in reality of two major subcities, more or less independent, plus a stillborn appendage to the south. By the middle of the twentieth century a third and new city had been added to the original complex, chiefly (but not exclusively, for here any simple scheme breaks down) to the north of the existing areas of settlement. Each of these cities was formed in the crucible of a different technology and was shaped by a different principle of social organization—which tended to confer upon each a fairly distinctive set of general characteristics. Thus, if the technological foundation of the first (the medieval core) was animate energy while that of the second (the colonial town) was steam, the energy that powered the third into existence was electricity. And if the organizing principle of the first had been religion and, within the Muslim majority, ethnicity, while that of the second had been the mutually repelling polarity between native Egyptian (Orient) and foreigner (Occident), the principle which governed distribution of population within the third city was chiefly economic—with rich and poor increasingly segregated. In many ways, these three models of urbanism still coexist in the city of Cairo, supplemented by a rural infusion about which more will be said later. However, time and process have tended to blur the boundaries between the three and to secrete transitional strips where once there had been unbridgeable barricades.

The three major geographic divisions of Cairo, then, constitute a basic framework within which the smaller subdivisions of the city fit (see Map XV). While to know the general character and historical development of these larger components is not to know, a priori, everything about the smaller quarters which comprise them, no understanding of the smaller "natural areas" can be gained in detail until the broader conditioning units have been understood.

The deepest stratum upon which today's city is built is the medieval. (As we have seen, settlements predating this period have disappeared, leaving as a cenotaph only some unstable mounds and the refuse of generations.) This intensively developed medieval "core city" is what will be referred to hereafter as the Eastern City. It is chiefly the elongated irregular rectangle that stretches from the Ḥusaynīyah projection just north of the Bāb al-Naṣr and Bāb al-Futūḥ southward to and including the Citadel and the Mosque of Ibn Ṭūlūn. On the west it is bounded roughly by the course of the Khalīj Street (for the canal is but a distant memory for the oldest inhabitants), while on the east it fades into the desert. Included also in this zone is the projection west of the Khalīj that encompasses the area originally occupied by the Fāṭimid port of al-Maqs and, with a leap and a break in contiguity, the former port of Būlāq, no longer literally but still figuratively an island with social and historic affinities to the Eastern City.

The *aqsām* (districts) of Cairo that comprise the Eastern City are: al-Jamālīyah, al-Darb al-Aḥmar, the northern portion of al-Khalīfah, the southern part of Bāb al-Sha'rīyah, and the eastern bank of Būlāq. Because these districts cannot easily be subdivided in the early censuses, the totals for each *qism* (district) will be combined to trace the growth of the Eastern City. However, it should be borne in mind that, as the recent period is approached, some of the totals are deceptively large since they begin to include portions of the nonmedieval fringe, i.e., the cemetery quarters to the east and south whose growth as residential zones dates essentially from the twentieth century. In a later analysis these developments will be treated separately.

Just west of the Khalīj begins the neo-medieval stratum, a narrow transitional belt parallel to the Eastern City. While it was originally settled in premodern times, its development was so impermanent and spotty that it was easily transformed into a more modern type of urban quarter when the need arose. Its transformation was facilitated by the ease with which older buildings could be displaced or supplemented by new additions dating from the last century. The *qism* of al-Mūski lies entirely within this belt, as do the easternmost portions of 'Abdīn and Sayīdah Zaynab, their combined extent comprising a transitional buffer strip between past and present.

The heart of the Western City, or what might be termed the post-Renaissance or Baroque stratum, occupies the land west of this transitional belt, almost to the river's edge. Its occidental limit is the Shāri' al-Qaṣr al-'Ayni, the major route leading to Miṣr al-Qadīmah, which was the westernmost street laid out in Ismā'īl's addition to the city. Beyond this core—along the riverfront overlooking the Nile, onto the islands of Rawḍah[1] and al-Jazīrah in the center of the stream, and beyond, along the shoreline of the river's west bank—lies a final addition to the Western City which dates from the twentieth century. At this point in the analysis the transitional belt, the Baroque strip, and the modern quarter will be combined and treated as parts of the Western City, although in a later analysis these substrata will be distinguished more carefully. Thus, in addition to the *aqsām* listed above (al-Mūski, 'Abdīn, and Sayīdah Zaynab), the districts of Azbakīyah, Qaṣr al-Nīl, as well as the western shore of Būlāq, are combined into the unit referred to as the Western City.

This rather simple division of the central portion of contemporary Cairo into two lateral halves, an eastern and a western, accounts effectively for all parts of that zone except the two discrete medieval ports of Būlāq and Miṣr al-Qadīmah. Būlāq has already been assigned to the medieval stratum and so perhaps should Miṣr al-Qadīmah. However, the isolation, until very recently, of the latter quarter and its combination with the agricultural zone south of the major settlement suggest that it be treated separately as an abortive Southern City.

The third major division of contemporary Cairo is the Northern City, a vast sprawling district extending eight kilometers in width from the Nile shore at Rawḍ al-Faraj to the sharply delineated desert edge beyond Heliopolis. To the south it is bounded by the Eastern and Western cities on a line that passes through the rail terminal of Bāb al-Ḥadīd. On the north it is bordered in highly irregular fashion by the rich agricultural lands of the Delta, into which it continues to make inroads. This city dates, almost exclusively, from the twentieth century, although in the path of its phenomenal tidal surge of expansion were isolated clusters of dwellings and even whole villages that were drawn into the stream of modernity, not, however, without deflecting its course here and there or without leaving small residual islands of resistance. The *aqsām* of Cairo which comprise this Northern City are al-Wāyli, Shubra, Rawḍ al-Faraj, and Miṣr al-Jadīdah (Heliopolis), which have sometimes been combined in different ways administratively and have progressively been subdivided as population continued to mount.

Before examining the development of this new city in greater detail, however, let us trace briefly the comparative growth of the Eastern, Western, and Northern cities during the past few generations, for only through such an approach can the significance of the Northern City's fabulous expansion be appreciated (see Map XV).

A little more than 100 years ago there was, for all intents and purposes, one and only one city—the Eastern—in which the vast majority of Cairenes lived. Even as recently as 1882, when the first official census of the city was taken, despite the radical additions made by Ismā'īl and the generosity of the boundary-makers in including a wide agricultural hinterland, this city (including Būlāq) still contained well over half of the population of Cairo. Of the close to 400,000 residents enumerated in that year, 213,427 were still following an essentially medieval style of life in the oldest stratum of the city. However, the new developments instituted by Ismā'īl and his successor had already begun to transform the transitional belt and to fill in the Baroque quarter, for in the Western City (including neo-medieval al-Mūski) there were almost 130,000 inhabitants, accounting for almost a third of the city's population. Miṣr al-Qadīmah, the aborted Southern City, contained 22,518 persons, a somewhat inflated total achieved only by adding the farmers of the southern agricultural fringe to the more urban population around the Qaṣr al-Sham' and the Fam al-Khalīj. In the enormous stretch of the Northern City, virtually untouched by urban development except in the southernmost tier adjacent to the older cities, there were only 34,000 residents, most of whom were simple agriculturalists who would have been surprised indeed to learn that, by a boundary definition, they had been accorded the dignity of being called *madanīyīn* (literally, "city dwellers" but connoting "civilized").

This situation was destined to change rapidly in the decades of modern expansion but between 1882 and 1897, when conditions of growth did not alter basically, the same relative strengths remained evident. The medieval stratum continued to house the major share of the city's population. By the latter year some 320,000 of the city's 590,000 residents, or 54 percent of the total, were found in these older quarters, all but one of which experienced substantial growth during that period when many of

[1] Rawḍah represents one of those parts of the city which experienced radical ecological succession. Up to the present decade it was functionally and socially linked with Miṣr al-Qadīmah. In recent census reports it constituted two tracts of the Miṣr al-Qadīmah *qism*. However, within the past decade its archaic and rural features have been swallowed up in a massive construction boom that has transformed the bucolic island into an integral part of Cairo's modern riverfront façade.

the "important" families removed themselves to the new sections of the city, permitting the conversion of their former homes into subdivided and densely packed tenements. Moderate growth was registered in the Western City, where the population increased to almost 160,000 (27 percent of the total), despite the proliferation of commercial uses that added daytime but not nighttime populations to these quarters. Even in Miṣr al-Qadīmah some small increase was also experienced, testimony to the general nature of the impulses to urban growth then making themselves felt.

But it was in the north that the first glimmerings began to appear of what was to be confirmed in the next decade as a transformation in the city's ecology. That region doubled its admittedly negligible population between the two census years, reaching in excess of 76,000 inhabitants by 1897. At that time the district of al-Wāyli included what was later to be designated Miṣr al-Jadīdah (still a thought, not a reality), while contained within the *qism* of Shubra was the entire area later to be divided between Shubra and Rawḍ al-Faraj.

The decade that bridged the turn of the century was also the decade that clearly signaled a basic shift in this balance between the old and new quarters. The Eastern City, although far from static (having increased in population by some 28,000), grew more slowly than the city as a whole, so that by the end of the decade it accounted for barely half of the city's dwellers. The Western City, on the other hand, gained population at a rate commensurate with the whole; by 1907 it still contained the same 27 percent of the city's then-larger population as it had in 1897. It was, however, in the newly settling Northern City that the greatest changes were to be observed. By then, population had mounted to over 112,000, constituting 16 percent of Cairo's 680,000 inhabitants. Virtually no growth at all was recorded for Miṣr al-Qadīmah, despite an extension of the southern limits of the city to include the distant suburbs of Ma'ādi and Ḥalwān.

These same trends continued into the next decade of growth, as Cairo's population approached 800,000. The Eastern City added little population, except in the two zones flanking the western business district at Azbakīyah. (These low-income zones of Būlāq and Bāb al-Sha'rīyah are still among the most densely packed quarters of today's city.) Thus, the proportion residing in the medieval quarters declined again, down to only 47 percent of the total, while the Western City barely held its own, containing by 1917 some 27 percent of the city's total, a share that had remained remarkably constant for twenty years. The rate of growth in the Northern City continued to gain momentum. By 1917, just prior to the urban boom decade that was to follow, the new "city" contained over 170,000 residents or *one out of every five* Cairenes. The Southern City remained stillborn, registering so negligible an increase that it could easily have been accounted for by a mere excess of births over deaths.[2]

As migrants poured into the city during World War I and the years immediately following, there was a dramatic expansion in every part of the city and a degree of residential mobility perhaps never before matched in Cairo's history. Within ten brief years the city absorbed more than 200,000 newcomers. Whereas in 1917 about 35 percent of Cairo's population had been born outside the city (i.e., were migrants), by 1927 this figure had risen to over 42 percent, despite the higher rate of natural increase that also contributed to urban growth. Migrants were drawn from all parts of Egypt and from abroad, but particularly attracted to the city at that time were numerous villagers who were already feeling the tightening man-land squeeze created by demographic pressures.

The mechanisms of absorption were twofold. First, the settled quarters of the Eastern City, while enjoying little new construction, were able nevertheless to crowd many of the new migrants into existing structures, raising both the area and room densities to levels then deplored as excessive, although they have since doubled! And second, people flocked into newer areas, both along the riverine portions of the Western City and even more on the expanding frontier of the Northern City. While some of the settlers in these freshly subdivided areas were recent arrivals to the city, either foreigners from abroad or, less commonly, Egyptians of rural origin, most were drawn from more interior portions of the city itself. The dwellings they vacated absorbed new inhabitants at densities far in excess of previous occupancy, which permitted all districts to contribute their share toward relieving the pressures caused by massive migration. Even the Eastern City, out of dire necessity, *created* its own frontier, namely, the adjacent funereal quarters whose tombs and hastily assembled mudbrick shanties gave shelter

[2] Note must be taken here of a major change in the boundary of Cairo and also of certain discrepancies in the reports of various censuses. Between 1907 and 1917 a large portion of the land on the western bank of the Nile was added to the city's jurisdiction, increasing its area from about 100 square kilometers to over 160 square kilometers. The increment in population that resulted, however, was far less than the increment in land, since the sections added to the city were then sparsely settled and still largely devoted to agricultural uses. (This may be why Clerget's analysis excludes this zone.) The *aqsām* of 'Abdīn, which gained the Jazīrah and some portion of the west bank, and Būlāq, which absorbed the settlement of Imbābah and its surrounding rural fringe, also on the west bank, benefited from this newly annexed territory. We would estimate that the former *qism*'s population was inflated by about 12,000-15,000 new residents by the territorial increase while the latter's was swelled by about 15,000-18,000 west-bank residents. However, exact numbers cannot be recovered, due to the widely varying reports of *aqsām* populations for given years as presented in successive censuses.

TABLE 5. MIGRANTS TO CAIRO:
POPULATION ENUMERATED IN CAIRO IN THE CENSUSES OF 1917, 1927, 1947, AND 1960, BY PLACE OF BIRTH

	Enumerated in Cairo in the Census of							
	1917		*1927*		*1947*		*1960*	
	Number	*%*	*Number*	*%*	*Number*	*%*	*Number*	*%*
Total	790,939	—	1,064,567	—	2,090,654	—	3,348,779	—
Population with known birthplace	787,461	100	1,058,428	100	2,085,987	100	3,331,078	100
Cairo-born	ca. 512,490[a]	65[a]	614,041	58	1,325,485	64	2,079,434	62
Born outside Egypt	76,658	10	81,835	8	59,009	3	57,378[b]	2
Egyptian-born migrants	ca. 198,313	25[a]	362,552	34	701,493	34	1,194,266	36
From urban governorates[c]	(22,293)	(3)	(28,717)	(3)	(58,998)	(3)	(102,587)	(3)
From Upper Egyptian provinces	(ca. 94,976)	(12)	(183,230)	(17)	(247,504)	(12)	(483,491)	(15)
From Delta provinces	(81,044)	(10)	(150,605)	(14)	(394,991)	(19)	(608,188)	(18)

SOURCE: Selected tables in the *Census of Egypt* for 1917 and 1927; the *Census of Cairo* (special volumes in 1947 and 1960). Computations mine, percentages rounded.

[a] In 1917 the boundaries of Cairo were enlarged to encompass the western bank of the river, an area which had hitherto been recorded with the Upper Egyptian province of Jīzah. Therefore, a sizeable but unknown proportion of the persons listed in the *Census of 1917* as residing in Cairo but having been born in Jīzah province actually were not migrants at all but "victims" of reclassification. I have attempted to correct for this by subtracting some 29,000 entries listed as migrants from Jīzah and adding them to the category, Cairo-born. Without this correction, the percentage of Cairo-born residents declines to 61. Logically, a similar correction should be made to compensate for Cairo's redistricting for the 1960 Census; this correction is more difficult and requires data by small areas which unfortunately I lack.

[b] Includes a large Syrian-born community temporarily in Cairo in connection with the political merger of Egypt and Syria under the then-common name, the United Arab Republic.

[c] Primarily but not solely urban.

to more than 10,000 of the city's burgeoning population by 1927.[3]

By that year, the city had passed the million mark in size and was changing unmistakably into the drabber dress of modernity. The medieval stratum was dwarfed in importance by later accretions within which some of the current strains between urbanity-ruralism and between modernity-traditionalism were already becoming apparent. By then, only two-fifths of the city's population lived in the fast-deteriorating older quarters to the east, and these were increasingly selected from among the city's poorest inhabitants. The remaining population, often but not always better endowed, was divided almost equally between the Western and Northern cities; but, in marked contrast, within these zones were also some of the least urbanized groups in the city, i.e., villagers who continued to till the same sod, oblivious of the administrative vagaries that now classified their farms as "city" and themselves as "urbanites." Apartment houses were supplanting or encircling single-family dwellings along the shoreline of the Western City and were accompanying the northeastward march of the major transportation axis that followed in the course of the filled-in bed of the Ismā'īlīyah Canal. To the north and on the west bank, whole communities were springing up where once there had been farms and orchards. In Heliopolis, first wrested from the desert only a score of years earlier, tens of thousands of residents demanded the local business services newly being offered there, and branches of downtown shops were opened to help serve their needs. It is notable that, in response to this enormous demand for urban living space, even the Southern City at Miṣr al-Qadīmah was the recipient of a backwater of urban growth that could not be fully contained within more desired parts of the metropolis. While increasing at a slower rate than other sections of Cairo, by 1927 it housed close to 50,000 persons.

In contrast with the preceding decade of expansion, the city registered only moderate gains during the economic crisis that dominated the 1927 to 1937 decade. But, significantly, those smaller gains it did make were confined totally to the newer parts of the city. The medieval core of the Eastern City appeared to have reached both

[3] For example, the Khalīfah "City of the Dead" (*Shiyākhāt* No.'s 27 and 30 in J. Abu-Lughod and E. Attiya, *Cairo Fact Book*, identification key) increased its resident population from about 3,500 in 1907 to 7,444 by 1927. In the former year most residents in this zone were employed in the stone quarries nearby or as custodians of the tombs. In contrast, many of the newcomers who settled in the zone between 1917 and 1927 had little reason, except the housing shortage, to choose this location, for few of them had jobs that tied them to the "local resources" of the district.

saturation level and a low ebb in attractiveness, for it had become an area if not of out-migration at least of apparent stagnation. (Later events were to prove it not dead but merely dormant.) The population in that zone was, at the end of the decade, no more than it had been at the beginning[4] but, because of the increases elsewhere, this represented a decreased proportion of the total. By 1937, only a third (34 percent) of the city's population lived in the Eastern quarters.

The reasons for this are not difficult to discover. The economic base of medievalism was fast disappearing and the monopoly which the medieval city had retained over the industrial structure of the city was beginning to vanish under the impact of changing technology. A dual urban economy began to appear in the Cairo of the 1920's, in which preindustrial firms shared the productive system with a newly evolving modern sector (then still confined to commerce but destined to spread to industry as well). As recently as 1917 one out of every four Cairenes engaged in the textile industry lived in the district of al-Jamālīyah (where the shops were concentrated) while other large minorities lived and worked in Bāb al-Sha'rīyah and al-Khalīfah—all parts of the medieval city. Metallurgists were concentrated in the districts of Būlāq, Bāb al-Sha'rīyah and al-Jamālīyah, while al-Darb al-Aḥmar (another medieval core quarter) housed a significant portion of all workers engaged in the important industries of "dress and toilet." Miṣr al-Qadīmah contained a disproportionate share of the labor force engaged in ceramics and leather goods while woodworkers were concentrated in Būlāq and Bāb al-Sha'rīyah.

By the 1920's, a small but growing modern sector of the Cairo economy had already been established and was in the process of being "indigenized," i.e., participated in by more than the foreign community. This trend continued even through the depression and, by 1937, it was evident that the structure of Egyptian industry was undergoing upheaval. Handicraft methods, though still persisting, were being supplemented more and more by mechanization, especially in the new industries being introduced. This economic transformation helped to seal Eastern Cairo's fate and to condemn her to decline by depriving many of her residents of their traditional livelihoods and by offering alternative opportunities elsewhere to those newcomers who otherwise might have been absorbed into the traditional urban economy.

[4] In each census year from 1917 onward, I have adjusted the figures of the Eastern City so that they include the entire eastern bank of *qism* Būlāq but *exclude* those portions located on the western bank (such as Imbābah and its hinterland). The latter's growth has been assigned to the Western City. This adjustment has been made by examining population figures for individual census tracts making up the various *aqsām* and recombining them in a more appropriate fashion.

In contrast to the Eastern City's stagnation, the Western City continued as before to enjoy healthy growth, while the expansion on the Northern City's fringe was spectacular. The population of the former grew to almost 350,000, while that of the latter approached 450,000, almost equaling the population of the Eastern City. Modest growth was recorded in the Southern City, but this was due not to indigenous factors but to the expansion of physically discrete suburbs whose development was tied to the new "commuter" train connections provided by the Cairo-to-Ḥalwān southern line. The year 1937 marks a watershed in the internal pattern of shifting dominance, as can be seen in Charts II and III.

The decade including World War II ushered in a city much altered in scale and quality. If the decade spanning the turn of the century marked one critical moment of discontinuity, certainly the decades at midcentury witnessed an even more profound alteration in the nature of the community. The change in scale is perhaps the most easily perceived transformation. By 1947 Cairo contained more than 2 million inhabitants, having added within the preceding decade of unprecedented expansion close to 800,000 more persons. This increment *alone* was roughly equivalent to the *combined* populations of Port Said, Ṭanṭa, Maḥallah al-Kubra, Suez, Manṣūrah, Asyūṭ, and Damanhūr, the third through ninth largest cities in the country in that year!

Where could this population go? Given the wartime restrictions on construction, it was perhaps inevitable that many of the newcomers should find their way into already densely settled areas where housing was, if not adequate, at least cheap. By the end of the decade, close to 670,000 persons were living in the old Eastern City where previously only 450,000 had lived, already tightly packed, at the beginning. Furthermore, this population had pushed or been expelled into the southern and eastern cemetery zones which, despite their lack of water and sewerage systems—not to mention such "luxurious" community facilities as schools and medical treatment centers—gave shelter to almost 50,000 "marginal" inhabitants.

In the Western City a similar intensification of land use and occupancy permitted 512,000 residents to live where only 350,000 had been ten years earlier. While some of this increase represented a "crossing" of the river into the overflow basin of the western bank, most was achieved either through the construction of taller apartment houses on the eastern shore and on the islands or through flat-overcrowding. The latter phenomenon resulted in rapid deterioration, especially in the zone just east of the Shāri' al-Qaṣr al-'Ayni, which increasingly began to mark a critical boundary between status zones.

Most of the new construction, however, was concentrated as before in the Northern City, which also began at

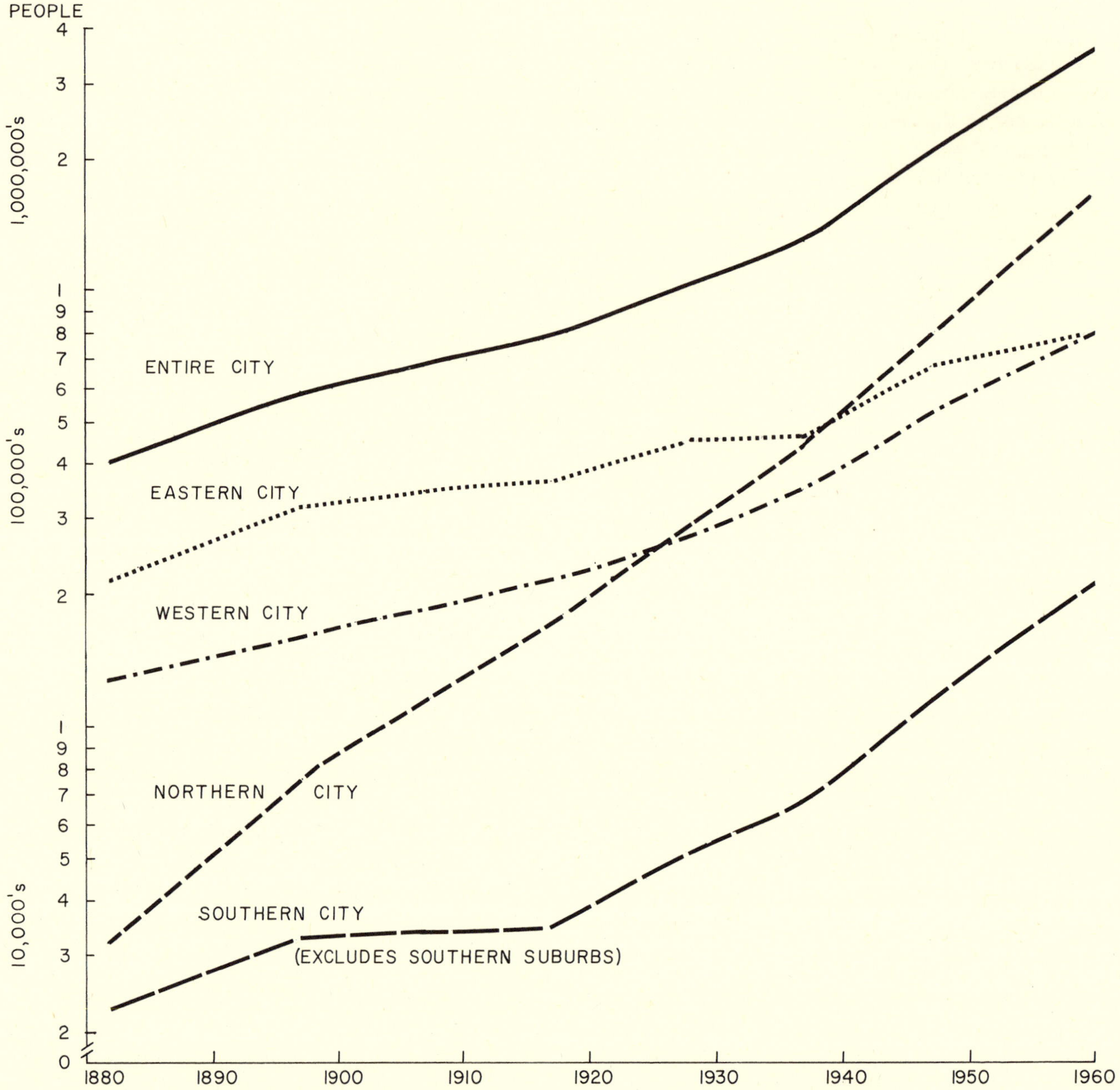

CHART II. Population Growth of Cairo and her Component "Cities," 1882-1960 (semilog projection)

this time to share some of the high density conditions that plagued the rest of the city. By 1947 this city contained close to 800,000 persons, an increment of almost 350,000 during the decade. Not only in density but in other characteristics as well the Northern City was beginning to lose some of its uniqueness. When the area had first been developed, it attracted a diverse but highly atypical population. For example, in 1917 only 70 percent of its residents were Egyptian Muslims, and many of these were agriculturalists; the *urban* population consisted disproportionately of native Christians (Copts) and of foreigners. By 1947, due to an influx of newcomers, many of them rural migrants who differed in income and ethnicity from the original settlers,[5] the zone, while remain-

[5] The outward movement of Copts from the center of the city coincides with the early expansion of the Northern tier, particularly within the district of Shubra. For example, in 1907, Copts were still largely concentrated in the region just north and west of the Azbakiyah Gardens which had been identified in the Napoleonic Expedition map as the Christian quarter. Over 20,000 Egyptian Copts lived there, as contrasted with only 7,000 in all of the yet-undeveloped Northern City. By 1927, however, the Northern City had become the clearly preferred residential zone for Copts. While their numbers had increased somewhat in the center of the city as well (up to 32,000 by 1927), this older colony was already dwarfed by the close to 40,000 Copts residing in the Northern City. My estimates are based upon manipulation of data contained in Clerget, *Le Caire*, II, Appendix B, Table IV,

ing the major area of Coptic residence, contained over 76 percent native Muslims and was no longer the exclusive if uneasily shared domain of middle-class urbanites (largely Christian) and poor farmers (almost totally Muslim); a substantial urban proletariat had been added.

Increasingly, also, ecological subdivisions within the vast region were becoming more pronounced. Differentiated were the low-income proletariat quarters concentrated along the Sāḥil (shore of the Nile) and in the area adjacent to the industrial-rail district of al-Sabtīyah. These zones took on more of the character of Būlāq, their slum neighbor to the south, from whose overcrowded buildings some of the newer residents were drawn. Rural migrants from Delta villages settled in the side streets of Shubra, interspersed with or displacing the Copts who had formerly preempted much of that district. Families drawn from middle- and low-income levels divided the *qism* of al-Wāyli into a checkerboard of small neighborhoods whose quality might vary with every block. An incipient upper-middle and *native* elite was clearly segregating itself in Heliopolis while, across the great divide of the major transportation axis that linked Heliopolis to the city, the area of Zaytūn contained a less exclusive and pretentious indigenous population. Despite the inroads into the countryside that had been made by the proliferation of urban structures, all along the periphery of the built-up edge of the city there still remained rural residuals. Villagers retained their claims in fringe areas that dipped, in some cases surprisingly deeply, into the very heart of the expanding city. The amorphous northern zone, which had previously spread like a protozoan across the width of the region, was coming into more concrete focus, revealing features and forms representing a wide variety of urban types.

Such phenomenal growth could not help but transform the physiognomy of the city. By 1947 the relative positions of the three component cities had clearly been reversed. The Eastern City, despite its heroic efforts and its bulging seams, was able to accommodate no more than 32 percent of the total population. The Western City, despite vigorous development along both shores of the Nile and on the islands, accounted for less than a quarter of the city's inhabitants. The aborted Southern City still contained the same minor 6 percent of the total she had housed in earlier decades. But the Northern City showed continued and growing strength. By then, some 38 percent of all Cairenes were living in these new quarters. Thus, the downstream movement of Cairo—which first began when Babylon-Fusṭāṭ supplanted Memphis and which continued throughout the centuries during which al-'Askar, al-Qaṭā'i', and finally al-Qāhirah were added on the north—found its ultimate expression in this final thrust into the fertile Delta—the Northern City.

The same trends continued unabated during the thirteen years between the censuses of 1947 and 1960. Although population expanded at a somewhat slower rate than it had during the war-boom years, in terms of absolute numbers the growth of the city was even more impressive. Almost 1,500,000 new urbanites were added to Cairo's population in the interim. By 1960, if we adjust the city's boundaries to be comparable to those that obtained in 1947,[6] Cairo contained almost 3.5 million persons living in the same area where 2 million had lived in 1947.

Scarcely any of that growth could be absorbed into the Eastern City which was already perilously overcrowded. It is perhaps a tragic tribute to her elasticity that she was able to give refuge to over 100,000 additional residents, but by then this included almost 80,000 who were living, legally or by subterfuge, in the cemetery zones which, in a surrealistic response to population pressure, had even begun to develop small commercial nodes near the points of "highest pedestrian count," the few communal water taps upon which all were dependent in this desert-dry city. But even that growth, which would have been significant during earlier periods of the city's history, could not assure the Eastern City of its continued importance

no pagination. In the absence of published information by census tracts in Cairo in 1927, I am dependent upon his figures, even though they lack sufficient explanatory notes. A similar movement of foreign nationals could also be observed during this period. Although the principal quarters favored by foreign nationals remained in the center of the Western City (in 1927, some 40,000 foreigners resided in al-Mūski, al-Azbakīyah, and 'Abdīn), many were also moving to the Northern zone where by 1927 they numbered close to 24,000. Estimated from figures given in Clerget, *op.cit.*, Appendix B, Table 11. The year 1927 seems to mark the apogee of this ethnic selection. In the decades that followed, the concentration of Copts and foreigners was greatly diluted by a comparable decentralization of the Muslim middle class and by an influx of village migrants, chiefly Muslim. More details can be found in J. Abu-Lughod, "Migrant Adjustment to City Life: The Egyptian Case," *American Journal of Sociology*, Volume 67 (July 1961), pp. 22-32.

[6] Between 1947 and 1960 the House Tax Boundary of Cairo was drastically altered. Ḥalwān, the industrial suburb to the south, which in the 1947 Census had been a separate enumeration district, was added to the Cairo Governorate, together with the agricultural zone which separated it from the main conurbation. On the other hand, the entire western bank, opposite and functionally integrated with the main Cairo complex, was ceded to the Upper Egyptian province of Jīzah. In order to retain comparable boundaries for analysis and because of my firm conviction that the metropolitan area of Cairo cannot logically be bifurcated in this manner, I have adjusted the 1960 boundaries to conform to those obtaining in 1947. Thus, population estimates presented here exclude Ḥalwān but include developments on the western bank of the Nile. This position appears to be receiving sympathetic attention in Cairo's Municipal Council, for it has been proposed that the older boundaries be readopted.

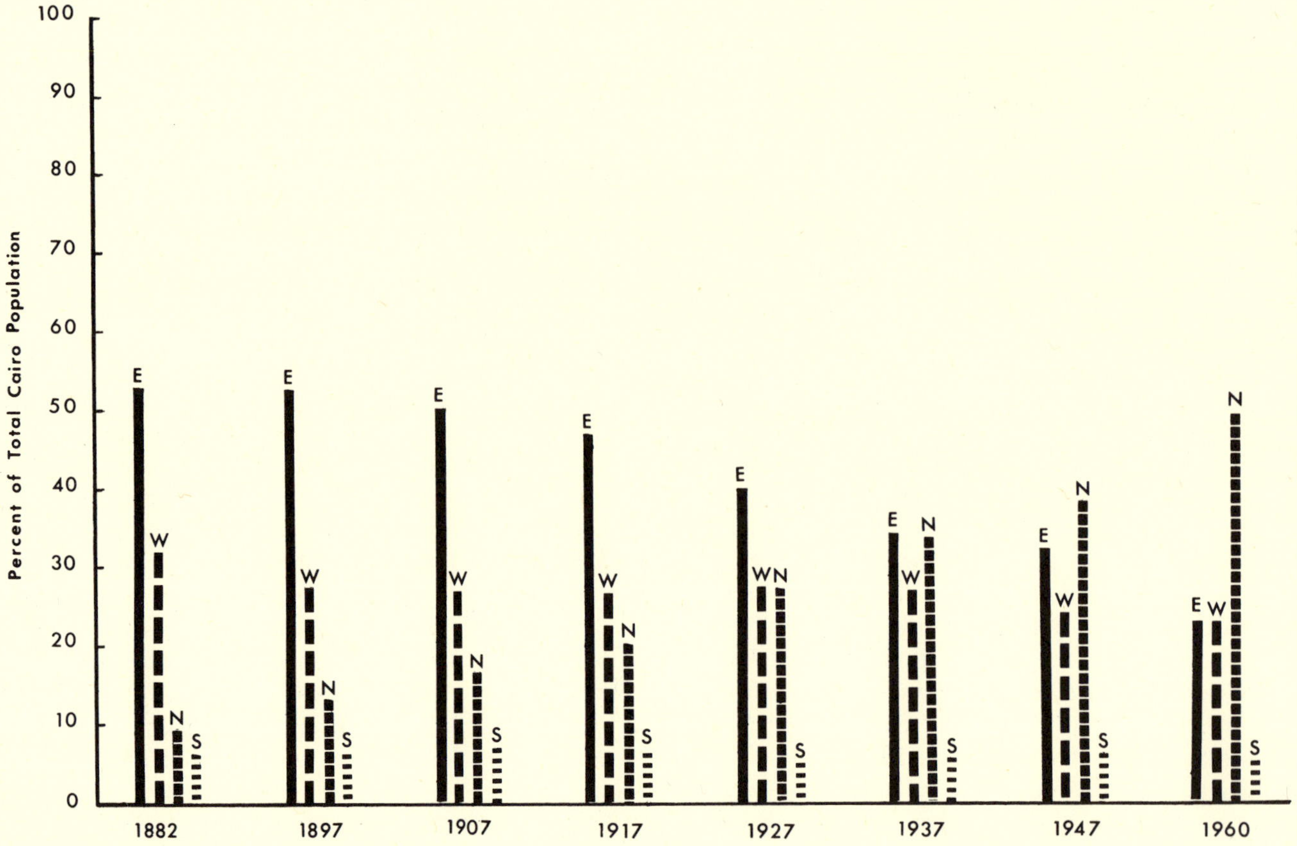

CHART III. Shares of Total Population Living in the Eastern, Western, Northern, and Southern "Cities" of Cairo, 1882-1960

in the expanding metropolis. By 1960, the proportion of Cairo's residents living in the medieval stratum and its funereal shadow city had dropped to less than one-fourth. And it had become clear that this would decline inevitably and even more precipitously in the years to come, unless the cemetery zones that continued to block physical expansion into the desert could be removed.

By this time the Western City also appeared to be approaching saturation point. No longer were there large undeveloped parcels that could easily be crowned with bristling apartment towers. Even the lushly gardened villas, which hitherto had been methodically replaced by skyscrapers, especially in the region fronting the Nile, were virtually gone. And as the central business districts of al-Azbakīyah (for those with Western tastes) and al-Mūski (for those with *baladi*, traditional, purses) became more exclusively commercial—business firms preempting not only the street floors that had always been devoted to shops but the upper stories which had once been residential—they too were less able to absorb additional residents.

What growth there was in the Western City came from only two sources: the piling up of densities (causing subsequent deterioration) in the southernmost and lower status areas of Sayīdah Zaynab and even eastern 'Abdīn; and second, the conversion to urban uses of the agricultural lands on the island of Rawḍah and those across the Nile on the western bank. The population residing on the western bank across from the city increased almost sixfold in the thirteen years between censuses, while the island of Rawḍah (illogically still linked administratively, although no longer functionally, with Miṣr al-Qadīmah) was virtually transformed from a rather bucolic refuge for some 22,000 residents into an urbane forest of tall apartment houses that contained over 56,000 inhabitants in 1960. The air on the island still reverberates from the ubiquitous pile drivers that will give homes for at least twice that many by 1970.

Nevertheless, despite this healthy expansion on the offshore islands and on the west bank, the Western City experienced a loss in relative importance almost as great as that suffered by the Eastern City. By 1960 no more than 23 percent of Cairo's population resided in the Western City, including the west bank, and the number of inhabitants scarcely exceeded those in the medieval core. Even with the new and projected housing projects that daily take on more concrete form in the residual rurban fringe to the west, this city has a limited future role in the ecology of Cairo.

In marked contrast to the relative decline of the two older cities was the continued growth of the Northern City which, by 1960, could claim with a fair degree of accuracy to have become the real Cairo, even though her undistinguished architecture and nondescript streets kept her still virtually invisible and off the beaten track for most outsiders. Ask any visitor to Cairo today to describe the city and he will tell you in great detail of the Western City that fulfills most of his commercial and residential needs, and of the Eastern City that fulfills his equally compelling cravings for the exotic Orient; he will probably forget even to mention the Northern City, despite the fact that by 1960 it already contained close to half of the total population of the city, a lead which continues to increase!

The expansion of this zone in only the past few decades represents a truly remarkable transformation in the ecology of the city for which none of our earlier incursions into history has prepared us. The region doubled in population in only thirteen years, increasing from a little under 800,000 in 1947 to in excess of 1,600,000 in 1960, and its growth seems only to have begun. To the north of the settled sections are located some of Egypt's most advanced and largest industrial establishments, many of them clamoring for additional subsidized low-income housing for their growing labor forces. At the edge of the eastern desert, in the vacuum between 'Abbāsīyah and Heliopolis, the new town of Naṣr City is being constructed which, when completed, will contain dwellings for half a million inhabitants as well as most of the government ministries, a vast commercial and recreational core, a new campus for al-Azhar University, and a zone for industrial development.

Recent building permits can be used to estimate relative growth rates since the Census of 1960 (see Table 6). Of the nearly 7,000 structures authorized by the Governorate of Cairo between July 1961 and April 1965, only about 450 were slated for the central zone of the city, both east and west, while another 585 were for structures in the newly revived Southern City at Miṣr al-Qadīmah. The fast-growing southern satellites of Ma'ādi and Ḥalwān were the location of another 1,245 of the building permit applications. The remaining 4,575, or fully two-thirds of all permits issued, were for apartment houses, villas, shops, and factories to be located in the Northern City—persuasive proof that the trend of northern expansion remains strong.

TABLE 6. BUILDING PERMITS ISSUED BY THE MUḤĀFAẒAH OF CAIRO BETWEEN JULY 1961 AND APRIL 1965, BY TYPE OF USE AND LOCATION

Location in the City	*Residential Uses*		*Trade and*	*Total*
	Villas	*Apartments*	*Industry*	*Structures*
Southern City	14	569	2	585
Southern suburbs of Ma'ādi and Ḥalwān	212	1,007	26	1,245
Western City (central)[a]	0	27	20	47
Eastern City	0	393	2	395
Northern City	332	4,217	26	4,575
TOTAL	558	6,213	76	6,847[b]

SOURCE: Table 6 has been compiled from the records of the Planning Division of the Section on Housing and Public Utilities, Cairo Governorate, and made available to the author through the cooperation of its director, Mr. Muḥammad Ḥāfiẓ 'Ali.

[a] Because the data were originally grouped somewhat differently from my classification, this section also includes Būlāq.

[b] There is a discrepancy between this figure and the total number of building permits issued, as obtained from another source, to which reference has already been made in the preceding chapter. I cannot account for this difference except to suggest that either the areas or the definitions of permits have been changed.

Nor is the available land in the north anywhere near exhausted, for there still remain substantial pockets of fertile farmland whose future disposition is not difficult to forecast. Despite the remarkably farsighted concern of Cairo's planners in trying to preserve this valuable greenbelt, which supplies much of the truck-gardening requirements of the city, it appears inevitable that the pressure of urban growth will continue to push the frontier deeper and deeper into the soft, yielding Delta, possibly even as far north as Qalyūb. The peculiar physiognomy of the land continues, like a vise or an iron mold, to force growth northward. Cairo had once been compared, in a flight of poetic fancy, to a diamond glistening in the handle of the Delta's wide green fan. To many an alarmed contemporary observer, she now seems more like an insatiable cancer threatening to devour the hinterland that feeds her.

If the nineteenth century unfolded the story of the Western City, the present century's story belongs properly to the Northern City. In the span of less than half a century a new city came into existence that contains, at the time of this writing, more than 2 million persons living on land that was, prior to World War I, almost entirely innocent of urban forms. Neither historical encrustations nor conscious planning served to mold or guide its development pattern. Growing in response to the manifold impulses generated by modernism—the muscular power flexed by industrialization and the gnawing hunger prodded by demographic derangement —it channeled itself unwittingly and perhaps even capriciously in dim response to the speculator's gamble and the transport engineer's ruled lines.

This process resulted, with rare exceptions (notably at Heliopolis), in spawning dismal stretch after stretch of yellow-grey tenements towering above shoddy yet gaudy commercial streets in endless procession—all of it neither quite Western nor really Oriental, neither wholeheartedly urban nor distinctively rural, neither particularly unsightly nor, again with few exceptions, especially elegant. Its pervasive dullness is enlivened only by the irrepressible vitality of the throngs of Cairenes who call this zone "home" and who have proved themselves equal to the task of infusing life even into these places chillingly described by today's planners as "the grey areas."

Despite a certain superficial sameness, however, the Northern City contains a population that spans almost the entire spectrum of Egyptian urban types and shelters within it a vast variety of neighborhoods characterized by distinctive life styles. Stretching northward from the center of the city are at least five sectors, each completely different from the other, reflecting the contrasting worlds of contemporary Cairo. Furthermore, despite the surface architectural resemblance of this new city to metropolitan communities elsewhere, the impress of culture has been deep. The Northern City, while perhaps lacking the exoticism of the medieval core and the *déclassé* elegance of the Westernized central business district, remains nevertheless distinctively Egyptian. It represents, however, as we shall see in the next chapter, an Egypt newly emergent rather than the Egypt of the past which has been the object of our study thus far.

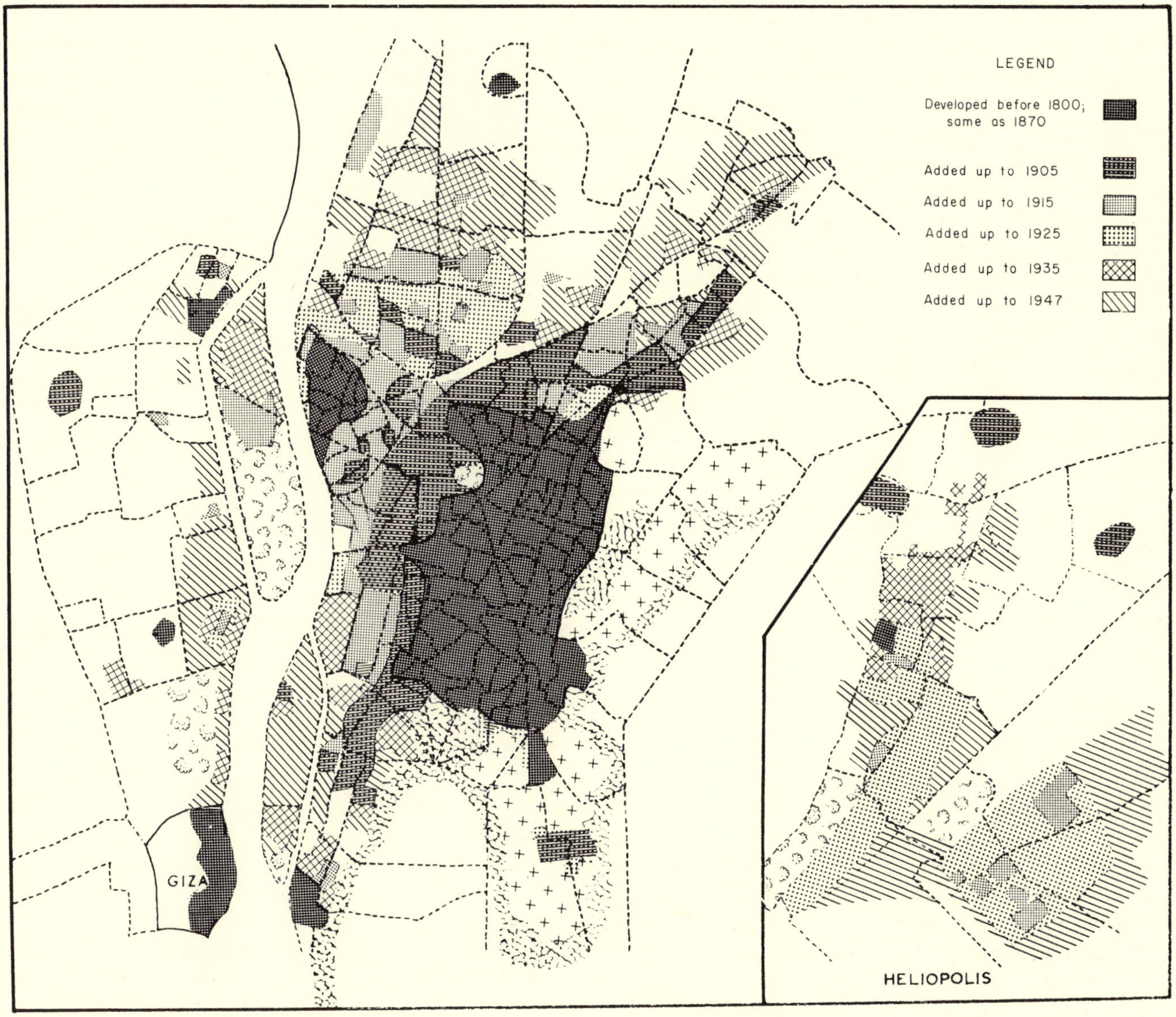

XVI. Segments of the city developed at stages of growth

12 The Anatomy of Metropolitan Cairo

CAIRO, like any other major metropolis, is much more than a congeries of physical subdivisions, salient landmarks and streets, and distributed land uses. It is, in the final analysis, more aptly described, in Louis Wirth's felicitous phrase, as a true "mosaic of social worlds." A generation ago he summarized the fundamental assumption of ecological studies by noting that:

> diverse population elements [within the city] . . . tend to become segregated from one another in the degree to which their requirements and *modes of life* are incompatible with one another . . . [while] persons of homogeneous status and needs unwittingly drift into, consciously select, or are forced by circumstances into, the same area. *The different parts of the city thus acquire specialized functions.*[1]

Now, while the history of Cairo's growth can help to explain why certain "social worlds" should be located where they are within the larger complex, only a more detailed examination of the people who actually live in the city—their characteristics and their ways of life—can help illuminate the nature of the diverse social worlds that coexist within the same city and that create, by their abrupt juxtaposition, the varied mélange that is contemporary Cairo.

Cairo, far more than any Western city of comparable size, is a city of contrasts and contradictions, of extremes and anachronisms. Egypt is a society deeply committed to a basic reorganization of its economy, its social structure, and its political community. Is it any wonder, then, that both the old and new orders (and their intermediaries) should exist side by side in its capital city? Cairo combines the passing traditionalism and agrarianism of an Egypt that has existed for centuries with the industrial modernism of an Egypt yet-to-be. Reflecting this, her population consists of diverse groups, some barely emerged from village life, some still immersed in the small worlds of traditional neighborhoods, some cut off from both village and neighborhood and adrift in the demimonde, some striving for mastery over the mechanical paraphernalia of the modern world, others seeking the harder mastery over its ideas and ideals, and a few, the most sophisticated, engaged in the challenging task of synthesizing the old and the new, the indigenous and the "imported."

[1] Louis Wirth, "Urbanism as a Way of Life," *American Journal of Sociology*, Volume 44 (July 1938), pp. 1-24, as reprinted in Hatt and Reiss, eds., *Cities and Society* (The Free Press of Glencoe, New York: 1961), quoted from p. 56 with italics added.

96. Village houses abut modern apartment building in 'Ajūzah i

97. *Mashrabīyah* and modern concrete juxtaposed in the 'Abdīn quarter

98. New National Library rises near semi-rural dwellings along Shāri' Abū al-Faraj in 1969

Given what we know concerning the ways people "divide up" cities, our knowledge of Egypt's present diversity should prepare us to expect the coexistence of many very different "cities within the city." This theoretical expectation is easily confirmed visually, for even the most uninitiated and casual visitor to the city cannot help but be struck by the rapid succession of urban neighborhoods that meet his eye as he traverses the city. It is a simple matter to acknowledge the existence of a Cairo mosaic; it is, however, a far more complex operation to summarize it by objective methods and to set forth the essential characteristics that distinguish the parts from one another. This, however, must be done if the city is to be understood.

A DIGRESSION ON METHOD AND MEANING

There are a number of equally valid ways to dissect a city and to subdivide it according to varying sets of criteria. The method ultimately selected depends essentially on the goal or goals of the investigator. For example, geographers conventionally classify subareas within the city according to the dominant uses of land; sociologists, on the other hand, are concerned with the social organization of the city rather than its physical plan and prefer to classify areas according to the dominant or "typical" characteristics of their residents. I have adopted the latter approach since my ultimate goal has been to identify those large segments of Cairo where residents share common social characteristics and follow particular life styles that mark them off from residents of neighboring communities, with whom they seldom interact. Within these "social worlds" there may be a wide variety of land uses which further subdivide the communities into smaller, more specialized quarters.

Just as there is nothing especially sacrosanct about the method and approach selected, there is nothing mystical or invariant about the final divisions. An investigator whose goal is to subdivide the metropolis into as many small, homogeneous and cohesive neighborhoods as are subjectively perceived by their residents might need to distinguish literally hundreds of subareas in order to describe adequately the social worlds of Cairo. My goal has been a different one. It has been to synthesize out of the multitude of the city's tiny cells and quarters the minimum number of major components necessary to account for basic social divisions within the city. The purpose in so doing is to relate these divisions to past patterns of growth and to suggest the direction of future changes in the metropolis. For this goal, the thirteen "cities within the city" which I have differentiated statistically represent a compromise between the infinite fragmentation that would have resulted, had every minor variation within the city been retained, and the too-gross generalization that would have resulted from treating Cairo as if the city were a unified or undifferentiated whole.

Because I believe so strongly that the product of an ecological "dissection" cannot be understood, much less evaluated and used, without reference to the methods that have been employed to arrive at it, I must, before presenting the results and their interpretation, digress a bit to describe briefly the techniques used to identify and locate the thirteen subcities of contemporary Cairo. Technical comments, however, have no place here. The reader interested in the details of the statistical procedures or in the raw and processed data themselves is referred to the Methodological Appendix to this volume and to the fuller explication available in another work.[2]

My first attempt to investigate the ecological organization of Cairo began in 1958 and was based upon the returns from the then-current *Census of Egypt, 1947*. Volume Fifteen of the series contained data for the Governorate of Cairo, including, in addition to the summary tables, four highly complex sets cross-tabulating a limited number of variables (such as age and sex, marital status, education, employment, family size, etc.) by the 216 census tracts into which the city was administratively divided.[3] A set of summary statistical measures (or indices) was devised, utilizing data contained in these tables, to capture significant dimensions of social differentiation within various quarters of the city. The results of this early study, including the statistical data processed for each census tract, maps showing the distribution of each variable in terms of the urban pattern, and computational formulas and explanatory notes for each of the

[2] A complete presentation of my method—its relationship to earlier techniques of ecological analysis and its rationale—and of the data upon which the conclusions are based, can be found in J. Abu-Lughod, "The Ecology of Cairo, Egypt: A Comparative Study Using Factor Analysis" (Unpublished Ph.D. Dissertation, University of Massachusetts: 1966). Some of these findings and their implications have been published in J. Abu-Lughod, "Testing the Theory of Social Area Analysis: The Ecology of Cairo, Egypt," *American Sociological Review*, Volume 34 (April 1969), pp. 198-212.

[3] The source volume for all 1947 data is the Arabic edition of Kingdom of Egypt, Ministry of Finance and Economy, *Census of Egypt, 1947*, Volume 15, *Governorate of Cairo* (Government Printing Office, Cairo: 1952). The four relevant tables cross-tabulating census information by census tracts are to be found on pp. 5-68. Administratively, the city of Cairo is divided into districts (*qism*, pl. *aqsām*) which are further subdivided into tracts (*shiyākhah*, pl. *shiyākhāt*). These roughly correspond in administrative function to the wards and precincts of an American city and are the units of political representation and police protection. They differ from American census tracts in that they are usually more than statistical units. Some, especially in the oldest quarters of the city, are physically and functionally derivative from the ancient *ḥārāt* and *durūb* which have had a long tradition of social cohesion.

indices employed, were published in the *Cairo Fact Book*[4] to which the reader may refer for additional details.

In 1957 the Egyptian government conducted its regular decennial census, and it was my intention to replicate the analysis that had been made of the 1947 data and to compare findings from the two years. Unfortunately, however, the quality of the returns left much to be desired and, after the first flurry of releases, no subsequent data were forthcoming. Instead, the census year was postponed until 1960. In that year a new census was conducted, and when the published returns became available in 1962, including a separate volume presenting data for the Governorate of Cairo,[5] it became possible to resume the study. Certain fundamental revisions, however, were required to maximize comparability between data from the two census years.

For one thing, between the two census dates the boundaries of the city as a whole and of some of its constituent census tracts had been altered. Thus, it became necessary to make adjustments. Some adjacent tracts had to be combined in one year or the other; certain peripheral tracts added to Cairo's jurisdiction after 1947 were eliminated while others, originally included with Cairo but later ceded to the province of Jīzah, had to be recovered and included. These adjustments made it possible to retain for final and comparative analysis 206 census tracts whose individual boundaries were comparable in the two separate data years and which, combined, accounted for virtually the entire official area of Cairo as it had been defined in 1947. Only a handful of peripheral tracts, whose boundaries either could not be determined or could not be made comparable, were actually eliminated from the study.

Not only the boundary and data units but the statistical indicators themselves had to be modified somewhat to make them comparable, since the forms in which data were reported, the categories retained for their presentation, and even specific items of information were not uniform in the two census reports. Indices which the 1947 analysis had suggested were relatively meaningless or those for which information was not available in 1960 were dropped or equivalent measures, after testing, substituted. For the final analysis some thirteen replicated variables were retained, most of which proved to be measuring the "same reality" in the two data years.[6]

The major difference between the present study and the earlier one, however, was a radical improvement in the technique of analysis itself. In the preliminary study I had followed conventional procedures by preparing separate maps showing the geographic distribution of each of the variables, as if they were independent of one another. These were to be visually superimposed in order to abstract from the congruencies those sections of the city (usually misnamed "natural areas") which appeared to contain populations with similar characteristics. Contiguous census tracts of roughly comparable "quality" were to be grouped together and distinguished from adjacent zones where populations with different characteristics appeared to be living. This was a time-honored method that had been used in virtually all prior ecological analyses employing census data.

For many years urban sociologists had been aware of certain defects inherent in this method but had been unable to devise a satisfactory alternative. It was recognized, for example, that subjective judgment was called upon to play too large a role in the determination of the number of districts and their boundaries, and that two investigators inspecting the same set of maps might reach quite different conclusions concerning the number and location of the subareas. Furthermore, stimulated by the formulations of the social area analysts after 1955, several empirical studies had been made in American cities which indicated that very different ecological patterns for the same city might be devised, depending upon which *clusters* of variables were selected for mapping. At least three separate clusters or dimensions had been identified—social class, type of family, and ethnic composition—each of which appeared in American cities to yield its own typical pattern of geographic distribution.[7] Earlier methods had assumed unidimensionality.

Parallel to this growing disillusionment with conventional ecological techniques was the development of an alternative approach which appeared to meet some of the objections concerning subjectivity and multidimensionality. This was factor analysis, which received its first successful application in the social sciences in the 1930's with L. L. Thurstone's investigation of mental capacities. Although as early as 1941 this technique had been adapted to the ecological problem of delimiting homogeneous economic regions in a state, the suggestion that it might prove equally valuable in analyzing the ecology of urban areas was not followed until almost twenty years

[4] See J. Abu-Lughod and Ezz el-Din Attiya, *Cairo Fact Book* (Social Research Center, American University at Cairo, Cairo: 1963), in Arabic and English.

[5] The source volume for all 1960 data is the Arabic edition of the United Arab Republic, Department of Census and Statistics, *The Population Census of 1960*, unnumbered volume on the Governorate of Cairo (Government Printing Office, Cairo: 1962).

[6] In one unavoidable case, namely, the rate of infirmity, the same apparent measure proved to be indicative of different realities, due to a change in census reporting of institutional populations. This difference, however, was not crucial in the results.

[7] An evaluation of the work of the social area analysts and a complete bibliography is included in J. Abu-Lughod, "The Ecology of Cairo, Egypt."

later, after the social area analysts had thrown into serious question the assumptions underlying more conventional methods of urban ecology. Only within the past few years has the method of factor analysis been used to analyze the ecological structure of cities outside the United States, of which Frank Sweetser's study of Helsinki[8] and mine of Cairo are among the first. Quite comparable methods were independently developed by the several investigators.

In brief, factor analysis identifies mathematical vectors capable of accounting parsimoniously for the relationships and independencies observed among many simpler variables. A factor is, therefore, a hypothetical "force" underlying and presumably accounting for the variance *common* to several variables which are highly intercorrelated. A separate general or group factor is hypothesized to account for each relatively independent cluster of intercorrelated variables.

When this technique is adapted to ecological research, each census tract is treated as an individual having certain characteristics measured by the indices. Correlation coefficients are computed between each and every index, yielding a matrix from which factors are extracted serially, each factor "removing" a measurable amount of the matrix's variance. The factors so extracted represent independent (orthogonal) forces but the analyst may choose to manipulate (rotate) their location in conceptual space in order to improve the usefulness of his factor solution. In my study I extracted seven factors, of which the first and most important accounted for about half of the total variance. This was the factor used to divide the city of Cairo into thirteen subcities.

The results of factor analysis are presented in the form of a table giving the "factor weights" (which may be thought of as the degree to which the separate variables correlate with the posited factor) of each separate empirical variable upon each hypothecated factor. Statistical manipulation of these entries and those contained in the original correlation matrix yields a method for weighting the value of variables in the individual census tracts in order to score each tract on each factor. These scores are standardized, i.e., expressed as ratios to the standard deviation of the distribution around the mean for all census tracts in a city, a technique which permits rather precise comparisons between census tracts in a city *within* the framework of the total city. The scores can also be transcribed onto maps which can then be used to subdivide the city into component subareas that are relatively homogeneous according to the dimension of differentiation identified by the factor.

While the above discussion may appear formidably technical to the lay reader (and insufficiently detailed to the statistician who should refer to the Methodological Appendix), it is important that the basic logic of the system be understood. The innovation lies in reversing the order of analysis. In conventional studies the distributions of the separate variables are mapped and then synthesized visually and subjectively. In the method followed here, synthesis of the separate variables occurs prior to mapping and is based upon fairly determinate mathematical relationships abstracted from the empirical data themselves. While the method is not totally free of subjective judgment—and, in fact, the naming and interpretation of the mathematical vectors remain solely the responsibility of the investigator—it does yield somewhat more trustworthy and objective results than can be obtained using more conventional techniques. Another investigator of Cairo's ecology, using the same data and the same technique, would reach very similar if not identical conclusions.

One final set of remarks concerns the "meaning" of the factors and their scores. In the discussion that follows, frequent references are made to the relative "position" or scores of different parts of the city, particularly on Factor I which has been identified as denoting variations in style of life. What is meant by this critical but composite variable? Strictly speaking, it is defined simply by its operational derivation, namely by the factor loadings of the various indices upon the first and most important factor. These are given in Table 7 for each of the data years. As can be seen, the operational definition has remained remarkably constant for 1947 and 1960, indicating that it is legitimate to make comparisons and analyze changes between the two time periods.

One may move from the operational definition to a more descriptive one by examining these factor loadings and putting them together into a coherent picture, fleshed out by a knowledge of the city and its social ways. Census tracts, and the composite subcities derived from their combination, that have high scores on Factor I measuring style of life are those portions of the city most easily identified as "modern urban." In these areas the residential structures are almost without exception "international urban" in design and use; the shops have glass-fronted display windows, stock a wide variety of merchandise, and adhere to a system of fixed prices. The inhabitants, except for domestic servants and the providers of local convenience services, are attired in Western clothes. Furthermore, a large majority of the men and a significant

[8] See the following articles by Frank Sweetser: "Factor Structure as Ecological Structure in Helsinki and Boston," *Acta Sociologica*, Volume VIII, Fasc. 3 (1965), pp. 205-225; "Factorial Ecology: Helsinki, 1960," *Demography*, II (1965), 372-386; "Ecological Differentiation in Helsinki, 1960" (in Finnish with English summary), Publication No. 42 of the Institute of Sociology, University of Helsinki, 1966. My data processing was completed during 1964-1965, so that Sweetser's work came too late to offer material assistance.

TABLE 7. FACTOR LOADINGS (AFTER VARIMAX ORTHOGONAL ROTATION) OF THIRTEEN REPLICATED VARIABLES ON FACTOR I STYLE OF LIFE, 1947 AND 1960

Variables or Indices	*Factor Loadings* *1947*	*1960*
Percentage of females in a census tract who are able to read (% literate females)	+.95	+.92
Percentage of females 16 years of age or older never married (typically late age for marriage)	+.91	+.95
Percentage of females enrolled in school/employed (equivalent, not identical measures)	+.72	+.85
Percentage of males in a census tract who are able to read (% literate males)	+.90	+.81
Fertility ratio (number of children under five per 1,000 women in childbearing ages)	−.81	−.89
Average number of persons per room in census tract (PPR)	−.80	−.81
Percentage of males 16 years of age or older never married (late marriage/migration)	+.67	+.76
Percentage of census tract population who are Muslims	−.65	−.56
Percentage of males who are unemployed in tract	−.68	−.31
Percentage of ever-married women who are currently divorced	+.42	+.52
Number of handicapped or infirm per 1,000 tract residents (changed reporting)	−.08	−.40
Number of inhabitants per square kilometer of census tract area (density)	−.18	−.02
Number of males per 100 females between ages of 15 and 50 in census tract	−.00	−.01

NOTE: The most significant factor weights have been underlined.

proportion of the women are not only literate but educated, work at occupations within the modern sector of the urban economy, and possess skills and/or property assuring them of a fairly adequate income. On the whole, their dwelling units are furnished in the European style and are large enough to be occupied at densities seldom exceeding one person per room. The nature of family life reflects some of these elements. Men and women tend to marry somewhat later than is typical in Egypt, frequently delaying marriage until the man is in his late twenties or early thirties and the woman is in the early or middle twenties. On the average, these couples tend to bear fewer children than is typical in Egypt, perhaps exercising control over the size of their families through birth control methods.[9] The children they do have, however, are enrolled in school without question and are often kept in school to a level of education that equals if not exceeds that of the parental generation. In 1947, reflecting socio-economic and life-style differences that had their roots in the nineteenth-century cultural bifurcation and even more in the insulation of the colonial period, a larger percentage of these residents than would be expected by chance alone carried foreign passports or professed a religion other than Islam. However, since the Revolution of 1952 and the sizeable exodus of foreigners in 1956 as an aftermath of the Suez War, these zones have become more properly the domain of the indigenous upper and middle classes of the city.

At the opposite end of the scale are those census tracts, and the composite subcities to which they belong, with extremely low Factor I scores. By maps one can determine that these are located almost exclusively at the rurban periphery of the metropolis; by reconnaissance one notes that they are more rural than urban in their appearance. Instead of the steel-girdered cement apartment buildings characteristic of the modern quarters, one finds lower, mudbrick or crudely fired brick dwellings, occasionally plastered over, gathered into small village-like clusters whose appearance is more reminiscent of rural settlements in the hinterlands than of any city, whether medieval or modern. Within the dwellings, furnishings are minimal—a few mattresses and quilts, some cooking pots, several glasses for tea, perhaps a trunk or two. Space is too valuable to be wasted in storage, for often one or two rooms must accommodate a family of ten or more. Commercial premises are infrequent and minimal, confined to providing the narrow range of necessities that corresponds to the limited buying power of the local residents who exist near marginal subsistence levels. The women in these zones, almost without exception, are attired in the same long black gowns, bright head kerchiefs and supplemental inky shawls that adorn their country cousins. The men still wear the flowing *jallābīyah* during leisure, even those who strip to undergarments to work in the fields or who may be required to wear uniforms or wrinkled trousers for more urban work. Only a minor percentage of these men can read and write, and it is a rarer handful per hundred among the women who can do even this much. With little or no formal schooling to interfere with other life plans, men and women marry young, most of the men by the time they are twenty, virtually all of the girls by the age of sixteen. Early and sustained child-bearing preoccupies the women, as attested by the extremely high fertility ratios in these zones—even higher than in the villages of the hinterlands, thanks to the greater availability of medical facilities in the metropolis. The men work at low-paid diverse jobs requiring little skill; only a few still farm full time, though some may supplement insecure employment by part-time farming. Until recently it was a rare child who attended school, and even now with the new compulsory education

[9] The single variable related most intimately to fertility differentials in Cairo is the educational achievement of the mother, as demonstrated in J. Abu-Lughod, "The Emergence of Differential Fertility in Urban Egypt," *Milbank Memorial Fund Quarterly*, Volume 43 (April 1965), pp. 235-253.

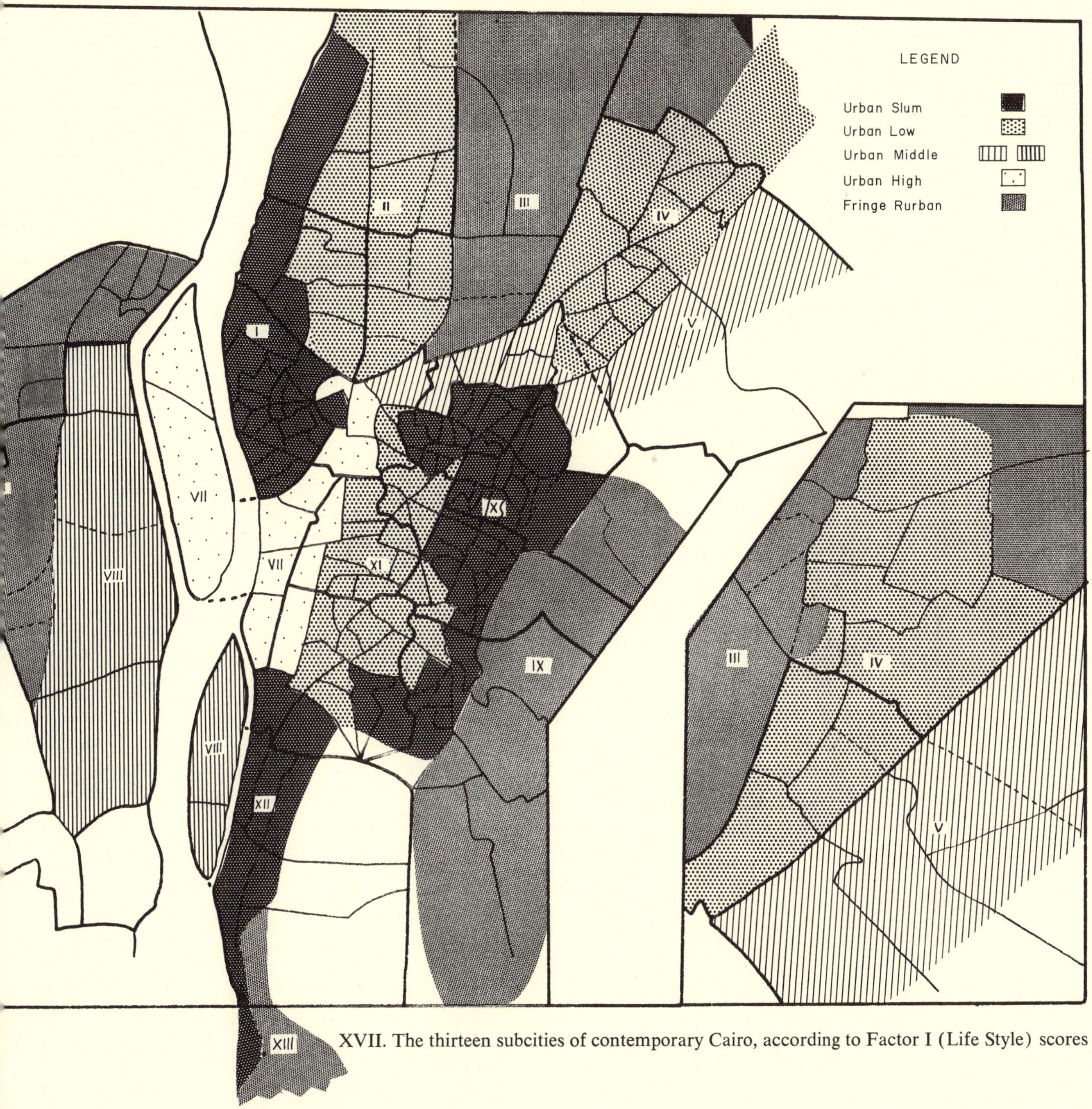

XVII. The thirteen subcities of contemporary Cairo, according to Factor I (Life Style) scores

laws the frequency with which girls are "overlooked" and the early ages at which most children disappear from the school system means a very low rate of school enrollment. The style of life in these quarters, then, despite their location within the urban boundaries of Cairo and despite the fact that farming no longer offers a livelihood to many residents, remains close to the rural model.

Between these two extremes are ranged most of the other variations within the city. Toward the bottom of the scale, although considerably above the rural fringe, are those areas nearer to the center of the city in which one still catches glimpses of a traditional style of urban living lineally descended from medieval Cairo, sustained by a dying economy based upon hand production, tiny scale of enterprise and inventory, and highly personalized relationships between proprietor and client. Toward the midpoint of the scale are areas of more modernized proletarian character, whose residents are moving into the wider realms of complex technology and industrial organization while still clinging to more traditional patterns in their homes and families. Somewhat above them socially are areas that help further to bridge the cultural gaps between old and new, dying and emergent, poor and rich. These are the variations to be explored in the section that follows. Throughout, however, it must be borne in mind that the statistics represent *real* people and are only significant in the context of their actual behavior and beliefs. Therefore, in this analysis of Cairo I shall attempt to tread a devious course, moving alternately between statistical abstraction and sensual reality, between numbers and maps and the more subjective descriptions to which they correspond.

THIRTEEN CITIES WITHIN THE CITY

Cairo is subdivided, according to Factor I which isolates style of life differences and which serves as an indirect indicator of *Weltanschauung*, into thirteen major subcities, whether "natural social areas" or not, each of which contains a population distinctively different, on the average, from that inhabiting the adjacent zones. As has been indicated, these differences in population characteristics are paralleled by differences in the physical appearance of the quarters, in the kinds of housing and shopping facilities available, and even in the dominant dress that adorns the inhabitants and perhaps symbolizes their belief systems.

Map XVII shows the boundaries of these major districts, as they have been delineated by combining adjacent census tracts with comparable 1960 Factor I scores.[10] Each city is identified by an arbitrarily assigned and colorless numeral, but nothing could be more vivid than the variations in life patterns contained in these numbered districts. Nor is their location within the metropolitan complex the result of arbitrary or capricious assignment. As will become increasingly clear, the character of each of today's cities within the city is inextricably linked to the developmental history of Cairo and to the successive transformations through which Egypt has passed. These trends also hold the key to the future, for the Cairo of tomorrow will be comprehensible only as an extension and modification of today's metropolis.

[10] The boundaries can only be approximate. I have reasonably good evidence to indicate that a number of census tracts, particularly those lying at the margins of one subcity or another, lack internal homogeneity. Rather, they combine portions of each of the adjacent districts; the true "natural boundary" lies somewhere within. However, since no block data exist to supplement the returns by census tracts, I have been forced to assign these marginal tracts *in toto* to one district or the other. In this I have been guided not only by the relative closeness of the score to the average of the adjacent districts but also by firsthand knowledge of the city. It must be admitted that another analyst might draw slightly different boundaries but I do not believe that a substantial revision could be suggested.

THE QUARTERS OF THE EASTERN CITY

Community X—Medieval Cairo Unreconstituted

If one were to overlay the map of today's subcities on a map showing the extent of al-Qāhirah during Fāṭimid, Ayyūbid, and early Mamluk times, one would find almost perfect correspondence in location and extent between the latter and Community X, which is almost all that remains of Cairo's extensive medieval heritage. At the heart of this subcity is the original walled nucleus, bisected longitudinally by the ancient *qaṣabah*, the main thoroughfare which still bears the name of Mu'izz li-Dīn Allāh, the Fāṭimid Caliph who ordered the construction of a city on this site. Only three gates and a few fragments of the wall still survive to mark its somewhat enlarged borders. One extension of this quarter protrudes northward beyond the wall and the massive twin gates of Bāb al-Futūḥ and Bāb al-Naṣr into al-Ḥusaynīyah—that extramural appendage with so vicissitudinous a history—and into the adjoining rickety residential *cum* cemetery quarter that grew up around the Tomb of Badr al-Jamāli, the *wazīr* who rebuilt Cairo's walls. Another segment pushes westward along Shāri' Bāb al-Baḥr (Gateway to the Nile Shore), through the *qism* of Bāb al-Sha'rīyah, until it terminates just short of the western business district of Azbakīyah, enfolding the now tightly landlocked, ancient port of Tendunyas (al-Maqs). Except for this bulge, the sharp line of the zone's western border follows the course of the old Khalīj Miṣri, even though the present noisy thoroughfare gives no hint that it was once a stream down which the Caliphs sailed in their golden barques with glistening sails to celebrate, with ceremony and display, the annual cutting of the dike at Nile flood.

99. The Ḥusaynīyah quarter just north of Bāb al-Futūḥ, a n
extension of Community X

). View of the southern part of Community X from the roof the Ibn Ṭūlūn Mosque

Farther to the south one notes a deep indentation, where the transitional belt (Community XI on the map) impinges upon the older quarter. Here was the site of the Birkat al-Fīl, around which the Mamluk amirs had built their sumptuous homes. The last surviving remnant of this lake was filled in only late in the nineteenth century, and nothing remains of former glory save a few palaces, dating from the last century, which are now used for schools and museums. In place of earlier landmarks are apartment buildings constructed to house modern bureaucrats who have sought residences convenient to the large governmental zone due west.

At its southernmost extremity, Community X encompasses the somewhat squalid residential and open-market zone that lies at the foot of Ṣalāḥ al-Dīn's Citadel, still perched on a spur of the Muqaṭṭam. Mounting the slopes, where rioting Mamluks often rose in protest, are newer barracks housing a modern and more disciplined army, and crowning the top is Muḥammad 'Ali's ostentatious copy of an Istanbul mosque. At the base of the Citadel, however, the district curves to the west to envelop the bustling quarter that now crowds against the only surviving fragment of Ibn Ṭūlūn's pleasure dome of al-Qaṭā'i'—his solemn, hollow mosque. It extends beyond, almost to the place where Baybars' famous Lion Bridge once spanned the Khalīj at its sharpest bend (a point now marked approximately by the Sayīdah Zaynab Mosque). Along the eastern edge the medieval quarter terminates abruptly and almost regularly at a dusty edge where once Ṣalāḥ al-Dīn's wall had held the line against the encroaching desert and where, even earlier, the Fāṭimid conquerors under Jawhar had once dug a moat.

The people who now live in this castoff shell of another age have more in common, however, than their physical legacy, even though they can scarcely be confused with the romantic figures who populated the imaginary city of a thousand and one nights. Gone are the caparisoned horses and their militant riders; gone are the pampered damsels secreted behind their *mashrabīyah* windows or borne in closed silken litters to the baths on ladies' day; gone, in short, is the ruling elite which this city once existed to serve. Only the servers are left, providing goods for each other's demands or those of villagers in town for the day, or the week, or for life. Tradesmen whose ancestors perhaps fashioned the opulent necessities of Mamluk households now cater to new patrons—the tourists. The destitute, once dependent upon the coin-scattering largesse of rulers and the food and lodging provided by *waqf*-endowed charities, now seek alms from casual passers or pensions from the government. The gangs of the *zu'ar* are reorganized for pocket-picking, shoplifting, and cigarette-butt scavenging. Only momentarily do optical illusions transform that white-turbaned *shaykh* into Sultan Mu'ayyad on his way to pray humbly for a full flood to end the famine, or that surly policeman examining a scale into an agent of the *muḥtasib*, or that hurrying veiled girl into a slave carrying a secret message from her mistress to her anxious lover around the corner. All is changed, but ghosts still linger.

To capture both a sense of the past and an overview of the contemporary state of the medieval city, one should simply traverse the entire length of the oldest surviving and most important street from the Middle Ages from its origin at the Bāb al-Futūḥ at the northern wall to its southern extension that reaches the foot of the Citadel. This was the *Qaṣabah* along which stretched the markets enumerated by Maqrīzi and along which marched the processions of centuries. Only vestiges remain of the warehouses, inns, shops, and workshops that once aroused the awe and envy of every visitor.

101. Al-Jamālīyah in Community X. Dome covers mausoleum of Sultan Qalāwūn

102. Wide square with al-Ḥākim Mosque at left

Entering by way of the imposing gate, one passes first the crenellated walls and minaret towers of the Mosque of Ḥākim (turn of the eleventh century) but also the more contemporary reminders of almost a millennium later, ragged and exuberant children, ubiquitous donkeys and some few camels (for here cars are useless), the open stalls with their woven straw containers overflowing with —depending upon the season—olives, dates, watermelons, or other bulk foods. Proceeding, one passes the Mosque of Aqmar (early twelfth century) and notices that the present congestion has increased. The road is mud where someone has emptied a pail of water, dry dust where no one has sprinkled. The nonsacred architecture is mud-brick, two-storied, and suggestive of a mud-colored Elizabethan street scene, with some projecting logs hinting half-timbered construction to shore up a past mistake. Occasionally one reads in the newspaper of the collapse of a building; its address is generally somewhere in Community X.

Farther along, two conflicting stimuli impinge almost simultaneously: on the right the breathtaking twin mosques of Sultan Qalāwūn and al-Nāṣir Muḥammad; on the left and a little ahead, the pounding tones of metal upon metal that herald the beginning of Sūq al-Naḥḥāsīn (the Market of the Brassworkers). Traffic now thickens—black-robed women, men in white and blue *jallābīyah*, and darting children in striped cotton nightshirts and pajamas. Everyone seems to be carrying something from somewhere to somewhere else, for the human head is the major delivery van in this zone.

The quality of the buildings becomes more substantial as the density of the foot traffic increases, indicating that one is approaching the zone of highest value in this hidden "downtown"—the place of the precious metals, the silks, the amber, the carpets, and that "modern highest use," the tourist trade. A detour into one of the tiny alleys to the west would reveal a world never glimpsed by the tourist. It is a dark and dense residential *cum* industrial *cum* commercial quarter, mud-spattered and garbage-strewn, penetrated by winding, narrow dirt paths, terminating here at the gate to a thirteenth-century *ḵhān*, terminating there at a cul-de-sac created by a house that bars a former street. Each step moves one farther back into the centuries, for if one penetrates deeply enough, one recognizes that this now largely Muslim-occupied zone was, as recently as a few decades ago, the Jewish ghetto into which poorer remnants of the "People of the Book" were still crowded, as they had been since first granted their quarter here on the site of the Gardens of Kāfūr which predated al-Qāhirah.

When you emerge again into the sunlight of the ancient *Qaṣabah*, you are abruptly disoriented by the sleek Levantine who beckons you into his gold shop—in French, or failing that, in English, then German and perhaps Italian or Greek. The tourist rarely if ever takes the detour through the western alleys to the right, for the bazaars of the Khān al-Khalīli magnetize from the alley to the east. Today's mundane needs are met for the residents of al-Jamālīyah (for such is the district's official name) in the ancient setting to the right and in its scattered and peripheral counterparts; in the self-conscious bazaar area to the left, yesterday's bibelots are offered to the tourist in contemporary shops with glass-fronted display windows.

If one continues along Mu'izz al-Dīn, however, the present century soon bursts full-blown upon unaware and dreamy senses. First comes one major cross street, Shāri' al-Mūski, the surgical incision begun by Muḥam-

103. Crossing Shāri' al-Azhar to the al-Ghūri Mosque at the entrance to al-Darb al-Aḥmar

mad 'Ali and completed by Ismā'īl, a raucous, *baladi*[11] but far from medieval street whose paved surface is all but obscured by the pedestrians and the sundry carts, carriages, cars, and taxis funneled into this one of few passable (?) streets in the old quarter. Then, after the myriad odors and noise from the spice, perfume, and cloth markets, comes a second latitudinal thoroughfare, the Shāri' al-Azhar, an even wider traffic and tramcar gash made in the 1920's to link the terminal at al-'Atabah al-Khaḍrā' on the west behind the Opera House with the tenth-century (much rebuilt) Mosque of al-Azhar, still visible, together with its University additions, near the edge of the desert to the east. These two intersections symbolize the symbiotic connection between the medieval city of Community X and the transitional and Westernized cities (Communities XI and VII) to the west, for they bring deep into the heart of the former the modern apartment structures, offices, and commerce of the latter.

The intrusion is but a narrow and shallow wedge, however. If one crosses the street, dodging careening taxis, lumbering carts, and clanging tramcars, one sees the al-Ghūri Mosque and *wakālah* at the corners. Passing between them, one reenters the medieval street and the life of Community X. Flanked by blankets and leather goods, one proceeds southward amid a thicker and more *baladi* crowd. Almost too soon one reaches the Bāb Zuwaylah, above which were once impaled the heads of deposed amirs. This gate signals the terminus of the walled city but not the end of Community X. The narrow cross street, Taḥt al-Rabb (Beneath the Apartments—one wonders whose), houses the ironmongers who once specialized in trappings for the elegantly adorned horses of proud Mamluks; today their descendants (?) forge less sumptuous charcoal burners, horseshoes, and tools. Some houses, with overhanging and almost touching balconies completely enclosed in delicate *mashrabīyah* screenings, pull one southward, past the quiet of old but solid residences and late Turkish mosques and the ghost *sūq* of the sword-makers toward the Citadel. Decay, decline, and a thinning out of commercial uses are the dominant features, but these are suddenly exchanged for openness and activity as one enters the large modern *maydān*, into which the Muḥammad 'Ali Boulevard and half a dozen other streets converge near the site of the old hippodrome (*qaramaydān*) where the Mamluk cavalry once wheeled and pranced to display its skill. Contemporary drivers need equal skill for their maneuvers. Skirting the unequal balance of the glorious Sultan Ḥasan Mosque and an undistinguished twentieth-century mosque, and glancing left to acknowledge the steep ascending path (Muḥammad 'Ali's fatal trap for his rivals) to the Citadel's summit, one plunges into the tenemented slum quarter to the west which obscures but can not totally conceal souvenirs from the past.

104. Taḥt al-Rabb Street looking westward from the Bāb Zuwaylah toward the Khalīj (now Port Sa'īd Street)

105. Melons and mosques. The sacred-secular mix of Community X

[11] This virtually untranslatable term, an adjective derived from the noun for community (country, city, town, village), now connotes native in contrast to Westernized; folk as contrasted with sophisticated; untutored and low class as opposed to refined; traditional as contrasted with modern.

106-108. Mosques and minarets dominate the skyline of the medieval city

109. Underneath the history, a residental slum

Three main observations can be abstracted from these kaleidoscopic impressions. First, the district is poor, a slum not only by Western but by Egyptian standards as well. Second, the area is traditional but it is also undeniably *urban*, albeit in a non-Occidental fashion. Residuals from urban life in the Middle Ages there may be, but residuals of rural life cannot be found. Third, the area is a vital complex of work and residence, sales and consumption, but its industry and commerce are molded on some preindustrial pattern of small scale, low mechanization, product but not division-of-labor specialization, frequent turnover but tiny inventories, personal rather than contracted negotiations. It is difficult to suppress the persistent, whispered thought, "Here is an anachronism." One suspects that, for all the vitality of the area, it is living on borrowed time. The insidious fact that the municipality of Cairo has recently enacted an "architectural control ordinance" designed to conserve and restore the historic character of the area suggests that artificial means may be required to prevent the borrowed time from running out.

In 1947 slightly under 400,000 persons inhabited Community X. By 1960 this population had risen slightly to 475,000. While such an increase is not insubstantial, especially considering the saturated level of physical development, it should be noted that of all the subcities in Cairo this one grew least, proportionately. In a metropolis that adds some 4 to 5 percent annually, both from migration and natural increase, to grow at so slow a rate is tantamount to decline. In 1947 almost one in five Cairenes lived in this city of the past; by 1960 it was only one in seven, and the proportion continues to grow smaller.

The Factor I scores of the fifty census tracts in Community X reflect the cross-product of poverty and urbanism. In 1947, the average Factor I score was —0.38;[12] some thirteen years later it was an almost identical —0.37, indicating that the relative position of the zone had not changed in the interim, despite its improvements in literacy and prosperity. Factor II scores, indicating the presence of many single males, were highest in the tracts that straddle the semi-modern business incursion along Shāri' al-Azhar and in the Azhar University quarters favored by students. Typically, the tracts in this community also had high scores on Factor III (indicating social disorganization) which identifies this zone as selectively attractive to the handicapped, the socially stigmatized, and those with no or illegitimate professions.

Commerce, industry, and services dominate the employment picture, but the future is bleak for the trades that have hitherto sustained the district. As recently as 1917 the zone still contained the heaviest concentration of industrial workers; however, since the competitive growth of modern industry and its final surge to dominance within the past few decades, this is no longer true. The older craftsmen may continue to live and work in al-Jamālīyah and al-Darb al-Aḥmar, but the new generation knows that the jobs of the future lie in the modern factories. And as the clientele of this business zone, drawn to it even now from other parts of the city, becomes more modern in its tastes and more secure in its finances, this economic avenue will also dry. The zone has shown a remarkable capacity for survival and a thousand years of history have not defeated it; possibly it will find some new support and survive yet a little while longer.

Community IX—The Funereal Quarters of the Eastern Fringe

If there is any section of Cairo that bears resemblance to the famous *bidonvilles* or shack towns surrounding North African cities or the squatters' *favellas* that ring South American centers, it is the cemetery cities that stretch in clustered concentrations along the eastern edge of the metropolis, all the way from Burj al-Ẓafar on the north to the tip of al-Khalīfah on the south. But whatever parallels the reader may attempt to construct in order to visualize this unique zone will be incorrect. Neither the image of a European-American cemetery (or even one in Turkey or the Fertile Crescent) nor of a *bidonville* will set one on the right track. There is literally no precedent —at least for its appearance and multiple functions, although there may be many legitimate precedents for its inhabitants and their problems. It is perhaps best, then, to empty one's mind totally and take a tour through the streets and perhaps a detour into history.

From the air the funereal fringe demonstrates a familiar rectangular and regular street plan with what appears to be an orderly procession of detached but roofless bungalows, a travesty on suburbia. Its openness

110-111. Aerial views of the tomb cities of Community IX

[12] In averaging the scores for 1947, N=48, since two tracts with high deviant scores on Factor I were omitted. These constituted the heart of the ancient Jewish ghetto of Cairo. The exodus of a large majority of Cairo's Jews began to occur in 1956 and was virtually complete by 1960. By that year, the two tracts had Factor I scores close to the average level of Community X and could be included in computing that average. Thus, in 1960, N=50.

112. Entering the Qayt Bay cemetery from the medieval city. Area has since been redeveloped

113. Orderly streets for the dead

114. Disorderly living quarters in al-Darāsah cemetery

115. Children enjoy the traditional swing, surrounded by the tombs of the Mamluks

and order are even more conspicuous in contrast with the crazy-quilt confusion of medieval Cairo which it adjoins. Coming down to earth, one exits from the bustling crowds of the medieval city into the dusty but straight and wide streets of the cemetery as if one had blundered upon a surrealistic stage set. Here is one writer's attempt to capture the ultimate sense of unreality engendered by a first visit:

> It is a lion-coloured, unlofty city, with streets like streets elsewhere, with the houses numbered, as though the postman might bring letters by the first delivery. But if he bangs the door and, no one opening, pushes

116. A restaurant coffee shop in the City of the Dead

in, he enters the parody of an ordinary house—two adjoining rooms, dust-carpeted, in each an oblong shape of stone or plaster. Under one floor lie the male members of the family; segregated in death in the adjoining cellar are the women.[13]

Remarkable as this description is, it misses the most surrealistic element of the scene, namely, that within this linear necropolis live perhaps 100,000 contemporary residents, not as bones in the cellar but as full-blooded if marginal inhabitants of a great living metropolis. Within this vast dusty quarter, wedged between the windmill hills that insulate it from the live city and the barren rockiness of the Muqaṭṭam chain of hills separating it from the eastern desert proper, unserved by municipal utilities, dependent upon a scattering of communal water taps, totally devoid of plumbing and sewers, largely unconnected, except illegally, to the electricity network, is a large resident population, some legitimately inhabiting the tomb-houses for which they bear custodial responsibility, others squatting in less-acknowledged state within other tomb buildings, still others inhabiting a multitude of jerry-built rural structures, some of which are taking on an air of substantial permanence. Here and there are commercial nodes—a small grocery stall, a barber, perhaps even an open-air "café"—all designed to mitigate the hard task of adapting a city of the dead to the needs of the living.

This linear city breaks down, in reality, into a number of subcities which constitute the functional arenas of a residential neighborhood. The northernmost concentration lies due east of the medieval core city and is most often referred to as the Qayt Bay cemetery, after the Mamluk Sultan whose tomb-mosque is found there, together with those of Barqūq, Ināl, and others who followed al-Nāṣir Faraj, the first to build in this zone. Farther south, approaching the sharp rise at the Citadel which divides the eastern from the southern cemeteries, is the subarea known as the Bāb al-Wazīr necropolis, deriving its name from a gate to Ṣalāḥ al-Dīn's wall extension, formerly there. Beyond the Citadel, entered through the ghost portals of yet another of Ṣalāḥ al-Dīn's additions (the Bāb al-Qarāfah or the Gate to the Tombs), is the so-called Great Qarāfah or the Tombs of the Caliphs (from which the quarter's name, al-Khalīfah, is derived) which stretches southward in a long lobe some two kilometers long and one kilometer wide, its outer limits described by the loop of a railroad line. The heart of this largest of all cemetery zones is the almost urban quarter around the shrine-mosque of Imām Shāfi'ī, to which Muslim pilgrims have been drawn for well over a thousand years. South of this dense concentration both

[13] Desmond Stewart, *Cairo* (Phoenix House Books, London: 1965), p. 25.

117. The Qayt Bay mausoleum mosque *ca.* 1840.

118. View of the same mosque in 1969. Note residences and shops

119. Densely settled urban quarter near the Imām Shāfi'i mausoleum today

the tombs and the residents are distributed more sparsely.

Who lives in these necropolises and why? I must confess ignorance, for to fathom the motives and adjustments of their residents would require a field study to supplement the statistical analysis. Some inferences, however, can be drawn even from the sparse statistics. First, it is possible to establish the general fact that until fairly recently the resident population of this enormous quarter was quite small and had fairly legitimate reasons for being there. In the Middle Ages, here were the *zāwiyah*s which offered hostel accommodations to pilgrims and *ṣūfi* mystics and, even then, the role of tomb custodian was known. Whole families might repair to the cemetery for a day or week to visit and commemorate their buried ancestors. On sacred holidays the cemeteries took on the air of a convivial community picnic, with vendors hawking edibles and sweets, children playing in the open spaces, their elders sociable and probably noisy. While the resident mystics have long since disappeared, the tomb custodians remain and have grown more numerous. Their ranks were supplemented in the early twentieth century by men employed in the lime kilns (in the northern portion) and the limestone quarries (in the south). Only a slight and gradual increase could be noted during the few decades following 1917, suggesting that the dynamics of the zone's settlement and its functions did not alter radically.

However, by 1947 population had mounted to over 50,000, indicating that the overcrowding and housing shortage induced during the war years had forced some Cairenes (or recent migrants to the city—I do not know which) to seek cheap or free housing in this peripheral zone, even if their employment did not require location there. Mining and quarrying still accounted for the largest proportion of employed males in each and every tract in the district, with services (presumably custodial care of the tombs) also important in the larger cemeteries; but employment was far more diversified than before and could not be adequately accounted for by the limited opportunities in the local vicinity. Men were engaged in transportation,[14] in trade, in construction, and even in personal services. The evidence points inescapably to the arrival of squatters uninvolved in the traditional economic base of the immediate district. Complete rural villages were constructed on open sites. As recently as 1959 such a squatters' village could be seen *in situ* just beyond the Mosque of al-Azhar at the edge of the Qayt Bay cemetery, although their mud huts were later forcibly removed by the government to make room for the major Ṣalāḥ Sālim Highway that now traverses what had been a totally rural setting. By 1960, with population up to 80,000-90,000, specialization of the labor force had virtually disappeared. No longer could the presence of local resources (tombs and quarries) account for the employment of more than an insignificant minority of the breadwinners. The zone had become just another place to live, "selected" only by those who had no alternative.

This change can be seen quite clearly in the relative decline of all census tracts in this subcity on Factor I between 1947 and 1960. The average Factor I score of tracts in Community IX during the earlier year had been −0.78, indicating a low status but not necessarily a rural-type population. On the contrary, there is reason to believe that this zone, unlike the other fringe areas, contained a population long adjusted to urban life and quasi-industrial employment. But by 1960 this score had dropped drastically to −1.54 (or one and a half standard deviations *below* the city's average), placing the cemetery zone on a par with the remaining rural fringe areas. It can be surmised, then, that the newer arrivals who swelled the resident population of the funereal cities between 1947 and 1960 were quite different from the original inhabitants. They must have been predominantly illiterate, poorer, and probably less well integrated into the urban economy; in addition, they had the family patterns of early marriage and high fecundity that betrayed their cultural affinity with rural Egypt, from which perhaps a great many had recently come.

The future of this city is moot. Cairo's planners eye the district covetously but in secret, for here is a logical direction into which the cramped city might expand, if

14 While the census does not provide information on the "type" of transportation, observation offers a hint. Nonmodern transportation in Cairo still depends upon the donkey- or mule-drawn cart. Only in the fringe areas can these animals be safely tethered *at home* for protection. The cemetery fringe areas, due to their proximity to the demanders of "nonmodern transport," namely the shops and industries in the medieval business district, have therefore proven especially attractive to persons in this occupation.

only the tombs could be removed! But the sheer size of the zone and the permanence of many of the tomb structures, as well as their high artistic merits, defy simple clearance, even if the revulsion against disturbing the dead could be overcome. On the other hand, there is the problem of the already-entrenched residents, as well as the new ones who have been added since the 1967 war, who live under conditions that cry for improved urban services. But if urban utilities are extended into the district to alleviate some of the real hardships, this cannot help but encourage further residential development, a prospect with dubious health consequences. To outlaw further settlement is extremely difficult, for so long as the metropolis remains severely overcrowded in its poorer districts, it is inevitable that some of her citizens will prefer the air and openness of the cities of the dead to the oppressive crush in the cities of the living.

Community I—The Baladi Slum of Būlāq

Bounded on the south by the major traffic artery that still insulates the former island from its physical but not social neighbor, the rococo "Gold Coast," truncated sharply on the west by the Nile that prevents contact with the plush island of Zamālik offshore, and attenuating northward along the coast of the Sāḥil, still a sometime riverport for small sailing vessels, is another urban slum of contemporary Cairo, Būlāq. Although lacking the venerable patina of the medieval city, Būlāq is nevertheless more comparable, in quality if not in age, to the old city whose port she originally was than to the rural or cemetery slums at the city's edge. Physically, her buildings are far superior to village-type constructions, for they are mostly made of cement and concrete rather than sun-dried mudbrick, and the zone contains a wide variety of industrial as well as commercial installations. Socially, too, poverty of the extreme type found in Egyptian villages or in Cairo zones of true marginal subsistence only tenuously connected with the urban economy is not marked here. Nevertheless, the qualities that undeniably make Būlāq an urban slum are those that define such districts elsewhere, albeit according to different sets of standards.

The urban character of Būlāq's slum state is seen most clearly in its density, for here, despite the generally unimpressive height of the buildings (two to four stories for the most part), are crammed one-tenth of the entire population of the city. In 1947, the 23 census tracts comprising this subcommunity contained over 267,000 persons, a figure that had increased to in excess of 350,000 by 1960. Since the total area of the district amounts to only 4.5 square kilometers, the overall density was almost 60,000 per square kilometer in 1947 and an astronomical 77,000 persons per square kilometer in 1960. (This is about four to five times higher than the density of big-city slums in the U.S.) While this is the overall density, when one takes into account that a large portion of Būlāq's land is for industrial, transport, or wholesale use,

120. Tramway terminal in northern Būlāq showing typical commercial uses

121. Doing the laundry in the Nile at Būlāq

122. Mosques, mares, and metal-working in Būlāq today

123. A main thoroughfare in Būlāq

124. An interior street of Būlāq near the Sīnān Pasha Mosque

one realizes that the true residential density, if it could be computed excluding the area used for nonresidential purposes and for streets, would be considerably higher. Indeed, some of the census tracts with the very highest densities in the city are to be found within the quarter of Būlāq. Small subdistricts having over 100,000 persons per square kilometer are not uncommon. Even the notorious hive-like quarters of urban India rarely reach such peaks! Given the modest heights of residential structures in this area, it is to be expected that Būlāq should suffer from extreme room-overcrowding. Indeed, here is a quarter in which whole families of twelve or even more members may sometimes be compressed into a single room; and here is a quarter in which the people, of necessity, must overflow onto the streets to carry out in public many of the functions that are generally confined in a Western city to the privacy of the dwelling unit.

Along the main artery of the quarter, the wide street of Shāri' Sittah-wa-'ishrīn Yūlyū, which is used by the buses, streetcars, and automobiles that must traverse the district in order to link the main Westernized shopping center of Azbakīyah with the island of Zamālik and the western shore of 'Ajūzah, this overflow often obstructs traffic. There is a constant ebb and flow of children—both ragged urchins and neat, tunic-clad school children; of women, almost uniformly in traditional black gown and veil but now often wearing more Western-style housedresses under their outer robes, carrying on head, shoulder, or hip a varied assortment of burdens ranging from laundry to edibles to infants; and of men, showing signs of increased urbanization—some still attired in the traditional garb of long, full *jallābīyah* and skullcap or turban but others in the white shirt and wrinkled trousers of the *faranji* (the foreigner). They gather in clots to gossip; they gather in the fly-specked coffee shops (for men only) that dot the area to while away the steaming hours over a small glass of too sweet and almost black tea, a newspaper (if they can read), or a slow game of backgammon; they gather to quarrel, with vigorous gestures and loud imprecations but rarely with physical force (at least among equals), or merely to watch the outcome of another's quarrels; they gather to haggle over a small purchase from a pushcart or to watch others. One senses that all these gatherings are fostered not so much by a gregarious nature as by the sheer pressures of people on space, making crowds even where crowds are not sought.

Off the main thoroughfare, in the tiny streets that take a labyrinthine and unpaved course to give access to the stores, dwellings, and tiny industrial shops that are freely intermixed in the quarter, the mass of humanity may thin out some. But it is here that the old men, circling with the sun in winter and the shade in summer in a slow progression of seats, the barefoot children, and the occasional tethered (or free-roaming) sheep or goat, are sufficient to remind one that, although they now live in an *urban* slum, many of Būlāq's residents have come from rural villages and have only recently begun the process of adapting to city ways. The major rural influx into the quarter dates from the years of World War II, and in 1947 the characteristics of the residents still reflected quite vividly the recent arrival of many of them. Since 1947, however, the process of cultural assimilation to urban ways has had a chance to blend in some of the more extreme rural types and, statistically speaking, to raise the relative socio-economic score of the district to within the urban range.

In 1947, the average score on Factor I of the 23 census tracts comprising the subcity of Būlāq was —.70, considerably below the theoretical "norm" for the city as a whole. By 1960 this score, while still in the lower portion of the distribution, had improved to —0.35. What do these scores tell us about the kinds of people living in Būlāq?

For one thing, they tell us that a large proportion of the men and an even more substantial proportion of the women are illiterate. Their children, numerous indeed as indicated by the universally high fertility ratios in the quarter, are likely to be somewhat better prepared for participation in the modern sector of the economy than are their parents, for many of them are enrolled in school and will complete at least the primary stage (six years), unless the loss of their parents or a complete catastrophe forces them onto the streets and into the army of unskilled boys prematurely "in the labor force." The girls are less likely than their brothers to be able to take advantage of the free public schools, for they are frequently needed at home to care for younger siblings and to relieve an overburdened mother. Some are entrusted as domestic servants in the households of the middle- and upper-class residents in the adjacent districts, where their youth limits their usefulness but where their jobs at least provide better food and lodgings than can be offered in their own homes. Their small wages are frequently paid directly to their families and some may be set aside to provide the girl with her basic dowry of bed quilts, cooking pots, and a personal wardrobe. Youthful marriage is typical in this area, the prelude to long years of almost constant pregnancy and childbearing, unless the alternate fate of divorce, unfortunately not uncommon in this district, befalls her.

Occupationally the residents of Būlāq do not rise above the semi-skilled level and most remain in the unskilled, brute force occupations. Men work in domestic service as cooks and waiters; work, often under Italian or Greek supervisors, in the small machine shops and automobile repair garages that are concentrated in the southern triangle of the zone; work as janitors in government or private office buildings, or in jobs associated with the wholesale warehouses, open storage yards, and transportation terminals also concentrated in the district. Local commercial establishments offering services to a local clientele probably also provide employment for some men in the quarter. Even so, there are many more people than there are jobs, and the district harbors a fairly substantial number of unemployed and "nominally employed" men, easily rounded up for emergency work on the Nile embankments when the river threatens to rise above normal, or for participation in a political demonstration when the government wishes to assemble an impressively large crowd to hail a visiting African statesman or to march on the embassy of an unfriendly power.

125. The future of Būlāq: slum clearance yielded the site for the new Television Building

The district is almost exclusively Muslim in its religious persuasion, with the exception of one tiny enclave at an old Italian Catholic school (census tract No. 126 on the key, in 1960 no longer significantly different from its neighbors as it had been in 1947), and the southernmost tip to which automobile repair shops, with their *déclassé* Italian and Greek mechanics, had gravitated. Few Egyptian Copts, even of lowest socio-economic status, have found this zone congenial, and its public edifices are almost exclusively mosques, including the shrine-mosque of Abū al-'Alā' and the multi-domed Turkish-style mosque of Sīnān Pasha (late fifteenth and sixteenth centuries respectively). Almost nothing remains of later public uses, for the port has long since disappeared and even the Museum of Antiquities, originally located in Būlāq, has been twice removed to its present site near the Hilton Hotel in the "Gold Coast." A few of Muḥammad 'Ali's industrial establishments still retain their original locations in Būlāq (most notably the Government Printing Office) although the plants have been renovated. Būlāq is a slum *because* it is an old area, but it retains little of historic interest or antiquarian charm.

126. The frontyard of Miṣr al-Qadīmah along the Corniche

128. New homes in old Miṣr

127. The backyard of Miṣr al-Qadīmah next to the Mosque of ʻAmr

129. Old homes crumble. A roof view in the walled compound of Miṣr al-Qadīmah

THE QUARTERS OF THE SOUTHERN CITY

Community XII—The Old Miṣr (Miṣr al-Qadīmah)

The reader will recall that, according to the Napoleonic map drafted at the turn of the nineteenth century, the urban region of Cairo consisted of the medieval nucleus somewhat expanded to include Birkat al-Azbakīyah, and the town's two distant and discrete port suburbs, Būlāq and Miṣr al-Qadīmah. One of these port suburbs has already been identified as an interior slum of contemporary Cairo; the second, which experienced a different but parallel evolution from its historic beginnings, is a zone of similarly depressed status. In a manner remarkable to observe, Cairo's premodern heritage surfaces spottily—in the three interior slum districts of al-Qāhirah, Būlāq, and Miṣr al-Qadīmah. Without a knowledge of the city's history, one could never account for the geographic distribution of these present-day slums.

Similar to the other major slums of the city, this zone, known as the "Old Cairo," owes its low state in part to its age, even though few of the buildings can trace a specific lineage in distant history. Only a tiny belt at the edge of the *kharāb* covering Fusṭāṭ is old, including the walled enclave of churches and Copts, synagogues and, formerly, Jews that make up the present complex at Babylon, and the Mosque of ʻAmr, which retains the site if not the architecture of the first mosque to be built in Africa after the Arab invasion. The remainder of the district, between this eastern limit and the river's bank, was constructed on land that had been added centuries after the founding of Fusṭāṭ. Nevertheless, later growth could not shake off the stigma of birth and tended to take on the character of existing uses. In 1800 this community was a separate "suburb" containing only 10,000 residents, many of whom were Egyptian Christians and Jews. A number of the more noxious industries of the metropolis

130. Squatter homes on the *kharāb*

131. Pottery kilns on the *kharāb*

were segregated there and, indeed, still are, including the abattoirs and the pottery kilns, although the latter no longer produce the lustre glass for which Fusṭāṭ was justly renowned. As urban expansion eventually engulfed the original nucleus and made it contiguous with the developments to its north, the district added population—but failed to better its degraded status.

The eight census districts that comprise this southern-situated slum contained a little more than 100,000 inhabitants in 1947, a number which had increased to 188,000 by 1960. Between the two census dates there occurred not only a marginal addition of population but also a replacement, with the departing Jewish community and foreign religious personnel more than compensated for by newcomers from lower educational and social levels. Excluding the tract that, due to its religious personnel, ranked far above the norm for the district in 1947, the average Factor I score for the seven remaining tracts was —0.45, placing the district on a par with the other two slum zones. After population replacement and new growth, however, the average of all eight tracts (for the one deviant had found its level) in 1960 had dropped to —0.54, making it by that year the most depressed of the three urban slum districts.

The many Cairenes who believe that Miṣr al-Qadīmah is still largely Coptic are carrying over from the past history of the district an anachronistic impression of its present character. Actually, only 8 percent of the population in 1947 was non-Muslim and this had dropped to 6 percent by 1960. Nevertheless, it is true that if there are Copts in the city who have failed to become absorbed into the educational and occupational modernization of Cairo, they are to be found concentrated in this zone from which the more upward mobile have departed. They can often be identified by their proud "badge" of community, elaborate blue byzantine crosses tattooed on the back of their hand or wrist.

The district differs from the two other slums in yet another way. Poverty in the zone is of a type closer to the rural than the urban mode, despite the generally high density of development. To some extent this results from the district's location on the fringe of the *kharāb*, since squatters have freely encroached into that desolate quarter, building their primitive mud huts on the mounds. To some extent it also results from the fact that the district blends into the true rural fringe to the south where agriculturalists predominate. The rural and quasi-rural population, however, is in the minority, and most residents are old-time urbanites who occupy dwellings that are of urban design, albeit of marginal quality.

Community XIII—The Southern Rural Fringe

Miṣr al-Qadīmah fades off imperceptibly on the south into a rich fluvial bed ideal for agriculture which, where it indents from the river almost to the edge of the Muqaṭṭam at the ancient village of Basātīn, occupies land once submerged under the Birkat al-Ḥabash (The Abyssinian Pond). The remainder of the zone hugs the river in a narrow strip that extends all the way to the industrial satellite of Ḥalwān. My statistical analysis has had to exclude the only nonrural settlement along the route and, indeed, the only true "suburb" Cairo has, namely the town of Ma'ādi, conceived by Britain's colonial architects and, during the British heyday, an exclusive residential enclave.[15] Ignoring this anomaly, however, the remainder

[15] Ma'ādi is now an upper-middle-class Egyptian community of private homes set amidst a cliché urban subdivision reminiscent of Geddes-Howard gone berserk. It was, unfortunately, one of the two census tracts that had to be eliminated from my statistical analysis because its boundaries and data could not be made comparable for the two census dates.

of the zone is chiefly rural. It is these portions that I have delineated as Community XIII.

As late as 1960 this zone of almost pure rural character had been bypassed in the process of urban expansion to the southernmost node of industrialism growing up at Ḥalwān. This can not long remain the case, however, for fingers of industrial development already stretch up from Ḥalwān, and cement factories, thermo-electric plants, and workers' compounds now abut alluvial fields still cultivated by *fallāḥīn* and irrigated by the water buffalo-powered *sāqiyah* (water wheel). Nevertheless, between 1947 and 1960 one would be hard pressed to discover any great evidence of the transformation or urbanization of the district. On the contrary, the average Factor I score of census tracts in this rural residual actually declined from —1.55 in the earlier year to —1.84 in the later year, placing the district below all other fringe areas.

On the other hand, direct preoccupation with farming and quarrying, formerly the dominant economic activities in these tracts, has tended to decrease markedly since 1947, indicating that, although life styles have altered little in the direction of either skill-improvement through literacy or increased equality between the sexes, the men at least are being drawn into urban service and industrial employment, albeit slowly and at the lowest paid and least skilled levels. This is a movement which cannot help but expose them eventually to the winds of change. What influences are not introduced by this exposure will undoubtedly force their way into the zone by more direct means, namely, by the location of industrial plants there. The strips bordering the railway and the newly improved highway that link Cairo with Ḥalwān are bound to become increasingly attractive to industrial uses which are already making their appearance. As this trend continues, one can expect a further influx of industrial workers, on the one hand, and the absorption of the resident labor force into the modern economy, on the other hand. When this happens, the Factor I scores of census tracts here will undoubtedly begin to rise to within the urban range. Other rural fringe areas may have their frontiers pushed back farther, but the southern fringe will probably become extinct.

THE QUARTERS OF THE WESTERN CITY

Virtually encircled on three sides by the ring of interior slums formed by the oldest quarters of al-Qāhirah, Būlāq, and Miṣr al-Qadīmah, the city which grew up in the early modern era as a counterthrust to medievalism could expand in only one direction—to the west, toward, then into, then beyond the Nile. Each successive thrust left a vertical striation in the social mosaic of Cairo. Closest to the medieval edge both physically and socially is Community XI, the transitional belt; then comes the Gold Coast, heart and façade of modern Cairo, denoted on Map XVII as Community VII; beyond it lies the Silver Coast of Community VIII, while still farther to the west remains an area just now being converted from rural to urban uses, the fringe area of Community VI. These four communities make up the Western City and are integrally and functionally linked in their development. The epitome of this city is the Gold Coast. Therefore, although it postdates the transitional belt in time of settlement, it deserves our attention first.

Community VII—The Gold Coast

In the space of less than 5.5 square kilometers of the most valuable land right in or adjacent to the center of the city is concentrated a significant proportion of Cairo's wealthiest and most Westernized residents. Once the rather exclusive domain of the "colonial" foreigner and the francophilic Egyptian elite, this zone has obviously undergone a dramatic transformation since the Revolution of 1952 and the foreign exodus of 1956. But despite these changes, it still ranks considerably above all other parts of the city and is both the subcity of Cairo most visible to foreign visitors and the district most frequently pictured on postcards and brochures designed to display Cairo's luxurious façade. Along the broad and fabled river, metallic green-blue under the winter sun, turbulently brackish through the summer swell that recalls a flood season now scientifically controlled and modulated, rise the glistening white piers of sleek apartment buildings and new hotels. Set amid lush tropical trees, the buildings are placed neatly into regular blocks and triangles defined by wide, paved, swept, and sidewalked streets. Taxis cruise the Corniche, the broad thoroughfare bordering the Nile (the revolutionary regime's first contribution to a Cairo yet-to-be), hunting well-dressed clients—domestic or from abroad—heading for the department stores and specialty shops "downtown," the plush cinema palaces, the Victorian ice cream parlors of Groppi, the Sporting Club or the races on the Jazīrah, or the "little" dressmakers and redolent, unbelievably numerous beauty salons upon which depends the superb grooming of Cairo's largest leisure class—the upper- and upper-middle-class matrons and their unemployed daughters being primed for marriage. Nannies, masquerading in blue or white uniforms, amble along in their backless slippers (the Achilles' heel that betrays proletarian origin), shepherding plump children in starched playclothes, perhaps as their grandmothers once minded the sheep and goats that still make an unexpected and incongruous appearance in the zone. Little boys dart hazardously out of the steamy tiny laundries that dot the area, balancing piles of freshly ironed sheets and linens on one palm,

132. Looking eastward from the Jazīrah to the Gold Coast

carrying in the other hand hangers (on loan only) on which are hung Paris-styled dresses that would scandalize their mothers and sisters at home. Cooks and *ṣuffrajis* (waiters) sally forth resolutely, *jallābīyahs* ballooning behind them, to replenish their inevitable woven baskets with food supplies from the markets. Idle *bawwābīn* (doorkeepers), resting from their daily chore of mopping hallways and lobbies, imitate the old men of Būlāq in their routine of shifting seats, but their finer garments and their occasional acts of rising to bow to an entering resident or to relieve one of a stray package distinguish them as "useful" members of the working force, in contrast to the dependents in Būlāq. Once, this subcity was a world unto itself—but that world is quickly passing.

The population of this zone is numerically less impressive than its influence, but its wealth has hitherto been sufficient to support a host of public and private facilities designed to insulate it quite effectively from the other social worlds of Cairo, of which many of its residents remain dismally ignorant. Some 65,000 privileged persons lived in the district in 1947. Since that time, the population has shifted somewhat, decreasing in the commercial quarters and expanding in the riverfront strips of high-

133. Maydān in the Westernized central business district

rise construction. By 1960 the district contained a population of over 82,000 but appeared finally to be reaching a saturation point that could be expanded only by building even higher. Many of the early villas had already been supplanted by apartment buildings, and those few remaining ones not being used as embassies and consulates

134. The Corniche Drive in front of the Semiramis Hotel

135. Apartment houses replace villas on the Jazīrah

showed the signs of neglect that presage a land use conversion.

No Cairo resident uses the term "Gold Coast" to describe this quarter. However, ordinary Cairenes carry within themselves a stereotype and an ambivalence toward the sections known as Azbakīyah, Sulaymān Pasha, Qaṣr al-Dūbbārah, Garden City, Qaṣr al-Nīl, and Zamālik that is unequivocally quite close to how Chicagoans of all classes view their North Shore Gold Coast. But unlike Chicago, where the slum symbolized the ethnic alien counterpoised against the white Protestant native aristocracy of the Gold Coast, in Cairo the Gold Coast is the "alien body" to which the native city has played exploited host (and reluctant beneficiary as well, for this is the quarter which employs a large minority in servile capacities).

In its insular days as a "colonial" city, about the turn of the century, the district was largely inhabited by foreigners and Christians, particularly in its most heavily developed commercial core at the Azbakīyah. Its slow expansion along the Nile shore and across the bridges onto the Jazīrah took place without disturbing either the dominance or the taste-setting role of the alien elements, although at least demographically this concentration was inevitably diluted as the district expanded and attracted followers of the twin and entwined magnets of royalty and colonial agents. By about 1917, Egyptian Muslims accounted for less than half of the population of the district, despite their presence in large numbers as a resident service population. By 1947, Muslim Egyptians constituted over 57 percent of the population but, of those who were in the district not as domestic servants but as fellow residents, many spoke French among themselves and patterned their values and way of life as closely as they could on their perhaps distorted image of a sophisticated and even parasitic West.

With the Revolution and then the aftermath of the Suez Crisis (1956), however, the district underwent a rapid population succession. In 1957 a high vacancy rate, brought about by the departure of significant numbers of foreign nationals, permitted the influx of many upwardly-mobile technocrats of the new regime, although some still shied away from the zone because of earlier antagonisms, preferring the more familiar quarters of Heliopolis and the Silver Coast. As a result, the ethnic composition of the Gold Coast's population altered radically in the direction of indigenization. By 1960, Egyptian Muslims constituted almost three-fourths of the population of Community VII, reflecting a new unification between elite and mass and a final extirpation of the more glaring aspects of alienism in the city. Arabic soon supplanted French on the streets and in the stores; even the once exclusive Jazīrah Sporting Club (island companion to the Turf Club that had been burned so eagerly in the street uprising in 1952 along with the old Shepheard's Hotel), the ultimate foreign citadel, bowed to its inevitable future as a recreational facility for Egyptians.

The alterations within the residential sections were paralleled by a similar metamorphosis in the "Westernized" central business district that included the census tracts of al-Tawfīqīyah, al-Azbakīyah, and its southern extension to Bāb al-Lūq (the notorious home of thieves and escaped prisoners in medieval times). In the shops, as a reflection of the changed nature of the clientele and often a changed ownership as well (some of the major ones sequestered by the government had been owned by prominent French-Jewish families), the alien goods, patterns, and prices that had discouraged the nonaristocracy from venturing into the shops gradually were removed and in their place were substituted items and actions designed to attract a less exclusive but also more typical class of buyers. Black-gowned or -coated women from the Eastern and Northern cities dared to windowshop along Shāriʿ Sulaymān Pasha, and aspiring girls and boys from lower-middle-class zones tried on new clothes in

136. Shāri' Qaṣr al-Nīl's shops shuttered for siesta

formerly august settings or tried on new personalities in the somewhat less well-tended premises of sequestered Groppi's. Recreational facilities also underwent a similar change, with movie houses that had formerly specialized in foreign films being converted to Arabic productions or to an expanding number of stages for the legitimate Arabic theater. Even the Opera House, last stronghold of Europe, billed fewer and fewer operatic and symphonic performances, more folk ballets and popular singers. The leisured and/or moneyed class had become both smaller and more broadly based in the new society.

Despite these radical changes, the relative position of the Gold Coast within the urban status pattern was sustained. In 1947, census tracts in this subcity had an average score on Factor I of +2.18, by far the highest of all subcommunities in Cairo. Even after the disappearance of the long upper tail of the distribution (which had been associated with European residents), the average in 1960 was still close to two standard deviations above the "norm" for the city, being +1.97 in that year, and was still substantially above the average for the second rank subcity of Heliopolis.

This high score, reflecting almost universal literacy, high rates of school attendance, delayed marriages and smaller families, expansive living quarters, and the host of related characteristics that help to define the degree to which residents of this zone are oriented toward the modern rather than the traditional patterns of evolving Egyptian life, can no longer be attributed merely to the presence of a polyglot foreign community. Statistically, this latter community has become both less significant numerically and more diversified socially (for it now includes embassy personnel of a variety of African and Asian powers as well as Europeans). In terms of its influence it no longer constitutes a closed social body dictating the terms of admission to aspirant Egyptians; rather, foreigners now adjust to or simply spurn the dominant community of upper- and upper-middle-class Egyptians who chiefly command this subcity.

137. Apartments replace grazing land on the ancient island of Rawḍah in the Silver Coast

Community VIII—A Parallel "Silver Coast"

If the Gold Coast preempts the central part of the east bank together with the island of the Jazīrah, a baser metal, perhaps silver, occupies the western bank and the southern island of Rawḍah. Of later origin, reflecting the tardy appearance and uncertain growth of a mediating middle class in Cairo, it has been growing in the quarters of 'Ajūzah, Duqqi, Jīzah (not the separate town but the zone near Cairo University and the Zoological Gardens), and Rawḍah in a manner that parallels the *other* middle-class zone at Heliopolis (Community V in the Northern City), namely, through land reclamation. However, while the northeastern middle-class city was carved out of the desert's border, this southwestern counterpart has gradually been encroaching upon the urban region's fertile green hinterland in its fight for *lebensraum*.

As recently as the late 1920's, the island of Rawḍah and the entire area on the west bank of the Nile, despite the existence of bridges crossing the waterway and the tramcar service that had been extended as far as the pyramids, was still being used primarily for agriculture. In this zone were some of Cairo's most prosperous and productive *'izab* (pl. for *'izbah*, a large, single-ownership "fief" including villagers who supplied the labor for generally absent owners), some held by members of the royal family, some by important "pashas," others in *waqf*. Only a few isolated clusters of urban uses were evident: the small village settlements at Imbābah (Minbabah of medieval manuscripts and later the site of the Mamluks' defeat at the hands of Napoleon), Mīt Kardak, Kafr al-Shawām, and Kafr Shaykh Ismā'īl; the similarly rustic concentrations of Mīt 'Uqbah, 'Ajūzah, Duqqi, and Maḥaṭṭat Būlāq al-Dakrūr. A handful of villas pressed themselves between the natural barriers of the river's shore and the tramcar line just a block to the rear. In

138. Maydān al-Taḥrīr

addition, there were a few recreational and institutional uses, generally occupying old palaces, including an Agricultural College, the faculties of Law and Engineering of the newly relocated Cairo University, a Shooting Club, the Zoo, etc.

Particularly since the 1940's, large sections of this formerly bucolic expanse have been converted to urban quarters capable of absorbing a growing proportion of Cairo's overflow population. Even Rawḍah, site of the ancient Nilometer, which had remained incongruously rural until very recently, has been the center of one of Cairo's most active building booms. The old villages are being displaced by dense arrays of elevator apartment houses; the flocks of black goats and grey sheep are disappearing. In place of corn crops, pile drivers are planting new steel foundations. Today, there are still sharp contrasts where the new has not yet totally supplanted the old, but one can safely predict that it will become increasingly difficult to locate such anomalies as the area completes its transformation.

In 1947, despite its vast area, there were fewer than 55,000 residents in the area delimited as Community VIII, including the student population around the Jīzah campus of Cairo University. Represented were such diverse elements as the fishermen squatters on the *waqf*-encumbered land at al-Ḥūtīyah, the scattered agriculturalists awaiting displacement, the urbane aristocratic residents of the narrow riverfront at Jīzah—whose expectations that the west bank also would become a Gold Coast had been foiled—and a large mass of lower-middle- and middle-class Egyptians attracted to the zone by its combination of locational convenience and moderate rents.

Some scant thirteen years later this population had quadrupled, reaching 220,000 according to the Census of 1960. Of all thirteen subcities of Cairo, then, Community VIII experienced the highest rate of demographic growth—most of it coming from an influx of Cairenes from across the river. The invading population resembled the middle-class Egyptians already in the district much more than they resembled either the defunct aristocracy (whose confiscated *'izab* provided the building sites for many of the new developments) or the displaced villagers. Favored by the upper-middle-class newcomers were the often elegant apartment houses close to the Nile at 'Ajūzah and near the Zoological Gardens in Jīzah; the remainder were content with the less commodious dwellings that lined and radiated out from the major highway to the pyramids.

The Factor I scores of census tracts in the community between 1947 and 1960 have been upgraded, reflecting the rapid conversion from semi-rural to urban and from poor to moderate and good residential uses. The average score on Factor I of the census tracts in Community VIII in 1947 was +0.68, which placed it considerably below the more established middle-class zone around Heliopolis, and put it roughly on a par with Shubra from which it differed primarily in terms of ethnic composition rather than social prestige. Whereas Shubra's distinguishing characteristic was its selective attractiveness to Egyptian Copts, the settlements on Rawḍah and the west bank were almost exclusively Muslim.

Community VIII maintained this characteristic feature through the post-1947 growth period. Even in 1960, when the average Factor I score of the tracts in the zone had increased to +1.13, some 95 percent of its residents were Egyptian Muslims. The zone, then, is best described as an emergent urban district catering to an emergent and native middle-class. Its future, bright indeed, will follow theirs, if the zone does not lose favor due to the relocation of the government offices from their present concentration at the southern edge of the Gold Coast to the new quarters in Naṣr City. However, other professional concentrations in the south, such as the University and the medical complex at Qaṣr al-'Ayni and Manyal, as well as the commercial center on the east bank, should help to sustain the locational advantages of the Silver Coast, even after the government offices have departed. In addition, since this area, together with the Gold Coast, has been the recipient of several new hotels for visitors to Cairo, it should begin to diversify its commercial services to take advantage of this potential source of prosperity. The prognosis is for Community VIII to continue its expansion into the residual rural fringe on the west, Community VI.[16]

Community VI—Imbābah and the Western Rural Fringe

The expansion of the Silver Coast back from the river's edge into the fertile flood plain between it and the desert's limit cut deeply into a formerly large rural fringe. This zone of fluid and contracting boundaries has no future at all. By the time of the next census, only a tiny rural portion will be left within the arc-shaped zone delimited on the north and west by the curving course of the major railroad to Upper Egypt and the irrigation canal that parallels it.

Because of its fluid condition one cannot locate a clear boundary for Community VI nor can one easily characterize the population. Two rather different types of population reside in the zone but, although they differ in the degree of their involvement with the urban economy, they do not feel as profound a gulf between them as the one which separates them both from the middle-class urbanites who have recently invaded. One subgroup of the population, concentrated largely to the north in the settlements around Imbābah, is urbanizing quite rapidly, but urbanizing on a pattern closer to the Būlāq prototype than to the Silver and Gold coasts that are its closer neighbors. Several nucleus villages in this subsection had long served as *entrepôts* for the produce of the western bank on its way to the city. Thus, many of the residents were occupied *not* in farming per se but in the associated activities of transport and marketing. However, as large industrial plants were located to the north of the bounding railroad, an urban proletariat was added to the nuclei populations. In addition, a public housing project built by the Ministry of *Waqf*, the so-called "Workers' City," added low-income but urban families to this subarea. By 1960, this urbanizing portion of the western fringe had

139. One side of the street: residual village of Mīt 'Uqbah, 1965

140. The other side of the street: new villa of Madīnat al-Muhandisīn, 1965

[16] I made a trip to Cairo during the summer of 1968, by which time this prediction had become a reality. Virtually nothing remained of the northern portion of the agricultural fringe nor of many of the cruder agricultural settlements. Only portions of Mīt 'Uqbah persisted, encircled by new apartment houses and villas.

doubled in population over 1947, containing by the latter year over 72,000 persons, many of whom, while of rural origin, had severed their dependence upon the rural economy and were engaged in unskilled service and industrial jobs. Many even "commuted" via streetcar or rowboat (a penny a trip) to their jobs in the city across the river.

The second subgroup in this community remains more rural, not only in origin and values but in occupation as well. In the residual rural zone beyond Imbābah and 'Ajūzah had been some of the most important agricultural estates in the Cairo vicinity, on which resided a large farming population. Gradually but decisively, especially after the rural reform laws broke up the pattern of large estates and the *waqf* reform laws returned mortmain land to government control or to the market place, this farmland began to be replanned for urban developments. Currently superimposed on this fringe are such urban schemes as Madīnat al-Muhandisīn (Engineers' City), for which roads have already been laid out and some substantial buildings constructed, and Madīnat al-Awqāf (City of *Waqfs*), still largely on the drawing boards. With their completion we shall witness a virtual displacement of the farming population which is, even now, moving to the more urban demi-slums of Imbābah's interior.

In 1947 there were about 60,000 residents in Community VI, and the average Factor I score of census tracts in this area was −1.08, making it one of the "better" fringe areas. Population more than doubled between census dates and by 1960 the zone housed some 150,000 persons—still drawn from the least urban types in the city. The average Factor I score for the constituent census tracts had dropped to −1.39 by the latter year. As shall be seen, not only this fringe area but all other rurban fringe communities of the city experienced a similar relative decline in Factor I scores between 1947 and 1960, the result of their having remained fairly untouched by the heightened urbanity that was upgrading other parts of the city.

The unity of Community VI is rapidly splitting apart, and an analysis of the "natural areas" of Cairo in 1970 or later will probably show a total realignment of the constituent parts. The northern section of Imbābah will undoubtedly remain an "island" of poor proletariat, functionally and socially linked more with Būlāq across the river than with the bourgeois districts that increasingly encircle it. The rural section to its west will have been almost totally displaced by a lower-middle- and middle-class zone dominated by minimum standard cooperative housing, while, toward the river's shore, some of the zone will have been redeveloped and joined to the substantial middle-class district to its south.

At this point in time, however, the realignment is not nearly so obvious as the anomalies that exist in the district because of the close juxtaposition between the area's past and its future. One frequently sees a squatter's mudbrick hut wedged between modern apartment buildings; the elaborate villa of a prosperous engineer across the street from a primitive village; goats and sheep herded down the elegant, tree-lined street that borders the Nile. This juxtaposition, as sharp and jarring as it is, is of a highly transitional character. The residuals are doomed and passing quickly.

Community XI—The Transitional Zone of Osmosis

If, to the west, the Gold Coast must be mediated against the countryside by a Silver Coast, to the east of the core there is an even greater need for transition. The polar elements of Cairo urbanism are the Gold Coast on the one hand and the medieval city on the other. Thus, the belt between them must serve as both a divider and a binder. Upon it impinge the conflicting impulses toward upgrading and modernization that press from the west and the impulses of deterioration that pound equally persistently from the east; throughout it blend the two competing patterns in a juxtaposition that with the years grows less and less uneasy. Once Cairo was bifurcated into two cities and the twain rarely met, even in the absence of a true physical buffer; social distance substituted efficiently for physical barriers. Today, however, the city grows more and more into one cultural unit. As the Gold Coast becomes increasingly "baladized" and the medieval city becomes more modernized, the transitional belt between them—neither fish nor fowl—widens to mediate between the narrowing social contrast.

A transitional district is always difficult to delimit and even more difficult to describe, since its prime characteristic is flux. Lacking internal coherence and stability, it is to be known chiefly by its rate of change and the marginality of its functions. The only historical element that unifies Community XI is the fact that, with virtually few exceptions, the zone coincides with the area settled between the fourteenth and the late nineteenth centuries, whereas the two districts it connects were intensively settled either before or after.

At the extreme northern edge, the transitional zone serves to insulate the Westernized central business district of al-Tawfīqīyah from the slums of Bāb al-Sha'rīyah that encroach precipitously. Here formerly was the official prostitution district of the city but, since the withdrawal of official supervision and the suppression of the "trade," its former denizens have scattered in either direction—depending upon class—and other uses have taken over. Farther south around the northern fringes of the Azbakīyah Gardens were only slightly more salubrious tourist attractions—dealers in authentic and spurious antiquities as well as gaudy mementos of contemporary Egypt—which depended heavily upon the clientele stopping at Shepheard's Hotel facing the Gardens. Since the burning of Shepheard's, this area no longer attracts the "best customers," although the nearby Continental Hotel still survives, somewhat *déclassé*. Many of the shops followed the major hotels westward to the Nile and Garden City, leaving the tattered edge at Azbakīyah even more run down.

The Azbakīyah Gardens themselves have suffered a sad decline since their dramatic landscaping in 1869. Once they were an exclusive domain, fenced and with an admission charge, in which white-uniformed nannies paraded pampered babies, to which Europeans and those with European pretensions flocked to listen to the military band concerts, and in which exotic parrots and brilliant tropical birds chattered from their well-tended cages. The fences have long since been removed and the admission charge dropped, a highway has been cut through its center, and, with the recent decline of the surrounding section, the park too has deteriorated. The grass is no longer lovingly manicured. Large brown areas show through the green cover along the more heavily traversed short cuts. Noisy and garish *al fresco* cafés and an outdoor Arab theater have encroached upon the site; the bird cages are empty. Homeless or away-from-home men sleep during the hottest noon hours upon its once-elegant slopes, and whole families picnic where they please, dining on round loaves of brown bread and onions and discarding nut shells, watermelon rinds, and cucumber ends where they please. Due east of the Gardens, where the Garden Rosetti had once offered a promenade ground to the otherwise tightly cooped Franks of the Mūski, and which had remained partially open until near the turn of the twentieth century, was a portion of Cairo's first Westernized business district. This had become so decayed by midcentury that it was recently cleared and redeveloped by the municipality.

Farther south, at the tramway terminal and interchange of al-'Atabah al-Khaḍrā', one enters the heart of the transitional business district, the link between the Western shops and the Oriental *aswāq*. It is an unattractive mélange having neither the modernity of the Western zone nor the exotic charm of the Eastern bazaars: a place of crudely fashioned but brightly colored imitations of Western products, of odd assortments of second-hand plumbing pipes, old containers or coiled rubber hoses in disorganized display on pushcarts. Here, too, the redeveloper has been busy upgrading.

South of this business zone one moves into the bustling but dingy working-class area around the 'Abdīn Palace—part offices, part shoddy commercial establishments, part lower-middle-class residences. The mixed uses of the palace itself perhaps symbolize the odd cross-breeding of cultural influences in this zone. Part of the palace contains government offices and, in the enormous square outside it, where 'Urābi presented his grievances, cheering crowds hailed the political speeches of a more successful ex-colonel, President Nasser. Another part contains an archival library indispensable for historical scholarship, but in one of the gardens of the palace—at least for a brief time—was a casino and nightclub with entertainment and a belly-dancer. Such incongruity within the palace is mirrored in the surrounding quarter.

Beyond and even farther to the south one comes upon the quarters of al-Nāṣrīyah, Darb al-Jamāmīz, and Ḥilmīyah, areas whose development was delayed in part by the natural features of this low-lying area, formerly spotted by ponds. (The first and third quarters are actually located on the sites of filled *birak*.) Accommodated in these sections are numerous civil servants employed in the government ministries along the western perimeter and large numbers of children in the residential schools and orphanages that abound here.

The entire transitional belt occupies a status position somewhere between the polar cities it mediates. In 1947, the average of Factor I scores of the census tracts in this belt was +0.58. By 1960 it had altered only slightly to +0.63. (Compare these to the +2 scores typical in the Gold Coast and the —0.4 scores of the medieval city.) These averages, however, conceal a wide range of subtypes and the apparent constancy of the overall score conceals rather major changes in the status and relative positions of constituent census tracts. Dynamic homogenization rather than stability has been the dominant fact.

In 1947, this "zone between zones" exhibited wider ranges within it and a more crazy-quilt pattern than it did by 1960, indicating that the process of blending the preindustrial with the modern city has been taking place rapidly and consistently. Extreme differences are decreasing. In 1947, although most tracts in the zone had Factor I scores between +.25 and +.75, a few deviated widely from this norm both above and below, the range for the entire community spreading between a low point of —0.73 and a high of +1.92! A graph showing the distribution of scores in Community XI was very irregular in outline. By 1960, however, the same 31 census tracts in the district had Factor I scores that followed a rather smooth and narrow distribution curve.

This trend toward homogeneity can be traced through the changes in specific scores. Tracts that had been below the average for the district as a whole in 1947 tended to upgrade their populations (Factor I scores) between 1947 and 1960, whereas tracts that had been above average tended to decline during the same interval. Thus, of the sixteen census tracts with Factor I scores of +0.5 or over in 1947, only five improved between 1947 and 1960 while eleven declined. On the other hand, of the fifteen tracts with Factor I scores below +0.5 in 1947, twelve improved their relative standing between 1947 and 1960 while only three declined. It is significant that the rare exceptions (high-scoring tracts whose Factor I scores improved) were to be found just adjacent to the Westernized central business district of the Gold Coast, and in some cases at least their change in score could be directly attributed to a municipal redevelopment project. The exceptions at the opposite end (low-scoring tracts that declined) tended to be located at the eastern extremity next to the medieval city into which they were being incorporated.

Thus, the hypothesized and long-overdue transition is taking place. The enormous gulf between the indigenous quarters of traditional urban life and the initially alien modern quarters associated with the colonial incursion—so marked at the turn of the century—is finally being bridged in Community XI, a zone of transition in more than one sense of the term. It is safe to predict that, by the next census, an even more complete blending of the two social worlds will have been achieved.

THE SUBCITIES OF THE NEW NORTH

Five sector cities stretch northward, spreading apart like the fingers on a hand from their common origin at Azbakīyah, to form the star-shaped and transport-linked city of the north. The "bone" of each finger is a radial transportation thoroughfare leading out from the city's center. Along the waterfront is the linear city of Sāḥil Rawḍ al-Faraj, actually an elongated tail that increasingly confirms its functional continuity with Būlāq; it has therefore been combined with that subcity in this analysis. The other four communities of northern Cairo must be described here to complete our survey of the metropolitan region.

141. Grain in transit at Rawḍ al-Faraj near Sāḥil

Community II—Shubra, Lower-Middle-Class Mélange

Radiating northward from the rear of Cairo's major railroad station at Bāb al-Ḥadīd, roughly circumscribed on the west by Shāri' Abū al-Faraj and on the east by the barrier of a major railroad to the Delta, is the sector of the city known generically as Shubra. The district derives its name from the major transportation axis that bisects it, the Shāri' Shubra which formerly joined Muḥammad 'Ali's palace with Birkat al-Azbakīyah but which now serves an even more critical function in linking central Cairo with the outlying and relatively new industrial complexes at Shubra al-Balad and Shubra al-Khaymah. The reader will recall the gradual transformation of this royal road into a fashionable carriage promenade and then into a streetcar axis, all prior to its urban development. Until World War I the sector was still largely agricultural, except for the few palaces and elaborate villas exploiting the access provided by the highway and for the buildings left unfinished by the 1907 panic. However, once fastened upon by the refinanced real estate speculators and jerry-builders of the first quarter of the century, its transformation was rapid and total. By 1947 some 282,000 persons were living in Community II; by 1960 this number had almost doubled to 541,000.

The sector city of Shubra contains wider variations than are to be found in other neighboring subcommunities, in terms of socio-economic status, ethnic composition and housing types. In general, there is a declining gradient of urban structures, of percent Copts and of socio-economic rank as one moves outward from the central origin point near the train station. This gradient, how-

142. The undistinguished skyline of Shubra

143. A main thoroughfare in Shubra

144. A less urbane side street in Shubra

ever, is not always consistent and, furthermore, has been pushing outward as the interior zones deteriorate and as the peripheral sites are converted from agricultural to urban uses. Poorer population from the interior city has been supplanting the middle class at the core just as the decentralizing urban population continues to supplant farmers at the periphery.

Perhaps the most significant fact about Shubra is that it has been the favored residential quarter for Cairo's Copts for half a century, having been the logical geographic extension of the original Coptic quarter just north of the Azbakīyah. Although Copts constitute perhaps a tenth of the total population of Cairo, within the inlying census tracts of Shubra their representation climbs as high as 45 to 50 percent. Perhaps a third of the population residing in the sector subcity of Shubra are Egyptian Christians, and just as mosques dominate the skyline of Būlāq and the medieval city, so churches are equally conspicuous in inlying Shubra. In only one census tract out of the eleven that make up this district does the population not contain a significant number of Copts, and this exception is the one containing Minyat al-Sīrij, an ancient outlying village that has been the recent recipient of some industrial plants and associated public housing.

Shubra, because of its diversity, is difficult to describe in simple fashion. In general, as one travels along the major thoroughfare one gains the definite impression of prematurely deteriorated modern urbanism. A solid phalanx of tall apartment buildings, whose nondescript character cannot be adequately conveyed to a reader who has not seen this yellow-grey area of Cairo,[17] lines the street. One is assailed by a continuous cacophony from rumbling tramcars, listing, overcrowded buses, donkey carts delivering vegetables from the rich agricultural lands to the north, and too-loud radio programs from the multitude of open-to-the-street commercial establishments that usurp the first floor front of most buildings. Pedestrians, neither so thickly compressed nor so slow moving as in Būlāq, fill the rest of the landscape. In marked contrast to the bustle of Shāri' Shubra are the quieter but less urbane side streets. Within these are highly diversified subsections. Some contain dignified although still undistinguished apartment buildings whose shabby hallways give little hint of the middle-class apartments within. Others, however, have a more bucolic mien, resembling the better dwellings to be found in villages and small towns throughout Egypt rather than the nearer but more urban prototypes. The occupants' ways of life reveal a similarly wide range. Lower-middle-class Coptic clerks with a high regard for their respectability congregate in some subsections; in others, recent arrivals from the rural Delta have imposed upon the unyielding urban environment the needs and necessities nurtured by a village style of life.[18]

[17] Testimony perhaps to the absolute nondescript quality of Shubra is that, among my hundred or more photographs of various parts of Cairo, I have almost none to exemplify Shubra. This unfortunate state of affairs can be explained in large measure by the fact that the area, populous as it is, is virtually invisible. It has so common a face that a photographer never immortalizes it.

[18] In J. Abu-Lughod, "Migrant Adjustment to City Life: The Egyptian Case," *American Journal of Sociology*, volume 67 (July 1961), pp. 22-32, the methodological problems of identifying ports of entry and the basis for the presumption that a great many rural migrants gravitated into Shubra during World War II are presented in greater detail. These findings as they apply to Shubra might be briefly recapitulated here. Within that district is the Khāzindār bus terminal, the end of the line for the provincial

The scores of the census tracts of Shubra on Factor I, then, are averages of the diversity within the district and, as such, are less indicative of a single way of life than are the average scores of other subcommunities in the city. Nevertheless, they permit us to rank Shubra with respect to other parts of the city and to evaluate its functional role within the urban complex. In 1947 the average Factor I score for census tracts in the sector of Shubra was +0.65, identifying the zone as one of moderate status, somewhat better than the norm for the city as a whole but lagging far behind the true middle- and upper-class districts near the Nile and toward the desert edge at Heliopolis. By 1960 the average score for the zone had improved to +0.95. This increase appears to be due to two complementary but independent trends: a conversion at the periphery from rural to urban uses, which has meant a population supplementation if not total displacement of low-scoring farmers; and a gradual assimilation of the rural migrants who temporarily swelled Shubra's less savory subquarters during World War II and have now become better adjusted to urban life and more securely integrated into the urban economy.

Community III—A Northern Agricultural Wedge

Cutting deep into the asymmetrical city is a residual wedge of farmland to remind us that, until recently, the northern section of Cairo, although officially classified as urban by a then-overgenerous boundary, really faded off quite sharply into the granary of the Delta. In this wide swath of land, at least equal in area to all of Shubra which abuts it on the west, lying between two major railroads that rigidly define its peripheries, almost totally devoid of transportation links to the center city, lived close to 100,000 "Cairenes" in 1947 and over 200,000 in 1960, under conditions which, except in the more urbane portions of Sharābīyah and Maṭarīyah, approximated those of any rural area in Egypt. (Another exception, added too late to appreciably affect the statistical results recorded in the Census of 1960, is to be found in several large public housing projects that have recently been constructed by the municipality in this sector.)

buses that link Cairo with the towns of the Egyptian Delta. These buses were the main means whereby Delta migrants reached the city during the war boom of the early 1940's. If the locations of the migrant associations organized by these recent arrivals are used as an indirect index to where migrants first settled, we find that many must have remained very close to their port of entry, the bus terminal itself. In the early 1950's, eight village associations had addresses within a quarter of a mile of the terminal, and sixteen were found within a half-mile radius of it. It is significant that all of these were associations for Delta villages; none represented Upper Egyptian village associations. The addresses of the latter tended, on the other hand, to be concentrated in the southern portion of Cairo.

145. Rural-style housing in Community III, since replaced by public housing

Although most of the land is in agricultural use, the occupational characteristics of the resident population are somewhat more diversified. Some 10 percent of the employed men in the entire zone were listed as full-time agriculturalists in the Census of 1947, a proportion that had declined to under 4 percent by 1960. On the other hand, most of the women with "occupations" (other than housewives) were listed as being engaged in farming, and many of the men were undoubtedly part-time agriculturalists in addition to their other employment. The railroads and railyards that define the limits of the district also offered major employment opportunities to the men. These have been supplemented in more recent years by the new industrial plants built and run by the government, which have attracted some of the residents to industrial employment.

The shift from agriculture to industry is easily documented. Despite the fact that population in the sector doubled between 1947 and 1960, the number of full-time agriculturalists actually declined. The number of industrial workers, on the other hand, doubled to match the population growth. This indicates a gradual transformation in the functions of this zone, but the transformation, except in the new public housing projects, is not yet evident either in housing characteristics or in style of life. Indeed, as the urban quality of the inlying areas of Cairo has improved over the years, all fringe areas, including this northern one, have declined relative to the improving norm. In 1947, the average score on Factor I for census tracts in this sector was −1.35; by 1960, despite the industrialization already evident in the zone, this score had dropped to −1.56. This does not necessarily mean that the zone deteriorated in the interval. Rather, it improved at a slower rate than most other sections of the city, thus leaving it farther behind in the race toward modernity.

Despite the involvement of many of the area's men in the expanding urban economy, the dominant way of life in this subcity has not yet altered much; it still remains closer to the rural than the urban mode. This can be recognized most easily by comparing the district with Būlāq, the not-too-distant urban slum, on two of the dimensions of differentiation. The zone ranks considerably below the urban slum quarter on Factor I, suggesting that illiteracy is almost universal, especially among the women, that it is only a rare child who is fortunate enough to attend school for any length of time if at all, that marriages are entered into at extremely early ages, and that large families are the norm. On the other hand, most of the *urban* forms of social disorganization, such as divorce, undisguised unemployment, and attractiveness to handicapped dependents, are relatively absent from this zone. The scores on Factor III (measuring relative "social disorganization") of census tracts in the agricultural wedge are considerably below those of the Būlāq census tracts, suggesting that while poverty may be more extreme on the periphery, its devastations are mitigated by a tightly organized social structure, in much the same way that the villages of Egypt, despite their physical deprivations, manage to maintain a stable and controlled social environment.

The future of this residual wedge is uncertain. Recognizing the need to assure sufficient truck-gardening activity to supply the growing metropolis with its daily requirements, and desiring to limit the physical sprawl of the urban area, the chief planner of Cairo has recommended that a greenbelt be established—a move that would protect this agricultural wedge, among other areas, from further urban encroachments.[19] On the other hand, the Ministry of Industry has tended to favor this zone, which is so well served by rail-lines and so temptingly open, for the construction of large-scale industrial plants, even when housing for employees must be provided as an adjunct to the plants. Given the conflict between the two goals, only political processes will determine the future disposition of the zone. Nevertheless, with the present stress on industrialization, it is very probable that industrial uses will usurp more and more of the agricultural land and that this sector city will eventually become the primary site of heavy industry and associated housing developments for industrial workers. It is perhaps appropriate that the city of the north, conjured into existence as it were at the beginning of Egypt's industrial age, should become the scene for the country's final mastery over modern industrialism. This quarter seems destined to pass from agrarianism to modern urbanism without going through the intermediate steps required in other parts of the city.

146. Rural-style housing in Community III, still not replaced

Community IV—A Strip City of the Urban Working Class

This city consists in reality of an elongated string of settlements (now almost continuous) that clustered one by one along the major transportation axis radiating to the northeast, toward the distant canal cities with which Cairo is linked by both a desert highway and a railroad.

147. Transition from rural to urban ways

[19] Conversations with Mr. Muḥammad Ḥāfiẓ 'Ali, Head of the Planning Subsection, Governorate of Cairo, during the summer of 1965. Some of his proposals to establish a greenbelt on the English pattern are contained in his publications. See, for example, his paper presented at a conference in Cairo in May, 1965, entitled *Al-Takhṭīṭ al-Ḥāli li Madīnat al-Qāhirah wa Ittijāhāt al-Mustaqbalah* [Contemporary Planning for the City of Cairo and its Future Trends] (mimeo., Cairo: *ca.* 1965).

148-149. Along the major axis

The subcity includes, as one moves outward from the point of origin, the settlements known as al-Wāyli, al-Dimirdāsh, Manshīyat al-Ṣadr, Qubbah, Qubbah Gardens, Kūbri al-Qubbah, Zaytūn, Ḥilmīyat al-Zaytūn, and finally, 'Ain Shams (where once, when it was the site of ancient Heliopolis, Plato had come to learn the wisdom of Egypt). While a few of these nuclei existed as villages or royal outposts before the present century, the process of conurbation and the gradual integration of the area with the central city were definitely twentieth-century developments contingent upon the electric tram and Metro lines installed there during the opening decades of the century.

Perhaps the most revealing fact about this strip city is the remarkable degree to which the census tracts that comprise it have Factor I scores clustering *at the dead center* of the distribution. If one were to look for an area representative of the theoretical "norm" or average for Cairo, one would find it here in this solid working-class zone in which some 187,000 Cairenes lived in 1947. In that year, the average Factor I score of the census tracts in the subcity was —0.10. Despite the fact that between 1947 and 1960 the area more than doubled its population, housing some 456,000 residents by the latter year, the community evidently selected its new population in the image of its existing residents, for in 1960 the average Factor I score of tracts in the zone was still —0.08.

But what does it mean to say that an area lies at the mid-range of the distribution as measured by its style of life scores? It certainly means more than saying that the area is what the "city as a whole" would be, if all its extremes were averaged! In ways, this community at dead center is the *bench mark* against which the deviations of other districts of Cairo, whether above or below, can be gauged. In ways, it is the *standard* of contemporary Cairo, against which one can estimate how much above par are the more elegant districts, how much below par are the slums, both rural and urban.

A problem which inevitably plagues cross-cultural comparative research is that the standards of the observer impinge upon the subject matter to distort judgment and even perception. This certainly occurs when the Western scholar tries to understand a phenomenon so different from his relevant experience as Cairo. To most Western observers (including myself when I first began to investigate the quarters of Cairo), the district here classified as solid working class would seem to be a slum; in many respects it is an Oriental version of such well-known prototypes as the South Side of Chicago, the Lower East Side or Upper Harlem of New York, the North End of Boston, or Bethnal Green of London—in short, any urban slum in an industrialized nation. The streets, although paved, are inadequately cleaned, and rubbish tends to accumulate more quickly than it can be cleared; children engage in their traditional rowdy street games, kicking cans, stones, or other ball-substitutes and hazarding accidents with cars and passers-by; tall buildings with walk-up flats or out-of-order elevators force unintended encounters; and windows opening on airshafts in tenement-type structures yield an auditory intimacy that permits one to follow in close detail the family squabbles of the neighbors. Children are admonished or called to dinner by mothers who lean over the edges of narrow balconies to signal them. The grocer across the street receives his orders by similar shouts. Whole conversations may be carried on at high pitch by neighbors with adjoining or opposing balconies, and one may often view through the open balcony doors of the flat across the street the life of a neighbor, as if it were being performed on a stage set. Meals are not particularly regular nor are the members of the household unvarying; whoever happens to be present at mealtime is fed; whoever happens to be there at nightfall is offered a mattress to sleep on. A kind of casual, noisy, sometimes violent but often just exuberant spirit fills the air—a quality that for hundreds of years in

150. Traditional and modern clothing coexist

151. Traditional goats herded in front of modern housing

152. Old and new façades intermixed

various parts of the globe has alternately attracted and repelled middle-class investigators and social workers. It is this quality that unites the district, for all the superficial distinctiveness of its odors and dress, with lower-class working districts throughout the world.

But these qualities and this way of life do not make Community IV a slum. The housing is too solid and the occupancy rates, although in excess of Western standards, are moderate in comparison with Būlāq, the medieval city, or Miṣr al-Qadīmah. The people, also, are too close to the middle of a pyramid of social status in Cairo to be classified as slum residents. Their educational level is not high, it is true, but neither is the average for the city as a whole. Their families are not small, granted, but neither could the typical Cairene family (average size 4.7 persons) be characterized as small by Western standards. In fact, on almost every variable, except the percent Muslims, which is higher in these census tracts than in the city as a whole, the rates found in this zone come very close to the overall average for the city. Again, quite typically, education is highly valued and a technical skill is much admired as a passport to security—but these values are chiefly projected onto the younger generation rather than applied personally to the parental one. Semi-skilled is the dominant labor force classification of workers living in this area. Commerce, industry, and services absorb most workers (scarcely any are in agriculture, despite the proximity to the fringe) and, although the data do not reveal at what levels, the likelihood of their being in the white-collar or managerial peaks of these industrial categories is slim indeed. The break with rural origins, however, has already been made by the residents of this zone, although they may occasionally receive relatives from the countryside, either as visitors or as new migrants whom they guide over the first hurdles of the urban transition.

It is here more than elsewhere in the city that one finds the crucible in which the Cairo of tomorrow—maturing beyond the ethnic fissions and life style ex-

153. The Heliopolis Cathedral and its upper-middle-class environs in Miṣr al-Jadīdah

tremes of yesterday—is being forged. Here, clerks, mechanics, electricians, and machine operators may live side by side with and even in the same extended family households as petty proprietors and simple workmen who follow older ways of making a living and more time-honored modes of involvement and association. The future, however, lies with the former. It is the emerging world of modern urbanism that serves as the focus for future orientations. While retaining emotional ties both with the past and with village Egypt, their goals and aspirations—of better jobs, of social mobility for their children, of advantageous marriages—are centered upon Cairo, their city of birth or adoption. A student of evolving Egyptian society would be wise to study this area, and perhaps the rest of the northern city as well, if he would understand some of the goals and problems of that society in transition.

Community V—A Sector City of the Old and New Middle Class

The final of our thirteen "cities within the city" is the large bulbous appendage to the northeast that consists of Heliopolis at the extreme, linked by a narrow thread with the northern edge of al-Azbakīyah from which it expanded sectorally. This zone parallels the working-class city (Community IV) in direction and shape, but lies south, rather than north, of the main route to the Canal. It is an extensive and fast-growing middle-class city—no small achievement in a society that is still filling in the middle ranks of its class pyramid, formerly so unevenly divided into an aloof elite and a massive peasant-proletariat.

Just as the middle class carved for itself a place in the social structure, so also it carved for its own use a residential quarter out of the desert limits of the city. A very narrow band connects this primarily peripheral district with its origin at the western business district but, with the exception of the few census tracts that constitute this connection, the remaining settlements all have in common a sharp border at the desert. Thus, although the district has, legally speaking, an area of over 40 square kilometers, much of it has still not been reclaimed from the desert. The actual functional and developed portion in which 172,000 persons resided in 1947 and 261,000 lived in 1960 is concentrated along the most interior strip abutting Community IV.

For those familiar with the neighborhoods of Cairo, much will be conveyed when it is noted that this middle-class district includes the census tracts of al-Ẓāhir and al-Fajjālah, skirts al-Wāyli to include the Faculty of Law Campus of 'Ain Shams University, takes in the new apartment house district at 'Abbāsīyah, includes Naṣr City, the new community now being reclaimed from the desert, as well as Heliopolis proper (Miṣr al-Jadīdah, the New Cairo), the prototype city that had been planned in similar fashion half a century earlier. The zone, while definitely of high status and prestige, was never particularly favored by the extremely rich, except by a minority who sought extensive sites on which to construct palatial single-family residences. And, despite its "foreign" origin, it never was quite as exclusive as the Gold Coast. With the exception of the older baronial halls and hotels and now a sprinkling of neat villas, the district, like most of Cairo, is dominated by multi-family flats. Unlike many other parts of Cairo, however, the apartments are spacious, newer, and more modern in design. Both the older middle class (disproportionately either Copt or foreign of Mediterranean rather than northern European origin) and the rising middle class (technocrats, among whom Muslim Egyptians are proportionately better represented) have mixed freely in this zone, although the older middle class tends to be concentrated in the interior portions while the newer middle class—latecomer to the zone—tends to be concentrated in the more peripheral sections.

In 1947 the average Factor I score of tracts in this subcity was +1.8, indicating that the zone deviated from the "norm" quite markedly, although it still ranked below the Gold Coast. By 1960 this average score declined somewhat to +1.5, although its relative rank among the thirteen subcommunities remained second. This decline, like that experienced even more drastically in the Gold Coast, could be attributed largely to the departure of the foreign communities of Cairo, already noted above. While a direct measure for this is lacking, the phenomenon can be partially traced in the decline of non-Muslims as a percentage of census tract population. Whereas in 1947, Muslims had constituted between 33 and 92 percent of the populations in the census tracts of Community V, by 1960 the range had shifted to between 42 and 94 percent. The median was 63 percent in 1947; 73 in 1960.

Despite the rather high representation of Christians and foreigners in this zone, however, the style of life—the dominant "tone" of this area—is set by the upper-middle-class Egyptian who has not been as alienated from his native identity as his francophile and somewhat more "sophisticated" counterpart in the Gold Coast. The

154. Roxy, the central business district of Heliopolis

old domestic virtues are highly prized here; social gatherings are still largely segregated by sex, even where there is no attempt to enforce such separation; kinship involvements still dominate leisure-time use; and eating is an organizing principle of life (although drinking alcoholic beverages remains an anathema). In this zone, possibly more so than any other, one sees symbolized the new aspirations of contemporary Egypt (perhaps this is one reason it has been favored by the elite of military officers), and one begins to discern the outlines of potential synthesis. It is apparent that this new synthesis will not simply ape the West in uncritical and uncomfortable fashion, even though competition for Paris-styled dresses executed by local seamstresses may be intense in the female gatherings and Parker pens the equal sign of prestige among the men. Nor will it reject out of hand what Western technology, now becoming Egyptian technology as well, has to offer. Rather, it will tend to extract the technological conveniences of industrial society (flush toilets, refrigerators, semi-automatic washing machines, television sets) from their value contexts and adapt them to indigenously defined goals.

Substantial confirmation of the modern as well as middle-class status of the district's residents is found in their occupational characteristics. They are almost exclusively engaged in commerce or professional services, with a high proportion occupying managerial and white-collar positions in both private and public enterprises. The zone's ability to attract members of the growing bureaucracy will probably intensify even more as the governmental ministries are progressively relocated in Naṣr City and as business uses further decentralize to serve the fast-growing peripheral quarters. And given the goals of the New Egypt, this zone cannot help but profit from some of the residual onus which still clings to its chief rival, the Gold Coast. A final factor that should assure continued growth is the relatively recent appearance of the private family car—formerly a monopoly of the very rich as carriages had once been of the royalty—as part of the market basket of consumer goods demanded and now more and more attained by Cairo's middle class. All peripheral zones should profit from this new release from the iron shackles that once bound developments to the streetcar tracks.

SOME BRIEF GENERALIZATIONS

The population of Cairo, diversified as it is, can be divided roughly into three main types—each following the tune of a different piper and each with a somewhat different prospect for the future. These three types are distributed within the metropolitan region according to a geographic pattern which is intimately connected with the past history of urban development in Cairo and which, for all its flux, shows a remarkable degree of persistence and reinforcement.

The three types that coexist within Cairo may be identified as (1) the rural; (2) the traditional urban; and (3) the modern or industrial urban.[20] Rather than being arranged stably on a single dimension or continuum, the first two types represent independent points of origin—both of which existed in preindustrial Cairo—which have been converging by different paths toward the new and third type, the emergent form of modern urbanism which, while it differs radically from the past, still retains enough distinctive features to differentiate Cairo from a Western metropolis. Each of the thirteen subcities of Cairo that has been delineated in this chapter approximates one of these three "models" or types, either in relatively pure form or in varying degrees of mixture.

Residuals of a rural way of life still remain in the present-day city, although these are gradually becoming less obvious as they become increasingly confined to peripheral quarters. It should be remembered that as recently as 1877, according to Ismā'īl's admittedly inaccurate Muqābalah survey, some 57 percent of Cairo's economically active population was engaged in farming; the remaining workers were absorbed in traditional crafts, administration, personal services, or brute labor, for the modern sector had not yet appeared. Some thirty years later the number of farmers within Cairo was still impressive, but, due to the growth of the city's population, they represented only about a tenth of the male labor force. Since that time there has been a steady decrease in the number of city residents engaged exclusively in agricultural work, and today, less than 3 percent of the city's males list themselves as full-time farmers.

Nevertheless, the break with rural patterns is far from complete. In the four peripheral or fringe communities

TABLE 8. THE COMMUNITIES OF CAIRO IN 1947 AND 1960

Communities Grouped by Type	Average Factor I Scores		Total Population in thousands[b]		Perc of To Popula	
	1947	1960	1947	1960	1947	1
Rural Fringes						
North (III)	−1.35	−1.56	100	200	11	
West (VI)	−1.08	−1.39	60	150		
Cemetery (IX)	−0.78	−1.54	50	90		
South (XIII)	−1.55	−1.84	23	42		
Interior Slums						
Būlāq (I)	−0.70	−0.35	267	350	37	
Medieval (X)	−0.38[a]	−0.37	391	474		
Miṣr al-Qadīmah (XII)	−0.45[a]	−0.54	103	188		
Urban Working Class—Low						
Zaytūn (IV)	−0.10	−0.08	187	456	9	
Urban Middle						
Transition (XI)	+0.58	+0.63	293	362	31	
Shubra (II)	+0.65	+0.95	282	541		
Silver Coast (VIII)	+0.68	+1.18	55	220		
Upper Middle or Better						
Heliopolis (V)	+1.80	+1.48	172	261	11	
Gold Coast (VII)	+2.18	+1.97	65	82		

[a] Several tracts omitted from computation, as noted in text.
[b] Total population as rounded and as used to compute percen is 2,048,000 in 1947. This is smaller than the official census tota the city due to elimination of several census tracts and roundin subtotals. Total population as rounded is 3,416,000 in 1960. Th different from the official census total because of changes in boun elimination of several census tracts, and the rounding of subtota
[c] Adds to less than 100 percent due to rounding.

identified by our analysis lived some 11 percent of the total population in 1947 and 14 percent in 1960 (see Table 8). While most of these residents were *not* agriculturalists, their ways of life were little differentiated, except perhaps by the occupation of adult males, from those typically found in the hinterland. Not only has ruralism persisted in these peripheral quarters but it has continually been reinfused even into the most interior quarters of the city by a continuous stream of migration. At least during the present century (for which we have records) and probably before that as well (for which records are lacking), about one-third of Cairo's population has consisted of persons born outside the city, primarily in villages. It would be unusual indeed if these migrants failed to influence the nature of life in the city by the patterns and needs they brought with them. Acculturation has been a continuing process, but even as yesterday's migrants blend, their places are more than filled by today's newcomers. While the proportion of migrants remains relatively constant, the absolute number to be absorbed has gone up drastically. And again, since the city has modernized much faster than have the villages, the gap between culture of origin and culture of

[20] See J. Abu-Lughod, "Varieties of Urban Experience: Contrast, Coexistence and Coalescence in Cairo," in *Middle Eastern Cities*, ed. Ira Lapidus (University of California Press, Berkeley: 1969), pp. 159-187.

destination has widened rather than decreased. All these factors suggest a continued although declining role for ruralism in Cairo.

Traditional urbanism, the second model that survives in today's Cairo, is even more important to an understanding of the city than ruralism, for it still guides the lives of a substantial proportion of the city's contemporary residents. While there can be no absolute definition of "traditionalism" applicable equally to all cultures, the meaning of the term within the Egyptian context is clear. It refers primarily to the persistence of economic activities, forms of social relationships, and systems of values which were once typical within the Cairo of a hundred years ago but which, since the advent of the twentieth century at least, have been increasingly challenged by newer ways of organizing production and sale, regulating identity and behavior, and setting definitions for the "good life."

Neither the "traditional" nor the "modern," as we have used these terms, is to be thought of as an invariant or unchanging "given"; rather, each lies at opposite ends of a continuum whose locus and range shift with societal changes. The traditional of today is not the preindustrial pattern of medieval times; it merely represents a much-metamorphosed set of survivals, adapted to the modern world, which demonstrates elements which one expects to become less and less vital as the city changes. The modern "type," as well, has a similarly relative meaning. When the modern sector of the economy first began to develop in Egypt, it was somewhat extraneous to the indigenous society, even though it had a significant impact upon the ecology of the city. To be modern meant, at that time, to be "foreign," either by origin or pretension. This meaning has changed over the years as the structure of Egyptian society has changed. Certainly by the 1920's, Egyptian participation in the modern sector of Cairo's economy was already established and, during the ensuing period, the role of foreigners and minority groups declined steadily. Today one can say quite easily that to be modern is to be no less Egyptian, as that identity is increasingly coming to be conceived and defined. The distinction—once ethnic and cultural—has now become one of technology, values, and socio-economic status, for the correlation between participation in the modern sector of the economy and the enjoyment of its greater material rewards is incontrovertible.[21] One of the major prerequisites for participation in the modern economy is, of course, education, which proved so sensitive an indicator of life style in our factor analysis. Education in turn provides the employment and therefore the income necessary to maintain housing standards that were another critical index to life style, and undoubtedly also influences the patterns of family life (later marriage, smaller families) associated with the style of life in Cairo called "modern."

According to these definitions, the heart of traditional urbanism in Cairo lies in the three interior slums that occupy land with the longest history of settlement: the medieval city, Būlāq, and Miṣr al-Qadīmah. While not all residents of these communities are "old urbanites" with a lineage to the Middle Ages (in fact, a sizeable minority have but recently come from the villages to occupy some of the lowest ranks), and while not all the residents are involved in the traditional enterprises concentrated in these zones, if there are transfigured remnants of premodernism still surviving in Cairo, they are chiefly to be found in these older quarters which, in 1947, contained some 37 percent of the total population of the city and in 1960, despite their inevitable decline, still some 30 percent.

Modern urbanism, on the other hand, is equally evident in the upper-income zones of Heliopolis and the Gold Coast, where the skilled managers and members of the liberal professions who operate on the growing edge of "modern development" in Egypt reside. In 1947 some 11 percent of Cairo's population lived in these distinctively modern quarters, a percentage that had declined to 9 by 1960, partly due to the exodus of foreigners but partly due also to the fact that these zones were no longer the *only* ones favored by the modernized segments of the population. As the base of modernism has broadened, so the quarters touched by its wand have grown more numerous. Much of the Silver Coast now shares qualities which formerly were to be found almost exclusively in the Gold Coast or Heliopolis.

[21] One rather sensitive index of modernization, at least in the field of economic activity, is the scale of operations. Just as preindustrial commerce and industry were organized around the family-sized firm, so modern enterprises tend to achieve their economies by increasing the average size of the establishment. I have computed, from data available in several tables included in *Annuaire Statistique, 1960/1961*, the rank correlation coefficient between the average number of workers per establishment and the average weekly wages paid in Egypt in January 1959 for 25 industry groups for which this information could be assembled. The Spearman rank correlation coefficient was +0.77, indicating a close association between scale and remuneration. Inspection of the rank order of industries by size confirms the distinction I have been drawing between the modern and traditional sectors of the economy. The largest firms were in industries such as electricity and gas, water, sanitation, extraction and processing of petroleum and its derivatives. At the bottom of the list, both in size and wage level, were such traditional industries as woodworking, extraction of stone and sand, leather processing and products, and the industries of food and beverages. In my "Varieties of Urban Experience: Contrast, Coexistence and Coalescence in Cairo," *loc.cit.*, more detailed estimates are presented on the differential involvement of Cairo's labor force in the modern and traditional sectors.

The rest of Cairo's population resides in the remaining communities where traditionalism and modernism still coexist somewhat uneasily. In each, however, the blend is in different proportions and in all the amalgam itself undergoes daily transformation. Especially in the working-class zone of Zaytūn and the lower-middle- to middle-class communities of Shubra, the transitional belt, and, to a lesser extent, the Silver Coast, the modern and the traditional remain intimately intertwined, even within the same families. A middle synthesis is being sought which holds the key to Cairo's future.

Physically, each of these subcities mediates between and modulates the contrasting worlds that flank it. Internally, as well, each contains contrasts which are due in part to generational changes, in part to shifts in upward social mobility, and in part to differences in place of birth or origin. The middle class is now embarking on drastic social change, and in these "grey" areas which the middle class calls home, both rural and traditional roots are being exchanged for the modern future promised by the Revolution. The dreams being nurtured here, the pains that are being felt as the price of change, and the conflicts that are being resolved by this group most caught in the cultural cross-currents now alive in Cairo, preview those which will beset an increasing number of Egyptians as their society is transformed by modernization. These zones are "transitional" in more than a physical sense. They are likely to represent more and more the Cairo of tomorrow. The student of that future city would be wise indeed to examine them with care.

This chapter has described the nature of Cairo today as she securely enters the age of industrial urbanism. While she has traveled far from her genesis as military-administrative outpost between river and desert, certain recurrent functions have unified her progress. Early in history she added to her initial function of defense that of commercial emporium, exploiting her strategic position at the crossroads between the African interior and the Mediterranean coast, and then later her site at the even more important nexus between Europe and the Orient. Since the time of the Fāṭimids she has also periodically served as the central governmental seat for important empires that extended far beyond the traditional limits of Egypt, the river valley region insulated by deserts. During the Fāṭimid, Ayyūbid, and Mamluk eras, the wealth of these empires was distilled to support her function as center of production and consumption. Even through the darkest days of Ottoman subjugation, when both commerce and control contracted, she kept alive a tradition of preindustrial urbanism, supporting an urban population which, while reduced in size from previous peaks, could never be dismissed as insubstantial. With the economic revival of Egypt in the nineteenth century, Cairo again played a role as consumption center and, after the opening of the Suez Canal, she again began to benefit from Egypt's key geographic position. Most recently, Egypt's political independence and her growing influence within the Arab world have enhanced the city's role as ideological and cultural center, while the current strides in industrial development have again restored to the city her function as productive center.

Throughout, Cairo's condition has been tied to the wider fate of Egypt and its surrounding region and to the central fact of Egyptian existence, the Nile. The changes now taking place in Cairo, vastly different as they may be from the past, are still linked to the country and the river. The new industrialization, which will have so marked an impact upon future development of the metropolitan region, is a national not a local policy and depends on the electric power generated by a harnessed Nile no less than the agricultural wealth of this ancient granary once depended upon its unfettered flood. Furthermore, many of the new industries depend for their raw materials upon expanding agricultural production for which the measured distribution of irrigation waters remains essential. Industrial Cairo, no less than preindustrial Cairo, retains a peculiar symbiotic relationship to the river basin economy of Egypt.

The Cairo that these new developments are ushering in will undoubtedly be a different city from the Cairo of the past or even today, but I cannot believe that the cultural and geopolitical continuity, sustained for more than 1,000 years of the city's existence, will suddenly be severed in the industrial age. The paradox of unchanging nature in the face of continual change finds an important illustration in Cairo. Nevertheless, many of the problems which the city faced during earlier moments in her history have been or are being solved. Parts of her heritage even now grow weaker and move closer to extinction. In their place are new problems and a new heritage, the broad outlines of which can already be discerned on the horizon. That significant improvements will occur in her material existence can readily be predicted. Whether this newer level of technical achievement will necessarily lead to greater convenience and a more satisfying social existence still remains problematical. Certainly, the examples of Western metropolitan centers which have preceded Cairo down the path to industrial urbanism offer at best only ambiguous answers.

13 Whither the City: A Prognosis

By 1975 the population of Cairo should exceed 7 million—excluding the residents in the northern industrial periphery at Shubra al-Khaymah and in that integral part of the metropolitan complex lying on the west bank of the Nile. This projection is conservative, being based upon an estimated annual growth rate of only 4 percent, an increment more and more easily assured by the rising rate of natural increase in the city, even in the absence of massive migration. In common with all previous projections of Cairo's growth, our estimate is likely to err in the direction of undercount. The actual population will be *no less*, short of unpredictable acts of God, but may be considerably more.

By that year Cairo will contain more than one-sixth (ca. 17 percent) of Egypt's population of 40 million; the metropolitan region as a whole may account for almost one out of every five Egyptians. Planning the living environment for so great a proportion of the country's population must, therefore, be a critical part of Egypt's plans for development, if she is to achieve her goals of sustained economic growth, higher income, and better living conditions. There is yet another reason why plans for the city cannot be separated from plans for the country. Cairo plays a dominant role in the modern economy, concentrating within her orbit much of the production, most of the communications, and virtually all of the coordinative networks that increasingly direct development. And from among her population are drawn much of the brawn and virtually all of the brains that run the modern economy. Although many of the latter may have been born in the hinterlands, they now live in Cairo and identify with that city, even when temporarily assigned elsewhere. Together with the twin magnet of Alexandria, Cairo represents an even more important fraction of Egypt than population alone would indicate.[1]

Perhaps in reaction against the previous exploitative role of the capital as the center of alien dominance, there has been a certain reluctance—which now seems to be passing—to give the city her due. For too long the countryside represented the Egypt of the Egyptians, whereas Cairo symbolized a parasitic growth whose conspicuous consumption was achieved through conscienceless mulcting of the *fallāḥīn*.[2] There existed an ambivalence—a pride in the greatness of Cairo but also a rejection of her symbolic association with "the government." Even after the revolutionary regime succeeded in making that government indigenous, some residual ambivalence remained. Improvements in the city were viewed suspiciously as luxuries which ought to be postponed until the farmers, who for too long had been totally overlooked and who still constitute the overwhelming majority of Egyptians, had been aided through preferential treatment. This early ideology has apparently now given way to a more balanced view. City and countryside are seen not so much as competitors as symbiotic outlets for balanced investment, the welfare of each dependent ultimately upon the other.[3] The city is too critical a link in the plans for economic development to be slighted for ideological reasons, the grounds for which, in fact, no longer exist.

Just as Cairo has become more rather than less important to the whole with every advance in Egypt's industrialization, so within the city itself a similar shift has been occurring which confers upon the modern quarters of Cairo increasing importance, as socio-economic development proceeds. In 1917, according to my estimates, only about 15 percent of the city's labor force was involved in the modern sector of the dual economy, and that insignificant proportion consisted largely of foreigners or Egyptians of minority status. By 1960 the balance had shifted so far that almost half of the labor force

[1] Some impressive figures have been compiled by the Egyptian economist, Saʿīd al-Najjār. See his "An Economic Analysis of the Metropolis," in *The New Metropolis in the Arab World*, ed. Morroe Berger (Allied Publishers, New Delhi and New York: 1963), pp. 142-165. For example, in 1957 Cairo consumed 48.3 percent of all the electric power in Egypt, in 1954 contained 39 percent of all establishments for gross trade, in 1960 accounted for 52.3 percent of all privately owned telephones in the country. Cairo, together with Jīzah and Qalyūbīyah, parts of her metropolitan sphere of dominance, accounted for 44 percent of industrial employment and 34 percent of "value added" in Egypt in 1957 (for firms employing a minimum number of workers). An analysis of the five-year plans for economic development, prepared by Alphonse Said and presented in mimeographed form to the same conference, indicated continued if not more intensive concentration of industrial development in Cairo.

[2] The generality of this phenomenon is suggested in Bert Hoselitz, "Generative and Parasitic Cities," *Economic Development and Cultural Change*, Volume 3 (April 1955), pp. 278-294.

[3] Some of this ambivalence and a major step beyond it is illustrated in a paper by the former head of Egypt's Higher Planning Institute, Ibrahim Hilmi Abdel-Rahman, "Relations between Urban and National Planning," in *The New Metropolis*, pp. 189-209. His concluding remarks (p. 209) represent a sophisticated view of the dilemma. "The physical problems of city planning, including space, design, transport and amenities, are not to be neglected but the country's resources and capacity for development must be the ultimate determinants. . . . It is only then that the modern city in Egypt will be able to execute its functions in a satisfactory manner."

of the city could be described as participating in the modern sector. By 1970, this should comprise some two-thirds of the working force.[4] Furthermore, most of Cairo's population already lives in quarters of the city that date from the present century. By 1970 the proportion living in the oldest zones should be no more, and probably less, than one-fourth. While the need to replan and perhaps preserve these sections remains great, it is also true that the need to service adequately the newer quarters and to preplan zones even now being converted from rural to urban uses grows more pressing.

The combined impact of these two trends—the higher percentage of Egyptians concentrating in Cairo and the larger percentage of Cairenes involved in the modern economy and residing in the zones of recent settlement—makes what happens in Cairo a prime test of what will eventually happen in the rest of the country. If Cairo is Egypt's showpiece to the world, she is also Egypt's testing ground for the future. What trials has she faced thus far and how has she sought to meet their challenge?

While others might compile a somewhat different list, it appears to me that several types of problems have salience at this juncture in the city's history. First, how can a metropolis of such great magnitude, occupying so central a position in the entire economy and power structure, be governed—especially in the face of its traditional lack of corporate identity and its prior inexperience in self-determination? Second, how in a situation of extremely limited financial resources and heightened competition between industrial investment and urban overhead can the city be kept from deteriorating to a dangerous point, in the face of the heavy demands which its rapidly increasing population places on housing, utilities, transport, and other public facilities? Third, given the present decision to depend upon public rather than private investment, how can major development and redevelopment be planned for and executed in the sphere of city building—traditionally the cumulative product of a multitude of private consumption-investments? Fourth, to what extent should housing—especially for low-income groups—be given priority in public investments, in view of the already severe housing shortage and the continued immigration from rural areas where housing standards fall far below those for urban areas? And finally, is there any way to deal with the problem of urban growth in Cairo that could maximize both Cairo's capacity to cope with her short-run problems of congestion and Egypt's future capacity to develop balanced regional economies?

Each of these questions has been the focus of study and debate in Egypt, and it would therefore be presumptuous for me to offer solutions or advice. The purpose of this chapter is more modest. I shall attempt to chronicle here some of the approaches explicitly attempted or implicitly espoused in Cairo's most recent efforts to deal with problems which will continue to challenge her in the years to come.

Within the past two decades considerable progress has been made in providing Cairo with greater control over her destiny and in assembling within a single administrative framework the multitude of separate agencies for decision-making which previously had been uncoordinated and diffused. The era of the private concession has been brought to a close. These separate empires of municipal servicing have finally been made a part of the city, responsible and hopefully more responsive to the overall needs of the community. This process was well under way even before the Revolution of 1952, which merely completed the task. For example, in 1947 when the concession of Lebon et Cie. expired, the government took over the company's installations for electric light, power, and gas within the Cairo District and has since operated the utility through a special administration.[5] The Cairo Water Works is similarly administered under the municipality and, while it has its own budget, this is subject to approval by the Cairo Council. Most recently, the transportation system of the city, which until 1956 still remained under the control of foreign concessionaires, became a nationalized concern under government and, most recently, army supervision.

With the elimination of the foreign concessions which since their inception had made decisions with important implications for city development within a goal context of private profit rather than public welfare, the door was opened to rational overall planning of the city's utilities and public services. This has, however, merely shifted rather than eliminated the arena of conflict. While the conflict between profits and general welfare has been resolved, it has been supplanted by a political conflict between the demands of local subareas for preferential treatment and technical evaluations of overall system requirements. In the absence of dispassionate planning the danger always exists that political power will be used as a new currency in place of monetary strength.[6]

[4] These estimates are my own and are extremely crude. They are based upon an analysis of labor force data in the censuses of Cairo and upon assignment of various industry groups (and their labor forces) to the modern *vs.* traditional sectors. Although I have detailed tables, I am simply making a rough approximation here.

[5] *Overseas Economic Surveys: Egypt, October 1951* (His Majesty's Stationery Office, London: 1952), p. 13.

[6] In a meeting of the Cairo Council which I attended in the summer of 1965, pressure was being exerted by the elected representatives of certain outlying districts of Cairo to have utility lines extended to constituents who had built dwellings in areas not yet cleared for subdivision by the Planning Department.

In addition to the private concessions, there had been another "government within a government," the Ministry of *Waqf*, which retained control over a significant proportion of Cairo's real estate and which, through its proceeds, had access to financial resources over which it exercised discretionary control. So long as this ministry stood in opposition to the colonially dominated national administration, arguments could be advanced that it represented a sacred rather than secular authority and, as such, could claim exemption from the regular framework of government. However, defense of its anomalous status became more and more tenuous as the government became indigenized and assumed responsibility for welfare functions that formerly had been performed through the institution of *waqf*. Under these conditions, how could funds available and indeed earmarked for welfare purposes be allowed to remain unintegrated with overall national plans for development and public services?

The first *waqf* reforms in the 1950's had affected family endowments only. The *waqf khayri* persisted and, at first, there was an attempt to maintain the autonomous administration of these properties. But while they were nominally left in the hands of the Ministry of *Waqf*, pressure was exerted to guide and cajole the admittedly compliant ministry to invest its funds in projects which fitted into the overall needs of the community, as those needs were defined by the government. The construction by the Ministry of *Waqf* of the Vagabonds' City at al-Marj and of several public housing projects for low-income tenants was undertaken during this interim period of coexistence.[7] In 1963, however, indirect influence was jettisoned in favor of incorporating this medieval survival into the framework of modern planning. A ministerial order issued in that year called upon the Ministry of *Waqf* to turn over all real estate properties under its jurisdiction to the governorates in which they were located, henceforth to be managed directly through the governorate offices. For the lands that were to be used for public purposes, the governorates were to recompense the Ministry of *Waqf* to 50 percent of the value of the property; for those properties taken but not required for public purposes, the governorates were to recompense to 90 percent of the value, the residual 10 percent being absorbed to defray the costs of administering the properties. I have been unable to determine the location and extent of *waqf khayri* properties that were, by this order, made available to the Governorate of Cairo for direct management and development. But even if it has not been substantial, the final elimination of this anomalous unit as a potentially competitive power and the addition even of scattered plots of land to the store of parcels over which the governorate exercises direct control cannot but strengthen the hands of Cairo's planners.

Local government and home rule also are no longer issues in Cairo, even though the process of trial and error still continues in search of a viable method for translating rights into daily practice. The peculiar role of Cairo in the national economy and the long tradition of national involvement in the governing of the capital have given rise to a system which deviates in fundamental respects from the pattern of local government that evolved in the United States. For that reason, the municipal structure of Cairo may appear somewhat unusual to the Western student. However, while the system seems to have its own special weaknesses, it also has a strong potential for solving certain serious problems which metropolitan areas in the United States, *because* of their excessive concern with home rule, have been unable to deal with effectively.

Ever since 1949 Cairo has had juristic personality. The Municipality (*Baladīyah*) created by Law 145 of that year was inaugurated in 1950 and assigned all the municipal functions that had formerly been under the jurisdiction of the *Tanẓīm* department of the Ministry of Public Works. In that same year a new Ministry of Municipal and Rural Affairs was established which absorbed the administrations for public services, local commissions, and the Cairo Main Drainage Department (which had formerly been under the Ministry of Health).[8] The law establishing the Municipality of Cairo, however, primarily changed the status of an anomalous level governing the city and added the formality of a town council; it neither solved the problems of overall coordination nor established true representative government. The relationship between the new *Baladīyah* and the other existing administrative unit, the Governorate (*Muḥāfaẓah*), remained relatively unspecified, although the former bore chief responsibility for housekeeping and planning (advisory) functions in the city whereas the latter, under the Ministry of the Interior, continued to be responsible primarily for the maintenance of law, order, and security. Under these conditions, the *Baladīyah* office, headed by an engineer in a capacity similar to a technician-city manager, enjoyed a certain amount of autonomy, albeit

[7] Among the construction projects attributed to the Ministry of *Waqf* during this period were 931 apartments and 378 shops and other buildings (at a cost of *LE* 2,557,800), as well as two "popular" (i.e., low-income) housing projects: one containing 1,584 dwelling units at a cost of *LE* 479,000, another with 1,007 dwelling units at a cost of *LE* 316,000. See *U.A.R.: Achievements and Future Development Plans* (Government Printing Office, Cairo: 1960), pp. 108-109. Again, in the United Arab Republic annual *Yearbook* [*Al-Kitāb al-Sanawi*], 1962, issued by the Ministry of Information (Cairo, April 1962), it is noted that the Ministry of *Waqf* constructed 1,097 low-cost rental units since the Revolution (p. 283) as well as 104 units of upper-middle-income housing (p. 285).

[8] *Overseas Economic Surveys* (1952), p. 2.

with strictly circumscribed powers and a very narrowly defined span of jurisdiction.

In 1960 a new law (No. 124 on Territorial Administration)[9] was promulgated, establishing a Ministry for Local Administration and outlining a uniform system of local government within the framework of the then-recently established National Union, a preliminary approach to representative government soon superseded by the Arab Socialist Union. This new law abrogated conflicting clauses in the 1949 Law and had the effect of merging the *Baladīyah* and *Muḥāfazah* of Cairo into a single entity, in which the former chief of the *Baladīyah* became an undersecretary directly responsible to the Governor of Cairo. Eventually the subsumed unit was renamed the Department of Housing and Public Utilities. This department was subdivided, as before, into separate sections to deal with planning and buildings, circulation (roads, bridges, and licenses), drainage, electrical and mechanical equipment, and public gardens, as well as an adjunct authority to deal with public housing. Other departments in the *Muḥāfazah*, on the same administrative level, include Education, Social Affairs, Youth, Welfare and Health.[10] While each of these divisions retains a stronger relationship to the relevant national ministry than would certainly be true in the United States—but not necessarily in France or other countries with centralized administrations—at least they are now gathered together under one roof where their decisions of planning and budgeting can be if not controlled at least coordinated.

Another important innovation of the 1960 Law was to empower the President of Egypt to establish the boundaries of all governorates (or *muḥāfaẓāt*, of which Cairo is one of twenty-four). Theoretically, at least, the power thus exists to constitute a metropolitan region for Cairo which would conform realistically to the functional unit required to plan the metropolis; this is a power which many Western metropolitan planners might well envy. Thus far the potentialities created by this law have not been exploited in a fashion designed to satisfy many persons deeply concerned with planning the future metropolis. The boundaries adopted for Cairo were those which had been in force since the 1950's, i.e., while they extended the limits of the Governorate southward to include Ḥalwān, they also left the western bank under the jurisdiction of the neighboring Governorate of Jīzah. Thus, the difficulties of achieving coordinated development on both sides of the river remain unabated. Quite a bit of informal coordination seems to take place, with observers attending relevant public and private meetings, with joint clearance required for certain projects, and with liaison officers from the concerned ministries maintaining contact to facilitate the exchange of information. Nevertheless, it seemed to this writer that there existed a strong feeling in 1965 on the part of many officials involved in planning for the metropolis that a redefinition of boundaries would be a wise next step. This step has, however, not been taken. Instead, a regional planning committee was set up by presidential decree (about which more will be said below) and charged with developing a plan for the wider region.

Another contribution of the 1960 Law was the inauguration of representative government in Cairo. The law called for the establishment of a council within each governorate, presided over by the governor of the province, on which were to sit both ex officio and popularly elected representatives. In conformity with these provisions, a Cairo Governorate Council (*Majlis Muḥāfaẓat al-Qāhirah*) was set up, consisting of 85 members. Of these, 26 plus the Governor himself are included in the council ex officio, i.e., by virtue of their important positions in the administrative apparatus of the government; 16 are special appointees to the council by virtue of their active participation in the Socialist Union and their particular technical competence (economists, lawyers, engineers, educators); the remaining 42 are representatives elected through the Socialist Union, 2 from each of the 21 districts (*aqsām*) into which the city is electorally as well as administratively divided.[11] While a local govern-

[9] An English digest of this law and the executive regulations accompanying it appear in Harold Alderfer *et al.*, *Local Government in the United Arab Republic, 1964* (Printed for the Institute of Public Administration by Al-Shaab Printing House, Cairo: undated but second edition), pp. 37-64. Amendments, designed chiefly to adapt the law to the Arab Socialist Union established in 1962, have subsequently been passed.

[10] As explained by Mr. Muḥammad Ḥāfiẓ 'Ali in a personal interview in July 1965. A slightly different list is given in Alderfer, *Local Government, 1964*, p. 9, where the major departments are given as: Finance, Education, Culture and Guidance, Supplies, Agriculture, Health, Labor, Social Affairs and Housing. This same list appears in the edition published in 1963. Whether our account is incomplete or the number of departments has been reduced since Alderfer's report cannot be determined.

[11] The 26 ex officio members include: an undersecretary of the Ministry of Public Works; Director-General of Cairo's Supply; Financial Supervisor for the Governorate of Cairo representing the Ministry of Treasury; Director of Security for Cairo representing the Ministry of the Interior; undersecretary of the Ministry of Agriculture; undersecretary of the Ministry of Housing and Public Utilities for the Governorate; Director-General of Northern Cairo for Social Affairs; undersecretary of the Ministry of Health for Cairo; representative of the Ministry of Transport and Communications; undersecretary for the Ministry of Economy; undersecretary for the Ministry of *Waqf*; undersecretary for the Ministry of Culture and National Guidance; representative of the Ministry of Industry; representatives from Cairo University, 'Ain Shams University, and al-Azhar University; Director-General of the Cairo Water Works; the Director-Generals of the four Educational Districts of Cairo; an undersecretary of the Ministry of Education; representative of the

ment council that consists only half of duly elected representatives of the residents of the city seems to fall short of Western ideals of popular self-government, the inclusion of these three classes of council members may be viewed as a transitional step which reflects certain realities in the decision-making structure of the metropolis that could be ignored only with serious consequences. Without the power to raise funds locally through self-taxation to anywhere near the level of required expenditures, how could a purely elective council realistically be empowered to determine the allocation of expenditures? Thus, the key to the problem of local government in Cairo, as elsewhere, seems to lie in the power of the purse.

The fact remains that the major portion of Cairo's financial resources comes *not* from locally raised taxes, over which elected representatives might legitimately be expected to exercise allocative control, but from nationally determined subventions and administratively determined allocations for specific functions. This being the case, it should not surprise us that the involved ministries expect to share in, if not to determine, expenditure decisions.

To demonstrate the degree to which Cairo's revenues are derived from sources over which it has no control and for which it remains at the mercy of other administrative bodies, I reproduce here (see Table 9) the revenues available to the Cairo Governorate in the fiscal years 1963-1964 and 1964-1965, together with their sources. Income is derived from three sources: (1) locally collected taxes, fees, incomes, loans, and other profits over which the locality has complete jurisdiction, within the governing ceiling limits established nationally; (2) Cairo's share of the Common Revenues, a central fund derived from surtaxes and custom fees which is redistributed among the various local administrations; and (3) an annual grant or subvention given to it through the Ministry of Local Administration as agent for functional units such as the Ministries of Education, Public Health, Social Affairs, Youth, etc.

As can be seen, the first source of revenue comes nowhere near meeting the needs of the budget and has been of declining significance to the city.[12] Nor is the second, meant perhaps to recompense the city for her formerly lucrative but no longer permissible *octroi* tax, a significant contributor to fiscal capacity. Most of the funds at the disposal of the city are made available to it through the Ministry of Local Administration which acts in concert with other involved ministries to work out capital and operating budgets for various locally administered but centrally financed programs.[13] Thus, debate on the

TABLE 9. REVENUES OF THE GOVERNORATE OF CAIRO BY SOURCE, FISCAL YEARS 1963-1964 (ACTUAL) AND 1964-1965 (ESTIMATED)

Source of Funds	*Amounts (in thousands of Egyptian Pounds) and Percentage of Total Revenues* 1963-1964 *LE* 000	%	1964-1965 *LE* 000	%
1) Locally Collected: Total	12,488.1	43	10,442.5	32
Of which:				
Cairo House Tax	1,210[a]	(4)	1,500.5	(5)
Tax on casinos, cafés, amusements	585		648	
Automobile fees	1,950		2,200	
Public accommodations	100		950	
Other taxes and fees	2,201		2,289	
Revenues from quarries	126.2		160	
Irregularly or singly imposed taxes, etc.	4,077		1,770	
Miscellaneous	816.9		925	
Special (capital investments)	500			
Housing revenues	700			
Proceeds from demolition and clearance of blight	222			
2) Cairo's Share of Common Revenues	427.8	1	1,260	4
3) Subvention from Ministry of Local Administration	16,258.2[b]	56	20,705.8	64
Total Revenues	29,174.1	100	32,408.3	100

SOURCE: Mimeographed releases from the *Muḥāfaẓah.*

[a] Formerly, the revenues from the Cairo House Tax were higher, but a graduated ceiling, with rates varying with the monthly rental of flats (reduced by government order), was established by the central government which resulted in reduced revenues.

[b] This includes over *LE* 10 million from the Ministry of Education and almost *LE* 3 million from the Ministry of Health—obviously earmarked for special purposes.

Agricultural Credit Bank; representative of the Ministry of Labor; Head of the Directorate of Youth and Sports; and Director-General of the Tourist Authority.

The 21 *aqsām* with elected representatives are: al-Azbakīyah, Sāḥil, Shubra, Rawḍ al-Faraj, al-Maṭarīyah, Būlāq, Qaṣr al-Nīl, Bāb al-Sha'rīyah, al-Darb al-Aḥmar, al-Jamālīyah, al-Zaytūn, 'Abdīn, al-Mūski, Ḥalwān, al-Ma'ādi, al-Wāyli, Miṣr al-Qadīmah, al-Sayīdah Zaynab, al-Khalīfah, Miṣr al-Jadīdah, and al-Ẓāhir. These represent extensions and subdivisions of census districts used in our statistical analysis and can be converted if desired into aggregates of data units.

[12] This trend can be seen more clearly if the analysis is extended backward to the period before the time covered in Table 9. In the fiscal year 1961-1962, according to the first edition of Alderfer, *Local Government* (1963), p. 12, the estimated revenues for the Governorate of Cairo totaled *LE* 28,647,968, of which only *LE* 11,801,968 or 41 percent was contributed through grants from the national government; *LE* 405,000 came from Cairo's share of common revenues. Of the remaining revenues locally raised, the taxes on land and buildings contributed almost *LE* 4,000,000, constituting some 14 percent of *all* revenues. New national legislation passed subsequently reduced House Tax revenues drastically, as can be seen by comparing this figure with later ones found in Table 9.

[13] "From the beginning of the fiscal year 1962/1963, the budgets of the following ministries were transferred to the budgets of the provincial councils: Education, Health, Social Affairs, Labour, Housing and Public Utilities, Agriculture,

budget, which plays so central a role in municipal council operations in American cities, is in Cairo still largely an ex post facto act of public approval for allocative decisions which have already been worked out, previously and sometimes quite heatedly, by the ex officio representatives of the various national ministries.[14]

Given the nature of fiscal realities, then, it should not surprise us that the Cairo Governorate Council should be heavily weighted on the side of the administrators who, seated closest to the dais, play a dominant role in meetings, chiefly as information-givers and clarifiers. But the important thing to note is that their power, formerly unlimited, is now shared with two other groups in a system which potentially can provide for checks and balances. First, the inclusion of the sixteen members selected on the basis of their particular competence appears to be an attempt not only to provide the council with expert opinion but also to constitute a senate of judges presumably aloof from the vested interests of both the administrative departments and the local subcommunities. The elected representatives, on the other hand, can defend the interests of their constituents, both by supporting and transmitting their petitions and by acting as watchdogs to prevent regional partiality. While this appears to be the theory behind the present constitution of local government in Cairo, the actual operation of the system cannot yet be judged. With time, with further decentralization of ministry budgets, and with a strengthening through exercise of the traditions of self-government, it is possible that real power could shift into the hands of the general technicians and the politically selected representatives, even without any formal change in organization; however, at this writing the shift is far from having been accomplished.

One measure of the strength of municipal government is its capacity to deal with crises. Such situations arise periodically in Cairo through an overburdening of municipal services and facilities—the joint product of the rapidly increasing population and the postponed investments in utility maintenance and extension. To what extent has the existing governmental structure been able to cope with these problems and to what extent has it been necessary to turn to extraordinary *ad hoc* and specially empowered agencies to meet emergencies as they arise?

Even the wealthiest urban community in the world would face severe difficulties if called upon to accommodate the magnitude of population increase which Cairo has experienced during the past few decades. The dimensions of the problem go far beyond numbers, however. Difficulties are compounded by the character of the population increase and by the effects of past investment inadequacies as well as current financial shortages. First, the type of natural increase which Cairo has been experiencing tends to expand the number of dependents requiring health and educational services although not yet contributing to economic growth; furthermore, growth from migration has come primarily from rural areas where illiteracy is greatest, health conditions poorest, and preparation for participation in the modern economy least adequate.[15] Thus, population increase raises the demand for public services and facilities at a rate which exceeds numerical growth. On the other hand, urban facilities and services were already severely inadequate when the present spectacular growth began. Utilities had not been extended systematically into the older and poorer quarters, and financial as well as material shortages during World War II had led to a postponement of even normal maintenance of existing facilities, not to mention their improvement and extension.

Thus, the current crises arise out of the need not only to keep pace with population increase but actually to outdistance it to meet remedial needs as well. All this, however, is to be accomplished at the very time when Egypt faces severe shortages of investment funds and especially the hard currency required to purchase heavy capital equipment, and at a time when necessity and prudence dictate concentration of investment in basic production rather than urban overhead. Is it any wonder, then, that situations of grave menace to health and safety have arisen requiring emergency attention? In these instances, the lumbering pace of existing municipal government and its limited power to requisition local funds and hard currency have rendered it impotent; hence the recourse to special *ad hoc* committees when the general welfare is threatened.

While it is not possible to describe or analyze these problems in detail here, perhaps one example will help to convey to the reader the nature and magnitude of the

Provisions and Supplies, Youth and Industry (in so far as it deals with quarries)." Special report by Kamel Mazen on "Administrative Problems of Rapid Urban Growth in the United Arab Republic," in United Nations, *Administrative Problems of Rapid Urban Growth in the Arab States* (United Nations, New York: 1964), p. 149. Whether this is more than a paper transfer cannot be determined.

[14] The Cairo Council meeting attended by this writer in summer of 1965, in which the annual budget was discussed and the Water Works' budget approved, was remarkable for its restraint and the degree to which interaction was one-sided. Information flowed from the dais, the rostrum, and the interior circle of ex officio members outward to the representatives of the *aqsām* seated at the rear. The rare comments by the latter tended to be in the form of respectful questions.

[15] The generality of this condition is amply documented in the U.N. seminar report on *Administrative Problems of Rapid Urban Growth in the Arab States.*

difficulties and the extreme lengths to which ingenuity has been taxed in solving some of them. In the spring of 1965 an event which had been forecast and feared for at least a decade finally occurred. Sewers in many parts of Cairo, especially in those lower quarters near the river and in the old beds of former water courses, backed up and overflowed, covering streets and filling basements with an odoriferous sludge. This created not only an aesthetic affront but a dangerous menace to health as well. The causes were complex, a combination of the gradually rising water table (endemic to lower Egypt) and the skyrocketing quantity of effluent to be handled by sewers and mains which were too small and too old and by drainage pumping stations that had been designed to carry a much smaller load.

The emergency came as no surprise to engineers in the Housing and Public Utilities Department of the Governorate, for in their numerous requests for funds and in their plans submitted annually they had stressed the need for undertaking major projects to renovate equipment, enlarge capacity, and add pumping stations. Each year these requests went unfilled, for the equipment needed to execute the projects required not only local funds and labor (which could have been provided) but an even scarcer resource, access to hard-currency reserves. Machinery had to be imported from abroad, but when the *Muḥāfaẓah* was unable to obtain hard-currency credits from the government, only patching operations on a reduced scale could be executed.[16]

Expeditious methods were required to deal with the new emergency. The President appointed an *ad hoc* committee to plan and execute the "100 Days' Project on Cairo Drainage," as the task became designated. Cabinet ministers, members of the National Assembly, representatives of the Arab Socialist Union, as well as technicians and functionaries, were appointed to the special committee, headed by the Minister of Electricity, which was granted extraordinary powers to requisition whatever resources—including scarce hard-currency credits—might be required to restore the drainage systems of Cairo and Jīzah to operating efficiency. On July 18, 1965, completion of their task was announced and on July 20, Prime Minister 'Ali Ṣabrī dedicated the new facilities. Among the projects undertaken were substantial replacements of defective or inadequate sewer pipes and mains as well as repairs, enlargements, and additions to the pumping stations at al-Maṭarīyah, Ghamrah, Jīzah, and Port Sa'īd (al-Khalīj) Street, at an estimated cost of a quarter of a million Egyptian pounds.[17] Recommendations for future projects and pumping stations were also made by the committee.

It is not known, however, whether their recommendations also directed attention to the underlying conditions that had led to the emergency or whether they suggested means for building into the day-to-day operations of the municipal government the powers necessary to avert future recurrences. This seems unlikely. Without such recommendations, however, a dangerous precedent has been set which cannot help but undermine the autonomy and self-reliance of the Governorate, although the latter has been a goal avowed by the government and supported both by legislation and executive directives. The attractiveness of this short-cut method to effective action in crisis situations cannot be denied, and the temptation to extend this principle into other areas seems to have become irresistible. The public transit system, for example, has also been subject to severe overload conditions, due to an enormously increased demand and usage coupled with the failure to replace, repair, or add to the rolling stock in sufficient force to meet it. Again, an emergency expedient was resorted to when the army was assigned the special task of coping with the mass transit crisis in the city.

A final example, designed to deal with problems of a somewhat different nature but according to the precedents established in these earlier efforts to "get around" the limited potency of existing units of government, was the issuance in early July 1965 of a republican decree by President Nasser forming a Higher Committee to supervise the planning of the Greater Cairo Region and the execution of necessary projects. According to a contemporary newspaper account,[18] the committee was entrusted with the responsibility for drawing up a comprehensive plan for the Cairo Metropolitan Region, including "all its public utilities and its requirements as a capital city," with setting a time schedule for the execution of plans, and with coordinating the efforts of all bodies concerned with executing these projects. The decree further stipulated—and herein lies the problem—that the committee's deci-

[16] According to an unreleased and therefore unofficial report prepared by the Department of Housing and Public Utilities entitled (translated) "The First Five Year Plan: Works Performed During the First Four Years; Expected Works to be Performed During the Fifth Year" (mimeographed in Arabic: 1965), sewage effluent in Cairo has been doubling every 10 years, and it is estimated that 40 years hence it will reach 40 million cubic meters per day! Despite this, no major additions to the system were made. Many of the sewer projects proposed and decided upon in 1958-1959 were not carried out because the Governorate could not obtain the hard-currency credits from the government which were essential to import the needed equipment (pp. 12-13).

[17] The fascinating account of this committee and its work can be found in the Cairo newspapers of the period. The completion of the project and its estimated cost are reported, for example, on page 1 of the Sunday edition of the *Egyptian Gazette*, July 18, 1965.

[18] As reported under the heading "Cairo Planning Committee," in the *Egyptian Gazette*, July 9, 1965, pp. 1 and 3.

sions are to be considered "final and will have to be observed by all Ministries, Governorates, organizations and authorities after being approved by the Prime Minister." The committee is to have its own independent budget, the funds being allocated to it by the Prime Minister himself, to whom and to the Deputy Prime Minister for Local Government and Services the committee is required to submit reports of its deliberations and decisions.

To what extent does this decree create a supergovernment independent of the Cairo Council and the operating departments of the Governorate? Although this appears to have been the interpretation of the ex-Governor of Cairo who resigned within a few days of this announcement, only time will tell whether the committee can even prove effective enough to seriously threaten existing units of government which, after all, are represented on the committee.[19] If, however, the committee does not succeed in its mission, this attempt to circumvent rather than strengthen normal administrative channels will have delayed rather than hastened the day of eventual adequate planning for the city. It is important in this respect to point out that the prerequisite legal powers to execute even the most carefully devised plans for the metropolis are still conspicuously absent.

Traditionally, large cities have evolved as the aggregate product of thousands or even millions of individual decisions coordinated loosely, if at all, through the operation of what urban ecologists have termed the "subconsensual" processes of spatial distribution. We have seen, in our analysis of the present social-physical organization of Cairo, that these processes have been far from ineffective in giving shape and coherence to the structure of the city. Where the state wishes to intervene in these processes to guide developments in certain desired directions or discourage decisions which would undermine planning goals, it has two options that are, of course, not mutually exclusive. First, it can participate actively in development, engaging in direct investment, physical planning, and construction; and second, it can use its legal powers of incentives and sanctions to manipulate the terms within which decisions of individual investors and consumers are made. Different systems place different emphasis upon these two techniques for guiding urban development. Although Cairo has apparently opted for heavy dependence upon the first, her planners have not ignored the second, even though the prerequisite powers have been slow in being granted. What are these indirect legal controls and to what extent are they at the disposal of responsible agents in the Governorate?

Among the minimum number of tools a modern municipality expects to have to control development are: building codes to set standards of safe and healthful construction; housing codes to control occupancy standards and minimum dwelling unit quality; zoning ordinances to assure conformity of land use to an overall plan for the city; subdivision regulations to confine new developments to approved areas and to assure conformity of site plans to current standards of adequacy; site control powers over nonprivate developers (usually governmental agencies exempted from the other types of controlling ordinances); and perhaps also general planning laws permitting the acquisition and/or reservation of lands required or anticipated to be required for given public purposes, such as schools, recreational facilities, the circulation system, utility installations, etc.

In American cities the existence of even the full roster of legal controls "on the books" has often failed to give assurance of effectiveness. First, most of these laws apply *only* to new construction or changed uses, not to existing structures or uses established before passage of the ordinances. Second, inspection and enforcement must be stringent enough and fines high enough to discourage violations. In Cairo these problems of securing compliance are compounded by inadequate or missing laws, the absence of sanctions and by the lack of long-range plans for metropolitan growth and land use which might serve as the ultimate referent for decisions and ordinances which are not ends in themselves but merely ways of achieving such ends.

Of these laws, Cairo by 1965 had only a building code and a law governing land subdivision. There was no housing code nor was there a general zoning ordinance, although in a few isolated quarters of the city, land use and architectural controls govern development. Among these are the zoning via deed restriction regulations in force in the two planned residential suburbs of al-Ma'ādi to the south and Heliopolis in the northeast, plus even more stringent regulations in the new town of Naṣr City, as well as the architectural control ordinance recently enacted to preserve the historic character of the Fāṭimid

[19] Among the members of the committee are the ministers of Housing and Public Utilities, Economy and Foreign Trade, the Treasury, Deputy Minister of Housing and Utilities, the governors of Cairo and Jīzah, the Chairman of the General Authority for Electric Power, the Chairman of the Cairo Transport Authority, the Chairman of the Central Organ for Statistics and Mobilization, undersecretaries of the ministries of Health and of Supply, the Director-General of the Cairo Water Works, professors of engineering and city planning from Cairo, 'Ain Shams, and Alexandria Universities, representatives from information, tourism, industry, transport and communications, as well as the Director of Planning of the Cairo Governorate (Mr. Muḥammad Ḥāfiẓ 'Ali), also appointed secretary to the committee.

City.[20] But it must be recognized that there does not exist any real basis for enacting an overall zoning ordinance, for the land use plan on which it must be based has not yet been drawn up or approved, nor in fact is a detailed land use map of the region, which would be required to draw up such a plan, available to the planners.[21]

In the absence of such overall regulations, the advisory powers vested in the Planning Department of the Governorate assume heightened significance as interim measures to prevent serious misjudgments which will interfere with effective planning at a later date. The site-control powers of the Planning Department, however, are not institutionalized. By convention, although not mandatory by law, the Planning Department has taken over the responsibility for approving all sites selected for planned use, including those selected for development by various government agencies. In the case of conflict, the issue is referred to the Cairo Council. According to its director, the Planning Department has been successful in about 60 percent of the conflict cases in obtaining the backing of the Council for its decisions and recommendations. However, the lack of any official powers and, consequently, the absence of any real sanctions that can be applied against offenders has inevitably invited numerous violations. Chiefly, these violations have been in the form of commencing construction before and without seeking to obtain clearance of the site for intended use. On the periphery, private developers and the Ministry of Industry have been the prime offenders; nearer to the center of the city, the Ministry of Tourism, which has been constructing numerous hotels and other accommodations to encourage the tourist industry, has frequently failed to consult the Planning Department about its intended constructions.

Before these weak legal powers can be strengthened, however, the goals toward which they are to be directed must be specified more clearly and receive official approval—a prerequisite still lacking in Cairo. It is true that in 1953 the Municipality commissioned a group of engineers and planners to formulate a master plan for the capital, and numerous committees were set up to handle specific aspects. Surveys were undertaken to accumulate needed data on the distribution of inhabitants, the location of industry, commerce, and other land uses, housing conditions, labor conditions, transport and communications problems, streets and highways, etc. These

[20] A zoning-architectural control ordinance was devised in 1965 to preserve the core Fāṭimid city against the encroachments of modernism. Full circle has been turned in the seven score years between Muḥammad 'Ali, who sought to change the Fāṭimid city into a more European model, and Cairo's contemporary planners who, secure in their modernism, seek to restore a museum of the past. The regulations govern the construction of new buildings in the area and the structural alterations of existing buildings. In addition to limiting the height of all buildings to four stories, including the ground floor, the ordinance specifies that the façades of all buildings in the historical district should be in a simplified Islamic style; should shade their exterior windows with *mashrabīyah* or some similar device (it will be recalled that it was these very *mashrabīyah* that Muḥammad 'Ali had outlawed as fire hazards); should be equipped with wooden doors or, where iron is used, it should be grilled in the Arabesque style. Counter to Muḥammad 'Ali's intent to "light up" his city, the ordinance specifically prohibits fluorescent and neon lighting and permits entrance-way lights only when they follow the lamp designs of the earlier period. Workshops are prohibited from fronting the streets; where they do, display windows must intervene between the shops and the thoroughfare. In only one area do the present regulations agree with those of Muḥammad 'Ali, namely in protecting the roadways from encroachments. Projections are limited on the ground floor to the entrance way only and may not exceed 15 cm. in width; on the upper stories, projections are limited to a specified proportion of street width. To enforce these regulations, a committee consisting of planners, archaeologists, and representatives from the ministries of Tourism, *Awqāf*, and Housing has been appointed by the Governorate to review designs and plans prior to the granting of building permits, and to pass even on the color of the cream whitewashing for exteriors and the "Oriental" quality of the interior decor of public places, such as restaurants and hotels, being constructed in the zone. Full provisions are found in "Building Regulations for Fāṭimid Cairo," mimeographed, undated, obtained from the Office of the Governorate of Cairo (in Arabic: 1965?). The *New York Times*, July 25, 1967, p. 17, contained an AP release indicating that, pursuant to this ordinance, a replanning of the famous Khān al-Khalīli is being considered. The Governor of Cairo had claimed that many of its buildings were unsafe and should be leveled. The Minister of Tourism, on the other hand, had protested that the bazaar was part of Egypt's medieval history and should therefore be retained. The controversy was resolved only by referring the matter to the National Assembly, which appointed its own engineers to investigate the situation. They recommended the demolition of only one-third of the famous complex, their recommendations being ratified by the Assembly which further specified that replacement structures must look the same as the old ones. Photographs are being taken before demolition to permit reproduction. This appears to be only an opening shot in a battle which will probably continue to be waged.

[21] In connection with the Master Plan of 1956, a large staff of university students was employed to gather detailed land use data through field surveys throughout the city. These data were transcribed by address on separate sheets which noted not only current usage but condition of buildings and other essential items. Organizing grids and codes were not used and no further processing (except a general map showing building conditions) was done. When I saw the sheets in 1959, they were dusty and beginning to deteriorate and were stored in a wooden cabinet far from the offices concerned with planning. An enormous amount of effort would be required to sort the sheets, to transcribe data for IBM analysis, and to prepare the land use map. By now, in addition, the data would be somewhat out of date. Another land use survey is now being undertaken in connection with the work of the new Higher Planning Committee.

surveys required two years to complete. Finally, in 1956 the Master Plan for the city was finished and subsequently published, but it has never been released. It is not officially binding, nor does anyone claim that its contents offer a realistic set of goals for the city or a reasoned program for their achievement.[22]

It may be that the Higher Planning Committee will succeed where the academic planners failed and that they will be able to assemble and process the required information and will be able to establish a mechanism for ongoing planning (rather than a static master plan outmoded by the date of its publication) that will be coupled with effective capital-budgeting both for long-range goals and short-run targets. Perhaps their recommendations will also include a delimitation of the metropolitan region which could, by Presidential order, be made coterminous with the Cairo Governorate.[23] And perhaps then it would be reasonable to hope for the legal powers that are so sorely needed to effectuate planning.

In the interim, however, some greater measure of control than now exists is necessary if the battle against undirected urban expansion is to be waged successfully. Whether this should be in the form of a general planning law on the English model, designating areas for urban expansion within a limiting greenbelt, both suitably zoned, as has been suggested by M. Ḥāfiẓ 'Ali,[24] or simply by further strengthening the site control powers of the *Muḥāfaẓah* until the plans are ready and given official sanction, we cannot say. We can only point to the serious fact that, with the city growing at the rate it is, each delay permits a hardening of patterns in the peripheral zones, i.e., in those areas which could benefit most from planning.

In the meantime, however, the government has become deeply committed to the path of direct investment and construction, not only in those areas where it has conventionally operated—such as the construction of roads, bridges, utilities, and community facilities—but also in areas formerly left to private investment. In its direct activities the government has been assisted by its rather extensive land holdings within the Governorate, in the form of state domains, *muḥāfaẓah* lands and *waqf* land over which it recently gained control, which have provided not only sites for construction but sources of revenue to finance further projects. The most important of these direct real estate operations has been in the field of housing which, since 1956, has become an important function of the Governorate in cooperation with the Ministry of Housing. These projects have helped to fill a vacuum of private investment which has generally fled the field of urban real estate.

We have already noted how Cairo entered the most recent decades of her history severely crippled by a serious housing shortage which required occupancy densities far exceeding accepted standards of adequacy. During World War II, when there was a virtual moratorium on construction, overcrowding became endemic. In the immediate postwar period private investment in housing, while vigorous, was confined almost entirely to providing luxury dwellings for that segment of the population already best accommodated in the city. When even this modest activity decreased in the 1950's, the overall shortage of housing became more acute and direct government investment was finally thrown into the breach. The task, however, is enormous, and the efforts thus far, heroic as they may be, have been tardy in beginning and paltry in comparison to the expanding needs.

In a 1965 appraisal of the housing problem in Cairo it was estimated that by the target date of 1970, some 40,000 new dwelling units would be required to take care of the population increase alone; another 30,000 dwelling units were required to reduce the existing levels of occupancy density; furthermore, another 70,000 dwelling units were needed to replace deteriorated or to-be-demolished units.[25] We have already seen that the number of building permits issued annually for residential structures in Cairo has averaged no more than 1,700 in recent years. Even if *all* these structures were built and if the average number of dwelling units provided in the apartment buildings was 10, the additions to the housing stock would run no higher than about 15,000 dwelling units annually. To what extent has direct government investment

[22] For the history of the first Master Plan, see United Arab Republic, Information Department, *Eleven Years of Progress and Development, 1952-1963* (Cairo, undated), unnumbered section on "The City of Cairo." In fairness, it must be pointed out that the Master Plan contained a number of recommendations that have already been carried out, such as the construction of several major highways, the Jāmi'ah Bridge, and the inauguration of a program of public housing. However, to illustrate the unrealistic assumptions upon which this plan was based, it need only be pointed out that it recommended a population "ceiling" for Cairo of 3.5 million—a size already approached when the plan was published.

[23] By so doing, the committee would, of course, terminate its legal *raison d'être*, for its existence is based upon a provision of the law of local government which permits the President to appoint special bodies where the problems to be solved exceed the boundaries of any one governorate.

[24] See Muḥammad Ḥāfiẓ 'Ali, *Al-Takhṭīṭ al-Hāli li Madīnat al-Qāhirah wa Ittijāhāt al-Mustaqbalah* [Contemporary Planning for the City of Cairo and its Future Trends] (mimeo., Cairo: *ca.* 1965).

[25] Department of Housing and Public Utilities, Governorate of Cairo, "Memorandum on Housing in the Governorate of Cairo" (mimeographed, in Arabic, undated but probably 1965), p. 10.

managed to bridge the widening gap between need and supply?

First, it is important to point out that before 1952 there was no housing policy in Cairo. The only publicly constructed housing project was Workers' City in Imbābah, with about 1,000 dwelling units. These had been rental units but, after the Revolution, they were sold to their occupants.[26] One of the recommendations contained in the Master Plan was that a program of public housing be commenced. The first project to be executed under this new program was a relatively small, middle-income development at Maydān Victoria in Shubra, followed by more ambitious schemes to reclaim the *kharāb* just below the aqueduct of al-Ghūri, where the projects of Zaynhum and 'Ain al-Ṣīrah were begun in 1957-1958. Another major development in the north, al-Amīrīyah, was also conceived at this early date, followed by two other minor projects, but there was as yet no coordinated program for housing.[27]

The Ministry of Housing drew up its first five-year plan to cover the period 1960-1965, allocating targets and finances to the local units charged with plan execution. In this first plan, the country-wide allocations for housing were as follows:

Low-income urban housing	45,200 d.u.'s at the annual rate of 9,000 d.u.'s	Estimated to cost *LE* 15,820,000
Middle-income urban housing	22,600 d.u.'s at the annual rate of 4,500 d.u.'s	Estimated to cost *LE* 18,000,000
Rural housing	500 d.u.'s at the annual rate of 100 d.u.'s	Estimated to cost *LE* 100,000

Cairo's share of this total allocation was quite high, amounting to some *LE* 11,000,000 of which *LE* 8,454,000 was specified for low-income housing and the remaining *LE* 2,500,000 for middle-income housing.

In line with this five-year plan, projects were rapidly undertaken by the *Muḥāfaẓah* to expand the scope and scale of their housing activities. By the end of 1964, with only one more year of the plan to run, they had spent close to *LE* 6 million on the construction of some 14,532 low-income dwelling units and close to *LE* 900,000 on slightly more than 1,000 middle-income housing units. During the final year of the plan, they anticipated completing an additional 1,750 dwelling units for low-income tenants, bringing expenditures up to about *LE* 7 million, including the cost of land acquisition and the installation of necessary public services. Despite the fact that middle-income projects, which required land clearance, got off to a relatively slow start, outstanding commitments for the final year of the plan were estimated at *LE* 1,736,000. Thus, to a large extent, the targets set in the plan have been met.[28]

TABLE 10. PUBLIC HOUSING CONSTRUCTED FOR LOW-INCOME TENANTS BY THE CAIRO GOVERNORATE THROUGH 1964

Name of Project	*Cost in* LE	*Number of Buildings*	*Number of Dwelling Units*
'Ain al-Ṣīrah	79,367	8	266
'Izbat Ḥarīdī	159,306	11.5	460
Al-Darāsah	71,043	5	200
Al-Zāwiyah al-Ḥamrā'	839,890	59	2,690
Al-Amīrīyah	495,951	42	1,008
Ḥalwān	1,210,267	86	2,760
Ramlat Būlāq	438,216	32	920
Jisr al-Baḥr al-A'ẓam	20,174	2	40
Al-Tur'ah al-Būlāqīyah	26,766	2	76
'Izbat Wahbī	29,717	2	90
Al-'Assān	182,660	15	452
Al-Qalali	25,369	2	60
Al-Amīrīyah	121,895	9	216
Maydān al-Maṭarīyah	40,578	3	100
Shāri' al-Ṣiḥḥah bil Maṭarīyah	77,796	7	220
Nādi al-Sabtīyah	301,544	19	410
Shāri' al-Khalīj bil Maṭarīyah	241,132	7.5	660
Al-Sharābīyah	439,601	32	1,160
Al-Ṭarīq al-Muwāzi	547,194	36	1,484
Gharb al-Yasār	79,800	5	150
Al-Abājīyah	410,603	38	1,120
Total Low Income	5,838,769	423	14,542[a]

[a] Of these dwelling units, 28 percent are one-room apartments; 54 percent are two-room apartments; and only 18 percent are three-room apartments, even though the assumed average size of occupant families is six and, in empirical studies, has been found to be closer to seven.

Tables 10 and 11 present information on the low- and middle-income housing projects which had been constructed in Cairo as of 1965. Most of the public low-income projects are rental units, although the government has sought to convert some to cooperatives; on the other hand, the middle-income projects have been conceived for cooperative ownership on attractive terms, even when they are initially rented. Demand for both types has been high, as one might suspect from the housing data pre-

[26] United Arab Republic Annual *Yearbook* [*Al-Kitāb al-Sanawi*], *1959* (Cairo, 1959), p. 623.

[27] There are serious and irreconcilable (for me) discrepancies between the various lists of public housing projects and their number of buildings and dwelling units, as issued by various subunits of the *Muhāfaẓah*. Information has been compiled with caution, therefore.

[28] This information, as well as that contained in Tables 10 and 11, has been taken from the unreleased and therefore unofficial report by the Department of Housing and Public Utilities, entitled "The First Five-Year Plan," pp. 51-55. (In Arabic.)

TABLE 11. MIDDLE-INCOME HOUSING UNDERTAKEN BY THE GOVERNORATE OF CAIRO DURING THE FIRST FOUR YEARS OF THE 1960-1965 FIVE-YEAR PLAN

Name of Project and Its Location	*Total Appropriation in* LE	*Spent in 4 Years* (LE)	*Number of Buildings*	*Number of Dwelling Units*
Shubra[a] (northwest)	348,734	93,949	4	264
land acquisition costs	(117,640)	(117,640)		
compensation to company	(40,063)	(40,063)		
public facilities	(1,650)	(1,650)		
Ma'arūf A (central)	354,915	249,539	3	275
Ma'arūf B (central)	658,994	51,304	none yet	none yet
Sayīdna Ḥusayn (east central)	97,718	32,480	3	48 plus offices
Bāb al-Sha'rīyah (east central)	195,000	6,405	3	134
Majlis al-Ummah (central)	51,391	—	1	27
Ḥalwān (southern)	104,993	84,276	7	67
Ṭajāri Ḥalwān (southern)	88,941	35,146	1	44
Al-Manyal (Rawḍah)	276,278	132,985	3	181
Total Middle Income	2,454,124[b]	893,160[b]	25	1,040 plus offices

[a] This was originally undertaken under another program, hence the compensations for earlier expenditures.

[b] These figures appear in the same source, but the sums of the entries in the table do not quite add up to the totals as reported. Either a typographic or transcription error in the original is possible.

sented earlier. Particularly for the middle-income project in Ma'arūf, located on prime downtown land which had escaped renewal only because it had previously been encumbered by *waqf*, the competition has been stiff. Priorities have been established to accommodate persons displaced by clearance operations, even when their incomes exceed the limits established for eligibility. Waiting lists are long and, in the case of the Ma'arūf project at least, it was necessary to resort to a public lottery for initial selection of tenants from among the long list of eligibles.[29] There is little doubt that these projects, extensive as they are, merely scratch the surface of the backlog of need and demand for housing in Cairo.

An even more ambitious program of direct government construction is envisaged during the second five-year plan for 1965-70. According to interviews granted by both the then-incumbent Minister of Housing and his Deputy Minister in July 1965, as reported in the press,[30] certain policy changes have been made which place greater emphasis upon rural housing and upon privately financed housing. In addition, more attention is to be paid to the possibility of repairing and renovating existing urban structures. What these new plans will mean for Cairo is not yet clear, but officials in the city anticipate an expanded program that would provide up to 56,000 additional dwelling units within the five-year period, of which about 50,000 would be for low-income families.[31]

In addition to these housing projects that have been or are being planned, built, and managed by the government, there are many other housing developments which have been or will be planned, constructed, and initially financed by special housing authorities but then sold in the form of cooperatives to occupant-owners. This method is favored for several reasons. First, it has the advantage of making available the large amounts of capital required to construct coherent developments. Second, it maximizes, through direct design, controls over the location and standards of developments which otherwise would be relatively unfettered by legal restrictions, given the inadequacy of the laws regulating housing and land use. And finally, this method extricates the government from having its funds tied up indefinitely in projects it must continue to administer and maintain. Presumably, as cooperative loans are paid off or transferred to other investment sources, the funds would again be available for new projects. This approach offers attractive possibilities which are now being exploited. Many of the housing developments on the west bank are being sponsored in this manner, as well as other more centrally located smaller projects for middle- and upper-middle-income groups.

By far the largest and most important of the government-sponsored projects is Naṣr City, a centrally planned and executed (but eventually self-liquidating) development designed to provide not only housing but employ-

[29] This information was provided by Mr. Al-Sabāḥi of the Ministry of Housing in an interview in the summer of 1965.

[30] As reported in accounts in the *Egyptian Gazette*, issues of July 18, 1965, and July 19, 1965.

[31] As reported to me in an interview with Mr. Muḥammad Ḥāfiẓ 'Ali, summer 1965.

155. Naṣr City, first blocks of apartment cooperatives

ment centers and community facilities as well. Because of its incredible scale it is far from typical of the other less ambitious direct activities hitherto undertaken. However, it appears to be a prototype for future experiments in government-sponsored community building. Should it prove successful, undoubtedly this will encourage other ventures along similar lines; should it encounter insurmountable difficulties, lessons for the future can be learned from its experience.

One of the recommendations included in the 1956 Master Plan for Cairo was that future growth be channeled into relatively self-contained satellite communities rather than be allowed simply to accrete along the urban margins. Another recommendation was that preference be given to desert sites rather than those at the fertile margins of the city, in order to improve the symmetry of the elongated metropolitan region and to preserve as much arable land as possible for agricultural purposes. Both of these recommendations appear to have been followed in the scheme for Naṣr City which was first put forth in organized form in 1958.

The site selected for the new community was the desert plateau, hitherto empty except for a mental hospital and the old British barracks inherited by the Egyptian army, lying between the outermost edge of ʻAbbāsīyah and Heliopolis. The community itself was envisaged in terms of a twenty-year plan leading eventually to the conversion of some 20,000 acres of desolate barren land into a thriving and relatively self-sufficient complex of residential, commercial, industrial, recreational, educational, and governmental uses, containing a resident population of perhaps half a million persons, most of whom would be connected in some way to the employment opportunities offered in the immediate locale. In many ways, this is a far more sophisticated and ambitious project than that conceived earlier by Baron Empain for Heliopolis, and there appears no reason to believe that it will prove any less successful.

156. Naṣr City, still under construction

Parallels not only to Heliopolis, which faced similar technical problems, but to even earlier prototypes suggest themselves. Cairo has had a long tradition of "royal cities" founded to mark the inauguration of new dynasties, and myths and symbolisms have grown up around their founding. This appears to be no less the case for Naṣr City. The fictions that Fusṭāṭ owed its site selection to the nesting of a dove in General ʻAmr's tent, or that al-Qāhirah was rechristened to counteract the ill-omened tug of a crow, seem to be matched by the now ritualized sentimentality that the site of Naṣr City was selected because it was in the very barracks of that zone that the Revolution of 1952 (whose secret watchword was *naṣr*, meaning "victory"), was conceived and successfully planned. Whatever the validity of this legend, it cannot be denied that Naṣr City has captured the imagination and enthusiastic support of the present regime.

The new city is being built jointly by the Ministry of Housing and the Ministry of Defense, the latter involved because much of the site belonged initially to the army which has retained its interest in it and which, when the old barracks are cleared within the next few years, will have to build new replacements. Administratively, the arrangement is as follows. The Ministry of Housing has under its jurisdiction a Building Authority for Cairo which, in turn, is composed of five societies: (1) Naṣr City; (2) Heliopolis; (3) al-Ma'ādi; (4) 'Ain Shams; and (5) Public Housing. Each of these societies is run by a board of directors. All plans made by the boards of these societies are submitted for approval to the Building Authority and in addition, in the case of major plans, may also have to be submitted directly to the Minister of Housing for his approval. The Chairman of the Board of Naṣr City in 1965 was a talented and dedicated retired general of the army corps of engineers, M. 'Arafah, who was associated with the project since its inception.

Despite the seeming independence of the Naṣr City Society from the formal government of the Cairo Governorate, the bonds are many and run deep. First, the original architect for the planned city, since replaced, was none other than the former chief of the Cairo *Baladīyah*, Muḥammad Riyāḍ. In addition, the current head of the Department of Housing and Public Utilities in the Cairo Governorate is ex officio a member of the board of directors of each of the five separate building societies as well as a member of the Building Authority. It would be a rare action that could escape his cognizance and he is viewed as a valued partner in planning.[32]

In addition to these personal links there are legal ones as well. The standards of construction and site design must conform to the minimum requirements established in the building code and subdivision regulations of the Governorate. According to General 'Arafah and to one of his chief architects, Khayri Rajab,[33] the designs for Naṣr City not only conform to these minimum standards but, in addition, are governed by even more stringent requirements as to land coverage limitations and setbacks, these being incorporated into deed restrictions running with the land. Furthermore, the Department of Housing and Public Utilities has been called upon to give technical assistance in the design of the community, particularly in coordinating the planned streets with those of the *Muḥāfaẓah*. This was essential, since the Governorate is financially responsible for half of the expense of constructing major thoroughfares in Naṣr City and is expected eventually to accept title to all public ways.

The final relationship between the Naṣr City Society and the Governorate lies in the ultimate disposition of the project. The Society has tried to minimize its permanent investment in the community, conceiving of its role as builder and then disposer of the project. To this end, land in most of the subareas is being marketed outright to private buyers and cooperative developers who will construct single-family dwellings and apartment houses using independent financial resources but conforming to the deed restrictions established by the Society.[34] The only direct construction undertaken by the Society has been the modest administration building and the blocks of eleven-story apartment buildings on a small off-center plot which the Society has been marketing to tenants on a cooperatively owned and managed basis. It intends to liquidate its investments in streets and street trees as soon as possible by getting the *Muḥāfaẓah* to accept the deeds and assume responsibility for maintenance. Large centrally located plots in each of the residential neighborhood units are being deeded directly to the Ministry of Education so that the latter can construct the necessary schools. General 'Arafah anticipated that within twenty years the Society would be able to turn over the completed community to the full control of the Cairo Governorate, thus freeing itself to undertake new projects.

These are the long-term prospects for the city; the immediate plans are somewhat more modest. The Society is now concerned with only the first phase of the development plan covering an area of some 7,000 acres. A fairly detailed site plan has been drawn up and approved for this nucleus which enjoys the most favorable location, being closest to access highways and existing mass transit routes and having the most hospitable terrain. Rights to the remaining 14,000 acres had not yet been granted as of 1965 and plans for them remain in the visionary stage. Map XVIII shows a rough sketch plan for the 7,000 acres currently being developed.[35]

[32] There are, as to be expected, the normal jealousies and conflicts, the usual injured feelings upon being overridden in judgment, between the Department of the Governorate, which has not always been enthusiastic concerning designs approved by the Board of Naṣr City, and the planners of the latter who have taken professional pride in their designs and resent adverse comments. These undercurrents, however, seem not to have risen to the level of direct confrontation nor have they interfered with the project's progress.

[33] I am indebted to these two gentlemen for their sacrifice of precious time in granting me long and fruitful interviews in the summer of 1965, and to the former, particularly, who permitted me to compare paper plans with the actual terrain and the progress thus far and, in fact, served as a gallant guide for a lengthy and complete tour.

[34] As we have seen, in the absence of overall zoning regulations for the city, deed restrictions have been the indispensable technique for whatever little control has thus far been exercised over land use and development in isolated sections of Cairo. Enforcement, however, remains difficult.

[35] Sketch Map XVIII has been prepared by compiling infor-

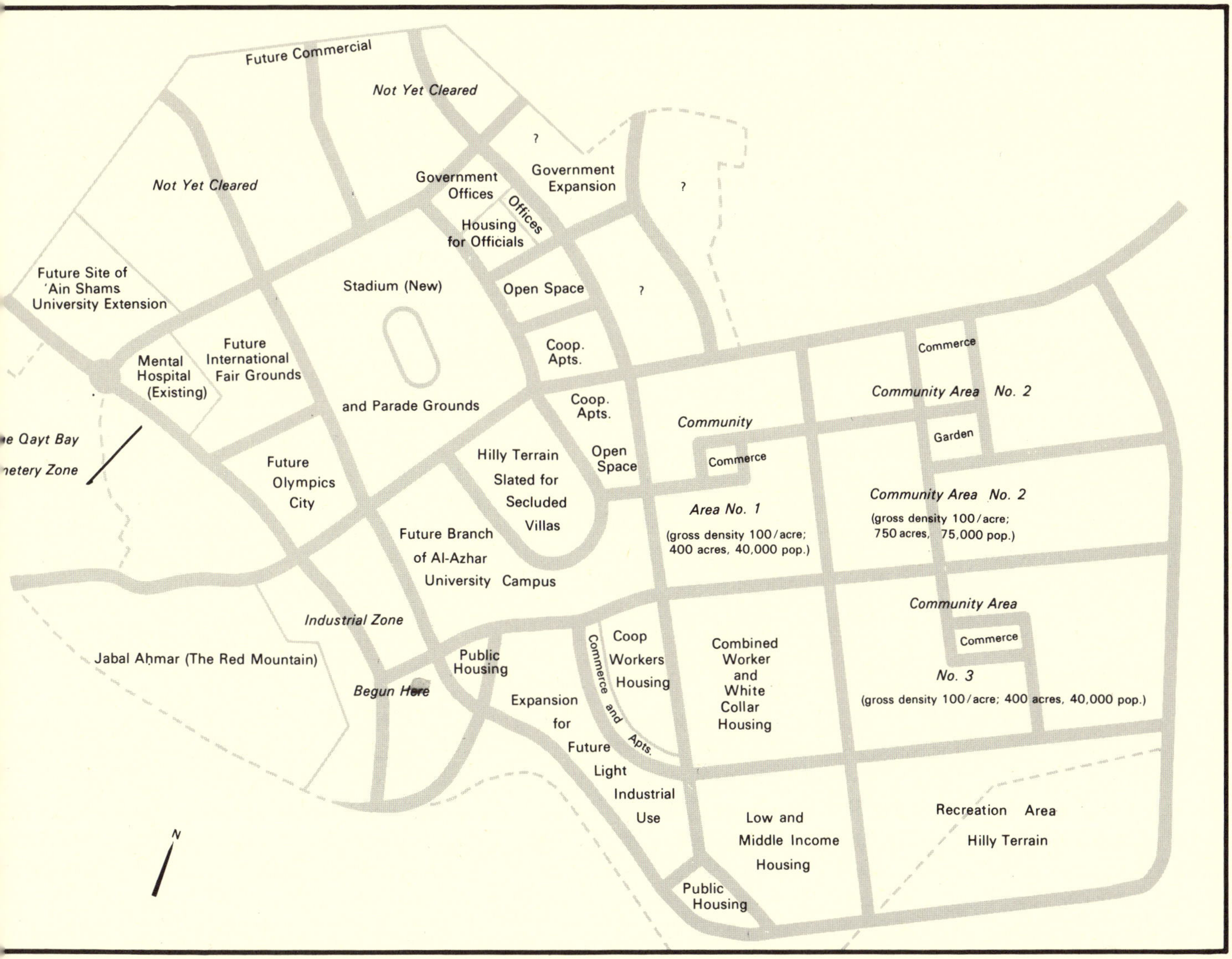

XVIII. Site plan of Naṣr City

The site is subdivided into three general zones which correspond roughly to three major categories of use. The most inlying portion of the site (northwest) contains a concentration of institutional and official uses—a true "royal city." The stadium (reminiscent of a hippodrome?) forms its core and constitutes, at present, its outermost limit, since the land intervening between it and the major thoroughfare that links Naṣr City to both Cairo center and Miṣr al-Jadīdah has still not been cleared or prepared for development. On its southwest flank are sites reserved for an International Fairgrounds (to be built once the existing mental hospital can be removed), an Olympics City, and, at the extreme corner nearest to the existing campus of 'Ain Shams, a parcel reserved for future expansion of that university.

The zone northeast of the stadium has already begun to take on more concrete existence, being the first occupied portion of the city. By the summer of 1965, several blocks of closely spaced tall apartment towers were substantially in place and, although interior finishing and exterior landscaping were far from completed, units were already being advertised for sale. Other completed structures included office buildings for several ministries, with more of these planned or being built. A small quarter nearby had all site improvements (sidewalks, paved

mation from several sources, none of which is without flaw and all of which may subsequently have been altered. A photographic reproduction of what appears to be a three-dimensional model of the original plan was included in an advertising brochure issued quite early by the Building Society. In addition, I was given a blue-line reproduction of the general site plan being used in the architects' office of the Society, showing major roads but no land uses. This plan covered a more extensive area than had been included in the advertising brochure. From these two "base maps," and on the assumption that the latter was probably more accurate and up-to-date than the former, the major outlines for the map were sketched. Information on present and planned uses came from observation and interviews, as well as additional maps on display in the office of the architect for the project.

streets, utilities, street lights, mailboxes), and its single-family detached houses, which in Egypt are always called "villas," were already occupied by a few higher ranking government officials. In addition, there were several other inhabited blocks containing semi-detached but low apartment buildings, each one accommodating from four to eight families. These sections were pleasantly landscaped with grass, flowers, and small shade trees, incongruously contrasting with the dusty expanses of surrounding desert. Nearby was a school building, a mosque under construction, and a small cluster of units obviously intended for commercial uses, although at the time only the government-run cooperative grocery store appeared to be functioning. One can only assume that at the time of this writing all these zones are fully inhabited.

The second major portion of the site, roughly to the south and west of the above quarter, is to be devoted chiefly to industrial, institutional, and recreational uses. At the southernmost extremity lies the intractable terrain of the "Red Mountain" (al-Jabal al-Aḥmar), an irregularly steep desert expanse, broken by outcroppings of reddish sandstone boulders and chunks of marbleized petrified wood, which rises to an elevation overlooking not only Naṣr City to the north and east but the remainder of Cairo as well. Due south one sees—two miles away—the companion peak of the Muqaṭṭam and Muḥammad 'Ali's citadel-mosque atop it, and in the flat intervening plain the exposed lines of the Qayt Bay cemetery city. It is on this peak that a casino-rest house is being built as a focus for a recreational zone; the surrounding hills are being terraced, irrigated, and planted with trees and groundcover.

The Red Mountain, however, has not hitherto been a place of recreation. Its chief value, rather, has been as a rich source of marble, sand, gravel, and other raw material for brick and concrete. Thus, in the industrial zone at its base are factories engaged in extracting and processing these materials. These are to remain and to be supplemented by other, hopefully less dust-raising, industries. On the foothills beyond is a large district being developed into an extensive campus for al-Azhar University. Some of these buildings were already being constructed as early as 1965 and the plans envisage a complex of classroom, laboratory, and dormitory structures to house the "secular" branches of the university (the Colleges of Arts and Sciences); the religious and literary schools will remain behind in the medieval city. The al-Azhar site is broken into at one corner by some very rocky irregular terrain. This area cannot be developed for anything except widely spaced villas and will require enormous investments in reforestation and groundcover. Each promontory has been tentatively marked off as the site for a single-family home and the minimum building plot has been set at one acre. It is hoped that this zone will be developed into a prestigious "garden city" for government officials of the highest rank.

The major use intended for the final third of the site is residential. As can be seen from the sketch map, three very extensive low-density "villa" communities, accommodating between 40,000 and 75,000 inhabitants each, are planned for this most peripheral portion, to be buffered from the industrial and institutional uses by multifamily housing for lower-income groups. By the summer of 1965, only the first community area had begun to receive site improvements, and lots had been platted and were being sold to private builders. At that time it was anticipated that all utilities and other improvements would be completed within two years and that the area would then be ready for development and occupancy.

Thus far, Naṣr City shows great promise. The amount of government backing available has enabled it to progress in a manner not matched by privately undertaken schemes. (Plans for a new town on the Muqaṭṭam to the southeast of the existing city, which were devised at about the same time as those for Naṣr City, have made far less progress, partly because government played a smaller role, partly because the zone abutted low-income areas rather than the more desirable residential quarters of Heliopolis.) The source of its strength, however, may prove a double-edged sword. Thus far, government agencies have been the exclusive investors in Naṣr City. The ministries have built their offices, the Ministry of Industry has invested in some of the new factories, housing for bureaucrats has been built by the respective ministries; and the cooperative apartments, which were originally intended for private construction, finally had to be built by the Naṣr City Society itself. Public investment, thus far, has therefore been the *sine qua non* of the new town. Its role, however, is soon coming to an end, and it remains for private investors to build the rest of the city. Will this investment be forthcoming, or will public funds again have to be thrown in the breach to stimulate the rate of the satellite city's growth? One recalls the era of Ismā'īl when the main lines for the modern Western communities of Ismā'īlīyah, Azbakīyah, and 'Abdīn were laid out in great hopes that private builders would immediately materialize. Demand, however, came only later, and for many years the new quarters remained improved but relatively empty. Will this also be true of Naṣr City? Certainly, the need for community development and additional housing is acute in Cairo today, but can capital be made available to private investors at a rate and under terms attractive enough to translate that need into effective economic demand? Public policy has favored direct public planning. Now the problem is: how can the public sector turn back to the private sector the responsibility for executing these plans according to schedule?

Cities develop and expand not only in response to edicts and to the intended consequences of master plans but also in response to conditions perhaps inadvertently created by many other decisions whose latent effects may be even greater than their manifest goals. Decisions concerning industrial location and transportation patterns may therefore shape the lines of the future city as much as, if not more than, the direct planning and construction of housing projects and even new towns.

Continued industrial location at both the southern and northern extremities of the metropolitan region will inevitably elongate the shape of Cairo, despite the attempts of her planners to encourage lateral expansion into the deserts. Even the ring roads designed to bypass the congested center of the city and to stimulate development at the eastern periphery, or the new bridges which will give added impetus to urbanization on the west bank, cannot hope to counteract the strong impulses toward a linear city dictated not only by terrain but by industrial location decisions. If and when the projected subway is built to connect the Bāb al-Ḥadīd railroad station north of the central business district with the terminus of the southern railway at Bāb al-Lūq south of the CBD, this cannot help but further contribute to the tendency to expand north and south, rather than east and west.

The forces pointing to this inevitability have been operative since the very founding of Cairo and we have traced this process throughout the entire history of the city. While the nature of these forces has perhaps altered with changing technology and shifting realities of political control, they have been neither eliminated nor reversed. In fact, as conurbation continues on an even greater scale, the magnets of distant cities both north and south gain increasing strength. Already, the magnet of Alexandria some 200 kilometers away pulls urban developments in its direction and, as we have suggested elsewhere,[36] should Egypt eventually develop its own "megalopolis," this will undoubtedly be located along the axis between the two most important cities of Egypt. To work against this trend may be futile; to work with it the better part of wisdom.

The satellite cities that have been so ardently advocated by Cairo's physical planners may offer a means for relieving some of the population pressure on Cairo while still not forfeiting the economies of scale desired by the economic planners. Technology permits this greater decentralization, for Egypt, perhaps more than most other nations, will depend upon electric power which elsewhere has been an important factor in urban decentralization. The strip between Cairo and Alexandria is already well served by highway, rail, and water connections, as well as a strong electricity grid. Satellite communities strung out along this axis may well offer an even more balanced solution to the realities of terrain and the problems of decongestion for the city than the solution that has been advanced to date, namely, ringing Cairo with satellites in circular orbit.

The social lines of tomorrow's Cairo are as important as her physical ones, but here both the forces and their results are somewhat less tangible. There can be little doubt that the trend toward social homogeneity, already observable, will continue to blend the disparate cultural and technological worlds into which Cairo, for at least the past one hundred years, has been subdivided. But as this social homogenization occurs, there will be increased economic differentiation within the unifying framework of industrial urbanism. Classes may well take the place of ethnic, religious, and birthplace communities in regulating the distribution of population in the city, but they cannot substitute for the organic social solidarity which the former units often provided in the lives of Cairo's inhabitants.

Some 600 years ago, the basic sociological dilemma was formulated by Ibn Khaldūn, and the issues he raised would now appear to have even greater applicability to the world of Cairo than they had in his day. He contrasted the moral strength and vitality of social units bound together by *'aṣabīyah* (an active principle of cognate solidarity in which the survival of each member was inextricably bound to the survival of the unit) with the effete, individualistic hedonism and passive bonds of larger more complex communities. While, literally, his comparison was between the tribal solidarity of the *badū* and the decadence of the urbanites of the medieval Arab world, we have already seen that even the latter units were nowhere as devoid of foci for group identity and solidarity as the form of urbanism now emerging in the modern world. What will the new organizing principles of Cairo's social life be and how will they shape the future face of the metropolis? As the smaller identities of "individual" and "family," on the one hand, and the larger identities of "Cairene" and "Egyptian," on the other hand, strengthen to compete with the middle-level identities of trade, quarter and religious sect or brotherhood, life paths should proliferate and intertwine for many subgroups in the city which have traditionally traveled in insular circuits. These new paths will mold the evolving city into a more complexly integrated organism—but its exact nature remains shrouded from our limited human vision. Perhaps this book must end appropriately on the same note that concludes all traditional Islamic endeavors to understand the ununderstandable:

And God Knows Best

[36] J. Abu-Lughod, "Urbanization in Egypt: Present State and Future Prospects," *Economic Development and Cultural Change*, XIII (April 1965), 313-353.

14 A Personal Postscript

In the summer of 1965 I made a "final" field trip to Cairo to gather information for the most contemporary period. By the end of May 1967, these additions and revisions had been incorporated into the manuscript. The concluding lines of the final chapter were typed and the manuscript mailed to the publisher. Although it was evident that there could never be a logical termination point for a biography of a living city, it appeared that the future of Cairo, at least for the next few decades, was clearly charted. National goals had been established and Egypt was making rapid progress in her social revolution. The problems facing the city were mere extensions of those already apparent and recognized, and were, furthermore, receiving concerted attention from a large and competent cadre of professionally trained and sophisticated Egyptian planners. It was, therefore, with a somewhat sanguine sigh of relief that I closed both the book and, so I thought, a chapter of my life.

Within only two weeks, however, war had again broken out in the Middle East. The future of Cairo was suddenly shrouded; there were even reports that the city was being bombed. It seemed that not only Cairo's but Egypt's fortune lay in the balance. These events set in motion changes that were far less predictable than the problems that had perplexed me in the final chapter. One year later, when shock had subsided, I returned to the manuscript, wondering whether or in what way it should be revised. Rather than attempt the impossible, I decided not to revise the book itself but rather to add a few brief notes concerning the impact of the present crisis upon Cairo. Return visits to the city during the summers of 1968 and 1969 were both reassuring and distressing. Reassurance lay in the fact that the supreme vitality of Cairo had again triumphed over adversity. Distress, however, lay in the fact that the still-smoldering war had imposed doubled difficulties upon the city.

One of the most important effects of the war and of continued hostilities along the Suez Canal has been a marked increase in the population of Cairo. Between half a million and a million Egyptians have been evacuated from the war zone, and although some have been relocated in other urban centers and in areas of land reclamation, many of them are now settled in Cairo. Public housing projects constructed initially for low-income Cairenes are being used to house some of the evacuees. Others have settled in the fringe cemetery cities where makeshift housing has supplemented public facilities. In every quarter of the city, however, is evidence of additional crowding, as families have doubled up to make room for relatives from the Canal towns. In the summer of 1969, official estimates of Cairo's population were as high as 6½ million, even though that number would not have been approached for several more years had growth remained at normal levels.

A second effect of the war has been a relative cessation of construction for tourism, for the tourist industry, upon which at least some of the future plans for Cairo were premised, has virtually disappeared. Many of the largest hotels under construction along the Nile Gold Coast remain uncompleted and the existing hotels report vacancies. Not only has demand disappeared but the need for construction to house the burgeoning population has deflected whatever activity was occurring near the city center to construction of housing on the periphery.

A third effect has been a tightened and more stringent budget for local improvements and developments. Many of the municipal schemes have been reduced to tabled plans and, although planning activities still go on, there is little immediate hope of putting the ideas into practice. The scheme to build a subway for Cairo is a case in point. Planning is going on, both in the Greater Cairo Planning Office and by foreign consulting firms, directed toward a rational underground transport system for the city, but expectations concerning the feasibility of executing these plans, if and when they are adopted, remain at a low level. With one mind, people plan for the future; with another, they fear that the plans will remain dreams for the distant tomorrow.

Despite these restrictions, despite halfhearted attempts to paint headlights blue, despite security measures prohibiting photography in the city and controlling internal population mobility, the city appears remarkably stable and prosperous. Many of the underlying trends in social transformation have continued despite the war. The homogenization of the city, perhaps even assisted by the abnormal times, has proceeded more rapidly than I would have predicted in 1960. This homogenization seems to be the joint product of two not unrelated trends. First has been an increased leveling off at the top, with conspicuous consumption less and less obvious. The older elite is scarcely visible any more, and with the temporary loss of stature of the new military elite, few have taken their place. Members of the older bourgeoisie have been emigrating from the country, their places being filled from the ranks. On the other hand, there has been an undeniable leavening from below. Consumption patterns, ways of dress, and leisure time activities which were once the prerogative of a somewhat Westernized middle class have been diffusing down the social structure. One rarely sees the *jallābīyah*, even in the most traditional quarters of the city, and many persons alternate with ease between Western and traditional dress (wearing trousers to work and putting on the *jallābīyah* only if required by the service character of their employment). Almost no women are veiled, and if one sees some black-gowned women, in most cases these turn out to be village women in for Friday shopping. Sharp social lines between the old and new cities are being rapidly erased and population flows more freely between the quarters. Downtown shops which formerly specialized in foreign goods now carry locally produced goods little differentiated from the lines handled elsewhere in the city. Rarely now does one see the pretentiously overgroomed; but rarely too does one see really destitute persons.

The overall appearance of the city reflects some of this social homogenization. The newer quarters of Cairo are somewhat shabbier than they were some ten years ago. They are also far more crowded, since all now dare to tread where once only the wealthier classes isolated themselves. The older quarters, however, are less depressed than they were some years ago, for public housing projects, slum clearance, and more equitable income distribution have been making their influences felt. Trades which formerly catered to a Western or Westernized clientele, such as furniture makers, now seem to do a thriving business among the indigenous working class of the city. Whereas fifteen years ago one was struck with the rural qualities of the city, today one is impressed with the urbanity of large quarters in Cairo. It is as if, in that intimate reciprocal relationship between the city and her national hinterland, Cairo has again forged ahead of the countryside, but her lead, as in the past, will again be drawn back to her roots.

Thus, the current crisis has in some important ways altered the city but in other equally important ways has scarcely affected her. The war has caused many projects for improvement to grind to a temporary halt; it has increased the city's responsibility for caring for an even larger proportion of the country's population and has led to attendant problems generated by numbers and density. On the other hand, the main thrust of the social revolution has not been deflected, however interrupted the economic revolution. The movement to Egyptian modernity has been sustained.

One final note. The publisher suggested to me that, perhaps in this somewhat dark hour of Cairo's history, it might appear insensitive to retain the word victorious in the title of a book about Cairo. I disagree profoundly. Al-Qāhirah still means "The Victorious"; Naṣr still means "victory." This name sustained her during the chaos of the late Middle Ages, during the inglorious defeat by the Turks, during the even more humiliating temporary capitulation to Napoleon, and during the long decades of colonial servility to a British High Commissioner. Survival, not temporary fortune, is the true measure of victory. In 1969, Cairo marked with subdued celebrations her thousandth anniversary. Few cities in the world share with her such longevity and sustained importance. That one can no more think of the world without its heritage of the great city of Cairo than one can think of the world without that city's silent sentinels—the pyramids—is perhaps the ultimate defense of

Cairo: City Victorious.

Appendix

Bibliography

Appendix A: A Methodological Note

THE variables selected for the original analysis of the *Census of 1947* were initially grouped under four headings which were considered related to the social dimensions suggested by the social area analysts, but no attempt was made to replicate the exact measurements employed by Shevky and Bell.[1] My efforts, rather, were directed toward developing measures that would be sensitive indicators of the unique social conditions of Cairo. Furthermore, my limited data precluded certain of the standard measures, as will be explained below. The major headings under which variables were grouped were demographic characteristics, family characteristics, socio-economic status characteristics, and ethnic identity. The final three categories were consciously predicated on the assumptions of social area analysis, although their ultimate combination was not attempted until the empirical interrelationships had been thoroughly investigated.

To summarize the demographic structure of each census tract, population pyramids were constructed from the age and sex distributions. Density of development was measured by computing the ratio of residents per square kilometer. In addition, because Cairo had experienced rapid growth resulting from rural-to-urban migration, it was felt that differences in the sex ratio might be found that would distinguish areas differentially affected by in-migration. Therefore, two final demographic measures, a general sex ratio and a sex ratio specific for the migration-prone ages between 15 and 50, were also computed.

To summarize the nature of family life in various quarters of the city, other indices were devised. Among these were the average size of family and the standard fertility ratio.[2] In addition, it was believed that some measure of marital status would be useful in describing the nature of family life, since significant cultural differences exist within the city that determine such matters as usual age at marriage and prevalence of divorce. To reflect these differences the percentage of females sixteen years of age and older who were listed as never married was computed and a similar rate of never-married males was derived.

These rates were presumed to measure somewhat different phenomena, justifying the inclusion of both. For females, eventual entrance into at least one marital union is virtually universal in Egypt. Therefore, the percentage of females in a census tract who have reached the age of sixteen or over but are still listed as "never married" represents in reality the proportion of women not yet married. Since this proportion decreases rapidly with age, the measure may be taken as an indicator of the "usual age of marriage" for females in a census tract. Given a normal age distribution, tracts having high percentages of never-married females contain populations in which females typically marry at older ages; conversely, those with low percentages of never-married females contain populations characterized by very early marriages.

The male rate, on the other hand, appears to be more complexly determined, being affected not only by the typical age at marriage but even more by the selective migration of single males. Transients, migrants who plan to return to their villages, and young, career-oriented males establishing residences apart from their families of origin tend to gravitate to sections of the city which provide housing and services suited to their special requirements. Their concentration in turn gives to certain census tracts high rates of "never-married" men, just as their selective out-migration from rural zones gives these areas typically low rates. There is absolutely no evidence that a similar selective process operates for females in Cairo, since the culture effectively bars single females from migrating singly and from living alone.

In the original study two additional indicators of marital status were computed, although these were later dropped and another measure substituted. These were the percentage of widowed and divorced men and a similar rate computed for women. Neither of these measures proved particularly sensitive. The male rate, for example, was found to be relatively constant throughout the city (in the neighborhood of 5 percent), a fact explainable by the ease with which widowed and divorced men remarry and by the nature of the census data which presented *current* marital status only. It was later omitted on the grounds of lack of discrimination. The female rate, on the other hand, did vary from one part of the city to another and was usually high enough (in the neighborhood of 20 percent) to discriminate. However, because it combined phenomena of very different meaning, I believed it could not be justified on conceptual grounds. Widowhood and the divorced state are perceived very differently and the attendant social condition of the indi-

[1] At the time (ca. 1958) I was deeply affected by the seminal study of Eshref Shevky and Wendell Bell, *Social Area Analysis: Theory, Illustrative Application and Computational Procedures*, Stanford University Series in Sociology, No. 1 (Stanford University Press, Stanford: 1955).

[2] The fertility ratio used differed slightly from that usually employed in American demography. It was the number of children under five years of age per thousand women 15-49. As will be noted, the age range of fecund females has been expanded, a decision justified by the actual behavior of Egyptian women. Childbearing begins earlier (the median age at marriage is 20, and the legal minimum of 16 is not always honored) and is sustained later in life.

vidual is therefore significantly affected. Young widows tend to remarry; current widows are therefore primarily older; on the other hand, currently divorced women are generally younger, unlikely to remarry, and poorly sustained by culturally approved support. The social stigma of divorce (and it should be borne in mind here that urban Egypt has a divorce rate that exceeds that of the United States and is one of the highest in the world) coupled with the financial deprivations that beset a divorced woman in a culture which provides few gainful legitimate ways of earning a living for ill-educated women, mean that divorced women represent a significant departure from traditional family life. I therefore decided to eliminate the general measure which combined widows and divorcées and to substitute, in later analyses, a new measure based on the ratio of currently divorced women per 100 ever-married women.[3]

Shevky had utilized, in addition to the fertility ratio, two other indicators of "urbanization" or "familism": the percentage of single-family dwellings, and the rate of female participation in the labor force. Neither of these indices was relevant to the Cairo case and no attempt was made to include them. For one thing, data on house types are not available in the Egyptian census. Furthermore, multi-family flats predominate in Cairo. Single-family dwellings remain rare. A few are scattered in upper-income districts where they have frequently been converted to institutional uses. At the periphery, they are found chiefly in Maʿādi and, most recently, in newer developments at the outskirts of Heliopolis and on the Silver Coast. However, they are also most likely to be found in the poorest quarters of the periphery as well, inhabited by farmers in the agricultural fringe and by tomb custodians and squatters in the Cities of the Dead. House type, therefore, is not yet indicative of family life or the values of familism, although recent beginnings in suburbanization suggest future differentiation more in line with Western developments.

Female employment, Shevky's final indicator of familism, is equally irrelevant thus far in Egypt. Few women work and those who do are drawn from both extremes of the social scale. According to a sample labor force study conducted by the Egyptian government in 1957, only 6 percent of all females over five years of age were employed in urban (nonagricultural) occupations, and except for a small number of professional and sales women, most were engaged in domestic service. This difficulty was compounded in the *Census of 1947* by an anomalous classificatory system which effectively prevented the computation of *any* meaningful labor force figures for females. Housewives engaged in caring for their own homes were, together with servants working for wages, classified as engaged in domestic service! Therewith went any opportunity to measure real labor force participation. Had domestic servants (including housewives) been excluded from the computation, most census tracts would have had a female labor force participation rate of zero, and none would have had more than 1 percent.

Under the general heading of socio-economic status were subsumed the largest battery of indices, although these were often indirect. Income and rent data, which should have occupied a central position in any index purporting to measure economic differentiation, were simply not available. Housing quality data, which might have served as a partial substitute, were similarly lacking, although it was possible to compute a measure of room overcrowding, the persons/room ratio, which I felt would indicate relative position in the housing market. In addition, I was able to examine a general land use map prepared during a 1956 field survey that had been conducted in conjunction with the abortive Master Plan of the city. Material from this map, which classified building quality as poor, good, or excellent, was later used to validate partially the patterns derived from the indirect statistical measures.[4]

Occupational data, which ideally also should have been included in an index of socio-economic status, were actually available by census tracts in 1947, but the gross categories employed in that particular cross-tabulation were of such dubious value that I reluctantly decided to abandon the attempt to develop an occupational index. All residents five years of age and older had been classified into nine categories shown in the table on p. 245.

Given these categories, it was virtually impossible to select any occupational index that would reflect relative status, skill or responsibility, without distortion from cultural or data-collection anomalies. The traditional distinction between blue collar and white collar was lost by a classification system which grouped workers in given industries, from top management to lowest unskilled employee, within a single category. Even commerce, which in Western industrialized societies at least is associated with literacy and white-collar status, does not imply a similar level of stratification in Cairo where the ranks of the commercially employed are swelled by petty marginal operators (see note a to the following table). My final decision, then, was to eliminate the occupational variable.[5]

[3] The use of "ever-married women" as the denominator represents my attempt to free the measure from contamination from the other index of marital status, namely, the proportion of adult females not yet married.

[4] This map was not available officially and I trust I shall be forgiven for having hastily transcribed the major outlines of the survey findings from a single copy on file at the planning office of the Cairo *Baladīyah*.

[5] In retrospect and after doing some additional research into the Egyptian class structure and the types of occupational cleavages resulting from the transition from a traditional to a modern

Category	Total Cairo Workers (in thousands)
Agriculture, hunting, fishing	23
Mining and quarrying	183
Building and construction	33
Transportation and related activities	51
Commerce[a]	140
Personal services[b]	755
Other services and professions	148
Persons unproductively employed[c]	289
Those with no employment[d]	178
Total: all persons 5 years or older living in Cairo in 1947	1,800

[a] This figure included, in addition to stockbrokers, wholesalers, and retailers of the conventional variety, the vast army of semi-employed Cairenes who watch cars for a penny, make tea on street corners, peddle shoelaces or broken bottles, and otherwise engage themselves in a host of commercial activities as imaginative as they are unrewarding.

[b] Here we find all the housewives of Cairo, as well as an undetermined (and undeterminable) number of paid domestic servants, from top chefs in fancy hotels to little boys who carry packages.

[c] This interesting category, as explained later, was comprised chiefly of children enrolled in school, although it probably also included beggars!

[d] Originally I interpreted this category as "unemployed" but it included, in addition to those persons seeking work, many others incapacitated by lack of physical or mental drive or who could not be classified, or whose occupations were unknown. This became clear when I compared the rates for 1947 with those of 1960. The consistent drop in rates was due not to higher employment rates but greater specification of the classification itself.

My methodological dilemma was a difficult one; namely, how to select measures indicating relative levels of socio-economic stratification in the absence of income, rent, and occupational data. Education, the conventional third component of most combined indices, had by default to carry most of the burden and no one is more aware than I am of the grave limitations this imposed on the validity of any combined index I could construct for socio-economic status.

economy, I have altered my first position and now firmly believe that *some* occupational index should have been included in the study, even if the index did not express a direct aspect of social stratification. If I were to conduct the study again, I would dichotomize the first seven categories into (a) those chiefly within the modern sector of the economy, namely transport, construction, commerce, and professional services; and (b) those chiefly within the traditional sector of the economy, such as agriculture, mining, and personal services. For any index, I would definitely use only the *male* labor force. The base for the rate would then be males classified in the first seven categories. This hindsight, however, comes too late to affect the study being reported here. Again, my only consolation lies in the fact that the *Census of 1960*, which I sought to compare with 1947, included so basically altered (and substantially improved) an occupational classification system that, had an index been derived from the original data, it could not have been replicated in the second census year.

The use of education as an index to status, however, is not without substantial justification, especially in the case of a newly industrializing country such as Egypt. Earlier research undertaken on the nature of Egyptian urbanization,[6] in which I had attempted to devise a scale of "urbanity" for Egyptian towns on the basis of demographic and industrial characteristics, had led me to the firm conviction that the single best index to way of life, values, degree of modernity, and social class position of subgroups in Egypt was the female literacy rate. No other variable appeared to occupy so pivotal a position in social differentiation. First, female literacy is associated with higher income, since only persons in comfortable circumstances can afford to spare girls from their farm and/or domestic duties (often by hiring a substitute, a young servant girl); only they can afford what appears to the outsider to be the "nominal" costs of books, clothing, and other materials required for school attendance. However, within the economic groups financially able to send girls to school, the decisive variable is value orientation. Along with a decision to educate females go many related cultural values, each of which implies a partial break with tradition and a preference for modernism. These in turn are significantly related to basic cleavages and distinctions in Egyptian social structure.

On the basis of this reasoning, then, a literacy index (constructed by computing the percentage of females five years of age or older in a census tract who could read and write) was placed under the rough heading, socio-economic status. A similar index, the male literacy rate, was also constructed. It seemed highly desirable to separate the two rates, not only because they were significantly different (male rates were generally three times higher than female rates) but because it appeared that even the size of the differential might reveal something about the double standard it implied. Whereas the female literacy rate can be viewed as an indicator of "conspicuous leisure," no such interpretation should be given to the male rate which I believe represents real differential power in the labor market.

My justification for selecting literacy rather than a more complex measure of educational attainment was a rather simple one. Only 57 percent of the males and 31 percent of the females of five years and older were classified as literate in Cairo in 1947, even after the exclusion of the "unknowns," most of whom may be presumed to be illiterate. Literacy rates ranged widely in the city, varying from a low of about 3 percent for females in certain agricultural fringe areas to a high of almost 90 percent for males in the highest status, most "Westernized" Gold

[6] Some of these findings appear in J. Abu-Lughod, "Urbanization in Egypt: Present State and Future Prospects," *Economic Development and Cultural Change*, XIII (April 1965), 313-343. The detailed study, however, has never been published.

Coast of the central city along the Nile. Had some higher educational level been selected, the result would have been to reduce the rates in a majority of census tracts to near zero, and the absolute numbers (particularly for females) would have been so small that meaningful rates could not have been computed, given the large number of unknowns and the relative unreliability of data on educational levels.

Change, particularly in the realm of education, has been taking place very rapidly in Egypt in recent decades, and each successive census has documented an impressive rise in literacy. Because of this, it was felt that the literacy rate based on almost the total population was a better reflection of the operation of *past* values than it was of contemporary ones. It therefore seemed desirable to include a measure of *current* educational differentials to supplement the literacy rate. Such a measure, for example, as percent of school-aged children (male and female) actually enrolled in school would have been an ideal one, but since these data were not available, a substitute measure had to be devised.

In my search for such a measure I was quite fortunate, for my struggles with the Egyptian census classificatory system for occupations had led me to an early insight. The unusual category of "unproductively employed," which accounted for a substantial proportion of Cairo's so-called labor force (really potential labor pool), upon closer examination of summary tables cross-tabulating occupation by age, was found to be comprised *almost* entirely of school-aged children. I then decided that some rough approximation of school enrollment rates could be obtained by dividing the number of persons five years and older listed as "unproductively employed" by the number of persons between five and twenty years of age in the census tract (per 100). This rate was computed separately for the sexes (ratios of male children in school and female children in school),[7] since the difference between the two, while less pronounced than the difference between male and female literacy rates, was still large enough to be affected by abnormal age and sex distributions.

Two additional measures, actually designed to tap the dimension Tryon had called "Economic Independence,"[8] were also included under the general heading of socioeconomic status: the handicapped rate (number of persons with reported mental or physical disability per 1,000 population),[9] and the rate of male unemployment.[10] It was hoped that these measures might reveal both economically depressed sections of the city and those sections to which a dependent population had gravitated.

The final category of ethnic identity included two variables which, while closely correlated with one another, were not merely reciprocals. The first was the percentage of Muslims residing in each census tract; the second was the percentage of non-Egyptian nationals in each tract. In order to demonstrate why both measures were considered necessary, I must digress somewhat to describe some of the basic communal cleavages in Cairo society.

In 1947 some 83 percent of the city's residents were Muslims, a lower proportion than was to be found in the country as a whole. Of the remainder, the largest majority were Egyptian Copts, adherents to a monophysite Christian sect who had resisted conversion to Islam. In addition, Cairo in 1947 still contained a fairly sizeable Jewish community, concentrated within three census tracts in the oldest parts of the city. Another small minority consisted of Protestant, Greek Orthodox, and Maronite Christians, largely from Syria-Lebanon, who held themselves aloof from other Christian sects. And

[7] I do not claim that my measure is numerically equivalent to the *actual* school enrollment figure; I simply claim that the measure would probably correlate very highly with real school enrollment and that therefore it allows us to locate census tracts with respect to their *relative* ranks on school enrollment. Obviously, a more direct measurement, were it available, would be superior.

[8] Robert Tryon, *Identification of Social Areas by Cluster Analysis: A General Method with an Application to the San Francisco Bay Area*, University of California Publications in Psychology, Volume 8, Number 1 (University of California Press, Berkeley and Los Angeles: 1955).

[9] It was recognized in advance that the 1947 Census had recorded institutionalized population by place of institution, rather than permanent residence. Therefore, I was aware that the several large hospitals in the Cairo metropolitan area would cause distortions in the rates for their census tracts. However, it was also believed that these rates would be so markedly higher than the norm that they could be easily identified. This proved to be correct. In later computations involving correlation coefficients between the handicapped rate and other variables, the three census tracts containing the major mental and two large general hospitals were omitted. What I could not have anticipated was that the procedure for dealing with the institutionalized population would be changed for the 1960 Census, a fact which reduced the value of replicating the handicapped rate.

[10] This was computed using the "no employment" category of 1947, which at the beginning I believed measured unemployment. It was gradually realized that the category was only partially composed of the strictly defined unemployed, i.e., persons actively seeking employment. The remainder were probably either so ill-defined (because their unemployment was being disguised behind some amorphous profession) or so withdrawn from the labor market that, while they constituted a dependent population, they would not be included in an economist's rate of unemployment. I therefore retained the category but interpreted it more broadly as an indicator of economic dependency and marginality to the productive system. Again, some loss in comparability occurred when the 1960 Census tightened its definition of unemployment. In the latter document, the unemployed were distinguished from the unemployable and the marginal employees, so that the rates in the latter year were substantially lower than those for the former.

finally, there were the foreign nationals—chiefly Greek and Italian but containing representatives of almost every nationality in the world—practically all of whom (except the Sudanese and the Turks) were non-Muslims. Thus, the identity between Egyptian and Muslim, while close, was not exact.

In 1947 the number of foreign nationals residing in Cairo constituted only 3 percent of the total, representing a substantial reduction from previous eras. Despite their small numbers, however, they exercised power disproportionate to their size. Furthermore, because of their tendency to concentrate within certain small areas of the city, they affected the ecological pattern of the city out of proportion to their numbers. It, therefore, seemed desirable to distinguish between those subareas that were non-Muslim by virtue of the presence of foreigners and those non-Muslim areas containing Copts, Jews, and other indigenous communities. Both religion and nationality, then, were included.

Thus, in my initial study undertaken in 1958, some 19 statistical measures were devised to summarize the differences between the populations residing in the 216 census tracts of Cairo. Conceptually, these variables were grouped into four general types—demographic, family, socio-economic status, and ethnic dimensions—but no attempt was made to combine them. Distribution maps were prepared for most of the variables, from which the general ecological outlines of the city began to emerge. Some of the distribution maps were remarkably similar in form; others were clearly deviant. From these visual impressions the idea occurred that there might be some way to construct composite maps; however, no methodology for doing so had yet presented itself. All that was clear at that time was that the logical constructs of social area analysis could not be justified. Only in 1962 was it determined that factor analysis was a reasonable way to arrive at a coherent synthesis.

In 1962, when the results of the *Census of 1960* were published, I immediately began to replicate those indices which had been of proven sensitivity in 1947, wherever comparable data were available. Before this could be done, however, it was necessary to obtain comparable boundaries, both of the census tracts in each year and of the city boundaries which had, in the meantime, been altered. In brief, the following corrections were made: (1) when a 1960 census tract boundary contained two 1947 census tracts, data for the earlier year were recombined and a new set of indices computed; (2) when a 1947 census tract had been subdivided into more than one tract in 1960, the data from 1960 were combined and a single set of indices computed; (3) peripheral tracts, where comparability was in doubt, were eliminated from the analysis; and (4) all tracts in 1960 beyond the 1947 boundaries of the city were eliminated and all tracts ceded to other districts in 1960 which had fallen within the city limits in 1947 were added. These operations resulted in a final total of 206 reproduced and exactly comparable census tracts retained for the study. Map XIX below shows the location of these replicated tracts.

Standardization of the indices remained the most difficult task. No one who has worked with serial census data needs to be reminded of the sad fact that the census exists for purposes other than the convenience of the researcher. Nor indeed can consistency from one census to the next be demanded when this would fixate data presentation at an unimproved level. Nevertheless, changes in definitions, methods of presentation, classification systems, and the like must all be taken into consideration in research involving more than one census date. Sometimes compromises are possible, in other cases measures must be dropped, and in still other cases the researcher can only hope that the inevitable distortions will not be great enough to invalidate his conclusions. All three techniques were necessary in this study. Table A-1 summarizes the variables initially computed and identifies whether they could be replicated in 1960, given the data in that census. Changes in definition and other *caveats* are presented as notes to the table.

These inconsistencies in the availability of data led inevitably to a truncation of the list of usable variables. A final set of only thirteen variables (see Table A-2) was used in the factor analysis that followed.

TABLE A-1. STATISTICAL INDICES POSSIBLE FOR CAIRO IN 1947 AND 1960

Index	*Available in 1947*	*Available in 1960*
Average persons/room	yes	yes
Average persons/family[1]	yes	yes
Density (persons/sq. km.)	yes	yes[2]
Sex ratio, all ages	yes	yes
Sex ratio, 15-49 only	yes	yes
Fertility ratio[3]	yes	yes
Percent females never married	yes[4]	yes[4]
Percent males never married	yes[4]	yes[4]
Percent ever-married females divorced	yes[4]	yes[4]
Handicapped persons/1000 population	yes[5]	yes[5]
Males unemployed[6]	yes	yes
Percent gainfully employed females	no[7]	yes[8]
Percent females literate	yes[9]	yes[9]
Percent males literate	yes[9]	yes[9]
Percent males 5-20 in school	yes[10]	no[8]
Percent females 5-20 in school	yes[10]	no[8]
Percent Muslims	yes	yes
Percent foreign nationals	yes	no
Population pyramid type	yes	yes

NOTES TO TABLE A-1

1 This variable was dropped because of a change in census procedure concerning the reporting of institutionalized population. In 1947, institutionalized population was reported by present location; in 1960, it was reported by permanent home address. Therefore, computations of persons per family varied widely. Short of recomputing an entirely new rate which would have excluded the "single person families" in both years, it seemed better to drop the index which, in any case, had not proved particularly valuable.

2 The densities for 1960 had to be computed using area measurements that appeared only in the *Census of 1947*. These were adjusted in gross fashion when tracts were combined or grouped. However, those cases where boundary changes were slight or marginal could not be corrected. Therefore, some of my density figures for 1960 undoubtedly contain errors but of small magnitude.

3 Between 1947 and 1960, Egypt experienced a radical drop in the infant mortality rate, the Cairo rate actually being halved. Therefore, there has been a major shift upward in the general fertility ratio which is quite sensitive to changes in the rate of infant survival. Despite this trend, I retained the fertility measure in this study, since it was used to determine relative positions of census tracts within the ecological structure rather than as an absolute measure.

4 In the *Census of 1947*, the base population for which marital status data were presented was the population sixteen years of age and older. Therefore, all the 1947 rates concerning marital status have this as a base. In the *Census of 1960*, the population covered in the table on marital status included all those fifteen years of age and older. My 1960 rates, therefore, diverge slightly from those computed for 1947, but the difference again appears to be minimal. The net result, *ceteris paribus*, would be to increase *slightly* the percentage of never-marrieds. The change in definition would not be likely to affect the divorced-women measure, since its base is "ever-married women."

5 See note 1 concerning changed treatment of institutionalized persons.

6 In 1947 the base used for presenting occupational data was the total population five years of age and older. In 1960, this base was revised to six years of age and older. Apart from a slight but constant change in all rates, this did not appear to be a serious contraindication to its retention. The change in definition of "unemployed" was a much more serious difficulty, and the results were not as successful as I had hoped.

7 This rate could not be computed in 1947 because of the listing of housewives as "employed in domestic service."

8 As an experiment I computed this rate in 1960. What I found was that it was primarily associated with high socio-economic status. Employed women were either educated themselves or were domestic servants who received room and board as part of their compensation. When the correlation coefficients between this variable and all other measures were computed, I discovered that they were almost identical to the coefficients obtained when the 1947 variable of females in school was correlated with the remaining variables. While the two variables appear superficially different, they evidently reflect a common (but amorphous) reality. I therefore decided to use females in school in the 1947 analysis and substitute females in paid employment in the 1960 analysis. No measure of school enrollment could be computed for 1960, due to the absence of data.

9 There was a rather drastic change in the age group for which literacy was reported. In 1947, literacy status had been given for all persons five years of age or older. In 1960, this information was given only for the population fifteen years of age and older. This was the largest shift in base population in the census. I made a number of independent investigations to determine to what extent the rates are changed for various subclasses of population by a change in population age base. The male rate appears to remain almost constant, dropping only slightly when the population between five and fifteen is omitted. The female rate, on the other hand, tends to decrease rapidly as the minimum age of the population base rises, reflecting the many decades during which females were neglected in the educational system. Although direct evidence is lacking, it is reasonable to assume that the population in the middle ranks of stratification is most affected by a change in the age base when the literacy rate is computed, for it was this group which neglected the education of the older generation of women but has taken enthusiastically to the schooling of its younger generation. Eliminating the effects of this recent interest and concern leads to an underestimation of the literacy level in all groups, but particularly in the middle group, i.e., the group undergoing the most marked transition. I therefore place a *caveat* before the use of the two differently defined literacy rates, but believe again that my use of the measure, to assign relative ranks *only*, removes some of the more glaring defects of noncomparability.

10 It will be recalled that this was merely an approximation and should be treated with care.

TABLE A-2. STATISTICAL INDICES ACTUALLY USED FOR CAIRO IN 1947 AND 1960

Index	*Comments*
Demographic	
1. Density	The population pyramid, w useful for identifying dev tracts, could not be used correlational analysis.
2. Sex ratio, 15-49.9	The general sex ratio dropped in favor of this specific ratio which pro more sensitive.
Family Characteristics	
3. Fertility ratio	Average family size was dropped.
4. Percent females never married	
5. Percent males never married	
6. Percent ever-married females divorced	Replaced two earlier measu
Socio-economic Status	
7. Persons/room ratio	
8. Percent females literate	
9. Percent males literate	
10. Percent females in school	Used for 1947.
Percent females employed	Used for 1960.
11. Handicapped rate	
12. Male unemployment rate	
Ethnic Identity	
13. Percent Muslims in tract	The loss of the important iable of foreigners could be helped, since this cr tabulation was omitted fr the 1960 returns.

Pearsonian product moment correlation coefficients (zero-order) between each and every variable for each of the two separate census years were computed, the results of which are reported in Matrix R reproduced as Table A-3. The r_r's were based on the total of 206 cases, except

TABLE A-3. MATRICES OF ZERO-ORDER CORRELATION COEFFICIENTS BETWEEN VARIABLES IN CAIRO; 1947 ABOVE THE DIAGONAL; 1960 BELOW THE DIAGONAL

Variables	*1*	*2*	*3*	*4*	*5*	*6*	*7*	*8*	*9*	*10*	*11*	*12*	*13*
1 (PPR)		.22	.05	.60	−.65	−.32	−.42	.11	−.65	−.70	−.51	.47	.44
2 (Den.)	.28		−.10	.24	−.18	.02	−.11	.07	−.09	−.17	−.18	.00	.13
3 (Sex)	−.03	−.05		−.19	.09	.15	.55	−.10	.04	.18	.13	−.23	−.02
4 (Fert.)	.73	.18	.02		−.81	−.48	−.66	.22	−.62	−.82	−.48	.47	.55
5 (FNM)	−.74	−.13	−.00	−.84		.42	.75	−.17	.81	.89	.63	−.59	−.51
6 (F. Div.)	−.29	−.09	−.12	−.54	.44		.41	−.05	.36	.40	.23	−.50	.04
7 (MNM)	−.52	−.05	.39	−.66	.78	.42		−.17	.68	.73	.55	−.59	−.33
8 (Hand.)	.50	.23	.02	.43	−.40	−.15	−.24		−.08	−.14	−.14	−.02	−.03
9 (M. Lit.)	−.74	−.22	−.04	−.64	.78	.31	.58	−.51		.89	.71	−.70	−.45
10 (F. Lit.)	−.84	−.23	.11	−.80	.90	.35	.71	−.50	.89		.67	−.67	−.64
11 (F.Sch.Emp.)	−.85	−.28	.08	−.85	.81	.45	.60	−.52	.71	.87		−.49	−.35
12 (M. Unemp.)	.43	.18	−.03	.39	−.37	−.19	−.23	.32	−.32	−.42	−.46		.24
13 (Muslim)	.51	.21	−.07	.47	−.47	.08	−.31	.17	−.37	−.50	−.45	.16	

Correlation coefficients, computed to six decimal places, have been rounded to the nearest one-hundredth for presentation only. Complete figures were retained for computations based upon these matrices.

those involving the handicapped rate in 1947, where three extreme cases were omitted to minimize the distortion they otherwise would have introduced. As can be seen, many of the variables demonstrated approximately the same intercorrelations in both years. Others showed variations which appear to be caused more by census redefinitions than by secular trends among the variables. To the extent that these gross similarities are found, it appears legitimate to use the data for time comparisons. Preliminary inspection of the correlation matrices indicated high intercorrelations within certain groups of variables which appeared somewhat independent of one another. On the strength of this observation, I decided to do a factor analysis for the purpose of extracting the underlying factorial structure that could account for the intercorrelations.

The data contained in Table A-3 were used as input for an IBM Library Program (No. 6.0.091) for Principal Axes Factor Analysis Using Hotelling's Iterative Procedure. Seven factors, accounting for more than 90 percent of the total variance in each year, were successively extracted from the original matrices and the sequential residual matrices. Table A-4 presents the sum of the squares and the percentage of variance accounted for in each data year by the four factors retained for later rotation. As can be seen, the solutions are quite comparable for both years and in each case the first four factors accounted for better than three-fourths of the total variance. Since subsequent factors added little marginal explanatory power, the study was confined to the first four.

One of the first items of interest in Table A-4 is the degree to which the first factor explains the variance contained in the correlation matrices, amounting to about half in both data years. This dominance of the first factor is not uncommon in principal axes factor solutions, but it should be noted that it appears even more dominant in these results than could be accounted for by the inherent bias of the method. A Thurstone centroid extraction, based upon fifteen variables for 1947 alone, had yielded a similarly dominant centroid factor, suggesting that, at least for the limited number of variables included in this study and for a city like Cairo, marked as it is by gross cultural variations, the major social differentiations reflected in ecological organization are almost unidimensional. This will be seen more clearly in Table A-5 which presents the factor loadings (before rotation) of each variable on the four basic factors.

TABLE A-4. VARIANCE ACCOUNTED FOR BY EXTRACTED FACTORS. CAIRO, 1947 AND 1960

Factor	*Sum of the Squares*	*Cumulative percent variance explained*
Factor I		
1947	6.25875360	48.14
1960	6.69599490	51.51
Factor II		
1947	1.40172870	58.92
1960	1.25691320	61.18
Factor III		
1947	1.20415960	68.18
1960	1.12635980	69.84
Factor IV		
1947	.99389126	75.83
1960	.99294947	77.48

As can be seen from Table A-5, the variables with the highest loadings on Factor I included the persons per room ratio (negatively related), the male and female literacy rates (positively associated), the female school enrollment and employment rates (again, positively related), and the handicapped and male unemployment rates (negatively associated with the factor). It had been hypothesized initially that all of these variables would indicate the relative socio-economic status of census tract populations, and in each case the direction of the association was in the hypothesized direction. This led me to identify Factor I tentatively as an underlying vector in-

TABLE A-5. UNROTATED FACTOR LOADINGS OF THE THIRTEEN VARIABLES. CAIRO, 1947 AND 1960

Variables	Factor loadings on Factor I	Factor II	Factor III	Factor IV
1947				
Persons/room	—.73745	.31617	—.05425	.16009
Density	—.20738	.21811	.64212	—.08549
Sex ratio	.23620	.72440	—.40088	.43319
Fertility ratio	—.84861	.03478	.14870	.08884
F. never married	.91990	—.08706	.00843	—.07265
Females divorced	.49957	.44923	.34784	—.32095
Males never married	.81402	.39056	—.13016	.16218
Handicapped	—.17090	—.16523	.53668	.70820
Males literate	.88930	—.10896	.19172	—.01099
Females literate	.96226	—.10756	.00796	.04548
F./Sch./Emp.	.73169	—.08374	—.02735	.00429
Males unemployed	—.73025	—.25448	—.34112	—.07412
Muslims	—.56829	.49374	.14593	—.34867
1960				
Persons/room	—.88117	.07536	.17530	.07254
Density	—.28939	.23222	.52830	—.44873
Sex ratio	.07894	.85297	—.17618	.43423
Fertility ratio	—.89163	.04241	—.17787	.07727
F. never married	.92180	.06336	.16389	—.16271
Females divorced	.46643	—.20945	.67811	.28060
Males never married	.74224	.48797	.27552	.06272
Handicapped	—.56190	.30773	.23128	—.22436
Males literate	.84351	—.08590	—.02477	—.10615
Females literate	.95776	.06647	—.03237	—.07347
F./Sch./Emp.	.92634	—.04257	—.00980	.04921
Males unemployed	—.48905	.20055	.14379	—.38395
Muslims	—.52476	—.18793	.47653	.49220

dicating high socio-economic status, although I later redefined it as life style for the following reason.

Variables that had been initially included in the study for the purpose of measuring *family* characteristics showed in some cases even higher loadings on this "socio-economic" factor than did some of the purer "status" variables, indicating that in Egypt variables reflecting differences in family life have not become disassociated from socio-economic status. In other words, class position in Cairo is a major determinant of family variations, higher socio-economic status being associated with higher educational achievement for women and a delayed age at marriage, which, in turn, are associated with decreased fertility after marriage. This lower fertility, despite the better survivorship rate of infants born to parents of adequate means, is great enough to carry over into a lower general fertility ratio.[11] This close association between socio-economic level and the usual age at marriage, as well as the fertility ratio, is seen in the high loadings these variables have on the first factor. (The fertility ratio loads —.85 in 1947 and —.89 in 1960 on Factor I; the percentage of women over fifteen-sixteen not yet married loads +.92 in 1947 and 1960 on Factor I.) Even the other two "family characteristic" variables, males never married and ever-married women divorced, while apparently related to other factors, still have surprisingly high loadings on Factor I, not all of which could be removed by judicious rotation.

Factor II was tentatively identified as reflecting the regions of concentration of single males in the city, for the two variables with the highest factor loadings are the sex ratio in the "migration-prone" years between fifteen and fifty and the percentage of never-married men. No other variables appear consistently and highly related in both study years.

The tentative identifications and possible interpretations of Factors III and IV were not readily apparent from the factor pattern before rotation. I shall therefore postpone a discussion of these factors and deal with them after describing the rotational procedures. Here it is sufficient to call the reader's attention to the interesting fact that several variables had "mirror image" loadings on the two factors—close in numerical value but opposite in sign. This phenomenon was used to advantage in the later rotation.

Graphs were prepared of paired factor loadings to investigate whether greater analytical strength could be obtained from rotation. It appeared that rotation would improve the factorial solution, but the question was whether to perform an oblique rotation (which might increase the chances for simple structure but at the expense of the independence of the factors) or, in the rotation, to retain the orthogonality of the factors, even if it meant a sacrifice in simple structure. In reaching a decision, I was guided by the ultimate purpose of the methodology, which was to make it possible to score each census tract in the city on *separate* factors or dimensions of differentiation. It seemed reasonable, therefore, to retain orthogonality so that the ecological patterns I later wished to plot could be treated independently of one another.

An orthogonal varimax analytical rotation was therefore performed, using as input the Factor Matrix (Table A-5) shown above. An IBM Library Program for Varimax Matrix Rotation (No. 06.0.094) was employed, which produced factor loadings after rotation as well as the communality values. Table A-6 presents the factor loadings after rotation.

As can be seen, rotation succeeded in clarifying the first two factors and, despite the fact that *no attempt* was made to maximize the congruence of the factor patterns in the two separate data years, the rotations and the resulting factor loadings for 1947 and 1960 are almost identical for the first two factors. In their clarified form, these were identified as a style of life factor and a demo-

[11] These interrelationships are explored quantitatively in J. Abu-Lughod, "The Emergence of Differential Fertility in Urban Egypt," *Milbank Memorial Fund Quarterly*, XLIII (April 1965), 235-253.

TABLE A-6. FACTOR LOADINGS AFTER VARIMAX ORTHOGONAL
OTATION, FIRST FOUR FACTORS ONLY. CAIRO, 1947 AND 1960

'ables	*Factor I*	*Factor II*	*Factor III*	*Factor IV*
7				
ersons/room	—.79729	.15413	.04176	.10578
ensity	—.18230	—.15882	.62386	.25010
:x ratio	—.00339	.96241	—.04026	—.03230
ertility ratio	—.81170	—.19695	.05784	.22442
. never married	.90979	.12432	.02920	—.12295
emales divorced	.41509	.19285	.64861	—.21259
'ales never married	.67027	.62446	.10211	—.09360
andicapped	—.08158	—.03843	.05444	.91377
ales literate	.90411	.06123	.13172	.03290
emales literate	.95300	.17389	—.02199	—.02689
/Sch./Emp.	.72218	.12896	—.03227	—.06262
ales unemployed	—.67654	—.28306	—.41322	—.12699
uslims	—.64538	.02370	.47823	—.25262
)				
rsons/room	—.81233	.01237	.38243	.07184
ensity	—.02761	—.09744	.80309	.21210
x ratio	—.01228	.96994	—.05049	.00360
rtility ratio	—.88699	.00812	.15943	—.16559
never married	.94565	.03891	—.07830	.04082
males divorced	.52479	.03387	—.08886	.67345
ales never married	.76006	.49095	.07998	.08011
andicapped	—.40349	.12986	.56591	—.11077
ales literate	.81462	—.06610	—.25443	—.03092
males literate	.92245	.09904	—.25851	—.01086
/Sch./Emp.	.85281	.06225	—.35614	.13841
ales unemployed	—.30705	—.03047	.54785	—.28845
uslims	—.55955	—.06128	.11579	.66695

graphic factor reflecting the prevalence of young single men.

The analytical rotation did not produce successful results for Factors III and IV which remained incomparable for the two census years and could still not be logically identified or interpreted. Rather than abandon the two factors, I attempted a graphic rotation to maximize comparability on at least one factor. The two axes were kept orthogonal to one another and tipped 45°. Transformation matrices were then computed[12] and each set of factor loadings on Factors III and IV was multiplied by the appropriate transformation matrix to yield new factor pattern matrices for Factors III and IV. This process produced a meaningful Factor III which was retained for the analysis. Factor IV was simply eliminated. The results of the graphic rotation and the new factor loadings for 1947 and 1960 on Factor III (revised) are presented in Table A-8.

TABLE A-7. FACTOR PATTERNS FOR FACTORS I AND II. CAIRO, 1947 AND 1960

Variables	*Factor I* 1947	*Factor I* 1960	*Factor II* 1947	*Factor II* 1960
Factor I				
Persons/room	—	—		
Fertility ratio	—	—		
F. never married	+	+		
Females divorced	+	+		
Handicapped		—		
Males literate	+	+		
Females literate	+	+		
F./Sch./Emp.	+	+		
Males unemployed	—	—	—	
Muslims	—	—		
Factor II				
Sex ratio			+	+
Males never married	+	+	+	+
On Neither				
Density				

TABLE A-8. LOADINGS ON FACTOR III (REVISED) AFTER GRAPHIC ROTATION. CAIRO, 1947 AND 1960

Variables	*1947*	*1960*
Persons/room	.1043	.3212
Density	.6180	.7178
Sex ratio	—.0513	—.0332
Fertility ratio	.1996	—.0044
F. never married	—.0663	—.0265
Females divorced	.3083	.4134
Males never married	.0060	.1132
Handicapped	.6846	.3218
Males literate	—.0346	—.1905
Females literate	.1164	—.2018
F./Sch./Emp.	—.0671	—.1540
Males unemployed	—.3820	.1834
Muslims	.1595	.5535

TABLE A-9. FACTOR PATTERNS FOR ORTHOGONAL FACTORS I, II, AND III (REVISED). CAIRO, 1947 AND 1960

Variables	*Factor I* 1947	*Factor I* 1960	*Factor II* 1947	*Factor II* 1960	*Factor III (revised)* 1947	*Factor III (revised)* 1960
Persons/room	—	—	0[a]	0	0	+
Fertility ratio	—	—	0	0	0	0
F. never married	+	+	0	0	0	0
Males literate	+	+	0	0	0	0
Females literate	+	+	0	0	0	0
F./Sch./Emp.	+	+	0	0	0	0
Females divorced	+	+	0	0	+	+
Handicapped	0	—	0	0	+	+
Males unemployed	—	—	—	0	—	0
Muslims	—	—	0	0	0	+
Density	0	0	0	0	+	+
Sex ratio	0	0	+	+	0	0
Males never married	+	+	+	+	0	0

[a] I have followed the usual procedure by counting any factor loading between ±0.20 as zero in evaluating the approximation to simple structure.

[12] The transformation matrices were, in this case, identical in the two years. Factors remained orthogonal to one another.

TRANSFORMATION MATRIX FROM GRAPHIC ROTATION (λ_{02})

	A″₂	B″₂	C″₂	D″₂
I	1.0	0	0	0
II	0	1.0	0	0
III	0	0	.7071	—.7071
IV	0	0	.7071	.7071

As can be seen from Table A-9, the three variables with consistently high loadings on Factor III in both census years were density (positive), the percentage of divorced women (positive), and the handicapped rate (also positive). The several other variables with significant loadings in single data years formed no logical pattern. In the light of this it appeared reasonable to interpret the third factor as indicating the presence of socially pathological conditions associated with the high density of urban residence. I believed that the factor could help locate high density zones in the city whose populations suffered from more than their share of the disorganization and dependency that often attends urban living for those at the economic margin. Density could be viewed not as a causal element in that disorganization but as a variable associated with the selective concentration of "problem persons" in inlying zones of the city. However, without further tests of validity, my identification of Factor III must remain tentative.

Now that I have presented the findings obtained through factor analyzing the variables included in the study, I must explain how these results were used to score census tracts by weighting the values on each variable for each tract and then combining them into a composite score or "index" to the factor. This step will require a fairly detailed description since few precedents existed at the time it was performed. The first operation in computing the factor scores was to convert the raw computed indices into standardized scores, that is, to express them in terms of their deviation from the mean value of all census tracts. To this end, means and standard deviations for each of the thirteen variables were computed for 1947 and 1960, based upon the distribution of values for each year separately. The results are presented in Table A-10. The two years were standardized separately because of the significant changes in value and distribution that occurred in the interim.

Two Z matrices of standardized scores were constructed on the basis of these results, showing for each separate census year the standardized scores for each census tract on each of the thirteen variables. The standardized score is a measure of the deviation of one value from the mean of all values expressed in terms of the standard deviation. Thus, for example, a census tract whose female literacy rate was exactly equal to the mean of all tract literacy rates would have a standardized or Z score of 0; one whose literacy rate exceeded the mean by a value exactly equal to the interval equivalent to one standard deviation would be scored $+1.0$; negative signs indicate deviations below mean value.

The standardized scores of each census tract were then weighted by means of a β matrix to obtain composite factor scores for each of the census tracts in each of the

TABLE A-10. MEANS AND STANDARD DEVIATIONS OF THE THIRTEEN VARIABLES. CAIRO, 1947 AND 1960

	1947		1960	
Variables	*Mean*[a]	*Standard Deviation*	*Mean*[a]	*Stand Devia*
1. Persons/room ratio (average)	2.17	0.65	2.43	0.
2. Density (000 persons/ sq. km.)	58	56	74	64
3. Sex ratio (males/ 100 females, 15-49 years of age)	109	37.3	105	18.
4. Fertility ratio (children under 5/1000 women, 15-49 years)	545	117	669	144
5. Females never married (%)	13.5	7.1	16.2	5.
6. Females divorced (% of ever-married females)	3.8	1.6	3.7	1.
7. Males never married (%)	29.9	8.6	28.8	6.
8. Handicapped/ 1000 population	8.7	5.9	5.7	3.
9. Males literate (%)	55.3	15.8	65.3	13.
10. Females literate (%)	29.7	17.2	36.3	16.
11. Females in Sch./ employed (%)	24.9	11.8	7.7	6.
12. Males unemployed	9.4	4.3	1.8	1.
13. Muslims	85.5	19.9	89.3	13.

[a] This mean (computed by averaging the census tract rates) is to be confused with the rates for the total city population, s tracts vary in size. No weighting was attempted.

NOTES TO TABLE A-10

Variable 1. The persons/room ratio measured almost the same phenomenon in both years, and the change in means reflects the real fact that between census dates the population of Cairo grew much faster than the housing stock. For the city as a whole, housing density (intensity of occupancy) has definitely increased.

Variable 2. The increase in average density reflects in part the heightened intensity of occupancy but is also the result of an expansion of the urbanized, built-up portion of the city into the rural fringe. The total density of the city in both years is substantially lower than this figure which averages the densities of census tracts, for the simple reason that the least densely settled tracts on the periphery of the city contain very small populations and very large areas, whereas the reverse is true for census tracts in the central core.

Variable 3. The change in sex ratios reflects a real change in the demographic structure of Cairo's population. Between 1947 and 1960, there has been an in-migration of the families of males who migrated singly in the war years prior to 1947, which has tended to equalize the overall sex ratio in the city for the first time since data became available (early nineteenth century). The sex ratio still remains slightly unbalanced in the migration-prone ages.

Variable 4. This variable changed most between census dates, reflecting a real change in the fertility situation in the city. The increase is due largely to the drop in infant mortality rates that occurred in the interim. However, other evidence indicates that there was actually an *increase* in fertility as well, which is in part traceable to an increase in the nuptiality rate, in part to the rural-to-urban migration of families of earlier migrant males, but may in part really be due to pure fertility factors.

Variable 5. This slight change is probably due chiefly to the change in age base of reporting.

Variable 8. The downward shift of the handicapped rate means is probably explainable in terms of the shift in census reporting procedures. The 1947 mean is distorted by the concentration of institutionalized persons within a few census tracts. This distortion is absent in 1960 where the census recorded institutionalized population by place of "usual" residence.

Variables 9 and 10. The population of Cairo has indeed become more literate between 1947 and 1960. The general trend is reflected in the improved means for both males and females in the latter year. However, it will be recalled that the age base for the reporting of literacy status was raised from five to fifteen years of age between 1947 and 1960. The effect of this redefinition of the age base would be to underestimate literacy in 1960. Therefore, the increase in literacy in Cairo was even greater than is evident from a comparison of census tract means.

Variable 11. No congruence between these two means should be expected since the variable is different in the two census years.

Variable 12. As can be seen, a rather marked difference in the means is evident. This does *not* reflect an enormous reduction in unemployment in Cairo between 1947 and 1960. Rather, it is merely additional proof that the census definition of the category "without work" has been drastically altered between censuses. This gross change, had it been noted earlier in the research process, would have been ample reason to eliminate this variable entirely. As it was, the weakness of the variable was not fully recognized until almost the entire project had been executed.

Variable 13. The change in mean percentage of Muslims reflects a real change in the religious composition of Cairo's population which is attributable to the exodus of two non-Muslim groups from the city in about 1956 and after. The Suez crisis of 1956, in which Israel attacked the U.A.R., had one repercussion in Cairo, namely, the mass exodus of the old Jewish community from the three census tracts that for hundreds of years had constituted the Jewish ghetto of Cairo. The Nationalization and Sequestration Laws passed shortly thereafter, confiscating the property of enemy aliens (French and British citizens but extending later to Swiss, Belgian, and other European nationals as well) served to encourage the exodus of other foreign groups. And finally, laws limiting the employment of noncitizens in industrial and commercial establishments led to a slower but steady exodus of Greeks and Italians. The net result has been a reduction in the size of the foreign community of Cairo, a commensurate decrease in the percentage of the population who are non-Muslims, and therefore, an increase in the proportion of Muslims, particularly in those areas most affected by the foreign exodus, which have, between 1947 and 1960, experienced "ethnic succession."

census years. The weighting was in accordance with the factor analytic solution described above and was derived logically from the interrelationships among the variables themselves, since the β matrix was itself the product of postmultiplying the transpose of the factor pattern matrix by the inverse of the correlation matrix.[13] Separate β matrices were derived for each census year and were used to weight the standardized scores for the appropriate year's data. The product of postmultiplying each β matrix by the appropriate *Z* matrix yielded a new matrix of factor scores (*F*), which showed the factor score of each census tract in the year on each of the three orthogonal factors that had been extracted from the original indices.

The final step in the method was to convert the factor scores into a geographic pattern for the metropolis. To this end, tract scores on each factor and for each data year were transcribed on separate base maps. Contiguous tracts were grouped together according to three criteria. First, I sought the smallest number of subcities necessary to summarize the critical differences. Second, I sought to maximize the average difference between adjacent subcities. And third, I sought to minimize the intra-subcity variations in tract scores.[14] In cases where tracts lay between two subcities, assignment to one or the other was made by testing the relative effects of differential assignment on the means and standard deviations of subcity scores; the best mathematical solution was then accepted. Only when there was no best mathematical solution was the conflict resolved by reference to my knowledge of the city.

At first, my attention was directed toward Factor I scores, for these were judged to have the greatest analytical power. From the 1947 data and, separately, from the 1960 data, subcities were delineated according to the criteria described above. In both years, the city subdivided into thirteen subcities which were almost perfectly congruent in outline. In those few cases (chiefly in the transitional belt) where interstitial tracts had been assigned to one subcity in 1947 but to an adjacent one in 1960, the conflict was resolved by accepting the 1960 best solution. In surprisingly few cases was this necessary. Map XVII in the text presents the results of this set of operations.

[13] The computation formula is: $S' \cdot R^{-1} = \beta$

Where S' is the transpose of factor loadings of the thirteen variables on the three factors, the values of which are shown in Table A-6 (Factors I and II) and Table A-8 (Factor III) above. There were two S' matrices, one for 1947 and one for 1960. Each was postmultiplied by its own *R*-Inverse Matrix.

Where R^{-1} is the inverse of the original matrix of correlation coefficients. Here I must acknowledge my own approximate solution which deviates from the ideal procedure. Because I retained only three factors which, combined, accounted for only two-thirds of the total variance of the original *R* (correlation coefficient) matrices, my residual matrices were too large to permit me to use the inverses of the original *R* matrices. Instead, a Reproduced *R* Matrix was computed by postmultiplying the Factor Pattern Matrix by its transpose ($S \cdot S'$). Then, the inverse of the Reproduced *R* Matrix was substituted for R^{-1}. The Reproduced Correlation Coefficient Matrix *R* should be viewed as the correlation matrix *that would have yielded* three and only three factors accounting for *all* of the variance; that is, the theoretical matrix having no variance deriving from unique factors or specific errors.

[14] Factor scores of tracts within a given subcity were averaged and the standard deviations from this mean computed. Differences between adjacent subcities were measured by their means; intra-subcity variations by the standard deviations.

In addition to Factor I, however, I prepared similar maps for the distribution of Factor II and III (revised) scores, although these maps do not appear in this book. They were more simply constructed and of a more tentative nature, since I felt that their validity had been less well established and that it would be going beyond their limitations to use them in more than very rough fashion. Primitive "social areas" were delineated by overlaying the few rough subcities derived from Factors II and III (revised) upon those established from the Factor I scores, but it was decided that, for purposes of the present book, they offered little additional value.

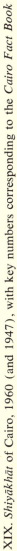

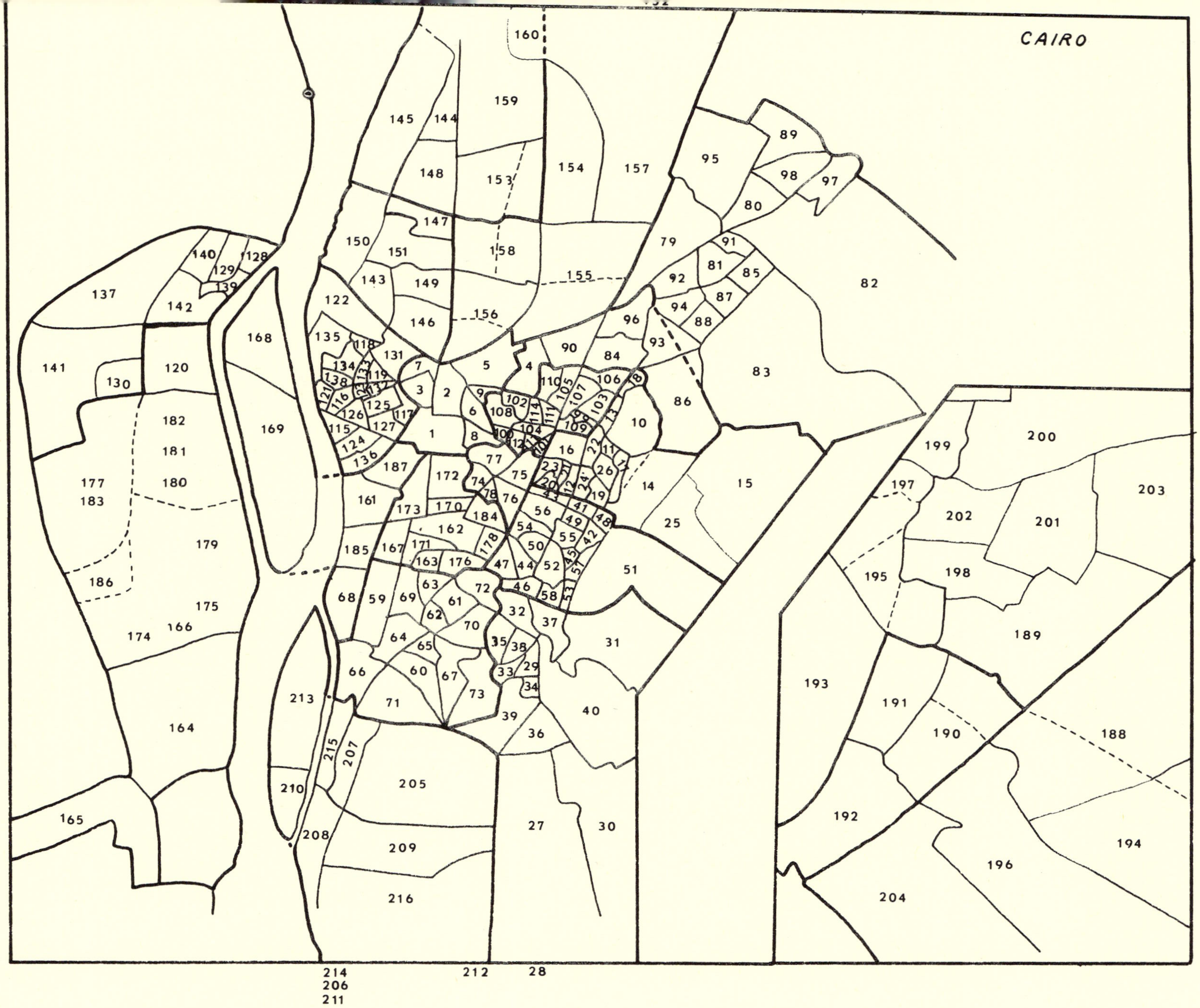

XIX. *Shiyākhāt* of Cairo, 1960 (and 1947), with key numbers corresponding to the *Cairo Fact Book*

Bibliography

GENERAL WORKS RELEVANT TO EGYPTIAN HISTORY AND DEVELOPMENT

al-Balādhuri, Aḥmad ibn Yaḥyā. *Futūḥ al-Buldān* [The Conquest of Countries]. Cairo: al-Mawsū'āt Press, 1901.

———. *The Origins of the Islamic State*, Philip K. Hitti, trans. *Studies in History, Economics and Public Law*, LXVIII, No. 183. New York: Columbia University, 1916.

Blunt, Wilfred Scawen. *Secret History of the English Occupation of Egypt; Being a Personal Narrative of Events.* New York: Alfred Knopf, 1922.

Breasted, James H. *A History of Egypt.* 2nd edn. New York: Charles Scribner's Sons, 1956.

Bréhier, Louis. *L'Égypte de 1798 à 1900.* Paris: Combet et Cie., 1901.

Brockelmann, Carl. *History of the Islamic Peoples.* Joel Carmichael and Moshe Perlmann, trans. New York: Capricorn Books, 1960.

Budge, E. A. Wallis. *Egypt.* New York: Henry Holt & Co., 1925.

Butler, Alfred J. *The Arab Conquest of Egypt and the Last Thirty Years of the Roman Dominion.* Oxford: The Clarendon Press, 1902.

———. *The Treaty of Misr in Tabari.* Oxford: The Clarendon Press, 1913.

Clot-Bey (Antoine Barthélemi). *Aperçu général sur l'Égypte.* 2 vols. Paris: Fortin, Massin et Cie., 1840.

Crabites, Pierre. *Ismail: The Maligned Khedive.* London: George Routledge & Sons, Ltd., 1933.

Creswell, K.A.C. *Early Muslim Architecture.* 2 vols. Oxford: The Clarendon Press, 1932 and 1940.

———. *The Muslim Architecture of Egypt: Ikhshīds and Fâtimids, A.D. 939-1171.* Oxford: The Clarendon Press, 1952.

———. *The Muslim Architecture of Egypt; Ayyūbids and Early Bahrite Mamlūks, A.D. 1171-1326.* Oxford: The Clarendon Press, 1959.

Cromer, The Earl of (Evelyn Baring). *Abbas II.* London: Macmillan and Company, 1915.

———. *Modern Egypt.* 2 vols. London: The Macmillan Company, 1908.

Darrag (Darrāj), Aḥmad. *L'Égypte sous le règne de Barsbay: 825-841/1422-1438.* Damascus: Institut Français de Damas, 1961.

de Chabrol, Volvic. "Essai sur les moeurs des habitants modernes de l'Égypte," *Description de l'Égypte: État moderne.* Tome II, Part II. Paris: L'Imprimerie Royale, 1822, pp. 361-578.

Dodwell, Henry. *The Founder of Modern Egypt: A Study of Muhammad 'Ali.* Cambridge, England: The University Press, 1931.

Douin, Georges. *Histoire du règne du Khédive Ismail, l'apogée, 1867-1873.* Rome: Istituto Poligrafico dello Stato per la Reale Società di Geografía d'Egitto, 1934.

———. *Histoire du règne du Khédive Ismail, les premières années du règne, 1863-1867.* Rome: Istituto Poligrafico dello Stato per la Reale Società di Geografía d'Egitto, 1933.

Elgood, Percival George. *Bonaparte's Adventure in Egypt.* London: Oxford University Press, 1931.

Enkiri, Gabriel. *Ibrahim Pacha, 1789-1848.* Cairo: Imprimerie Française, 1948.

Gibb, H.A.R. and Harold Bowen. *Islamic Society and the West.* Vol. I, Part I. London: Oxford University Press, 1950.

———. *Islamic Society and the West.* Vol. I, Part II. London: Oxford University Press, 1957.

Hallberg, Charles. *The Suez Canal: Its History and Diplomatic Importance.* New York: Columbia University Press, 1931.

Herold, J. Christopher. *Bonaparte in Egypt.* New York: Harper and Row, 1962.

Heyworth-Dunne, James. *An Introduction to the History of Education in Modern Egypt.* London: Luzac, 1939.

Hitti, Philip K. *History of the Arabs, from the Earliest Times to the Present.* 5th edn. revised. New York: The Macmillan Company, 1951.

ibn Iyas, Muḥammad ibn Aḥmad. *An Account of the Ottoman Conquest of Egypt in the Year A.H. 922 (A.D. 1516), Translated from the Third Volume of the Arabic Chronicle of Muhammed ibn Ahmed Ibn Iyas, an Eyewitness of the Scenes He Describes.* Colonel W. H. Salmon, trans. London: Royal Asiatic Society, 1921.

al-Jabarti. *Merveilles biographiques et historiques, ou Chroniques du cheikh Abd-el-Rahman el Djabarti.* Chefik Mansour *et al.*, trans. 9 vols. Cairo: Imprimerie Nationale, 1888-1896.

John, Bishop of Nikiu. *Chronique de Jean, Évêque de Nikiou.* (Amharic, French.) Hermann Zotenberg, ed. and trans. Paris, 1883.

———. *The Chronicle of John, Bishop of Nikiu.* R. H. Charles, trans. London: Williams and Norgate, 1916.

Lane, Edward William. *Egypt.* British Museum Manuscript No. 34,080.

———. *An Account of the Manners and Customs of the Modern Egyptians, Written in Egypt During the Years 1833, -34, and -35.* First edition in two volumes. London: Charles Knight and Co., 1836.

———. *The Manners and Customs of the Modern Egyptians.* Reprinted from the 1860 third edition. London: J. M. Dent and Sons, 1908 and subsequently.

Lane-Poole, Stanley. *A History of Egypt in the Middle Ages.* London: 1925.

——. *Saladin; and the Fall of the Kingdom of Jerusalem.* New York and London: G. P. Putnam's Sons, 1898.

Lloyd, Lord (George Ambrose). *Egypt Since Cromer.* 2 vols. London: The Macmillan Company, 1933-1934.

al-Maqrīzi, Taqi al-Dīn Aḥmad. *Kitāb al-Sulūk li Ma'rifat Duwal al-Mulūk* [History of the Mamluk Sultans]. M. Ziadeh, ed. 2 vols. Cairo: Dār al-Kutub al-Miṣrīyah, 1936-1958.

Marlowe, John. *A History of Modern Egypt and Anglo-Egyptian Relations, 1800-1953.* New York: Praeger, 1954.

Mas'ūdi, 'Ali ibn Ḥusayn. *Les prairies d'or.* C. Barbier de Meynard and Pavet de Courteille, Arabic text ed. and trans. into French. 9 vols. Paris: Société Asiatique, Imprimerie Nationale, 1861-1917.

Mathews, Joseph. *Egypt and the Formation of the Anglo-French Entente of 1904.* Philadelphia: University of Pennsylvania Press, 1939.

Mengin, Félix. *Histoire de l'Égypte sous le gouvernement de Mohammed-Aly.* 2 vols. Paris: A. Bertrand, 1823.

Milner, Sir Alfred. *England in Egypt.* Revised edn. London: Edward Arnold, 1899.

Mubārak, 'Ali. *Al-Khiṭaṭ al-Tawfīqīyah al-Jadīdah.* 20 vols. Cairo: Būlāq Press, 1888.

Muir, Sir William. *The Mameluke or Slave Dynasty of Egypt, 1260-1517 A.D.* London: Smith, Elder & Company, 1896.

Popper, William. *Egypt and Syria Under the Circassian Sultans, 1382-1468 A.D.; Systematic Notes to Ibn Taghri Birdi's Chronicles of Egypt.* Vols. 15 and 16 of the University of California Publications in Semitic Philology. Berkeley and Los Angeles: University of California Press, 1955 and 1957.

Ragatz, Lowell Joseph. *The Question of Egypt in Anglo-French Relations, 1875-1904.* Edinburgh: F. Pembroke, 1922.

Sadeque, S. Fatima, ed. *Baybars I of Egypt.* Dacca [London]: Oxford University Press, 1956.

Sāmi, Amīn. *Taqwīm al-Nīl* [Almanac of the Nile]. Vols. I, II, and III in three parts. Cairo: Dār al-Kutub al-Miṣrīyah, 1936.

Sauvaget, Jean. *Introduction to the History of the Muslim East; a Bibliographical Guide.* Based on the second edition as recast by Claude Cahen. Berkeley and Los Angeles: University of California Press, 1965.

Spüler, Bertold. *The Muslim World; A Historical Survey.* Part II, *The Mongol Period.* F.R.C. Bagley, trans. Leiden: E. J. Brill, 1960.

Stripling, George W. *The Ottoman Turks and the Arabs, 1511-1574.* Urbana: University of Illinois Press, 1942.

al-Ṭabari. *Ta'rīkh al-Rusul wa al-Mulūk* [Annals of the Apostles and Kings]. 9 vols. de Goeje edn. Leiden, 1877-1901.

ibn Taghri Birdi, Abū al-Maḥāsin. *History of Egypt, 1382-1469 A.D.* William Popper, trans. University of California Publications in Semitic Philology. Serial vols. 13, 14, 17, 18, 19, 22, 23. Berkeley and Los Angeles: University of California Press, between 1954 and 1960.

Tignor, Robert. "Public Health Administration in Egypt Under British Rule, 1882-1914." Unpublished Ph.D. Dissertation, Yale University, 1960.

——. *Modernization and British Colonial Rule in Egypt, 1882-1914.* Princeton: Princeton University Press, 1966.

Wiet, G. "Le voyage d'Ibrahim Pasha en France et en Angleterre, d'après les archives européennes du Palais d'Abdine," *Cahiers d'Histoire Égyptienne*, Vol. I (1948), 78-126.

Young, George. *Egypt.* New York: Charles Scribner's Sons, 1927.

Zaky, Mohamed Hassan. *Les Tulunides.* Paris: Busson, 1933.

GEOGRAPHIES, GUIDES, AND TRAVEL ACCOUNTS RELEVANT TO CAIRO

Adams, Francis W. L. *The New Egypt; A Social Sketch.* London: T. Fisher Unwin, 1893.

Adler, Elkan N., ed. *Jewish Travellers.* London: George Routledge & Sons, Ltd., 1930.

Affagart, Greffin. *Relation de Terre Sainte, 1533-1534.* J. Chavanon, ed. and annot. Paris: Librairie Victor Lecoffre, 1902.

Anis, M. "British Travellers' Impressions of Egypt in the Late 18th Century," *Bulletin of the Faculty of Arts*, Cairo University, Vol. 13, II (1951), 9-37.

Baedecker, Karl. *Egypt and the Sûdân; Handbook for Travellers.* 7th edn. New York: Charles Scribner's Sons, 1914.

——. *Egypt: Handbook for Travellers.* Leipsig: Karl Baedecker Pub., 1895.

——. *Guide to Egypt.* 2nd edn. Leipsig: Karl Baedeker Pub., 1885.

Balls, William Lawrence. *Egypt of the Egyptians.* New York: Charles Scribner's Sons, 1916.

ibn Baṭṭūṭah, Muḥammad ibn 'Abdullah. *The Travels of Ibn Batuta.* H.A.R. Gibb, trans. 2 vols. Cambridge: Cambridge University Press, 1958-1961.

Bénédite, Georges A. *Le Caire et ses environs.* Paris: Hachette, 1909.

Blount, Henry. *A Voyage into the Levant: A Brief Relation of a Journey Lately Performed by Master Henry Blount, Gentleman, from England by the Way of Venice, into Dalmatia, Sclavonia, Bosna, Hungary,*

Macedonia, Thessaly, Thrace, Rhodes and Egypt into Gran [sic] Cairo: with Particular Observations Concerning the Moderne Condition of the Turks and Other People Under That Empire. 4th edn. London: Printed by R. C. for Andrew Crooke, 1650.

Browne, William George. *Travels in Africa, Egypt and Syria from the Year 1792 to 1798.* London: T. N. Longman & O. Rees, 1799.

Charmes, Gabriel. *Five Months at Cairo and in Lower Egypt.* William Conn, trans. London: R. Bentley and Son, 1883.

Cunningham, Alfred. *To-Day in Egypt: Its Administration, People and Politics.* London: Hurst & Blackett, Ltd., 1912.

de Beauveau, Henri. *Relation journalière du voyage du Levant.* Nancy: Iacob Garnich, Imprimeurière Ordinaire de Son Altesse, 1615.

de Forbin, Count. *Travels in Egypt, Being a Continuation of the Travels in the Holy Land, in 1817-18.* London: Sir Richard Phillips and Co., 1820.

de Guerville, A. B. *New Egypt.* London: Heinemann, 1906.

de Montulé, Edward. *Travels in Egypt During 1818 and 1819.* London: Phillips and Co., 1821.

Denon, Vivant. *Voyages dans la basse et la haute Égypte.* 2 vols. London: Samuel, 1809.

de Planhol, Xavier. *The World of Islam.* Ithaca: Cornell University Press, 1959.

Description de l'Égypte. Text and Plates. 20 vols. Paris: Imprimerie Imperiale, 1809-1813; also 22 vols. Paris. Imprimerie Royale, 1818-1828.

de Thevenot, Jean. *The Travels of Monsieur de Thevenot into the Levant.* A. Lovell, trans. 3 vols. London: H. Clark, 1686-1687.

de Vaujany, H. *Description de l'Égypte. Le Caire et ses environs.* Paris: E. Plon et Cie., 1883.

Dopp, P. H. "Le Caire: Vu par les voyageurs occidentaux du Moyen Âge," *Bulletin de la Société Royale de Géographie d'Égypte.* Vol. 23 (June 1950), pp. 117-149.

Ebers, Georg. *Aegypten in Bild und Wort.* 2 vols. Stuttgart: Hallberger, 1878-1880.

[Anonymous.] *Egypt: Familiar Description of the Land, People and Produce.* London: William Smith, 1839.

Evliya, Effendi. *Narrative of Travels in Europe, Asia, and Africa in the Seventeenth Century.* Joseph von Hammer, trans. 2 vols. London: William H. Allen & Co., 1846-1850.

Fay, Eliza. *Original Letters from India (1779-1815).* E. M. Forster, ed. New York: Harcourt, Brace and Company, 1925.

Fedden, Robin. "Notes on the Journey from Rosetta to Cairo in the Seventeenth and Eighteenth Centuries," *Bulletin de la Société Royale de Géographie d'Égypte,* Vol. 21 (1943-1946), pp. 99-107.

Fermanel, Fauvel, de Lavney and de Stochove. *Voyage d'Italie et du Levant, de Messieurs Fermanel, . . . , Fauvel, . . . , Baudouin de Lavney et de Stochove.* Rouen: Chez Jean Viret, 1670.

Fullerton, William Morton. *In Cairo.* London and New York: Macmillan and Company, 1891.

Gargiolli, Carlo. *Viaggi in Terra Santa di Leonardo Frescobaldi e d'altri del Secolo XIV.* Florence: G. Barbera, 1862.

George of Cyprus. *Georgii Cyprii, Descriptio Orbis Romani.* Heinrich Gelzer, ed. Lipsiae, 1890.

Grey, Mrs. William (Maria Georgina). *Journal of a Visit to Egypt, Constantinople, the Crimea, Greece, etc. in the Suite of the Prince and Princess of Wales.* New York: Harper and Bros., 1870.

Guides Joanne. Le Caire et ses environs. Paris: Hachette et Cie., 1909.

Henniker, Sir Frederick. *Notes, During a Visit to Egypt, Nubia, The Oasis, Mount Sinai and Jerusalem.* London: John Murray, 1823.

ibn Jubayr. *The Travels of Ibn Jubayr.* R.J.C. Broadhurst, trans. London: Jonathan Cape, 1952.

Khusraw, Nāṣir-i. *Sefer Nameh, Relation du voyage de Nassiri Khosrau en Syrie, en Palestine, en Égypte, en Arabie, et en Perse, 1035-42.* Charles Schefer, ed. and trans. Series 2, Vol. 1. Paris: Publications de l'École des Langues Orientales Vivantes, 1881.

———. *Safar Nameh.* al-Khashāb, Arabic trans. Cairo: Cairo University, 1945.

Lamplough, Augustus, and R. Francis. *Cairo and Its Environs.* London: Sir Joseph Causton & Sons, 1909.

Legh, Thomas. *Narrative of a Journey in Egypt and the Country Beyond the Cataracts.* Philadelphia: M. Thomas, James Maxwell, 1817. London: Murray, 1817.

Light, Henry. *Travels in Egypt, Nubia, Holy Land, Mount Libanon, and Cyprus in the Year 1814.* London: Rodwell and Martin, 1818.

Millard, David. *Journal of Travels in Egypt, Arabia, Petrae, and the Holy Land During 1841-42.* Rochester, New York: E. Shepard, 1843.

al-Muqaddasi, Muḥammad ibn Aḥmad. *Aḥsan al-Taqāsīm fi Ma'rifat al-Aqālīm* [The Best Divisions in the Knowledge of the Countries]. M. J. de Goeje, ed. 2nd edn. Leiden: E. J. Brill, 1906/1909.

———. *Aḥsan al-Taqāsīm fi Ma'rifat al-Aqālīm.* English trans. Publ. by Asiatic Society of Bengal, New Series, No. 899. Calcutta: Baptist Mission Press, 1897.

Niebuhr, Carsten. *Voyage en Arabie et en d'autres pays circonvoisins.* (Trans. from German.) F. L. Mourier, trans. 2 vols. Amsterdam: S. J. Baalde, 1776-1780.

Norden, Frederick Ludvig. *Travels in Egypt and Nubia.* Dr. Peter Templeman, trans. 2 vols. London: Lockyer Davis and C. Reymers, 1757.

Penfield, Frederick Courtland. *Present-Day Egypt.* Revised and enlarged edn. New York: The Century Company, 1903.

Platt, Raye and Mohammed Hefny. *Egypt: A Compendium.* New York: American Geographical Society, 1958. Photo-offset, typed.

Poole, Sophia, with E. W. Lane. *The Englishwoman in Egypt; Letters from Cairo, Written During a Residence There in 1842, 3 and 4.* Philadelphia: Zieber, 1845.

Prescott, Hilda Frances Margaret. *Once to Sinai: The Further Pilgrimage of Friar Felix Fabri.* London: Eyre and Spottiswoode, 1957.

Reynolds-Ball, E. *Cairo of To-Day*, Black's Guide Books. London: Adam and Charles Black, 1899.

Roberts, David. *The Holy Land . . . Egypt and Nubia.* 3 vols. London: Moon, 1842-1849.

Rushdi, Rashad. "English Travellers in Egypt During the Reign of Mohammed Ali," *Bulletin of the Faculty of Arts*, Cairo University, Vol. 14, II (1952), 1-61.

St. John, James Augustus. *Egypt and Mohammed Ali: or Travels in the Valley of the Nile.* 2 vols. London: Longman, Rees, 1834.

Savary, Claude. *Lettres sur l'Égypte.* 3 vols. Paris: Onfroi, 1785-1786.

Senior, Nassau William. *Conversations and Journals in Egypt and Malta by the Late Nassau William Senior.* M. Simpson, ed. London: Sampson, Low, Marston, Searle, and Rivington, 1882.

Sherer, Moyle. *Scenes and Impressions in Egypt and in Italy.* London: Longman, Hurst, Rees, Orme, Brown and Green, 1825.

Sonnini, C. S. *Travels in Upper and Lower Egypt: Undertaken by Order of the Old Government of France.* Henry Hunter, trans. Vol. I. London: John Stockdale, 1799.

Strabo. *The Geography of Strabo.* Horace Leonard Jones, trans. Vol. VIII. London: William Heinemann, Ltd., 1932.

Tafur, Pero. *Pero Tafur, Travels and Adventures, 1435-1439.* Malcolm Letts, ed. and trans. London: George Routledge and Sons, Ltd., 1926.

Thenaud, Jean and Domenico Trevisan. *Le voyage d'outremer de Jean Thenaud suivi de la relation de l'Ambassade de Domenico Trevisan auprès du Soudan d'Égypte.* 2nd edn. Charles Schefer, ed. and annot. Paris: Leroux, 1884.

Thompson, Charles. *The Travels of the Late Charles Thompson, Esq.* Vol. III. London: J. Newbery and C. Mickelwright, 1744.

Toussoun, Prince Omar. *La géographie de l'Égypte à l'époque Arabe.* Vol. VIII, Mémoires de la Société Royale de Géographie d'Égypte. Cairo: Imprimerie de l'Institut Français d'Archéologie Orientale, 1926.

Volney, M. (pseud. for Constantin-François Chassebeuf). *Travels through Syria and Egypt, in the Years 1783, 1784, and 1785. . . .* (Trans. from French.) 2 vols. London: G. G. J. and J. Robinson, 1787.

Wilkinson, John. *A Handbook for Travellers in Egypt (Being a New Edition, Corrected and Condensed of "Modern Egypt and Thebes").* London: John Murray, 1847.

———. *A Handbook for Travellers in Egypt (A New Edition with Corrections and Additions).* London: Murrays, 1867.

———. *Modern Egypt and Thebes: Being a Description of Egypt, Including the Information Required for Travellers in that Country.* 2 vols. London: John Murray, 1843.

Wilson, Colonel. *Picturesque Palestine, Sinai and Egypt.* New York: D. Appleton Company, 1883.

Ya'qūbi, Aḥmad ibn Waḍiḥ. *Kitāb al-Buldān* [Book of Countries]. M. J. de Goeje, ed. Leiden: E. J. Brill, 1892.

———. *Kitāb al-Buldān*, Gaston Wiet, trans. *Livre de les pays.* Cairo: Imprimerie de l'Institut Français d'Archéologie Orientale, 1937.

Yāqūt, ibn 'Abdullah al-Ḥamawi. *Mu'jam al-Buldān* [Geographical Dictionary]. Vols. I, IV, V. Beirut, 1957.

Zincke, Foster Barham, Vicar of Wherstead. *Egypt of the Pharaohs and of the Khedive.* London: Smith, Elder and Company, 1871.

DEVELOPMENT OF SOCIAL AND ECONOMIC INSTITUTIONS RELEVANT TO EGYPT AND CAIRO

Alderfer, Harold, M. F. el Khatib, and M. A. Fahmy. *Local Government in the United Arab Republic.* Cairo: Institute of Public Administration, UAR, and the United Nations, 1963, 1964.

Artin, Yacoub Pasha. *Essai sur les causes du renchérissement de la vie matérielle au Caire dans le courant du XIXe siècle (1800 à 1907).* Cairo: Imprimerie de l'Institut Français d'Archéologie Orientale, 1907.

Ayalon, David. *Gunpowder and Firearms in the Mamluk Kingdom, a Challenge to Mediæval Society.* London: Vallentine, Mitchell, 1956.

———. "Studies in al-Jabarti I: Notes on the Transformation of Mamluk Society in Egypt under the Ottomans," *Journal of the Economic and Social History of the Orient*, Vol. III, Part 2 (August 1960), pp. 148-174.

———. "Studies in al-Jabarti I: Notes on the Transformation of Mamluk Society in Egypt under the Ottomans," *Journal of the Economic and Social History of the Orient*, Vol. III, Part 3 (October 1960), pp. 275-325.

———. "The System of Payment in Mamluk Military Society," *Journal of the Economic and Social History of the Orient*, Vol. I, Part I (August 1957), pp. 37-65.

———. "The System of Payment in Mamluk Military Society," *Journal of the Economic and Social History of the Orient*, Vol. I, Part 3 (October 1958), pp. 257-296.

Baer, Gabriel. *Egyptian Guilds in Modern Times*. Jerusalem: The Israel Oriental Society, 1964.

———. *A History of Landownership in Modern Egypt, 1800-1950*. London: Oxford University Press, 1962.

———. "Waqf Reform in Egypt," *St. Anthony's Papers*, No. 4. London: Chatto and Windus, 1958, pp. 61-76.

Berger, Morroe, ed. *The New Metropolis in the Arab World*. New Delhi and New York: Allied Publishers, 1963.

Boak, A.E.R. "Guilds, Late Roman and Byzantine," *Encyclopedia of the Social Sciences*, Vol. VII. New York: The Macmillan Company, 1932, pp. 206-208.

Bowring, John. *Report on Egypt and Candia*. London: Her Majesty's Stationery Office, 1840.

Brunschvig, Robert. "Urbanisme médiéval et droit musulman," *Revue des Études Islamiques*, Vol. 15 (1947), pp. 127-155.

Cahen, Claude. "L'evolution de l'iḳṭā' du IXe au XIIIe siècle," *Annales: Économies, Sociétés, Civilisations*, VIII (January-March 1953), 25-52.

———. *Mouvements populaires et autonomisme urbain dans l'Asie Musulmane du Moyen Âge*. Reprinted from *Arabica*. Leiden: E. J. Brill, 1959.

———. "Réflexions sur le waqf ancien," *Studia Islamica*, XIV (1961), 37-56.

Chehata, Tawfiq. "La concession du service public: Étude comparée de droit administratif Français et Égyptien." Entire issue of *L'Égypte Contemporaine*, Nos. 197-198 (March-April 1941), pp. 205-496.

Coulson, Noel James. *A History of Islamic Law*. Edinburgh: University Press, 1964.

Crouchley, A. E. "A Century of Economic Development, 1837-1937," *L'Égypte Contemporaine*, Vol. 30, Nos. 182-183 (February-March 1939), pp. 133-155.

———. "The Development of Commerce in the Reign of Mohamed Ali," *L'Égypte Contemporaine*, Vol. 28 (1937), pp. 305-368.

———. *The Economic Development of Modern Egypt*. London: Longmans, Green and Company, 1938.

Debs, Richard. "The Law of Property in Egypt: Islamic Law and Civil Code." Unpublished Ph.D. Dissertation, Princeton University, 1963.

Delcroix, M. M. "L'Institution municipale en Égypte," *L'Égypte Contemporaine*, Vol. 14, No. 65 (April 1922), pp. 278-323.

Earle, E. M. "Egyptian Cotton and the American Civil War," *Political Science Quarterly*, Vol. 41 (1926), pp. 520-545.

Fahmy, Moustafa. *La révolution de l'industrie en Égypte et ses consequences sociales au 19e siècle (1800-1850)*. Leiden: E. J. Brill, 1954.

Fischel, Walter J. "The Spice Trade in Mamluk Egypt; a Contribution to the Economic History of Medieval Islam," *Journal of the Economic and Social History of the Orient*, Vol. I, Part 2 (April 1958), pp. 157-174.

Gardet, Louis. *La cité Musulmane; Vie sociale et politique*. Paris: Librairie Philosophique J. Vrin, 1954.

Goitein, S. D. "New Light on the Beginnings of the Kārim Merchants," *Journal of the Economic and Social History of the Orient*, Vol. I, Part 2 (April 1958), pp. 175-184.

———. "The Rise of the Near Eastern Bourgeoisie in Early Islamic Times," *Cahiers d'Histoire Mondiale*, III (1957), 583-603.

Government of Egypt, Ministry of Finance. *Budget of the Egyptian Government, 1922-23*.

———. *La législation en matière immobilière en Égypte*. Cairo: The National Press, 1901.

al-Giritli, 'Ali. "Taṭawwur al-Niẓām al-Maṣrafi fi Miṣr" [The Development of the Banking System in Egypt], *Buḥūth al-'Īd al-Khamsīni* [50th Anniversary Special Issue of *Miṣr al-Mu'āṣirah*]. Cairo, 1960.

Heffening, W. "Waḳf," *Encyclopedia of Islam*, Vol. IV. Leiden: E. J. Brill, 1934, pp. 1096-1103.

Hourani, George Fadlo. *Arab Seafaring in the Indian Ocean in Ancient and Early Medieval Times*. Princeton: Princeton University Press, 1951.

al-Husaini, Ishaq Musa. "Ḥisba in Islam," *The Islamic Quarterly*, Vol. 10 (July and December 1966), pp. 69-82.

Institute of Public Administration, United Arab Republic. *Development of Local Government in the United Arab Republic*. Cairo, October 1959.

Issawi, Charles Philip. *Egypt at Mid-Century: An Economic Survey*. London: Oxford University Press, 1954.

———. *Egypt in Revolution: An Economic Analysis*. New York: Oxford University Press, 1963.

Kamel, Mazen. "Administrative Problems of Rapid Urban Growth in the United Arab Republic," *Administrative Problems of Rapid Urban Growth in the Arab States*. New York: United Nations, 1964.

Landes, David S. "Bankers and Pashas: International Finance in Egypt in the 1860's," *Men in Business*. W. Miller, ed. Cambridge: Harvard University Press, 1952, pp. 23-70.

———. *Bankers and Pashas: International Finance and Economic Imperialism in Egypt*. Cambridge: Harvard University Press, 1958.

Lapidus, Ira Marvin, ed. *Middle Eastern Cities*. Berkeley: University of California Press, 1969.

———. *Muslim Cities in the Later Middle Ages*. Cambridge: Harvard University Press, 1967.

Legrand, F. *Les fluctuations de prix et les crises de 1907 et 1908 en Égypte*. Nancy: J. Coubé, 1909.

Le Tourneau, Roger. *Les villes musulmanes de l'Afrique du Nord*. Algiers: La Maison des Livres, 1957.

———. *Fez in the Age of the Marinides*. Bessie A. Clement, trans. Norman: University of Oklahoma Press, 1961.

Lévy, Edwin. 'Les événements de 1907 et la situation actuelle de l'Égypte," *L'Égypte Contemporaine*, Vol. 3 (November 1912), pp. 503-530.

Levy, Reuben. *The Social Structure of Islam, Being the Second Edition of the Sociology of Islam*. Cambridge: Cambridge University Press, 1957.

Lewis, Bernard. "The Islamic Guilds," *The Economic History Review*, VIII (November 1937), 20-37.

Lybyer, Albert H. "The Ottoman Turks and the Routes of Oriental Trade," *English Historical Review*, Vol. 30 (October 1915), pp. 577-588.

Marçais, Georges. "L'urbanisme musulmane," *5e Congrès de la Fèderation des Sociétés Savantes de l'Afrique du Nord*. Algiers, 1940.

———. "La conception des villes dans l'Islam," *Revue d'Alger*, II (1945), 517-533.

Marçais, William. "L'Islamisme et la vie urbaine," *L'Académie des Inscriptions et Belles-Lettres, Comptes Rendus*, Paris (January-March 1928), pp. 86-97.

Massignon, Louis. "Les corps de métiers et la cité Islamique," *Revue Internationale de Sociologie*, Vol. 28 (1920), pp. 473-489.

———. "Guilds, Islamic," *Encyclopedia of the Social Sciences*, Vol. VII. New York: The Macmillan Company, 1932, pp. 214-216.

———. "Şinf," *Encyclopedia of Islam*.[1] Vol. IV. Leiden: E. J. Brill, pp. 436-437.

Overseas Economic Surveys: Egypt, October, 1951. London: His Majesty's Stationery Office, 1952.

Piloti, Emmanuel. *L'Égypte au commencement du quinzième siècle d'après le traité d'Emmanuel Piloti de Crète (Incipit 1420)*. P. Hermann Dopp, ed. and annot. Cairo: Fuad 1st University, 1950.

Poliak, A. N. *Feudalism in Egypt, Syria, Palestine and the Lebanon, 1250-1900*. London: Royal Asiatic Society, 1939.

———. "Les révoltes populaires en Égypte à l'époque des Mamelouks et leur causes économiques," *Revue des Études Islamiques*, Vol. 8 (1934), pp. 251-273.

al-Qalqashandi, Aḥmad ibn 'Ali. *Al-Qalqachandi: Les institutions des Fâtimides en Égypte*. Marius Canard, ed. Algiers: La Maison des Livres, 1957.

Rivlin, Helen Anne B. *The Agricultural Policy of Muhammad 'Ali in Egypt*. Cambridge: Harvard University Press, 1961.

Schacht, Joseph. *An Introduction to Islamic Law*. Oxford: The Clarendon Press, 1964.

Sékaly, A. "Le problème des wakfs en Égypte," *Revue des Études Islamiques*, Vol. 3 (1929), pp. 75-126, 277-337, 395-454, 601-659.

Shaw, Stanford. *The Financial and Administrative Organization and Development of Ottoman Egypt, 1517-1798*. Princeton: Princeton University Press, 1962.

Sjoberg, Gideon. "The Preindustrial City," *American Journal of Sociology*, LX (March 1955), 438-445.

———. *The Preindustrial City, Past and Present*. Glencoe: The Free Press, 1960.

Stripling, George William Frederick. *The Ottoman Turks and the Arabs, 1511-1574*. Urbana: The University of Illinois Press, 1942.

Tomiche, Nada. "La situation des artisans et petits commerçants en Égypte de la fin du XVIIIe siècle jusqu'au milieu du XIXe siècle," *Studia Islamica*, XII (1960), 79-98.

Tyan, Émile. *Histoire de l'organisation judiciare en pays d'Islam*. 2nd edn., revised and corrected. Leiden: E. J. Brill, 1960.

United Nations. *Administrative Problems of Rapid Urban Growth in the Arab States*. New York: United Nations, 1964.

Von Grunebaum, Gustave. *Islam: Essays in the Nature and Growth of a Cultural Tradition*. Memoir No. 81. The American Anthropological Association, 1955.

Wiet, Gaston. "Les communications en Égypte au Moyen Âge," *L'Égypte Contemporaine*, Vol. 24 (1933), pp. 241-264.

———. "Les marchands d'épices sous les sultans Mamlouks," *Cahiers d'Histoire Égyptienne*, Series VII, Fasc. 2 (May 1955), pp. 81-147.

Wittek, Paul. "La féodalité musulmane," *Revue de l'Institut de Sociologie* (January-March 1936), pp. 97-101.

Ziadeh, Nicola. *Urban Life in Syria Under the Early Mamluks*. Beirut: American Press, 1953.

STUDIES OF CAIRO

Abbate, W. *Les origines du Caire: Ésquisse historique sur Babylone et Fostatt*. Cairo, 1891.

Abou El-Ezz, M. S. "Some Aspects of Migration in Cairo," *Bulletin de la Société de Géographie d'Égypte*, XXXII (1959), 121-141.

Abu-Lughod, J. and Ezz el-Din Attiya. *Cairo Fact Book*. Cairo: Social Research Center, American University at Cairo, 1963.

Abu-Lughod, J. "The Ecology of Cairo, Egypt: A Comparative Study Using Factor Analysis." Unpublished Ph.D. Dissertation, University of Massachusetts, 1966.

———. "Migrant Adjustment to City Life: The Egyptian Case," *American Journal of Sociology*, LXVII (July 1961), 22-32.

———. "A Tale of Two Cities: The Origins of Modern Cairo," *Comparative Studies in Society and History*, VII (July 1965), 429-457.

———. "Testing the Theory of Social Area Analysis: The Ecology of Cairo, Egypt," *American Sociological Review*, Vol. 34 (April 1969), pp. 198-212.

———. "Varieties of Urban Experience: Contrast, Coexistence and Coalescence in Cairo," *Middle Eastern Cities*. Ira Lapidus, ed. Berkeley: University of California Press, 1969, pp. 159-187.

Adham, Moustafa Bey Munir. "Le Caire au XVe siècle d'après les données de Maqrizi," *Bulletin de la Société Géographie d'Égypte*, XIII (1924-1925), 131-180. (In Arabic.)

Becker, C. H. "Cairo," *Encyclopedia of Islam.*[1] Vol. I. London: Luzac, 1913, pp. 815-826.

———. "Bābalyūn," *Encyclopedia of Islam.*[2] Vol. I. London: Luzac, 1958, pp. 844-845.

Boulad, Émile. "La voirie et l'esthétique de la ville du Caire," *L'Égypte Contemporaine*, Vol. II, No. 5 (January 1911), pp. 33-51.

———. *Les tramways du Caire en 1919*. Cairo: Imprimerie Barbey, 1919.

Butler, Alfred J. *Babylon of Egypt; A Study in the History of Old Cairo*. Oxford: The Clarendon Press, 1914.

Carnoy, Norbert. *La Colonie Française du Caire*. Université de Paris, Faculté de Droit. Paris: Les Presses Universitaires de France, 1928.

Casanova, Paul. *Essai de reconstitution topographique de la ville d'al Foustât ou Misr*. Cairo: L'Imprimerie de l'Institut Français d'Archéologie Orientale, 1913.

Clerget, Marcel. *Le Caire; Étude de géographie urbaine et d'histoire économique*. 2 vols. Cairo: Imprimerie E. & R. Schindler, 1934.

Colombe, Marcel. *La vie au Caire au XVIIIe siècle*. Cairo: Conférence de l'Institut Français d'Archéologie Orientale, 1951.

ibn Duqmaq. *Kitāb al-Intiṣār li Wāsiṭāt 'Iqd al-Amṣār* [*Description de l'Égypte*]. Karl Vollers, ed. Cairo: Imprimerie Nationale, 1893.

Faraj, Fu'ād. *Al-Qāhirah*. 3 vols. Cairo: Dār al-Ma'ārif, 1946.

Fourmont, Cl. C. *Description historique et géographique des plaines d'Héliopolis et de Memphis*. Paris: Chez Duchesne, 1755.

Greene Pasha (Dr.). "The Sanitation of Cairo," *The Provincial Medical Journal*, Vol. VII, No. 73 (January 2, 1888), pp. 9-10.

Guest, A. R. "The Foundation of Fustat and the Khittahs of that Town," *Journal of the Royal Asiatic Society* (January 1907), pp. 49-83.

——— and E. T. Richmond. "Misr in the Fifteenth Century," *Journal of the Royal Asiatic Society* (October 1903), pp. 791-816.

———. "Cairene Topography: El Qarafa according to Ibn Ez-Zaiyat," *Journal of the Royal Asiatic Society* (1926), pp. 57-61.

Ḥāfiẓ 'Ali, Muḥammad. *al-Takhṭīṭ al-Ḥāli li Madīnat al-Qāhirah wa Ittijāhāt al-Mustaqbalah* [Contemporary Planning for the City of Cairo and Its Future Trends]. Cairo: mimeo, 1965.

Haswell, C.J.R. "Cairo Origin and Development. Some Notes on the Influence of the River Nile and Its Changes," *Bulletin de la Société Royale de Géographie d'Égypte*. Vol. XI, Nos. 3 & 4 (December 1922), pp. 171-176.

Ibrāhīm, Shiḥātah 'Īsa. *Al-Qāhirah*. Cairo: Dār al-Hilāl, n.d. 1959?

Jomard, Edme-François. "Description abregée de la ville et de la citadelle du Kaire," *Description de l'Égypte: État Moderne*. Tome II, Part II. Paris: L'Imprimerie Royale, 1822, pp. 579-783.

Khoury, R. "Le Caire au Moyen-Âge," *Cahiers d'Histoire Égyptienne*, Vol. 5 (1953), pp. 302-338.

Kirkwood, Kenneth Porter. *Preface to Cairo: A Survey of Pre-Cairo in History and Legend*. Ottawa: Mutual Press, Ltd., 1958.

Lane, Edward. *Cairo Fifty Years Ago*. Stanley Lane-Poole, ed. London: John Murray, 1896.

Lane-Poole, Stanley. *The Story of Cairo*. London: J. M. Dent & Sons, Ltd., 1902.

al-Maqrīzi, Taqi al-Dīn Aḥmad. *Al-Mawā'iẓ wa al-I'tibār fi Dhikr al-Khiṭaṭ wa al-Āthār* [Lessons and Considerations in Knowing the Structure of Countries (Cities)]. 2 vols. Cairo: Būlāq Press, 1853.

Margoliouth, D. *Cairo, Jerusalem and Damascus, Three Chief Cities of the Sultans*. New York: Dodd, Mead & Co., 1907.

Martin, Germain. *Les bazars du Caire et les petits métiers arabes*. Cairo: Université Égyptienne, 1910.

Ministry of Municipal Affairs and the Municipality of Cairo Planning Commission. *Master Plan of Cairo*. Cairo: Government Printing Office, 1956.

el-Naggar, Said. "An Economic Analysis of the Metropolis," *The New Metropolis in the Arab World*. Morroe Berger, ed. New Delhi and New York: Allied Publishers, 1963.

Niyāzi, Muṣṭafa. *Al-Qāhirah: Dirāsāt Takhṭīṭiyah fi al-Murūr wa al-Naql wa al-Mūwāṣalāt* [Cairo: Planning

Studies in Traffic, Transport and Communications]. Cairo: Anglo-Egyptian Library, 1958-1959.

Pauty, E. *Les palais et les maisons d'époque musulmane au Caire.* Cairo: Imprimerie de l'Institut Français d'Archéologie Orientale, 1932.

Pyramid [pseud.]. "The Drainage of Cairo," *The Provincial Medical Journal,* Vol. XIV, No. 162 (June 1, 1895), pp. 298-301.

Raymond, André. "Essai de géographie des quartiers de résidence aristocratique au Caire au XVIIIème siècle," *Journal of the Economic and Social History of the Orient,* Vol. VI, Part 1 (May 1963), pp. 58-103.

Rhoné, Arthur. "Coup d'oeil sur l'état du Caire, ancien et moderne," extracted and reprinted from issues of *La Gazette des Beaux Arts.* Paris: A. Quantin, 1882.

Russell, Dorothea. *Medieval Cairo and the Monasteries of the Wādi Natrūn.* London: Weidenfeld and Nicolson, 1962.

Salmon, Georges. *Études sur la topographie du Caire—La Kal'at al-Kabsh et la Birkat al-fîl.* Cairo: Imprimerie de l'Institut Français d'Archéologie Orientale, 1902.

Scanlon, George. "Preliminary Report: Excavations at Fustat, 1964," *Journal of the American Research Center in Egypt,* IV (1965), 7-30.

Schemeil, Marius. *Le Caire: sa vie, son histoire, son peuple.* Cairo: Dār al-Ma'ārif, 1949.

Sladen, Douglas Brooke. *Oriental Cairo: The City of the "Arabian Nights."* London: Hurst and Blackett, Ltd., 1911.

Stewart, Desmond. *Cairo 5500 Years.* New York: Thomas Y. Crowell Co., 1968.

———. *Cairo.* London: Phoenix House Books, 1965.

Toy, Sidney. "Babylon of Egypt," *The Journal of the British Archaeological Association,* 3rd Series, Vol. I (January 1937), pp. 52-77.

Wensinck, A. J. "Misr," *Encyclopedia of Islam.*[1] Vol. III. London: Luzac, 1913, pp. 520-521.

Wiet, Gaston. *Cairo: City of Art and Commerce.* Seymour Feiler, trans. Norman: University of Oklahoma Press, 1964.

Zaki, 'Abd al-Raḥmān. *Al-Qāhirah . . . 969-1825* [Cairo: Its History and Heritage, 969-1825]. Cairo: Dār al-Ṭibā'ah al-Ḥadīthah, 1966.

Zwemer, S. M. "The City of Cairo according to the Census of 1917," *Moslem World,* Vol. 10 (1920), pp. 266-273.

OFFICIAL AND STATISTICAL REPORTS RELEVANT TO CAIRO

Government of Egypt, Ministry of Finance. Annual *Almanac.* Būlāq: Government Press, issued annually between 1902 and 1946.

———, ———. Budget of the Egyptian State. Cairo: Government Press, 1920 and *seq.*

———, ———. *La législation en matière immobilière en Égypte.* Cairo: National Press, 1893 (reprinted 1901).

———, ———. *Census of 1897.* Not available to me except as figures summarized in later censuses.

———, ———. *The Census of Egypt Taken in 1907.* Cairo: National Printing Department, 1909.

———, ———, Statistical Department. *The Census of Egypt Taken in 1917.* Cairo: Government Press, 1921.

———, ———, Statistical and Census Department. *The Population Census of Egypt, 1927.* Cairo: Government Press, 1931.

———, ———, ———. *The Population Census of Egypt, 1937.* 2 vols. Cairo: Government Press, 1942.

———, Ministry of Finance and Economy, Census Department. *Census of Egypt, 1947.* General summary volume plus separate volume for the Governorate of Cairo. Cairo: Government Printing Office, 1952.

United Arab Republic, Department of Census and Statistics. *The Population Census of 1960.* General summary volume plus separate volume for the Governorate of Cairo. Cairo: Government Printing Office, 1962.

———, ———. *Annuaire Statistique, 1960/1961.* Cairo: Government Printing Office, 1962. These were issued every two years, beginning about 1914, until this last edition.

———, Ministry of Information. Annual Yearbooks, *Al-Kitāb al-Sanawi,* from about 1958 through 1965. Būlāq: Government Press.

United Arab Republic, ———. *Eleven Years of Progress and Development, 1952-1963.* Cairo: Information Department, 1963.

———, ———. *Overall Five Year Plan for Economic and Social Development, 1960-1965.* Undated.

———, ———. *U.A.R.: Achievements and Future Development Plans.* Cairo: Government Printing Office, 1960.

Government of Egypt, Ministry of the Interior, Bureau of Statistics. *Essai de statistique générale de l'Égypte, années 1873 . . . 1877.* Cairo: Imprimerie de l'État-Major Général Égyptien, 1879.

———, ———, Department of Public Health. *Births and Deaths in the Principal Towns of Egypt During the First and Second Quarters of 1907-1908.* Cairo: National Printing Office, 1908.

———, Ministry of Public Works. *Règlement pour le service du Tanzim.* Decree of August 26, 1889. Cairo: National Press, 1903.

Government of Egypt (and later, United Arab Republic), Statistical Department. *Quarterly Return of Births, Deaths, Infectious Diseases, Marriage and Divorce,* issued four times each year until 1960.

——, Ministry of *Waqf. The Mosques of Egypt.* Giza: The Survey Department, 1949.

Governorate of Cairo, Department of Housing and Public Utilities. "Building Regulations for Fāṭimid Cairo." (In Arabic.) Mimeographed release, undated (1965?).

——, ——. "The First Five Year Plan: Works Performed During the First Four Years: Expected Works to be Performed During the Fifth Year." (In Arabic.) Mimeographed report, 1965.

——, ——. "Memorandum on Housing in the Governorate of Cairo." (In Arabic.) Mimeographed release, undated (1965?).

Government of Great Britain. *Egypt No. 1 (1909): Reports by His Majesty's Agent and Consul-General on the Finances, Administration, and Condition of Egypt and the Soudan in 1908.* London: His Majesty's Stationery Office, 1909.

Government of Great Britain. *Egypt No. 1 (1920): Reports of His Majesty's High Commissioner on the Finances, Administration, and Condition of Egypt and the Soudan for the Period 1914-1919.* London: His Majesty's Stationery Office, 1920.

——. *Egypt No. 1 (1921): Reports by His Majesty's High Commissioner on the Finances, Administration, and Condition of Egypt and the Soudan for the Year 1920.* London: His Majesty's Stationery Office, 1921.

OTHER POPULATION STUDIES

Abdel-Aty, S. H. "Life Table Functions for Egypt Based on Model Life-Tables and Quasi-Stable Population Theory," *Milbank Memorial Fund Quarterly,* XXXIX (April 1961), 350-377.

Abu-Lughod, J. "The Emergence of Differential Fertility in Urban Egypt," *Milbank Memorial Fund Quarterly,* XLIII (April 1965), 235-253.

——. "Urbanization in Egypt: Present State and Future Prospects," *Economic Development and Cultural Change,* XIII (April 1965), 313-343.

——. "Urban-Rural Differences as a Function of the Demographic Transition," *American Journal of Sociology,* LXIX (March 1964), 476-490.

el-Badry, Mohammed. "Some Aspects of Fertility in Egypt," *Milbank Memorial Fund Quarterly,* XXXIV (January 1956), 22-43.

——. "Some Demographic Measurements for Egypt Based on the Stability of Census Age Distributions," *Milbank Memorial Fund Quarterly,* XXXIII (July 1955), 268-305.

Cleland, W. Wendell. *The Population Problem in Egypt: A Study of Population Trends and Conditions in Modern Egypt.* Lancaster, Pennsylvania: Science Press, 1936.

el-Darwish, Mahmoud Mohamed. "Analysis of Some Estimates of the Population of Egypt Before the XIXth Century," *L'Égypte Contemporaine,* XX (1929), 273-286.

Farid, I. A. *Population of Egypt.* Cairo, 1948.

Hamdan, Gamal. *Studies in Egyptian Urbanism.* Cairo: Renaissance Bookstore, 1959.

Rizk, Hanna. "Fertility Patterns in Selected Areas in Egypt." Unpublished Ph.D. Dissertation, Princeton University, 1959.

Said, Alphonse. "The Growth and Development of Urbanization in Egypt." Cairo: Social Research Center, American University at Cairo, 1960 mimeo.

Index

Index